Foreword by
Brian Fagan

ARCHÆOLOGY

THE ESSENTIAL GUIDE TO OUR HUMAN PAST

Smithsonian Books
Washington, DC

◄ The rock tomb of Achaemenid king
Darius I (550–486 BC) at Naqsh-i Rustam
near Persepolis, Iran.

This book was designed and produced by
Quintessence Editions Ltd.
The Old Brewery
6 Blundell Street
London N7 9BH

Senior Editor	Elspeth Beidas
Editors	Rebecca Gee, Carol King,
	Frank Ritter, Fiona Plowman
Designer	Josse Pickard
Production Manager	Anna Pauletti
Editorial Director	Ruth Patrick
Publisher	Philip Cooper

Published in North America by Smithsonian Books

This book may be purchased for educational, business, or sales promotional use.
For information, please write: Special Markets Department, Smithsonian Books,
P.O. Box 37012, MRC 513, Washington, DC 20013

Cataloging-in-Publication Data on file at Library of Congress

ISBN 978-1-58834-591-2

Manufactured in China, not at government expense

21 20 19 18 17   5 4 3 2 1

For permission to reproduce illustrations appearing in this book, please
correspond directly with the owners of the works, as seen on page 574.
Smithsonian Books does not retain reproduction rights for these images
individually or maintain a file of addresses for sources.

CONTENTS

FOREWORD

Archaeology is one of the great scientific triumphs of the past century. What began as little more than a treasure hunt has become a highly sophisticated multidisciplinary enterprise that combines anthropology, climatology, history, and a host of sciences to help tell the story of humanity over more than four million years. We archaeologists are unique in our ability to study human societies over immensely long periods of time. Not for us the deeds of political leaders or the minutiae of a century's events. The great fascination of archaeology comes from its remarkable chronological range, from human origins across the millennia and into the details of the Industrial Revolution, World War I trench warfare, and even Hollywood movie sets from the 1920s.

Today's archaeology is an enormous, complex enterprise, which makes it much harder for outsiders to explore our discoveries. This guide is a welcome and richly illustrated pathway through the intricacies of our past, as revealed by the very latest research, for a general readership. There are dozens of books that cover aspects of the past. Encyclopedias of archaeology abound, but none of them describes for everyone what archaeology does and what we know about the past from its researches. Established authorities contribute to the story in this volume in a remarkably seamless narrative, accessible to all.

Archaeology tells a complex story, written as a narrative of exploration. Eloquent text complemented by lavish illustrations takes us from human origins through prehistory, then through the ancient civilizations and historic times. Finally, we explore more recent developments, with global coverage of conflict archaeology, cultural tourism, indigenous peoples, slavery, and other contemporary concerns. I am impressed with the ways in which the expert authors have filled out the overall narrative with featured sites that cover a breathtaking range of locations and topics. What other guide to archaeology has stand-alone features on early humans, Lascaux cave paintings, Tutankhamun, the Chinese terracotta soldiers, and Ironbridge, a masterpiece of the Industrial Revolution? Where else will you find essays on Great Zimbabwe, Rapa Nui, Stonehenge, and Taxila? Inevitably, a far-ranging narrative of this kind raises questions in the reader's mind. Carefully highlighted key issues, such as the reasons why states arose, answer some of these questions.

After a tour through the world's greatest and most interesting archaeological sites, the closing section rounds the book off with a lively, balanced account of topics fundamental to our field, including basic theory, dating the past, and how we survey and excavate. But there is more, much of it on cutting-edge developments, such as the use of DNA and ways of studying individuals like King Richard III. Rightly, there is discussion of non-intrusive archaeology. The American archaeologist Kent Flannery once remarked that archaeologists are the only social scientists who murder their informants.

He is technically correct, for archaeological excavation permanently destroys the archives of the past. In recent years, excavation has become much more of a strategy of last resort. We now rely increasingly on remote sensing methods instead of excavation. Subsurface radar, laser imagery, and satellites allow us to probe beneath the ground and to examine ancient landscapes around such iconic sites as Angkor Wat in Cambodia. There are features on genetic coding, isotope studies that examine diet, and the remarkable travels of prehistoric people like the Amesbury Archer from southern England and Ötzi the Bronze Age Iceman from the Alps. The book closes with a tantalizing glance at the decipherment of ancient scripts.

The pages of this comprehensive guide weave a complex tapestry not only of the past itself, but of the ways in which archaeologists everywhere are studying it. In addition to its accessibility, this book is important for being truly international. Archaeology began in Europe and the Mediterranean, and only became global during the later twentieth century. That it is now possible to tell a world-wide story in these pages for a general audience is a testimony to how far archaeology has come since the days of Austen Henry Layard, Arthur Evans, and Howard Carter. Today's archaeologists work on the shoulders of giants, who lacked the tools that we now possess. No longer is archaeology the romantic adventure of yesteryear, nor do its practitioners behave like the fictional Indiana Jones. Yes, the subject still has a whiff of adventure, but behind it lies a fascinating world of captivating detail and meticulous detective work. Archaeology is a compelling doorway into the past that celebrates spectacular discoveries and painstaking inquiry. I enjoyed every page of this engrossing book.

Brian Fagan

Author and professor emeritus of anthropology
at the University of California, Santa Barbara

INTRODUCTION

As far as we know, human beings are unique creatures in that we are interested in our past—a phenomenon that British antiquarian William Camden (1551–1623) called a "back-looking curiositie." And for the great majority of that past, and certainly for any period that predates writing, archaeology is our principal—and usually only—source of knowledge.

Archaeology is a vast and varied subject, covering everything from the crude stone tools of at least 3 million years ago to the materials thrown away yesterday. It encompasses the entire world, from the seabed to mountain tops, and from jungles to deserts. Clearly, no single book could possibly contain all the detail of such an enormous phenomenon—each of the contributors could easily have filled the book with an account of their own regions or periods of expertise—so this book can only try to present the big picture. What may be found here is a broad overview of the major cultures and sites of the archaeological world, as well as some of the more general subjects covered by the modern discipline. It is hoped that the book will encourage readers to pursue the study of archaeology and delve more deeply into those aspects of the subject that they find of particular interest.

The term "archaeology" derives from the Greek *arkhaiologia* (discourse about ancient things), but today it means the study of the human past through those material traces of it that have come down to us. The greatest challenge of the subject is that, for most of the things that ever happened in the past, very little evidence has survived, and of this evidence only the tiniest fraction is ever recovered by archaeologists, and it is difficult to know what portion of that is correctly interpreted or identified. But countless archaeologists rise to that challenge and maintain steadfast optimism that they can reliably reconstruct some aspects of the human past.

The discipline of archaeology arose primarily in Europe. By medieval times, people were becoming intrigued by "magic crocks," probably cremation urns that mysteriously emerged from the ground through ploughing. Similarly, flints worked by humans and polished stone axes were constantly turned up as farmers ploughed their fields; these were usually interpreted as elf-shot or thunderbolts. The realization then slowly dawned in more enlightened minds that all these finds were in fact crafted by ancient peoples. At around the same time, discoveries of Greek and Roman sculpture began to be collected and displayed by wealthy families.

It was in the sixteenth century that some scholars in northwest Europe recognized that information about the ancient past could be obtained from the study of field monuments; thus, antiquarians in Britain, Scandinavia, and elsewhere started to visit and describe ancient monuments. The next two centuries saw these activities being pursued more systematically and increasing numbers of excavations were carried out. While these were mostly intended simply to retrieve objects from the ground, a few pioneers were already treating the work like a careful dissection, noting the relationships of artifacts to different layers in the soil, and realizing that, in general, objects from upper layers must be younger than those from layers below. There also arose a craze for barrow-digging, or excavating the burial mounds of northwest Europe or North America. This was primarily a leisure pursuit for gentlemen, clerics, doctors, lawyers, teachers, and the like, who would usually employ laborers to dig into the sites with picks and shovels.

▼ A page from a chronicle of 1610 features a fanciful illustration of the Neolithic monument of Stonehenge in Wiltshire, England. Antiquaries are seen directing investigations, and bones are being dug up by laborers in the foreground.

It was really only in the early to mid-nineteenth century that true archaeology took over from antiquarianism, in the sense of attempting to be systematic and scientific about the vestiges of the past. This was the period when, through discoveries in western Europe of stone tools associated with bones of extinct animals, it was gradually realized and accepted that humankind had a formidable past. By the end of the nineteenth century, true archaeology was already flourishing, with many of the "greats" hard at work — such as Petrie in Egypt, Koldewey at Babylon, Schliemann in the Aegean, and Pitt-Rivers in Britain. By now, for most enthusiasts, archaeology was far less of a treasure-hunt and more a means of answering specific questions.

Through the twentieth century, thanks to the efforts of a series of major figures — Wheeler in Britain and India, Reisner and Woolley in the Middle East, Uhle and Kidder in America, Bordes and Leroi-Gourhan in France — archaeology became a massive, multidisciplinary enterprise, drawing on the skills of innumerable experts of different kinds: geophysicists, aerial photographers, zoologists, botanists, chemists, geneticists, and a whole range of scientists able to date different materials. Today, science-based archaeology is very much to the fore, and archaeologists are now taking part in some of the most prominent debates of our time, such as climate change — examining the effects of rises in sea-level and the consequences of global warming.

Overall, several major trends have emerged in archaeological studies since they began, and especially in recent decades. First, the work has become far slower, more painstaking and, inevitably, more expensive. Instead of tackling the stratigraphic layers with pickaxes, archaeologists carefully shovel the soil, scraping or brushing it away and recording each step in the sequence, and everything is sieved to prevent any scrap of information from being lost.

▲ British archaeologist Leonard Woolley (1880–1960, right) and British author, archaeologist, military officer and diplomat T. E. Lawrence (1888–1935) with a Hittite bas-relief in basalt from the Herald's Wall at Carchemish, Turkey, in 1913.

Second, we are now acquiring vastly increased quantities of material of all kinds, to the extent that severe storage problems are created. As a result, it is sometimes wiser to leave evidence in the ground, rather than expose it to deterioration in unsatisfactory storage conditions. After an excavation, the study and analysis of finds may take decades rather than years; in fact, the processing and study of the results may take up the rest of the excavator's life. This kind of timescale imposes a limit on what can and should be taken out of the ground. Further, the great cost in money and human effort of a major excavation has ensured that few big digs are now undertaken. For example, the excavation of the Upper Paleolithic rock-shelter of L'Abri Pataud (Pataud Shelter) by Hallam Movius between 1958 and 1964 yielded 2 million objects, and doctoral theses are still being written about this material today. Few Paleolithic sites in France have been dug on this scale since then, and only a few sites—such as the caves of the Sierra de Atapuerca, near Burgos, in Castilla y León, Spain, with their abundant content of nearly 1-million-year-old fossils— are sufficiently well funded to maintain annual excavations.

Third, the accepted dates for many phenomena—the appearance of farming or pottery, the arrival of people in Europe, the New World, or Australia—have been pushed steadily back in time, and may well continue to retreat. And fourth, thanks to new technology, archaeologists are now able to do far more with far less material. For example, the organic samples needed for radiocarbon dating are tiny, while pigment analysis can be carried out with equally tiny samples, or even—thanks to portable spectrometers—with no physical contact at all. Also, satellite imagery, advanced computers, GPS, and genetic and chemical analyses have revolutionized many aspects of our studies of the past. In view of the rapidly accelerating developments in these and other technological approaches, it boggles the mind to try and imagine what people will be able to learn fifty or one hundred years from now. A century ago, a potsherd was simply studied in terms of its manufacture, shape, decoration, and likely date. Today we can assess the precise contents of its paste, the source of its raw materials, the temperature at which it was fired, when the firing occurred, and, if the pot bears residues, what it formerly contained.

Our "back-looking curiositie" has also grown to become one of the foremost factors in world tourism, and indeed the economy of some countries relies heavily on archaeological tourism as a source of income: notable examples include Greece, Peru, Mexico, and Egypt. Unfortunately, warfare or terrorist events can have a devastating impact not merely on archaeological sites or monuments but also in deterring tourists from visiting. For obvious reasons, in countries like Afghanistan, Iraq, and Syria, archaeological tourism has been virtually nonexistent for years now, while, far worse for the historical record, ideological extremists have set about destroying or vandalizing monuments and museum collections. Even in Egypt, which has remained relatively unaffected by such hostilities, the fear of terrorist attacks alone has had a major impact. In 2010, the year before the "Arab Spring," 14.7 million tourists visited Egypt. Tourism made up 11.3 percent of the country's gross domestic product and employed 1.3 million people. But only 3 million tourists visited during the first half of 2016—only half of the previous year's equivalent.

However, ideological extremists do not stop at destroying monuments of the past, such as the Bamiyan Buddhas in Afghanistan or the temples of Palmyra in Syria. They also participate actively in the traffic in antiquities, looting sites and museums to obtain objects for sale to unscrupulous buyers in the West. This phenomenon is by no means limited to the Middle East; it is also common in other, more stable parts of the world, such as Latin America. Even China, which imposes draconian penalties on traffickers, is losing many of its antiquities to the West. Peasants in many countries stand to make enormous profits by

▼ A cast of the Venus of Pataud. Measuring 7 by 5½ inches (18 x 14 cm.), it is just one of the millions of finds unearthed by American archaeologist Hallam Movius (1907–87) during his excavation at the Upper Palaeolithic site of L'Abri Pataud, in the village of Les-Eyzies-de-Tayac, south-west France.

selling their heritage to wealthy collectors, as do the middle-men who identify the buyers and smuggle the artifacts out to them.

The past has become big business, in many different ways. In the modern age of generally cheap air transport, people are able to travel farther and more often than their predecessors, and hence they can visit the great archaeological sites of the world relatively easily. Sadly, their increasing numbers are posing a serious threat to many sites and monuments, which are in real danger of being "loved to death." The primary concern must be to preserve the sites for future generations, and unfortunately this means that tourist visits have to be severely restricted—and in some cases totally stopped—at certain sites. That is why only about fifty of the caves of Spain and France that were decorated in the Ice Age are open to the public, and the numbers of people admitted per day, and the time allowed inside, are carefully controlled. Access to Stonehenge in England or to the rows of stones at Carnac, France, is likewise restricted to prevent wear by hundreds of thousands of pedestrians per year. Major sites, like Pompeii, Italy; Machu Picchu, Peru; and Angkor Wat, Cambodia, are forever swamped by countless visitors. Even on Easter Island, remote in the Pacific Ocean, the increasing number of tourists has necessitated many restrictions on which paths can be taken and where visitors are allowed.

Archaeology has to weigh the right of the public to see the cultural heritage against its paramount duty to protect and preserve that heritage—and it can be very hard to strike the right balance. Difficult decisions often have to be taken, some of which are resented by the public because archaeologists are usually able to retain access to sites that become off-limits to others. A tried solution to this problem—one that can only exacerbate as mass tourism expands further—is to create accurate facsimiles of some of the most threatened sites, such as the caves of Lascaux and Chauvet-Pont-d'Arc in France, and that of Altamira in Spain. Also, virtual reality technology is making

▲ In September 2015, the jihadist ISIS destroyed the UNESCO-listed Temple of Bel in the ancient city of Palmyra, Syria. Here, a photograph taken of the temple in its relatively intact state in March 2014 is compared to how it looked in 2016.

▲ In a studio in Toulouse, France, an artist works on a full-sized reproduction of the cave paintings found in the Chauvet-Pont-d'Arc cave, in the Ardèche, France. The facsimile, called Caverne du Pont-d'Arc, opened to the general public in 2015 and is the largest cave replica ever built worldwide, bigger than the facsimile of the Lascaux cave.

it possible to make virtual visits to many sites, and this option is likely to be expanded in the future to incorporate holograms and other effects.

New technology is also having an unprecedented and very positive impact on archaeological studies in many different ways. A whole new world of digital archaeology is opening up awe-inspiring prospects for the future. For example, digital imaging and 3D printing have made possible an accurate and detailed recreation of the destroyed Arch of Triumph at Palmyra, and could likewise be used to restore or replace antiquities elsewhere, such as those attacked for various reasons or damaged by natural disasters. As long as there is some photographic or other recording of the precious relics of the past, there is potential for them to be "restored."

In another exciting recent development, it has become possible to read texts that were thought destroyed. For example, a 1,500-year-old Jewish scroll, found at Ein-Gedi in Israel, was charred in a fire and thought unreadable, but X-ray scans and sophisticated computer programs have "unfurled" it virtually and made it legible. It is now hoped that this method can be applied to a cache of charred Roman scrolls found at Herculaneum, Italy.

In many places, modern archaeology has become a race against time because rapidly expanding construction and urbanization are threatening to destroy sites before they can be investigated. In Scandinavia, Alaska, and elsewhere, receding sea ice and glaciers are opening up previously inaccessible areas and exposing numerous artifacts. These are often astonishing finds, beautifully preserved organic materials that would have disintegrated in warmer climes, but that are now thawing and at risk of destruction. In its totality, this priceless and irreplaceable archive is being destroyed faster than archaeologists can locate and retrieve it.

Archaeology in the future will be a more anonymous activity than in the past, when it was dominated by big personalities. The relatively recent phenomenon of consulting and involving indigenous peoples in the study of their ancestors will be developed further. Androcentric views of the past will give way to equal emphasis being placed on the roles and activities of women and children. Also, there has been a growing realization that the ways in which archaeological data were presented to the public in the past were subject to all kinds of bias—expressing the prejudices and beliefs of the society, religion, politics, or world view of the scholars involved. Inevitably, the scholars were influenced by their background, upbringing and education, their social status, their interests, teachers, friends, and enemies, all of which colored the versions of the past that they put forward. Today's archaeologists recognize their responsibilities in this domain, try to be more conscious of these factors, and endeavor to be more objective in their work.

Archaeology is undeniably a "luxury" subject in that it is not crucial to human existence. Nevertheless, it interests an enormous number of people and, as we have seen, is an important component in the economies of many countries. As long as it can go on stimulating and giving pleasure to the masses, its public funding and support will continue to flourish. Archaeology is the only discipline that can tell us about 99 percent of the human past, and can deliver insights into the big questions about our development—when, where, and how we originated; the human colonization of our planet; the development of technology, art, and writing; and the origins and spread of agriculture, complex societies, and urbanization. Only archaeology provides the long-term view of the human trajectory, and at the same time captures the interest of the whole world with spectacular finds such as Ötzi the Iceman or China's Terracotta Army. Few other studies can make such a boast.

▼ Only 2¾ inches (7 cm.) long, this burned Torah scroll from *c.* 600 CE was excavated from a Holy Ark at a synagogue at Ein-Gedi on the Dead Sea in 1970. With the aid of a micro CT 3D high-resolution scanner and digital imaging software, it was revealed to contain verses of the Book of Leviticus.

1 | Deep Prehistory
4 MILLION — 10,000 BCE

From the gnarled remains of our very earliest ancestors in Africa to the glorious rock art of fully modern people, this chapter traces the evolution of the human family tree up to modern humans, or *Homo sapiens* (wise man). The archaeological evidence uncovered from this period helps to address such key questions as: Where do we come from? When did the first humans evolve? What makes us distinctly human?

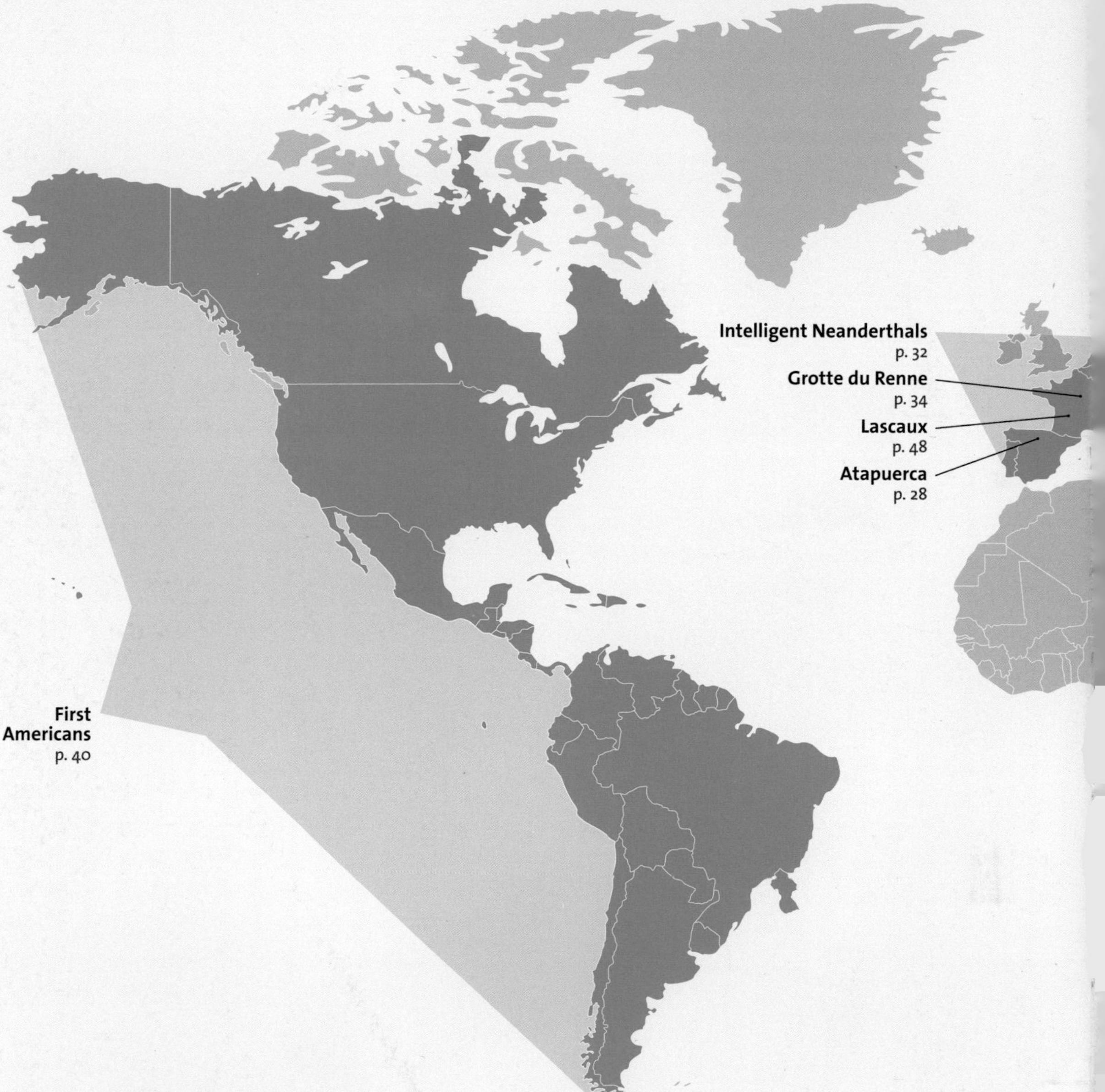

Intelligent Neanderthals
p. 32

Grotte du Renne
p. 34

Lascaux
p. 48

Atapuerca
p. 28

First Americans
p. 40

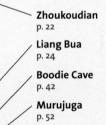

BEFORE HUMANS

1 A reconstruction of what *A. afarensis* may have looked like, based on the hominid skeleton of Lucy. It is on display in the Museum of Human Evolution in Burgos, Spain.

2 A 230-foot (70-m) trail of hominid footprints fossilized in volcanic ash at Laetoli, Tanzania. It was dated to 3.7 million years ago using potassium–argon dating and stratigraphic analysis of the geological strata.

3 The discovery of the skull of the Taung Child, *A. africanus*, was evidence of a new genus, *Australopithecus*, that was ancestral to modern humans.

In 1924, workers in a lime quarry in Taung, South Africa, uncovered a small, fossilized skull (see image 3). Raymond Dart (1893–1988), the anatomist who examined it, concluded that it was a child, and that its mix of apelike and human features suggested a type ancestral to humans. He named the Taung Child *Australopithecus africanus* (African southern ape), but it took more than two decades before its status as a possible human ancestor was generally acknowledged. It is now thought to be about 2.8 to 3.3 million years old.

Seven species of *Australopithecus* are now recognized, almost all from east Africa and South Africa. They have small brains of 18 to 37 cubic inches (300–600 cu. cm.) approximately one third of that of modern humans. They walked upright, but they were probably not the first bipedal hominins. In general, australopithecines had smaller canine teeth than apes, but retained relatively large molars for grinding tough foods in a largely or exclusively plant-based diet. However, there is considerable cross- and sometimes intra-species variation, and the genus displays a mosaic of apelike and humanlike traits.

Especially in early research, a key distinction was made between gracile (slender) and robust (heavily built) specimens. Robust types, from South Africa, Kenya, and Ethiopia, are now usually placed in the genus *Paranthropus*. These are still sometimes described as "australopiths," a broad term that includes other early, humanlike primates from east and northeast Africa. Among them are (from oldest to youngest) *Sahelanthropus tchadensis*, *Orrorin tugenensis*, two species of *Ardipithecus*, and *Kenyanthropus platyops* (see p. 18).

KEY EVENTS

7–6 Million years ago	4.2–3.9 Mya	3.8–2.9 Mya	3.7 Mya	3.67 Mya	3.5–3 Mya
Emergence of *S. tchadensis* and *O. tugenensis*, the earliest hominins, close to the time that humans and chimpanzees diverge.	*A. anamensis*, the oldest member of the genus *Australopithecus*, appears in northern Kenya and Ethiopia.	*A. afarensis*, the species to which the fossil Lucy belongs, is present in northeast Africa.	Footprints are left in soft mud by *A. afarensis* at Laetoli, Tanzania. They are of two adults, with a third set possibly belonging to a child.	The age of Little Foot, an australopithecine of uncertain species, found in deposits at the Sterkfontein Caves, South Africa.	The age of *A. bahrelghazali*, found in Chad in 1995; the only australopithecine fossil found outside east/northeast and South Africa.

The oldest documented species in the genus *Australopithecus* is from Kenya and Ethiopia. *A. anamensis*, from 4.2 to 3.9 million years ago, probably lived in a part-woodland habitat, and was probably the ancestor of the next oldest species, *A. afarensis*, from 3.9 to 2.9 million years ago. This is the species to which the famous Ethiopian fossil known as Lucy (see image 1) belongs. Don Johanson (b. 1943) and colleagues found 40 percent of the skeleton of Lucy, a young adult, in 1974. In life she probably stood about 3 feet 7 inches (110 cm.) tall and weighed about 66 pounds (30 kg.). Males may have been about 50 percent larger. This sexual dimorphism is much diminished in humans. *A. afarensis* is a mixture of apelike and more humanlike features, especially adaptations for upright walking—a development that preceded an increase in brain size. Various traits, including reduced tooth size and arm length, nevertheless suggest an evolutionary move forward from its primate forebears.

Other important australopithecines from more northerly areas of Africa include *A. garhi*, from about 2.5 million years ago. It resembles *A. afarensis* but has some strongly apelike features, including large molar teeth. Regardless, it was found in association with animal bones showing cutmarks and rudimentary stone tools. This may make it a candidate for being one of several australopithecine species possibly in the direct line of human evolution. However, some researchers take the view that the australopithecines were a dead-end side branch on the evolutionary tree, and were not direct human ancestors.

Since the discovery of the Taung Child, hundreds of *A. africanus* specimens, among other hominin fossils, have been found in a group of sites north of Johannesburg. The oldest may date to 3.3 million years ago; most are about 2.1 to 3 million years old. They are similar in many ways to the more ancient *A. afarensis*, but have some more human traits, including a larger braincase and a flatter face. However, they also have some apelike features, such as long arms relative to leg length. Along with *A. garhi*, *A. africanus*, and a newly discovered species, *A. sediba* (see p. 18), have also been suggested as human ancestors.

The changing morphology of the australopithecines relates partly to a more terrestrial, rather than arboreal, way of life. Adaptations for tree dwelling and climbing—such as flat, mobile feet and ankles, and long, curved digits—reduce through time. The Laetoli footprints in Tanzania (see image 2), probably made by three *A. afarensis* and then preserved by falling volcanic ash, have provided important data on foot anatomy, including the development of arched feet. The relation of skeletal changes to habitat and changing climates is not well understood. It may relate to increased flexibility in areas of mixed woodland and grassland, with early australopithecines taking advantage of a wider range of dietary possibilities and responding to rapidly changing environments.

The australopithecines have been of huge importance in studies of human evolution, not least because it was the discovery of *A. africanus* that first directed attention to Africa as the continent where humans evolved. **AS**

3.3 Mya	3.3–2.1 Mya	c. 2.8–2.75 Mya	c. 2.5 Mya	c. 2 Mya	1924
Artifacts that may be the oldest known stone tools are made. The makers may have been australopithecines or *K. platyops*.	The probable dates for the southern species *A. africanus*. Dates here are less secure than for east Africa, because of the fossils' location in limestone deposits.	The age of the oldest fossil attributed to the genus *Homo* (species unknown), a partial jaw from Ethiopia. It coexisted with australopithecines.	The dating of *A. garhi*, from the Afar Depression in Ethiopia, one of several australopithecine species possibly ancestral to humans.	The age of two individuals of a new species, *A. sediba*, discovered in South Africa's Cradle of Humankind World Heritage Site in 2005.	The first australopithecine, the Taung Child, from South Africa, is identified by Raymond Dart as a possible human ancestor.

Recent *Australopithecus* Finds 3.6–2 MILLION YEARS AGO

Kenyanthropus platyops, found in Kenya in 1999, dates to between 3.5 and 3.3 million years ago. It is a puzzling hominin specimen with a relatively flat face, whose classification is complicated by distortion of the skull during fossilization. Some researchers believe it belongs to the *Australopithecus* genus or that it is a variant of *A. afarensis*, which also lived at this time.

With fossil-rich areas now well known and fossil-bearing strata well mapped, new finds keep on coming. Two australopithecine finds from South Africa's Cradle of Humankind World Heritage sites in Gauteng Province have been twenty-first-century sensations. In 2008, a new species, *Australopithecus sediba*, was found near Malapa Cave. Two individuals were retrieved: an adult female and a juvenile male. Dated to just under 2 million years ago, *A. sediba* displays the expected mosaic of humanlike and older characteristics. It is of interest because it indicates advanced upright walking, more similar to humans than other australopithecines. Some modern features of the hand (shorter fingers and a longer thumb) suggest it may have used tools and could be ancestral to *Homo erectus*. Some researchers regard it as a new variant of *A. africanus*. Another find known as Little Foot, from the nearby Sterkfontein Caves, came to light when four small ankle bones in a museum were re-examined in 1994. Paleoanthropologist Ronald J. Clarke (b. 1944) recognized them as those of an upright-walking species. The remainder of the skeleton was relocated, embedded in rock. Still not fully described, its species remains undetermined. Various unique features have led Clarke to suggest it represents a new species, *A. prometheus*; others regard it as *A. africanus*.

In Ethiopia, *A. afarensis* finds in 2000 and 2005 include a three-year-old female from Dikika that is more than 100,000 years older than the Lucy fossil. Kadanuumuu (Big Man), a partial skeleton from the same area, is older still, at 3.58 million years ago. Its significance lies in the information it provides about the locomotion of *A. afarensis*. Dikika, and the Kenyan site of Lomekwi, have also provided evidence of tool use by australopithecines. **AS**

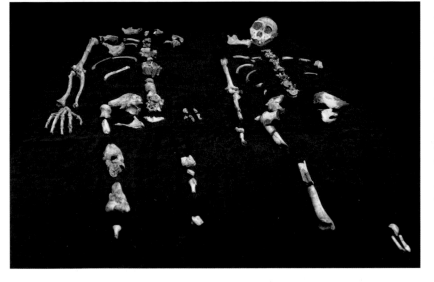

CAVE COMPLEX

The Cradle of Humankind World Heritage Site is 31 miles (50 km.) north of Johannesburg and covers 116,139 acres (47,000 ha.). It contains more than thirty sites, including the Sterkfontein Caves, in a limestone cave complex that has yielded hundreds of important hominin and other fossils. The caves' complex geology and stratigraphy make dating the fossils here more difficult than in east Africa, where remains occur in ash deposits that are easier to correlate with local volcanic eruptions.

UNDERSTANDING VARIATION

Some australopithecines are known from numerous specimens, some relatively complete, allowing assessment of age- and sex-linked skeletal variations. This is the case with *A. sediba*, represented by a juvenile and an adult. Some, however, are represented only by one individual and fragmentary remains. For example, *A. bahrelghazali* is known only from a lower jaw fragment and a single tooth from another individual. It has affinities with *A. afarensis* and is remarkable for its location in northern Chad, over 1,243 miles (2,000 km.) west of the other known specimens.

EARLY STONE TOOLS

Stone tool use and manufacture were long considered the hallmark of humanity and the earliest evidence of cultural behavior. It has since emerged that prehuman species and even chimpanzees used tools. Previously, the oldest stone tools were thought to belong to the Oldowan industry, attributed to *H. habilis*. Oldowan artifacts were first discovered at Olduvai Gorge in Tanzania, and have been recovered from several localities in eastern, central, and southern Africa. At Gona, Ethiopia, these date to about 2.5 million years ago. However, there is now evidence for pre-Oldowan tool use.

Near the Dikika Baby site, researchers found fossilized animal bones with what appear to be cutmarks and hammering damage consistent with stone tool use, though no actual tools were found. Somewhat less controversial are approximately 150 large, very crude artifacts from Lomekwi 3, Kenya. At 3.3 million years old, they are 700,000 years older than the Gona artifacts, though there are some questions about their antiquity and the dating of the associated deposits. Possible makers were *A. afarensis* or *K. platyops*. Cutmarked bones from Bouri, Ethiopia, dated to about 2.5 million years ago, may have been made by *A. garhi*. These finds have caused debate because they imply that perhaps australopithecines were not as primitive as some once believed. They have also revolutionized our understanding of technological evolution, challenging the notion that making stone tools is one of the defining attributes of the human species.

BECOMING HUMAN

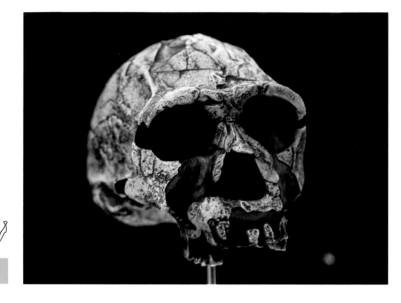

1 *H. erectus/ergaster* lived in eastern and southern Africa between 1.9 and 1.4 million years ago.

2 The 609,000-year-old Mauer 1 mandible, found in Germany in 1907, is a specimen of *H. heidelbergensis*.

The evolution of the genus *Homo* and the relationships of the many species of human known from the fossil record worldwide are matters of intensive study. *Homo erectus* is a key species in the debates about the classification of human fossils and early population migrations around the globe. *H. erectus* originated in east Africa perhaps 2 million years ago but is found in numerous sites across Europe and Asia. Some paleoanthropologists hold that the African *H. erectus* was the direct ancestor of the Asian specimens and is therefore a distinct species, rather than a regional variation. Accordingly, the name *H. ergaster* is often used for the African examples.

Researchers generally agree that an initial migration of *H. erectus/ergaster* (see image 1) into Asia took place by 1.8 million years ago. This migration, perhaps across the land bridge of the Sinai Peninsula, is known as Out of Africa I. The site of Dmanisi, in Georgia, has yielded a subspecies of *H. erectus* fossils dating to about 1.8 million years ago. East Asian and Indonesian sites contain further specimens dating from about 1.7 to 1 million years ago.

Another key player in the story is the species *H. heidelbergensis* (see image 2), which had emerged in Africa by approximately 700,000 years ago. It is thought to have descended from *H. ergaster*, but has a larger braincase and made more sophisticated tools. Not all scientists accept that it is a separate species from *H. ergaster*. According to one interpretation, *H. heidelbergensis* spread into Europe perhaps 300,000 to 400,000 years ago, with one branch giving rise to the Neanderthals (see p. 30) and another to the Denisovans. The latter, recently

KEY EVENTS

c. 2 Mya	By 1.8 Mya	*c.* 1.8 Mya	*c.* 1.7 Mya	*c.* 750–680,000 Ya	*c.* 700,000 Ya
Homo erectus (upright man) evolves in Africa, where it is also known as *H. ergaster*.	Out of Africa I: the first humans (*H. erectus/ ergaster* populations) emigrate from Africa, spreading to Europe and Eurasia.	*H. erectus*–type individuals, now classified as a Eurasian subspecies, have established themselves at Dmanisi, in Georgia.	Early evidence for the initial dispersal of *H. erectus*, found in 1965 at the site of Yuanmou, China.	Specimens of *H. erectus* individuals present in Zhoukoudian, Beijing, discovered in the 1920s and originally known as Peking Man.	The appearance of *H. heidelbergensis*, an early human generally believed to be intermediate between *H. erectus* and *H. sapiens*.

discovered in Siberia and known only from two teeth and a finger bone, have provided genetic information that indicate that Denisovans were related to Neanderthals but constitute a new species of archaic humans.

The species *H. sapiens* relates to a more recent migration, according to most researchers. Anatomically modern humans are thought to have evolved in Africa from *H. heidelbergensis*, approximately 200,000 years ago. Between 100,000 and 50,000 years ago, they spread from Africa to Europe and Asia, where they replaced the local populations, eventually becoming behaviorally modern humans, or *H. sapiens sapiens*.

The Out of Africa II hypothesis is also known as the recent African origin model, to distinguish it from a competing interpretation, the multiregional hypothesis. This proposes that all humans are descended from the *H. erectus* migrations from Africa after about 1.8 million years ago, and regional differences are due to natural selection, related to local conditions.

The evidence for human origins is anatomical (skeletal characteristics), archaeological (associated artifacts, inferred behavior) and genetic. Genetic evidence seems to support the recent African origin model, because the small variations in the genetic makeup of modern humans suggest a shorter period in which to diversify and, therefore, a more recent origin. Anatomical evidence is more ambiguous and subjective: How different do two specimens have to be to classify them as separate species? Attention has focused on the presence of features such as heavy brow ridges and the absence of a chin (archaic), as opposed to a large braincase and small teeth (modern). *H. heidelbergensis* shows archaic and modern traits, and is usually regarded as a transitional form between *H. erectus* and the anatomically modern *H. sapiens*.

However, new finds continually challenge older interpretations. Recent work on Chinese human fossils has also thrown up puzzling anomalies. In multiple Chinese sites there are specimens, some dating from as early as 900,000 years ago, that would conventionally be seen as transitional between *H. erectus* and *H. sapiens*. Given their early dates, the implication is that there may be another explanation for the mix of modern and archaic features.

For some researchers, the Chinese finds lend support to the multiregional hypothesis, perhaps even providing evidence that Asian populations descended from an Asian *H. erectus*–like ancestor, such as Peking Man (from Zhoukoudian, near Beijing; see p. 22), that was unrelated to African *erectus*-type populations. Against this is the fact that genetic studies show that Chinese DNA is largely derived from modern humans of African origin.

Presently, the Out of Africa hypotheses still holds sway: modern humans are all Africans. New research usefully directs attention to possible weaknesses in the arguments. It may be that the competing arguments are not entirely mutually exclusive. Genetic studies are one avenue of research that will shed new light on the key questions in the future. **AS**

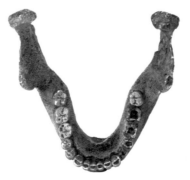

200–100,000 Ya	100–50,000 Ya	c. 50,000 Ya	1891	2003	2010
In Africa, the appearance of anatomically modern humans. *H. sapiens sapiens*, as distinct from archaic humans.	Out of Africa II: *H. sapiens* groups who had evolved in Africa spread out and replace populations elsewhere.	Two of the three fossil remnants of the Denisovans, in Siberia, date to this time, though a third may be considerably older.	An early *H. erectus* find in Java, popularly called Java Man, is initially named *Pithecanthropus erectus*.	A skeleton of an unusually small female at Liang Bua in Indonesia is found and said to represent a new species, *H. floresiensis* (see p. 24).	The groundbreaking find of the remains of the genetically distinct Denisovans in Siberia is announced to the world.

Zhoukoudian PLEISTOCENE EPOCH

Archaeologists exploring relics in Zhoukoudian in 2011. Ashes, charred seeds, and burned bones and rocks were found at the Peking Man cave in 1929, leading to the assumption that Peking Man knew how to use fire. In 2015, excavations uncovered a fireplace, with ashy soil, burned rocks and bones, which proved the control of fire.

One of the most important excavation projects in China since the first surveys in 1918 and 1921 is the Pleistocene site of Zhoukoudian in the Fangshan District, 26 miles (42 km.) southwest of Beijing (also known as Peking). Adequate water supplies and natural limestone caves in this area provided an optimal survival environment for early humans. It yielded the largest known collection of fossils of Peking Man, who lived in the Middle Pleistocene (700,000 to 200,000 years ago).

The hominid remains were found by Swedish geologist and archaeologist Gunnar Anderson (1874–1960) within a series of scree- and loess-filled clefts in a cliff of sedimentary rocks (limestone). In 1921, he became intrigued by the so-called dragon bones that local people found in the clefts, and discovered some quartz pieces that could have been used as early cutting tools. This discovery lent credence to his theory that the bones were human fossils. In 1927, Canadian anthropologist Davidson Black (1884–1934) retrieved a hominin molar from the site, the first of this kind in the Asian world. Black studied the upper molar found in 1921 and concluded that it belonged to a human species, *Homo erectus pekinensis*. U.S. geologist Amadeus William Grabau (1870–1946) gave it the moniker Peking Man.

From 1927, more scientists became involved in the project and a cooperation of various institutions was established. Chinese geologist Pei Wenzhong (1904–82) joined the excavation and made the most important discovery of all in 1929. In a branching cave, Pei found the first and almost complete skull cap of Peking Man in the red sandy clay. This was the final proof that convinced researchers that Peking Man really existed. **MP**

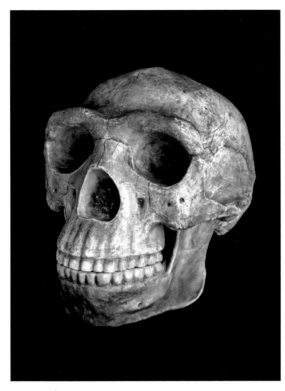

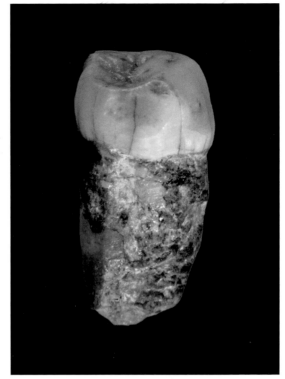

SKULL

Peking Man's skull was flat in profile with a small forehead. He had a keel along the top of the head to attach jaw muscles; thick skull bones; heavy brow ridges; and a large, chinless jaw. He had a cranial capacity averaging 61 cubic inches (1,000 cu. cm.); some skulls reach 79 cubic inches (1,300 cu. cm.)—nearly the size of a modern human's.

TEETH

Peking Man was among the best-documented extinct hominids before the loss of almost all the material during World War II. From the original excavations, only some teeth have survived in the paleontological collections of Uppsala University, Sweden. They represent the first four specimens of Peking Man ever collected.

DRAGON BONE HILL

Since the systematic excavation of the Peking Man site in 1927, more than twenty localities have been found. The most important is the Peking Man cave—the place where Peking Man first settled—in Dragon Bone Hill. The site was originally a natural limestone cave, although the roof had collapsed, spreading a layer of breccia and rubble across the top of the deposits. Excavations from 1927 to 1937 yielded traces of human habitation and identified 200 human fossils. More than 10,000 stone tools and animal fossils from 200 different species also came to light.

The upper cave is situated in the upper part of Dragon Bone Hill. It was discovered in 1930, and excavated three years later. The cave was divided into an upper level, serving as living quarters, and a lower level used for burials. Three well-preserved skulls and a skullcap were found, together with pelvic bones and femurs. Anthropologists have attributed these finds to a late *H. sapiens*.

Liang Bua 190,000 – 50,000 BCE

The discovery of *H. floresiensis* at Liang Bua and evidence of much earlier occupation at Mata Menge is surprising, because Flores was never connected to mainland Southeast Asia. Even at times of lower sea level, the water crossing was at least 15 miles (24 km.). How hominins managed to achieve this feat is unknown.

Liang Bua is a limestone cave on the island of Flores in Indonesia. In 2003, the discovery of a nearly complete skeleton of an unusually small adult female caused controversy. The bones were about 18,000 years old but were claimed to represent a new species, *Homo floresiensis*, nicknamed "hobbits." *H. floresiensis* stood 3 feet 6 inches (1.06 m.) tall and had a brain about a third the size of a modern human's. The remains were associated with stone artifacts and faunal remains, including *Stegodon*, the pygmy elephant. Bones and teeth from up to twelve other individuals have been found, and the first analyses suggested that *H. floresiensis* had survived at Liang Bua until 10,000 BCE.

The recent date for the bones was problematic because it implied that the small-bodied and small-brained hominins survived on Flores long after the spread of modern humans out of Africa. Consequently, several researchers argued that the bones were from a diseased individual. However, continuing excavations and new dating methods have resulted in a better understanding of the stratigraphy and chronology of the Liang Bua cave. The deposits associated with *H. floresiensis* remains actually date to between 190,000 and 50,000 BCE. Direct dating of three arm bones using the uranium–thorium method gave results between 87,000 and 66,000 years old, confirming the older date for the hobbits and that they may have died out before modern humans arrived on Flores.

In 2014, excavations at Mata Menge in central Flores uncovered a partial hominin jaw and several teeth. At 700,000 years old, these fossils are much older than the Liang Bua specimens but are also small. The excavators suggest the Mata Menge remains may come from a population ancestral to *H. floresiensis*. **CB**

STONE TOOLS

The stone artifacts found with
H. floresiensis remains include
simple flakes and cores made
on cobbles of volcanic tuff
brought from the riverbed a
few hundred yards from the
cave. The earth was washed
and sieved to extract even tiny
fragments of stone. Deliberately
shaped tools are rare, but
include perforators. Use-wear
analysis shows that the flakes
were used for working wood
and other plant materials. The
artifacts are broadly similar to
the much older artifacts from
Mata Menge.

INSULAR DWARFISM

One possible explanation for
the small size of *H. floresiensis*
is insular dwarfism—reduction
in size of larger animals as a
result of selective pressures
on a population whose range
is highly restricted, as on an
island. This phenomenon is
well known and has occurred
many times throughout
evolutionary history. This
selection can affect sensory
organs such as the brain,
which may explain the
small endocranial volume
of *H. floresiensis*. One of the
best-known examples of
insular dwarfism is the pygmy
elephant, also found on Flores.

A CONTROVERSIAL SPECIES

The unexpected and startling discovery of *H. floresiensis*
sparked immediate controversy and skepticism. The
unusual anatomical features of the remains and their
young age did not fit into any existing interpretations
of either human evolution or archaeological evidence
from mainland Southeast Asia.

Some anthropologists suggested that the so-called
hobbits did not represent a new species at all, but could
be explained as modern humans who were diseased or
had congenital abnormalities. A range of conditions have
been proposed, including microcephaly, various forms
of dwarfism, Down's syndrome, and hypothyroidism.
Proponents of the hypothesis that the bones represent
a new species point to analyses of anatomical features,
comparing them with other early hominins. The

configuration of the shoulder girdle, for example, is
similar to that of *H. ergaster* (see p. 20), while the foot
bones show a mixture of modern and primitive traits.

The revised dating of Liang Bua suggests that
H. floresiensis is indeed a new species. How this new
species fits into the human evolutionary tree is less
clear. One possibility is that the small hominins on
Flores may be descendants of *H. erectus*, with insular
dwarfism explaining their small size. However,
comprehensive comparison of *H. floresiensis* with
fossil remains of Asian *H. erectus* and African hominins
suggests that they are most closely related to older
African *H. habilis*. This raises the possibility that the
first migration out of Africa may have involved more
than one species.

FIRST EUROPEANS

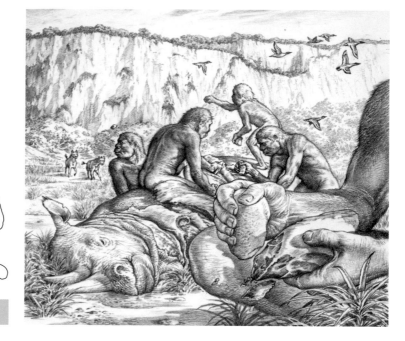

1 This artwork depicting *H. heidelbergensis* behavior is based on fossil evidence discovered in 1994 at a quarry in Boxgrove, West Sussex, United Kingdom. The Boxgrove remains (dubbed Boxgrove Man) date to 500,000 years ago and consist of a tibia and incisors.

2 A large Acheulian pointed hand ax found at Furze Platt in Berkshire, United Kingdom, in 1919. The hand ax is about 400,000 years old and is carefully worked on both sides. It is over 1 foot (30 cm.) long and weighs over 6 pounds (2.8 kg.).

3 A skull of an elderly adult from Dmanisi, Georgia. About 1.8 million years old, the Dmanisi humans are the most primitive found outside Africa. At Dmanisi they were active around a lake edge, using crudely worked Oldowan-style stone tools to butcher carcasses of animals.

Humans were present at the edge of Europe about 1.8 million years ago, where *Homo georgicus*, a species with similarities to earliest African *Homo*, had adapted to a forested Mediterranean-like environment at Dmanisi, Georgia. Crania of at least four individuals are well preserved (see image 3), and microwear traces on teeth show that they retained the mixed diet rich in fruit and nuts of their African cousins, although cutmarks on the bones of large mammals show that they were scavenging meat.

A more advanced human first reached southern Europe about 1.4 million years ago, probably from Africa. At least two human species occupied Europe from this time, before one of them evolved into the Neanderthals about 1 million years later. *H. antecessor* is recognized only from deposits approaching 800,000 years old at Atapuerca, Spain (see p. 28). Fossils of the younger species *H. heidelbergensis* are known widely, from the United Kingdom to Greece. These fossils may represent stages of an evolutionary line from *H. antecessor* through *H. heidelbergensis* to *H. neanderthalensis*. Some, such as a 0.35-million-year-old skullcap from Ceprano, Italy, display primitive traits similar to African and Asian *H. erectus*, and it seems possible that this confusing picture indicates that Europe saw dispersals of several archaic human species—when climate allowed—during the Lower and Middle Pleistocene.

KEY EVENTS

1.8 Mya	1.4 Mya	1 Mya	1 Mya	900,000 Ya	800,000 Ya
Primitive humans, *H. georgicus*, are present at the gates of Europe, at Dmanisi, Georgia.	Earliest humans (probably *H. antecessor*) are present in southern Europe.	Sporadic appearances of the Acheulian culture (defined by hand axes) occur in southern Iberia.	Humans obtain bison by hunting at Untermassfeld, Germany.	Humans briefly disperse as far north as the United Kingdom, where footprints and stone tools have been discovered at Happisburgh, Norfolk.	Climate change, already unstable, is more pronounced as glacial/interglacial cycles appear at the Lower to Middle Pleistocene boundary.

Pleistocene climate was unstable, and the earliest humans entered Europe during windows of opportunity when conditions were relatively mild, and probably followed the establishment of forested Mediterranean-like environments, becoming locally extinct as conditions declined once more. In open grasslands plant foods were rare, but large herbivores were abundant. Meat and fat were crucial to survival in high latitudes, with their short growing seasons and cold winters; unlike plants, herbivores were available year-round, and humans became increasingly reliant upon them in Europe. They had to compete with powerful predators, such as giant hyenas, for prey. It is possible that scavenging the leftovers from these carnivores' kills originally helped human survival, but early archaeological sites show that hunting was at least already supplementing scavenging as their survival strategy. Cannibalism seems to have been a recurrent practice by *H. antecessor*, possibly as a result of attacks between different groups as they competed for resources.

Stone tools and cutmarked animal bones show that humans were present as far north as the area around Burgos in northern Spain by 1.2 million years ago. They used small flakes of coarse stones as tools, some of which were shaped into cutting edges to butcher meat and notched to work wood. Similar tools were used at Dmanisi, and before 1 million years ago to butcher carcasses of bison on a river floodplain at Untermassfeld in Thuringia, Germany.

The large, solitary carnivores became extinct about 800,000 years ago, from which time competition lessened and increasingly abundant herbivores such as bison may have made hunting more viable for humans. A new immigrant, *H. heidelbergensis*, was more widespread and abundant in the landscape from this time. Between 1 million and 600,000 years ago, evidence shows that *H. heidelbergensis* had made innovations that further improved its survival in Europe. The hand ax—a large, teardrop or almond-shaped cutting tool characteristic of the Acheulian culture (see image 2)—probably appeared in the Levant or Africa by 1.5 million years ago, and became commonplace in Europe about 650,000 years ago, such as at Notarchirico, Italy. These earliest hand axes and their heavy-duty chopping counterparts—cleavers—were relatively simple.

After 600,000 BCE, the Acheulian spread north of the Pyrenees, and by 500,000 years ago it was widespread from sites such as Boxgrove in the United Kingdom (see image 1) to Germany and farther east. It is tempting to think of a more successful, larger-brained human with improved hunting prowess and better toolkits. Sources of high-quality flint were preferred for shaping relatively small and finely made hand axes, and evidence of fire—for warmth, protection, and cooking—if not abundant, appears on several archaeological sites. At Beeches Pit in Suffolk, England, and Schöningen, Germany, controlled use of fire is evident 400,000 years ago. *H. heidelbergensis* seems to have been an efficient hunter of even the largest animals such as elephants in southern Europe and rhinos in the north. **PBP**

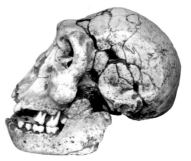

600,000 Ya	500,000 Ya	400,000 Ya	400,000 Ya	380,000 Ya	300,000 Ya
The Acheulian spreads widely north of the Alps as *H. heidelbergensis* adapts to northern latitudes.	At Boxgrove in West Sussex, United Kingdom, *H. heidelbergensis* hunts a variety of large animals, including rhino and horse, on a floodplain.	Remains of over twenty *H. heidelbergensis* adults accumulate in the Sima de los Huesos (Pit of the Bones) at Atapuerca, Spain.	Evidence of controlled use of fire is present at an open-air camp at Beeches Pit, Suffolk, United Kingdom.	*H. heidelbergensis* is obtaining meat from elephants at Aridos, Spain, and elsewhere.	Humans hunt at least twenty horses with wooden javelins around a lake edge at Schöningen, Germany.

Atapuerca PLEISTOCENE EPOCH

The Galeria cave at Atapuerca seems to have been a natural trap into which animals such as horse, bison, and deer fell from above. Here, they were not only scavenged by predators but also butchered by hominins up to 500,000 years ago, who left behind only the ribs and vertebrae along with their hand axes.

One of the foremost collections of archaeological sites, the Sierra de Atapuerca in northern Spain has been under excavation for almost forty years, yet the work will continue for centuries due to the wealth of its sites. A railroad trench was cut into the sierra long ago, and it exposed a series of limestone caves. Already they have proved to be the largest known repository of fossil humans from the Middle Pleistocene.

The Gran Dolina cave has a stratigraphy of 59 feet (18 m.), spanning a period from more than 1 million to 120,000 years ago. Here, five primitive stone artifacts were found in a layer initially dated to at least 700,000 years ago, but they were dismissed by scholars who refused to believe that humans were in Europe 500,000 years ago. Only human bones constitute undeniable proof of human presence, and in 1994 teeth and bone fragments from at least four individuals were found associated with a hundred stone tools, including hammerstones, flakes and cores made from quartzite river pebbles and flints. Paleomagnetism dated this layer (TD6) to between 800,000 and 1 million years ago. These hominin remains are archaic, with primitive dental traits reminiscent of African australopithecines, and they have been dubbed *Homo antecessor*. Some even bear cutmarks, which suggest early cannibalism. Stone tools subsequently recovered from the lower TD4 layer, associated with animal bones, are thought to be about 1 million years old.

In 2016, an immense new site, the Cueva Fantasma, was opened up, and it has already yielded a fragment of human cranium dating to at least 200,000 years ago. It is expected that the site will prove to contain a wealth of Neanderthal occupation, while its stratigraphy will probably extend downward as far as that of the Gran Dolina. **PGB**

SIMA DE LOS HUESOS

The Sima de los Huesos (Pit of the Bones) has proved to contain the remains of at least twenty-eight individuals, dating to about 430,000 years ago and assigned to *H. heidelbergensis*. This pit has yielded more than 6,700 bones, approximately 90 percent of all pre-Neanderthal remains in Europe. They include well-preserved skulls, with large brow ridges, a complete pelvis (nicknamed Elvis), and even foot and hand bones, as well as the tiny bones of the inner ear.

EXCALIBUR

Among the bones found in the Pit of the Bones was a remarkable unused, finely flaked quartzite hand ax, dubbed Excalibur, which may, therefore, be one of the world's earliest grave goods. Many theories have been put forward to explain the presence of so many bodies in the Pit of the Bones. They were not dragged here by carnivores and they seem to be in position, but this is not a habitation site, so it is thought that this was an early method of disposing of the dead over several generations.

HOMO HEIDELBERGENSIS

Although it is not yet clear where or how the few fragments of *H. antecessor* fit into the human family tree, the abundant remains of *H. heidelbergensis* from the Pit of the Bones—more than 6,700 bones so far—have revealed a great deal about these pre-Neanderthals. No fewer than seventeen skulls have been reassembled from fragments, and they are the oldest known fossils to show clear Neanderthal features in the skull, although DNA analysis of samples from two thigh bones had some genetic differences from Neanderthals. They are early members of that lineage, but their specific name is still undetermined.

The Pit of the Bones is the first site where sufficient skeletal material has been found to study a population rather than individuals. They appear to have been more robust than modern humans, with males between 5 feet 7 inches (1.7 m.) and more than 6 feet (180 cm.) tall, and weighing an average of 140 pounds (63.5 kg.).

The teeth are very worn from chewing plants, but there are no cavities and overall the bones show very little sign of illness or trauma. Right-handedness seems to have dominated. Males and females are equally represented, with size differences similar to those of today, and most are adolescents and young adults aged between thirteen and twenty-two. Older people were probably disposed of elsewhere.

The deformed skull of a twelve-year-old girl suggests that the people cared for her, while the remains of an elderly man with severe back problems, who could not have fended for himself, likewise point to protection by the community. Conversely, one skull may have undergone two episodes of blunt force trauma, with fatal wounds perhaps inflicted by a hand ax or wooden spear. If so, this would be the earliest known example of lethal interpersonal violence.

NEANDERTHALS

1 First introduced by Neanderthals, Levallois points were a lethal improvement in the technology of killing. Hafted to spear shafts, these razor-sharp tips opened a lethal wound in the prey.

2 A brain as large as that of a human today sits behind the jutting face of a Neanderthal. The pigment markings and feathers are based on recovered crayons of red ocher and manganese, and cutmarked wing bones of raptors.

3 This reconstruction of a pit at the site of La Chapelle, France, is where the hypothesis of a Neanderthal burial was raised for the first time. However, the rarity of graves suggests that this was not common for Neanderthals.

The first truly indigenous Europeans, the Neanderthals, evolved from *Homo heidelbergensis* as a biological response to the cold, unstable climates of northern latitudes. They were not the only mammal to have to adapt to northern conditions—other large animals such as mammoths and rhinos also evolved physiological ways of coping with cold, dry winters and the abundance of meat in open grasslands. European fossils of *H. heidelbergensis* display traits characteristic of Neanderthals as early as 400,000 years ago, such as at Atapuerca's Sima de los Huesos (Pit of the Bones; see p. 28) in Spain, and the classic Neanderthal form had appeared by 250,000 years ago. They were a widespread species: from their European heartland they spread as far as southwestern Siberia, were abundant in the Middle East, and were sporadically found as far east as Uzbekistan.

The sequencing of the Neanderthal genome has clarified their biological relationship with humans of today. More than 400,000 years separate the two species, reflecting their evolution in northern latitudes as a response to cold, highly seasonal environments, parallel to human evolution farther south. They may be ancestral to some modern humans; a very small degree of interbreeding with *H. sapiens* is evident, although the two species probably hardly ever met. Their low genetic diversity reveals a picture of low population numbers, small groups, and considerable isolation, and archaeology reveals regional pockets in which they were relatively common, such as southwest France and the Middle East.

KEY EVENTS

400,000 Ya	300,000 Ya	250,000 Ya	125,000 Ya	80,000 Ya	75,000 Ya
Anatomical traits characteristic of Neanderthals appear in *H. heidelbergensis*, as seen in fossils at Atapuerca's Sima de los Huesos.	The flake-tool-based Middle Palaeolithic appears, for example at Orgnac 3, Aven d'Orgnac, France. This includes stone spear points.	Neanderthals are capable of targeting single species in highly organized hunting and scavenging episodes, as at La Cotte de St. Brélade, Jersey.	Neanderthals hunt juvenile rhinos at a warm spring at Taubach, Germany.	Neanderthals are particularly abundant in the Middle East, for example in Israel and Syria.	Several Neanderthals are deliberately buried under the rock shelter of La Ferrassie, France.

Classic Neanderthals had evolved by 250,000 years ago. They had a pronounced brow ridge, jutting face, and thick teeth, and they were ruggedly built and barrel-chested, with arms and legs that were short relative to their bodies. This mix of traits indicates the adaptation of an archaic human body to the cold, dry environments of northern climes, although a degree of regional diversity reveals biological flexibility. They have often been characterized as highly predatory carnivores. Isotopic measurements of their bone and teeth reveal that 80 to 90 percent of their dietary protein was obtained from meat, and numerous archaeological sites show that they were efficient hunters of large herd animals, such as horse, bison, and reindeer, and the more solitary animals like rhinos and deer. Bones from campsites show that they filleted meat and obtained marrow by smashing bones open. At La Cotte de St. Brélade, Jersey, they were butchering mammoth and rhino as early as 250,000 years ago.

Their diet did not just consist of large animals, but included small resources such as tortoise, birds, rabbits, and hares, and river fish such as trout and salmon. Groups near the Mediterranean coast gathered shellfish and beached seals and dolphins. Stone-tool cutmarks on bones show that large animals were skinned for pelts and small animals for fur. While their relatively simple tools were probably not capable of fine tailoring, tannins preserved on a stone tool at the 240,000 year-old site of Neumark Nord in Germany show that skin or fur was made waterproof by this treatment. Pollen and plant remains and microscopic starches preserved on the surfaces of teeth show that berries, nuts, and wild grasses were gathered when in season.

Neanderthals used bones and stones such as flint to create a flexible set of tools. By 300,000 years ago they were using the Levallois technique (see image 1) to control the size and shape of flakes detached from cores, and a variety of edge shapes to create cutting, whittling, and piercing tools. The appearance of the stone point—which was hafted to wooden shafts with mastics of birch tar and bitumen—marks an important development in killing technology.

Neanderthal brains were as large as those of humans of today, but it is difficult to understand how they were using them and how similar to modern humans they were mentally. Excavations at Fumane cave in northern Italy have shown that they often used red (ocher) and black (manganese) pigments and the feathers of raptors such as black eagles and crows, as well as eagle claws and marine shells for display (see image 2). This reveals that they were closer in their behaviors and perhaps intelligence to H. sapiens, and could be evidence of symbolism (see p. 32). Some Neanderthals buried their dead in simple graves (see image 3). Cannibalism occurred occasionally too, probably for survival in harsh periods, rather than anything ritual. It is possible that Neanderthals created art; simple engraved lines preserved on bedrock in Gorham's Cave, Gibraltar, cannot be explained in any functional way, suggesting that this was as much a part of their behavior as pigments and feathers. **PBP**

50,000 Ya	50,000 Ya	43,000 Ya	41,000 Ya	40,000 Ya	1856
A Neanderthal at Umm-el-Tlel, Syria, hunts a wild ass with a spear and leaves a fragment of a flint spear point embedded in the neck.	Ocher stains on a marine shell at the Aviones and Antón caves, Spain, and indicates the transport and use of red pigments.	The bodies of eight Neanderthals come to rest in El Sidrón cave, Spain. They are skinned or disarticulated, and one of them has had its brain consumed.	At least two Neanderthals are buried at the Feldhofer cave in Germany's Neander Valley.	Neanderthals have become extinct everywhere, as later revealed at the Grotte du Renne (Reindeer Cave), Burgundy, France (see p. 34).	Two Neanderthals are excavated in the Feldhofer cave, Neander Valley. They give their name to the species H. neanderthalensis.

Intelligent Neanderthals MIDDLE PALEOLITHIC

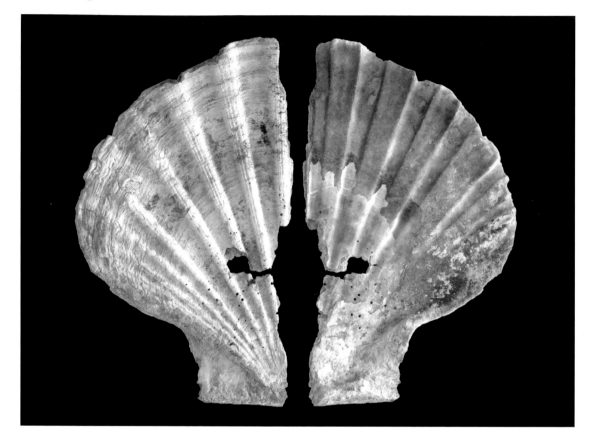

In southeast Spain, Aviones cave and Antón rock shelter have yielded seashells used as necklaces and paint cups dating between 50,000 and 37,000 years ago. Antón cave has a pierced scallop painted with orange pigment made of yellow goethite and red hematite from 3 miles (5 km.) away. Aviones has two pierced cockleshells painted with red hematite.

For decades it was assumed that Neanderthals had little intelligence, with no culture, no art, no aesthetic sense. But evidence has accumulated to show that Neanderthals did produce art, or at least decoration, in a variety of media. The earliest piece of evidence was a limestone block, found above a child burial in the rock shelter of La Ferrassie in Dordogne, France, which was decorated with a series of small carved cup marks, mostly in pairs, that were placed apparently at random. More recently, various incised patterns on smaller stones have been found, such as a series of nested arcs on a flint cortex from Quneitra, Israel, dating to about 54,000 years ago. There are also numerous incised bones from the period, such as from Prolom II cave in Crimea. The Bulgarian cave of Bacho Kiro has a bone fragment from about 37,000 years ago that has a zigzag motif engraved on it.

The use of red ocher increased markedly in the Neanderthal period. At the Dutch site of Maastricht-Belvédère, concentrations of a hematite-rich liquid have been found in a layer dating between 250,000 and 200,000 years ago; the ocher must have been imported from dozens of miles away. During the period from about 200,000 to 30,000 BCE, such pigments become abundant in occupation deposits and burials, which occurred for the first time. Pigments have been found in seventy Neanderthal sites. The richest collection comes from the French cave of Le Pech de l'Azé I, dating to between 60,000 and 50,000 years ago; it comprises more than 500 pieces of manganese dioxide (black/blue) and iron oxide (red), scores of which were rounded into a crayon shape, as if they had been used on a soft surface, perhaps human or animal skin. The French caves at Arcy-sur-Cure have yielded 41 pounds (18.5 kg.) of ocher, many of the pieces bearing signs of wear. Some were in a hearth, suggesting Neanderthals were heating them to change their colors. **PGB**

CAVE ART

Recent dating of calcite on top of motifs in some north Spanish caves suggests that Neanderthals may have produced some simple cave art, such as red dots or hand stencils. In Gorham's Cave, Gibraltar, a deeply incised abstract motif has been found on bedrock, and may date to more than 39,000 years ago. It was said to be covered by an undisturbed archaeological layer containing Neanderthal artifacts. Specialists who have studied the marks have estimated that the engraving would have required 200 to 300 strokes with a stone cutting tool.

MASK OF LA ROCHE-COTARD

La Roche-Cotard is a Neanderthal site located in the Loire Valley, France. The so-called mask of La Roche-Cotard is a block of retouched flint from the site, with a natural conduit into which a piece of reindeer bone was carefully inserted and wedged into place with small stones, thus forming what look like bone eyes in a stone face. Dating of the layer suggests an age of more than 75,000 years ago. The cave that yielded the mask has finger markings, dots and ocher marks on the walls that can safely be attributed to Neanderthals.

FEATHERS AND BONES FOR DECORATION

Bird-bone evidence suggests that Neanderthals also used feathers for decoration. Several caves in Gibraltar contain a large number of wing bones with cutmarks on them. There is no meat on the wings, so the Neanderthals must have been doing this to detach the large flight feathers, and there is even an apparent preference for raptor and corvid species with dark or black plumage. Moreover, the Croatian site of Krapina has yielded eight white-tailed eagle talons, which appear to have been worn as jewelry. In addition, a series of perforated objects—mostly animal bones and teeth—are known from sites around Europe.

The richest collection comes from the Grotte du Renne at Arcy-sur-Cure in Burgundy, France. It includes wolf and fox canines made into pendants by incising a groove around the top, at least one sawn reindeer incisor, a bone fragment with a wide carved hole, a sea fossil with a hole bored through its center, and a fossil shell with a groove cut around the top. These can all be attributed to Neanderthal craftsmanship, as they come from a layer of the cave from c. 34,000 BCE, containing a Neanderthal temporal bone. They were carved and pierced using Neanderthal techniques, and were not stolen, traded, or copied from the work of newly arrived modern humans. Other such objects have been found in several contemporaneous sites. Their discovery led to a change in archaeological thinking, evident in the fact that recent likenesses of Neanderthals made for museum displays tend to bear body paint.

Grotte du Renne UPPER PALEOLITHIC

The entrance to the Grotte du Renne, which contains evidence of late Neanderthal and early modern human occupation. Its rich Level X contains a Châtelperronian occupation, from which evidence of bone- and tooth-working is apparent, and illustrates what Neanderthals were capable of doing.

The Grotte du Renne, one of several at Arcy-sur-Cure in Burgundy, France, has been central to the understanding of Neanderthal extinction. Deposits accumulated between 50,000 and 35,000 years ago contain evidence relating to late Neanderthal and early modern human (*Homo sapiens*) activity. Debate has focused on its rich Châtelperronian Level X. Stone tools in this level fit technologically with the Middle Paleolithic tools lower in the sequence, yet display a degree of standardization that foreshadows the overlying Upper Paleolithic. Because of this, the Châtelperronian here and elsewhere in France, and other contemporary groupings such as Italy's Uluzzian, are often referred to as transitional in that they represent a technological advance over more typical Middle Paleolithic toolkits. In addition, the Grotte du Renne contains pendants made of animal teeth, finely made bone points, and evidence of the manufacture of disks from flat bones, all of which are far more characteristic of the succeeding Upper Paleolithic. Human teeth and fragmentary cranial bones found in Level X are clearly Neanderthal and, as with other "transitional assemblages," show that Neanderthals were the manufacturers and may be the key to understanding Neanderthal extinction.

Neanderthals had become extinct everywhere by 40,000 years ago. The reasons for this are unclear. Climatic severity and instability are possible factors and drove other animals to extinction, but Neanderthals had survived these before during their long existence. The small size of their populations may have rendered them particularly susceptible to climate change or changes in the availability of the prey that they were dependent upon for survival. **PBP**

FOCAL POINTS

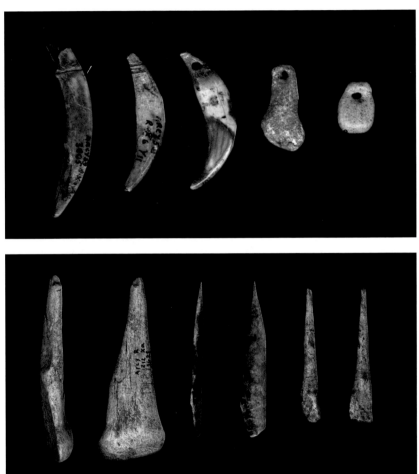

PENDANTS

These pendants—made of fox canines and carved bone, scored and pierced for suspension—are from the Châtelperronian levels of the Grotte du Renne. Used for personal display, examples of Neanderthal pendants are remarkably rare. The Grotte du Renne was excavated between 1948 and 1966, and half a century later the collection from here remains the most important known. Similar objects appear much earlier among African and Middle Eastern *H. sapiens* groups.

TOOLS

These pointed tools made from animal bones were found in the Châtelperronian levels at the Grotte du Renne. The awls were probably used for working soft materials such as skins. They are very rare from earlier, Middle Paleolithic sites, and their presence in the Châtelperronian suggests that in the last few thousand years of their existence, the Neanderthals were improving on ways of working hides and manufacturing clothing, adding to the complex picture of Neanderthals.

RADIOCARBON DATING AND NEANDERTHAL EXTINCTION

Establishing the pattern of Neanderthal extinction depends mainly on radiocarbon dating, which is the most precise of all dating methods applicable to this time range. Radiocarbon dating measures the amount of radioactive carbon left in organic samples such as bones and charcoal, and it has been applied widely in Paleolithic archaeology. Dating of Neanderthal fossils and animal bones from European Middle Paleolithic and transitional sites shows that Neanderthals had begun to disappear from some regions of Europe by 60,000 years ago. The process of extinction occurred from then on, varying from region to region, until they existed only on the edges of their original geographical range in isolated pockets—such as in the south of Iberia or the northern Balkans—for another 20,000 years.

Contrasting radiocarbon dates from Early Upper Paleolithic sites thought to be indicative of the earliest members of *Homo sapiens* in Europe generally do not overlap with those of the last Neanderthals. This suggests that real contemporaneity and contact between Neanderthals and *H. sapiens* was remarkably rare, and perhaps did not occur outside central Asia. In most regions, Neanderthals seem to have become extinct before the arrival of modern humans, and it seems very unlikely that their extinction was due to competition or violence at the hands of our own species. Genetics supports this view; it reveals only very small degrees of interbreeding, with the result that modern humans possess around 2 percent of Neanderthal genes—one would expect more if contact and interaction were more common. There is also no convincing evidence in the form of toolkits, fossils, or other behaviors that the two species met and exchanged things between them.

HOMO SAPIENS: BECOMING MODERN

1 The presence of ocher-working as early as 100,000 years ago at Blombos cave, South Africa, and from 80,000 years ago elsewhere indicates it was widespread.

2 The Laetoli Hominid (LH) 18 cranium from Ngaloba, Tanzania, displays traits characteristic of *H. sapiens*, including a large brain and reduced brow ridges.

Archaeological, skeletal, and genetic evidence points to the primacy of Africa in the origins of *Homo sapiens*, an evolutionary process that culminated c. 200,000 years ago. As with the Neanderthals in northern latitudes, *H. sapiens* evolved gradually from the Middle Pleistocene species *H. heidelbergensis* (in Africa sometimes known as *H. helmei*). Fossils from about 250,000 years ago begin to show anatomically modern human traits, although they retain characteristics of their Middle Pleistocene predecessors. Two crania from Omo, Ethiopia, dating to close to 200,000 years ago bear traits that are characteristic of *H. sapiens*, such as a chin, small brow ridges and braincases, and faces that are essentially modern in size and shape. By 160,000 to 100,000 years ago, human fossils that are anatomically modern are found across the continent, from Jebel Irhoud in Morocco to Ngaloba in Tanzania (see image 3) and Klasies River Mouth cave in South Africa, although a degree of regional difference can be seen among these, which may represent distinct subspecies. Adult and juvenile crania from the campsite of Herto in Ethiopia have been classed as *H. sapiens idaltu*, and were possibly defleshed in an early episode of ritual activity.

As a species, modern humans are alone with the Neanderthals in having brains that are huge relative to body size; this is metabolically costly and must reflect the importance of cognitive evolution and may be closely related to the rise of language and symbolic activity. Modern humans' long-limbed and tall body proportions reflect their subtropical evolution, stemming from a

KEY EVENTS

300,000 Ya	250,000 Ya	200,000 Ya	160,000 Ya	130,000 Ya	100,000 Ya
Backing (blunting) of tools, probably for hafting, is present in the Middle Stone Age Lupemban culture of south-central Africa.	African fossils assigned to *H. heidelbergensis* (or *H. helmei*) dated to this time display traits later characteristic of *H. sapiens*.	*H. sapiens* characteristics are visible, as evidenced later on two crania from Omo, Ethiopia.	Human cranial remains from Herto, Ethiopia, dating to this period belong to *H. sapiens*. They display stone-tool cutmarks indicative of defleshing.	Diets in South Africa are broad-spectrum and have a major marine component, including fish, mammals such as Cape fur seals, and shellfish.	At Blombos cave on South Africa's Cape coast, *H. sapiens* are producing pigment by grinding red ocher using marine shells and stone grinders.

biological adaptation to keeping cool by convecting heat off the surface of the skin; and relatively gracile (thin) limb bones show that tools were beginning to take some of the strain off the body in daily tasks. In this sense, modern humans' parallel evolution to that of the Neanderthals contrasts with the latter's rugged, short-limbed bodies.

African *H. sapiens* fossils are associated with the African Middle Stone Age (MSA), elements of which are present in South Africa as early as 500,000 years ago. Hafting may have been practiced by 300,000 years ago; and MSA stoneworking had spread to east Africa by 300,000 years ago, and over the entire continent by at least 100,000 years ago. MSA sites show evidence of greater skills of stone tool manufacture; regional stylistic differences in tools such as spear points that may reflect cultural preferences; and the transport over long distances of high-quality stones that were particularly suited to shaping, perhaps through exchange. Traces of plant gums, fat, and ocher on stone tools from 70,000-year-old deposits at Sibudu cave in South Africa show that these were securely hafted. Microliths—small, shaped weapon tips—appeared as early as 65,000 years ago and represent an innovation in hafted weapon technology, maximizing the economy of good raw materials and minimizing the effort of repair when elements of weapons broke.

MSA humans regularly hunted large animals, such as zebra, wildebeest, eland, and smaller antelopes, and collected or trapped small animals, including tortoises and reptiles. Marine resources were particularly important on the southern coast, where fish, shellfish such as mussels and limpets, and occasional marine mammals were highly nutritious and provided omega-3 oils that may have been important to the evolution of modern humans' large brains. River fish were exploited inland. At Katanda in the Democratic Republic of the Congo, large catfish were speared with bone-tipped weapons as early as 90,000 years ago. Grinding stones and plant remains show that modern humans' African ancestors practiced a broad-spectrum diet from the early MSA onward.

An explosion in the use of colored pigments such as red ocher and other indications of jewelry and, perhaps, symbolism occurred at least 100,000 years ago. A long archaeological sequence at Blombos cave on the coast of South Africa shows the processing of ocher into pigments using pestles of marine shell and grinders of stone, and the proliferation of ocher crayons bearing engraved designs (see image 1). By 75,000 years ago, these were commonplace in the South African MSA, and about 60,000 years ago, ostrich eggshell containers were decorated with similar designs (see image 2). Shells perforated for suspension have been found as far north as Algeria and Israel by 100,000 years ago, suggesting that jewelry was part of the first modern human dispersal out of Africa by this time. Beadworking may well be one of modern humans' earliest surviving crafts. **PBP**

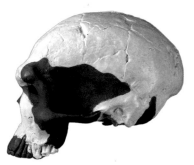

100,000 Ya	77,000 Ya	70,000 Ya	70,000 Ya	65,000 Ya	60,000 Ya
Pierced shells from South Africa to Algeria indicate that beadworking is being practiced across the continent at this time.	On Stillbay stone-tool sites, finely made stone points are transported over long distances, reflecting adaptation to dry grassland environments.	Sites of the Howieson's Poort lithic technology tradition in South Africa show evidence of composite weapon systems being used.	Hafting of stone tools takes place, as demonstrated at Sibudu cave, South Africa.	Small stone microliths appear at Mumba, Tanzania.	Fragments of ostrich eggshell containers decorated with incised lines are used at Diepkloof rock shelter, South Africa.

OUT OF AFRICA

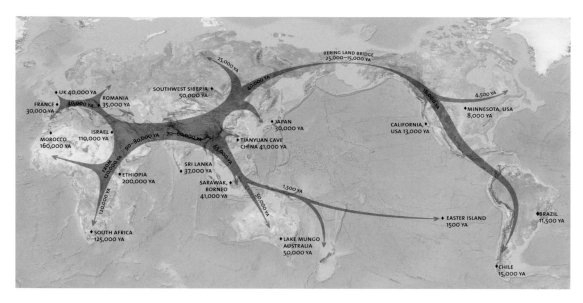

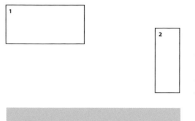

1 Human dispersals were complex, as shown by this map based on the location of sites where fossils of *H. sapiens* were found.

2 The fossilized bones of a 90,000-year-old *H. sapiens* female and child from the Qafzeh cave site in Israel.

Early explorers such as James Cook (1728–79) were surprised to find humans in every corner of the world. The global distribution of modern humans can be traced to several early dispersals of the species from Africa, beginning about 100,000 years ago. Genetic evidence shows that this great dispersal occurred in several waves, separated by thousands of years, in which small groups of *Homo sapiens* dispersed from Africa and adjoining areas. This occurred against the backdrop of unstable climate, as shifts from cold, arid periods to warm, wet periods opened and closed up habitable environments on a global scale. When opportunities arose, humans spread, exploiting plants, animals and workable stones on routes that took humans first eastward. Features that were highways in some periods—like India's Indus river or Thar desert—became barriers in others, forcing the pattern of temporary, shifting dispersals across vast scales. As a result, large areas of the Old World (Afro-Eurasia) were populated as early as 60,000 years ago. The routes followed by these early pioneers are unclear. The coast—and its diverse and nutritionally rich resources—may have formed dispersal highways for large-brained humans dependent on the fatty acids available from shellfish, although coastal sites are few, and it seems that ecologically diverse inland regions were important too.

The entire African continent was populated by *H. sapiens* about 110,000 years ago (see image 1), although this was not permanent, and populations likely fluctuated in response to unstable climates. Increased aridity across Africa at this time probably rendered much of west, east, and north Africa inhospitable,

KEY EVENTS

110,000 Ya	80,000 Ya	65,000 Ya	60,000 Ya	50,000 Ya	50,000 Ya
Earliest *H. sapiens* in the Near East, at Skhūl and Qafzeh caves. Stone tools from Arabia suggest a presence here, too.	Neanderthals replace modern humans in the Levant as climate worsens and the latter become locally extinct.	Microlithic stone tools in India, like those from Africa, suggest regional innovations in weapon technology.	A second dispersal of *H. sapiens* eastward out of Africa, as genetics and archaeology later indicate.	*H. sapiens* is present in India, China, Australia, southwest Siberia, and the Balkans.	*H. sapiens* in north and west Australia use ground-edge axes at Boodie cave on Barrow Island (see p. 42) and Carpenter's Gap in the Kimberley.

with an expanded Sahara desert driving groups in the north of the continent eastward out of Africa into temperate grasslands of the Middle East. Anatomically modern humans began to take the highway out of Africa—the Nile Valley—and were burying their dead in the caves of Israel's Mount Carmel and Lower Galilee (see image 2) between 110,000 and 90,000 years ago. Here, they used ocher, hunted gazelle, and included objects such as deer antlers and boar's tusks in graves. But this dispersal did not last. As the climate deteriorated, they became locally extinct, replaced by Neanderthals who dispersed into the region from the north. But they did not simply return to Africa; populations sharing similar toolkits to Middle Stone Age Africans had appeared in Arabia around the same time, although they also disappeared when climate worsened.

Modern humans had spread as far east as India and China by 50,000 years ago—possibly earlier, but understanding is hampered by a poor fossil record in these and surrounding countries. A 41,000-year-old skeleton from Tianyuan cave in China has several archaic features, which suggests a degree of inheritance from earlier dispersals, reinforcing the picture of regions getting populations repeatedly. By this time, humans had spread to Borneo, which in times of lowered sea levels became part of the land mass of Sundaland. A human cranium and limb bones from the Great Cave at Niah in Sarawak, Borneo, were found with worked bones and evidence of complex foraging technologies; and they are contemporary with hand stencils on rock surfaces in Indonesia, suggesting that art had become part of human behavior. Even in periods of lowest sea levels, reaching the land mass of Sahul—Australia, New Guinea, and Tasmania—would require a sea crossing of 12 to 18 miles (20–30 km.), and rudimentary sea craft. This had been achieved by 50,000 years ago, when humans were being buried in sand dunes at Lake Mungo in southeastern Australia. Crayons of red ocher and examples of rock art belonging to this period reveal a long time-span before Aboriginal culture.

The archaeology of the period 50,000 years ago changes considerably, indicating new levels of behavioral organization. The earliest evidence of modern human presence in northern latitudes appears, all with regional variants of this emerging Upper Paleolithic archaeology. They are present as far as southwest Siberia by 50,000 years ago, and in the Balkans about the same time, spreading across Europe by 42,000 years ago.

By at least 16,000 years ago humans had spread to the Americas (see p. 40), probably over the dry land mass that is now the Bering Strait, although genetics indicate a complex ancestry for modern Americans that likely reflects several subsequent dispersals. Only over the last few thousand years had humans spread to the last habitable regions—the Pacific Islands—where explorers such as Cook were to encounter their distant descendants. There is much to learn about the spread of *H. sapiens* across the world, and the picture will continue to get more complex as new sites are discovered. **PBP**

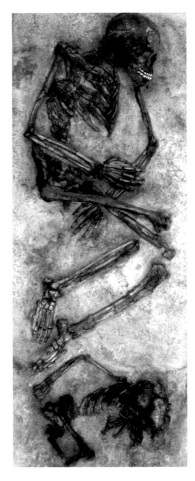

41,000 Ya	40,000 Ya	16,000 Ya	15,000 Ya	2,000 Ya	1,500 Ya
The presence of *H. sapiens* in Sundaland, as the cranium from the Great Cave at Niah in Sarawak, Borneo, later reveals.	*H. sapiens* are found as far north as northwest Europe and northern Siberia. The Upper Palaeolithic lasts 30,000 years.	Probable date for the first human dispersal into the Americas.	At Monte Verde, Chile, hut structures contain stone tools and medicinal plants, attesting to complex hunter-gatherer groups in South America.	Human presence established in Fiji and Tonga, requiring navigational skills.	First human presence in Hawaii, New Zealand, and perhaps Easter Island (see p. 378).

First Americans 20,000 BCE onward

Because of the vagaries of preservation, most evidence pertaining to the earliest Americans comprises stone artifacts such as projectile points or tools used in preparing food. Only rarely do archaeologists uncover any organic materials.

For most of the twentieth century, archaeologists thought that they had achieved consensus on the peopling of the New World and that by about 13,000 years ago ancient Native Americans, identified by the distinctive Clovis projectile point, had spread over large parts of North America. These earliest peoples had come across the Bering Strait while it was still a land mass connecting northeast Asia to northwest North America. They then migrated south in the continent's interior, down the Ice-Free Corridor, formed as the two major glacial masses retreated north into the Arctic Circle or west into the Rocky Mountains. The Clovis people were followed by the Folsom people, named after their own type of point and one similar in morphology to the Clovis. The Clovis were primarily big-game hunters of the mammoth; the Folsom hunted a now-extinct form of bison. Archaeological evidence pertained mostly to hunting practices, so less is known about other components of their diet or lifestyle.

However, in the last three decades of the twentieth century, archaeological evidence from North and South America, augmented by the field of genetics, cast doubt on almost every element of the consensus. In 1973, excavations were initiated at the Meadowcroft Rockshelter in the eastern United States. In this deeply stratified site, archaeologists found evidence of human remains that may be as early as 19,000 years ago. These dates were controversial: some archaeologists believed that the radiocarbon samples were contaminated by coal-bearing groundwater. A cluster of associated open and rock-shelter sites, the best known of which is Pedra Furada in the Piauí region of Brazil, has also raised the level of controversy. Here, stone artifacts have been found in levels that predate 20,000 years ago. The Monte Verde site near Puerto Montt in southern Chile also raised controversy when it was found in 1997. Human occupation there may be as early as 18,500 years ago. The site boasts well-preserved organic remains, such as wooden artifacts, berries, and fruits. However, even if the earliest dates for these sites are discounted, other sites indicate a well-established pre-Clovis occupation of the New World. **PD**

DEGLACIATION

Glacial geology gives archaeologists a time frame for the opening of glaciated regions in the northern half of the continent. Deglaciation would be necessary for humans migrating into the interior. Associated rises in sea level at the end of the Ice Age would also have a profound effect on the feasibility of coastal travel and habitation. This shows strata markers at the Meadowcroft Rockshelter in Washington County, Pennsylvania, which may be the oldest known site of human habitation in North America.

CLOVIS POINTS

Clovis points, which date to about 13,000 years ago, are some of the most exquisitely made stone tools on the continent—this example was discovered in North Carolina. These lanceolate points are made by the bifacial percussion flaking technique, whereby both sides of the point are thinned using the percussion and the pressure method (flakes are pushed off the point rather than being struck off with a hammer). The base of each point is fluted (a flat flake has been removed). The function of the flute is unclear.

COASTAL MIGRATION

What route the earliest Native Americans took as they spread through North and South America is debatable. As an alternative to the interior route, a coastal-migration route has been hypothesized since the 1980s. But this could not be corroborated because sea levels rose at the end of the Ice Age—perhaps up to 328 feet (100 m.) above their Ice Age maximum—and ancient coastal settlements would have been submerged. Now a coastal route to the south is looking more likely as sites like Monte Verde and other putative pre-Clovis sites along the west coast—such as those excavated on Santa Rosa Island off the coast of California—have forced archaeologists to rethink the route by which humans arrived in the New World. Archaeologists also have evidence of boat technology from sites along the coast of Japan perhaps as early as 30,000 years ago, and there is some indication of similarities in stone artifacts between northwestern North America and the east Asian coast.

Boodie Cave 50,000 – 5000 BCE

Marine resources occur throughout the Boodie Cave site from about 42,000 years ago and reflect the marine economy of the first arrivals in Australia. Layers with more shell correspond to periods when rising sea levels brought the coastline closer to the site. Animal bones, shellfish remains, stone tools, and pebbles used as cooking stones have been found.

Boodie Cave is a large limestone cave on Barrow Island off the coast of northwest Australia. More than 6 feet (2 m.) of stratified deposits document occupation at the site from about 50,000 years ago. The deposits contain thousands of stone artifacts, and excellent preservation means that animal bones and shellfish remains survive in large quantities.

Barrow Island is now more than 31 miles (50 km.) from the mainland, and seems to have been abandoned some 7,000 years ago, when it was cut off by rising sea levels at the end of the last Ice Age. Twenty thousand years ago, however, at the height of the Ice Age, the island was one of several hills and knolls in a broad coastal plain, and the sea was more than 31 miles (50 km.) west of Boodie Cave.

The dietary remains at Boodie Cave are extremely well preserved. Clearly, the inhabitants had a rich diet that included land animals such as wallaby and kangaroo, hunted in the vicinity of the cave, and marine resources brought from the more distant coastline. These included turtle, crocodile, porpoise, and sea urchin as well as shellfish. The most recent levels of the site have the greatest quantity of shellfish and represent the period immediately prior to Barrow Island being cut off from the mainland.

The excavators recorded tens of thousands of waste flakes from shaping stone tools. Two flakes from ground-stone axes were recovered from levels dated to about 15,000 years ago. Most of the artifacts at Boodie Cave were made from local silicified limestone, but small numbers were made from volcanic and metamorphic rocks that probably came from ranges now on the mainland, hundreds of miles away. Large quartzite cobbles were also brought to the site for use as cooking stones. **CB**

⊙ FOCAL POINTS

GROUND-EDGE AXES

Once believed to be a Neolithic invention, evidence of ancient ground-edge axes occurs in several sites in northern Australia, indicating technological innovations by fully modern *Homo sapiens* at the eastern end of the out-of-Africa dispersal route. The oldest of these come from Carpenter's Gap, a limestone cave and shelter complex in the Napier Range in western Australia, and are more than 40,000 years old. The Boodie Cave fragments are the oldest evidence of this technology found outside the northern third of the continent.

SHELL TOOLS

A number of shell beads have been excavated at Boodie Cave from levels dated to about 12,000 years ago. These are made from tusk (*Dentalium* sp.) shells and resemble beads from the site of Riwi Cave in the Kimberley, 310 miles (500 km.) from the ancient coastline and dated to more than 30,000 BCE. Other worked shell has also been found at Boodie Cave, including baler (*Melo* sp.) shell fragments shaped for use as scoops or spoons, indicating the resourcefulness of the site's inhabitants. Another baler shell fragment was marked with incised lines.

COLONIZING SAHUL

At times of lower sea level during the last Ice Age, Australia, New Guinea, and Tasmania were connected to form the continent known as Sahul. Modern humans reached Sahul by c. 50,000 BCE. Several archaeological sites are now reliably dated to 45,000 BCE or older. The first landfall must therefore be earlier, possibly 60,000 years ago or more. This is at the limit of radiocarbon dating. Moreover, the earliest sites must have been close to the edge of the now-drowned continental shelf.

There is no doubt that colonizing Sahul involved sea voyaging, because there was no land bridge connecting Sahul with southeast Asia even when sea levels were at their lowest. At least ten crossings—some out

of sight of land—were required, indicating that these first colonists were accomplished voyagers and their journeying was planned rather than accidental. Traces of this early marine lifestyle are unusual and Boodie Cave offers a rare glimpse into the lives of some of the first arrivals on Sahul. There is much debate regarding the nature of the watercraft used and the motivations of the first colonists.

Sites dated to 35,000 BCE or older are widely dispersed across the continent, from New Guinea to Tasmania, including the central desert core. The first Australians must have been highly adaptable to be able to spread so rapidly into new environments.

A CULTURAL EXPLOSION

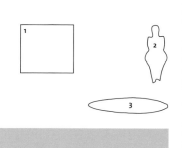

1 An engraving of a human head
discovered at the cave of La Marche in
Lussac-les-Chateaux, Vienne, France. It
is one of dozens of human depictions
found engraved, along with numerous
animal figures, on limestone slabs that
were brought into the cave from outside.

2 Ceramic technology was developed at
Dolní Věstonice, Czech Republic, about
27,000 years ago. The female body was
a frequent subject for Ice Age sculptors.
This model of a mature woman, known
as the Venus of Dolní Věstonice, is the
oldest ceramic figure in the world.

3 A Paleolithic bullroarer from La Roche
Cave at Lalinde, Dordogne, France, with
incised patterns and incrusted pigment
(ocher). The instrument is made from
antler. It would have been attached to a
cord and swung through the air to make
a roaring sound.

Although there was a variety of artistic activity in earlier periods (see p. 32), it was with the advent of anatomically modern humans around 40,000 years ago that artistic evidence became truly abundant—not just in the well-known cave art (see p. 46), but also in terms of portable art objects, ornaments, and music-making. Obviously, however, the surviving evidence represents only the tip of the iceberg, since song, dance, hairstyles, tattoos, scarification, and body-paint are completely gone, along with anything produced on perishable materials such as wood, bark, fibers, or feathers.

Ice Age art studies are uniquely fortunate in that, alongside the images on rocks and cave walls, there are many thousands of portable images. These are found on stones, bones, antlers, and ivory, which have been far easier to date because often they have been found stratified in datable layers. They have served as a template for the changes in technique, content, and styles through this period, from about 40,000 to 11,000 years ago. The depiction of an animal on a piece of that animal, such as red deer images on deer shoulder blades, or a whale on a whale tooth, is a frequent occurrence. Such objects were found long before the discovery of cave art—the earliest known find occurred in the 1820s. It was one such discovery in 1864, of an engraving of a mammoth on a piece of

KEY EVENTS

40,000–10,000 BCE	1833 CE	1852	1864	c. 1864	1908
Ice Age portable art and jewelry are created.	A harpoon engraved to resemble a budding plant and an antler baton decorated with a possible bird are found at Grotte Veyrier in Haute-Savoie, France.	A reindeer foot bone engraved with hinds is discovered at Chaffaud in Vienne, France.	A mammoth image engraved on mammoth tusk is found at La Madeleine, a rock shelter with distinct layers of deposits in Dordogne, France.	The first Ice Age figurine, a statuette of a young girl in mammoth ivory, is discovered at Laugerie Basse in Dordogne, France.	A limestone statuette of a female figure is found during excavations near Willendorf, Austria, and named the Venus of Willendorf.

mammoth tusk at La Madeleine in Dordogne, France, which first proved that humans had coexisted with, and depicted, now-extinct animals.

Among the most famous pieces of portable art are the female figurines found from France to Russia, known as venuses, and often made from mammoth ivory. Most of them date to the Gravettian period, about 27,000 years ago. Around that same period, there was a mass production of small terracotta figurines in several sites in the Czech Republic, including one of the earliest known ceramic objects, the Venus of Dolní Věstonice (see image 2).

Another major category of portable art is the plaquette, a flat slab of stone. Hundreds of these have been found in some sites, bearing engravings and, in a few cases, painted figures. At Parpalló in Spain, more than 5,000 were unearthed, spanning the entire period, and with more than 6,000 decorated surfaces. Those from the French site of La Marche bear images of Ice Age animals such as reindeer and bison, but, uniquely, humans dominate the art here, with portraits and caricatures of people (see image 1) 14,000 years ago.

Ice Age people also loved ornaments, and a mass of jewelry from the period has been discovered made from animal teeth, bones, ivory, shells, and fossils, which had been incised, sawed or perforated. Many such artifacts have been found in burials. Among the valued items were stag canines, a rarity that must have been a sign of prestige and wealth. Seashells, too, were prized and widely traded, and Mediterranean specimens have been found in Germany, 621 miles (1,000 km.) away. Mammoth ivory beads were sometimes produced in huge numbers, such as at the Russian site of Sungir, where an adult and two children each had approximately 3,500 of them, arranged in rows all over the head and body. They were probably strung on sinew and sewn onto clothing.

Finally, musical instruments are rare, but did exist. In some caves, lithophones in the form of a series of hollow stalactites were clearly played, as shown by percussion marks on them. A few bullroarers (see image 3) have been found, along with bone whistles and a whole series of so-called bone flutes that are more like penny whistles or recorders. Some flutes were quite sophisticated, as is evident from one ivory specimen from Geissenklösterle, Germany, which was made in two halves that had to be stuck together. **PGB**

CAVE ART

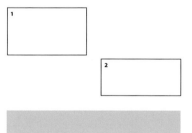

1 A rock engraving of an aurochs in the Côa Valley in northeastern Portugal. The art was discovered while building a dam.

2 The paintings of two spotted horses at the cave of Pech-Merle in southern France are surrounded by dots and stencilled black hands.

More than 400 decorated caves and rock shelters from the last Ice Age (c. 40,000 to 11,000 years ago) are currently known in western Eurasia. The first major discovery—the astonishing decorated ceiling in the Spanish cave of Altamira—came in 1879, yet few could believe that supposedly primitive Stone Age savages could have produced such an impressive work of art. Eventually, decorated caves were found in southern France in circumstances that proved their antiquity, so that the existence of this phenomenon was officially accepted in 1902. Since then, hundreds of discoveries have been made, primarily in France and Spain.

Walls and, more rarely, ceilings were decorated in different ways: the simplest was to make fingermarks in soft surfaces. Engravings are the commonest form of decoration, but bas-reliefs are also known. Only the caves of the French Pyrenees have so far produced any works in clay, from bas-reliefs to haut-reliefs and even a clay statue—the reclining bear of Montespan.

Pigments were applied using fingers or mineral crayons. Brushes were sometimes used, although none has survived. Many images, most notably hand stencils, were produced by spitting paint from the mouth or possibly by blowing air across liquid paint. There were two colors available, red and black.

KEY EVENTS

c. 40,000–11,000 BCE	1879 CE	1895	1902	1912	1922
Most Ice Age cave art is created.	Amateur archaeologist Marcelino Sanz de Sautuola (1831–88) discovers paintings on the ceiling of the cave of Altamira in Cantabria, Spain.	Engravings found in the cave of La Mouthe in Dordogne, France, finally prove the existence of Ice Age cave art.	Cave art is officially accepted as authentic after art is found in the caves of Les Combarelles and Font-de-Gaume in Dordogne, France.	The first work in clay is found in the cave of Le Tuc d'Audoubert in Ariège, France. It shows two modeled bison.	Cave paintings are discovered at Pech-Merle in Lot, France.

One of the characteristic features of Ice Age cave art is the use of 3D via the incorporation of existing rock shapes. For lighting they had lamps, mostly made from hollowed stones or even flat stones, although a beautifully carved and engraved sandstone specimen has been found at Lascaux in Dordogne, France (see p. 48). Animal fat or bone marrow was the usual fuel, with juniper or moss as a wick. Artists also used burning torches and lit fires on cave floors. The flickering flames could make the animal images seem alive, while moving a light source could make engravings appear and disappear.

The vast majority of images produced are animals—almost always adults from a small range of species, primarily horses (see image 2), bison, and aurochs (wild ox); secondary animals include deer, ibex, and mammoths, while the rarer species depicted include carnivores and rhinos. Humans were very rarely drawn, though there are exceptions (see p. 44). There is also a wide range of signs—dots, lines, and geometric shapes. The more elaborate of them are limited in space and time, and are thought to be tribal or ethnic markers.

Many theories have been put forward to explain cave art, from "art for art's sake" to hunting magic to totemism and shamanism, but none stands up to scrutiny. No single explanation can account for such a varied phenomenon that spans such a vast amount of space and time. Moreover, numerous discoveries made since the 1990s—especially in Portugal (see image 1)—have shown that most Ice Age imagery was made in the open air, often on rocks along rivers. Cave art, for so long considered characteristic of the period, was more likely a marginal phenomenon that has survived so well because it was protected and preserved by the stable underground environment. **PGB**

1923	1940	1968	1990s	1994–95	2003
A clay statue depicting a headless bear with a bear skull at its feet is found in the cave of Montespan-Ganties in Haute-Garonne, France.	The greatest of all Ice Age decorated caves—Lascaux in Dordogne, France—is found by a dog and four teenage boys in September.	The Tito Bustillo Cave in Asturias, Spain, is discovered. Its paintings are an example of the rare use of purple pigment.	Open-air rock art is discovered in the Côa Valley, Portugal.	Discovery of the caves of Chauvet in Ardèche, France, and La Garma in Cantabria, Spain.	Cave art is found in England, at Creswell Crags in Nottinghamshire.

Lascaux LATE UPPER PALEOLITHIC

No fewer than 158 mineral fragments were found in various parts of the Lascaux cave, together with crude mortars and pestles, stained with pigment, and naturally hollowed stones still containing small amounts of powdered pigment. There were scratches and traces of use-wear on thirty-one of the mineral lumps.

NAVIGATOR

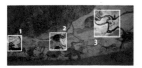

The greatest of all Ice Age decorated caves was discovered in 1940, near the village of Montignac in Dordogne, France. Although fairly small, Lascaux contains about 1,500 animal images, with far more engravings than paintings, and a bewildering variety and quantity of apparently abstract or geometric motifs known as signs. One particularly sophisticated technique used was the gap left between legs and the body, which tells the brain that certain limbs are on the far side. In addition, one large horse figure was painted upside down around a rock, so that the artist could never see the whole figure at once, yet it is in perfect proportion.

For such an important site, Lascaux is very poorly dated, largely because its contents were cleared out in 1948 without any archaeological investigation. It has been treated as a homogeneous collection of figures, all produced within a maximum of about 500 years; but specialists have discerned different phases of decoration. There is some heterogeneity of style in the cave, and a great deal of superimposition. A single date of 17,190 years ago for the cave came from charcoal in the passage, while later dates of 16,000 and 15,516 years ago were obtained from charcoal down the well shaft. One spear-point fragment from an excavation in the shaft has been directly dated to 18,600 years ago. Some of Lascaux's art can be attributed to the traditionally accepted date, but this does not prove that it is a coherent entity spanning only a few centuries. The cave is dominated by its score of aurochs figures, yet in southwest France bones of the aurochs are absent in that period. It is probable that Lascaux is not a homogeneous whole but belongs to a number of different periods. **PGB**

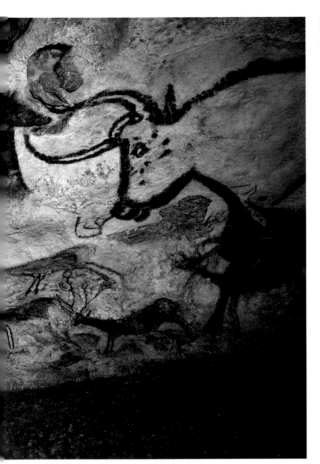

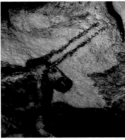

1 LICORNE

The poorly named *Licorne* (unicorn) seems to have two horns. It is probably a fantasy creature comprising parts of different animals and perhaps even some human traits. Such figures are rare in Ice Age cave art, as are scenes. There are no landscapes and no vegetation.

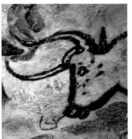

2 HORSES

Lascaux is dominated by its hundreds of horse depictions, both painted and engraved. The Hall of the Bulls was originally decorated with numerous horses, as well as stags, a few bison, and a bear. Black pigments dominate, followed by yellows, reds, and white.

3 AUROCHS

The Hall of the Bulls earned its name when a series of huge aurochs bulls were added to the walls, often superimposed on existing images. The biggest figures in all Ice Age cave art, some are 16 feet (5 m.) long. Extinct since the seventeenth century, the aurochs is the ancestor of domestic cattle.

PIGMENTS

Lascaux has fifteen hues derived from the four dominant colors, those of ocher having been modified by heat. Yellow ocher, when heated beyond 482 degrees Fahrenheit (250°C), passes through different shades of red as it oxidizes into hematite. A further stage in pigment preparation, in Lascaux at least, involved the mixing of different powdered minerals, since unmixed pigments are rare there. Clearly, the artists were experimenting and combining their raw materials in different ways. Traces have been found of reindeer antler in some pigments; it is thought to be a pollutant caused by stirring the pigments in water with a piece of antler, or by carving antler artifacts close to where painting materials were being prepared.

AUSTRALIA

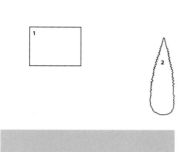

1 The complex network of Brewarrina fish traps, constructed of rocks in the shallows of the Barwon river, is the largest known in Australia. It was built to catch fish as they swam upstream.

2 This serrated weapon was made from bottle glass by Australian Aborigines c. 1960. At the base end of the spear head are remnants of the gum that was applied to attach the spear to its shaft.

Australian Aboriginal societies today are diverse, with a rich and creative spiritual life. At the time of European settlement in the late eighteenth century, there were at least 250 languages spoken and many more dialects. Ethnographic and historical evidence attests to a range of distinctive adaptations to Australia's climatic and environmental diversity, from the tropical north through the desert core to temperate Tasmania in the far south. Archaeological evidence shows that the dynamism and innovation of Aboriginal groups observed by Europeans in the late eighteenth and nineteenth centuries were typical of the more than 50,000 years of human occupation in Australia.

The first Australians were clearly highly adaptable and spread rapidly throughout the continent, including the arid center. Over time, increasingly diverse regional economies developed, particularly following the most extreme aridity of the last Ice Age in c. 20,000 BCE. Archaeological evidence suggests that significant economic, technological, and social changes occurred over the past few thousand years, particularly since c. 5000 BCE. There is debate among Australian archaeologists about how best to explain these changes. Some prefer to see increasing population and response to a changing environment as important factors. Certainly, regional populations had to adapt to the loss of large areas of territory because of rising sea levels at the end of the last Ice Age, including those that inundated vast areas of the continental shelf and severed the land bridges connecting Tasmania and New Guinea to Australia. In many coastal regions, this process would have been clearly perceived by local

KEY EVENTS

Before 50,000 BCE	45,000 BCE	40,000 BCE	20,000 BCE	11,000 BCE	9000 BCE
Sahul, made up of New Guinea, Australia, and Tasmania, is colonized by seafarers from Southeast Asia.	Ground-edge axes are in existence. A flake from one is later found at Carpenter's Gap 1 in the Kimberley and is the oldest evidence of this technology.	Mungo Man is buried and Mungo Lady is cremated; she is one of the oldest cremations in the world.	Finger flutings are made deep underground in the soft limestone walls of Koonalda cave, South Australia.	Cheetup cave, Western Australia, is first occupied. This site has the oldest evidence of the processing of toxic cycad seeds.	Wooden artifacts, including boomerangs and barbed spears, are used in Wyrie Swamp, South Australia.

populations, and the memory of it is preserved by many Aboriginal groups in their mythology. Others characterize change in the past few thousand years in terms of increasing social and economic complexity. However, it is likely that complex social behavior characterized the early colonizing population, as suggested by early archaeological evidence for art (see p. 52), personal adornment, and long-distance exchange.

New features appeared in Australian sites between about 4000 and 2000 BCE. In southern Australia, small backed implements became common. These tools were most likely spear barbs and had one edge deliberately blunted. Analysis of the backed tools associated with the skeleton of Narrabeen man, discovered in Sydney and dated to c. 2000 BCE, showed that they were spear barbs and that he was probably the victim of a ritual spearing. Over the central third of the continent, different forms of spear point appeared, including elaborately pressure-flaked forms in the Kimberley. In historic times, these were often made of glass (see image 2) or porcelain. Flaked adzes, used for wood-working, also became more common and more specialized in form in the desert, while ground stone hatchets became widespread over most of Australia.

Aboriginal hunter-gatherers were by no means at the mercy of their surroundings and there is plenty of evidence that they were skilled environmental managers. The sophisticated use of fire as a land management tool is perhaps the best-known example of this, and Aboriginal people have even been described as "fire-stick farmers." Furthermore, elaborate processing methods were used to remove toxins from poisonous plants such as cycads. Complex fish trapping systems were developed in many areas, too (see image 1). The best known of these is in the Budj Bim area, at Lake Condah, where weirs, channels, and holding ponds were used to trap and store eels at least 6,500 years ago and probably earlier.

Exchange was an important feature of Aboriginal life and commonly fulfilled important social and ritual purposes. Many types of material objects, as well as ceremonies, songs, and stories, were exchanged—often over great distances. The long-distance movement of stone tools, particularly axes, shell beads, and ocher, is well documented archaeologically.

Australia does not fit easily into the picture that prevails in many parts of the world, where major environmental changes associated with the end of the Ice Age led to the emergence of agriculture and the development of urban societies. Australia is unique in that it was the only continent occupied exclusively by hunter-gatherers until European settlement. It thus provides a singular perspective on variability in hunter-gatherer societies in space and time. In most parts of the world, these societies were pushed into marginal environments. The persistence of the hunter-gatherer way of life in Australia leads to questions about ideas of inevitable "progress" toward social and economic complexity. **CB**

6000–4000 BCE	4600 BCE	2500 BCE	2000 BCE	1606 CE	1700
Rising sea levels stabilize, and land bridges connecting Australia, New Guinea, and Tasmania are finally severed.	Complex fish trap systems exist at Lake Condah, probably continuing older practices.	Small flaked tools, including backed implements and bifacial points, become common and widely distributed in Australian sites.	The dingo arrives in Australia, probably brought by seafarers from Asia.	Willem Janszoon (1570–1630) has the first recorded European encounter with Aboriginal people in Cape York.	Macassan traders from Indonesia begin regular visits to northern Australia in search of trepang (sea cucumber), a popular delicacy in China.

Murujuga c. 20,000 BCE – c. 1800 CE

Murujuga has great spiritual significance for the Ngarda-Ngarli people, who are the custodians of the area today. They believe that the engravings are the work of the Marga—ancestral creative beings from the Dreaming—made as reminders of the law, and that they have a duty to care for them. Ceremonies still performed in the region today can be recognized in the art.

Murujuga (known as the Burrup Peninsula) is part of the Dampier Archipelago on the northwest coast of Australia. It has the richest concentration of rock art in Australia—perhaps even in the world. The rocky slopes are covered in petroglyphs, and archaeologists estimate that there may be millions of individual engravings. This art is extremely diverse and includes human and animal figures as well as tracks and geometric motifs. Land animals such as kangaroo and wallaby; reptiles such as lizards and snakes; birds; and aquatic species such as turtles, fish, and crabs are all depicted. Many of them are extraordinarily detailed and can be identified to species level.

Today, Murujuga is the largest island in the Dampier Archipelago. During the last Ice Age, when sea levels were much lower, the area was a range of rocky hills far inland. Archaeological excavations have shown that it was certainly occupied at this time. The rock art itself is very difficult to date. At Murujuga, however, studies of weathering in conjunction with style and subject matter allow a relative chronology to be constructed. Much of the most recent, least weathered art depicts marine species and relates to the recent past after the formation of the archipelago. Many human figures from this period connect to contemporary songs and stories. The more weathered motifs clearly predate the sea-level rise. Some of these are very large and prominent engravings of kangaroos and emus. Others show human figures that differ stylistically from the more recent motifs. Particularly intriguing are the deeply weathered and highly distinctive "archaic faces." These may be the oldest depictions of faces in the world. Similar motifs are found throughout central Australia and suggest long-distance cultural connections, perhaps dating back to the initial spread of modern humans through the continent, before 30,000 BCE. In addition to rock art, there are many other sites including shell middens, fish traps, surface artifact scatters, quarries, and flaking floors. There are also stone arrangements and numerous standing stones. Many of the standing stones are Thalu sites, which are linked to ceremonial activities associated with increasing resources. **CB**

EXTINCT ANIMALS

Depictions of extinct animals can provide clues for dating rock art. On Murujuga, there are a number of images of thylacines and Tasmanian devils—both of which have been extinct on mainland Australia for at least 3,000 years. Other engravings are thought to portray extinct species of kangaroo. In addition, emu are no longer found in the area, but they are common in earlier phases and therefore may date to a time when the islands were still part of the mainland.

TECHNIQUES

The petroglyphs on Murujuga were produced by removing the weathered surface of the local granophyre by pecking, abrading, or scratching, in order to create a contrast with the unweathered rock beneath. Some engravings are deeply pecked and create an intaglio effect, whereas others are shallower. Over time, the freshly pecked surface gradually weathers back to the original color of the rock, thereby providing relative age estimates for the engraved art.

ROCK ART IN AUSTRALIA

Paintings and engravings are found across most of Australia, wherever suitable rock surfaces exist. However, there is considerable regional diversity in style, motif, and techniques. For example, petroglyphs are common in the Pilbara region of Western Australia, where different areas demonstrate a variety of styles and motifs. On Murujuga the range of styles and motifs is unusually large, and there are numerous examples from different areas of the Pilbara and as far away as the Western Desert. Consequently, archaeologists have suggested that Murujuga could have been an important meeting place for different groups of people.

The discovery of ocher crayons at Madjedbebe in the Northern Territory, dated to c. 50,000 BCE, and a roof-fall fragment with ocher at Carpenter's Gap 1 in Western Australia, dated to c. 40,000 BCE, suggest that art was practiced by the first Australians. However, exact dates for rock art are rare. A painted motif on a fragment of rock at Nawarla Gabarnmang in the Northern Territory dates to c. 26,000 BCE. At Koonalda cave in South Australia, finger markings on the limestone walls were made deep underground. These are attributed to approximately 20,000 BCE by radiocarbon dating of charcoal from torches used to light the cave.

In many regions, changes in style can be identified through time by studying the superimposition of motifs. Depictions of contact subjects, such as ships, introduced animals and people wearing European clothing, indicate that local rock art traditions were practiced in many areas well after the arrival of Europeans. In Arnhem Land in the Northern Territory, for example, the most recent rock art dates to the late twentieth century, but similar styles of art continue in the region today on bark and other media.

2 | From Hunters to Farmers

10,000 – 3000 BCE

During the Mesolithic period, humans started transitioning towards a settled way of life, and in the Neolithic period, people began to farm in earnest. This change in economy took place at different times and followed different trajectories, depending on the region. However, it was typically accompanied by similar traits: growing competition, the need to mark land, and emerging social differentiation—setting the stage for the great civilizations that were to follow.

Neolithic Orkney
p. 116

Hunter-gatherers
of the British Isles
p. 66

Irish Passage Graves
p. 128

Stonehenge
p. 130

Eythra
p. 112

Temples of
Malta and Gozo
p. 114

Social Complexity
in the Archaic
p. 72

Real Alto
p. 120

The Chinchorro
p. 74

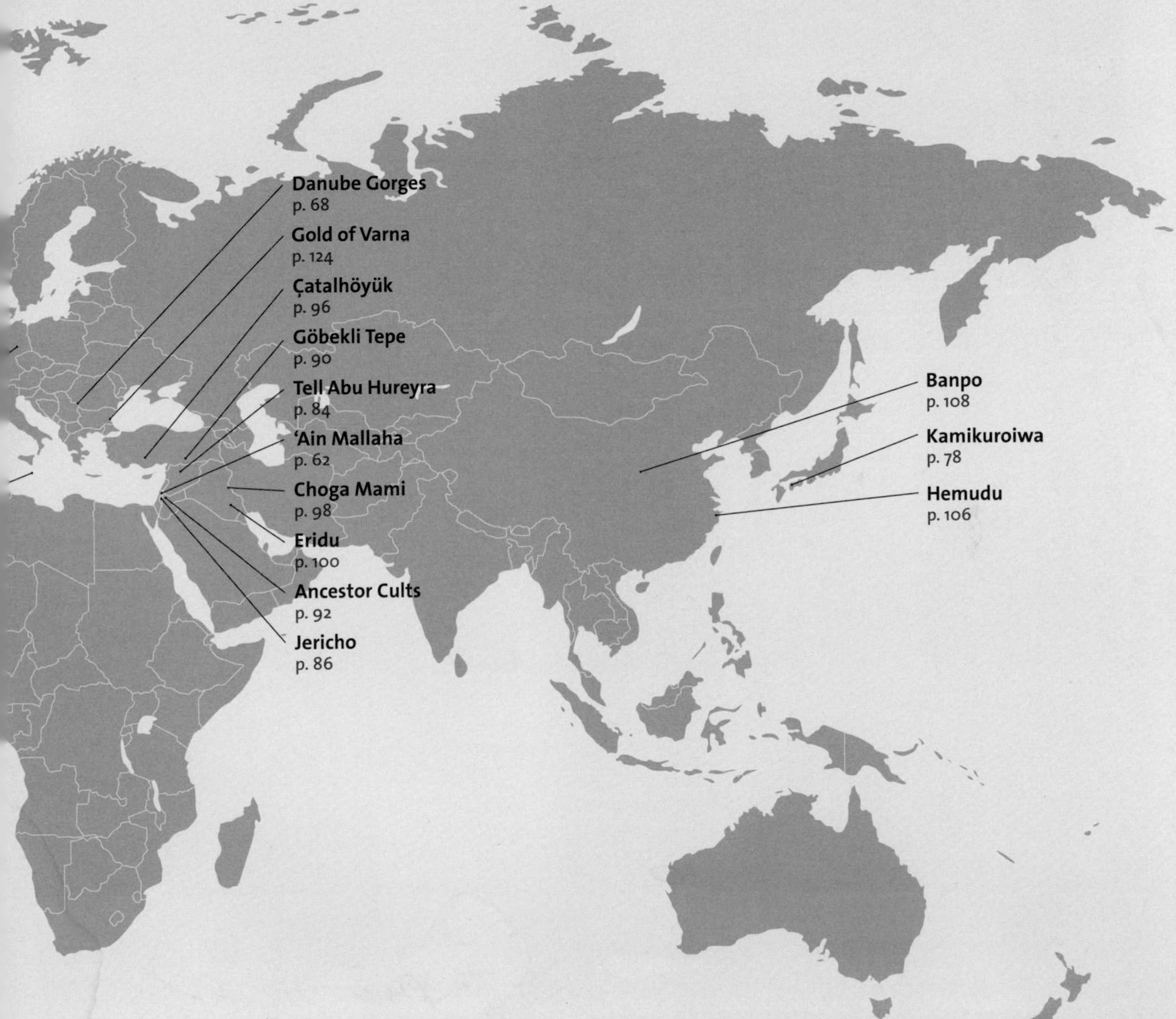

Danube Gorges
p. 68

Gold of Varna
p. 124

Çatalhöyük
p. 96

Göbekli Tepe
p. 90

Tell Abu Hureyra
p. 84

'Ain Mallaha
p. 62

Choga Mami
p. 98

Eridu
p. 100

Ancestor Cults
p. 92

Jericho
p. 86

Banpo
p. 108

Kamikuroiwa
p. 78

Hemudu
p. 106

ANCIENT CLIMATE CHANGE

1 The Franchthi Cave in southern Greece, which had been far inland during the Ice Age, is now on the coast.

2 This carved bone comb was found on Gotland, Sweden's largest island.

3 At a Mesolithic cemetery of the Ertebølle culture at Vedbæk, Denmark, red ocher was spread over this woman and her infant; she possibly died in childbirth.

Approximately 20,000 years ago, the ice sheets that had covered much of North America and Europe began to retreat as the climate gradually warmed. The frigid conditions that had so challenged Neanderthals (see p. 30) and modern humans (see p. 38) abated over the next 10,000 years. Leaving their refugia in southern Europe, people followed the herds of reindeer back into northern Europe, and in North America new habitats became available to recently arrived humans. Advances in technology and cognitive capacity that began under glacial conditions could now be fully realized, resulting eventually in the most significant transformation of the human condition since the species began: the shift from mobile hunting and gathering to agriculture.

The melting of the Cordilleran and Laurentide ice sheets in North America and the Scandinavian ice sheet in Europe released vast quantities of water into the world's oceans. Global sea levels rose and remodeled the world's coastlines (see image 1). At the same time, the land that had been under the ice, now released from incalculable amounts of pressure, rebounded upward. In North America and Eurasia, postglacial hunter-gatherers encountered new landscapes. Tundra was relatively familiar from their previous experience, and they could follow and ambush herds of reindeer. Over time, however, shrubs and trees began to cover formerly frozen regions as more temperate conditions

KEY EVENTS

c. 18,000 BCE	c. 14,000–10,000 BCE	c. 10,900–9800 BCE	c. 9800 BCE	c. 7000–3000 BCE	c. 6200 BCE
Deglaciation begins in the northern hemisphere.	Northern Europe is recolonized by hunter-gatherers in pursuit of reindeer; forests grow in former tundra areas.	The Younger Dryas sudden cold spell temporarily reverses the warming trend.	The Holocene, or Postglacial, period begins.	The postglacial thermal maximum is reached. Average temperatures are up to 35.6 degrees Fahrenheit (2°C) warmer than today.	A temporary cooling occurs in Eurasia due to the sudden release of freshwater from Hudson Bay in North America.

prevailed. The result was a more complicated landscape that contained many resources for the humans who inhabited it. In addition to large herbivores such as red deer, also known as elk, smaller animals could be hunted and trapped. Vast flocks of waterfowl flew overhead, while rivers and lakes teemed with fish. Along coasts and some interior rivers, shellfish were found in abundance. In the forests, nuts and berries could be gathered by everyone in a hunting band.

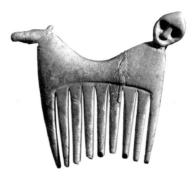

People developed new ways to take advantage of these resources. Like their Ice Age precursors, they were still highly mobile but certain locations were used more persistently for habitation. Caves and rock shelters continued to serve as living places, as they had during the Ice Age. Increasingly, however, settlements were established out in the open. At prime locations, such as rapids for fishing, campsites were occupied seasonally. People congregated at these locations, exchanging news, obtaining materials for tools, and acquiring mates.

New technology was developed to take advantage of the changed conditions. Nets, traps, and snares were used for catching small game and fish. In both the Americas and in Europe, the bow and arrow became an important hunting weapon. Wood, bone, and antler were worked into all sorts of novel implements, and there was also room for artistic expression, as seen in the carving of designs on bones (see image 2). In addition, people began to pay more attention to how they buried their dead. Certain locations were used repeatedly for burials with elaborate rituals, including sprinkling red ocher over the corpse (see image 3), lining graves with stones, decorating the body with ornaments such as shell beads, and including items such as animal parts and stone tools in the burial. Bodies were arranged in different positions: lying flat, contracted with the legs drawn close to the chest, or even sitting.

Archaeologists call these societies Mesolithic in northern Europe (see p. 64); Epipaleolithic in southern Europe, the Middle East, and North Africa; and Archaic in the Americas (see p. 70). All these terms describe postglacial hunter-gatherers who were generally mobile but often returned to specific locations, relying on a broad spectrum of wild resources, including mammals, fish, birds, shellfish, and plants. These societies persisted until the emergence of agriculture, which took place at various times in different regions following a long period of experimentation with different types of plants and animals.

After having given them scant regard for many years, archaeologists now recognize that these postglacial hunter-gatherers represent the transition between the hunting bands of the Ice Ages and the settled agricultural settlements of later prehistory. Today, archaeologists see these societies as crucial for understanding the great transformation caused by the development of agriculture. In order for people to make the shift from hunting and gathering to agriculture, several social and technological transformations had to occur. These include some sense of property and ownership, the ability to store and preserve food, and a detailed accounting of kin relationships. **PB**

c. 6000 BCE	c. 4000 BCE	c. 3900 BCE	c. 3500 BCE	c. 1800 BCE	c. 200 BCE
Doggerland in the North Sea basin finally disappears.	The transition to agriculture is made across northern and western Europe: foragers become farmers.	The arid event known as the 5.9 kiloyear event prompts worldwide migrations to river valleys.	Watson Brake—the earliest mound complex—is built in Louisiana.	Archaic foragers in riverine southeastern North America propagate wild plants: chenopods, sunflowers, and marsh elder.	Maize cultivation begins in eastern North America.

FARMING AROUND THE WORLD

1 Petroglyphs dating from the northern European Bronze Age (2000–600 BCE), found in Bohuslän province, Sweden, depict oxen and a human ploughing.

2 This reproduction of a rock painting from the Ain Dua area of the Jebel Uweinat mountain range in the eastern Sahara (in what is now Libya) shows bovine livestock and humans. Life flourished in the desert during two wet periods: the first occurred 12,000–8,000 years ago, and the second, 7,000–5,000 years ago.

3 This wooden sickle dates from the pre-dynastic period of Egypt, c. 6,000 years ago. The "blade" of the harvesting tool consists of a number of flints, each given a sharp, serrated edge, inset into the wood.

For several million years, people obtained all of their dietary requirements from hunting, fishing, and collecting wild foods. Today, almost everyone in the world obtains most, if not all, of their diet from plants that are cultivated and animals that are raised under human control. In relative terms, this complete transformation of how humans obtain food was remarkably sudden, quick, and complete. However, it did not happen at the same time around the world, nor did the change take place everywhere initially. It involved different types of plants and animals in specific areas.

Archaeologists debate why and how people made this change. For a long time, they assumed that hunter-gatherers were so successful that it must have taken a very powerful force, such as climate change or extreme population growth, to make them take up agriculture. Some thought that people unwittingly became dependent on certain wild resources and were eventually obliged to cultivate them. Others invoked social reasons for people taking up cultivation, such as the need to produce extra food for use in ceremonies and feasts. In the end, the shift from hunting and gathering to agriculture may never be fully explained. In recent years the focus of research has shifted to documenting the evidence for domestication through high-precision radiocarbon dating, detailed archaeobotanical and archaeozoological investigation, and archaeogenetics.

The world of early farming can be divided into two types of regions: first, relatively small areas in which wild species of plants and animals were domesticated independently and from which their use spread; and second, much larger areas in which agriculture was introduced, either by the spread

KEY EVENTS

c. 11,000 BCE	c. 9000 BCE	c. 8000 BCE	c. 7000-6000 BCE	c. 6700 BCE	c. 6000-5000 BCE
Rye grains at Tell Abu Hureyra, Syria, show signs of domestication.	Wheat is domesticated in southwestern Asia.	Sheep, goats, barley, lentils, and peas are domesticated in southwestern Asia.	Farming spreads from the Fertile Crescent to Europe and Africa.	Maize and squash begin to be domesticated in southwest Mexico.	Millet, rice ,and pigs are domesticated in China.

of farming populations or by the adoption of domestic plants and animals by hunter-gatherers. The areas of pristine initial domestication were the heartlands of today's major agricultural systems. In southwestern Asia, in the so-called Fertile Crescent, Natufian hunter-gatherer communities began to experiment with cultivation even before the end of the Ice Age. Rye grains at Tell Abu Hureyra, Syria, dated to *c.* 13,000 years ago, show signs of being domesticated. Domesticated wheat appeared *c.* 11,000 years ago, followed by barley, lentils, peas, sheep, and goats during the following millennium, and finally cattle (see image 2) and pigs *c.* 10,000 years ago. Natufian hunter-gatherers had long been experimenting with various species of plants and animals, and had ruled out many others as potential candidates for domestication. In China, the intensive exploitation of millet and rice began *c.* 10,000 years ago, and both were eventually domesticated between 7,000 and 8,000 years ago. Zebu cattle were independently domesticated in southern Asia by *c.* 8,000 years ago. In New Guinea, bananas, taro, and yams were cultivated by 6,000 years ago after several millennia of intense management of wild forms. The earliest sorghum was cultivated in Africa *c.* 4,000 years ago.

In the New World, the key cultivated plants, maize and squash, were first domesticated *c.* 9,000 years ago in central Mexico, although it took several millennia before their valuable traits were firmly established. Beans soon followed. An array of plants and animals were domesticated in South America, including potatoes *c.* 5,000 years ago, and llamas *c.* 4,000 years ago. In the interior river valleys of eastern North America, a variety of seed plants, such as squash, sunflower, marsh elder, and goosefoot, appear to have undergone changes linked to domestication between 5,000 and 4,000 years ago.

From these areas of initial domestication, the use of crops and livestock spread outward. In some areas, this happened quickly. Cereals, cattle, sheep, and goats spread from southwestern Asia to Europe, northern Africa, and central Asia within a couple of millennia. Maize spread north from central Mexico to the southwestern United States by *c.* 4,000 years ago, but only reached its eventual growing limits in eastern North America *c.* 1,000 years ago. Yams, pigs, and taro were taken across the Pacific by seafarers who colonized the islands of Oceania and Polynesia.

Over time, people used animals not only for meat but also for milk, wool, and pulling power. They diverted water to irrigate arid lands for growing crops, and used ploughs (see image 1) to break up heavy soils, as well as scythes and sickles (see image 3) for harvesting. They learned how to select and breed desirable characteristics, which led to additional "improved" varieties of the initial domesticated species. Further plant and animal types were domesticated for their specific characteristics, such as horses for riding in central Asia *c.* 5,000 years ago, and camels in Asia and Arabia *c.* 4,500 years ago. **PB**

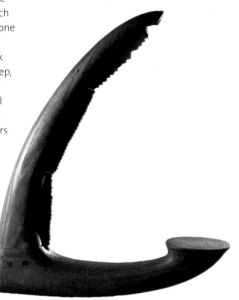

c. 5500–5000 BCE	c. 5000–4000 BCE	c. 3400–2500 BCE	c. 3000–2000 BCE	c. 2600–2000 BCE	c. 2100 BCE
Farming spreads throughout central Europe.	Bananas, taro, and yam are cultivated in New Guinea after several millennia of management.	Domestication of the potato begins in Andean South America.	Squash, sunflower, marsh elder, and goosefoot are cultivated in riverine zones of eastern North America.	Llamas are domesticated in highland South America.	Maize is grown in the southwestern United States region. Maize growing reaches northeastern North America c. 1000 CE.

TOWARD FARMING AND SEDENTISM

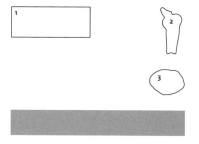

1 A reconstructed Kebaran knife, made of wood with inset blades of flint was used for cutting wild plants (16,000 BCE).

2 This bone handle of a sickle, now without its flint microlith blades, was carved in the form of a gazelle—the main prey of its Natufian makers. Found in Hanahal cave, Mt. Carmel, Israel, it dates to 10,000 BCE.

3 A Natufian grindstone shaped from a limestone block (9800 BCE).

The Last Glacial Maximum ended around 18,000 BCE as temperatures began to rise and aridity to decrease (see p. 56). Plants that had survived in pockets of favoured conditions (refugia) began to spread, along with animals dependent on them, and people exploiting them. These regions included the Levant, particularly the Jordan valley, where grassland vegetation spread, including cereals, as well as oak woodland on the adjacent mountains. A mosaic of environments offered opportunities for hunter-gatherers to spread and multiply: the Kebaran culture (c. 18,000 to 12,500 BCE) bears witness to the expansion made possible by the growing resources of this favored region. Plant foods became increasingly important, including cereals such as wheat and barley, seeds, pulses, roots, fruits, nuts, and leafy plants. New equipment was developed, including grindstones to process them. Microliths (tiny worked flints) were used alone or as components set into hafts to create knives (see image 1), scrapers, and sickles, and arrows, spears, and harpoons for hunting. Sheep, goats, and especially gazelle, wildfowl, and smaller creatures were hunted, snared, or trapped. Lakes and rivers offered fish and shellfish. Kebaran hunter-gatherers generally moved with the seasons to exploit these resources where they were available, establishing a series of camps to which they returned annually. In a few particularly favored localities, such as Ohalo near the Sea of Galilee, Israel, they might stay in one camp for most or all of the year.

Around 12,500 BCE this became more common. The Natufian culture began living year-round in sedentary settlements, such as that at 'Ain Mallaha, Israel (see p. 62), making expeditions to obtain additional resources, such as stone for tools. Wild cereals, occurring in dense stands, now played a major part in the diet, being not only eaten when ripe but gathered in quantity and stored: storage pits were a new feature of these settlements. This shift from procuring

KEY EVENTS

18,000 BCE	18,000 BCE	16,000–13,500 BCE	14,000 BCE	c. 13,000 BCE	12,700–10,700 BCE
Ohalo II, Israel, is occupied. It is a very early example of sedentary settlement, with huts constructed of tamarisk, oak, and willow branches.	The Late Glacial Maximum peaks; temperatures then begin to rise, rainfall increases and sea levels rise, flooding coastal areas.	The Kebaran culture in Levant increasingly exploits plant foods. Plant-processing equipment, such as grindstones, become more common.	Tiny amounts of central Anatolian obsidian found in Levantine sites indicate that exchange networks are already operating over long distances.	A man is buried at the hunter-gatherer base camp of Neve David, northern Israel, in a grave lined with stone slabs and covered by a stone mortar.	Temperatures and rainfall rise very rapidly to around modern levels; the conditions bring a great expansion of vegetation and animals.

food as required to storing it was a major economic change, foreshadowing agricultural development. Dogs, the first animals to be domesticated, assisted in hunting. Studies of Natufian hunter-gatherers' bones show they were well fed and healthy, but suffered tooth decay due to their carbohydrate-rich diet.

Sedentism had major consequences. Mobile, nomadic life restricts people's possessions to what can be carried: small, light, essential or highly valued objects. Other things were made where people camped but discarded when they moved on, though they could be retrieved if people returned to the camp each year. Sedentary settlement, however, enabled people to accumulate possessions, including large, heavy objects like grindstones (see image 3)—a spur to creativity (see image 2). Mobile foragers had to carry their infants, acting as a brake on family development: year-round sedentism removed this constraint, allowing population increase, which could be supported as natural resources increased. In the Levant, the Last Glacial Maximum had seen a few sites clustered in favored pockets; the Kebaran, still in small groups, spread through the mountain foothills of the Jordan valley and adjacent areas, reaching from the north Syrian plain to the Negev and Sinai; the Natufian spread farther, settling in the North Euphrates area and filling out the Levant.

This favorable picture was not typical of all West Asia, much of which had been virtually depopulated in the Last Glacial Maximum. Occupation in Anatolia expanded first in coastal areas and the Taurus mountains, parts of the interior being colonized by 14,000 BCE: small amounts of obsidian from central Anatolia found in the Levant bear witness to occupation of that region and to the development of exchange networks trading desirable commodities, such as shells from the Mediterranean and Red Sea. The Zagros region, to the east, abandoned in the Late Glacial Maximum, was recolonized as temperatures rose: here, too, hunter-gatherers engaged in broad-spectrum foraging, intensively hunting wild sheep, collecting shellfish, fishing, hunting small mammals, and gathering plant foods, including cereals and pulses.

Favorable conditions ended abruptly around 10,900 BCE, when temperatures plunged and extreme aridity set in: this climatic reversal (the Younger Dryas period) was triggered by the release into the Atlantic of huge quantities of icy meltwaters from the North American ice sheets. For around 1,100 years, glacial conditions returned to West Asia. Many settlements were abandoned, communities returning to the earlier pattern of seasonal movement, and population declined. Exceptionally, Tell Abu Hureyra in Syria (see p. 84) was occupied throughout the cold phase: here, as the availability of local plant foods declined, those that remained were exploited more intensively. Rye, in particular, was able to tolerate the cold, dry conditions; it shows genetic signs of having been cultivated—the first evidence of agriculture. **JM**

12,500–9500 BCE	11,500–9600 BCE	11,000 BCE	10,900–9800 BCE	10,000 BCE	10,000 BCE
Natufian sedentary culture dominates in the Levant: it is supported by a wide variety of foods and produces an increasing range of artifacts.	The village of Tell Abu Hureyra on the Euphrates river has 100 to 300 people. Its semi-subterranean houses are occupied year-round.	Abu Hureyra's response to worsening climatic conditions entering the Younger Dryas is intensive exploitation of rye, causing genetic changes in the plant.	The Younger Dryas, a temporary reversion to colder conditions, sees many communities reverting to the more mobile lifestyle of previous ages.	Shanidar cave and Zawi Chemi in the Zagros mountains, Iraq, are occupied by hunter-gatherers dependent particularly on hunting sheep.	A woman is buried in the cave of Hilazon Tachtit, Israel, with body parts of many animals: her special treatment suggests she was a shaman.

'Ain Mallaha 12,000–9600 BCE

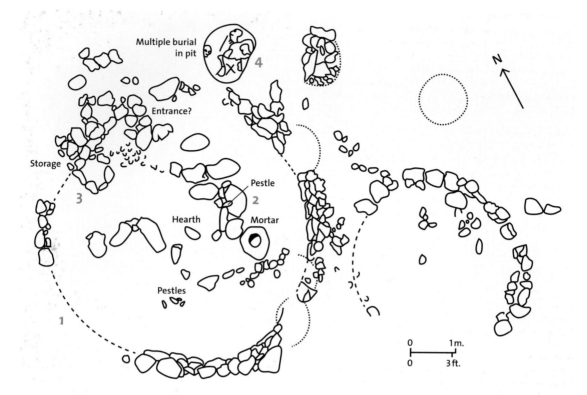

This plan records two houses from the second building phase of 'Ain Mallaha. A large hearth lies at the center of the larger of the two houses, and grinding equipment, including pestles and a large mortar, is scattered across its floor. In this phase the houses, though smaller than those of the initial occupation, were generally similar in appearance.

Situated near a freshwater spring in the basin of Lake Huleh in northern Israel is a substantial Natufian settlement, 'Ain Mallaha (also known as Eynan or Einan). A French team began excavations there in 1955, and the site produced the first substantial architecture known to be associated with the Natufian period. The settlement, c. 2,150 square feet (200 sq. m.) in extent, was occupied from c. 12,000 to 9600 BCE, during which its layout was altered several times. The site, located on a hillside and arranged in terraces, was occupied by between fifty and a hundred people. The location took advantage of the resources of a range of ecological niches: Lake Huleh itself, its marshy fringes, the lake basin's steppe grassland, and the surrounding hills. From here it was possible to catch fish, reptiles, amphibians, and tortoises; hunt wildfowl, small animals such as hare, deer (red, roe, and fallow), wild boar, and particularly gazelle; and gather a wide variety of plants including terebinth, almonds, and wild cereals such as barley. That plant foods had become important in the settlement's diet is indicated by the high levels of decay to be found in the inhabitants' teeth, a consequence of their carbohydrate-rich diet. Also found at 'Ain Mallaha was a variety of stone tools, including flint sickle blades, lunate flint arrowheads, whetstones, and small weights from fishing nets. One person was buried here with the body of a dog—one of the earliest domesticated dogs known in the region.

The first two phases of occupation at 'Ain Mallaha saw the construction of large houses, between 10 and 26 feet (3 and 8 m.) in diameter. Several of the buildings were very carefully laid out following geometric principles to form a perfect arc or circle—arguably the beginning of architectural design. In the final phase, however, the settlement shrank and the houses became more flimsy: this coincided with the drastic change to cold, dry conditions brought by the Younger Dryas period, when life became harder. By the time conditions improved, c. 9600 BCE, the settlement was abandoned. **JM**

👁 FOCAL POINTS

1 SEMI-SUBTERRANEAN HOUSES

Typical houses at 'Ain Mallaha were semi-subterranean. A pit was dug, around 1 foot 6 inches (0.5 m.) deep, and lined with drystone masonry walls, or cut into a slope. The stone walls also provided the perimeter on the outer side. The houses were roofed, probably with wood, brushwood, and thatch, supported where necessary by large wooden posts. Typically, two or three steps led from the doorway down into the semi-subterranean part of the house.

2 FOOD-PREPARATION FACILITIES

The Natufians were hunter-gatherers who prepared their foods inside their homes, using their central hearth for cooking. Pestles and mortars were used to make plant foods more digestible. It has been observed that the establishment of Natufian villages coincided with the appearance of commensual species: house mice and sparrows, both of which evolved to depend on food foraged from the kitchens and storage areas of humans.

3 STORAGE CONTAINER

Storage facilities were an important feature of the houses at 'Ain Mallaha and at other Natufian sites. The larger house of this pair had an internal storage container constructed of stones. As in many parts of the site, there were a number of circular pits around the outside of the house, lined with stones or mud plaster: these were probably used for storage.

4 BURIAL PIT

Many of the pits had been used as graves for single individuals. Others, however, contained the collected bones of several people, removed from their original graves after the bodies had decomposed. This sheds an interesting light on developing funerary practices, foreshadowing the later ancestor cult. It is assumed that such pits were initially used for storage and only later came to serve as burial pits.

▲ Grindstones, mortars, and grinders appeared during the Late Glacial period as plant foods became important in the diet. Deep mortars like this Natufian example (10,000 BCE) of basalt from 'Ain Mahalla were used with a pestle for pounding nuts. Flat grindstones were used with oval grinders to process grain into flour. At the Ohalo II site in Galilee, a piece of basalt yielded evidence of even earlier grinding of barley, in c. 21,000 BCE.

NATUFIAN BURIALS

Although burials occur much earlier, regular cemeteries only began in the Natufian period. A cemetery of around twenty-eight people in a cave at Hilazon Tachtit in Galilee included the exceptional burial of a disabled woman aged around forty-five, probably a shaman. Her rock-cut grave was lined with stones, shells, a gazelle horn, and tortoise shells, covered by ash. Her body was covered with symbolic animal parts: a golden eagle's wing, the skulls of two martens, the tail of an aurochs (wild cow), a boar's front leg, and a severed human foot. The remains of a funerary feast—the source of the numerous tortoise shells—had been heaped over her.

EUROPEAN MESOLITHIC

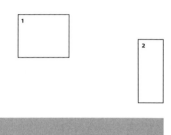

1 This reconstruction of a fish trap is based on evidence found at the Mesolithic site at Nämforsen, Näsåker, Sweden. Large fish caught in the closed and tapered end stood little chance of turning and swimming against the current to escape.

2 A fish leister has three points lashed to a wooden shaft. Barbed wooden or antler side pieces gripped the fish firmly, while the middle skewer pinned it in place. This example belonged to a Copper Inuit group.

The retreat of the Scandinavian and Alpine glaciers dramatically changed the environment of northern Europe. A warming climate, rising sea levels, and the removal of the weight of the glacial ice transformed the landscapes north of the Alps from periglacial tundra into forests and lakelands within a few millennia. By c. 7000 BCE, much of Europe was covered by dense woodlands—populated by forest animals including red deer, wild pigs, and wild cattle—and the rivers, lakes, and seas were full of fish. South of the Alps, the climate of the Mediterranean zone also warmed and coastlines changed.

The interplay between sea-level rise (eustasy) and rebounding land surfaces (isostasy) is illustrated by the history of the Baltic Sea. First, water from melting ice accumulated to form a giant lake. When the retreating ice reached a point where the lake could overflow across central Sweden, about 11,500 years ago, the ice lake became the brackish Yoldia Sea, a bay of the Atlantic Ocean. Isostatic rebound, however, blocked the connection some 10,700 years ago, turning the Yoldia Sea into the Ancylus Lake. Several centuries later, a new connection to the ocean was formed via the Danish straits. The resulting Littorina Sea was again a brackish body, which over time developed into the modern Baltic Sea.

In the deciduous forests of northern and central Europe, Mesolithic hunter-gatherers developed tools and techniques to get the most out of rich environments. A good example is a fishing spear called a leister (see image 2),

KEY EVENTS

c. 9800 BCE	c. 8700 BCE	c. 8500–7000 BCE	c. 8000–7500 BCE	c. 8000–7500 BCE	c. 7400–6200 BCE
The Holocene, or Postglacial, period ends and thus the Mesolithic begins.	Ancylus Lake is formed in the Baltic basin due to isostatic rebound in central Sweden.	Mesolithic bands visit lakeside sites such as Star Carr in England and Friesack in Germany.	The Pesse dugout canoe, the world's oldest known boat, is made in the Netherlands.	Mesolithic bands camp at Howick in northeastern England and Mount Sandel in Ireland (see p. 66).	Complex Mesolithic societies flourish in the Danube Gorges (see p. 68).

which was a compound tool, thrust down from above onto a fish. Across shallow tidal bays in Denmark, wooden fences allowed fish to swim in with the tide and trapped them when it went out. At low tide, the traps could be retrieved and the fish removed. Several fish traps have been found along the River Liffey in central Dublin, and on river sites in Sweden (see image 1).

The Mesolithic period in Europe saw a profusion of watercraft, particularly dugout canoes, as rivers, lake belts, and straits became arteries of communication. Many dugouts have been found in waterlogged deposits across northern Europe, along with other equipment such as paddles. Watercraft allowed people to stay in the same place longer, since they no longer had to relocate in search of resources. Instead, they could travel in their dugouts along coastlines and slow-moving rivers, and return with what the band needed. Around the Mediterranean, Mesolithic seafarers were able to cross open seas to reach islands such as Melos, where they obtained obsidian to make tools.

The attachment by Mesolithic people to particular locations is seen in the appearance of cemeteries, to which the hunters returned repeatedly to bury their dead. People were buried with distinctive rituals. At Skateholm in Sweden and Téviec in France, deer antlers were often placed over the body before the grave was filled. Other grave goods included shell beads and flint projectile points. Oleni Ostrov cemetery in Russia has yielded more than 400 Mesolithic burials, which contained carved representations of animals on wood and bone.

Harvesting of marine resources across northern Europe after c. 6000 BCE resulted in many sites being located on coastlines or along estuaries, with substantial accumulations of shells and debris. These include the classic "kitchen middens" of the Ertebølle culture in Denmark and similar shell mounds along the Atlantic coast from the British Isles to Portugal. The largest middens run parallel to the shore and comprise many separate episodes in which shells, animal bones, and hearths have built deposits up to 6.5 feet (2 m.) thick.

Around the Baltic, Mesolithic sites have yielded very early pottery, from c. 5500 BCE onward. It appears in two basic forms: thick-walled, pointed-base, sack-shaped vessels and small oval bowls termed lamps. For many years, archaeologists believed that the hunter-gatherers of the Baltic acquired pottery-making from agriculturalists farther south, despite the fact that the techniques and forms of both societies bore little resemblance to one another. More recently, it has been suggested that pottery manufacture reached the Baltic via northern Eurasia in a hitherto-unsuspected tradition of pottery-making that reaches back to eastern Asia several millennia earlier.

After having been neglected by archaeologists for many years, the Mesolithic period in Europe has emerged as being of considerable importance for understanding the transition from hunting and gathering to agriculture, particularly in northern Europe. It now seems clear that, in areas such as Scandinavia and the British Isles, the last hunters became the first farmers. **PB**

c. 6900 BCE	c. 6000 BCE	c. 5500–4500 BCE	c. 5000 BCE	c. 5000–4300 BCE	c. 4000 BCE
The first domestic plants and animals appear at Franchthi cave in southern Greece.	Pottery production appears along the upper Volga in western Russia.	Mesolithic people leave footprints along the Severn Estuary in southwest Britain.	Pottery production reaches the Baltic.	A settlement of hunters, fishers, and gatherers is established at Tybrind Vig, Denmark.	The foraging way of life is disrupted and the Mesolithic peoples of northern and western Europe adopt domestic plants and animals.

Hunter-gatherers of the British Isles *c.* 8000−5000 BCE

Star Carr is a Mesolithic camp site in Yorkshire, England, that dates from 9000 to 8500 BCE. The site was first excavated in the 1940s. When excavations were resumed in 2006, new trenches were opened. The camp was along the boggy shore of a lake that has since vanished, and the waterlogged conditions have preserved large quantities of wood and bone.

The lands along the Atlantic coast of Europe and the neighboring seas were rich in the resources on which Mesolithic hunter-gatherers thrived. Until *c.* 6500 BCE, Britain was connected to the European continent, and thus it was an extension of the lowland plain between the Atlantic and Russia across which foraging bands roamed. Coastal zones were attractive for settlement but rising sea levels drowned many coastal sites. Bouldnor Cliff is a submerged site on the coast of southern England, where traces of Mesolithic occupation were discovered in 1999 when divers observed a lobster toss out some pieces of worked flint from its burrow 36 feet (11 m.) below the water surface.

Mesolithic sites of the British Isles take many forms. The most celebrated is the wetland site of Star Carr in Yorkshire, first excavated from 1948 to 1951. Its most prominent feature is a large platform of worked and unworked timbers at the edge of an ancient lake, unique for this period. Other Mesolithic sites include short-term camps, longer-term occupations with substantial houses, and coastal middens (refuse heaps) with the remains of shellfish and other marine foods. In the Aveline's Hole cave in Somerset, the corpses of several dozen individuals were placed unburied just before 8000 BCE. Human burials dated to the Mesolithic have been found in other British caves as well.

Throughout northwestern Europe, the characteristic chipped stone tools of the postglacial hunter-gatherers are known as microliths and consist of very small pieces of flint. Microliths were assembled into composite tools: a spear point might consist of one small pointed microlith on the tip of a wooden or bone shaft, with other microliths embedded down the sides to form barbs.

Ireland was separated from Britain by rising sea levels soon after the glacial retreat. Some game animals, such as red deer, did not make it across before the connection was cut. Nonetheless, the rivers and coasts of Ireland supported mobile groups of Mesolithic hunter-gatherers at low population densities. Migratory fish such as salmon were an important component of the diet. Fish traps made from hazel have been found along the River Liffey in Dublin, as well as along lakes and estuaries elsewhere in Ireland. **PB**

MESOLITHIC SETTLEMENTS

Many Mesolithic sites in the British Isles consist of little more than scatters of flints, but some with more substantial dwellings have been found. Two sites with well-defined traces of houses are Mount Sandel, on a bluff overlooking the Bann River in Northern Ireland, and Howick on the North Sea coast of Northumberland. At both sites, circular houses were framed with stakes or saplings, then covered with hides or reeds. Hearths inside the houses contained charred hazelnuts and bones.

FOOTPRINTS

At several points around the British coastline, footprints dated to the Mesolithic have been found in intertidal estuarine silts. Goldcliff East, on the Severn Estuary in Monmouthshire, has yielded footprints from adults and children, dated between 6000 and 4700 BCE. Archaeologists believe the footprints were made by people collecting shellfish and crustaceans from tidal pools and beach surfaces. The many children's footprints show they were active members of the foraging community.

DOGGERLAND

In 1931, the crew of the trawler *Colinda* hauled up their nets from the bottom of the North Sea to find that they had snagged a lump of peat from the sea floor, a frequent occurrence. Since peat only grows in the open air, this area must have been exposed land in the past. As the men prepared to pitch the lump overboard, it broke open and out fell a barbed antler harpoon. This artifact, clearly fashioned by a human hand, was eventually placed in a museum in eastern England, where it caught the attention of a Cambridge doctoral student, Grahame Clark (1907–95). He recognized it as being similar to harpoons found in Denmark. The find provided additional evidence that in *c.* 8000 BCE it was possible to walk from Denmark to England, with only a few shallow rivers to wade across. Low worldwide postglacial sea levels meant that the edge of the Atlantic Ocean was far to the north, and the English Channel was a river draining westward.

In recent years, the ancient land surface now covered by the North Sea has become known as Doggerland, after the Dogger Bank, a prominent bathymetric (ocean-floor) feature. The land must have been home to Mesolithic communities like those found at Star Carr and other British sites. Further evidence is provided by large quantities of animal and human bones that have been dredged up from the sea floor. Computer models based on data generated by petroleum prospection and gravel dredging have made possible the reconstruction of a vast lowland landscape, with rivers and marshes full of habitats favorable for hunter-gatherers.

Rising sea levels between 7000 and 6000 BCE ultimately inundated Doggerland. Its disappearance may have been hastened by a tsunami caused by an underwater landslide off Norway *c.* 6200 BCE.

Danube Gorges 7400–5900 BCE

Several of the Danube Gorges sites in their later phases feature many small houses of trapezoidal plan. At the center of each is a stone-lined hearth surrounded by paving stones. At the roofed site of Lepenski Vir, Serbia, the houses are arranged around a central open space, suggesting a remarkable degree of planning and structural sophistication.

After meandering south across Hungary and northern Serbia, the Danube river forces its way through the Carpathian mountains in a series of gorges called the Iron Gates before emerging in Romania and wending its way to the Black Sea. In those gorges, on both the Serbian and the Romanian sides of the frontier, a series of remarkable Stone Age settlements have been found. They belonged to the hunters and fishers, and eventually to the farmers, who lived along the Danube over 8,000 years ago.

The most famous of the sites in the Danube Gorges is Lepenski Vir, which was excavated in haste before it was submerged behind a hydroelectric dam built in the late 1960s. Excavations revealed several successive settlements of what appear to be highly successful hunter-gatherers drawn by the abundant fish that congregated around a whirlpool in the Danube. Additional sites were identified at Padina, Hajdučka Vodenica and Vlasac on the Serbian side of the border; more sites were found downstream in Romania, of which Schela Cladovei is the best known. Each site is slightly different, which complicates the task of interpreting them as a group.

Dating the Iron Gates sites has been a challenge because the stratification of the multilayer sites is complicated and often disturbed. Also, a characteristic of radiocarbon dating called the freshwater reservoir effect, in which "old" carbon in water is taken up by organisms, yields earlier dates than the actual calendric ages of the finds in question. However, recent excavations with strict stratigraphic control have established a reliable chronological framework that dates sedentary hunter-gatherer occupation in the Gorges between 7400 and 6200 BCE, followed by a transitional period between 6200 and 5900 BCE, when the foragers made contact with agriculturalists. **PB**

BURIAL SITES

The Mesolithic settlements in the Danube Gorges include one of the largest concentrations of hunter-gatherer burials in Europe. One of the most important sites is Vlasac, Serbia, where extended skeletons were interred lying parallel to the river. Cremation burials are sometimes also present, mixed among the bones.

CARVED BOULDERS

Found among the houses at Lepenski Vir were numerous carved sandstone boulders. Standing up to 2 feet (60 cm.) in height, many are engraved with simple geometric patterns of zigzag lines; others are representations of humanoid figures, including hybrid fish–humans, such as the so-called Siren (5600–4300 BCE).

FORAGERS AND FARMERS TOGETHER?

Lepenski Vir and its neighboring hunter-gatherer sites in the Danube Gorges stand out from the poor record of Mesolithic hunter-gatherers elsewhere in southeastern Europe. Their density and complexity, and the appearance of domestic plants and animals in their upper layers, suggest that the hunter-gatherers found such rich habitats that they settled down and developed characteristics associated with sedentary farming communities—such as permanent architecture and sculpture—while retaining the basic outlines of hunter-gatherer life.

The big question is what happened in the years between *c.* 6200 and 5900 BCE. Neolithic farming communities were already present elsewhere in the Danube region, where they had not yet encountered such thriving groups of hunter-gatherers. The appearance of domestic plants and animals during this period, coupled with even earlier evidence for the use of domestic plants in the dental tartar of the people

at Vlasac, indicates a period of interaction, perhaps of trade, between foragers and farmers. During this period, however, continuity in burial practices suggests that the population occupying the Danube Gorges was not replaced. However, contemporaneous infant burials adjacent to a number of the houses at Lepenski Vir recalls a practice common in sedentary farming communities in the Balkans and Anatolia.

Eventually the hunter-gatherers of the Danube Gorges, as elsewhere in southeastern Europe, were absorbed into the farming communities that spread through the Balkans at the start of the sixth millennium BCE. The slopes of the Gorges were unsuited to agriculture, so people moved to the wide floodplains on which crops could be grown. By 5900 BCE, most of the trapezoidal buildings were abandoned, and the farmers' practice of burying the dead in a crouched, rather than extended position, became predominant.

THE ARCHAIC IN THE AMERICAS

1

1 A copper falcon sculpture (200 BCE–1 CE) by the Hopewell Culture, excavated from a Native American burial mound near Chillicothe, Ohio.

2 A notched flint atlatl projectile point from the Desert Archaic culture in the American Southwest.

The Archaic culture (or period) is one of the most widespread and longest-lasting cultural manifestations on the American continent. It is found virtually all over North America from 8000 to 2000 BCE, although in some areas the Archaic way of life lasted until Europeans arrived and all indigenous cultures on the continent were fundamentally changed. It is often compared to the European Mesolithic, sandwiched as both are between the end of the Pleistocene and the beginning of food production.

The origin of the Archaic culture lies in the profound climatic changes at the end of the last Ice Age, specifically rising temperatures and increased aridity. As the large game animals of the late Pleistocene and early Holocene became extinct, people switched to hunting and gathering animals and plants: rabbit, antelope, deer, birds, and fish; roots, tubers, seeds, and nuts. An important innovation was the introduction of the atlatl, a throwing stick used to propel a spear, which increased hunting efficiency. Projectile points used with the atlatl are typically notched, either in the sides of the point or at its corners (see image 2). In addition to traditional chipped stone technology, the Archaic saw the appearance of ground and polished stone tools. These fulfilled a variety of functions, from grinding seeds and vegetal matter to felling trees.

KEY EVENTS

10,000 BCE	7000 BCE	7000 BCE	5000 BCE	5000 BCE	4500 BCE
Ongoing climatic change at the end of the Pleistocene creates a warmer and drier climate, necessitating major adaptive shifts by human populations.	The occupation of Koster, Illinois, begins and lasts until the Mississippian culture (1200 CE).	Hunters and gatherers begin to occupy Modoc Rock Shelter, Illinois.	The Chinchorro culture of northern Chile and southern Peru (see p. 74) develop the earliest mummification technique.	Corn domestication is established in Mexico, developed from the wild grass teosinte.	The city of Uruk (in modern-day Iraq; the oldest such settlement in the world) is founded.

By the end of the Archaic period, the first experimentation with ceramics had begun. In addition, as population size and density increased, Archaic peoples became more sedentary; they built more permanent villages and larger structures. The extensive mound complex of Watson Brake in Louisiana, constructed by Archaic hunter-gatherers, is an example of this trend. Late Archaic peoples also improved their food cultivation techniques as a precursor to the full-blown domestication of plants such as corn, beans, squash, and amaranth. This transition did not, however, take place in all areas of the continent, nor at the same time. Multicomponent sites such as Koster and Modoc Rock Shelter (see p. 72), both in Illinois, with thousands of years of occupation levels, are useful in showing the processes involved in the diffusion and adoption of cultivation.

Owing to its extreme geographical range, there is much variation in the Archaic. For example, the Desert Archaic culture is found in a huge expanse of the American Southwest, from northern Mexico to southern Colorado and Utah, and its sites have yielded a large number of well-preserved artifacts because of the extreme aridity of the environment. Archaeologists have recovered wooden digging sticks—used for extracting roots from the ground—nets utilized for catching small game, yucca sandals, baskets, tanned hides, and split-twig figurines, the last made by folding a single split twig (often willow) into the desired shape, usually a bighorn sheep or deer.

The Old Copper culture (or complex) is found along the southern coastline of Lake Superior. From c. 4000 BCE onward, Archaic peoples began making various copper artifacts. At first these were utilitarian in nature, such as knives, projectile points, fish hooks, and perforators. Later, copper technology was applied to the creation of personal ornaments, which some archaeologists have interpreted as symbols of social status and inequality. Old Copper culture miners removed huge amounts of copper from deliberately excavated pits, dug as far as 30 feet (9 m.) into the bedrock. These pits are surrounded by thousands of hammerstones, which were used to extract the ore. It has also been suggested that miners may have extracted ore by heating the veins and then dousing them with cold water, thereby splitting the rocks. The copper would have been cold-hammered into shape rather than being smelted. In addition, annealing (the process of alternately heating and cooling the copper) was used to make the metal more workable. Copper technology spread to many parts of the continent, including the Hopewell culture of Ohio (see image 1).

Finally, it should be noted that the use of the term Archaic is problematic. It can be employed to describe a specific culture (a particular way of life) or to delineate a specific time period. Given that the Archaic way of life had a varying duration depending on the geographical area, it is perhaps best to restrict the use of the term to a specific set of cultural adaptations. Nevertheless, Archaic is still often employed as a chronological unit. **PD**

4000 BCE	3600 BCE	3500 BCE	3000 BCE	2000 BCE	c. 1500 BCE
The Old Copper culture begins to use copper to make a variety of everyday objects.	Cuneiform (wedge-shaped) writing is invented at Uruk. It is now the oldest example of its kind in the world.	Construction begins at Watson Brake, northern Louisiana, the oldest earthen mound complex in North America.	The earliest Egyptian pyramids follow from the unification of Lower and Upper Egypt.	Some parts of North America witness increasing experimentation with plant cultivation and ceramic technology.	Copper technology is applied to personal ornamentation.

Social Complexity in the Archaic 7000 BCE onward

Excavations at the Koster archaeological site near Eldred, Illinois, during the 1970s were remarkable for the public interest they attracted. The couple who owned the farm where the dig took place, Theodore (1907–92) and Mary Koster (1908–2001), let members of the public watch.

Archaic peoples were hunters and gatherers. Rather than living in settlements all year round, they moved from camp to camp, their movements dictated by the seasonal availability of resources. Moreover, hunters and gatherers tend not to burden themselves with lots of material possessions. For these two reasons, Archaic hunting-and-gathering sites are much more difficult to locate than large permanent settlements. However, sometimes the forces of nature fortuitously bury these sites and they remain hidden until chance reveals them.

One important example, the Koster site, is located in the lower valley of the Illinois River, approximately 30 miles (40 km.) north of the confluence of the Illinois and the Mississippi. The site lay under farmland, thus contributing to its excellent preservation. The site goes to a depth of 30 feet (9 m.). Alluvial deposits sealed in its different occupations and allowed its primary excavator, Stuart Struever (b. 1931), to catch a rare glimpse of how the Archaic culture changed over time.

Excavations revealed twenty-five different occupations, from Early Archaic (6700 BCE) to the Mississippian period (c. 1200 CE). The Early Archaic Horizon 11, dated to c. 6400 BCE, is particularly important, as it contained evidence for an intensive occupation longer than temporary hunting camps. In this horizon were found a midden (a refuse-disposal area), storage pits, hearths, and human burials. More recent Archaic burials were found on the bluffs overlooking Koster, all with suggestions of a social inequality in how they were treated at the time of death. The excavators also found five domesticated dog skeletons deliberately interred in pits.

The excavations at Koster are important for many reasons. The stratified well-preserved levels provided much knowledge on the development of Archaic culture over thousands of years. Struever also employed a multidisciplinary approach to analyzing the site and its remains. Every effort was made by the excavation team to involve the public, and the site received more than 10,000 visitors a year when it was excavated in the 1970s. **PD**

👁 FOCAL POINTS

MODOC ROCK SHELTER

The Modoc Rock Shelter Archaic site is located in southern Illinois. Late Pleistocene flooding initially undercut the base of a cliff at the edge of the Mississippi River valley, providing shelter for Archaic hunter-gatherers. Over time the rock shelter was filled with alluvium as the Mississippi River flooded, and this preserved a number of Archaic occupations, both short-term and long-term base camps. The earliest occupation level dates to c. 7000 BCE; the latest aboriginal occupation dates to 2000 BCE.

WATSON BRAKE

Located in northern Louisiana, the Watson Brake Archaic site has the earliest earthen mounds yet found on the continent. The site was first occupied about 6,000 years ago. From c. 3500 to 3000 BCE its occupants constructed eleven mounds as high as 25 feet (7.5 m.), arranged in an oval pattern. These mound constructions show that hunter-gatherers were capable of the type of communal organization that is usually associated with sedentary agricultural communities.

🕐 ARCHAEOLOGIST PROFILE

1931–64

Stuart Struever was born in Illinois. He attended Dartmouth College, graduating in 1953. Five years later, he entered the doctoral program at the University of Chicago. His dissertation focused on the Woodland Period of the American Midwest. His doctoral advisor was Lewis Binford (1931–2011), who advocated New Archaeology (later renamed Processual Archaeology) and argued for a multidisciplinary, science-based approach to the study of the past.

1965–83

Struever joined the faculty at Northwestern University. He continued research in the Woodland Period, settlement patterns and the origins of agriculture. From 1969, he led the team that excavated Koster. Struever saw the importance of helping the public understand—through hands-on participation—why archaeology makes a vital contribution to society and to understanding the past. He founded the Center for American Archeology from its Kampsville campus while it conducted excavations at Koster.

1984–94

Struever retired from Northwestern University. He moved to southwestern Colorado, where he continued his interest in public involvement in archaeology. His leadership led to the foundation of the Crow Canyon Archaeological Center, which is still one of the most important research and public-outreach organizations in the United States. Struever retired from this institution in 1992. He remained involved in the field of archaeology in various roles, including fundraising for Crow Canyon. Struever served as Northwestern University's chairman of the department of archaeology, editor of *Studies in Archaeology and Memoire*, and as a board member on national humanities and science committees. He was president of the Illinois Archaeological Survey and the Society for American Archaeology.

1995–PRESENT

The Society for American Archaeology presented Struever with its Distinguished Service Award in 1995. The society then awarded him a Presidential Recognition Award in 2003.

The Chinchorro *c.* 5000–1200 BCE

The Atacama Desert is the most arid in the world and one of the most difficult landscapes for human life. It is only habitable thanks to resources provided by seasonal rivers that descend from the Andes, as well as springs, mists, and the sea. The Chinchorro society would have experienced climatic conditions very similar to those of the present day.

The Chinchorro culture, which first appeared *c.* 5000 BCE and persisted for more than four millennia, is one of the most significant and oldest pre-Hispanic societies that has been found on the edge of the Atacama Desert, which extends along the coasts of southern Peru and northern Chile. This hunter-forager-fisher society is well known for the mummified bodies of its elaborate funerary tradition, which spread from the region of Ilo in the far south of Peru to Antofagasta in Chile. German archaeologist Max Uhle (1856–1944) is credited with identifying that the greatest concentration of mummies was to be found in northern Chile, especially in the Arica-Camarones region.

The Chinchorro funerary tradition is characterized by clusters of human burials that mummified naturally in the dry desert environment. The bodies, in groups of three to nine individuals, were set out side by side on their backs with their limbs extended. Great care was taken in the postmortem treatment of the bodies, which conformed in method to two successive traditions: black mummies (from 5000 to 2800 BCE) and red mummies (from 2000 to 1500 BCE). In addition, three other types of mummies were also common: bandaged mummies, mud-coated ones, and those wrapped in reed cords. The ritual mummification of bodies almost certainly had a role in ancestor worship.

Apart from the burials, Chinchorro material culture is scarce. The people were sedentary fishermen, hunters and gatherers who lived in semi-subterranean circular houses. Their way of life, material culture, and funerary practices suggest a relatively egalitarian society. It is remarkable that a society that was so ancient and had so little in the way of natural resources and technology should form complex ideas about death and develop such a sophisticated knowledge of the treatment of human bodies. **HT**

FOCAL POINTS

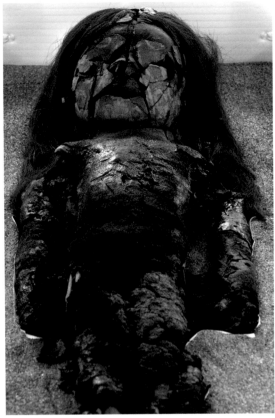

BLACK MUMMIES

To create a black mummy, a buried body was unearthed and reassembled after the soft tissue had decayed. The organs were removed but the skin was retained, sometimes laid alongside animal skins. The cavities were filled with botanical material and clay. Later, the skull and skeleton were reassembled; cords were used to tie them to wooden sticks. The faces of the dead were then recreated using grey manganese mud.

RED MUMMIES

Red mummies were less elaborate than the black ones. Here, the body was more directly disrupted as organs, parts of muscles, and the skull were extracted through cuts in the skin. A wooden frame was created for the body and inserted underneath the skin; the body cavities were filled with various materials. The head was replaced, and wigs of human hair were added. Finally, the whole body excepting the face and hair was covered with ocher pigment.

ARCHAEOLOGIST PROFILE

1856–91

Max Uhle was born in 1856 in Dresden, Germany. He obtained his doctorate in Linguistics at the University of Leipzig in 1880, going on to work in Dresden's Royal Museum of Zoology, Anthropology, and Ethnology. He moved to Berlin in 1888 to work at the Royal Ethnographic Museum of Berlin, led by Adolf Bastian (1826–1905). In 1892 he was commissioned to travel to South America to make collections for the museum.

1892–1916

Arriving in Buenos Aires in 1892, Uhle went first to northwest Argentina, before entering Bolivia in 1893 with the primary intention of investigating the site of Tiwanaku, once the seat of the pre-Columbian Tiwanaku culture. Starting work for the University of Pennsylvania in 1895, he moved to Lima and excavated at Pachacamac in 1896. In 1899 he visited and excavated at Huacas de Moche. He was director of archaeology at the National History Museum, Lima, between 1905 and 1911. Then, in 1912, at the invitation of the Chilean government, Uhle moved to Santiago de Chile, where he founded and directed the Museum of Ethnology and Anthropology.

1917–1944

In 1917, Uhle carried out systematic excavations in Arica, northern Chile, discovering and scientifically recording hundreds of Chinchorro mummies. Then, at the invitation of Jacinto Jijón y Caamaño (1890–1950), Uhle moved to Ecuador, in 1920. There, he excavated in places as important as Tomebamba (1921–22) and Cochasqui (1933). Uhle returned to his homeland in 1933, dying there in 1944.

JAPANESE MESOLITHIC

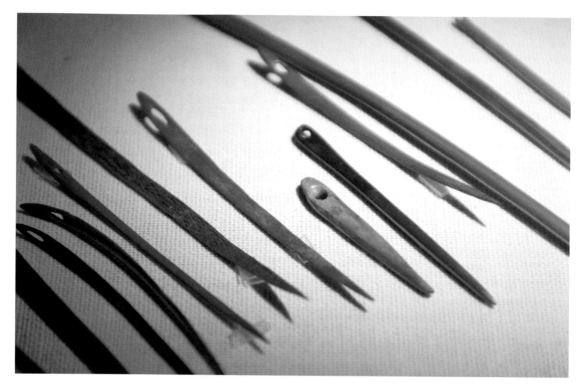

1 Jōmon-period bone needles from the Sanmaru Museum in Aomori Prefecture.

2 A pit-house reconstruction at the Sannai-Maruyama Early to Middle Jōmon settlement in Aomori Prefecture.

3 A conical terracotta *fukabachi* (deep bowl) from the Early Jōmon period.

The Mesolithic culture followed the Paleolithic era, and developed with diverse local adaptations to special environments. In the case of Japan, these two archaeological periods overlap in time, and archaeologists needed to define different concepts for these cultures in the archipelago.

Between 10,500 and 7500 BCE, the Japanese archipelago saw a brief and unusual drop in temperature. The sea fell to between 65 and 131 feet (20 and 40 m.) below its present level, leading to a period of rapid warming. Alpine forest receded, and wild animals retreated to the mountains. Climatic changes help to account for the existence of a Mesolithic, when much of the abundant fauna of earlier times became depleted by the expanding human population of the archipelago. Humans started to live in caves, still hunting and gathering for food. The introduction of the bow and arrow is regarded as a local response to a decrease in game available for food.

No written records are available to aid in interpretation, so it is archaeology alone that helps to determine the various cultural distinctions within Japanese prehistory. Archaeologists therefore examine pottery, stone tools, pit

KEY EVENTS

c. 10,500–8000 BCE	c. 8000–5000 BCE	c. 7500 BCE	c. 5000–3500 BCE	c. 5000–3500 BCE	c. 5000–4000 BCE
The Incipient Jōmon period, the prehistoric era of tribes and Stone Age hunter-gatherers.	Large amounts of seafood refuse are deposited in shell mounds.	Japanese pottery appears. Pots are made by hand using the coiling method to build up coils of soft clay.	People start to live in pit houses. There are clear cultural differences between people on various islands.	Tools, stone awls, scrapers, and axes are used. Storage pits appear.	Potters in Kanto produce *ka'en-shiki* (fire flame)-type pottery, so called because the coils of clay resemble leaping flames.

dwellings (see image 2), human remains, and burial systems. Periods are marked by typological terms, mostly determined by Western archaeology, which are not always applicable to Japanese prehistory. Some terms are more useful in their Japanese form, such as the Jōmon period, which takes its name from a style of pottery (see image 3) found throughout the Japanese archipelago. The term was first used in 1877 by U.S. zoologist Edward S. Morse (1838–1925) to describe pottery decorated with *jōmon* (cord-pattern) impressions. The Jōmon period is divided into six phases: Incipient (*c.* 10,500–8000 BCE), Initial (*c.* 8000–5000 BCE), Early (*c.* 5000–2500 BCE), Middle (*c.* 2500–1500 BCE), Late (*c.* 1500–1000 BCE), and Final (*c.* 1000–300 BCE).

The Incipient Jōmon includes the transition between the Paleolithic and Neolithic eras, when hunter-gatherers lived in simple surface dwellings and pottery production began. During the Initial Jōmon period, the sea level rose and the southern islands of Japan, Shikoku, and Kyūshū were separated from the main island. Food supplies increased and were processed with stone tools, such as knives and axes. The Early Jōmon period is known for its shell mounds (mounds of edible mollusk shells and other refuse that indicates human occupancy), while its pottery is similar to finds in Korea, which probably indicates early exchange between the islands. People lived in small villages, and archaeological excavations have brought to light bone needles (see image 1) and ceramic storage vessels. The Middle Jomon people started to live in larger communities. They relied on fishing; on hunting bear, rabbit, or duck; and on gathering nuts, berries, and mushrooms; but there was a slow change toward an early cultivation of plants. Burials took place in shell mounds, and early female figurines are found in caves such as Kamikuroiwa in Ehime Prefecture on the island of Shikoku (see p. 78). The people of the Late and Final Jōmon periods settled closer to the coast, employed new techniques in fishing, and performed communal rituals in several spheres of life. Regional differences became apparent and rice domestication was introduced.

Archaeological finds indicate that weaving of fibers was unknown during the Jōmon period. However, the manufacture of woven baskets appears to have begun in the Early Jōmon period. Bone needles and thimbles have been recovered from various sites. Mulberry bark was often woven into cloth, while ornaments made of seashells, stone, clay, and horn appeared in the later periods. Throughout the Jōmon period, the manufacture of ceramics saw major changes. From urnlike and cylindrical containers with simple cord designs, pottery developed to include vessels with complex patterns of raised lines and decorative projections on the rims or handles.

In the later Jōmon period, the typical pit house featured a superstructure supported by five or six posts over a central fireplace, and had an average of five occupants. Some villages had stone platforms, probably for ceremonial purposes, as well as storage pits. **MP**

c. 5000–2500 BCE	*c.* 2500 BCE	*c.* 2500–1500 BCE	*c.* 1500–1000 BCE	*c.* 1000–300 BCE	*c.* 300 BCE
The first contacts are made with the Korean peninsula, leading to similarities in the pottery produced.	There is an increase in population and the production of handicrafts.	People start to cultivate plants and are sedentary for longer periods of time.	People assemble stones in circles at various sites for important rituals.	Climate changes causes a decline in population.	The Jōmon period ends. There is a transition to the Yayoi period; it lasts to the third century CE, and is marked by a new pottery style.

Kamikuroiwa 14,000–300 BCE

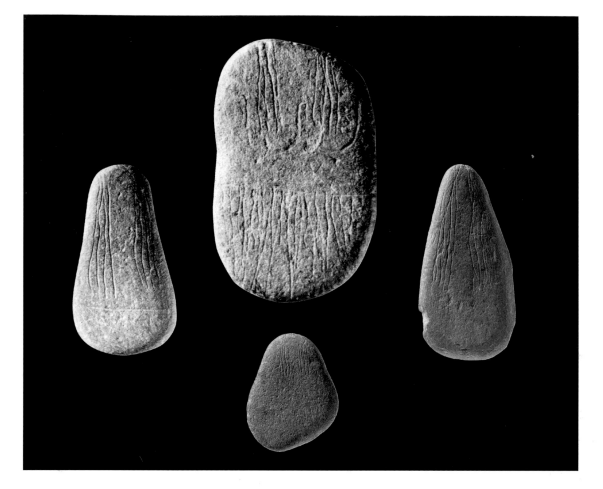

Some of the so-called Venuses from the Kamikuroiwa site in western Japan. The stone figurines are about 15,000 years old. They are small enough to fit in the palm of the hand.

The Kamikuroiwa archaeological site is a limestone rock shelter, located in the township of Kumakogen, in Ehime Prefecture on the island of Shikoku in western Japan. It is a small-scale site, eroded from a slope of coal-bearing rock situated on the right bank of the Kuma River. Facing southwest, it is 29 feet (9 m.) wide, 13 feet (4 m.) high and 6 feet 6 inches (2 m.) deep.

Local landowners found the site in 1961. It underwent five excavation campaigns until 1970 and is still an important subject of study for archaeologists. Research on the material unearthed has proved that the site dates from the Incipient to the earliest Jōmon periods, a time corresponding to the latest Palaeolithic and Mesolithic in Europe. The rock shelter was used continuously until the Kofun period (250–552 CE). People probably lived there seasonally, from spring to fall, because of the considerable temperature drop in the intermontane areas.

The numerous artifacts and items brought to light included large amounts of pottery, stone implements, stone Venuses that probably served as fertility talismans, and animal remains. Human bones from twenty-eight individuals have been excavated, and constitute the largest collection of specimens from any single site dating to the earliest Jōmon period. The remains include those of three adult males, eight adult females, and seventeen children or adolescents. The deceased were found in the extreme rear of the rock shelter. Given that the shelter was used for daily life, this means that the burials took place in the vicinity of the living. **MP**

👁 FOCAL POINTS

Excavations at the Kamikuroiwa rock shelter began in 1961, well guarded by policemen and observed by curious locals. Five excavations were undertaken up to 1970. The small shelter is located at an elevation of 1,377 feet (420 m.) and the sun shines into it in the afternoon. Artifacts have accumulated to a depth of 6 feet 6 inches (2 m.) inside the shelter. Kamikuroiwa is considered a major archaeological site of the Jōmon period, and has been designated a National Historic Site.

DOG REMAINS

In 1962, two sets of dog remains were excavated from Kamikuroiwa. For nearly half a century these bones were thought to be lost, but they were rediscovered in 2011. Most buried dog bones have been found in a flexed position, with the complete articulated skeleton preserved. This is also true of the dog bones found at Kamikuroiwa. The remains correspond to a time from the end of the Initial Jōmon to the beginning of the Early Jōmon period, so constitute one of the oldest dog burials in Japan.

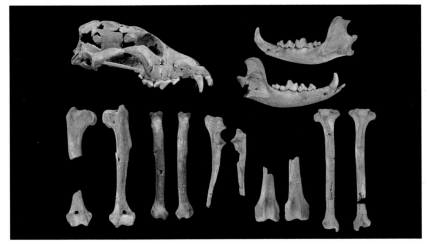

POTTERY, ORNAMENTS, AND STONE FIGURINES

The pottery excavated at Kamikuroiwa consists of more than ten pieces of linear-relief pattern pottery, five pieces of plain pottery, and four forms of cord-patterned ware. Altogether there are no more than twenty pieces from any era, so the amount of pottery excavated from the Incipient Jōmon era is extremely small. Carbon was detected adhering to even the oldest pottery, proving that the vessels were used for stewing and boiling.

Ornaments were found inside cord-patterned earthenware near the human bones, which suggests that they were adornments for the dead. They mostly date from the earliest Jōmon period: there were round beads made of shells, rod-shaped earrings, necklaces of small beads, and bracelets made of deer antler or boar tusks. Some round beads were also made of fish bones. Only a few small stone beads and triangular stone pendants were found in the shelter. All the shells were seashells from conchs, cowrie, or cone snails.

Thirteen stone figurines, the Kamikuroiwa Venuses, have been found at the rock shelter. Each is made on a small cylindrical rock shaped to portray the human form, either female or male. Fine lines have been scratched on the stones. Some of the incisions depict human figures with hair, breasts in the upper part, and lattice and saw-tooth markings in the lower part, probably representing a skirt. There are also stone figurines with a large or sometimes slender upper body, in which the gender is not clear. Although other relics with depictions from this time are known, no similar stone figurines have been found anywhere else.

NEW GUINEA: PLANT DOMESTICATION

1   A satellite view of Kuk in the New Guinea Highlands. The site consists of 287 acres (116 ha.) of swamps.

2   The drainage and management system at Kuk is not unique. Similar features, including ditch networks, have been identified at several other sites in the region, such as Warrawau, Tambul, and Mugumamp.

The identification of early agricultural systems in highland New Guinea highlights the complexity of defining agriculture and documenting the slow transformation from hunting and gathering to farming. Complex systems of management of plant resources through the manipulation of the environment can be traced back thousands of years in New Guinea. These systems predate the separation of New Guinea from Australia by rising sea levels. Indeed, complex practices of resource management have been identified in parts of Australia, too, most notably the use of "firestick farming."

The evidence for New Guinea as an independent center of plant domestication comes from several different strands, including linguistics and plant genetics, as well as archaeology and the reconstruction of past environments. Direct archaeological evidence is quite sparse because many of the crops grown were not cultivated from seeds but through vegetative propagation. The remains of these types of plants are rare archaeologically, although advances in the microscopic analysis of starch grains and phytoliths are beginning to provide direct evidence of the presence of key species.

Archaeologists believe that a wide range of plants cultivated in Southeast Asia and the Pacific originate from New Guinea, including taro, yams, bananas, breadfruit, and sago. The exact timings of many of these domesticates are unclear. However, linguistic evidence indicates that both bananas and sugarcane had spread to the islands of Southeast Asia in the early to mid Holocene. Most archaeological evidence for the domestication of plants comes

KEY EVENTS

Before 50,000 BCE	c. 40,000 BCE	Before 10,000 BCE	10,000–9500 BCE	c. 7000 BCE	5000–4490 BCE
Sahul is colonized, and archaeological evidence for occupation has been found in most regions of Australia and in New Guinea.	The sites of Buang Merabak, in the Bismarck Archipelago, and Kosipe, in the New Guinea Highlands, are occupied at this time.	A wide range of plants are used in the New Guinea Highlands, with evidence of burning for hunting and plant exploitation.	The first evidence of plant and animal domestication in Western Asia dates back to this period.	Phase 1 at Kuk provides evidence of erosion and management of the swamp margin.	Evidence of drainage channels and raised beds from Phase 2 at Kuk, probably for the cultivation of a range of plants, dates back to this period.

from the pioneering excavations at Kuk Swamp in the Upper Wahgi Valley (see image 1), conducted by Jack Golson (b. 1926). The oldest phase at Kuk dates back to approximately 10,000 years ago. The excavations identified soil erosion resulting from local forest clearance, and indicated environmental management at the swamp margins. A range of earth features were uncovered, including stake holes, some of which may be associated with the exploitation of various tuberous plants. Starch residues on stone artifacts suggest that plants used include both taro and yam. It is not clear whether the species were wild or domesticated forms. Nor is this unequivocal evidence of deliberate plant cultivation. However, soil and pollen evidence from other sites in the New Guinea Highlands indicates forest clearance at about the same time, and it is likely that the practice of maintaining and enlarging forest clearings to promote plant growth had a long history.

The earliest undoubted evidence of cultivation comes from Phase 2 at Kuk, just under 7,000 years ago. Here, a network of short channels defines small islands, or raised beds (see image 2). These channels retained water during dry times, but also drained surplus water into larger channels. The features can be interpreted as a system of manipulation of the swamp margin to allow multiple crops with different requirements to be grown together. Taro would have been planted within the channels, whereas sugarcane, banana, and other dry-land plants were grown on the raised beds. At the same time, ground stone axes became relatively common in sites in the region. This probably reflects more extensive forest clearance, which is apparent in pollen diagrams. As in Phase 1, microscopic analysis of residues on stone tools confirms that taro and yam were grown. Beginning approximately 4,350 years ago, Phase 3 at Kuk signals a new period of intensive wetland management and drainage, marked by a series of ditch networks.

There is no evidence for the independent domestication of animals in New Guinea. The main domestic animals in the area today (pigs, dogs, chickens) came from Southeast Asia, most probably brought by Austronesian-speaking Lapita people in c. 1500 BCE. Before then, New Guinea subsistence was based on a range of complex practices involving the cultivation and management of different species of plants, as well as hunting animals. In the Bismarck Archipelago, off the northeast coast of New Guinea, there is archaeological evidence for the transportation of various animal species to the islands. This practice is first documented as far back as 18,000 BCE, with the appearance of phalanger (a type of possum) at several sites in New Ireland. By the time that substantial evidence for forest clearance and swamp management appeared in the highlands, in c. 5000 BCE, a number of animal species, including a small wallaby, had been introduced to various islands in the region as far as the Solomon Islands. The reasons for this are unclear, but the animals could have been introduced as food or for other useful resources such as fur. **CB**

c. 4500 BCE	2400–2030 BCE	c. 1350 BCE	50–750 CE	1550–1700	1930s
Ground stone axes are used in the highlands at Manim 2.	Phase 3 at Kuk is marked by extensive networks of linear drainage channels.	Austronesian speakers associated with the Lapita cultural complex reach Melanesia, bringing domestic animals.	Phase 4 at Kuk has evidence of more intensive drainage networks, representing more intensive and specialized cultivation.	Phase 5 at Kuk is associated with the cultivation of the sweet potato introduced from South America.	An expedition led by Australian explorer Michael Leahy (1901–79) first encounters the people of the New Guinea Highlands.

NEOLITHIC REVOLUTION

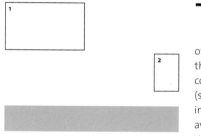

1 Houses in a Pre-Pottery Neolithic village, Beidha, Jordan, reconstructed on original foundations (7200 to 6500 BCE). Their inhabitants grew barley and wheat, bred goats, and hunted wild animals.

2 Neolithic farmers ground crops such as wheat and barley with querns like this reconstructed example from Beidha.

The first steps toward the development of farming took place in the Epipaleolithic period in West Asia, as Natufian villagers in the Levant and adjacent areas developed a sedentary way of life involving intensive use of wild plants, food storage, and year-round reliance on local resources. During the cold and arid Younger Dryas period (10,900 to 9800 BCE) some communities, such as the inhabitants of Tell Abu Hureyra in modern Syria (see p. 84), began to cultivate the surviving cereals, causing genetic changes in the plants. When conditions eased after 9600 BCE, and cereals increased in availability, dense stands of different wild cereals occurred in various parts of West Asia. To harvest these required a few days' intensive labor but yielded enough grain to provide staple support for the harvesting family for the year.

While the development of farming is often regarded as "progress," it was not inevitable, obvious, or necessarily desirable. Farming can support more people in a given area, but it is more labor-intensive than foraging and so reduces leisure time. Early farming provided a less varied diet than foraging and was therefore less healthy: early farmers were smaller than contemporary hunter-gatherers and suffered tooth decay and deficiency diseases. Later, as population size and density increased, endemic diseases also developed.

KEY EVENTS

11,000 BCE	9600–7000 BCE	9400 BCE	9150–8950 BCE	c. 9000 BCE	c. 9000 BCE
Rye and possibly wheat show genetic evidence of domestication, probably due to deliberate planting, at Tell Abu Hureyra on the Euphrates.	The Pre-Pottery Neolithic (PPN) period in the Levant; the time span divides into PPNA (c. 9600–c. 8500 BCE) and PPNB (c. 8500–c. 7000 BCE).	Villagers at Tell Abu Hureyra cultivate cereals and hunt gazelle; they herd sheep after 8300 BCE.	Emmer wheat is grown by the first settlers at Tell Aswad, modern-day Syria: it must have been domesticated earlier somewhere else.	People growing wheat settle at Tell Aswad, near Damascus; by 7500 BCE the village is substantial, covering around 12 acres (5 ha.).	The village of Jericho, (see p. 86) abandoned during the Younger Dryas cold spell, is reoccupied; growing to around 10 acres (4 ha.), it is enclosed by a wall.

Why, then, did farming happen? Many scholars argue that population increase was the catalyst: sedentism (see image 1) encouraged population growth, leading to the need for greater yields from the settlement's habitat, thus encouraging the planting of cereals (see image 2) and other staples on suitable patches of local land where they did not grow naturally. Groups also moved out and founded new communities, eventually reaching areas where the desired or required resources, such as cereals, were scarce or absent, also encouraging deliberate cultivation. Certainly, once farming became established, people progressively colonized all the regions in which dry farming was possible, and developed technology to enable them to farm in regions beyond. Settlements grew ever larger, from at most several hundred people c. 10,000 BCE to some with thousands by 7000 BCE, although the majority were still small. The population-growth argument is compelling, but there may have been other reasons to create a food surplus: perhaps in order to engage in competitive feast-giving, or support community or intercommunity construction of monumental shrines.

Beginning in c. 11,000 BCE, but mainly after 9500 BCE, cereals were domesticated in their areas of natural occurrence—barley and emmer wheat in Syria and the Jordan valley; einkorn wheat in the Karacadag region of southeast Turkey. Other plants were also domesticated in various parts of West Asia, and exchange networks rapidly spread them through the regions in which they could be grown. By 8000 BCE, these included pulses such as pea, chickpea, lentil, and bitter vetch; figs; and flax for oil seeds and for making linen fiber.

Animal husbandry also developed in different regions, sheep being domesticated in the Zagros region as early as 9000 BCE and goats by 8000 BCE; pigs in Anatolia by c. 8500 BCE and cattle by 6000 BCE. The move to farming was not sudden but gradual. Intensively using, and relying on, wild cereals and pulses that could be stored led people to deliberately planting them, watering and tending them, and clearing competing vegetation to increase yields. This resulted in changes to the plants, some of them intentional. Once farming was set in train, it was hard to retreat from it and revert to foraging. Farming supported populations beyond the capacity of foraging, and clearing natural vegetation reduced the wild resources available for foraging. Domesticated plants depended on continued human intervention for their propagation; and farming communities developed ties with their land. The development of territorial ideologies is a major change associated with the beginning of farming.

Domestication and later agricultural advances have supported a continuing rise in world population, but poor management and overexploitation could always locally reverse this trend. At 'Ain Ghazal, for example, excessive tree clearance and overgrazing caused soil erosion, reducing farmland, and the site declined. **JM**

8500 BCE	8500 BCE	c. 8000 BCE	c. 8000 BCE	7500 BCE	6000 BCE
Farmers colonize Cyprus, using boats to bring domestic crops and animals, and also wild fallow deer. They establish villages such as Shillourokambos.	A cat buried at Shillourokambos indicates that wild cats, drawn to hunt vermin attracted by stored grain, have by now become domesticated.	Farmers in the Levant and eastern Turkey are raising domesticated emmer and einkorn wheat, barley, and pulses, plus flax for its oilseeds or fibers.	Domestic sheep and goats are herded in the Zagros (Iran and Iraq) and Taurus (Turkey) regions, at sites such as Ganj Dareh (Iran).	A full mixed farming economy, with cereals, pulses, and domestic animals, is established across the dry-farming regions of West Asia.	Olives are intensively exploited at Mersin in Turkey and slightly later at Kfar Samir, now a drowned site off the Carmel coast of modern-day Israel.

Tell Abu Hureyra 11,500–7000 BCE

Abu Hureyra's rectangular mud-brick houses were rebuilt repeatedly on the same base, thereby suggesting ownership by a family over generations. The old house was demolished down to a few courses of brick and the room stubs infilled with clay—often covered by a layer of stones—to create a flat surface on which the new house was constructed.

◆ NAVIGATOR

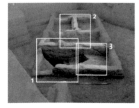

Tell Abu Hureyra was established in c. 11,500 BCE, during the Natufian period, favorably situated to exploit the Euphrates river and its backswamps, forested alluvium, plateau steppes, and open hilly woodlands. The wide range and abundance of plants and animals enabled a hunter-gatherer community to live there year-round. Early settlers constructed circular semi-subterranean pithouses; later they built circular houses on the ground surface. They hunted, mainly gazelle, and gathered a great range of plants, including at least thirty varieties of cereals and other seeds. In c. 11,000 BCE, probably in response to diminishing resources as the cold, dry conditions of the Younger Dryas developed, they also began to cultivate rye and perhaps wheat.

From 9400 BCE, as warm, moist conditions returned, the settlement rapidly expanded and became one of the largest villages known in West Asia at the time. Domestic cereals—rye, three varieties of wheat, and two of barley—now provided most of the villagers' plant foods; domestic pulses—lentils, peas, and vetches—were also important. Some wild leafy plants, roots, and fruits were still gathered. Hunting still relied mainly on gazelle, although sheep were also eaten. After 8300 BCE, however, domestic sheep and goats became the main source of meat, as in many contemporary farming sites. By this time the villagers were building rectangular mud-brick houses, close together, separated by narrow alleys and small courtyards. The main room, in the middle of the building, contained a central hearth and often a separate oven on a platform beside one of the walls. By 7300 BCE, the population had increased to between 5,000 and 6,000. However, thereafter it declined, and the site was abandoned in c. 7000 BCE. **JM**

◉ FOCAL POINTS

1 PLASTER

Plaster was a major Pre-Pottery Neolithic invention. Limestone was burned to make lime, which was then mixed with water to create a plaster that dried to concrete hardness. This was used mainly for floors, but also to make "white-ware" containers, the precursors of pottery in the region.

2 WALLS

The rectangular houses were divided by internal walls: the example seen here had five rooms. All of its walls were two mud bricks thick, although some houses had external walls three bricks thick. High sills connected these rooms and may originally have held doors.

3 PLASTER FLOOR

Lime plaster often covered the house floors. Floor plaster, hard and easy to keep clean, was either left white or colored using readily available pigments: soot for black, ocher for red. The floor was generally renewed several times: clay was spread over the old surface before the new floor was laid.

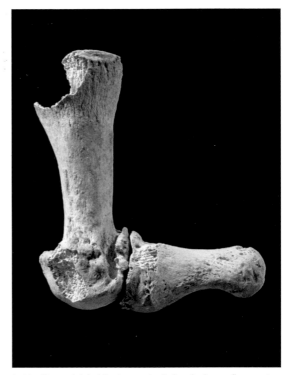

▲ Abu Hureyra's inhabitants were buried under house floors or in abandoned houses. Their skeletons reveal that they were generally well fed, but that the diet exacted a price from women, who spent many hours a day grinding grain: kneeling, pressing the ground with their toes, and pushing strongly with their arms and back. Well-developed arm muscles and deformed knees, vertebrae, and toes bear witness to their labors.

THE FLOTATION MACHINE

The 1960s and 1970s saw a major focus on investigating the origins of agriculture, led by Eric Higgs (1908–76). Traditional excavation methods rarely recovered small bones or plant material: at Abu Hureyra, experiments with technology to address this problem were conducted.

Excavated soil was sifted to recover small remains missed by diggers. Four wheelbarrow loads of soil from each deposit were passed through a froth-flotation machine devised to recover plant material. The soil was poured into a sieve submerged in water to separate denser material from carbonized seeds and other plant remains. A frothing agent and paraffin helped this light material to float; air was bubbled through to separate the material. The denser fraction was then wet-sieved through a coarser-meshed sieve, thus recovering small bones and bone fragments, beads, and microliths (chipped stone tools). The material collected by dry and wet sieving and flotation greatly increased knowledge of early agriculture.

Jericho 10,000–7000 BCE

In the early Pre-Pottery Neolithic A period, Jericho's first houses were replaced by more substantial circular ones, still semi-subterranean, of mud brick on stone foundations. The houses were surrounded by a massive wall, beyond which a wide, deep moat extended down into the bedrock.

♦ NAVIGATOR

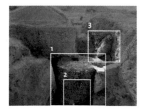

Famous from the Bible, the settlement of Jericho (modern Tell es-Sultan) in Palestine attracted archaeologists' attention early on. By 1936, John Garstang (1876–1956) had established that an early farming settlement existed beneath the Bronze and Iron Age city, but it was the work of Kathleen Kenyon (1906–78) here in the 1950s that revealed unexpectedly spectacular details of Jericho's early history.

Around 10,000 BCE, during the Natufian period, people and the animals they hunted were attracted here by the local springs, which also watered abundant vegetation. Settlement began in circular semi-subterranean houses, and, after a break, the site was reoccupied in the early Pre-Pottery Neolithic A (PPNA) period. The settlers now grew wheat, barley, and pulses, but still hunted gazelle. Remarkably, they built a very substantial wall around the settlement, with a huge tower. There was no need for defense against enemies at this time, so it may be that the wall was intended to divert flood waters away from the village. The wall and tower also may have been created by the community to reinforce group identity and unity; or the wall may have formed a boundary, preventing refuse dumped outside from accumulating within the settlement.

The wall and tower fell into disrepair in the later Pre-Pottery Neolithic B period, during which substantial rectangular mud-brick houses were built, their interiors divided into three by mud-brick piers that may have supported the roof. Often, one of these three rooms contained a sunken hearth. Jericho was abandoned around 7000 BCE, though it was reoccupied during the Pottery Neolithic period (6400–4500 BCE) and later. **JM**

FOCAL POINTS

1 TOWER

A huge tower of boulders and mud was constructed against the inner face of the wall's west side. From here, approaching people and herds of animals could be observed—perhaps the tower's purpose. Alternatively, the tower, which dominates the settlement, may have played an important part in ceremonial activities.

2 DOOR AND STAIRCASE

On the tower's eastern side, a door opened into a passage leading to an internal staircase of twenty-two stone steps, each made of a single slab at least 3 feet (1 m.) wide. This gave access to the top of the tower, which is 27 feet (8 m.) from the base. The door was blocked when the tower was abandoned in the PPNB period.

3 PERIMETER WALL

A wall, built of large stones set in mud mortar, was constructed around the settlement in the PPNA period. Great community organization and cooperation were required to bring the materials a mile (1.6 km.) from the adjacent mountains. The wall was gradually extended upward, eventually reaching 16 feet (5 m.) high.

◄ Jericho was well placed to participate fully in the exchange network of its period. Salt and bitumen from the nearby Dead Sea, turquoise from Sinai, cowries from the Red Sea, and Anatolian obsidian from Çiftlik have all been discovered there.

ARCHAEOLOGIST PROFILE

1906–30

Kathleen Mary Kenyon was the daughter of Sir Frederick Kenyon (1863–1952), later director of the British Museum. After studying history at Oxford, she gained experience of excavation at Great Zimbabwe (see p. 476) in 1929.

1930–51

Working at Verulamium, England, with Mortimer Wheeler (1890–1976) and Tessa Verney Wheeler (1893–1936), she embraced their systematic methodologies in excavation, stratigraphy, and archaeological recording, later introducing these to West Asian archaeology. She served as acting director of the Institute of Archaeology in London during World War II.

1951–58

Appointed honorary director of the British School in Jerusalem, Kenyon began systematic excavations at Jericho in 1952, uncovering the early farming settlement, including its impressive wall and tower. Her establishment of the site's stratigraphy provided a clear chronology of the development here, from the earliest, pre-farming settlers to the Iron Age.

1958–78

Kenyon's excavations in Jerusalem (see p. 232), from 1961 to 1967, investigated the city of David. She was appointed principal of St. Hugh's College, Oxford, in 1962. Following her retirement in 1973, she devoted herself to writing.

FARMING AS A CULTURAL CATALYST

1

2

1 Two human figures dance with an animal on a carved limestone slab from Nevali Çori, an early Neolithic settlement on the middle Euphrates, in Şanliurfa province, Turkey.

2 This stone figurine of a ram, dated around 7500 BCE, was found in the substantial early Neolithic village of Tel Motza, Israel. It had been placed with another animal figure in a large building that probably served a ritual function.

The development of farming brought significant changes in many aspects of life, not just in the foods eaten and the means used to obtain them. Sedentism similarly brought changes well beyond the simple abandonment of a mobile way of life. Supported by cultivated crops and domestic animals, and encouraged by the reduced interval between births that sedentism allowed, farming populations grew in size and density. At the same time, only some parts of the landscape were suitable for cultivation (in contrast to the great diversity of environments that hunter-gatherers exploited): this concentrated population into particular environmental zones.

Hunter-gatherer communities were generally small, managing social relations at a family level. Kinship and other ties allowed individuals to move between groups, which eased social tensions and encouraged fluid community composition. Settled farming communities, however, were tied to their cultivated land and had to manage far more social interactions, without the luxury of moving away when interpersonal problems arose. Kinship was still crucially important, but new social mechanisms were needed to manage community relations. Archaeological evidence of these is hard to pin down, but clues may be found. Some unusual buildings in settlements were probably used by community members for discussions of local matters or celebrations. Others were shrines (see p. 90), bringing the community together through shared rituals. Special treatment after death might mark individuals who had a special role in the community, such as a leader, shaman, or chosen ancestor.

KEY EVENTS

9600 BCE	9000–8700 BCE	9th millennium BCE	c. 8350 BCE	8000 BCE	8000 BCE
A stone shrine is built at Göbekli Tepe, Turkey: equally elaborate shrines may have previously existed in (now-perished) wood.	Three unusual circular, subterranean structures are built in Jerf al-Ahmar village, Syria. Their decoration and contents suggest a ritual function.	Beads, pins, and awls are made by cold-hammering native copper (naturally occurring pure copper) at Çayönü Tepesi in southeast Anatolia.	An enormous stone wall and tower built at Jericho, Palestine, show that villagers are able to collaborate and complete massive community projects.	Cloth found in Nahal Hemar Cave, Israel, is made by twining linen threads; contemporary evidence of tabby woven textiles survives at Jarmo, Iraq.	Bones are collected in a "house of the dead" at Dja'de al-Mughara, Syria. This one of the ways in which ancestral remains are curated in Neolithic West Asia.

Together, farming and sedentism spurred the development of ideas of territorial ownership and inheritance: emphasizing and validating these ideas often involved ways of linking the living with their ancestors (see p. 92)—by burying the dead beneath houses, curating their remains (such as skulls or mummies), or erecting funerary monuments. Correctly identifying the living and their affiliations was also important, both in asserting land ownership and in managing social relations, with kinship as a major element in both. Sedentism allowed the accumulation of possessions and encouraged the development of craft activities, and many objects were designed to mark identity and affiliation, including personal ornaments such as beads.

Some materials used to make jewelry and other objects were acquired from afar through social exchange networks. Obsidian, identifiable to source, marks the distance these could travel. Even in the Natufian period, tiny amounts of central Anatolian obsidian were reaching sites in the Levant; over time the volume of obsidian circulating in Neolithic West Asia from multiple sources grew hugely, as did the distances it could travel. Many other materials were also in circulation, such as gemstones and shells.

Plant fibers, used to make cord and simple cloth in late Paleolithic times, now included cultivated varieties, and new textile manufacturing and decorative techniques were developed. Food storage was important, including the use of pits and boxes built into houses; separate containers, including baskets and textile bags; and carved stone or wooden vessels, and ones of artificial materials, particularly pottery. The use of fire to bake clay objects had been discovered in the Paleolithic period; pottery was made in East Asia by 18,000 BCE, and repeatedly invented at different times in other parts of the world, but not until 7000 BCE in West Asia. Pottery transformed cuisine, allowing food to be boiled and stews, broths, porridge, and gruel to be created, whereas before that food was only roasted over the fire or baked on hot stones.

Architecture was also born from sedentism. Constructing permanent houses encouraged not only experimentation with new building materials, such as mud brick and plaster, but also artistic creativity: painted house walls became common in many cultures. Shrines and monuments created with enormous effort and decorated in many ways (see image 1) appear widely in the early postglacial period, associated mainly with farming communities, but sometimes with sedentary communities depending on other, locally abundant, resources. Artistic creativity is also seen on a smaller scale, in the creation of figurines and other portable objects—both those related to ritual (see image 2) or other cerebral aspects of life and ones used in embellishing the purely functional, such as the figures carved on Kebaran sickles. These were nothing new: art and the decoration of everyday objects were known in the Paleolithic period, but the range, quantity, and diversity were greatly increased, and the pace of invention was much quicker. **JM**

8th millennium BCE	8th millennium BCE	7000–6500 BCE	6500 BCE	Early 6th millennium BCE	5000 BCE
Lime plaster, concrete-hard and sometimes painted, is used in West Asia to cover floors and make "white-ware" vessels.	Skulls, possibly representing selected ancestors, are given reconstructed features of lime plaster with shells for eyes, and are put on display.	Some West Asian farming settlements now extend over 25–50 acres (10–20 ha.) and have populations numbered in thousands.	Cattle skulls and cattle horns are incorporated into the decoration of rooms in the enormous settlement of Çatalhöyük in Turkey.	A bracelet of copper beads strung with cotton thread proves that cotton has begun to be cultivated in the village of Mehrgarh, Pakistan.	Chinchorro sedentary hunter-fisher-gatherers in Peru and Chile use complex processes to reassemble their dead as mummies (see p. 74).

Göbekli Tepe 9600–8200 BCE

The Göbekli Tepe shrine is arranged as a series of circular unroofed enclosures, 35 to 100 feet (10 to 30 m.) in diameter. At least twenty such circles have been identified here by geophysical survey, and six have been excavated. Each has drystone walls into which are set a number of T-shaped pillars. Two larger T-shaped pillars stand in each circle.

◆ NAVIGATOR

A large mound at Göbekli Tepe near Urfa in Turkey had attracted mild interest over the years because of the large stone blocks scattered over its surface, but it was not until 1995 that it was actually excavated—to reveal an astonishingly early shrine with extraordinary art and architecture.

The joint Turkish−German excavations, directed by Klaus Schmidt (1953−2014), uncovered small, rectangular structures with monolithic pillars in the most recent levels, dated to c. 8200 BCE; however, as the excavators penetrated deeper, they discovered a shrine complex with much larger monumental monolithic pillars dating back to 9600 BCE or earlier, making it the earliest known shrine in the world. More than 200 monolithic pillars have been identified. Quarrying and transporting these was an incredible achievement. Around 500 people would have been needed to move each stone, quarried on the adjacent plateau, a quarter of a mile (0.4 km.) away: given the low population density of the time, this had to represent the communal endeavors of a number of groups. Butchered bones, mainly of gazelle but also of red deer, boar, cattle, sheep, goats, and birds, including vultures, cranes, partridges, and ducks, were found across the site; these may represent the remains of food that people consumed while here.

Despite the numerous bones, there are no traces of habitation. At this time the region was inhabited by people who lived by hunting and gathering. Wild einkorn wheat was abundant here (this region has been identified as the one where it was first domesticated). One novel theory suggests that large numbers of hunter-gatherers assembled here annually at around the time that the dense stands of wild wheat were ripening. They would have hunted their animal competitors, while also collaborating to raise the shrines and engaging in ritual activities. After harvest, the groups would have dispersed, taking the grain back to their separate base camps elsewhere. **JM**

1 CENTRAL PILLARS

The pair of large, T-shaped pillars in the center of each enclosure may have been intended to symbolize human (or divine) figures, the crossbar representing the head and the upright the body. This is suggested by the depiction on some pillars of arms, hands, and possibly clothing. The arrangement of the central pillars facing each other perhaps reinforces the idea.

2 CONCENTRIC WALLS

After a drystone circle had been in use for a number of years, perhaps for one or two generations, it was replaced. The old wall was buried and a new, smaller circle erected within it. Eventually the whole circle was infilled and a new circle erected in another part of the mound. Later, small, rectangular enclosures were erected over the infilled remains of the earlier circles.

3 SIDE PILLARS

Set at intervals within each circular wall is a series of monolithic, T-shaped limestone pillars. These pillars are enormous: one example, found incompletely quarried and perhaps abandoned as being too ambitious, was 23 feet (7 m.) high and weighed as much as 50 tons; most are up to 16 feet (5 m.) high with weights ranging from 10 to 20 tons.

▲ All the T-shaped pillars bear carvings, mainly in relief but occasionally in the round. Though a huge range of creatures is shown—including gazelles, donkeys, ducks, and flocks of cranes—the emphasis is generally on dangerous animals in threatening poses, and on maleness: snarling lions, leopards, and foxes; menacing bulls and rampant boars; snakes and scorpions; and vultures with their wings spread and heads poised to peck.

OTHER EARLY SHRINES

Göbekli Tepe is the earliest and most impressive of a series of shrines created by people in this region. The later village of Nevali Çori, 20 miles (32 km.) away, had a sunken square enclosure with a plastered floor, edged with a drystone bench faced and capped with stone slabs, with pillars set at intervals. In its center was a monolithic T-shaped pillar, originally one of a pair, carved with arms. Stone pillars were erected within a square sunken building at Çayönü Tepesi, farther north in Anatolia. Jerf al-Ahmar in Syria, contemporary with Göbekli Tepe, had a sunken circular enclosure edged by a stone bench faced with decorated slabs and set at intervals with massive wooden posts. Many of the carved creatures that appear on Göbekli Tepe's monolithic slabs, especially bulls and vultures, reappear at Çatalhöyük (see p. 96), millennia later, suggesting continuity of early belief systems.

Ancestor Cults 8800–6500 BCE

Some of the Jericho skulls, probably chosen to represent ancestors, were given special treatment. Disinterred after the flesh had decomposed, they were coated in plaster to remodel the head and features. Hair and facial hair were painted on, and cowrie or bivalve shells inserted as eyes. Plastered skulls were displayed on house floors or in community buildings, or reinterred in pits.

The remarkable Pre-Pottery Neolithic (PPN, c. 9000–7000 BCE) village of Jericho in Palestine (see p. 86), was excavated between 1952 and 1958 by Kathleen Kenyon (1906–78). Among the surprising finds from its later phase, PPNB, were a number of extraordinary skulls. Following death and decomposition of the bodies, the skulls of certain individuals had been removed and their features remodeled in lime plaster, with cowrie shells to represent their eyes. The skulls had then been displayed. Similar skulls later found at other sites confirmed that the practice was common in the PPNB period. It followed a simpler practice of occasional skull detachment that began before 10,000 BCE.

In 1974, road building at 'Ain Ghazal in Amman, Jordan's capital, unearthed remains of a substantial PPN settlement, excavated from 1982. One pit, found in 1983, contained plaster figurines, half life-size, with cowrie-shell eyes, that were clearly created as part of the same ritual tradition as the PPN plastered skulls. The figures had been carefully stacked in a purpose-dug pit, which had then been filled in. The worn state of the figures, some of which had broken feet, suggested that they had been frequently used, probably in rituals. When no longer required, they were ceremonially buried rather than discarded. A second pit brought the total of figurines found at 'Ain Ghazal to twenty-eight, some being complete figures and some represented by head and torso only; they were dated to between 7200 and 6500 BCE. Burial practices in the settlement varied. Some bodies were dumped in refuse pits. Others were interred under floors; often their skulls were removed later, some being plastered and kept on display, while others were reburied in separate pits, divorced from their bodies. All this evidence suggests that the PPN people practiced an ancestor cult to affirm their ties and rights to their ancestral land. **JM**

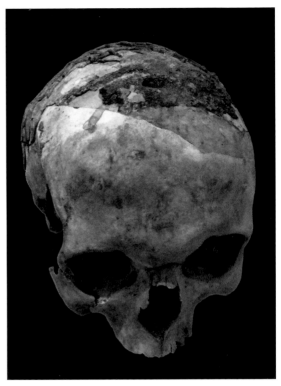

HALF LIFE-SIZE FIGURINE

The 'Ain Ghazal figurines consist of a framework of twine-tied reeds covered with plaster. Some are plain; others have painted bands on their faces and bodies, perhaps representing clothing. Some are full-length, around 36 inches (90 cm.); others are simply armless torsos. Many are gender-neutral; others clearly female.

DECORATED SKULL

The arid cave site of Nahal Hemar, Israel, housed skulls that were not plastered, but had a net pattern drawn in bitumen on the back of the cranium. Also present were wooden figurines; textiles made by twining linen threads or weaving; baskets; mats; and masks in the form of elongated human faces, made from painted stone.

RESTORATION OF THE FIGURINES

When discovered in 1983, the 'Ain Ghazal figurines had long since lost their organic framework of reeds, leaving only rigid but fragile empty plaster shells. Over time, soil accumulating above had compressed and cracked the figurines, shifting or destroying some thinner pieces, while chemical changes had cemented the mass of them together. Their discovery posed a major problem: broken into thousands of fragments, they retained their form only while they lay in the ground; if disturbed, they would crumble into meaningless flakes. British conservator Kathryn Walker Tubb was asked to tackle the problem: little did she realize that it would be a decades-long task.

The figurines could not be dealt with in situ, so the whole block of soil containing them was cut out and shipped to the Institute of Archaeology's laboratories in London. Exhaustive photographic records were made before the meticulous work of deconstructing and restoring the surviving remains was started. The task began with cleaning the figurines' delicate plaster surfaces and the friable pigment used to decorate them. The soil was removed under a microscope, millimeter by millimeter, using scalpels, needles, dental probes, soft brushes, and other precision tools, as well as laser cleaning devices. Perspex rods were inserted to provide a rigid framework and were packed around with cotton to replace the decayed reed original. Displaced plaster pieces were gently moved back into their original positions. The task was like building a complex, three-dimensional jigsaw puzzle. Missing pieces were replaced with an appropriately distinct but unobtrusive modern material.

When all the conservation had been completed on a figurine, it had to be carefully lifted and mounted for study and display. Such work is extremely slow, difficult, and painstaking—but the results are magnificent and potentially highly informative.

WEST ASIA

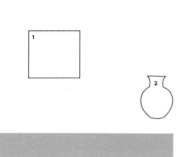

1 An earthenware vase decorated with incisions, deriving from the Hassuna culture and dating from 6500 BCE.

2 Found at Tell Hassan, Iraq, this ceramic vase, painted with geometric and zoomorphic patterns, was made by the Halaf culture in the late fifth millennium BCE.

By the seventh millennium BCE, farming was well established as a way of life in the region extending from the Levant through northern Mesopotamia to the Zagros foothills, Iran and Iraq in the east, and Turkey in the west. Emmer, einkorn, and hulled barley, the original domesticated cereals, were now joined by evolved, improved, or hybrid forms such as naked barley and bread wheat, and the range of crops was growing.

Sheep, goats, pigs, and cattle were herded; present in most areas, their ratios depended on local environmental circumstances, though sheep and goats predominated. Animals were still hunted, but in small numbers. Domestic animals were initially kept for meat, but by 6500 BCE they were also being milked. Most humans cannot digest milk protein (lactase) beyond infancy, so at first milk was processed into yogurt and cheese, as residues in pots reveal. Over time, many people in areas where milk products were used, including West Asia and Europe, acquired a genetic mutation that produced lactose (the enzyme infants use to digest lactase) throughout life, enabling them to drink milk.

From 7000 BCE, pottery began to be made, at first quite crude but developing by 6500 BCE into well-made painted or incised Hassuna ware (see image 1) in northern Mesopotamia; different wares were made in other regions. Metal

KEY EVENTS

7400–5500 BCE	7000 BCE	6500 BCE	6200 BCE	6000 BCE	5600 BCE
At Çatalhöyük, Turkey, the farming settlement of houses with painted walls, entered from the roof, eventually grows to 33 acres (13.5 ha.).	Copper ore is smelted to extract metal for manufacturing objects by hammering and annealing. Melting and casting in open molds begins c. 5700 BCE.	Milking of animals begins: residues in pottery from Anatolian sites show that milk was being processed, probably into yogurt or cheese.	The settlement at Tell el-'Oueili is the first indication of farming communities in southern Mesopotamia.	Halaf pottery with highly geometric polychrome painted designs is made right across northern Mesopotamia.	A village is established at Choga Mami (see p. 98) in central Mesopotamia, using a small canal to make farming possible since rainfall was insufficient.

ores, particularly copper, were being smelted by 7000 BCE, to be melted and cast into simple shapes in open molds by 5700 BCE. By the mid-fifth millennium, two-piece molds were in use, allowing more complex shapes to be cast. The ceramics and metallurgy reflected pyrotechnological advances, with kilns achieving ever greater temperatures. After 6000 BCE, extremely fine Halaf ware (see image 2) appeared across northern Mesopotamia, made by people who built domed circular houses (*tholoi*), sometimes with a rectangular annex. In general, however, houses were rectangular, made of mud brick or pisé (packed earth), often having a large room with small rooms opening off it for storage. Most settlements were small, but in the regions where agriculture had first developed, the Levant and eastern Anatolia, some settlements grew to enormous size: these included Basta and 'Ain Ghazal (Jordan), Abu Hureyra (Syria), Beisamoun (Israel), and, most famously, Çatalhöyük (Turkey, see p. 96). Occupied by thousands of people and located in particularly favorable locations for agriculture and interregional exchange, these megasites were eventually abandoned for various different reasons, but perhaps partly because there were as yet no adequate social mechanisms to cope with tensions arising among large numbers of people coexisting without an overriding authority.

Around 6200 BCE, there was a massive fall in global temperatures and an increase in aridity that endured for up to 400 years. Farming communities became smaller but more widespread, and animal husbandry increased in importance in some regions, now including transhumance (taking herds to higher or inland grazing during the summer months and back to lowland or coastal pastures in the winter). Perhaps in response to the drier conditions, people also developed simple water-control mechanisms such as small canals to irrigate crops, enabling them to settle beyond the region of rain-fed agriculture. In southern Mesopotamia, the high agricultural potential under irrigation spurred rapid population growth.

Exchange networks between communities flourished from early times and became more developed between 7000 and 3000 BCE. The range of goods included foodstuffs such as olives, and raw materials such as copper ore, obsidian, turquoise, and shells, as well as some manufactured goods. Technologies and ideas also spread. The development of the slow-wheel in southern Mesopotamia saw mass-production of Ubaid pottery in the later fifth millennium, with distribution extending to northern Mesopotamia and south through the western Gulf. Metallurgy was also advancing: a hoard of copper objects found at Nahal Mishmar, Israel, shows that lost-wax casting of complicated shapes was now well developed. The Nahal Mishmar finds relate to a local shrine, and religious installations of various forms were now appearing. In some areas, such as southern Mesopotamia, shrines began an unbroken sequence of development into historical times. **JM**

5400–5000 BCE	5400 BCE	5000 BCE	4900 BCE	5th millennium BCE	Late 5th millennium BCE
Evidence from the analysis of a residue in a jar found at Hajji Firuz Tepe, Iran, shows that resinated wine is now being produced.	A small, one-roomed shrine is the first in a sequence of increasingly elaborate temples built at Eridu, Iraq (see p. 100).	A clay model boat from Tell Mashnaqa, Syria, resembling southern Mesopotamian boats made of reed bundles, suggests river traffic along the Euphrates.	A large building with a number of rooms at Tell Kosak Shamali, Syria, is used as a workshop, probably by several potters.	Olives, intensively exploited by 6000 BCE, are now fully domesticated in the southern Levant; olives and olive oil are used there in quantity.	Bitumen with reed and barnacle impressions, and a painted depiction of a boat in Kuwait, both attest to the use of seagoing sailing boats made from reeds.

Çatalhöyük 7400–5500 BCE

Çatalhöyük's mud-brick houses were tightly packed together without streets—the roofs provided a walkway across. A hole in each roof led down a ladder into the house below, which probably accommodated a family of up to ten people. A house might last for up to 100 years, before being half-demolished and a new house built on the filled-in stub.

NAVIGATOR

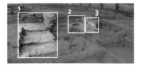

The Neolithic mound of Çatalhöyük in Anatolia was discovered by James Mellaart (1925–2012) and others in 1958; till then, it had been thought that occupation began in Anatolia only after the Neolithic period. Excavating the site from 1961, Mellaart uncovered closely packed houses containing extraordinary art, as well as material shedding light on early Neolithic life. After 1965, excavations ceased but the site's fame lived on, and Ian Hodder (b. 1948) restarted work here in 1993. Since then, use of modern techniques has revealed far more information about the life of the inhabitants.

Çatalhöyük was first occupied around 7400 BCE by people who were already farming. They grew wheat, herded sheep and goats on higher ground nearby, and caught fish and water birds in the surrounding marshes. Aurochs (wild cattle) were hunted, their meat being eaten probably in communal ritual or celebratory feasts. The villagers made tools of flint and obsidian, as well as pottery for domestic use and figurines. By 6500 BCE, they were also keeping cattle, for meat and for milk, processed into yogurt or cheese. Çatalhöyük's inhabitants took part in contemporary exchange networks, acquiring shells for jewelry from the distant Red Sea. From the Göllü Dag and Nenezi Dag sources in Cappadocia they obtained obsidian, a material both useful and extremely attractive. It was highly prized in the Neolithic period for making tools, beads, and other objects.

As the settlement grew in size, reaching 335 acres (13.5 ha.), some people moved out to set up villages elsewhere on the Konya plain, including Çatalhöyük West Mound, but still buried their dead in the main settlement and probably joined in community activities there. Occupation in the West Mound continued after the main settlement was abandoned. **JM**

1 PLATFORM

The interior of the room was largely occupied by low platforms built of brick and covered with plaster. On one stood the oven in which the household's cooking was done. Others were used for daytime activities and for sleeping at night; or for holding baskets to store things in daily use.

2 GRAVE

The platforms also served as tombs: burial pits were dug beneath the house floor; after interment the platform was rebuilt and replastered. Bodies were buried tightly contracted, probably wrapped in a mat. Graves were single or multiple, and could contain as many as sixty individuals.

3 PLASTERED WALL

The interior walls were covered with white-washed plaster, renewed annually. Frequently the walls were decorated with elaborate geometric patterns or figurative scenes. In some houses, bulls' horns, separate or attached to the skull, were fixed to the walls or used in other decorative ways.

EXPLAINING EARLY MEGASITES

As a settlement, Çatalhöyük's size seems anomalous: it housed 3,500 to 8,000 people at its peak. It is generally thought that, as a settlement's size rises, so does its complexity: that mechanisms for managing large numbers of people and their interactions would require leaders to emerge, while other factors would encourage craft specialization and other social, economic and occupational differentiation. Thus complex settlements (towns) should emerge when numbers reach a certain level, and cities (even more complex settlements) when they climb still higher and demands and opportunities increase. In terms of size, Çatalhöyük is a town, but in organization and function it is a hugely overgrown village, composed entirely of small, self-sufficient households. A few other similarly huge early Neolithic West Asian settlements are known. They are a puzzle: what social mechanisms enabled so many people to live together in such close proximity and apparently in harmony? Shared religious beliefs may be one answer.

Choga Mami 6300–5000 BCE

Distinctive pottery styles allow archaeologists to identify cultural groups. Samarran ware, typically with patterns, animals, people, and birds painted in dark colors, was made in central Mesopotamia by people practicing simple irrigation, while farmers growing rain-fed crops farther north made different styles of pottery.

The village of Choga Mami in central Iraq, covering 15 acres (6 ha.), was excavated by Joan (b. c. 1930) and David (1927–2004) Oates from 1967 to 1968. It was established in the Samarran period; this began c. 6300 BCE at the related site of Tell es-Sawwan, a large village surrounded by a substantial mud-brick defensive wall and external ditch, with houses and material very similar to those at Choga Mami.

Choga Mami and other sites of the region yielded Samarran pottery, a ware associated with sites lying beyond the limits of rain-fed agriculture in central Mesopotamia. Flint tools at Choga Mami included an increasing proportion of sickle blades through time, an indication of the importance of agriculture. The inhabitants of Choga Mami, Sawwan, and other Samarran sites grew emmer and einkorn wheat, bread wheat, three varieties of barley and pulses, as well as flax, a thirsty crop. The large size of the grains recovered from Samarran sites indicates that the plants were grown using irrigation, which helped the farmers to achieve a higher yield. Direct evidence of irrigation was found associated with Choga Mami. Otherwise, the villagers mainly herded sheep and goats, but they also kept a few pigs and still hunted gazelle. Domestic cattle do not make their appearance in Choga Mami until the late Samarran period.

Development of irrigation and water-control techniques encouraged the spread of settlement into adjacent regions beyond the limits of rain-fed agriculture, including southern Mesopotamia and the Deh Luran plain in Iran. Lizard-headed figurines show links between the late stages of the Samarra culture at Choga Mami (the Choga Mami Transitional phase) and contemporary sites in southern Mesopotamia, such as Eridu (see p. 100) where the Ubaid culture was beginning to develop.

The later levels at Choga Mami were removed by erosion, so the only surviving traces of the post-Samarran period come from surface finds of pottery, and from wells dug down into Samarran levels from the now-vanished ground surface. **JM**

ALABASTER FIGURINE

Samarran sites produced attractive figurines. At Choga Mami, tall thin female figurines of terracotta wore jewelry similar to that found in the settlement. Beautiful alabaster figures with eyes and eyebrows outlined in bitumen were made at the contemporary settlement of Tell es-Sawwan, Iraq.

HOUSES

Choga Mami's houses were rectangular, with external buttresses, and were divided by partition walls into two or three rows of three to four rooms. They were built of long, cigar-shaped bricks, laid in courses that alternated headers and stretchers. The lowest courses were often externally plastered to protect them from weather.

WATER MANAGEMENT

Choga Mami was founded in a region slightly beyond the zone where rainfall was sufficient for cultivation, so its inhabitants had to devise ways to supply their crops with water during the growing season. Small water channels were uncovered in the excavations here, cut to bring water from the Gangir river at the point where it transitions from the mountain to the plain. During most of the Samarran period these small channels provided simple fan irrigation; in the late phase, however, they were replaced by a single larger canal, around 20 to 26 feet (6 to 8 m.) wide and up to 3 miles (5 km.) long, following the slope's contours and watering a more extensive area. This system continued in use over the next two millennia, its location shifting slightly as the occupation level rose. Tell es-Sawwan also shows evidence of irrigation, using water from the Tigris river. Contemporary sites farther northwest on the Mandali plain had simple irrigation canals, as did most later sites on the Deh Luhran plain, farther east in Iran.

Water-control technology was a key development because it allowed farmers to spread into lands beyond the range of rain-fed or flood-based agriculture. Simple techniques enabled people not only to water their crops but also to divert and, if appropriate, store potentially damaging excesses of floodwater. In southern Mesopotamia (Babylonia), the Tigris and Euphrates flooded annually, watering land and depositing fertile alluvium; but these floods occurred at just the wrong time of year, when cereal crops were ready for harvest. Thus, they threatened the crops and did not supply water when needed. Water-control techniques were a prerequisite for agricultural colonization of this richly fertile environment. By the third millennium BCE, Babylonia had evolved, from simple beginnings, a sophisticated system of flood control, with canals, reservoirs, dams, sluices, and regulators that controlled the rate of flow in the channel.

Eridu 5400–2000 BCE

Little evidence of housing was found at Eridu. Today's inhabitants of the Iraqi marshland build magnificent structures from tied bundles of reeds, and this was probably the case in antiquity, too. Later Sumerian art shows reed-built farm buildings. An architectural reed bundle is the symbol of the goddess Inanna, indicating the importance attached to this architecture.

Eridu (Tell Abu Shahrein in modern-day Iraq), legendarily the world's first settlement, first attracted antiquarian attention in the nineteenth century, but full excavations were carried out only from 1945 to 1949, jointly led by Seton Lloyd (1902–96) and Fuad Safar (1911–78). A ziggurat (stepped tower), built by kings of the Ur III dynasty around 2050 BCE, dominated the site, but it became clear that by then Eridu was an empty shell, revered for its past sanctity but unoccupied. Its heyday had been far earlier, with its occupation stretching back to the later sixth millennium BCE. The settlement declined during the early fourth millennium BCE, surviving only as a religious center.

Around 1000 pit burials, 200 of which were excavated, provide direct evidence of the inhabitants. The graves contained the remains of single individuals or family groups, each accompanied by a pottery jar, dish, and cup. Some bodies wore jewelry, including obsidian beads. One young man was buried with his dog across his chest, with a bone in its mouth. Eridu's pottery included beautiful painted vessels. Further, in this region virtually devoid of stone, people made imaginative use of clay to create tools, including very hard, surprisingly efficient baked-clay sickles and "bent nails" (pestles).

Southern Mesopotamia in the sixth and fifth millennia BCE was a region criss-crossed by small rivers and streams, and its southern portion, Sumer, was probably largely marshland. A model sailing boat found here reflects the importance of water transport to the people of the region. Sheep and goats were kept by farmers in Eridu and other Ubaid settlements, but in this wetland region cattle became the favored domestic animal: later artwork depicts people milking cattle and churning milk to produce butter and make cheese. Fishing, hunting wildfowl, gathering marsh plants, harvesting dates, and eventually cultivating date palms also played an important part in Eridu's economy. **JM**

FOCAL POINTS

CLAY FIGURINE

Probably of religious significance, clay figurines found in Eridu burials are long and thin, often with breasts and other female characteristics, and elongated lizard-head faces with eyes resembling cowrie shells. Bitumen, clay blobs, and incised striations represent clothing, jewelry, scarification, or tattooing.

THE SHRINE AT ERIDU

Eridu's earliest shrine was a single room with a recessed niche for the altar and a pedestaled offering table facing the entrance. In time the shrine's design was extended into a rectangle. With the later addition of side chambers, the shrine assumed the standard tripartite form of Mesopotamian temples.

THE SANCTITY OF ERIDU AND ITS SHRINES

Eridu held a special place in ancient Sumerian religious belief. It was thought that, in the beginning, primordial waters separated into the Ocean and the freshwater Abzu and that the Earth originated as an accumulation of silt where these waters met. Eventually the gods came into being. Enki, god of the Abzu and responsible for all the waters of the Earth, filled the empty world and assigned every part its role and attributes. People were created to serve the gods, and Eridu was made as a place for them to dwell. Eridu in antiquity was situated between desert, alluvial plain, and marsh, and occupied an island of higher ground within a depression 20 feet (6 m.) deep that held a freshwater lake, taken by the Sumerians to be the Abzu. It was at Eridu, therefore, that they built Enki's shrine.

Babylonia's bountiful but unpredictable environment led its inhabitants to rely on religious authorities who could mediate between humanity and the inscrutable gods. Shrines became the focus of community activity,

receiving offerings of produce from the surrounding people, who also labored to construct temples of ever-increasing magnificence. Eridu's excavations revealed a sequence typifying this. A small, one-roomed shrine, 10 feet (3 m.) square, was constructed around 5400 BCE. This was demolished and repeatedly rebuilt in a larger, more elaborate form. Many inhabitants of the region would have congregated here for particular ceremonies. Numerous fishbones from the shrine in its later versions suggest offerings of fish or ritual feasts.

By 3500 BCE, the shrine stood on a platform and was surrounded by subsidiary buildings—probably priests' residences, administrative offices, workshops, storerooms, and treasuries—the whole enclosed by a stone wall. Later these were all razed to create the platform for the last, most magnificent incarnation of the temple. Eridu remained a place of pilgrimage, venerated throughout Mesopotamian history.

AFRICAN PASTORALISTS

1

2

3

1 In this aquatint (1805) by Samuel Daniell, Khoekhoe pastoralists in South Africa prepare to move to new pastures.

2 Rock paintings of cows at Laas Geel, Somalia, suggest their central importance in the Neolithic economy of the artists, probably 5,500–4,500 years ago. The cows have remarkable stylized bodies, prominent udders and lyre-shaped horns. The neck is often decorated with multicoloured stripes.

3 This camping scene, engraved in Wadi Tiksatin in the Messak, Libya, is one of the few portrayals of a cow being milked.

In many ways less well known than hunter-gatherers or farmers, pastoralist peoples in Africa were an important presence over many millennia. "Pastoralism" is a much-debated term, but it generally refers to an economy based mainly on the herding of domestic animals, which also loom large in cultural and religious life. (Some peoples are herders without this being the primary or central element of their subsistence strategies.) Traditionally, prehistoric pastoralism has been linked to the Neolithic, a term originally coined for the last part of the European Stone Age, transitional to the introduction of farming, but of questionable utility for materials elsewhere. In its original usage, it also refers to the making and use of ground stone tools and pottery as part of a Neolithic cultural package. However, the situation in Africa is rather different. One significant difference is that, unlike in the Middle East, herding and pottery both long preceded plant cultivation.

The study of early pastoralists is hampered by the fact that the traces that mobile peoples leave on the landscape may be relatively ephemeral. In South Africa, for example, despite numerous historical accounts of Khoekhoe peoples with large cattle herds, known sites are remarkably few and far between. Other lines of evidence, such as genetic information on the development of lactase persistence (tolerance of lactose beyond infancy), provide insights into the origins of the consumption of milk from domestic animals. Linguistic evidence and the presence of domesticated livestock in rock art are additional clues.

KEY EVENTS

c. 10,200–4500 BCE	c. 9000 BCE	c. 8000 BCE	c. 7000–6000 BCE	c. 5000 BCE	c. 3500–2500 BCE
Prior to farming, the Neolithic, beginning in the Middle East, marks the advent of cereal cultivation and the keeping of domestic animals.	A period of increased humidity transforms the Sahara desert into a verdant environment, with greenery and lakes.	Early cattle remains in Egypt date to this time, but whether they are wild or domesticated cattle remains unclear.	Early sheep arrive in Africa from the Levant, perhaps at the same time as a variety of Asian cattle.	Analysis and dating of the residues of milk lipids in pottery vessels indicate dairying and consumption of milk products in the Libyan Sahara at this time.	The early Holocene humid phase ends and desertification of the Sahara resumes.

Inevitably, the origins of African pastoralism are tied to the origins of domesticated animals. Of the principal animals herded, none were domesticated from African species (but there is evidence for the management and corraling of wild Barbary sheep in Libya in *c.* ninth millennium BCE). Cattle, sheep and goats as well as camels were all introduced species, but controversy persists about when and from where. Ten-thousand-year-old cattle bones from Egypt may not have been domesticated animals, and some maintain that the first imports came via the Levant approximately 8,000 to 9,000 years ago. Sheep and goats may have been introduced at a similar time along the same route. There is also genetic evidence that suggests that there may have been a domestication of one cattle type in North Africa approximately 10,000 years ago. However, camels were a later introduction, appearing in North Africa by the early first millennium CE.

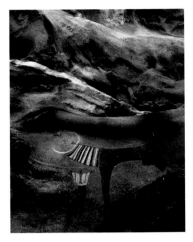

Key areas in the archaeology of African pastoralists include the Sahara, east Africa, and southern Africa. Knowledge of these sites indicates that pastoralists in different times and places varied considerably in their use of animals, mobility, ways of life, and material culture. In east Africa, early herder assemblages dating from *c.* 2500 BCE onward, often containing ground stone bowls but with varying pottery and lithic assemblages, are described as Pastoral Neolithic. Images of domestic animals in Saharan rock art are particularly evocative and informative, and suggest the important role that domestic stock played in cultural and religious as well as economic life. Sheep and cattle are well represented in the art (see image 2). Some images of cattle emphasize the udders, and there are a few depictions actually showing cows being milked (see image 3). The prominence of sheep and cattle in this body of art testifies to the importance of domestic animals, economically and beyond.

Pastoralists in southern Africa have been the subject of intensive research in recent years, throwing up interesting and important questions. Until recently it was thought that the Khoekhoe (see image 1; formerly known by the highly pejorative term Hottentots) originated in northern Botswana, bringing sheep and pottery with them in waves of southward migration over the past two millennia. An alternative hypothesis suggests that it was Later Stone Age hunter-gatherers who first acquired sheep approximately 2,000 years ago, in a southern African Neolithic period. This does not exclude some southward migrations of Khoe speakers, but provides another explanation for the scarcity of identifiable Khoekhoe pastoralist sites. Nevertheless, hunter-gatherers persisted, and it has been counter-argued that their notions of individual property inhibited their adoption of pastoralism.

The study of African pastoralism and its origins is poorly understood in several ways, but the important role of this way of life over many millennia is clear: pastoralism is a flexible economic strategy that is well suited to marginal environments and the vagaries of changing climates. **AS**

c. 3000–2000 BCE	c. 2200 ya	c. 2000 ya	300–400 CE	2nd–5th century	15th–19th century
The earliest evidence for herders in east Africa probably relates to the movement of peoples in response to growing aridity in the Sahara region.	Domestic caprines (either sheep or goats), are present at Leopard Cave, a Later Stone Age cave site in Namibia.	Domestic sheep reach the southernmost tip of Africa, as indicated by bones from Later Stone Age coastal cave sites.	Camels are introduced to North Africa, where evidence shows them being used by Berber nomadic pastoralists by the mid first millennium CE.	Early Iron Age peoples, cultivators of plants and keepers of domestic animals, disperse rapidly southward from east Africa.	Travelers to southern Africa describe Khoekhoe with large herds, but early stock-keeping may have been small-scale and focused on sheep.

FARMERS IN EAST ASIA

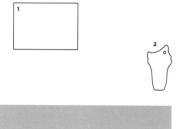

1 These Neolithic comb-pattern pottery vessels from Korea, incised with short, slanted lines, have typical pointed bases.

2 Decorated with geometric motifs, this flat-based ovoid terracotta jar originates from Japan in the second millennium BCE.

In East Asia (China, Korea, Japan), the term Neolithic primarily means the presence of pottery vessels. East Asian pottery technologies were developed at approximately the same time (before 13,000 years ago) in three different regions—South China, the Japanese archipelago, and the Amur River basin in the Russian Federation—and these clay vessels are the oldest in the world made for utilitarian purposes.

The Neolithic period in China (c. 8500–2070 BCE) is characterized by the development of settled communities along the main river systems, the Yellow (central and northern China) and the Yangtze (southern and eastern China; see p. 106). These communities relied primarily on farming and domesticated animals rather than on hunting and gathering. Recent studies of the earliest traces of agriculture have established a chronology for the emergence of plant cultivation as a productive economy. However, there was a division between the northern millet-growing cultures and the southern rice-growing cultures, between dry-land and wet-land farming systems. The earliest emergence of millet cultivation in China was found at the Cishan site, in Hebei province. Excavations of pit buildings yielded a wide range of pottery and tools, indicating a fully developed agricultural village dating to the sixth millennium BCE.

KEY EVENTS

c. 10,000–7000 BCE	c. 8000–5000 BCE	c. 7500 BCE	c. 7000–5000 BCE	c. 6000–5000 BCE	c. 5200 BCE
The rise of farming leads to a more settled lifestyle, evidenced by pottery found in rock shelters in Zhejiang and Guangxi provinces, China.	Gradual climatic warming raises sea levels. The Japanese islands of Shikoku and Kyūshū are separated from the main island of Honshu.	Jōmon pottery cooking vessels are handmade using the coiling method and decorated by pressing plant fibers into the moist clay.	Small agricultural villages, such as Cishan and Peilingang, are established in China.	The first distinctive pottery styles, such as Yunggimun (raised design pottery), appear in Korea.	The cultivation of domesticated rice begins in China in the Yangtze valley.

The first Neolithic site to be scientifically excavated was the village of Yangshao, Henan province. During the Yangshao period (*c.* 5000–3000 BCE), economic patterns and innovations varied. Hunting, fishing, and gathering became less important, but still existed in some areas. In the painted designs of the Banpo ceramics (see p. 108), fish, deer, frogs, birds, human faces, and fishnet patterns were popular. Bamboo, wood, basketry, weaving, and pottery underwent major changes, and metallurgy, jade, and lacquering industries appeared. People started to live in villages with a sophisticated arrangement of houses, ditches, pottery kilns and common graveyards.

The period that subsumes the Neolithic in Korea lasted from *c.* 6000 to 1500 BCE. Small settlements of hunters, fishers, and foragers were established in coastal areas or near rivers, such as the Amnok in the north and the Naktong in the south. These partly subterranean village sites are characterized by their stone tools, fishing utensils and handmade pottery. Combed-pattern pottery (known as *Chulmun*; see image 1) appeared in *c.* 5000 BCE in the Chongchon River valley in the north and the Han River in the south. An important site of a typical Chulmun settlement was excavated at Amsa-dong, southeast of Seoul. Neolithic remains include comb-pattern pottery and stone tools such as axes, arrowheads, and fishing net weights. Acorns and grinding stones, hand-held ploughs, and stone scythes were also found. These remains indicate that hunting, gathering, and incipient agriculture were all practiced.

In Japan considerable regional and temporal variation in the so-called Jōmon period (*c.* 10,500–*c.* 300 BCE) has been recognized. Jōmon pottery is characterized by its cord markings, which became more elaborate toward the end of the period (see image 2), and the oldest examples of Jōmon pottery were found in the Odai Yamamoto I site, in Aomori Prefecture of North Honshu island. This site indicates that East and Northeast Asia are key areas for understanding the context of changing human environmental interaction. People were semi-sedentary and were living mostly in pit dwellings arranged around central open spaces. From 6000 BCE, large settlements appeared, sometimes with more than a hundred pit dwellings. Food was still obtained by gathering, fishing, and hunting, and plant and food processing tools such as stone hoes have been found. The existence of Jōmon agriculture as such is still debated. From 7000 to 4000 BCE, plant husbandry—for example, barnyard millet or bottle gourd—was present in some areas. The discovery of the Sannai-Maruyama site (occupied between 3500 and 2000 BCE) confirms the existence of food planning and forest management. In the last stage of the Jōmon period, the climate cooled and food became less abundant. As part of the transition to the following Yayoi period (300 BCE to 300 CE), it is believed that domesticated rice, grown in dry beds or swamps, was introduced into Japan. A broad suite of plants including barley, wheat, millet, and other dry crops was also a significant component of the new agricultural system. **MP**

5000–4500 BCE	*c.* 5000–4000 BCE	*c.* 5000–3000 BCE	*c.* 5000–1000 BCE	*c.* 4500–3750 BCE	3500–2000 BCE
Farming and plant cultivation spreads into Korea and the Japanese archipelago.	Potters in the Kanto and Chubu regions (eastern Japan) begin to produce pots with flame-shaped rims, a feature typical of the Middle Jōmon period.	Named after the village in Henan province, the Yangshao culture thrives in the Yellow river basin.	Comb-pattern earthenware becomes the most representative type of pottery from Korea's Neolithic period.	Banpo, a Neolithic village located east of Xi'an in Shaanxi province, is inhabited.	The Liangzhu culture emerges around the mouth of the Yangtze river. It is an agricultural society and represents the end of the Neolithic period.

Hemudu   *c.* 5500 – 3300 BCE

The excavation site at Yuyao in eastern China showed that the Hemudu people lived in wooden houses on stilts.

The archaeological site of Hemudu is located in Yuyao in Zhejiang province. It lies about 3 feet (1 m.) above sea level, in the lower reaches of the Yangtze River. It also gave its name to the Hemudu culture, which was situated in the Ningbo-Shaoxing Plain along the south bank of Hangzhou Bay. The discovery of the Hemudu site in 1973 resounded throughout the world because it yielded the earliest evidence of rice culture. The top cultural layer of the ruins dates to 5,000 years ago, while the lowest layer dates to 7,000 years ago, and Hemudu marks the beginning of the Middle Neolithic in China.

Because of the waterlogged condition of the Hemudu site, organic materials were well preserved. The people of Hemudu used to live in a column-fenced style of compound, built above ground level using earth mounds, posts, and beams. More than 4,000 wooden remains—such as round wooden posts, square posts, beams, pillars, and wooden boards—have been found, all related to house and storehouse building. The most impressive structure consists of 220 long round posts placed side by side to form a building of more than 1,722 square feet (160 sq. m.). A shallow wooden-framed well was also discovered, which is the oldest water well with a vertical structure known in China.

Hemudu pottery is highly diverse and shows traces of daily use. Excavations yielded cauldrons, tripods, portable cooking and heating vessels, steamers, cups, bowls, jars, basins, plates, stemmed dishes, and pot supports, all made of porous, charcoal-tempered black pottery. Cord marks were impressed on the body for decoration, but this decoration may also have strengthened the body and increased thermal efficiency.

Some graves included jewelry and ornaments, including earrings, tubes, beads, and pendants made of stone such as jade. Incised bone hairpins, and polished teeth of tiger, bear, boar, and water deer have been excavated, as well as artifacts made of antler, ivory, and boar tusk. **MP**

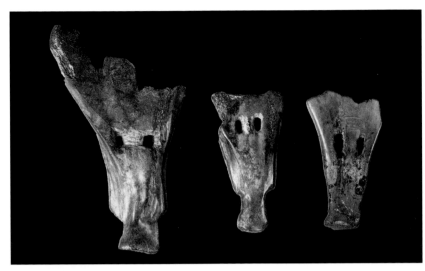

TOOLS

Various tools were found at Hemudu, including those made of bone. Some are crafted from large mammal scapulae in the form of spadelike implements, but their use is debated.

No textile fragments were uncovered at the site; however, implements relevant to weaving—such as bone needles, spindle whorls, and small wooden and bone tools that were probably components of looms—suggest that there must have been sophisticated textile production. It is thought that craftsmen could have used hemp or some kind of grass for ropes or mats.

CARVINGS

Hemudu people appear to have had a rich spiritual life, evidence of which can be seen in their fine bone and ivory carvings, such as this butterfly-shaped ivory artifact. Measuring about 6 by 2 by ½ inches (16 x 6 x 1 cm.), it is decorated with two birds facing the sun, indicated by five concentric circles. Some have suggested that the carving is a symbolic representation of life. Other objects, like bone daggers, were incised with depictions of a long-tailed bird, showing a high degree of artistry and providing some insight into a mythical realm.

HEMUDU FOOD RESOURCES

The Hemudu people lived amid rich wetlands, in a warm and humid environment that they shared with an abundance of animals and plants, providing a broad spectrum of resources for hunting and gathering. Among the tremendous amount of plant material found at the Hemudu site are water chestnuts, acorns, bottle gourds, *Euryale ferox* (water lily), jujube, and various weed seeds—the latter mostly stored in oval pits. More than sixty-one species of animals were identified, but dog, pig, and water buffalo were the main domesticated animals.

However, what distinguished the Hemudu people was their appetite for rice. Excavations, including water sieving and flotation, have yielded the world's earliest evidence for rice cultivation, and the large quantity and quality of rice consumed by the Hemudu culture find no equal elsewhere in the Chinese archaeology. Organic materials at the site were well preserved because of the waterlogged conditions. Thick deposits of rice grains, husks, and straw formed an accumulation layer, from 8 inches (20 cm.) to more than 39 inches (1 m.) deep. The rice has been identified as the long-grained variety *Oryza sativa* var. *indica*. The organic remains, together with the discovery of paddies and planting tools, prove that rice farming was already quite advanced, with the people of Hemudu also using rice husks and rice straw in their pottery manufacture.

Banpo *c. 4500 – 3750 BCE*

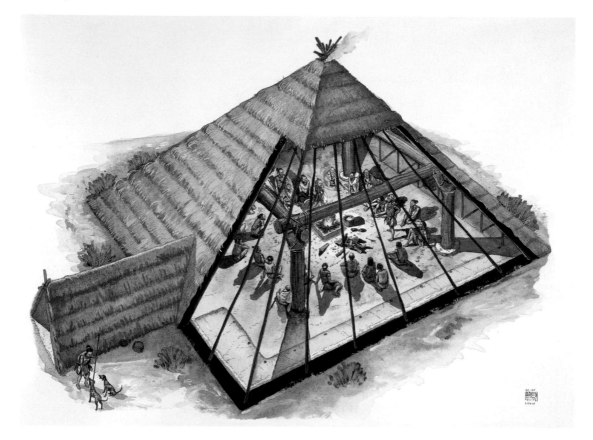

A typical house in the Neolithic village at Banpo in central China had a hard-baked clay floor and a porch with an overhanging roof of thatch to provide shade.

The archaeological site of Banpo village is located east of Xi'an in Shaanxi province in the Yellow River valley. It is one of the most significant Neolithic sites in the world and belonged to the Yangshao culture. The village was occupied from *c.* 4500 to 3750 BCE and covered approximately 12 to 15 acres (5 – 6 ha.). More than 10,000 stone tools and artifacts, six large kilns, 250 tombs, storage pits, and almost 100 house foundations have been excavated at the Banpo site.

Archaeologists from the Institute for Archaeology of the Chinese Academy of Science working at the site obtained the first detailed data on the layout of the Neolithic village. The dwelling area was enclosed by a circular ditch that served as a drainage channel and a line of defense. Within this area, pit buildings with sunken floors of various shapes and sizes—some round, others square—were arranged around a central plaza. There were approximately 100 houses clustered in about five groups, with bigger houses in the center surrounded by smaller ones. The houses were dug to 3 feet (1 m.) below ground level, and the excavated soil was used for the foundations of the walls. The carefully constructed wooden walls were covered with a thatched roof. Clay and wattle were used on the walls for insulation. The spatial clustering of the houses is an indication of a planned development of the village, of kin grouping and the organization of the society into clans.

Agriculture in the Yellow River valley was based on millet. The people of the culture also planted vegetables such as leaf mustard and cabbage. There was advanced development of animal husbandry, including raising pigs, dogs, cattle, chickens. Fishing and hunting were also significant elements in daily life. Bone implements such as arrowheads and harpoons were found among the burials. Agricultural tools included shovels, stone axes, hoes, and stone knives. **MP**

CRAFTS

Bamboo, wood, stone, ceramics, basketry, and weaving underwent major developments at Banpo. While the majority of ceramics were produced by the coiling technique, the use of the potter's wheel can be observed in circular marks on the bottom of some vessels, indicating that they were cut off from the wheel with threads. The pottery was decorated with animal motifs, geometric designs, dragons, and human faces that may be deities. This bowl found at Banpo dates to between 5000 and 4000 BCE, and is decorated with an image of a human face and fish.

BURIALS

Outside the dwelling enclosure were located pottery kilns and a graveyard with tombs arranged in clusters. Adults were buried in a cemetery outside the village, while children were buried in large urns within it. Burial objects included bone beads, bone hairpins, shell knives, and pottery vessels. Fragments of textiles were found on human remains and attached to artifacts. What the clothes looked like Is unknown because of the fragments' state of decomposition. Some of the pottery is decorated with cord or textile prints, which gives an idea of some fabrics.

YANGSHAO CULTURE

Banpo village is one of the best-known ditch-enclosed settlements of the Yangshao culture (c. 5000–3000 BCE). One of the most important cultures of the Chinese Neolithic era, it consisted of hundreds of settlements along the Yellow River and Wei River regions, and ⟨…⟩tche across the northwestern plains from Shaanxi ⟨…⟩ central China to Gansu province in the west. ⟨…⟩o culture in central China can be divided ⟨…⟩n phases: Banpo (c. 4800–c. 4300 BCE) ⟨…⟩ou (c. 4000–c. 3500 BCE). It is named after ⟨…⟩e first excavated representative village of this

culture, which was discovered in 1921 in Henan province by the Swedish archaeologist Johan Gunnar Andersson (1874–1960). He had trained as a geologist, and he used his geology to observe stratigraphic patterns and scan the landscape to find the remains of Yangshao culture.

Results and interpretations, first published in the periodicals of the Geological Survey of China and in Sweden, had a long-lasting effect on the development of prehistoric archaeology in China. Hence Yangshao was for a long time the center of the assumed cradle of Chinese civilization.

THE NEOLITHIC IN EUROPE

1 This nineteenth-century etching is from
a study of the Swiss lake dwellings
conducted by French archaeologist
Gabriel de Mortillet (1821–98) in c. 1858.

2 Decorated with typical bands of incised
lines, this simple Linear Pottery bowl was
produced between 5300 and 4900 BCE.

After emerging in the Middle East, the use of domestic plants and animals
spread to western Anatolia and across the Aegean to south-eastern
Europe. Neolithic communities appeared on the floodplains of Thessaly
and Crete just after 7000 BCE and then in northeastern Greece around 6500 BCE.
Within 3,000 years, farming had reached almost every part of Europe, except
where the climate made it impossible. This spread of plants and animals was
helped by the fact that the climate in Europe was distinctly warmer during
much of the seventh and sixth millennia BCE, except for a cold snap in 6200 BCE.

From Greece, agriculture dispersed rapidly along two main pathways. One
route went west from Greece along the Mediterranean coasts to Italy, southern
France, and eventually Spain and Portugal, reaching the Atlantic by 5000 BCE.
The other line followed the rivers of interior Europe, especially the Danube, to
the north and northwest. Eventually, it reached northern Poland and eastern
France in c. 5300 BCE. At this point, the spread of farming halted for more than
1,000 years before continuing into southern Scandinavia and the British Isles.

Archaeologists debate the processes by which farming developed across
Europe. In some areas, it is clear that the establishment of farming communities
occurred through the movement of farming populations, who colonized areas
that were sparsely settled by hunter-gatherers. The motivations for this action
are unclear, but it is known that it took place over multiple generations. In
other areas, particularly in northern and western Europe but also in interior
localities such as the Danube Gorges, domesticated plants and animals were
taken up by hunter-gatherers who incorporated them into the foraging economy
and settled down. Along the Mediterranean coasts, watercraft permitted

KEY EVENTS

c. 6800 BCE	c. 6400 BCE	c. 5500 BCE	c. 5400 BCE	c. 5000 BCE	c. 4300 BCE
The first farming communities are established on the Aegean coasts of Greece and Crete.	Farming communities begin their breakout from Greece, west toward the Atlantic and north to the Danube.	Linear Pottery culture emerges in the area of Lake Balaton in Hungary and begins its spread north and west.	Neolithic communities using shell-impressed pottery reach Spain and Portugal.	The dispersal of farming throughout central Europe halts for several centuries.	The first Neolithic sites are settled in the Alpine foothills.

long-distance contacts through which domestic plants and animals spread to diverse communities of hunter-gatherers, and enclaves of farmers sprang up.

Although not used by the very earliest farmers in Greece, pottery soon came to be a key marker of Neolithic communities, enabling the identification of the earliest presence of farmers. In the Adriatic basin and on the coasts of Italy, France, and Spain, the pottery associated with the dispersal of domestic plants and animals has impressed decoration, most commonly made using shells, but occasionally with a comb or other sharp object. In central Europe, the first farmers decorated their thin-walled pots with incised lines (see image 2), hence the name Linear Pottery given by archaeologists. Linear Pottery sites are found along small streams draining the hills of Austria, the Czech Republic, Germany (see p. 112), Poland, the Low Countries, and eastern France. These settlements comprised clusters of timber dwellings called longhouses and are sometimes enclosed by ditches. Linear Pottery farmers grew wheat, peas, and lentils, and raised mostly cattle, along with sheep, goats, and pigs. Lipid residues on pottery fragments indicate that they used the cattle for milk as well as for meat.

After a delay of nearly a millennium, hunter-gatherers in the British Isles and southern Scandinavia adopted agriculture around or just after 4000 BCE. Again, the use of watercraft permitted the movement of livestock and grain from one native community to another. Although there may have been small-scale movements of people from Continental Europe into these areas, the principal agents of the adoption of agriculture were the hunter-gatherers. Isotopic studies of human bones show a fairly rapid shift from marine to terrestrial resources, while lipid residue analysis of pottery indicates that dairy products were adopted immediately by the earliest farmers in the British Isles. Around the same time, hunter-gatherers in the foothills of the Alps also adopted agriculture and settled on lake shores in Switzerland and neighbouring areas. These are the celebrated Swiss lake dwelling sites (see image 1), once believed to have been built on pilings over the waters but now known to have been on the shorelines of lakes whose levels later rose. The remarkable preservation of organic objects at these sites has provided an insight into the plants, animals, and tools of the early Alpine farmers during the fourth millennium BCE.

By 3000 BCE, farming settlements such as Skara Brae had appeared in the Orkney Islands (see p. 116) in the far northwest of Europe, at the environmental limit of prehistoric agriculture. Within a relatively short period of time, a set of animals and plants whose wild forms occurred only in very limited areas in the Middle East was being herded and cultivated thousands of miles from their places of domestication. The Neolithic farming communities of Europe not only laid the foundation for the technological and social innovations that followed during the Bronze Age and Iron Age, but also provided the economic basis for the emergence of the great Mediterranean civilizations of Greece and Rome. **PB**

c. 4100 BCE	c. 3900 BCE	c. 3600 BCE	c. 3300 BCE	c. 3100 BCE	c. 3000 BCE
Farming communities are established in northern Germany and the Rhine-Meuse Delta in the Netherlands.	Agriculture spreads to Denmark and southern Sweden, reaching the Dal River within a few centuries.	The earliest monumental architecture on Malta (see p. 114) is constructed.	Ötzi the Iceman is killed in the Alps. His mummified remains are discovered in a glacier in 1991.	Neolithic occupation is established at Skara Brae, Orkney Islands.	Communal graves give way to single graves in round barrows. Often the remains of other family members are later placed with the "primary" person.

Eythra *c.* 5300 – 4800 BCE

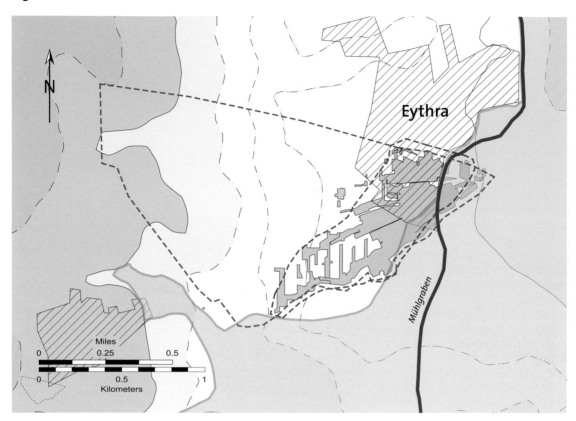

In the excavated area (outlined in red) of the huge Neolithic settlement at Eythra, dozens of Neolithic houses have been discovered along with two major earthworks and wells. Only a few of the houses were occupied at the same time. Houses that fell into disrepair were abandoned and pulled down. Later, a new house might be built on the same spot.

One of the main areas settled by the first farmers of central Europe was in central Germany, not far from Leipzig. In this area, enormous deposits of lignite—brown coal—are being strip-mined, causing the removal of acres and acres of topsoil. Archaeologists are able to work in advance of the strip-mining to expose traces of the settlements of the first farmers dating between 5300 and 4800 BCE. One such settlement complex is located along the White Elster river just south of Leipzig at Eythra.

An area of about 75 acres (30 ha.) at Eythra is covered with traces of Neolithic settlement, and the excavators say that the boundaries of the settled area have not yet been reached. About 300 whole or partial outlines of houses have been exposed so far. Settlement by the makers of Linear Pottery began in the northeastern part of the site and spread toward the west and southwest. Even a portion of the area would be equivalent to the largest known Linear Pottery sites elsewhere in central Europe. A large ditched enclosure dating to the late sixth millennium BCE and a series of concentric ditches, called a rondel, dating to the beginning of the fifth millennium BCE have also been uncovered.

Perhaps the most interesting features at Eythra are two wood-lined wells. Before the 1990s, wells were unknown on Linear Pottery sites, but since then about a dozen have been discovered. Burial deep in waterlogged ground has preserved the timbers and organic materials at the bottom of the wells. Archaeologists were unwilling to believe their age at first, as the carpentry work at the corners used sophisticated joinery. With a river nearby, why did early farmers need to dig wells inside their settlements? Perhaps they wanted a water supply close to their houses, in case they were attacked. It is also possible that this part of the river had become contaminated from human and animal waste. Another possibility is that the farmers needed a lot of water—for making beer from their grain, for example—and did not want to carry it from the riverbank. **PB**

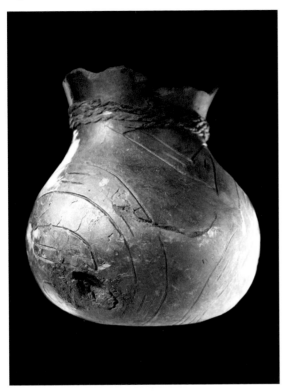

POTTERY

This ceramic vessel from the bottom of a well at Eythra, with the remains of a rope still attached, shows the curving, incised lines that give the Linear Pottery culture its name. Such pottery is found throughout central Europe, from Ukraine to France and from Hungary to Poland. Over time, the incised lines give way to similar decoration done with short strokes. Both types are found at Eythra.

WELLS

The wells at Eythra are deeply buried in the fine-grained soil known as loess. Their lower parts are below the water table, thus permitting the wood to be preserved. Oak trunks were split into planks, probably using stone or bone wedges. Then the ends were worked by Stone Age carpenters, who made notches to lock the planks together or connected them with mortise-and-tenon joints.

LARGEST BUILDINGS IN THE WORLD

The earliest farmers of central Europe built timber structures several times longer than they are wide, which are referred to as longhouses. The longhouses of the Linear Pottery culture could reach 100 feet (30 m.) long and 20 feet (6 m.) wide. Such dimensions made them the largest free-standing structures in the world in the second half of the sixth millennium BCE, long before the pyramids and temples of Egypt, the Middle East, and the Aegean were built. These houses were built of timber rather than clay or stone, as this was the most abundant building material in central Europe. Large trees, usually oak or pine, were cut with stone axes and placed upright in postholes, whose dark traces are found in the light-colored subsoil. In addition to the timbers that formed the outside walls, there were usually three interior rows of posts. The spaces between the posts were filled with interwoven twigs, called wattle, on to which clay plaster was applied. Large

pits adjacent to the houses were the source of the clay. Little is known about the roof construction: it is assumed that the roof was pitched along the long axis of the house, but the roofing material can only be guessed. Most reconstructions use thatch, but the wells at Eythra and other sites show a hitherto-unsuspected ability to make planks, which might explain the massive interior posts. Estimates of how long a timber longhouse could have lasted vary widely, between twenty and fifty years. In addition to the constant repair of deteriorating building materials, its inhabitants would also have needed to deal with rodents and insect infestation. Longhouses beyond repair were abandoned and torn down, often with their replacements built nearby. The rebuilding and clustering of longhouses resulted in dense settlement layouts like the one found by archaeologists at Eythra, even though only a few houses were occupied at any time.

Temples of Malta and Gozo Fifth millennium BCE

This statue is from the temple complex at Tarxien near Valletta, Malta. The temple was built in *c.* 3000 BCE and has four main parts. In the south temple, the elliptical apses are decorated with carved reliefs, some depicting animals. The statue shows the lower part of a female and is estimated to originally have been 6 feet 6 inches (2 m.) high.

The Maltese archipelago lies in the Mediterranean Sea between Sicily and Tunisia. Its three largest islands—Malta, Gozo, and Comino—are the only ones that are inhabited. Neolithic farmers reached Malta in *c.* 5000 BCE after crossing about 50 miles (80 km.) from Sicily, leaving traces of their presence at Skorba. They quickly cleared the sparse tree cover and established a farming economy; but, as a result, they lacked wood for building boats, so they maintained contact with Sicily to procure more.

In *c.* 3600 BCE, the inhabitants of Malta and Gozo began to build monumental structures using large pieces of the local coralline limestone as the major architectural elements and walls, with smaller pieces of softer globigerina limestone for decorative features and paneling. These monumental structures are referred to as temples, and they have been studied since the nineteenth century. About thirty temple complexes are known on Malta and Gozo. Their most visible feature is a symmetrical lobed plan, in which semicircular apses (domed or vaulted recesses) are arranged off a corridor that is entered from a large forecourt through a doorway formed with a large stone lintel. Typically, the apses are between 16 and 26 feet (5–8 m.) in diameter. The apses and corridors are decorated with carved reliefs of geometrical patterns, spirals, animals, and human forms. Three phases of temple construction have been distinguished. The Ġgantija, named after a large temple complex on Gozo, runs from 3600 to 3200 BCE, while the Saflieni, named after a vast underground burial complex, is from 3300 to 3000 BCE. The final phase, the Tarxien, lasted from 3150 to 2500 BCE, after which construction came to an end. **PB**

HAĠAR QIM

Located on a hilltop on the south coast of Malta, Haġar Qim is arguably the best preserved of the Malta temples. It was built earlier than Tarxien, dating from 3600 to 3200 BCE. It consists of a single main temple, with four apsidal chambers along with several additional rooms opening off a main corridor. A large pair of seated figures is carved into the limestone facade. Access to the interior at Haġar Qim is more restricted than at the other temples. The visitor must pass through rectangular openings cut through limestone slabs, and some apses are screened by walls. One apse has a small oval hole through which the rays of the rising sun pass on the summer solstice.

ĠGANTIJA TEMPLE

The temple at Ġgantija on the island of Gozo has two parts. Dating to 3600 BCE, the southern part is probably the oldest of the Maltese temples. It consists of five large apses opening from a central corridor, which was faced with globigerina limestone. Some have niches that resemble closets, and the apse walls, which reach 26 feet (8 m.) high, were covered with clay and lime plaster. The smaller northern temple was added to the complex in c. 3100 BCE. It also has five lobes, but they are smaller. The two temples are surrounded by a perimeter wall of large, upright limestone slabs. Nearby, the Brochtorff Circle is a burial complex of natural underground caves, surrounded by a walled enclosure.

HYPOGEUM AT HAL SAFLIENI

The Neolithic temple builders of Malta and Gozo buried their dead in immense underground catacombs, or hypogea. The hypogeum of Hal Saflieni, located 330 feet (100 m.) from the Tarxien temple complex, is one of the largest. This underground mortuary complex contains the remains of more than 7,000 people in over seventy crypts carved out of the limestone. It appears that natural caves were then expanded as more space was needed for burial, digging downward to form several more levels.

The individuals buried at Hal Saflieni had been allowed to decompose above ground. Then their bones were gathered and taken underground to be placed in one of the burial crypts. Copious amounts of red ocher (iron oxide) were sprinkled on the bones. In addition to the burial crypts, larger chambers appear to have been used for rituals. Their walls were carved to match decorative elements of the temples above, including

lintels over entrances to adjacent chambers that evoke the entrances through the facades of the temples, and carved running spirals like those found at Tarxien. Red ocher was used for painted decoration on the walls. A reclining figure of a plump woman, known as the Sleeping Lady, was found in the largest chamber, which evokes the standing female figure in the temple above ground.

The hypogeum at Hal Saflieni is clearly coupled with the temple complex at Tarxien. In a similar way, the Brochtorff Circle hypogeum at Xaghra on Gozo is linked with the temple at Ġgantija. An interesting finding at the Brochtorff Circle is that the general state of health of the 800 or so individuals buried there declined over the duration of its use. This suggests that people may have been under dietary stress that possibly led to the end of temple construction.

Neolithic Orkney Fourth – third millennia BCE

The Maeshowe passage grave dominates the landscape of Neolithic Orkney. Dating to the first quarter of the third millennium BCE, it has been suggested that it took 100,000 person-hours to build. Its central chamber is entered via a passage 36 feet (11 m.) long. The passage and chamber were covered by a mound 115 feet (35 m.) in diameter and 24 feet (7.3 m.) high.

The windswept Orkney Islands lie 10 miles (16 km.) off the northern tip of Scotland. Today, as was probably the case in the past, few trees are found on their rocky landscape, which is used primarily for grazing livestock. The surrounding ocean is a challenge to navigate even now, and is prone to gales and high waves, although it is home to abundant sea life. Despite these harsh conditions, Neolithic people made their way to Orkney during the fourth millennium BCE. By 3000 BCE, they had established settlements whose economy was based on herding and fishing—with faint traces of cultivation—and built megalithic monuments. Together, the Orkney sites make up a complex domestic, ceremonial, and mortuary landscape at the edge of Neolithic Europe.

Since wood was scarce on Orkney, the principal Neolithic building material was stone, which was laid dry to form walls and chambers. Slabs of flagstone were used for walls and floors. It was also used to construct interior fittings in domestic areas.

In 1999, a cluster of major Neolithic monuments on the largest Orkney island, Mainland, was declared a UNESCO World Heritage Site known as Heart of Neolithic Orkney, taking note of the fact that monuments are found on other islands in the archipelago. Four major sites make up the Heart of Neolithic Orkney: Maeshowe, a passage grave; the Stones of Stenness, a henge; the Ring of Brodgar, a stone circle; and Skara Brae, a settlement of eight stone houses. Although not formally part of the UNESCO World Heritage Site, the Ness of Brodgar and Barnhouse Neolithic residential and ceremonial sites lie nearby. **PB**

RING OF BRODGAR AND STONES OF STENNESS

Henges and standing stones are familiar prehistoric monuments throughout the British Isles. Orkney has two such monuments that were integral to the ceremonial landscape. The Stones of Stenness on Mainland are thought to be one of the oldest monuments on Orkney, dating to just after 3000 BCE. Four large stones survive from an elliptical arrangement of up to twelve. The nearby Ring of Brodgar is a henge 341 feet (104 m.) in diameter, in which twenty-seven stones of an estimated original sixty still stand. The Ring of Brodgar is believed to be one of the younger Neolithic monuments on Orkney, dating to the second half of the third millennium BCE.

NESS OF BRODGAR

The Ness of Brodgar lies between the Stones of Stenness and the Ring of Brodgar on Mainland. In contrast to the other sites, it is quite large, covering more than 6 acres (2.5 ha.). The earliest occupation at Ness of Brodgar began in c. 3300 BCE and continued through several phases for approximately a millennium. One building built in c. 2900 BCE is much larger than the others, measuring 82 feet (25 m.) long and 65 feet (20 m.) wide. It has been interpreted as a ritual complex, and when it was demolished several hundred cattle were slaughtered to mark the event. In 2010, archaeologists found proof that the Neolithic occupants used paint to decorate their buildings.

SKARA BRAE

The Orkney Neolithic site of Skara Brae is a settlement on Mainland along the Bay of Skaill. After it was abandoned, Skara Brae was covered by drifting sand and sod until it was exposed by a gale in the nineteenth century. V. Gordon Childe (1892–1957) excavated the site from 1927 to 1930 and other archaeologists have studied it since.

Skara Brae now presents a subterranean warren of structures surrounded by mounds of sod-covered refuse. Many accounts of Skara Brae report that Neolithic people burrowed into a refuse deposit left by an unknown earlier settlement to build their houses, which were then insulated from the harsh climate by the organic debris. Recent investigations suggest this is an oversimplification. It seems likely that the houses were built as free-standing structures, and then over a number of generations they became embedded in the debris of their inhabitants before the site was abandoned.

Today, Skara Brae consists of eight rectangular dwellings, each 15 to 20 feet (4.5–6 m.) across, interconnected by narrow passageways. Each house has a central stone hearth. In some houses, smaller alcoves branch off from the central space. How the houses were roofed is not known; possibly whale ribs were laid across the openings and covered by hides.

Skara Brae was the first Orkney site at which the remarkable stone furniture around the walls of the central rooms was observed. Directly opposite the entrance to each house is a stone shelf construction that evokes a dresser, albeit without drawers. These may have served as storage shelves for pots of food and milk. On either side of the hearth are stone boxes that have been interpreted as beds, although this function is not certain. Stone pits in the floors were caulked with clay to make them watertight and may have been used to store shellfish.

THE FIRST FARMING IN THE AMERICAS

1 Near Nazca, Peru, the pre-Columbian Cantayoc Aqueducts are still accessed and maintained via spiral entrance holes that the Spanish called *ojos* (eyes).

2 This nineteenth-century illustration depicts a group of mound builders at harvest time, gathering their crops of maize and squash.

3 These maize grinding stones were discovered at Besh-Ba-Gowah Archaeological Park, Arizona, a site occupied by the Salado peoples from *c.* 1225 to 1400.

As a worldwide phenomenon, farming arose more or less simultaneously in many parts of the world, which led early scholars to propose that the domestication of plants and animals occurred in relatively few areas but then spread rapidly though the processes of diffusion. However, it is now clear that the processes of domestication occurred independently in many places, including in the Americas. As communities became more confident in a stable food supply, ensured by domestication, settlements became more permanent, ultimately leading in some areas to the earliest civilizations. Archaeologists have isolated three primary areas in the Americas where farming first took hold: Central America (or Mesoamerica), South America (see p. 120), and the eastern United States. The emphasis in all three areas was on the domestication of plants; domesticated animals never achieved the same level of importance as they did, for example, in Europe.

Central America is a region of great ecological diversity that includes high mountains, lowland plains, temperate and tropical forests, and desert. Many plants were domesticated in this region, but perhaps the three most important were maize, squash, and beans (the last was domesticated somewhat later than the first two). The domestication of plants occurred in different regions, the precise processes varying from area to area. For example, some plants, such as maize, were probably domesticated in one locale and then spread through Central America and beyond by various means; others, for example some species of bean, may have been domesticated independently in different places.

KEY EVENTS

10,000 BCE	8000 BCE	6700 BCE	5300 BCE	4700 BCE	4300 BCE
The end of the Pleistocene period ushers in a global warming period that leads to the development of farming.	In highland Central America, squash and bottle gourd are domesticated.	The domestication of maize and squash, together with beans, becomes the basis of the great New World triad of cultivated plants.	The appearance of slash-and-burn farming in lowland Central America increases crop yields.	The earliest evidence of irrigation canals in northern Peru indicates communally organized planning and execution.	Domesticated maize is introduced to the highlands of Central America, the first leg in the remarkable global spread of this plant.

In the lowlands of Central America, both maize and squash had been domesticated from their wild prototypes by 8,700 years ago. It is likely that the earliest farming was done in small plots close to individual houses (see image 2). However, by 7,300 years ago (some scholars place this development much later), farmers had developed the slash-and-burn technique whereby forests were cleared of their vegetation to create fields, and then the vegetation was burned before the crops were planted, the ash temporarily increasing the fertility of the soil. Typically, farmers would move on to a new area after a few seasons and repeat the process.

In the highlands of Central America, squash and bottle gourd (used as a receptacle rather than as a food source) had perhaps been domesticated as early as 8000 BCE. Domesticated maize had spread into the highlands by 4300 BCE, and the turkey was domesticated from its wild progenitor about 2,000 years ago. As in Central America, a wide array of plants was domesticated in South America, which reflected its great ecological diversity. The domestication of squash took place as early as 10,000 years ago. However, the period 3000 to 2000 BCE seems to have been crucial in the intensification of native plant cultivation, much of which occurred in the Andes. Potatoes were first cultivated in the highlands of Peru and Bolivia (about 4,500 years ago). Quinoa (a grain crop grown for its seeds) was domesticated at about the same time. Recently, archaeologists have recovered evidence of irrigation canals (see image 1) dating possibly as early as 4700 BCE in northern Peru, close to the Pacific coast. In the tropical lowlands, a variety of squashes and peppers were domesticated along with sweet potato, pineapple, and avocado, to name but a few. Two animals were domesticated in South America. The first, the guinea pig, is still a food source in the Andes, whereas the llama and alpaca were domesticated as pack animals approximately 4,500 years ago.

The earliest domesticated plants in the eastern United States form a crop complex that was the result of long-term independent experimentation with planting and seed storage. The first to be cultivated was the squash, in c. 3000 BCE. This was quickly followed by the domestication of sunflowers (c. 2800 BCE) and marsh elder (c. 2400 BCE). These plants were ultimately superseded in economic importance by maize, but that crop was not introduced into the region until approximately 2,000 years ago.

Although the Pueblo societies of the American Southwest were not a primary center of plant domestication, it is worth noting that they relied on a triad of maize, beans, and squash. The earliest evidence for domesticated maize (see image 3) in the Southwest is dated to approximately 2000 BCE. The plant arrived there from Mexico, presumably by the process of diffusion, although the precise route is still unclear. By this time, the plant was being hybridized to survive the new climatic conditions in which farmers planted the crop. **PD**

4000 BCE	3400 BCE	3000 BCE	2500 BCE	2000 BCE	2,000 years ago
Peppers are cultivated in both Central America (Panama) and South America (Ecuador).	A period of intensive cultivation of new plants in South America begins.	Squash is domesticated in the eastern United States, quickly followed by sunflowers and marsh elder.	The potato is domesticated in South America and spreads throughout the world to become an important dietary staple.	Domesticated maize arrives in the American Southwest and subsequently becomes the staple underpinning the rise of complex societies.	The turkey, a native species found in both North and Central America, is domesticated in Central America.

Real Alto *c.* 3800 – 1800 BCE

Among the most striking elements of Valdivia material culture are the anthropomorphic figurines made with fired clay. They are generally found incomplete, although there are also intact examples. They usually represent female figures standing erect with arms over their abdomens or chests. The complexity in the depiction of hairstyles in these figurines has been related to the existence of rituals in the Valdivia villages.

The archaeological site of Real Alto is located on the peninsula of Santa Elena on the southern coast of Ecuador. One of the best-known sites of the Valdivia culture, it received the attention of archaeologists in the 1970s, especially the U.S. scholar Donald Lathrap (1927–90) and the Ecuadorian researcher Jorge Marcos (b. 1932). The site extends over 40 acres (16 ha.) and is recognized by the elevations on the relatively flat surface of this area, and by a large quantity of ceramic sherds and faunal remains, especially mollusks.

Real Alto was a village consisting of a number of circular houses with some main public buildings built around open spaces or plazas. The architecture was predominantly mud and plant materials. A great quantity of food processing (mortars and grinding stones) and debris have been found on the site's floors and middens. Like other Valdivia sites, Real Alto is characterized by one of the earliest ceramic wares on the Pacific coast. In addition to pottery, the most significant and iconic objects are the anthropomorphic figurines — almost always feminine — made of fired clay.

A series of platforms with public structures has been excavated at this site, which were possibly community meeting spaces or even the homes of community leaders. In addition, a custom that is in evidence here was to bury the dead inside the settlement in a flexed position, although with few or no grave goods. Even the presence of human sacrifices has been discovered. Although Real Alto was one of the largest towns in the Valdivia culture, its political organization was quite simple, perhaps led by those who did not distance themselves economically or politically from the rest of the social group. **HT**

👁 FOCAL POINTS

ORGANIZATION OF VILLAGE SPACE

The organization of space in such an early village as Real Alto has attracted the attention of archaeologists. In spite of being a relatively simple economic and political society, the village arrangement suggests an important capacity to coordinate populations. Originally, the huts were organized in a U shape but as the population grew, this was replaced by a rectangular layout. In addition, it has been suggested that the orientation of the village plan was related to the observation of the movement of the sun.

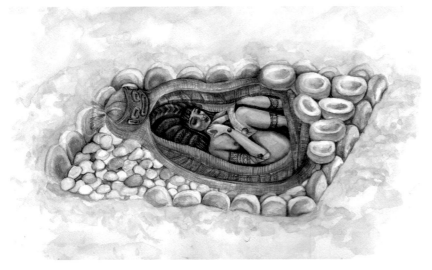

EXTRAORDINARY BURIAL

The B15 burial was that of a woman about thirty-five years old, arranged in a foetal position inside a pit covered with grinding stones and broken mortars. It was accompanied by a large fragment of ceramic with incised decoration, red boulders, and whole grinding stones. The Valdivia culture is particularly renowned for the development of the earliest ceramics in Ecuador. The woman was buried in an *osario* (charnel house mound) where other human burials were also found, some of them the result of sacrifices.

🕐 ARCHAEOLOGIST PROFILE

1932–71

Jorge Marcos was born in Guayaquil, Ecuador. Although interested in archaeology from a young age, he chose to study English literature at Harvard University. In 1967, he joined an expedition during which he carried out his first fieldwork with archaeologist Carlos Zevallos Menéndez (1909–81). A few years later, Marcos attended the International Congress of Americanists in Lima, Peru, where he met Donald Lathrap.

1972–89

In 1972, Marcos embarked on his doctoral studies in anthropology at the University of Illinois. He studied with Lathrap, with whom he excavated the site at Real Alto between 1974 and 1976. He then went on to obtain a Ph.D. in anthropology in 1978. Two years later, Marcos was invited by the Escuela Politécnica del Litoral (ESPOL) to create an archaeology program.

1990–99

Between 1991 and 1993, Marcos carried out research on materials of the Valdivia culture in Europe. Until 1997 he taught at the Universitat Autonoma de Barcelona and the Complutense University of Madrid, both in Spain. The following year, he became a senior fellow at Dumbarton Oaks in Washington, D.C.

2000–PRESENT

Marcos returned to Ecuador in 2000 and conducted archaeological research on pre-Hispanic hydraulic technologies. Between 2007 and 2009, he served as undersecretary of heritage at the Ministry of Culture of Ecuador. Between 2009 and 2013, he directed the Cerro Hojas-Jaboncillo archaeological project in the province of Manabi. Marcos is currently a director of the archaeology program at ESPOL.

COPPER AND GOLD

1 This heavy gold Bronze Age comb was found as part of a hoard in Caldas de Reyes, Galicia, Spain. Its weight would have made it impractical to use.

2 The Copper Age Rinaldone culture from west-central Italy was renowned for its metalwork, including tools such as these copper axes.

3 Archaeologists have informed the reconstruction of buildings at the Copper Age Los Millares settlement, Almeria, Spain.

Although pure or native copper was hammered into shapes nearly 10,000 years ago in eastern Anatolia, Turkey, the use of copper that derived from smelted ores appeared first in southeastern Europe during the sixth millennium BCE. Smelting means that copper ore, usually malachite, is heated to about 2,000°F (nearly 1,100°C) in order to separate the metal from various impurities. The smelted copper can then be hammered into sheets or bars for further shaping, or it can be melted and cast in molds.

Copper is a very soft metal, so its initial use was for ornaments and for clunky tools such as axes (see image 2), which could be used for cutting but would get dull very quickly. One good thing about copper is that it can be melted down and reworked, so it could be continuously recycled if desired. Yet the primary attraction of copper was for its bright orange surface. Although when aged, copper takes on a green patina; when new it is attractive and therefore desirable. Copper ornaments were made to be seen.

Since copper had to be mined, smelted, and worked into finished products, as well as transported at some stage of the process from the maker to the user, it had a high cost in terms of labor. Consequently, although copper ore was relatively plentiful in particular regions, it was outside those regions that the finished copper products acquired their value. Ancient people desired copper and went to great lengths to obtain it and display it. One of these areas was a broad section of eastern Europe during the fifth and fourth millennia BCE, where archaeologists speak of a Copper Age that began in c. 4500 BCE and flourished

KEY EVENTS

c. 8000 BCE	c. 6800 BCE	c. 5500–5000 BCE	c. 4560–4450 BCE	c. 4400–4200 BCE	c. 3900–3800 BCE
The first cold-hammering of native copper takes place in eastern Anatolia, Turkey.	The practice of farming makes its first appearance in Greece.	Farming spreads throughout central Europe.	The cemetery at Varna on the Black Sea coast is in use at this time.	Copper ornaments are buried in graves at Brześć Kujawski and Osłonki in northern Poland.	The transition to agriculture takes place in the British Isles and southern Scandinavia.

during the forth millennium BCE. Mines in the Balkans, such as at Aibunar in Bulgaria and Rudna Glava in Serbia, yielded copious amounts of copper ore. Copper artifacts are found in burials, such as those at Varna (see p. 124), and in deposits where they were placed for safekeeping or as offerings. An immense amount of copper was in circulation, and some of the largest and heaviest copper artifacts are large cast axes with holes for a shaft.

The demand for copper extended to the north and to the west during the fifth and fourth millennia BCE. Many of the graves found at Brześć Kujawski and Osłonki in northern Poland contain copper ornaments obtained from sources more than 500 miles (800 km.) away lying south of the Carpathian Mountains. A millennium later, Ötzi the Iceman was carrying an ax that had been cast from pure copper when he died in the Alps (see p. 546).

By 3000 BCE, the mining and smelting of copper had become an important activity in the Iberian Peninsula. Large fortified settlements such as Los Millares (see image 3) have yielded evidence of copper smelting, while burials contain copper objects. Eventually, the use of copper was brought to the British Isles during the second half of the third millennium BCE. The copper knives found with the Amesbury Archer (see p. 136) are believed to have come from Spain or western France. The Amesbury Archer was also buried with gold ornaments. Gold was another highly desired metal in prehistoric Europe, although much rarer in the archaeological record. Unlike mined copper, gold was obtained from stream deposits as flakes and nuggets, then concentrated to be put in the hands of expert goldsmiths (see image 1). It is very rare during the fifth millennium BCE, which makes the tremendous quantity of gold found at Varna even more remarkable, but it then appears sporadically during the millennia that followed. Sometimes hoards or deposits of multiple objects are found, such as the one at Hotnitsa in Bulgaria that comprised four amulets, thirty-nine spiral rings, and a spiral bracelet weighing nearly 11 ounces (310 g.). High temperatures were not necessary to produce gold. Rather, it was hammered into sheets or into small figures that could then be used to decorate clothing and to apply to the surface of objects made from wood or pottery.

Ultimately, being able to display copper and gold ornaments and copper tools spoke to the other members of the community. It revealed knowledge of how the metal could be acquired and what was necessary to provide in return. If the corpse of a relative was adorned with this scarce and desirable metal, which would then disappear from public view for ever when it was buried, this sent a strong message about the household's ability to acquire wealth through luck, skill, and the control of assets. The role of copper and gold in mortuary rituals was as part of the burial performance, less in honor of the dead person and more for the surviving relatives to make a statement to the rest of the community. **PB**

c. 3300 BCE	c. 3200 BCE	c. 3200–2300 BCE	c. 2900 BCE	c. 2400 BCE	c. 2380–2290 BCE
Otzi the Iceman dies while carrying a copper ax in the Alps.	The Newgrange passage grave is constructed in Ireland (see p. 128).	The Copper Age of southern Spain flourishes at sites such as Los Millares.	Construction begins on the first stage of Stonehenge in southern England (see p. 130).	The mining of copper begins at Ross Island, County Kerry, Ireland.	The Amesbury Archer dies in southern England.

Gold of Varna   Fifth millennium BCE

The spectacular and mysterious Grave 43 is the iconic Varna burial, whose reconstruction is the centerpiece of the public presentation of the site at the Varna Museum of Archaeology.

The city of Varna on the Black Sea coast of Bulgaria is known as a resort town, but it was the development of an industrial zone inland that led to the discovery of the most spectacular cemetery of the fifth millennium BCE in Europe. In 1972, workers came across prehistoric burials, some of which had gold artifacts and other interesting grave goods. In 1974, Grave 36, with its profusion of gold artifacts, was discovered, and soon thereafter Graves 41 and 43, which were also rich in gold, were found. These finds put the Varna cemetery on the map of important Copper Age sites. By the end of excavations in 1991, 294 Copper Age graves had been excavated at Varna. Recent high-precision dating places the use of the cemetery between 4560 and 4450 BCE.

The most lavish burial with a skeleton was Grave 43, which contained the supine skeleton of a man between forty and fifty years old. He stood 5 feet 9 inches (1.75 m.) tall. He was buried with 990 gold objects that weighed more than 1 pound (1.5 kg.), including beads, rings, appliqués, plaques, lip plugs, earplugs, and arm rings. Other ornaments including several tubes of sheet gold were lined up as if they were covering a wooden shaft topped with a stone macehead, which has been interpreted as a scepter. The gold veneer covering the wood made it appear as if the shaft was of solid gold. A *Spondylus* (thorny oyster) bangle was also covered with gold foil. An unusual gold tube found in the vicinity of the man's hip has been termed a penis sheath, although not all archaeologists agree with this interpretation. Other objects in Grave 43 included ceramic vessels, copper axes, a copper chisel and awl, and flint blades, one of which was 15 inches (39 cm.) long.

The man in Grave 43 was someone of status, and he has been referred to as a chieftain or a king. Analysis of the Varna skeletons for isotopes of Nitrogen-15 and Carbon-13, reveals he was one of a small number of individuals with abundant grave goods that appear to have had an enriched diet, which included more marine protein than the population as a whole. This raises questions as to whether in the coastal community of Varna he had special access to marine foods or he traveled extensively along the Black Sea, resulting in more opportunities to consume fish. **PB**

✦ NAVIGATOR

👁 FOCAL POINTS

1 SHELLS

More than 1,000 bracelets, beads, and pendants made from the shell of the marine mussel *Spondylus gaederopus* were found at Varna. It comes from the Aegean Sea. In addition to *Spondylus*, 12,000 shells of a smaller marine mollusk *Dentalium*, also from the Aegean, were found.

2 GOLD

More than 3,000 gold objects, together weighing 13 pounds (6 kg.), have been found in sixty-two of the graves at Varna. The weight of gold in just four graves accounted for over 80 percent of the total. Varna's gold probably came from placer deposits near the Turkish border with Bulgaria.

3 TOOLS

While the gold artifacts are clearly the most memorable category of finds at Varna, significant numbers of copper, flint and shell artifacts were found in the burials as well. Many of the copper objects are cast hammer-axes, while the flint tools are made from long blades of high-quality material.

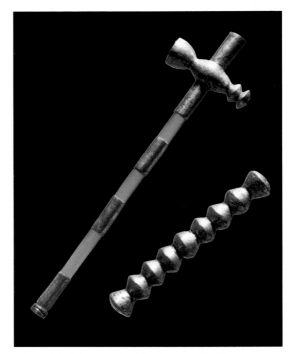

▲ A surprisingly large number (about 15 percent) of the graves at Varna were cenotaphs—symbolic burials that lack human remains. Their significance is unknown, but they are interpreted as symbolic graves of members of the Varna community who died elsewhere and could not be brought back for burial. Much of the gold is found in three cenotaphs: Grave 1 with 216 objects, Grave 4 with 339, and Grave 36 with 857. Interestingly, each of these three graves also contained a scepter (the one seen here from Grave 36), which is considered to be a symbol of authority. Three other cenotaphs had gold-ornamented clay masks placed where the head of the deceased would have been.

GOLD GRAVE GOODS

Graves at Varna are usually found in rectangular pits between 1 foot (30 cm.) and 8 feet (2.5 m.) deep. About 85 percent of them contained skeletons, either in an extended or a contracted position, while the rest were symbolic graves. Only five lacked any grave goods, and some contained hundreds of artifacts. The amount of gold found at Varna is the earliest such concentration of this metal, not equaled until the royal cemetery at Ur in Mesopotamia (see p. 146) a millennium later.

Archaeologists are still trying to understand the meaning of the Varna cemetery. While other cemeteries in southeastern Europe have abundant grave offerings, Varna stands out as spectacular. In addition to the symbolic significance of the burials as performance by the descendants of the deceased individual, the Varna community represents one of the first instances in which differences in status, power, prestige, and wealth were expressed in such an elaborate way.

Unusually, the Varna cemetery is not directly associated with a known settlement site nearby. It has been suggested that several contemporaneous settlement sites along a nearby inlet of the Black Sea, now a landlocked lake, may be associated with the cemetery, but they are now submerged and unstudied.

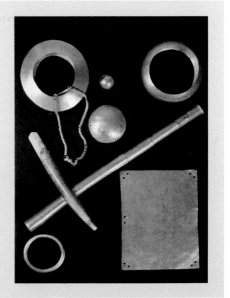

EUROPEAN MEGALITHS

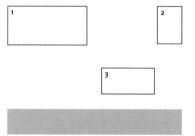

1 The chamber of Poulnabrone tomb contained the bones of about thirty-three individuals that had been allowed to decompose elsewhere before being gathered and placed in the tomb.

2 The standing stones at Carnac are at the center of a remarkable concentration of megalithic monuments in the Gulf of Morbihan in southern Brittany.

3 All of the Barnenez chambers and passages were covered with an immense cairn of small stones, 236 feet (72 m.) long and up to 26 feet (8 m.) high.

Among the most evocative features of the landscape of western and northern Europe are the ancient monuments constructed from large blocks of stone, known collectively as megaliths. The tradition of building megalithic monuments began in c. 4500 BCE in Brittany and continued to the final centuries of the third millennium BCE, when the monuments at Stonehenge in southern England were erected. They are thus associated primarily with the early farming societies of the Neolithic period.

Megaliths can be divided into mortuary monuments and standing stones, both of which were associated with ritual and ceremonial activity. Their construction was made possible by the geology of northern and western Europe, where rocky outcrops and fields strewn with boulders provided the primary building materials. Large stones of an appropriate shape and size were chosen, transported to the site of the planned megalithic monument and maneuvered into place. Megalithic engineering required considerable labor, probably draft animals and an assortment of rollers, levers, ropes and ramps. Some of the most celebrated megalithic monuments served as tombs, for which there is a complicated taxonomy of forms. Some of the simplest are known as dolmens, in which a few upright stones form a chamber that was then capped with a single immense capstone. One of the best-known dolmens is the Poulnabrone tomb (see image 1), located in County Clare in western Ireland. Recent radiocarbon dates indicate that the Poulnabrone dolmen came into use soon after 3800 BCE.

KEY EVENTS

c. 4400 BCE	c. 4000–3800 BCE	c. 3800 BCE	c. 3500 BCE	c. 3200 BCE	c. 3100–2600 BCE
The Barnenez passage grave is constructed in Brittany.	The transition to agriculture takes place in the British Isles and Scandinavia.	The Poulnabrone dolmen is built in Ireland and the first interments are made.	Construction of megalithic tombs begins in Scandinavia.	The Newgrange passage tomb is constructed in Ireland (see p. 128).	The Skara Brae settlement is occupied on Orkney, Scotland.

More elaborate megalithic burial monuments are known as passage tombs (see p. 128). Barnenez, on the coast of Brittany in France, is one of the earliest passage tombs (see image 3), dating to the fifth millennium BCE. It contains eleven separate chambers, each entered by its own passage from the exterior. The other major category of megalithic monument comprises standing stones, often called menhirs. They can occur singly or as part of a group of similar stones, sometimes in a circular pattern or as a linear alignment. Their significance is not entirely understood, although menhirs, stone circles and alignments probably served as focal points for ceremonies and rituals.

In c. 3300 BCE, Neolithic communities in the Carnac region in southern Brittany began erecting long rows of standing stones (see image 2). These were smaller than the large menhirs put up almost a millennium earlier, but there are thousands of them. At le Ménec, more than a thousand stones are arranged in ten roughly parallel rows that stretch for about three-quarters of a mile (1,200 m.). The Kermario alignment also has about a thousand stones in seven main lines and three partial ones about two-thirds of a mile (1,000 m.) long. Other alignments of menhirs fit the same general pattern. The function of the Carnac alignments is unknown, but it has been suggested that they were paths for ceremonial processions that led to stone circles where rituals took place.

The most celebrated megalithic monument is, of course, Stonehenge. It has a lengthy developmental history (see p. 130). When it is viewed in comparison with all the other megalithic structures of northern and western Europe, many similarities can be found. If the landscape around Stonehenge is taken into account (see p. 526), the processional interpretation of Carnac is echoed in the other monumental constructions that have been discovered. Megaliths remain a mysterious category of archaeological monument, but advances in archaeological techniques continue to discover new pieces to add to the puzzle. **PB**

c. 2900 BCE	c. 2900 BCE	c. 2800 BCE	c. 2600 BCE	2500–2000 BCE	c. 2200 BCE
The Standing Stones of Stenness are set up on Orkney.	Construction begins on the first phase of Stonehenge.	The Maes Howe passage grave is constructed in Orkney.	Work begins on the final version of Stonehenge.	Chambered tombs known as wedge tombs are built in western and southwestern Ireland.	The Ring of Brodgar standing stones are erected on Orkney.

Irish Passage Graves 4000 – 3000 BCE

The clusters of passage tombs in prominent locations in Ireland, such as Newgrange in the Boyne Valley, defined landscapes of ceremony and ritual. Their construction, the rituals performed at them, and occasional remodeling formed connections between ancestors, the cosmos, the living community that built them, and its descendants.

Although megalithic tombs are found in many parts of western and northern Europe, the Neolithic mortuary monuments of Ireland provide outstanding examples of their variety, architecture, geographical distribution, and artistic expression. They reached their zenith in the second half of the fourth millennium BCE in the form of several concentrations of passage tombs in which a narrow corridor leads into a chamber, with the whole construction buried under a mound of stones and earth.

Four major passage-tomb cemeteries form a belt across Ireland, from the Atlantic coast to the Irish Sea. Each comprises up to thirty passage graves. Starting in the west, the Carrowmore cemetery is found on the Cúil Irra peninsula in County Sligo, above which looms Knocknarea mountain with its immense cairn known as Queen Maeve's Tomb, presumed to cover a Neolithic passage tomb but never excavated. About 19 miles (30 km.) to the southeast on the peaks of the Bricklieve Mountains lie the Carrowkeel group of passage tombs. In County Meath, 47 miles (75 km.) to the east, the Loughcrew passage tombs and their cairns cover several hilltops. Finally, a short distance from the eastern coast of Ireland, at a bend in the River Boyne, lies a group of tombs dominated by the large mounds of Knowth, Dowth, and Newgrange. Additional solitary passage tombs, such as Fourknocks and the Mound of the Hostages on the Hill of Tara, are nearby.

Cremated human bones, burial offerings, designs on the stones, and the alignment of chambers and passages to significant sunrises and sunsets made the passage tombs points of convergence of the past, present, and future. These monuments would have held many layers of meaning for the community that built them and for its descendants. **PB**

PASSAGE-TOMB ARCHITECTURE

Upright slabs define the walls of an entrance corridor like this at Loughcrew. Capstones laid across the uprights form the roof. At one end, the passage widens into a circular chamber; smaller chambers extend from its sides. Large chambers are roofed using a corbeling technique, with flat stones laid in courses that meet at the top.

MEGALITHIC ART

Irish passage tombs saw the emergence of a distinctive art style made by pecking and carving designs on stones that formed parts of their structures or that marked the perimeters of the cairns. A classic motif is flowing and interlocking spirals such as this one at Newgrange, as well as sunbursts and zigzags.

NEWGRANGE AND THE WINTER SOLSTICE

Although it looks like no other passage tomb, Newgrange in the Boyne Valley is the most famous of the Irish megalithic graves. Located close to Dublin, it is visited by thousands of tourists annually. Its huge mound is a dramatic sight in its hilltop location. The current appearance of Newgrange is the result of a reconstruction in the 1970s, in which white quartz and granite cobbles lying around the entrance were interpreted as the collapsed remains of a facade. This reconstruction is controversial, and many archaeologists believe it to be fanciful or worse.

Yet it does not obscure the megalithic architecture of the interior, in which a passage 62 feet (19 m.) long extends from the entrance to a central chamber with three side chambers. The top of the corbeled roof of the central chamber reaches 12 feet (3.6 m.) above the floor. At the entrance lies a large stone covered with spirals and other geometric designs.

A remarkable feature of Newgrange is that for six mornings, from December 18 to 23, at 8:58 a.m., the rising sun shines directly down the passage, eventually reaching the chamber. The light enters the interior of the tomb through a special opening above the entrance. Clearly the winter solstice had significance for the builders of Newgrange, even if in many years the rising sun is obscured by clouds. Consider the planning involved: in a previous year, the direction of the rising sun and its angle would have been marked out before any construction could begin. During construction, the builders would have observed these markings and positioned the stones accordingly. Perhaps they made modifications in subsequent years to refine the effect. Today, more than 30,000 people apply to be one of the few who enter the tomb on one of the six mornings to see first-hand how the sun illuminates the passage and chamber.

Stonehenge 2900 BCE onward

Between 2620 and 2480 BCE, Stonehenge was extensively remodeled. First, the immense trilithons, consisting of two massive uprights and a lintel made of sarsen stone, were put up in a horseshoe arrangement. Around them was a circle of upright sarsens and lintels. Finally, the bluestones were relocated from the Aubrey Holes to the interior of the monument to form additional circular arrangements. Several more standing bluestones were erected along a gap in the bank through which the monument is entered.

Located on the Salisbury Plain in southern England, Stonehenge is arguably the most recognizable archaeological monument in the world, apart from the Pyramids at Giza. Almost every archaeologist makes the pilgrimage there at least once in a lifetime. It is celebrated in art, literature, and popular media. Stonehenge has also been adopted as a focal point by those in modern society seeking a spiritual touchstone.

Over the past 400 years, antiquarians and archaeologists have been fascinated with Stonehenge, but even after many different investigations the site has been reluctant to answer all the questions that surround it. Stonehenge is one of a number of circular ditched stone monuments in the British Isles that are known as henges. The term comes from an Old English word for hanging, because the most visible structural elements of Stonehenge were thought to resemble gallows. Over the years, archaeologists have been able to untangle the sequence in which Stonehenge was constructed, starting in c. 2900 BCE and ending several centuries later. They have also been able to trace the sources of the stones used for the major architectural elements. New discoveries within the enclosure have added to the understanding of the activities that took place there. The astronomical alignments of Stonehenge have been the subject of close examination, as well as considerable speculation. Finally, the landscape around Stonehenge has been surveyed, and recently subjected to geophysical prospection with magnetometry and ground-penetrating radar (see p. 526). The result has been the discovery and excavation of many new sites that are contemporaneous with Stonehenge itself, but, as with all new discoveries, this work has raised more questions than it has answered. **PB**

THE FIRST STONEHENGE

In *c.* 2900 BCE, work began on a ditch and bank about 330 feet (100 m.) in diameter. Around the interior perimeter of the bank, fifty-six holes were dug, known as the Aubrey Holes after their discoverer John Aubrey (1626–97). They were once thought to have been the footings for timber posts, but recent investigations have shown that they were the sockets for short upright stones, called bluestones, which were subsequently pulled out. At this time, the interior of Stonehenge functioned as a cemetery.

BUILDING STONEHENGE

The engineering skills of the builders of Stonehenge are illustrated by the immense size of the stones that comprise the trilithons and the sarsen circle, as well as the fact that posts on top of the upright stones fit into holes on the underside of the lintels. The upright stones had to be levered into position and slid into the holes. Then the lintels had to be raised higher than the tenons on top of the uprights and moved horizontally until their mortises were directly over the tenons, and finally lowered.

SOURCE OF THE BLUESTONES AND THE SARSENS

One of the most significant aspects of Stonehenge is the effort that went into the acquisition of the stones used to build it. The bluestones at the center of the monument have been traced to the Prescelly Hills of southern Wales. These hills are about 150 miles (240 km.) from Stonehenge. The stones were quarried there, then probably transported by boat up the Bristol Channel and as far as possible up rivers on rafts, then finally hauled overland to the Salisbury Plain. A Stonehenge bluestone can weigh up to 4 tons (3.6 metric tons). Although moving a mass that weighs as much as a modern car would have been a challenge, stone quarrying and moving skills would have been developed during the previous centuries in the construction of dolmens and passage graves.

As large as the bluestones are, they are puny in comparison to the massive sarsen stones that form the trilithons and the post-and-lintel circle. Not only

are they up to 30 feet (9 m.) long, but they weigh 25 tons (22.7 metric tons). These blocks of sandstone came from the Marlborough Downs, about 20 miles (32 km.) north of Stonehenge. Many hypotheses have been advanced for how they were transported. Simple rollers would not have been effective, and constructing a smooth road that could then be coated with winter ice also seems dubious. One hypothesis is that some sort of heavy-duty cradle that ran on greased timber rails was used to traverse the rolling terrain. However the stones were moved, the amount of human and animal power that was brought to bear must have been immense. Hardwood levers would have been important tools, as would ropes, probably made from bark. An individual or a group of leaders would have needed to organize and manage this effort over many years, and perhaps over several generations.

3 | The Rise of Civilizations

3000–1000 BCE

As Bronze Age technology developed, so too did new, ever more socially complex ways of living. Social control, religious authority, craft production, and other non-agricultural activities became concentrated in centers of population where rulers resided, creating cities and leading to the rise of great urban civilizations. Starting around 3000 BCE, especially in the fertile river valleys of Mesopotamia, Egypt, Pakistan, and China, the first fully formed, class-divided, urban-based societies emerged.

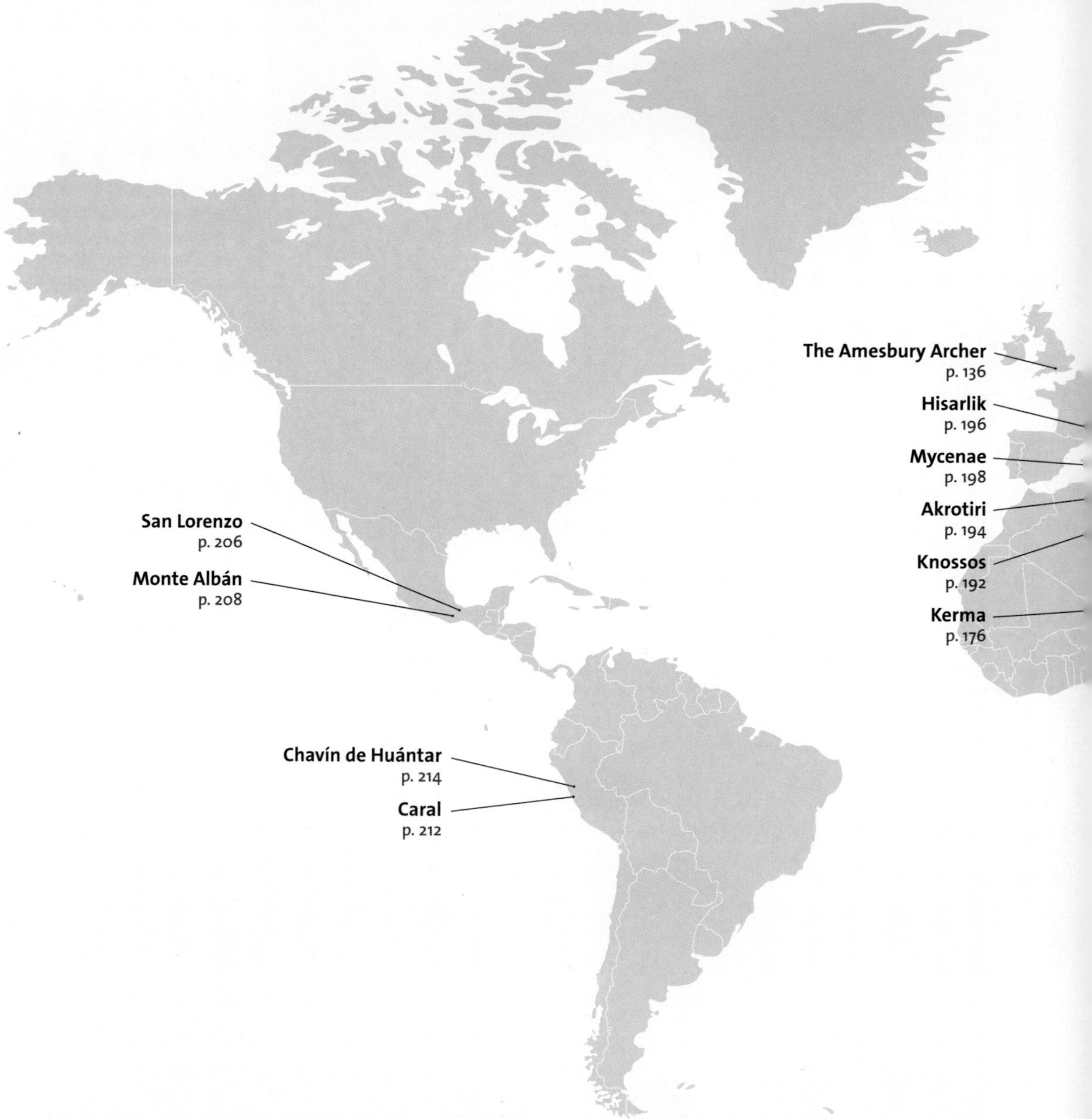

The Amesbury Archer
p. 136

Hisarlik
p. 196

Mycenae
p. 198

Akrotiri
p. 194

Knossos
p. 192

Kerma
p. 176

San Lorenzo
p. 206

Monte Albán
p. 208

Chavín de Huántar
p. 214

Caral
p. 212

BRONZE: AGENT OF TRANSFORMATION

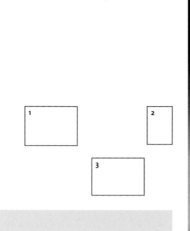

1 A bronze *zun* or wine vessel dating from the Shang dynasty (*c.* 1600–*c.* 1046 BCE), is shaped in the form of an elephant with uplifted trunk. The tip of the trunk features a crouching tiger and phoenix head, and on the vessel's surface are cloud and thunder, *kui* (dragon), and ogre mask designs.

2 First uncovered in 1987, these Bronze Age copper workings at Great Orme in Llandudno, North Wales, are believed to be the largest prehistoric mines so far discovered in the world.

3 Made from bronze and gold, the Trundholm sun chariot (1400 BCE) was found in 1902 in a peat bog on Trundholm moor on the northwest coast of the island of Zealand, Denmark. It is thought that the two sides of the disk may have functioned as a calendar.

Bronze, an alloy of copper and tin, became the prime industrial metal throughout Europe between 3000 and 2000 BCE. Copper and tin do not usually occur in the same places in nature, so the two metals were mined at their respective sources, smelted, and then brought together to be alloyed. The resulting bronze was cast and hammered into artifacts; some had crude precursors in stone, bone, and wood, and some were completely new in their forms and complexity—particularly in the case of ornaments and weapons. Bronze artifacts were much more durable than their equivalents made of pottery, flint, bone, or copper. Bronze tools and weapons maintained a sharp edge and were not deformed by impacts. If they eventually broke or wore out, they could be melted down and recast into new or updated forms.

For the production of bronze, long-exploited copper sources, such as mines in the Carpathian mountains and the Alps, were expanded. New sources were found in Wales (see image 2) and Ireland; Mount Gabriel on the Mizen Peninsula in southwest Ireland is one site of caverns from which copper ore was extracted, and where stone hammers used by the miners may still be found. Copper was mined in Cyprus (whose very name is derived from the Greek word for copper), Turkey, the Levant, and Iran. Tin was much more scarce, coming primarily from the mineral cassiterite. In Europe, Cornwall in Britain appears to have been a major supplier, as well as Spain, Anatolia, and minor sources in central Asia. In China, deposits of cassiterite along the Yellow River supplied the tin required to make the famous Shang bronzes (see image 1).

KEY EVENTS

c. 3500 BCE	*c.* 3300 BCE	*c.* 3200 BCE	*c.* 2580 BCE	*c.* 2300 BCE	*c.* 2000 BCE
Copper and tin are deliberately alloyed for the first time in the region east of the Mediterranean.	Ötzi the Iceman dies in the Alps. Interred with him is a copper ax.	The Bronze Age begins in the Aegean region.	The Great Pyramid of Giza is built in Egypt.	The Amesbury Archer is buried in England along with his copper knives (see p. 136).	Bronze Age innovations spread to northern Europe.

Prehistoric metallurgists learned that 10 percent tin produced the very hard bronze best suited for weapons, while bronze made with 6 percent tin could be hammered into sheets and used for body armor. More than 10 percent tin produced a bronze that was brittle and easily broken.

Possession of metal objects had long been a marker of status (see p. 122), but the demand for bronze, the requirement for expertise and knowledge, and the need to extract and transport raw materials had a transformative effect on prehistoric society and the avenues by which individuals could acquire power and wealth. Communities around mines demanded goods and commodities in exchange for the copper and tin they controlled. Transportation of ingots and discarded metal objects for recycling grew in importance. For example, a ship wrecked off Ulu Burun, Turkey (c. 1300 BCE, see p. 152), was carrying 10 tons of copper ingots and one ton of tin ingots; more than 400 bronze objects found on the seabed at Langdon Bay, England, are thought to be the remains of a shipment of scrap metal headed from France to Britain for recycling.

Products made of bronze were highly valued throughout the ancient world, and the drive to acquire them stimulated the production of other commodities that could be used in exchange. For instance, an immense number of fine bronze artifacts have been found in Denmark (see image 3), even though the country lacks natural sources of copper and tin. During the 2nd millennium BCE, agricultural products, wool, hides, and dried fish were produced there on a far greater scale than before, and captives from raiding were sold as slaves in exchange for copper and tin as well as finished bronze products. **PB**

c. 1800 BCE	c. 1600 BCE	c. 1500 BCE	c. 1300 BCE	c. 1200 BCE	c. 500 BCE
Rich burials in such places as Leubingen, eastern Germany, provide evidence for differentiation in status in central Europe.	The volcano on the island of Thera (Santorini) erupts.	Large quantities of bronze objects begin to be made in China during the Shang dynasty period.	A ship sinks off the Ulu Burun headland of Turkey. It is loaded with ingots of copper and tin.	In Europe and the Middle East, iron begins to replace bronze in the manufacture of tools.	A massive bronze vessel, made in a workshop in southern Italy, is placed in a tomb in Vix, northern Burgundy, France.

The Amesbury Archer   *c.* 2380 – 2290 BCE

The abundance and variety of objects in the grave suggest that the Amesbury Archer held a position of high status within his society. The stone anvil, or cushion stone, may provide a clue as to how he attained this status. Although he was buried far from any source of metal, he may have been adept in the finishing of copper and gold objects made by other hands.

In Amesbury, 3 miles (5 km.) south of Stonehenge in southern England, a new school was being built in 2002. Archaeologists investigating the site before construction came across the grave of an adult male surrounded by artifacts. The skeleton was in a contracted position, lying on its left side, with the head pointed toward the northeast. Subsequent analysis showed that the man was between thirty-five and forty-five years old and about 5 feet 9 inches (1.75 m.) tall. He had injured his knee early in life and probably walked with a permanent limp. Radiocarbon dating of his bones determined that he lived right on the boundary between the Stone Age and the Bronze Age.

The Amesbury Archer lived at a time when metals were just coming into use in northwestern Europe. In southeastern Europe copper was already being alloyed with tin to make bronze, but this technology would not reach the British Isles for another three centuries. The source of the copper used in the knives found with the Archer appears to have been Spain, which signaled that the Archer was part of a network of communities that spanned different parts of western Europe. When these interregional connections finally brought bronze metallurgy to northwestern Europe at the end of the third millennium BCE, it was rapidly adopted as a marker of status.

Other items in the grave included two wrist guards, a stone that may have served as an anvil, four boar tusks, and two small gold objects interpreted as hair ornaments. Five drinking vessels without handles, known as bell beakers because of their resemblance to an upturned bell, were positioned around the body. Placed upon the body were seventeen barbed flint arrowheads—an exceptional number for a single burial. **PB**

WRIST GUARDS

On one wrist of the body was a perforated polished flat stone; another one lay nearby. These stone objects are traditionally interpreted as bracers, or wrist guards, designed to protect the hand holding the bow from the sting of the bowstring. However, some archaeologists question this idea and suggest instead that they functioned as indicators of status. Whether or not this theory is correct, the abundance of archery equipment in the grave led to the interred man being dubbed the Amesbury Archer.

BODY AND ARTIFACTS

The contracted body of the Amesbury Archer was surrounded by around a hundred objects. The black object near his back is the cushion stone he used to finish metal objects. The dark areas visible on either side of his head and at his feet mark the sites of bell beakers. Close to both beaker locations by his head, but not easily discerned, are caches of flint arrowheads. One of the wrist guards is visible lying alongside one arm. Several metal objects were also present in the grave.

CLUES FROM THE TEETH

In recent years, studies of the mobility of ancient peoples have benefited enormously from analysis of teeth from prehistoric graves. The key lies in the isotopes of oxygen and strontium that the teeth contain. Tooth enamel forms in childhood, and its proportions of oxygen and strontium isotopes can show where the person grew up. People take in oxygen from drinking water, and in warmer regions the proportion of oxygen-18 to oxygen-16 is higher than in colder regions. Strontium, on the other hand, originates in the local geology and proceeds up the food chain to people. Different regions have different proportions of strontium-87 to strontium-86, and these can be mapped.

The oxygen isotopes in the Amesbury Archer's teeth show that as a young teenager he lived in a cold climate. Although this could lie in a zone stretching from Scandinavia to the Alps, the northern areas are ruled out by the strontium isotopes. Together, the oxygen and strontium isotopes indicate that he spent his youth in central Europe, perhaps in the foothills of the Alps. Only as an adult did he reach England.

In 2003, a year after the discovery of the Archer, a group burial containing eight bell beakers was discovered nearby, on Boscombe Down. The grave contained the remains of five related adult males, a teenager and one or two children. The teeth of the Boscombe Bowmen tell a different story. Their strontium isotope ratios point toward areas in the west of Britain, while their oxygen isotope ratios constrain that area to Wales and the Lake District. Moreover, the chemical fingerprints between their premolars and their third molars are different, suggesting that each lived in one place until age six and another until age thirteen. Neither place lay in the area near Stonehenge where they were buried.

DEFINING CIVILIZATION

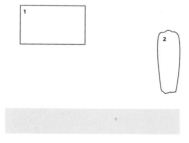

The first primary civilizations emerged independently at different times: in Mesopotamia (see p. 142) and Egypt (see p. 154) in the late fourth millennium; in the Indus basin (see p. 178) by 2600 BCE; in China (see image 1 and p. 184) in the early second millennium BCE; and in Mesoamerica (see p. 204) and Andean South America (see p. 210) later in the second millennium. Secondary civilizations also emerged, partly influenced by their already civilized neighbors. Each was unique, but there were also shared features.

Chief among these was social complexity. Civilizations generally show marked social stratification, an elite minority controlling access to certain resources denied to others or limited in their distribution. These included luxury goods used to display status; religiously imbued objects, situating the elite between the gods and the rest of society; and necessities, such as food, which gave the elite a higher standard of living and greater life expectancy. The elite also monopolized power and controlled the activities of the rest of society to some degree, backed by physical force, religious beliefs, or social norms. Social complexity also included occupational specialization: Many members of society were no longer primary food producers but worked as artisans, traders, priests, administrators, soldiers, or in other specialist roles.

Such social complexity was only possible with high economic productivity: primary producers supporting large, dense populations and creating a surplus. This productivity was possible where environmental potential intersected with society's ingenuity and drive to exploit it. In many cases, this was in major river

1 This excavated prehistoric site, Lajia in Qinghai province, northwest China, speaks of a period of disastrous flooding that is associated with the establishment of the Xia dynasty (c. 2070–c. 1600 BCE) and the beginning of Chinese civilization.

2 Found in the nineteenth century, this Olmec ceremonial ax is made from ritually significant imported blue-green jade. Its symbols include early glyphs.

KEY EVENTS

3400 BCE	3200 BCE	3200 BCE	3100 BCE	3000 BCE	2800–1800 BCE
Uruk emerges as the first city in Sumer; Sumerian colonies and outposts are established in other parts of West Asia, probably to control trade.	Tablets bearing simple writing appear in Uruk. Words include numbers, commodities, and ration disbursement.	Labels bearing probable town names are buried in tomb U-j at Abydos, the first evidence of writing in Predynastic Egypt.	Cities emerge across Sumer. Tablets with more developed writing reflect complex temple administration and deployment of produce.	Upper and Lower Egypt are unified, traditionally by legendary King Menes. Early kings are buried in tombs at Abydos.	A major settlement at Caral, Peru, with monumental architecture by 2600 BCE, has wide-ranging economic and ritual connections.

valleys where irrigation agriculture produced heavy yields. Water management in other situations could also significantly raise productivity: for example, by swamp drainage to create raised field systems, employed in both Mesoamerica and South America. Integrated mixed economies, combining the farmed or foraged resources of different environments, also provided high productivity in some places. Whereas primary civilizations developed through local high productivity, secondary civilizations could arise by exploiting opportunities for trade with already existing states, by controlling access to highly prized resources.

The management of trade was another feature common to civilizations. In most cases, emerging states had a real or perceived need for commodities that were not available locally: Some utilitarian, such as hard stone for tool-making, many more for religious purposes (see image 2), monumental constructio, and elite or community display. Although surplus agricultural or foraged produce could be used as trade goods, more commonly the latter were manufactured goods, such as fine pottery, textiles, olive oil, wine, perfumes, or materials traded from elsewhere—their value increased with distance from the source. The organization of foreign trade and domestic craft production to supply trade goods was a key factor in the growth of elite power in many early states.

In some early civilizations, the managerial elite derived its power from its religious authority. Kings or priests were attributed the ability to intercede between the human and divine worlds, directing society in line with the gods' wishes and acting on behalf of the people to please the gods. Often this involved creating monuments to honor the gods, such as temples and other structures magnificent in their size, complexity, and decoration. Elsewhere, authority was secular, vested in elite war leaders, aggrandizing the state at the neighbors' expense. Labor might then be expended on monumental defenses and exotic goods on the trappings of war. However, ancient civilizations were often not polarized; rulers might exercise both divine and secular authority.

Managing a state's economic complexities led to the development of writing, to record movement of goods and labor deployment. Some civilizations managed without written accountancy but invented writing for other reasons, such as recording royal events or consulting the gods. Once writing had been invented, it generally developed into a multipurpose tool, used to record history, literature, and propaganda; mark ownership; and for correspondence.

Archaeologically, the most obvious feature of civilizations is urbanism: the emergence of cities. These took many forms: for example, tightly concentrated within city walls; discrete clusters of public buildings and housing loosely distributed over large areas of garden landscape; or a center focused on public activities, closely surrounded by specialist satellite settlements performing other urban functions, such as craft production. Cities' functions, however, were generally similar: administrative, religious, ceremonial, royal, industrial, residential, cultural, and as service centers for their region or state. **JM**

2600 BCE	c. 2500 BCE	2100 BCE	2000 BCE	1500 BCE	1200 BCE
The transformation of settlements in the Indus region, with the creation of new or refounded cities, heralds the beginning of Indus civilization.	Indus beads buried with Sumerian royalty at Ur attest to trade between the Indus civilization and Sumer.	The start of the Xia dynasty, legendary predecessors of the historical Shang dynasty in China.	Palaces at Knossos, Malia, and Phaistos on Crete mark the emergence of state societies in the Bronze Age Aegean.	San Lorenzo emerges as the first Olmec ceremonial and urban center. Olmec influences are present through much of Mesoamerica.	Chavín de Huántar is founded in Peru (see p. 214). It becomes a ceremonial center, uniting much of Andean South America in a shared cult.

Hierakonpolis 3700 – 3500 BCE

Hierakonpolis (ancient Nekhen; modern Kom el-Ahmar or Red Mound) lies 50 miles (80 km.) to the south of Thebes (Luxor) on the west bank of the Nile. It is one of Egypt's largest and best-preserved Predynastic (late prehistoric) settlement sites. It spread over an area running 1½ miles (2.5 km.) north to south and over 1¾ miles (3 km.) from east to west.

Hierakonpolis in Egypt was continually occupied from at least 4500 BCE. At the height of its prosperity, from 3700 to 3500 BCE, it was a wealthy city centered on an extensive administrative and cultic or ceremonial center. The city included many houses, shrines, potters' workshops, and waste dumps, and there is evidence of an extensive brewing industry capable of producing an estimated 300 gallons (1140 L.) of beer per day. The industrial zones brought wealth to Hierakonpolis, with expensive raw materials being imported, crafted into desirable artefacts and traded on at a profit. Egypt's oldest known house, a potter's home dated to c. 3600 BCE, was preserved at Hierakonpolis because the craftsman accidentally burned it down.

Hierakonpolis was first excavated systematically by James Quibell (1867–1935) and Frederick Green (1869–1949). They discovered a temple dedicated to the falcon god Horus, which yielded the Main Deposit, a cache of unknown date that included Predynastic and Early Dynastic votive material, including hundreds of ivory, stone, and faience artifacts, many of which had been manufactured at up to ten times life-size.

Excavations from 1967 onward have done much to clarify the extent of early urbanism in Predynastic Egypt. It seems likely that Hierakonpolis, designated Egypt's first capital city, was home to local rulers who became the kings of a unified Egypt in c. 3100 BCE. However, following unification a new bureaucratic center, White Walls, was established at the apex of the Nile Delta near modern Abusir. This city would creep southward as the Nile shifted its course until it lay opposite the Saqqara cemetery. It would become known as Mennefer or, in the more familiar Greek version, Memphis. Despite continued royal interest in the cult of Horus, Hierakonpolis declined as Memphis flourished, though later Egyptian tradition would regard Hierakonpolis as one of its most venerable cities. **JT**

THE NARMER PALETTE

Found close to the Main Deposit in Hierakonpolis temple, the Narmer Palette is a ceremonial carved stone that records scenes of the first king of the unified Egypt, Narmer, executing an enemy and marching with his army. A falcon, likely to be an early depiction of the god Horus, is also shown leading a captured enemy.

HIERAKONPOLIS FORT

The oldest freestanding mud-brick building in the world, Hierakonpolis's so-called Fort is a massive rectangular enclosure built by the second dynasty king Khasekhemwy in *c.* 2690 BCE. Not appearing to have had any military function, it is likely to have been in some way connected to the king's funerary cult.

CEMETERIES AND TOMB 100

As would be expected of a long-surviving settlement, Hierakonpolis was surrounded by many cemeteries of different ages. The Predynastic cemeteries have yielded the earliest evidence for artificial mummification, dating to *c.* 3600 BCE. The bodies' heads and hands were padded with linen and then wrapped in linen bandages. The cemeteries included burials of animals too, including baboons, dogs, a triple burial of a bull, cow, and calf as well as the only known elephant burial in Egypt, also dating to *c.* 3600 BCE. Egypt's first stone-cut tomb was created at Hierakonpolis and dates to *c.* 3100 BCE.

Included among the many elite human burials here was Tomb 100: the only Predynastic tomb with painted decoration preserved on its plastered walls. Today, Tomb 100 is lost, but its wall art survives in copies, and painted fragments are preserved in Cairo Museum. Egyptologists believe that this was the tomb of a local king, but the painting belongs to an age before writing, so we cannot be certain of its interpretation. Depicted at the tomb were six large-scale boats complete with cabins and some crewmen but no oars. Five of the boats are white; the sixth is black. Given its location, it seems probable that it represents a funeral cortège, because boats were strongly associated with funerals throughout the dynastic age. Although the river appears as a safe, controlled environment, the riverbank is chaotic and dangerous; present there are images of wild animals, hunters, men fighting, and men bound and dying. The riverbank images of combatants also include Egypt's first smiting scene: a powerful individual raises a club or mace to strike an enemy who grovels before him. This would become a defining image of Egyptian kingship; it features on the Narmer Palette (also recovered from Hierakonpolis), and it would be displayed on exterior temple walls throughout the dynastic age.

MESOPOTAMIA

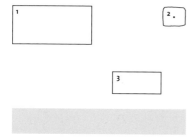

1 The mid-third-millennium BCE Standard of Ur was found in a royal tomb in Ur. This mosaic panel (Peace) depicts preparations for a banquet celebrating a victory shown on the reverse (War).

2 On this votive plaque, King Ur-Nanshe, founder of Lagash's first dynasty c. 2500 BCE, symbolically carries the first hod of bricks to build a shrine and attends a banquet celebrating its inauguration.

3 The ziggurat of Ur (Tell al-Muqayyar, Iraq), built by King Ur-Nammu c. 2100 BCE.

Major developments in fourth-millennium BCE West Asia, particularly in Sumer (southern Babylonia), had far-reaching consequences. The invention of the potter's wheel, enabling fine pottery to be efficiently mass produced, reflects growing craft specialization and organized labor. Wheels were used in transport, too, creating carts. Animals (oxen and recently domesticated donkeys) were now used for traction and to carry loads. Together these revolutionized productivity in many fields, including agriculture where animals drew the newly invented plough, expanding the land that could be cultivated. This period also saw the emergence, through selective breeding, of woolly sheep (see image 1), on which by the later fourth millennium Sumer based an officially controlled textile industry, of great importance throughout Mesopotamian history, providing domestic clothing and a principal export.

Towns developed in parts of West Asia during this period. In Babylonia, where water management was necessary but gave high productivity, huge population growth increased social complexity and cities emerged by the late fourth millennium. The administrative demands of managing labor and offerings (taxes) were met by innovations that culminated c. 3200 BCE in the emergence of writing in Uruk (see p. 144). Surplus production and community labor were used by the Sumerian authorities to create monumental architecture and irrigation works, support craft production, and promote trade.

At first, authority rested with the temple establishment, but by the early third millennium kings (see image 2) were also wielding power and leading the

KEY EVENTS

c. 3800 BCE	c. 3400 BCE	c. 3200 BCE	c. 3100 BCE	c. 2900–2600 BCE	c. 2600–2450 BCE
Administrative devices develop: accounting tokens enclosed in clay balls, cylinder seals (3600 BCE), and tablets with token impressions (3500 BCE).	Sumerian colonies are established on the upper Euphrates, supplementing Sumerian trading outposts in northern Mesopotamia.	Uruk emerges as the first city. Elaborate, often remodeled architecture in Eanna precinct is associated with clay tablets bearing the first writing.	Sumer has a number of cities, including Uruk. Writing becomes more sophisticated, trading colonies are abandoned, and there are signs of warfare.	Early Dynastic I to II period in southern Mesopotamia sees city-states ruled by kings and is the time of the legendary hero Gilgamesh.	The Early Dynastic IIIA period sees border conflict between Umma and Lagash (the first historically documented war) and royal burials at Ur.

city-states that were crystallizing around cities such as Ur (see p. 146) along Babylonia's rivers. After 2500 BCE, powerful rulers sought hegemony beyond their own city-state, claiming divine support for their expanded rule. The last, Lugalzagesi (r. *c.* 2340–2316 BCE), was defeated by Sargon (r. *c.* 2334–2279 BCE), who emerged in Akkad (northern Babylonia), conquering the south and creating Mesopotamia's first major territorial state, organized into provinces under Akkadian governors. Sargon and his successors waged external campaigns, gaining substantial booty and probably establishing bases to control trade (see p. 148), a major preoccupation of Babylonia, whose agricultural wealth was balanced by an absence of materials such as metal ores, stone, hardwood timber, and gemstones. Sea trade with the Indus civilization (see p. 178) flourished, reaching its peak in the later Ur III Empire (*c.* 2112–*c.* 2004 BCE), which saw great architectural and literary flowering (see image 3).

Declining agricultural fertility in Sumer saw a northward shift of population and power in the early second millennium, northern Babylonia becoming the regional focus thereafter. Trade networks with the north gained in importance, now including the Mediterranean. Assyria (northern Mesopotamia), the middle and upper Euphrates region, and the northern Levant became equal players with Babylonia: this period saw fierce competition between powerful regional states, in which occasionally one gained wider control. Finally, Hammurabi, king of Babylon from 1792 BCE, gradually conquered his neighbors to secure a Babylonian empire extending north to Mari (see p. 150). The collapse of the Ur III Empire had seen a significant change, economic organization shifting from tight state control to considerable private enterprise. The political situation stabilized by the mid-second millennium, when the north was united under Mitanni and Babylonia was ruled by the Kassite dynasty, who revived Gulf trade, sponsored architecture, promoted traditional culture, and maintained irrigation works—a key royal responsibility upon which Babylonia's renewed agricultural prosperity depended. **JM**

c. 2500 BCE	*c.* 2450–2334 BCE	*c.* 2334–2193 BCE	*c.* 2112–2004 BCE	From 2004 BCE	*c.* 1792–1750 BCE
The cuneiform writing system is fully developed and used for economic records but also royal inscriptions, lexical texts, and a range of literature.	The Early Dynastic IIIB period sees territorial conflicts, leading to the claim by Lugalzagesi of Umma and Uruk to exercise kingship over all Babylonia.	Sargon of Akkad conquers Sumer and unites Babylonia in the Akkadian Empire with administrative standardization and a standing army.	The third dynasty of Ur reunites Babylonia. There is stifling bureaucratic efficiency in state-controlled agriculture, industry, and trade.	Smaller states compete and private enterprise grows. There is economic decline in Sumer. Gulf trade is much reduced and eventually ceases.	Hammurabi reigns and conquers neighboring states to create the Babylonian Empire, which declines after his death, falling in 1595 BCE.

Uruk 4800 – 2900 BCE

The Warka Vase, discovered in 1934, was part of a collection of precious temple objects. It shows people bringing offerings to the city's goddess Inanna: those already given are piled behind her. The temple, the controlling authority in the late fourth-millennium Sumerian towns and emerging cities, was supported by offerings of produce and labor from its citizens.

NAVIGATOR

U ruk (Warka, Iraq) is credited as the world's first city, emerging in the late fourth millennium BCE. A German team has been excavating here, almost continuously, since 1912. Uruk was favorably located to exploit the varied resources of marsh, farmland, and desert margins and waterborne routes through Sumer and north along the Euphrates. Other Sumerian towns flourished in the fourth millennium, but Uruk grew more rapidly, reaching about 1,350 acres (550 ha.) by 2900 BCE. It was founded as two villages *c.* 4800 BCE, each focused on a shrine. Since farmers first settled in Babylonia, shrines had been community foci, built by communal endeavor and supported by offerings of produce. The power and administrative responsibilities of religious leaders grew as the population expanded: religious centers grew into towns, focused around the temples. In Uruk, the An temple and Eanna, Inanna's precinct, were repeatedly rebuilt and expanded; buildings probably included shrines, decorated spaces for public celebrations, workshops, administrative buildings, storerooms, and priestly residences. The authorities used offerings and produce from temple lands to issue rations to people undertaking corvee labor, building temples and irrigation works, or working as temple dependents, especially making textiles for export to obtain valued raw materials. Many finds are administrative: seals, sealings, accounting tokens, and from 3200 BCE onward, written tablets. **JM**

1 INANNA

The 39-inch (1 m.) high alabaster vessel was found in a deposit dated *c.* 3000 BCE, but may be older. By then Inanna was Uruk's principal deity. The Sumerians saw civilization as the *me*, a set of defining attributes. In one myth, the gods entrust these to the god Enki for safekeeping. However, Inanna tricks them from him and gives them to her city so that it may reap the benefits of civilization. This surely reflects Sumerian recognition of Uruk's importance in the development of civilized life.

2 OFFERINGS

The lower tiers of decoration symbolize the city's local sources of wealth: the river that provides the water upon which everything, including agriculture, depends; plants, perhaps representing the versatile date palm and barley, Sumer's agricultural staple; animals, an alternating frieze of ewes and rams, signifying pastoral abundance; and bearers of vessels containing offerings (possibly grain and certainly fruit) to sustain the goddess and her household of priests, servants, administrators, and workers.

ORIGIN OF WRITING

From early times, simple tokens were used for recording in West Asia. In the fourth millennium BCE, as administrative activity increased, accounting used them more systematically: tokens recording individual transactions were strung on strings or enclosed in clay balls, sometimes with the tokens impressed on the outside. By 3500 BCE, clay tablets bearing such impressions appeared, making tokens redundant. In *c.* 3200 BCE at Uruk, a further step was taken, drawing representations of tokens with a stylus on clay tablets: the beginning of writing. At the same time, the variety of signs proliferated, representing different things, including number signs. The first written tablets bear simple records: one or several entries listing quantities of a commodity, such as measures of grain, and a sign for "ration disbursement" (a head and a bowl). By 3100 BCE, the entries were more complex and writing was known in cities beyond Uruk.

◀ To compensate for Sumer's deficiency in raw materials, the Sumerians were inventive in using what they had—for instance, building in mud brick, lesser woods such as poplar and willow, and reeds. Some fourth-millennium temples, at Uruk and elsewhere, and a court in Uruk's Eanna precinct were imaginatively decorated with patterns made in cone mosaics, as this reconstruction at the Pergamon Museum in Berlin shows. Baked clay cones with painted bases were embedded end-out in the plaster of pillars and walls, decorating and strengthening them.

Ur and the Royal Graves 3000 – 1750 BCE

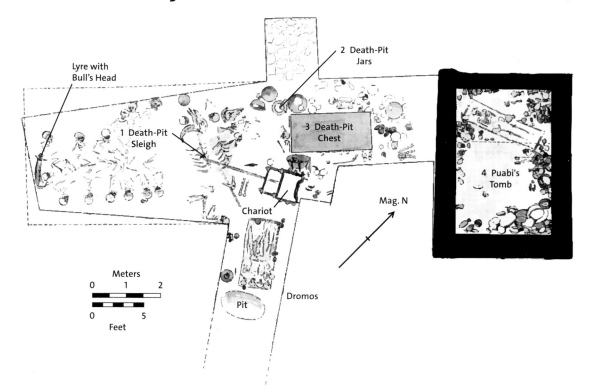

Leonard Woolley published this plan of Royal Tomb (RT) 800 at Ur. The black-bordered rectangle (right) represents the vaulted stone tomb chamber of Queen Puabi, an unknown queen, adjoined by a much larger death pit filled with grave goods such as gold cups and musical instruments, and the bodies of twenty-three attendants.

The ziggurat of Ur, built by Ur-Nammu around 2100 BCE, is highly visible on the flat Babylonian plain in southern, Iraq, so Ur (Tell al-Muqayyar) attracted early antiquarian attention. Between 1922 and 1934, Leonard Woolley (1880–1960) directed major excavations here. He found a cemetery soon after starting, but moved elsewhere on the site to enable his inexperienced team to develop the expertise needed for such delicate excavation work. Returning to the cemetery in 1927, he exposed around 2,000 burials, mainly mid Early Dynastic in date (c. 2600–c. 2450 BCE), including sixteen richly furnished Royal Graves. The latter generally comprised a vaulted or domed stone chamber in which the principal burial was placed, with a wealth of grave goods, and a much larger grave pit containing other funerary offerings and the bodies of retainers. One, the Great Death Pit, holds seventy-three bodies in one grave, along with jewelry, weapons, and musical instruments. Such human sacrifices are unknown in other Mesopotamian burials and their significance and cultural context remains a puzzle.

Ur is the most explored Sumerian city. Woolley excavated its sacred precinct, including the ziggurat and the *giparu*—residence of the priestess of Ur, a post occupied around 2300 BCE by the Akkadian princess Enheduanna, whose surviving hymns make her the first named author in history. Woolley also uncovered the impressive vaulted tombs of the Ur III kings (2112–2004 BCE); the western harbor; substantial residential areas, particularly Old Babylonian (early second millennium BCE) housing; and remains showing that settlement began here in the fifth millennium. Ur, on the Euphrates river, emerged as a city in the early third millennium, when the head of the Gulf was around 150 miles (240 km.) farther north, so Ur lay close to the sea. Carnelian beads, lapis lazuli, and other exotic materials found in the royal graves indicate that Ur derived much of its importance from its command of sea trade on the Gulf. The trade reached its peak under the Ur III dynasty, when Ur was the capital of an empire controlling all of Babylonia, Elam (southwest Iran) to the east, and southern Assyria. **JM**

 FOCAL POINTS

1 DEATH-PIT SLEIGH

At the center of the death pit was a fine wooden sleigh, of which only the mosaic panels and decorative gold and silver lion and bull heads survive, along with the electum rein-ring, a model donkey. Around it lie the bodies of four or five attendant grooms and the pair of oxen that drew it.

2 DEATH-PIT JARS

Three large silver jars in the death pit probably held beer. Each was furnished with a reed drinking tube: this one was encased in silver and decorated with rings of gold and lapis lazuli. Beer was served in such jars at banquets, with each participant using a personal drinking tube to drink.

3 DEATH-PIT CHEST

Puabi's death pit was located on top of the deeper death pit and tomb of an unknown king. This was looted, probably by the workers preparing Puabi's grave. A clothes chest was positioned to hide the hole dug by the robbers. Such "recycling" of grave goods was not uncommon at this time.

4 PUABI'S TOMB

Puabi's body, laid on a wooden bier within the tomb, wore a cape of beads of lapis lazuli, carnelian, agate, gold, and silver. On her head, an elaborate diadem of beaten gold featured delicate leaves and flowers. One male and two female attendants, and a mass of goods, were buried with her.

▲ This goat is from the Great Death Pit. Its fleece is of shell and lapis lazuli, as are the facial details, its eyes of copper, and its belly of silver sheet. Gold covers the rest of its wood and plaster frame.

FOUNDATION PEG

Most of the temples in Ur's sacred precinct were built by the Ur III kings. They recorded their pious works on inscribed metal pegs placed in temple foundations: these depicted the king carrying the first basket of soil. These kings also built ziggurats in Sumer's major cities: in form, a three-tiered stepped pyramid, surmounted by a shrine.

Ebla 3000 – 1600 BCE

The early palace was built on the high mound's western slope. Its mud-brick walls survive 23-foot (7 m.) high in parts. A large courtyard for public activities was flanked by domestic and administrative quarters, including a large southern storeroom. A basalt staircase on the courtyard's eastern side led to the palace's upper levels, now gone.

⬥ **NAVIGATOR**

Around 3100 BCE, the Sumerians withdrew from their northern trading outposts. Although in Babylonia cities continued to develop, urbanism in the north was largely abandoned for a time. By 2600 BCE, however, northern city-states were emerging, from southeastern Anatolia and Syria to Assyria. Italian excavations from 1964 under Paolo Matthiae (b. 1940) at Tell Mardikh, a major mound in northwestern Syria, have revealed a wealth of information about the mid-third-millennium political, economic, and cultural situation in this region, previously regarded as a backwater until the arrival of the conquering Akkadians in the twenty-third century BCE. One of the Akkadian kings, Sargon or his grandson Naram-Sin, burned down Ebla's palace, firing the clay tablets in the palace archives, thus preserving a rich record of life in twenty-fourth-century Ebla.

Ebla was the center of a large and powerful city-state, controlling a vast area including many vassal states, which paid it silver and copper tribute; metalworking was a major industry supervised by the Ebla palace. Ebla competed with Mari (see p. 150) for control over the upper Euphrates region. The state was ruled by a king, aided by his queen and princes; a council of elders (heads of leading families) was also influential, presided over by a hereditary royal vizier. Much of Ebla's third-millennium palace was uncovered in the excavations, revealing public, administrative, and domestic areas, grouped around an open courtyard. It was built on the city's central mound, surrounded by the lower town. Most of the city's inhabitants would have been direct dependants of the palace: ration texts refer to several thousand officials, hundreds of women textile producers, and other workers. In other parts of the city, temples, burials and later palaces were exposed, within substantial city walls: an equally splendid earlier second-millennium palace was burned down by invaders around 1600 BCE. **JM**

⊙ FOCAL POINTS

1 THRONE PLINTH AND STAIR

At the northern end of the audience hall or chamber, a raised plinth is believed to have been the base for a throne. Close to this, in the courtyard's northeastern corner, was a square tower in which there was a four-flight internal staircase. It is thought that this led to the upper story, perhaps to the private residential apartments of the incumbent royal family. The staircase therefore provided restricted access to this area of the palace.

2 ADMINISTRATIVE AREA

A small room set within the audience courtyard and several adjacent rooms housed the palace archives. Texts in each room related to different administrative activities, including the management of agriculture and the distribution of rations to the palace's dependent workers. One room also had writing equipment, including a stone to smooth the damp clay surfaces of the tablets and styluses with which to impress cuneiform signs upon them.

NEIGHBORS AND TRADE

Ebla was strategically placed to control trade in metal ore from Anatolia, timber from Lebanon, and goods from Egypt. When its big commercial rival, Mari, extended its military influence, Ebla deemed it wise to pay tribute. This cuneiform tablet records a letter from Mari king Enna-Dagan regarding the tribute. When Sargon of Akkad united southern Mesopotamia, he also campaigned against and defeated Mari, Ebla, and other places vital for trade. His grandson Naram-Sin again defeated Ebla, indicating that Akkadian control was difficult to maintain. The Ur III Empire solved the same problem of keeping trade routes open by making allies of Ebla and Mari.

◄ A reconstruction of the archive room in the courtyard, where clay tablets were stored on wooden shelves. Impressions of the shelves are still visible in the walls of the ruins. When the Akkadians sacked the palace, the shelves burned and the serried rows of neatly filed tablets collapsed onto the floor. This archive related to Ebla's all-important textile industry, using wool from huge palace flocks.

Mari and Kanesh *c.* 2900 – 1755 BCE

The throne room at the center of the Palace of Zimri-Lim at Mari, Syria, where visitors were received and public business conducted. North of this and on the upper story were the royal apartments. The rooms to the south included administrative offices, storerooms, kitchens, a schoolroom, and workshops for various craft activities.

The chance find of an ancient statue in 1933 led a French team to excavate the site of Tell Hariri in Syria. This, they discovered, was the important ancient city of Mari. Mari lay in a narrow stretch of the middle Euphrates valley, with restricted agricultural land, but strategically located for trade: the Euphrates was the major highway giving southern Mesopotamia access to the metal ores of Anatolia, the timber of the Lebanese mountains, and the Mediterranean Sea, linking the Levant with Egypt, a trade route even in the third millennium BCE. Mari was also the terminus of a caravan route from the Mediterranean coast across the formidable Syrian Desert, passing through the major oasis town of Tadmor (later Palmyra). A settlement existed at Mari from the early third millennium BCE; by 2400 BCE, this had temples and a substantial palace and was the centre of a kingdom vying with Ebla (see p. 148) for regional domination. In the early second millennium BCE, Mari's ruling dynasty was allied with the king of Yamhad, which controlled much of the northwest. In 1796 BCE, it was conquered by the Amorite king Shamshi-Adad (r. *c.* 1813 – *c.* 1781 BCE), who created an empire across northern West Asia: Mari became the capital of a province governed by Shamshi-Adad's son, Yasmah-Addu, a lazy and self-indulgent young man, according to his father's enraged letters found in the Mari archives. After Shamshi-Adad's death, the original dynasty was restored under Zimri-Lim, an ally of Hammurabi, ruler of Babylon, whose meteoric rise he assisted. Hammurabi, however, turned on him in 1757 BCE and in 1755 BCE burned down the palace, destroying Mari but preserving an archive of clay tablets that provide insight into life at Mari. **JM**

FOCAL POINTS

PALACE WALL PAINTINGS

Many rooms in the palace at Mari were decorated with paintings. One, near the palace entrance in the shrine to Ishtar (goddess of love and war), showed offerings being made to Ishtar and the sun god Shamash (above). An intermediate courtyard had a large scene depicting an important religious ceremony in the palace garden in which Ishtar reinvested the king with the symbols of office. The king's apartments were decorated with hunting scenes.

MARI TEXTS

About 25,000 cuneiform tablets were found at Mari, mostly from Zimri-Lim's reign. These include letters about both personal and business matters, sent between Zimri-Lim and his queen Shibtu, who ran the palace while he was absent on campaign. Others, from his daughters—married off to other rulers as diplomatic pawns— often contain complaints. Most are administrative—for example, recording supplies to the kitchens and for religious ceremonies.

KANESH AND ASHUR'S TRADE

The city-state of Ashur on the Tigris river (in modern Iraq) had limited agricultural land but was well placed for trade. In *c.* 1910 BCE, merchants from Ashur established a major trading outpost, or *karum*, in the Anatolian town of Kanesh, capital of a small kingdom. For three generations, these merchant families operated a trading network with Kanesh as its hub, from here overseeing operations in the *karums* they established in other towns. Each family had its head office in Ashur run by senior family members. Here too lived their women, intimately involved in the trade, making and obtaining textiles—a major export to Anatolia—and managing much of the home end of the trade. Meanwhile their husbands and brothers worked in Kanesh and other stations, and their sons and nephews learned their business in junior posts, journeying with the donkey caravans carrying Mesopotamian textiles and Afghan tin to Anatolia and returning with Anatolian silver.

In *c.* 1830 BCE, Kanesh was sacked and the merchants' houses destroyed, ironically preserving the records of their activities. More than 25,000 clay tablets have been excavated, bearing witness to every aspect of the trade and life in general. There are invoices listing consignments of goods, records of entry or exit taxes, instructions on the goods' disposal, and loan and repayment agreements. There are also letters from home, giving family and local news, reporting the dispatch of requested goods, and complaining about late or inadequate payments of the silver the women needed to run their households and supply more textiles. There are reports from merchants in other *karums*, describing successful transactions and local difficulties. One sequence details the worsening affairs of an illegal iron-smuggling company, which ends with an unfortunate subordinate being arrested.

Ulu Burun c. 1300 BCE

A unique find was a gold cup found between a Canaanite amphora and Mycenaean drinking cup. The date and origins of the gold cup have been difficult to ascertain. Some objects may have been destined to be melted down and the metal reused.

The most significant shipwreck site to shed light on Late Bronze Age trade in the eastern Mediterranean was found in 1982 off the headland of Ulu Burun, south of Kaş in modern southwestern Turkey. It was excavated between 1984 and 1994 by a team from the Institute of Nautical Archaeology, initially led by George Bass (b. 1932). Scientific dating suggests that the ship sank shortly before 1300 BCE.

The preservation of the cargo has been the main focus of study, because only a few fragments of the ship's hull have survived. A major element of the cargo was copper and tin, the components of bronze, with approximately 10 tons of copper ingots and 1 ton of tin ingots found. Ingots of colored glass destined to be made into finished goods such as beads were also carried, along with logs of African blackwood. Animal products included tortoise shells from a lute, unworked elephant tusks, and ostrich eggs. An item of trade not previously suspected was opercula (cuticles) from murex shells, which were a by-product of the purple dye industry. Some of the more unusual raw materials carried in 150 amphorae of the type known as Canaanite were the yellow pigment orpiment and over 1 ton of terebinth resin. Foodstuffs and spices were present: coriander, cumin, safflower, sumac, almonds, olives, figs, grapes, and pomegranates.

A range of luxurious finished goods included bronze bowls, ivory cosmetic boxes, a pair of small cymbals, drinking cups made from faience in the shape of rams' heads, and shell finger-rings. Metal finished goods comprised tools, daggers, spears, and swords, including a fragmentary sword of a type with parallels in southern Italy and Sicily, which, although possibly carried for scrap, suggests contact with the western Mediterranean. **GM**

POTTERY

One of the large storage vessels on the shipwreck contained eighteen pieces of Mesopotamian pottery, mostly from Cyprus. The pots in the storage jar included small jugs, bowls, and lamps. It is possible that other Cypriot pottery found nearby fell out of the storage jar during the shipwreck. Aegean pottery was also found, including Mycenaean stirrup jars, used to transport perfumed oil. The humbler components were perhaps for non-elite markets.

SHIP RECONSTRUCTION

The Bodrum Museum of Underwater Archaeology in the Castle of the Knights of St. John, Turkey, has a gallery devoted to the Ulu Burun ship. The museum has created a display of finds from the wreck, together with a full-size replica, 49 feet (15 m.) long, which shows how the cargo would have been carried, including the so-called oxhide-shaped copper ingots stacked in four rows. The oxhide shape allowed ingots to be carried on the backs of horses or mules easily.

SHIPWRECKS AND LATE BRONZE AGE TRADE

Late Bronze Age shipwrecks from the eastern Mediterranean have made a substantial contribution to the knowledge of the nature of trade in this period. The cargoes carried have provided information on small-scale commerce and, in the case of the Ulu Burun cargo, possible information on gift exchange between elites. In particular, wrecks have provided valuable knowledge of maritime trade in copper and tin.

The Cape Gelidonya A shipwreck, to the east of Ulu Burun, was excavated in 1960, 1987, and 1988 by a team led by George Bass. The main cargo was copper, more than sixty ingots in total, with tin ingots also carried. Brushwood dunnage had been placed underneath the cargo to cushion it and protect the hull timbers. Broken ingots and bronze tools, in well-preserved baskets, were probably carried as scrap. Late Minoan pottery dated the wreck between *c.* 1200 and 1150 BCE. Finds from the ship suggest that one of the people on the ship was an itinerant smith, carrying his tools and

several sets of weights, which would have enabled him to conduct commercial operations in virtually every area of the eastern Mediterranean.

A contemporary shipwreck was found in 1961 off Point Iria in the northeastern Peloponnese, Greece, and excavated between 1990 and 1994. The cargo, however, was different in nature from that of the Cape Gelidonya ship, and consisted almost entirely of pottery—mainly amphorae and stirrup jars used for transporting a variety of commodities and originating in Cyprus, Crete, and the Greek mainland.

The high-status manufactured objects and large quantity of metals in the Ulu Burun cargo may reflect the exchange of gifts between rulers described in the Amarna Letters found at the roughly contemporary Egyptian New Kingdom city of Amarna (see p. 166). If this were the case, the cargo suggests that the ship would have been carrying out an ambassadorial mission to an Aegean ruler.

RISE OF THE PHARAOHS

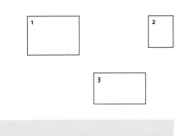

1 The Great Sphinx and the Pyramid of Khaefre on the Giza Plateau on the outskirts of Cairo. The limestone statue is believed to be a portrait of the king.

2 The Valley Temple of Khaefre at Giza dates to *c.* 2558 BCE. Made from pink granite, it is part of the pharaoh's funerary complex and is linked to the pyramid by a causeway.

3 The Step Pyramid at the Saqqara necropolis is the first monumental stone building ever constructed. It was built as a tomb for King Djoser of the third dynasty.

The arrival of agriculture in *c.* 5450 BCE converted the Egyptian people from hunter-gatherers to farmers and encouraged the development of permanent settlements for the living—villages—and the dead—cemeteries. While the dynastic Egyptians built their houses and palaces of mud brick, they built their tombs of stone in the hot, dry desert.

King Djoser (r. *c.* 2667–2648 BCE) of the third dynasty built a funerary complex that included a stone step pyramid (see image 3), underground galleries and a series of open courts lined with shrines. Pyramid building would be the defining characteristic of the next 500 years. The constant demand for limestone, granite, wood, charcoal, grave goods, and supplies for the workforce stimulated the economy and encouraged the craftsmen to perfect their skills. Meanwhile the workers, summoned from villages along the Nile valley and delta to work for three or four months in the royal cemetery, were united in one huge project. Snefru (r. *c.* 2613–2589 BCE), first king of the fourth dynasty, built Egypt's first straight-sided pyramid. Snefru's son Khufu (r. *c.* 2589–2566 BCE) built his Great Pyramid complex at Giza (see p. 158); nearby, Khufu's son Khaefre (r. *c.* 2558–2532 BCE) built a slightly smaller pyramid (see image 2) and the Great Sphinx (see image 1). This prosperity could not last, and the sixth dynasty saw a decrease in pyramid size. The bureaucracy had grown unwieldy, and the land was experiencing increasing dryness, which was affecting the crops. As confidence in the royal family declined, the local governors grew powerful. Central authority collapsed and Egypt fragmented into a series of petty states.

KEY EVENTS

c. 3050 BCE	*c.* 2667 BCE	*c.* 2613–2184 BCE	*c.* 2055–1650 BCE	*c.* 1525 BCE	*c.* 1504 BCE
Egypt becomes one land ruled by a king or pharaoh. The first kings build mud-brick mastaba tombs in the Abydos cemetery (see p. 156).	King Djoser builds a funerary complex, including a six-step pyramid, in Saqqara. This is the world's first substantial stone building.	Old Kingdom rulers build large-scale pyramid complexes in northern Egypt.	Middle Kingdom rulers build pyramids that, although apparently made entirely from stone, have mud-brick cores.	King Amenhotep I (r. *c.* 1525–1504 BCE) is probably the first New Kingdom monarch to build a rock-cut tomb in the Valley of the Kings (see p. 160).	King Thutmose I (r. *c.* 1504–*c.* 1492 BCE) begins the conquest of Nubia and the Levant, laying down the foundations of the Egyptian Empire.

The governors of the Valley and the Delta started to form alliances until two dominant dynasties emerged: a northern dynasty based at Herakleopolis and a southern dynasty based at Thebes (modern Luxor). Both dynasties aspired to reunite Egypt but that honor fell to the Thebans, who vanquished their rivals.

Middle Kingdom Egypt (*c.* 2055–1650 BCE) underwent a renaissance. But these were difficult times in the Mediterranean world, and as Egypt grew prosperous a steady flow of foreigners arrived, anxious to settle in the Nile Delta. This reignited discontent among the local governors. A succession of weak kings sparked the collapse of central authority.

Egypt was again divided. The south was ruled by a dynasty based at Thebes, while the Palestinian Hyksos kings ruled the north from Avaris (modern Tell el Dab'a) in the eastern Delta. Again, a series of Theban monarchs sailed northward to fight. Ahmose (r. *c.* 1550–1525 BCE) was able to expel the Hyksos, chasing them across the Sinai Peninsula into Canaan. In honor of this achievement, he is considered the first monarch of the New Kingdom (*c.* 1550–*c.* 1069 BCE). Successive New Kingdom pharaohs annexed Nubia and much of the Middle East, until the Egyptian Empire stretched from the Sudan to Syria.

The reign of Ramesses II (r. *c.* 1279–1213 BCE) started with a series of international campaigns and then matured into an age of peaceful prosperity. But his death left Egypt unsettled. The Mediterranean coast was menaced by pirates, the Delta was threatened by Libyans, and the southern and eastern empires were starting to crumble. As the empire shrank, the loss of taxes from the vassal states combined with the closure of the international trade routes to wilt the Egyptian economy. Poor harvests led to a high inflation, while official corruption led to civil unrest and a series of strikes in the Theban necropolis. The twentieth dynasty ended with Egypt once again a divided land. **JT**

c. 1390–1352 BCE	c. 1349 BCE	c. 1327 BCE	c. 1279 BCE	c. 1184 BCE	c. 1099 BCE
The reign of King Amenhotep III. During this time Egypt is the greatest superpower in northeast Africa and the eastern Mediterranean.	King Akhenaten (r. *c.* 1352–1336 BCE) devotes himself to the Aten sun god. He builds a new royal city at Amarna (see p. 166) in Middle Egypt.	King Tutankhamun (r. *c.* 1336–1327 BCE) dies and is buried in a nonroyal tomb in the Valley of the Kings.	The long reign of King Ramesses II sees Egypt competing for influence in the Near East with the Hittites of central Anatolia.	King Ramesses III (r. *c.* 1184–1153 BCE) defends Egypt against incursions by the Libyans and the Sea People. He is later assassinated.	King Ramesses XI (r. *c.* 1099–1069 BCE) starts to build, but then abandons, his Valley of the Kings tomb. He is eventually buried in northern Egypt.

Royal Tombs at Abydos *c.* 3100 – 2686 BCE

The extensive Abydos necropolis lies on the desert edge, on the west bank of the River Nile, 80 miles (128 km.) downriver from ancient Thebes, now Luxor, in southern Egypt. The necropolis was used for burials for more than 3,000 years, from Predynastic times until the Roman Period.

Egypt's earliest kings built their tombs in the Umm el Qa'ab region of the Abydos necropolis. Their mastaba tombs were substantial, flat-topped, free-standing structures incorporating a subterranean burial chamber covered by a low, brick-covered mound that was itself hidden beneath in a larger mound. Two stelae (inscribed stone slabs) recorded the name of the deceased king. Early archaeologists, unimpressed by the size of these tombs, classified them as cenotaphs. They believed that all the Early Dynastic kings were interred in the western desert at north Saqqara, close by the bureaucratic center of Memphis and the cult center of the sun god Re at Heliopolis. It is now realized that the mud-brick tombs were just one element in the kings' much larger Abydos funerary provision. Near to the northeast of the Umm el Qa'ab, closer to the cultivated land, they also built massive ritual enclosures defined by mud-brick walls.

The first dynasty royal tomb complexes included subsidiary graves provided for the king's retinue: his servants, harem women, and favorite animals, including dogs and lions. The deceased, who were partially mummified in natron-coated cloth, were buried in short wooden coffins with their own grave goods, and their names were carved on crude limestone stelae. The funerary complex of King Djer included 318 of these additional burial chambers, many of which were occupied by women. Most of the secondary graves were disturbed in antiquity, so it is impossible to determine how their occupants died. But, because the tomb architecture suggests that they were all sealed at the same time, it is possible that they were human sacrifices: servants either killed or compelled to commit suicide to accompany the dead king on his journey to the afterlife. If this is the case, it was a short-lived ritual. The second dynasty Abydos tomb complexes of the kings Peribsen and Khasekhemwy lack any form of subsidiary burial. **JT**

👁 FOCAL POINTS

MOTHER OF POTS

The Abydos necropolis has been the subject of virtually unbroken excavation since 1859. During the first (c. 3000–2890 BCE) and second (c. 2890–2686 BCE) dynasties it was a royal burial ground. As the Early Dynastic royal cemetery became an established place of pilgrimage, increasing numbers of visitors brought offerings in pots. The broken fragments of many thousands of pots now litter the ground, giving the area its modern name Umm el Qa'ab, meaning mother of pots.

TOMB OF KING DEN

The mud-brick tombs of Egypt's earliest kings have suffered extensive damage. The tomb of the first dynasty king, Den, for example, has lost its impressive superstructure, while its substructure has been looted and burned, firing the normally gray mud bricks and turning them red. Much of what can now be seen is modern reconstruction. Den's tomb was the first to incorporate significant amounts of stone and a stepped entrance; his burial chamber is paved in red and black Aswan granite.

PILGRIMS AT ABYDOS

By the twelfth dynasty (c. 1985–1773 BCE) the Umm el Qa'ab had been recognized as the burial place of the god Osiris, and excavations were conducted within the first dynasty cemetery to try to identify his tomb. Eventually King Djer's tomb was converted into a cenotaph for Osiris.

Ideally, every Egyptian would have liked to have been buried close to Osiris, but this was impossible. Instead, Abydos became a place of pilgrimage, with many ordinary Egyptians visiting to dedicate *mahat*: mud-brick shrines holding limestone stelae and/or statues, which could act as small-scale cenotaphs. The *mahat* were set up overlooking the route that linked the temple of Osiris to his tomb, so that they could "see" the procession of the statue of Osiris as it was taken from the temple to his tomb for a ritual of resurrection and thereby gain benefit for their owners' afterlives. The stelae, which have survived in the

hundreds, are the most important source of information for the funerary beliefs, occupations, and family connections of nonroyal Egyptians at this time.

Kings, too, established *mahat* at Abydos, although their monuments were on a larger scale. The twelfth dynasty king Senwosret III (r. c. 1870–1831 BCE) built a cenotaph temple. The eighteenth dynasty king Ahmose continued this tradition by building a cenotaph for his grandmother, and other New Kingdom monarchs followed suit. The most impressive surviving *mahat* are the temples built by the kings of the early nineteenth dynasty. Seti I (r. c. 1294–1279 BCE) built a small *mahat* for his father, Ramesses I, and an enormous one for himself, together with a subterranean complex that mimicked the tomb of Osiris. His son, Ramesses II, completed Seti's temple and also built his own, smaller version.

Pyramids at Giza *c.* 2589 – 2503 BCE

The Pyramid of Khaefre at Giza. The Giza cemetery lies on a plateau in northern Egypt, close to the Old Kingdom capital city, Memphis. It became a royal necropolis when the fourth dynasty King Khufu chose Giza as the site for his pyramid complex. Khufu's successors Khaefre and Menkaure also raised their pyramids at Giza.

Khufu's Great Pyramid is a true, or straight-sided, pyramid standing 481 feet (146.5 m.) high. Its sides are oriented almost exactly toward true north, and its base is almost completely level. The pyramid was once cased in fine Tura limestone, but this covering was removed, primarily during the Middle Ages. Khufu's pyramid was originally surrounded by a courtyard bounded by a limestone wall. The main access to this area was via a causeway that linked Khufu's mortuary temple to his low-lying valley temple, which is now lost under the modern suburb of Nazlet el Simman.

Khufu's son, Khaefre, built his mortuary complex to the south of the Great Pyramid. His pyramid is smaller than Khufu's but is built on higher ground and this, plus its slightly steeper angle, makes it appear larger. Khaefre's pyramid had a subterranean burial chamber that was built, lined, and roofed in a large, open trench before the pyramid was built on top. His complex comprises a pyramid, mortuary temple, causeway, and valley temple, and is the most complete of the three at Giza. Khaefre's pyramid retains some of the original polished limestone casing on its tip. The Great Sphinx, Egypt's largest statue, crouches beside the Valley Temple of Khaefre, facing toward the rising sun. It is carved from a natural rocky outcrop covered in places with a stone-block veneer, so the Sphinx shows differential weathering due to the three limestone strata included in its body.

Khaefre's son, Menkaure, also chose to build at Giza. His pyramid was aligned with those of his father and grandfather, although, because space was now somewhat limited, it was built at a much smaller scale. To compensate, the bottom layers of his pyramid were cased in expensive red granite. His burial chamber yielded a basalt sarcophagus carved with elaborate paneling. In 1838, this was sent to the British Museum, but it was lost at sea when the *Beatrice* sank off the Spanish coast. **JT**

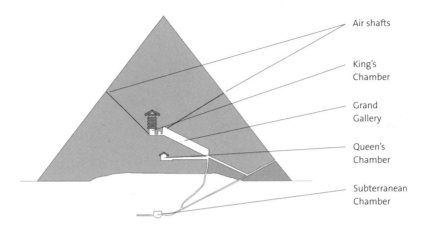

Air shafts

King's
Chamber

Grand
Gallery

Queen's
Chamber

Subterranean
Chamber

KHUFU'S GREAT PYRAMID

Khufu's pyramid houses three chambers. From the entrance on the north face, a passageway drops to the Subterranean Chamber, an unfinished room of ritual significance. The ascending passage leads to the Grand Gallery and allows access to the Queen's Chamber; a room of unknown ritual purpose. The Grand Gallery leads up to the King's Chamber. Air shafts (narrow passages oriented toward the Pole Star and the constellation of Orion) lead from the King's Chamber and Queen's Chamber.

WOODEN BOAT

Two narrow, rectangular pits dug parallel to the south side of Khufu's pyramid held dismantled wooden boats that were discovered in 1954. While one boat remains sealed in its tomb, the easternmost boat was conserved and fully reassembled by master conservator Hag Ahmed Youssef (1912–99), and is currently displayed in a museum alongside the pyramid. Five other boat pits were empty when examined. Khufu may have hoped to use this boat to sail to his afterlife.

BURIAL OF QUEEN HETEPHERES

Khufu's pyramid complex included a small satellite pyramid to the southeast of the main pyramid. Three larger queens' pyramids, complete with mortuary chapels, lay to the east of this satellite pyramid. All three queens' pyramids were robbed in antiquity.

In 1925, a survey team led by U.S. Egyptologist George Reisner (1867–1942) discovered a shaft hidden beneath a layer of plaster to the east of the Great Pyramid. The shaft proved to be 89 feet (27 m.) long, and was filled with limestone blocks. After weeks of excavation the team entered the chamber at its base. Here they discovered the stored remnants of the burial equipment of Queen Hetepheres, mother of Khufu. Her grave goods included an alabaster sarcophagus and her sealed alabaster canopic chest complete with linen-wrapped internal organs still soaking in embalming fluid. It was to take almost two years to

empty the tomb; only then did the team learn that Hetepheres' sarcophagus was empty. Hetepheres' burial equipment included thousands of fragments of pottery and a precious collection of wooden furniture including a dismantled canopy, a bed, two chairs, and a sedan chair. The wooden elements of these pieces had decayed but enough of their golden coverings remained to allow them to be restored. More personal items included gold razors and knives, small alabaster pots containing perfumes and kohl, and jewelry stored in a wooden box covered with gold leaf.

Reisner believed that his team had discovered the reburial of Hetepheres' looted tomb. More recently archaeologists have suggested that it may have been Hetepheres' intended tomb—a pyramid occupied before its superstructure could be completed—but this does not explain the absence of Hetepheres' body.

Valley of the Kings c. 1550 – 1099 BCE

Looking down on the remote, dry valley known today as the Valley of the Kings, or Biban al-Moluk, on the west bank of the Nile opposite the Karnak Temple of Amen at Luxor. Here were hidden the rock-cut tombs of many of Egypt's New Kingdom monarchs. The sacred Theban mountain acted as a natural pyramid protecting their burials.

The west bank of the Nile at Thebes (modern Luxor) is riddled with tombs of all ages, some royal and some private. Starting in the eighteenth dynasty, the New Kingdom pharaohs chose to be buried in the remote Valley of the Kings. Most of their tombs were emptied in antiquity, and the contents dispersed. The first-century-BCE historian Diodorus Siculus understood that the valley had once been a cemetery, but it was not until 1707 that Claude Sicard (1677–1726) recognized the true nature of the necropolis. The first significant work in the valley was conducted by Italian archaeologist Giovanni Battista Belzoni (1778–1823), who in 1816 found the tomb of the eighteenth dynasty pharaoh, Ay. Excavations and explorations have continued into the present day, and include a spectacular recent discovery in 1989, when the Theban Mapping Project, led by U.S. Egyptologist Kent R. Weeks (b. 1941), identified an enormous tomb prepared for the burial of the sons of Ramesses II. Work on this tomb—today designated KV 5—is still in progress; so far more than one hundred chambers have been revealed.

In 1827, English Egyptologist John Gardner Wilkinson (1797–1875) surveyed the twenty-one known tombs in the valley. Each tomb was given a number, allocated on the basis of its position. His system has continued to be used, with the tombs now being numbered according to the order of their discovery, so that in 1922 Tutankhamun's tomb became KV (or King's Valley) 62. When in 2005 the next tomb was discovered by a team led by U.S. Egyptologist Otto Schaden (1937–2015), it became KV 63. Just twenty-five of the KV tombs are royal tombs. Many of the others were built for Egypt's nonroyal elite, while some are not even tombs; KV 54, for example, is a stone-lined pit. **JT**

In November 1922, English archaeologist Howard Carter (1874–1939), financed by Lord Carnarvon (1866–1923), discovered the near-intact tomb of the eighteenth dynasty king Tutankhamun. The tomb had been buried under flood debris and forgotten by the tomb robbers. The king still lay inside, surrounded by a nearly intact set of grave goods. However, many Egyptologists were disappointed by the contents of the tomb, because it lacked the texts that would explain the complex history of the boy-king's reign.

VALLEY OF THE QUEENS

During the nineteenth dynasty the Valley of the Queens was known as the Place of Beauty and was developed as an elite cemetery for some of the more important royal wives and their children. The cemetery was first recorded by Scottish Egyptologist Robert Hay (1799–1863) in 1826, with official excavations, conducted by Ernesto Schiaparelli (1856–1928), the Italian director of Turin Museum, starting in 1903. In 1904, Schiaparelli discovered the beautifully decorated tomb of Queen Nefertari, dating to *c.* 1259 BCE.

FATE OF THE ROYAL MUMMIES

Toward the end of the nineteenth dynasty, Egypt entered an economic decline. Thieves were preying on the elite cemeteries, and Thebes suffered sporadic raids by Libyan nomads. By the late twentieth dynasty, Thebes was in a state of civil war and the Valley of the Kings was insecure. Abandoning his unfinished tomb (KV 4), Ramesses XI moved north. His would be the last royal tomb built in the valley.

With peace restored, the High Priests of Amen had the responsibility of restoring the plundered royal tombs. It was clear that as soon as the burials were restocked with grave goods, the robberies would start again. The priests decided on a change of plan. If the promise of hidden treasure was attracting thieves to the tombs, the removal of that treasure should solve the problem. As a bonus, the valuables collected from

the tombs could be used to swell the depleted state coffers. So the royal tombs were opened and emptied. The kings were taken from their sarcophagi and moved to temporary undertakers' workshops dotted around the valley. Here they were stripped of their bandages and jewelry, rewrapped, labeled and placed in plain wooden coffins. The mummies were then stored in chambers throughout the necropolis. These collections were inspected, moved and amalgamated, until there were two major royal caches: one in the tomb of the High Priest Pinudjem II at Deir el-Bahri (DB 320) and one in the tomb of Amenhotep II (KV 35), who reigned from *c.* 1426 to 1400 BCE. Both caches were discovered in the late nineteenth century, ending speculation about the missing mummies of the pharaohs.

ANCIENT EGYPTIAN SETTLEMENTS

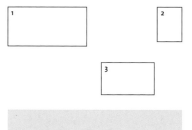

The Egyptians built almost all their domestic architecture from sun-dried mud brick, locating their villages, towns, and cities in the cultivated land close to the Nile. This was necessary because the Nile was not only an unfailing source of water and fish; it also served as Egypt's main highway, linking the settlements to create one long, thin land. The Egyptians traveled by boat rather than by chariot, and even the sun god Ra used a boat on his daily journey across the sky.

Mud was a sensible choice of building material because it was cheap, plentiful, and easy to work. The eighteenth dynasty king Akhenaten, who reigned from c. 1352 to 1336 BCE, proved so at Amarna (see p. 166) by raising the entire city from nothing in four or five years. The mud-brick buildings (see image 3) were cool in the summer heat, and warm in the chill of winter. Plastered, painted, and occasionally tiled, they looked magnificent. They were not, however, expected to last forever. Tombs, which were expected to last forever, were located in desert cemeteries above the Nile flood line, and were either built from stone or cut into rock. Unfortunately, over the centuries, almost all the mud-brick architecture has been lost; it has either crumbled and dissolved into mud, due to rising groundwater (see image 1) and the annual flooding of the Nile, or has been flattened beneath fields and later buildings. The decayed mud brick creates *sebekh*, an extremely fertile soil, so many ruined ancient buildings have been spread over modern fields (see image 2). This practice has now ended, and it is illegal to dig for *sebekh*. The problem of

1 One of the most important cities of Middle Egypt from the Old Kingdom onward, the remains of Herakleopolis Magna have been attacked by both stone robbers and the raised water table.

2 The most obvious remains of the city of Bubastis are the tumbled blocks of its central temple area, mainly the work of Ramesses II and later pharaohs.

3 The view over part of the city of Elephantine shows a complex of mud-brick administrative buildings erected during the Middle Kingdom.

KEY EVENTS

c. 3300 BCE	c. 2667 BCE	c. 2589 BCE	c. 2345 BCE	c. 1985 BCE	c. 1877 BCE
Egypt's first cities appear; the best preserved of these is Hierakonpolis in southern Egypt.	Memphis is the administrative capital of the Old Kingdom (c. 2686–c. 2160 BCE). Kings and their courtiers are buried in the Saqqara cemetery.	King Khufu builds his Great Pyramid at Giza. The workers who labor on his monument are housed close by the building sites.	During the late Old Kingdom, the town of Ayn Asil flourishes in the Dakhla Oasis.	The Middle Kingdom pharaohs found the now-lost city of Itj-tawy, close to the entrance to the Fayyum.	King Senwosret II, who reigns from c. 1877 to 1870 BCE, builds a pyramid at Lahun. His workforce is housed in the purpose-built town of Kahun.

settlement loss is particularly obvious in the moist Nile Delta, which was once home to many flourishing settlements, including Per Ramesse, a magnificent city built by Ramesses II, who reigned from *c.* 1279 to 1213 BCE.

The settlements that have survived tend to be atypical; built in unusual, often desert-edge locations for specific purposes, and often employing a higher-than-usual percentage of stone in their construction. The Middle Kingdom (*c.* 2055–1650 BCE) pyramid workers' village of Kahun, the New Kingdom (*c.* 1550–*c.* 1069 BCE) workers' village of Deir el-Medina (see p. 164), and Akhenaten's short-lived city of Amarna are the best-known examples of this atypical settlement type. The first archaeologists to work in Egypt saw little reason to excavate these badly preserved sites when the tombs, rich in grave goods and decorated with lively scenes of daily life, seemed to offer all the information about real people that could possibly be required. Their concentration on tombs was in part a response to the antiquities legislation that allowed excavators to retain a percentage of their finds. No one would dig for broken pottery in a mud-brick ruin if they could obtain golden grave goods by excavating a cemetery. Relatively recent legislation banning the export of excavated finds from Egypt has freed excavators to investigate less obviously attractive sites. However, because of their early bias, there are relatively few significant old excavations at major settlement sites. The work of Flinders Petrie (1853–1942) al Kahun and that of Bernard Bruyère (1879–1971) at Deir el-Medina are the most significant exceptions. Today, in contrast, archaeologists place less emphasis on funerary archaeology and have a greater interest in domestic or everyday sites of all types, from fortress towns to quarrymen's encampments. **JT**

c. 1650 BCE	*c.* 1525 BCE	*c.* 1349 BCE	*c.* 1333 BCE	*c.* 1279 BCE	*c.* 1099 BCE
The Hyksos kings rule northern Egypt from the eastern Delta city of Avaris while a native dynasty rules southern Egypt from Thebes (modern Luxor).	King Amenhotep I (r. 1525–1504 BCE) and his mother Ahmose Nefertari are celebrated as the founders of the village of Deir el-Medina.	King Akhenaten abandons Thebes and Memphis, and dedicates a new city at Amarna, Middle Egypt, to the god known as the Aten.	King Tutankhamun abandons Amarna, reinstating Memphis and Thebes as Egypt's administrative and religious centers.	King Ramesses II builds the splendid new city of Per Ramesse in the eastern Delta.	As Thebes grows increasingly insecure, tomb building ceases in the Valley of the Kings and the Deir el-Medina village is abandoned.

Village of Deir el-Medina *c.* 1550 – 1069 BCE

The village of Deir el-Medina was established to accommodate the workmen employed in building tombs in the Valley of the Kings and the Valley of the Queens. It was situated in the desert, on the west bank of the Nile, at Thebes (modern Luxor). Deir el-Medina was occupied for almost five centuries.

The pyramids had been built by a temporary workforce of many thousands, summoned to work for pharaohs under a system of national service. The rock-cut, painted tombs in the Valley of the Kings needed a different approach. They were built by a dedicated workforce of artists housed in a purpose-built village defined by a thick wall. In its heyday, this village was home to a permanent population of approximately 120 families. The workmen knew their village simply as "the village." Its modern name, Deir el-Medina, or Monastery of the Town, is a reference to the much later Coptic church and monastery built at the site.

Deir el-Medina was built in the desert, away from other settlements and above the water table, which meant that it was unable to support itself. This made many aspects of daily life difficult, since everything—food, clothing, raw materials, and of course, every drop of water—had to be imported. Attempts to dig a well failed, leaving a large hole known today as the Great Pit.

Deir el-Medina has been the focus of archaeological work by excavators of many nationalities. Ernesto Schiaparelli (1856–1928) conducted the first formal excavations at the site between 1905 and 1909, focusing on the village cemeteries. Schiaparelli's excavated finds are today housed in the Turin Museum, alongside many unprovenanced artifacts acquired via collectors. Bernard Bruyère excavated for the French Institute of Oriental Archeology in Cairo from 1922 to 1940 and 1945 to 1951. He concentrated on both the village itself and the structures in its environs, such as the private chapels, the cemetery, and the refuse dump, which yielded a large amount of written material. **JT**

FOCAL POINTS

VILLAGE HOUSES

VILLAGE HOUSES

The village houses were built by the state, with changes to the original plan being the responsibility of individual householders. The first houses to be built lacked foundations and were built of mud brick. Later houses had stone rubble foundations, with stone lower courses and mud-brick upper courses. The roof was constructed from palm-tree trunks and plastered. It was strong enough to form a floor, extending the usable space within the house. The houses varied in size.

PRIVATE TOMBS

Away from their official employment, the Deir el-Medina workmen were able to put their particular skills to good use. Not only did they provide themselves with elaborate and beautifully decorated family tombs, which they built just outside the village wall; they also sold their specialist labors to the residents of Thebes, offering a range of funerary artifacts. This partially reconstructed private tomb is topped by a pyramid-shaped chapel capped with a limestone pyramidion.

DEIR EL-MEDINA OSTRACA

Between 1 and 10 percent of the population of ancient Egypt could read and write, so only the most important matters were committed to writing. At Deir el-Medina, however, the exceptionally literate workforce habitually recorded the details of their daily lives. They wrote and drew not on papyrus but on ostraca: smooth chips of local limestone, which could be picked up anywhere, used, then discarded when unwanted. When Deir el-Medina was abandoned at the end of the twentieth dynasty, the villagers left a large collection of these writings and drawings behind.

The written records show that absenteeism was rife in the workforce. Almost any excuse was considered acceptable, and workmen missed work to brew beer or because their womenfolk were unwell. Those who did bother to turn up spent the eight-day working week living in temporary camps close to the tombs.

They returned to the village for a two-day weekend. This meant that, back in the village, the wives of the workers were left to their own devices. They cared for their children, cooked, cleaned, and ran small businesses bartering surpluses on the open market.

The ostraca provide a glimpse of family life. The Papyrus Deir el-Medina 27, for example, tells of a humble workman who was engaged to marry the daughter of a fellow workman. When he learned that his bride-to-be had been seduced by a wealthy man, Mery-Sekhmet, he reported the matter to the court officials. Most unfairly—perhaps they were influenced by Mery-Sekhmet's wealth—they ordered that the wronged man be punished with one hundred blows with a stick. It was only when one of the foremen took up the case that justice prevailed and Mery-Sekhmet was made to swear that he would leave the girl alone.

Royal City of Amarna c. 1347 BCE

The North Palace, Amarna. The city (ancient Aktetaten) was designed by the eighteenth-dynasty pharaoh Akhenaten as a home for his favored god, the Aten. It was situated on the east bank of the Nile in Middle Egypt, almost equidistant from the southern capital Thebes (modern Luxor) and the northern capital Memphis.

Amarna was an elongated city laid out along a long, fairly straight road, known today as the Royal Road. This ran parallel to the river, linking the North Palace—the private home of the royal family that now lies largely under modern fields—to the southerly Maru-Aten cult center. The city center housed the administrative center, or Great Palace. The King's House was situated opposite the Great Palace and linked to it by a mud-brick bridge passing over the Royal Road. Surrounding the house were the offices and archives of the civil service. It was here, in 1887, that archaeologists discovered the Amarna Letters—an archive of clay tablets representing the remains of Akhenaten's diplomatic correspondence written in the cuneiform script. There were two significant temples dedicated to the Aten sun god: the Great Temple was the place where the king and queen made offerings to their god, while the Small Temple probably served as a mortuary temple for the royal family. To the north and south of the central city were the suburbs that housed Akhenaten's courtiers.

The royal tomb lay in a dry valley, or wadi, in the eastern cliffs. It was discovered and looted sometime during the early 1880s, making it difficult to determine who was actually buried there. Two groups of rock-cut tombs were provided for Amarna's elite, with seventeen tombs lying to the north and twenty-seven tombs to the south of the royal wadi. Only twenty-four of the elite tombs were inscribed and none has yielded a mummy, suggesting that few were occupied. As Akhenaten had banned many of the traditional gods, the elite decorated their tomb walls with images of the royal family going about their daily duties. **JT**

AMARNA BOUNDARY STELAE

The limits of the new city and the surrounding agricultural land were defined by a series of massive inscriptions, or stelae, carved into the limestone cliffs of the east and west banks. The stelae display texts outlining Akhenaten's plans for his new city, and images of the royal family worshipping the Aten.

BUST OF NEFERTITI

The Amarna workshop run by the sculptor Thutmose specialized in the creation of royal images in stone and plaster. When, the court left Amarna, following the death of Akhenaten, Thutmose abandoned his unwanted sculptures. It was here, in 1912, that the bust of Queen Nefertiti (*c.* 1347), Akhenaten's consort, was found.

PHARAOH AKHENATEN

Akhenaten (r. *c.* 1352–1336 BCE) inherited his throne from his father, the eighteenth dynasty king Amenhotep III (r. *c.* 1390–1352 BCE). Initially, he too was known as Amenhotep (Amen is Satisfied), but his growing dedication to the sun god known as the Disk or the Aten persuaded him to change his name to Akhenaten, (Living Spirit of the Aten). Akhenaten's god represented the light of the sun rather than the sun itself. Akhenaten was not a monotheist. He remained comfortable with references to a range of solar deities, including the sun god Re. But if Re and his family were acceptable, the state god Amen of Thebes was not. Akhenaten set about erasing all memory of Amen by closing his temples and attacking his name and image in all official contexts.

Inspired by the Aten, Akhenaten built a new city on virgin land in Middle Egypt. Ancient Akhtetaten (Horizon of the Aten) is known today as Amarna. It has been estimated that at least 20,000 people followed Akhenaten to Amarna. While his people seem to have been free to come and go as they pleased, Akhenaten vowed never to leave his city.

Akhenaten's official portraits show him with a startling range of features; a thin, elongated face and a feminine body with breasts, wide hips, and a narrow waist. Interpretations of this image have varied, with some archaeologists seeing it as a truthful depiction of a king suffering from illness, others as an attempt to depict a religious belief through art.

The Amarna experiment ended soon after Akhenaten's death. Early in the reign of Tutankhamen (r. *c.* 1336–1327 BCE), Amarna city was abandoned and the traditional pantheon restored. When the Ramesside kings of the nineteenth dynasty (*c.* 1295–1186 BCE) recorded a list of Egypt's kings, Akhenaten and his immediate successors were omitted. Effectively, the Amarna period vanished from official history.

EGYPTIAN TEMPLES

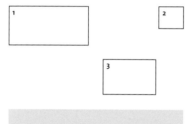

1 The first pylon of the stone mortuary temple of Ramesses III at Medinet Habu, Thebes, leads to an open courtyard. The pylon is decorated with scenes of the king triumphing over Egypt's enemies.

2 A relief at the temple of Karnak showing the king making an offering to the gods.

3 The Great Hypostyle Hall at the temple of Karnak was decorated by Seti I (r. *c.* 1290–1279 BCE) and by Ramesses II (r. *c.* 1279–1213 BCE).

The Egyptians acknowledged at least 1,500 deities, many of whom were worshipped formally in temples. Technically, the king of Egypt was the only mortal who could communicate with the gods and so was the only one who could make the daily offerings in their temples. It would have been impossible for him to be present at every ritual in every temple, so he appointed deputies, or priests, to act on his behalf. However, scenes carved on to the temple walls always show the king acting as priest (see image 2).

The temple was considered to be the house of the god. In a similar way, the tomb was considered to be the house of the spirit of the deceased. Temples and tombs therefore echoed the accommodation provided in domestic housing. In each, there were the equivalents of the bedroom, reception area, and storerooms. As in any private home, strangers were kept outside: a thick mud-brick enclosure wall separated the controlled environment of the temple from the chaotic outside world. The innermost sanctuary, where the king or high priest worshipped on behalf of Egypt, was an intensely private place.

Egypt's earliest temples were built from ephemeral materials and took the form of reed huts and open enclosures. As the dynastic age progressed, the relatively simple temple structure was transformed first into a mud-brick temple and then, during the Middle Kingdom (*c.* 2055–1650 BCE), into a stone temple. By the start of the New Kingdom (*c.* 1550 BCE), it had become customary to build state temples, known as houses of eternity, in stone (see image 1). These new stone temples retained elements of the original shrines and

KEY EVENTS

c. 3000 BCE	*c.* 2667 BCE	*c.* 2613–2184 BCE	*c.* 1956 BCE	*c.* 1870 BCE	*c.* 1831 BCE
Colossal statues of the god Min stand in the temple complex at Coptos.	As part of his pyramid complex at Saqqara, Djoser builds dummy stone chapels, replicating simple reed and matting temples that have not survived.	Old Kingdom rulers build stone mortuary temples as part of their pyramid complexes. The building of cult temples is mainly left to local communities.	Senwosret I begins a major program of temple building and restoration in Egypt. The best preserved of these is the White Chapel at Karnak.	Senwosret III restores the temple of Osiris at Abydos. He also re-establishes the processional festival of the god from the temple to his tomb.	Amenemhat III develops the Faiyum region, including the creation of stone and mud-brick temples to local gods, some of which survive today.

provided large expanses of stone wall for kings to decorate with propaganda messages. Although all temples differed, it is possible to determine a basic plan. The enclosure wall was pierced by a pylon, or gateway, which allowed access to the complex. Beyond the pylon lay one or two open courts. One or two halls led to the sanctuary at the rear of the temple, grouped around which were subsidiary rooms used for storing ritual artifacts.

Each temple could be interpreted as the island of creation that, mythology taught, emerged from the waters of chaos at the beginning of time. This was reflected in their architecture and decoration; the ceiling, for example, might be decorated to represent the sky, while a frieze around the base of the walls might illustrate plants growing up from the soil. The hypostyle hall (see image 3) was filled with massive stone columns arranged in rows; these were not designed to support the roof, but to recreate the island vegetation. The capitals of the columns might be palm-shaped, lotus-shaped, or papyrus-shaped.

Traditionally, Egyptian temples have been divided into two types, according to their use. A cult temple, such as Luxor Temple (see p. 172), was prominently situated within a town or city and housed the cult statue of the temple god. A mortuary or memorial temple, such as Hatshepsut's Djeser-Djeseru (see p. 170), was situated in the desert, within or near the royal cemetery. A part of the king's funerary complex, but not necessarily physically connected to the tomb, it was primarily associated with the cult of the deified ruler. Recently, it has been acknowledged that the distinction between cult and mortuary temples is difficult to justify, because all temples had varied and interconnected functions. In particular, a mortuary temple might also be home to a resident state god. **JT**

Djeser-Djeseru *c.* 1473 BCE

Hatshepsut's temple takes the form of three ascending terraces set back against the cliff. The tiered porticoes are linked by a long, broad stairway that rises through the center toward the shrine of Amen. The temple was originally accessed through a garden, and defined by a thick limestone wall.

The mortuary temple of Hatshepsut (r. *c.* 1473–1458 BCE), Djeser-Djeseru (Holiest of Holies) is set in a natural bay in the cliffs on the west bank of the Nile at Thebes (modern Luxor). It is the focal point of the temple complex Deir el-Bahri, meaning Monastery of the North, whose name is a reference to the mud-brick Coptic monastery that was established at the site during the fifth century CE. Hatshepsut's conspicuous temple was only one part of her mortuary provision. It was here, she hoped, that her priests would make offerings to her divine being until the end of time. The other part of her mortuary provision—the rock-cut tomb designed to hold her body—was hidden from public view in the nearby Valley of the Kings.

Djeser-Djeseru was a multifunctional temple with a complex of shrines devoted to various deities. In addition to the mortuary chapels provided for Hatshepsut and her father, Thutmose I, there were twin chapels dedicated to the deities Hathor and Anubis and an open-roofed chapel dedicated to the sun god Re-Harakhte. Cut into the living rock of the cliff, the main shrine was devoted to the god Amen. The temple served as the focus of the Feast of the Valley, an annual festival of death and renewal. During this festival, the people of Thebes would visit the cemetery to enjoy a meal with their ancestors.

Hatshepsut used her temple walls to display the highlights of her life and reign. Here, there are depictions of obelisks being raised, enemies being defeated, the visit to Punt, and, importantly, Hatshepsut's conception and birth. The uppermost level of the temple was fronted by a portico, whose twenty-four square-cut pillars were each faced by a colossal painted limestone statue of Hatshepsut in the role of Osiris, god of the dead. **JT**

HATHOR-HEADED COLUMNS

Deir el-Bahri bay was associated with the cult of the mother-goddess Hathor in her role as goddess of the west. Hathor appears several times in the temple decoration, including on the columns, suggesting that Hatshepsut, as a female king, may have felt a particular affinity with this powerful goddess.

CHILD OF AMEN

Hatshepsut was the daughter of Thutmose I. But, in a story depicted on her temple wall, she claims to be the child of Amen. Disguised as the king, Amen seduces the queen with his perfume, and nine months later a baby is born. Amen knows that his beloved child is a daughter, but he is happy for her to rule Egypt.

THE FEMALE PHARAOH HATSHEPSUT

Hatshepsut was the daughter of King Thutmose I (r. c. 1504–1492 BCE), consort to her half-brother, Thutmose II (r. c. 1492–1479 BCE), and first regent for, then co-ruler with, her stepson, Thutmose III (r. c. 1479–1425 BCE). After a short period of experimentation that involved combining her female body with kingly (male) regalia, her formal portraits invariably depict the female pharaoh with a male body, wearing the king's kilt, crown, and false beard. Her intention was not to appear as a man, but as a king.

Although her reign started with a successful series of brief military campaigns, Hatshepsut's foreign policy was based on trade rather than war. Scenes in the Deir el-Bahri temple show details of her hugely successful expedition to Punt, a now-vanished trading center on the east African coast. Gold, ebony, baboons, and myrrh trees were brought back to Egypt, and the trees were planted in the gardens of the Deir el-Bahri temple.

Hatshepsut undertook an extensive building program throughout Egypt. In Thebes, this focused on the temples of the god Amen. Her supreme architectural achievement was the Deir el-Bahri temple. This was, however, just part of her funerary provision. Her tomb was constructed in the nearby Valley of the Kings, where she remodeled her father's tomb so that she could be interred beside him.

Following Hatshepsut's death, Thutmose III ruled alone for thirty-three years. Toward the end of his reign an attempt was made to remove the traces of Hatshepsut's co-rule. Her statues were torn down, her monuments defaced, and her name erased from the official king list. Early scholars saw this as a vengeful attack, but it is more likely that Thutmose was simply ensuring that the succession would run from Thutmose I to Thutmose III without any female intervention.

Luxor Temple *c.* 1390 – 1213 BCE

The pylon of Ramesses II features two granite seated statues of the king, some 50 feet (15 m.) high, flanking the gateway. Originally, there were also four standing statues of Ramesses II, but only one remains intact.

Luxor Temple is located on the east bank of the River Nile at Thebes (modern Luxor). Its ancient name was Ipet-Resyt, meaning "southern harem." This refers to the fact that the temple was connected by a processional route to the much larger temple of Karnak, home of the god Amen (Hidden one), which lies 1.8 miles (3 km.) to the north. Luxor Temple was dedicated jointly to the god Amen and to the concept of the divine king.

An earlier temple had stood on the spot, but the main building phases of Luxor Temple took place during the reigns of the eighteenth dynasty king Amenhotep III (r. *c.* 1390–1352 BCE) and the nineteenth dynasty king Ramesses II (r. *c.* 1279–1213 BCE). It was Amenhotep who built or remodeled the rear parts of the temple, making it a suitable resting place for the great state god Amen of Karnak, who visited Luxor Temple every year for the Opet Festival. During this festival, crowds of worshippers would watch the god's sacred boat, with his statue hidden from view, as it was carried in procession along the great road between Karnak and Luxor, or as it sailed along the Nile. Amen was accompanied by his wife, the goddess Mut, and their son Khons, who were also carried in sacred boats. Once at Luxor Temple, a series of rituals was performed, some of which were for the benefit of the *ka* (spirit) of the living king.

At the end of the eighteenth dynasty, several kings, including Tutankhamun, Ay, and Horemheb, carried out minor additions to Luxor Temple. However, it was during the reign of Ramesses II that the second great phase of building took place, in which he added a courtyard and a massive pylon, or gateway. The latter is a typical feature of New Kingdom temples; it was partly a space for royal propaganda and partly an indication that access to the temple was strictly controlled. Ramesses II covered the Luxor Temple pylon with scenes of his military victories. In front of the pylon, the king added further impressive works in the form of colossal statues of himself and a pair of tall granite obelisks. One of these obelisks was removed in 1831 and now stands in the Place de la Concorde in Paris. Luxor Temple continued in use until well into the Greco-Roman Period. **JT**

◉ FOCAL POINTS

COLOSSAL STATUES

Luxor Temple contains a number of colossal hard-stone statues of Ramesses II. Six of these statues were positioned in a row in front of the pylon, and others were placed between the columns in the first courtyard of the temple. Here, they could be approached and worshipped by the general population who were expressly forbidden entry to the inner sanctums of the temple. Deep within Luxor Temple, the cult statue of the temple god Amen was serviced by specialized priests.

USURPATION

It was relatively common for the monuments of earlier kings to be claimed as their own by later rulers. In this example from Luxor Temple, a carved relief of a king making an offering bears the distinctive features of Tutankhamun, who reigned from 1336 to 1327 BCE. However, the accompanying royal name (written in an oval cartouche) has been re-carved after Tutankhamun's death, so that it now displays the name of the later king Horemheb, who ruled from 1323 to 1295 BCE.

RAISING AN OBELISK

Obelisks were cult objects created as a stone representation of the first beam of light. They were tall, thin, square, hard-stone shafts, which tapered to a pyramid-shaped point. Traditionally erected in pairs before the entrance to a temple, obelisks were finished with tips covered in gold to reflect the sunlight. They were dedicated to the temple god by the king, and their shafts contained columns of hieroglyphs detailing their erection and dedication. However, obelisks were also regarded as divine beings; they were given personal names, and offerings were made to them.

The successful cutting, transportation, and erection of an obelisk was a remarkable feat of engineering for a society reliant on river transport and human power and ingenuity. Some successful examples measured more than 98 feet (30 m.) in height, while the "unfinished obelisk," which had to be abandoned

in the Aswan granite quarry after it developed a fatal crack, would have stood more than 135 feet (41 m.) tall.

The mortuary temple built by Hatshepsut (see p. 170) includes a scene detailing the transportation of a pair of obelisks from the Aswan quarry, at Egypt's southern border, to Thebes. The two obelisks are lashed to wooden sleighs and lie on a sycamore wood barge as they are towed along the Nile by a fleet of small boats. This is an important civil and religious event— the barge is accompanied by three ships transporting priests who are kept busy blessing the proceedings. When the obelisks arrive in Thebes, there is yet more celebration; a bull is killed, and offerings are made to the gods. The bases of these two obelisks may still be seen at the eastern end of the Amen temple at Karnak. Texts reveal, unusually, that these two obelisks were entirely covered in gold foil.

AFRICA BEYOND EGYPT: NUBIA

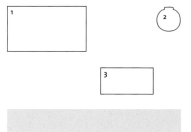

1 The Great Temple of Ramesses II
(r. c. 1279–1213 BCE) at Abu Simbel in
Lower Nubia (now southern Egypt).

2 A jar, decorated with lion masks and
lotus flowers, from Tomb 1090, Faras,
Lower Nubia (first–second century CE).

3 Traditional graves of Old Dongola, Upper
Nubia (now Sudan), which was founded
in the fifth century CE.

The name "Nubia" refers to a geographical location—the region immediately to the south of ancient Egypt—rather than the ethnicity or language of the peoples who lived there. Nubia started at the First Nile Cataract (ancient Egypt's traditional southern border) and ended in the region of the Sixth Cataract, to the north of modern Khartoum. Lower Nubia lay in the north, between the First and Second Nile Cataracts, and is today part of Egypt. The archaeology of this region is relatively well known, but is now almost entirely lost under the waters of the human-made Lake Nasser. Upper Nubia lay in the south, between the Second and Sixth Cataracts, and is today part of Sudan. The archaeology of this region survives, but is less well known.

Archaeologists have identified three distinct cultural groups that coexisted in Nubia from c. 2400 BCE to Egypt's conquest of Nubia in c. 1550 BCE. The C-Group culture flourished in Lower Nubia as early as c. 2400 BCE. They shared certain features with earlier Nubian cultures, but probably originated in sub-Saharan Africa. Although they were transient pastoralists who accorded their cattle great economic and symbolic importance, they also developed settlements. Their dead were buried in cemeteries, where they lay in pits topped by gravel, within a ring of stones (see image 3). C-Group cemeteries have been found as far north as Hierakonpolis (see p. 140) in southern Egypt.

KEY EVENTS

c. 2696 BCE	c. 2500 BCE	c. 2400 BCE	c. 2278 BCE	c. 2125 BCE	c. 1956 BCE
The Egyptian pharaoh Khasekemwy (second dynasty) undertakes a brief military campaign to subdue Nubia.	The Upper Nubian city of Kerma begins a continuous period of occupation that lasts until 1450 BCE.	The C-Group culture flourishes in Lower Nubia.	Harkhuf, Egypt's Overseer of Foreign Lands, makes trips to Nubia and returns with various exotic gifts for the pharaoh.	The collapse of centralized control at the end of Egypt's Old Kingdom causes Egypt to abandon previously settled areas in Nubia.	Pharaoh Senwosret I (twelfth dynasty) colonizes parts of Nubia and builds a large mud-brick fortress at Buhen.

The Pan-Grave culture, identified by its cemeteries of shallow, circular graves, appeared in c. 1800 BCE. The Pan-Grave people are thought to have been nomads from the Eastern Desert, and many Egyptologists believe that they were the mercenary soldiers known as Medjay in Egypt. Pan-Grave cemeteries and pottery have been found in northern Nubia and at many sites in Egypt. The Kerma culture developed from preexisting cultures in the region of the Third Cataract. As Egypt fragmented in c. 1600 BCE, the ill-defined entity known as the Kingdom of Kush, a state centered on the city of Kerma (see p. 176), grew in influence, spreading in the region between the First and the Fifth Cataracts.

From c. 1500 BCE onward, the New Kingdom pharaohs undertook the systematic conquest of Nubia. Lower Nubia, a previous Egyptian colony, was quickly subdued, but Upper Nubia—Kush—put up a long resistance. Three distinct phases of Egyptian construction have been identified in occupied Nubia. First, Egypt enlarged the fortresses that had been built during the Middle Kingdom, and secured settlements in Upper Nubia. Second, there was a shift from military control to more obvious colonialization. As fortified temple-towns emerged to the south of the First Cataract and north of the Fourth Cataract, Egypt's kings built temples (see image 1) around existing settlements in Lower Nubia, and new temples in Upper Nubia. Third, there came a time of consolidation. Nubia was now a part of the Egyptian empire, and items subsequently found in the region's graves reflect this (see image 2).

The collapse of the New Kingdom in c. 1069 BCE led to a period of independent Nubian cultures and development of the Second Kingdom of Kush in Upper Nubia. Two phases are identified: the Napatan Empire (c. 900–300 BCE) saw burials south of the Fourth Cataract at Gebel Barkel, Kurru, and Nuri; and the Meroitic Empire (c. 300 BCE—300 CE) saw burials beyond the Fifth Cataract at Meroë. The twenty-fifth dynasty Kushite kings ruled Egypt but eventually the city of Meroë fell to Ezana of Axum (c. 320–c. 360 CE) and was abandoned. **JT**

c. 1870 BCE	c. 1650 BCE	c. 1550 BCE	c. 1279 BCE	c. 1069 BCE	c. 747 BCE
Pharaoh Senwosret III targets Upper Nubia in a series of ruthless military campaigns. He is worshipped as a god by Egyptians in Nubia.	Egypt's Middle Kingdom collapses. The Kerma people gradually start to occupy the abandoned Egyptian fortresses.	Pharaoh Kamose (seventeenth dynasty) creates a protective buffer zone between the Kingdom of Kush and Egypt.	Pharaoh Ramesses II (nineteenth dynasty) builds or extends seven temples in Nubia, including the two temples at Abu Simbel.	Egypt's New Kingdom collapses and Nubia once again gains independence from Egypt.	A line of Nubian kings gain power as Egypt's twenty-fifth dynasty.

Kerma *c.* 2500 – 1450 BCE

The city of Kerma with its Western Deffufa (above) is located 30 miles (50 km.) to the south of the Nile's Third Cataract, in Upper Nubia (modern Sudan). One of the earliest urbanized communities in Africa outside Egypt, Kerma was occupied continuously from *c.* 2500 to 1450 BCE, when it was invaded and destroyed by the New Kingdom Egyptians.

Kerma, in Upper Nubia, was first excavated by George Reisner (1867 – 1942) from 1913 to 1916. He interpreted the extensive settlement to be a fort controlled by an Egyptian governor; today, it is known that Kerma was the principal city of the important Nubian Kingdom of Kush. The local economy was based on agriculture and animal husbandry, supplemented by hunting, gathering and fishing. However, Kerma stood at the crossroads of routes linking Egypt, the Red Sea, and central Africa, and trade in precious goods including gold, ebony, ivory, and cattle brought great wealth to the city. Kerma's wealth, and links with Egypt, are reflected in the wide range of grave goods recovered from its cemetery. These include typically Nubian artifacts (pottery and copper vessels), typically Egyptian artifacts (copper daggers and stone statues), and locally manufactured, Egyptian-style artifacts (furniture and jewelry).

Four main phases of occupation have been identified: Early Kerma (*c.* 2500 – 2050 BCE), Middle Kerma (*c.* 2050 – 1750 BCE), Classic Kerma (*c.* 1750 – 1580 BCE), and Late Kerma (*c.* 1580 – 1450 BCE). The city started as a relatively small-scale walled settlement of round huts and granaries made of wood and reeds. Later it gained fortifications including a wall standing 33 feet (10 m.) high. The most prominent building was a large mud-brick temple known today as the Western Deffufa (*deffufa* being a local word denoting any substantial mud-brick ruin). The Deffufa stood at the heart of a city composed of rectangular stone houses, workshops, and traditional round huts with conical roofs. Other important buildings of the city included a palace and a royal audience hall. **JT**

KERMA POTTERY

The potters of Kerma were skilled craftspeople, able to create distinctive and technologically sophisticated pieces that demonstrated an excellent understanding of firing techniques. Classic Kerma pottery is distinguished by its black top and red base, separated by a band varying in color from purple to gray. This jug, which was recovered from the cemetery at Kerma, may be emptied via the long, thin spout protruding from its shoulder. Recognizable types of Egyptian pottery found alongside it in the same grave date it to c. 1650–1550 BCE.

STATUE OF LADY SENNUWY OF ASYUT

A tumulus tomb in the Kerma cemetery yielded this statue of an Egyptian, Lady Sennuwy, and a broken statue of her husband, Hepdjefa. They were residents of Asyut during the reign of Senwosret I (c. 1956–1911 BCE). It is likely that the statues arrived in Kerma during the Second Intermediate Period (c. 1650–1550 BCE), possibly sent as gifts by the Hyksos rulers of northern Egypt.

KERMA CEMETERY

The extensive cemetery of Kerma lies on a low hill, approximately 2½ miles (4 km.) northeast of the Western Deffufa. The cemetery was used throughout the lifespan of the city, and it is estimated that it includes approximately 40,000 burials. Most of the graves consist of oval or rectangular burial chambers dug into the subsoil and covered with low mounds, or tumuli. Within the burial chamber, the unmummified dead lay contracted on wooden beds, facing north. They wore leather clothes and were covered by animal skins. Their graves have yielded goods such as bronze mirrors, ostrich-feather fans, and in the male burials, bows. Several burials included sacrificial dogs and sheep, the latter sometimes with headdresses and pendants hanging from their horns. Using cattle skulls to mark the grave was a particular feature of Middle Kerma burials; one exceptionally large tumulus is associated with 4,500 skulls. Sometimes the skulls were arranged to suggest a herd, with cows and calves placed at the front, and bulls and oxen at the back.

At the southern end of the cemetery were eight exceptionally large tumuli. Dating to the Classic Kerma phase, they represent Nubia's largest known burial structures. Dubbed the Royal Tumuli, they were plundered in antiquity, but there is evidence that they once housed exceptionally rich burials. One of the deceased originally lay on a glazed quartz bed, while another lay on a bed of slate. Broad central corridors in three of the large tumuli have yielded the remains of several hundred men and women interred simultaneously with the main burial. These and others in subsidiary graves dug around the tumuli may have been sacrificed.

INDUS CIVILIZATION

1 The archaeological site of Harappa in Punjab, Pakistan, was first excavated in the 1850s but its significance was not recognized until the 1920s.

2 Part of a greenstone, steatite, and gold necklace, with pendants of agate and jasper, found in a hoard buried in a silver vessel at Mohenjo-daro, Pakistan.

3 This terracotta figurine from Harappa with earstuds, choker, necklace, girdle, and elaborate headdress decorated with flowers, probably shows how Indus women dressed.

Farming settlement began in the Indo-Iranian borderlands by the seventh millennium BCE, and by the fourth millennium there were many flourishing villages in this region, practicing mixed farming, making wheel-turned pottery, and casting copper. Pastoralists exploited grazing on the Indus plains, and some people from the uplands began to settle here, their numbers increasing after 3200 BCE. Mutually profitable relations were established with the hunter-fisher-gatherer communities of the greater Indus region, who acquired domestic livestock and manufactured goods, in return supplying wild resources not easily accessed by settled communities: these relations later strengthened. Regional cultures developed among the Early Indus farming settlers. Some settlements, including Harappa (see image 1) in Punjab, Pakistan, and Kalibangan in Rajasthan, India, grew into towns. Craft specialization began to develop, and trading relations were established with the people of the Aravalli Range to the south, where copper was abundant. Contacts with southern Oman probably reflect the movements of sea fishermen.

In c. 2600 BCE, a major transformation occurred. Regional cultures gave way to considerable cultural uniformity throughout the greater Indus region, from Gujarat and Makran in the west to Punjab in the north and Haryana in the east. Many settlements were abandoned or destroyed; some were rebuilt, and many new settlements were founded. These followed a planned layout that involved cardinally oriented streets and a division between a walled area, or citadel— generally raised, with probably official buildings—and a residential lower town. Settlements, however, show considerable variation and individuality— for example, in the layout and range of buildings on the citadel.

KEY EVENTS

3800–3200 BCE	By 3500 BCE	3200–2600 BCE	2600–2500 BCE	2600–2450 BCE	By 2500 BCE
Farming settlements are well established in Baluchistan, Pakistan; pastoralists begin to settle on the environmentally very different Indus plains.	A settlement is founded at Harappa in Punjab. Continuously occupied, it grows into a major city with a population of perhaps 60,000.	The Early Harappan period sees farming communities spread throughout the Indus plains and Gujarat. Some towns develop, including Dholavira.	Many settlements are destroyed or abandoned but many new planned settlements are founded, including Mohenjo-daro.	Indus beads in the Royal Cemetery at Ur attest to long-distance trade contacts, perhaps through Oman with which Mesopotamia and Indus now trade.	After centuries of contact by fishermen, Indus develops closer relationships with settlements in Oman, supplying Indus goods in exchange for copper.

Urban life was highly developed. The largest city, Mohenjo-daro (see p. 180), was centrally located to the whole civilization in Sindh; other cities each dominated a region of the Indus realm and managed access to the world beyond: Dholavira (see p. 182) in the west; Ganweriwala central to the now-dry Saraswati valley south of the Indus; Harappa in the north; and Rakhigarhi in the east. The regions also had towns, often with specialist trading or industrial functions, industrial villages, and rural agricultural settlements.

Craft production was highly organized: raw materials were worked intensively near their source, or in major centers, by highly skilled artisans, and their products were circulated throughout the Indus realm. Imported metals and some other materials were also worked; and the production of faience, terracotta (see image 3), high-quality pottery, and other artificial materials shows the Indus mastery of pyrotechnology.

Trade flourished with local neighbors and farther afield. The rich metal deposits (gold, tin, and copper) of Afghanistan, coupled with its lapis lazuli, mined at Badakhshan, drew the Indus people to establish a trade route north and a trading outpost at Shortugai, building a typical Indus town; this enabled them to monopolize access to the lapis lazuli, which the Indus people hardly used themselves but exported to Mesopotamia, where it was highly prized. Mesopotamian texts and archaeological finds show that Indus exports to Mesopotamia included a range of timbers, copper, gold, tin, agate, and carnelian, especially as beads (see image 2); they do not provide evidence of what the Indus people received in return, but woolen textiles and silver both seem possible. Indus merchants also traded with Oman, where they obtained copper, and Bahrain. The management of internal industry and distribution and external trade was probably facilitated by use of the Indus script (see p. 554).

After c. 2000 BCE, the Indus civilization began to decline, and after 1800 BCE, most towns and cities were abandoned. Evidence of disease, such as cholera and malaria, suggests one reason for this: concentrations of people creating conditions in which diseases thrived. The flow of water in the Saraswati, a major river south of the Indus, probably began to drop, reducing the area of arable land that it could water. The adoption of new crops—Chinese rice and African millets—around this time may have encouraged some farmers to colonize lands in the Deccan and the east, to which these summer crops were better suited than the winter-grown Indus staples, wheat and barley; Gujarat, which continued to thrive, was suited to both. Political upheavals in distant Mesopotamia undermined trade, state-sponsored activity giving way to smaller scale private expeditions, with probable knock-on effects on their Indus trading partners. All these and other factors may have contributed to the decline, which saw change but not collapse. Urban life disappeared, along with such features as writing, mass production, and cultural uniformity, but their place was taken by flourishing regional cultures. **JM**

2500–2000 BCE	After 2500 BCE	c. 2300 BCE	c. 2100 BCE	2000–1800 BCE	1800 BCE
The peak of Indus civilization. Cities and towns flourish, with high living standards and interregional circulation of fine craft products.	Outpost towns are established in Makran at Sutkagen Dor to facilitate sea trade and in Afghanistan at Shortugai to obtain valuable minerals.	Akkadian texts attest to the presence of Indus ships in Mesopotamian ports, showing that Indus merchants operate throughout the Gulf.	Gulf trade is at its height between the Indus civilization and Ur III Empire in southern Mesopotamia, where some Indus merchants now reside.	Towns and cities decline, sometimes the victims of disease. The changing water regime and agricultural practices alter the pattern of life.	The urban way of life disintegrates, but regional cultures emerge and flourish in Gujarat, the Kachi Plain, and the Ganges-Yamuna Doab.

Mohenjo-daro 2600 – 1900 BCE

Looking west across the northern area of the citadel at Mohenjo-daro. In Indus times, the Indus River flowed close to the city's west side, putting it at risk of flooding: the site was probably not habitable until massive brick platforms were constructed, upon which the city was built.

⬥ NAVIGATOR

Investigations of a possible Buddhist stupa at Mohenjo-daro in Sindh, Pakistan, in 1922 exposed material that was clearly much earlier, including inscribed steatite seals. Published in the *Illustrated London News* in 1924, the material and architecture quickly drew comparisons with third-millennium-BCE Sumer (see p. 142), providing a tentative date that was confirmed by John Marshall (1876–1958) and others in the 1920s and 1930s, and then Mortimer Wheeler (1890–1976) in 1950. More recent work has focused on determining the extent of the city, about 600 acres (250 ha.), well beyond the originally identified so-called Citadel and Lower Town mounds; investigating the lowest levels, largely thwarted by the high water table; and understanding the Marshall-era excavations, conducted and recorded in a manner now considered inadequate. The deep soundings show that Mohenjo-daro was founded on virgin soil as a planned city, central to the Indus realm, in *c.* 2600 BCE. High platforms were constructed to keep the city above the Indus River's flood level. On the western citadel platform were built the Great Bath and associated buildings, with a pillared hall, probably for public assemblies, in the south. Nothing resembling a palace or temple was found either here or in other Indus cities: their absence is one of the Indus civilization's many puzzling features. On the larger eastern mound were built the cardinally oriented broad streets and narrow lanes of the Lower Town. Houses opened from the lanes, avoiding the dust of the main thoroughfares: a passage led into an internal courtyard, where much of life was lived. Off this opened various rooms, generally including a bathroom paved with baked bricks and sometimes the equivalent of a toilet. **JM**

⊙ FOCAL POINTS

1 GRANARY

This massive building was interpreted as a granary; evidence suggests this is unlikely, though it may have been a warehouse. A roofed platform runs along its northern side, while the main structure was a platform supporting nine brick podia.

2 GREAT BATH

The citadel mound's dominant feature was the Great Bath, believed to have been a religious installation connected with ritual bathing. The rectangular basin was skillfully constructed of layers of baked brick and bitumen, rendering it watertight.

3 COLLEGE

The College building probably housed the priests associated with this sacred facility. It had many small rooms and at least seven entrances as well as several courtyards, one with a fenestrated walkway. Two staircases led to an upper story.

◄ Numerous private and public wells supplied Mohenjo-daro with fresh water: about 700 have been found in the excavated portion of the city. They were built of wedge-shaped baked bricks. A network of brick drains removed waste water from the bathrooms of city houses, running along the streets under stone-slab covers to empty outside the city. Sumps retained solid waste, and were periodically cleaned out.

SKILLED ARTISANS

Indus artisans used fine materials. For example, whereas in earlier and later times tools were made from local flint, in the Indus period they were made of high-quality flint from mines in the Rohri Hills (Sindh). While most settlements made goods for wide distribution from a few local materials, the full range of craft activities was undertaken at Mohenjo-daro—including some otherwise known only at Harappa, such as making inscribed copper tablets. Many artisans worked at home, for example making seals, silver, or steatite objects, shell inlays, or beads. Mohenjo-daro had industrial quarters with workshops making faience, beads, weights, and stoneware bangles and working flint, steatite, shell, and copper. Noxious industries, such as cleaning out conch shells before they were used to make bangles, took place on the city's outskirts.

Dholavira and Lothal 3000 – 1500 BCE

Along two sides of Dholavira city, at least sixteen huge reservoirs were constructed to conserve and store water for domestic, industrial, and agricultural use in the city's arid setting. The reservoirs were partly dug down through soil, to be lined with brick and plaster, and partly cut down through bedrock—a mammoth undertaking.

The old idea that the Indus civilization had twin capitals at Mohenjo-daro (see p. 180) and Harappa has been abandoned as more has become known. It now seems that each region was served by a major city. Dholavira, discovered in 1967 and excavated from 1989, dominated Gujarat in the southwest; it is situated on an island off the northeast coast of Kutch, itself a huge island in Indus times.

Many settlements in Gujarat were industrial centers, their products including salt, tools, inlays, and ornaments made from seashells and beads from locally abundant gemstones such as agate and chalcedony (transformed into carnelian by heating). Agriculture and pastoralism provided local subsistence. This region was also the Indus terminus for sea trade, which continued after the unified realm collapsed. Dholavira was the integrating authority for this regional activity, controlling communications and the movement of goods from the local area overseas and to the rest of the Indus realm.

Unusually, stone was plentiful in Gujarat so Dholavira often used stone instead of brick for construction. Little is known of the citadel's buildings. In front of it was a large esplanade; to its north was a walled residential area, the Middle Town, from which an eastern gate led into the more extensive Lower Town. Although the town lacked drains, an elaborate water-catchment and drainage system was installed in the Citadel. Surrounding the city to the west and north, within its walls, were enormous reservoirs— a remarkable feature. When the Indus civilization declined, Dholavira was briefly abandoned. Parts were then reoccupied, but no longer as a city; the new inhabitants salvaged building materials and tipped refuse into the reservoirs. **JM**

CITADEL GATEWAYS

In Dholavira, impressive gateways gave access to the Citadel. Leading to a staircase and flanked by guard rooms, each gateway featured stone pillars made of ring-shaped sections that were laid one on top of the other and anchored to the column base by a wooden pole that ran through their center. A wooden signboard bearing nine signs in the Indus script once stood above the north gateway: the gypsum signs survived because the board was taken down and laid on its face, protecting them.

RESIDENTIAL AREAS

A wide main thoroughfare ran through Dholavira's Middle Town, where streets were laid out on the traditional cardinally oriented grid plan. The Lower Town, added after 2200 BCE, developed more haphazardly. The outer city wall, which was 60 feet (18 m.) thick, was extended to include the Lower Town, increasing the walled city's area to around 250 acres (100 ha.). A gate allowed the authorities to control movement between the Middle and Lower towns.

LOTHAL: A GATEWAY TOWN

Like many Indus towns, tiny Lothal, 10½ acres (4.2 ha.) in area, on the Sabarmati river in southern Gujarat, operated as a specialist element of the Indus organizational machine. Part of the town was residential, probably housing workers, and there was further housing outside the walls. Much of the town, however, was taken up by industrial facilities: a factory making beads from local gemstones, including storerooms and a courtyard where the work was undertaken; a copper smithy; workshops making steatite seals and objects of shell and ivory; and kilns to fire pottery, heat gemstones to make them easier to work, and refine and melt copper.

A small citadel mound, in the town's southeast corner, included houses, probably occupied by administrators; a line of twelve bathing platforms; and a large raised podium supporting sixty-four brick-built square blocks in rows separated by aisles, probably originally roofed with wooden beams. The latter feature is interpreted as a warehouse: material found here included many clay sealings bearing the imprint of storage jars and packaging material such as cords, woven cloth, and matting. A large brick-revetted basin alongside the town has been interpreted as a dock, although awkwardness of access argues against this.

Lothal, situated near the southwest extreme of the Indus realm, acted as a gateway town to the exterior world, particularly the North Gujarat Plain. This was inhabited by hunter-gatherers, whose seasonal movement gave them access to distant resources. By engaging with the hunter-gatherers, the Indus people could acquire materials such as ivory, wax, honey, and resin, in exchange for manufactured goods and grain. Lothal managed this network, receiving and making goods and dispatching them in both directions.

CHINA'S FIRST CIVILIZATIONS

1 This bronze bust with angular human features and large ears dates to between the twelfth and eleventh centuries BCE. It is one of thousands of artifacts unearthed at Sanxingdui, Sichuan province.

2 Oracle bones dating to the Shang dynasty. The animal bones are inscribed with ideograms that record questions to which the court of the royal house of Shang sought answers by divination.

3 A gray earthenware ritual wine vessel, or *zun*, dating to the Late Shang dynasty. Its shape and decoration reflect the influence of bronze ware and it is an example of the Shang's craft skills.

The Shang dynasty (c. 1600 – c. 1046 BCE) is the first recorded in Chinese history with archaeological and written evidence. The dates given for the founding of the Shang vary from c. 1760 to 1520 BCE. Archaeological evidence can prove the beginning of the dynasty as not later than 1600 BCE. The area where the Shang people resided was located along the Yellow river, in present-day Henan province in east-central China. It became the center of the most advanced political and military power of this time, which has been considered the world's fourth greatest early civilization.

Shang historiography changed radically when oracle bones (see image 2) were first identified in 1899. Oracle bones were usually scapula of large animals or turtle shells inscribed with ideograms that were used to divine the future. The inscriptions on the bones are early examples of Chinese writing and they provided evidence for Shang society. When the inscriptions were deciphered in 1917, they helped in tracing the origin of the geographical center of Shang, which was located at the modern village of Xiaotun, near the city of Anyang (see p. 188). Excavations conducted there from 1928 to 1937 unearthed the Yin ruins at the site of Yinxu and created what is known as "Shang archaeology."

The kings of Shang are believed to have occupied several capitals, including one at modern-day Zhengzhou (see p. 186) and, from the fourteenth century BCE onward, Anyang. Most of the excavated cities and tombs of the Shang people are well preserved, and demonstrate the religious and ritual framework within which political and court life was organized. Excavations at Anyang and

KEY EVENTS

c. 2000 BCE	c. 1700–1500 BCE	c. 1600 BCE	1600 BCE	c. 1600 BCE	1400–1200 BCE
Metal is used to make knives, awls, bells, and smaller vessels.	The Erlitou culture flourishes at modern-day Yanshi, Henan province, and is possibly the center of the Xia dynasty (c. 2070–c. 1600 BCE).	The Shang dynasty controls a large area in the northwest of China. The dynasty exists for eight generations under the reign of twelve kings.	Large-scale human sacrifices and the ceremonial burial of valuable artifacts begins in Shang tombs.	Construction of the Shang capital at Zhengzhou begins. A large, walled city, it covers about 6,178 acres (25 ha.).	Inscriptions on Shang oracle bones mention ritual dances and musical instruments, including *zhong* bronze bells and *gu* drums.

Xiaotun have revealed building foundations indicating a transformation from moderate-size settlements to royal capital cities with palatial-size structures. The Shang built houses on rammed earth floors, using beams for the construction. Walls of wattle and daub and thatched roofs were erected.

Ruling the vast area occupied by the Shang was not possible without a sophisticated political system. The Shang lived in an enormously stratified society. Shang kings appointed local governors to control the empire and the chief labor was in agriculture. Honoring the dead was also essential: respect was shown toward ancestors in accordance with their role, status, and rank in life. There are no detailed written sources on how ceremonies for the forefathers were celebrated, but finely cast bronze ritual vessels for food and wine have been discovered that are evidence for the special emphasis and care expended on offering food to ancestors.

A large number of Shang tombs have been excavated, revealing an abundance of grave goods. The tombs are mainly aligned north–south and have several common features. Typically, they are shaft tombs with four pathways leading to a base, containing chambers made of large timber logs that house a coffin. Human and animal sacrifices were placed in these chambers, as well as grave goods such as jades and bronzes. The Shang were renowned for their high-quality bronze casting and jade carving. A great number of surviving items indicate that Shang craftspeople had developed refined production methods and it is likely they had large workshops. Each craftsman had a specific task, such as smelting copper and tin to obtain bronze, making ceramic molds, casting the bronze artifacts, or forming and finishing the objects. Using piece-mold casting was unique in the ancient world and meant decorative patterns could be carved or stamped on the inner surface of the mold before it was fired to achieve sharp, intricate designs.

Pottery artifacts of hard gray earthenware (see image 3) have been key in defining Yinxu culture. Grayware vessels were produced in large numbers for a variety of purposes in homes, palaces, and graves. They were made using a mixture of techniques: coiling for the bodies, molds or hand-modeling for the legs and handles, and wheel-turning for ring feet and rims. Hard white and glazed pottery was used for burial goods in the tombs of the wealthy.

Bone, ivory, and marble played a major role in Shang culture. Bone came from many animals, especially oxen, which were of great importance in Shang life. Oxen were slaughtered for ritual offerings, and their shoulder blades used for divination.

In 1986, archaeologists discovered remarkable artifacts in Sanxingdui, Sichuan province, dating from c. 1200 to 1000 BCE. Gold, jade, elephant tusks, and refined bronzes (see image 1) in the shape of humanoid figures and heads were found, suggesting there was a metalworking culture in western China contemporaneous with the Shang, now known as the Sanxingdui culture. **MP**

1300–1050 BCE	c. 1300–1050 BCE	c. 1200 BCE	c. 1200–1045 BCE	c. 1200–1000 BCE	c. 1046 BCE
Yin (modern Anyang) becomes the new capital of the Shang.	Shangdi is considered the most powerful Shang deity and the greatest ancestor, controlling harvests, the weather, and victory in battle.	Construction of the Fuhao Tomb, believed to be the queen or consort of the first king, Wu Ding (r. 1250–1192 BCE), certain to have reigned in Yin.	Cracking animal bones or turtle shell by applying heat and then interpreting the resulting stress cracks becomes a major divination device.	Bronze humanoid figures and heads are produced at what is now Sanxingdui, Sichuan province.	Decline of the Shang dynasty. The Zhou people from the northwest of China establish a new dynasty.

Zhengzhou 1600 – 1300 BCE

Almost one hundred human skulls as well as a row of sacrificial pits for dogs have been discovered within the palace area at Zhengzhou. The workshops and residential areas were outside the city walls. Two larger copper foundries with ceramic molds were found outside the north wall section.

Modern Zhengzhou in Henan province, in east-central China, is the site of the royal capital Bo of King Tang (c. 2070 – c. 1600 BCE), the founder of the Shang dynasty. It was the largest walled urban city in the Early Shang dynasty—also known as the Erligang culture—covering 61.77 acres (25 ha.). The massive city wall, with a circumference of about 4 miles (7 km.), enclosed an area of more than 741 acres (300 ha.). It included the royal palaces that formed the major part of the city. Archaeologists discovered a palace foundation in the northeast of the city, extending over more than 15 acres (6 ha.). The city also had residential areas, farming settlements, cemeteries, and a variety of workshops.

The core wall of Zhengzhou was about 33 feet (10 m.) wide, adding about 16 feet (5 m.) more on each side with sloping layers of earth. The preserved height is 16 to 30 feet (5 – 9 m.). Eleven gaps were discovered in the wall, most of which were used as gates. The inner structure of the city is not well preserved in all parts, but large pounded-earth platforms, ranging in size from 1,076 to 21,528 square feet (100 – 2,000 sq. m.) indicate they originally served as house foundations.

One house, probably serving as a residential palace, has been given a hypothetical structure using the excavated foundations as a basis for reconstruction. This foundation stretches from east to west for more than 213 feet (65 m.), and north to south for about 43 feet (13 m.). Postholes, accurately set in a row every 6 feet 6 inches (2 m.), were dug into the pounded earth, creating an interior space of about 29 feet (9 m.) in depth. The building had nine rooms, double-eave rooftops, and a surrounding corridor. **MP**

CITY WALLS

The city walls were usually built using the *hangtu* pounded-earth technique, which was inherited from the Neolithic period, but improved during the Shang dynasty. Foundation trenches were dug below the surface. The wall was constructed in two sections: thin layers of earth were placed in wooden frames and pounded until solid with a final layer on top. Sloping layers on either side were laid against this construction.

BRONZE CONTAINER

No traces of Shang royal patronage were found inside Zhengzhou's city walls. But archaeologists discovered three sites outside the perimeter, probably sacrificial deposits or hoards, containing *fang-ding* containers like this one unearthed in 1974. The bronze vessels measure 32 to 39 inches (81 cm.–1 m.) in height and weigh 115 to 190 pounds (52–86 kg.). Dated to the Early Shang period, their large scale means they must have been royal possessions.

ANCIENT CITIES DISCOVERED NEAR ZHENGZHOU

Important discoveries in the vicinity of Zhengzhou have also been made other than the site of the royal city. The Xiaoshuangqiao site, dated to the Early Shang period, and located 12 miles (20 km.) northwest of Zhengzhou, covers about 3,558 acres (1,440 ha.). It includes a city wall, animal and human sacrificial pits, sacrificial graves and the remains of a bronze foundry. Three large bronze architectural fittings that must have belonged to magnificent buildings were discovered in ditches close to the foundry. In addition, large numbers of bronzes, ceramics, and stone artifacts such as jade (nephrite) have come to light. Characters written in red pigment on ceramic vessels and oracle bones discovered at the site are the earliest handwritten documents in Shang history. The function of the site is debated. Some suggest that Xiaoshuangqiao was a ritual complex attached to the royal capital at Zhengzhou, while others believe that when Shang kings abandoned their capital, they relocated to Xiaoshuangqiao and it became a new political centre.

The second walled city to have been discovered is Yanshi, located 41 miles (66 km.) west of Zhengzhou. Yanshi is smaller than Zhengzhou and covered an area of 470 acres (190 ha.). Its walls were extremely thick, while the city gates were very narrow. Chariot tracks have been found inside the city. Archaeologists have suggested that Yanshi could have had a defensive function. Palatial foundations were located inside the inner wall and several well-fortified, multistory structures in the inner city relating to the palace complex have been interpreted as arsenals or warehouses. It is thought that the inner city probably served as an elite citadel.

Anyang 1250 – 1050 BCE

The archaeological remains of Yinxu comprise two sites: the palace and royal ancestral shrines area and the royal tombs area, covering a total of 1,023 acres (414 ha.). The first excavations began in 1928 and excavation is ongoing.

The archaeological site of Yinxu, close to Anyang in Henan province, northeast central China, is Yin, the ancient capital of the Late Shang, built on the banks of the Yellow river. It underwent uninterrupted development and expansion from c. 1300 to 1050 BCE. Oracle-bone inscriptions and historical records provide proof that it was a Shang capital, referring to the Shang dynasty king Pan Geng moving his capital from Yan to Yin. The structure of Yinxu is different from that of earlier Shang cities because it lacks a city wall and is more diffuse—the political and ritual center of Yinxu was located at Xiaotun. A great number of palaces, which are probably the prototypes of later Chinese architecture, have been discovered at Yinxu. Most important for the understanding of early construction activity is the palace and royal ancestral shrines area, which has more than eighty house foundations of rammed-earth with remains of timber structures. The defensive ditch surrounding the city also functioned as a flood-control system, and a drainage system ran throughout the palace and temple area.

Yinxu is part of a broader regional complex. The banks of the Yellow River were densely populated, and up to now more than thirty sites have been located and some have been excavated. Hundreds of Late Shang graves have been located in Yinxu and other contemporaneous sites. Most of the tombs are very small, containing only a few burial goods, indicating that there was a dramatic increase of sociopolitical and economic stratification in the area around the royal city. Although the majority of the sites around Anyang have been badly looted, they are nevertheless important, and the structure and layout of Yinxu greatly influenced the planning and construction of subsequent cities. **MP**

STONE ARTIFACTS

Finds of soft jade (nephrite), such as this decorated comb with a feline figure, were limited to rich burials. Marble, limestone, sandstone, slate, and quartz have been identified among the many stone artifacts. They were used to create musical instruments, vessels, and animal sculptures placed in royal tombs.

TOMB OF FUHAO

Since archaeological work began in Yinxu, more than 4,000 tombs and 1,500 sacrificial pits have been excavated. These tombs provide important research material for the analysis of social structures and burial customs of the Shang. The Shang cemeteries were lineage cemeteries, where members of clan were buried in the same place. The largest grave in the Yinxu area is located at the Xiaotun excavation site, and through inscriptions on many of the bronze vessels was identified as the tomb of Fuhao, the consort of the Shang king Wuding, the twenty-third king of the Shang who lived c. 1200 BCE. Fuhao was involved in state matters, led military campaigns against the enemies of the Shang, and conducted ritual ceremonies. Her tomb had not been touched by grave robbers and provided a full assemblage of ritual vessels and objects. The tomb measures only 18 by 13 by 26 feet (5.6 by 4 by 8 m.) but was richly furnished with 1,928 burial objects, including bronze ritual vessels and jade artifacts.

BRONZES

Bronze vessel types, such as this urn, were discovered. Fragments recovered from pits and houses document the process of bronze casting. More than 20,000 mold fragments have been found, revealing the abundant variety of vessel types produced.

BRONZE AGE GREECE

1 The throne room and hearth of the
Mycenaean Palace of Nestor at Pylos.

2 A Kamares ware vessel (1800–1700 BCE)
from the site of Phaistos in Crete.

The Bronze Age in Greece is considered to last from *c.* 3100 until *c.* 1070
BCE. Archaeologists have identified three distinct societies that have the
modern names Helladic for the Greek mainland, Minoan for Crete, and
Cycladic for the islands in the central Aegean. Helladic is from *Hellas*, the Greek
name for Greece, and Minoan is derived from the legendary King Minos, whose
palace was at Knossos (see p. 192). Hisarlik, or Troy (see p. 196), is included in
this chapter, although the archaeology is overwhelmingly Anatolian. Its fame
derives from Greek epic poetry, which mentions cities such as Mycenae and
Tiryns, which are attested archaeologically in the Greek Bronze Age.

The Early Bronze Age saw many technological advances. In addition to the
spread of the use of metals, this era saw advances in domestic and funerary
architecture and artistic achievement. Architectural development is manifest
on the mainland, most marked in the Early Helladic II period. A striking
example is the House of the Tiles, the largest building at Lerna, on the coast of
the northeastern Peloponnese. Protected by fortification walls, it was a corridor
house, consisting of two main rooms and would have originally had an upper
story. In northern and eastern Crete, a new type of tomb was developed, known
as the house tomb. Particularly elaborate examples were found on the island of

KEY EVENTS

c. 3100 BCE	*c.* 2700 BCE	*c.* 2200 BCE	*c.* 2000 BCE	*c.* 1800 BCE	*c.* 1600 BCE
The start of the Bronze Age in Greece, when bronze replaces stone as the main material for tools and weapons.	Skilled artisans in the Cyclades carve figurines and stone vessels with bold, simple forms from local marble.	Destruction by fire of the House of the Tiles at Lerna, which had been built 500 years earlier.	Palaces emerge on Crete at three main sites: Knossos and Malia in the north, and Phaistos in the south.	Although handmade pottery continues to be made, the fast wheel is in use, particularly on Crete, where fine wares include Kamares ware.	Spectacular burials occur at several sites on the Greek mainland, especially the Shaft Graves at Mycenae, and signal major changes in social organization.

Mochlos, some multiroomed, with the use of different colored stone. Some had plentiful grave offerings, including stone vases and delicate gold jewelry. Artistic excellence was also apparent on the Cyclades in this period, with a range of stone vases and figurines sculpted from marble. Most of the figures are female (see image 2), although a few male figures are to be found.

The Middle Bronze Age on Crete is marked by changes in the organization of society evidenced by the rise of centers that were the focus of political and economic power, conventionally called palaces. The use of the term *palace* is misleading, because it implies that its main purpose is to serve as an elite residence. Evidence suggests that the palaces on Crete, and later on the mainland, were the administrative, economic, religious, and creative focus of a the state. Art flourished and the creation of Kamares ware pottery (see image 3) began at palatial workshops. However, the first Minoan palaces were destroyed by earthquake and rebuilt *c.* 1700 BCE. Although not as spectacular as the palatial society of Crete, the archaeology of the Middle Bronze Age on mainland Greece demonstrates changes in society. The site of Kolonna on Aegina, in the Saronic Gulf, was fortified in this period. The start of the Late Bronze Age on Crete is considered to be the peak of Minoan civilization. In addition to magnificent art and architecture associated with the palaces, Minoan influence spread to many Aegean islands, especially the Cyclades, as well as the west coast of Anatolia. This era came to a violent and abrupt end in the middle of the second millennium BCE, when many of the major sites on Crete were destroyed by fire.

On the Greek mainland, spectacular burials at the start of the Late Bronze Age, especially at Mycenae (see p. 198), are evidence of major changes in social organization. This period subsequently saw palaces built on the Greek mainland, initially at the site of the Menelaion in Lakonia, and subsequently at other sites in the Peloponnese, including Tiryns, Mycenae, and Pylos (see image 1), as well as Thebes in central Greece, and as far north as Dimini in Thessaly. Many Mycenaean sites were heavily fortified with defense systems that were clearly designed to impress as well as to protect. Although not as large as their Minoan counterparts, Mycenaean palaces were also multifunctional, with an administrative system recorded using the Linear B script (see p. 552), storage facilities, workshops, and provision for communal feasting. Archaeology indicates a network of overseas contacts in this period, with contact between the Greek mainland, the Cyclades and Dodecanese islands, Hisarlik and the Black Sea area, Anatolia, Cyprus, the Levant, Egypt, and Italy, with evidence from both land and shipwreck sites, including Ulu Burun (see p. 152) in Turkey.

The collapse of the Mycenaean palace economies *c.* 1200 BCE led to changes in the material culture, the most marked being the disappearance of the Linear B script, although there was some reoccupation of palace sites. The Greek Bronze Age is considered to come to an end *c.* 1070 BCE, with the adoption of iron as the dominant metal for weapons and tools. **GM**

c. 1500 BCE	*c.* 1450 BCE	*c.* 1400 BCE	*c.* 1300 BCE	*c.* 1200 BCE	*c.* 1070 BCE
A volcanic eruption destroys the island of Thera and buries the town of Akrotiri (see p. 194) in a thick layer of ash and pumice.	The Minoan palace system ends violently with major fires at sites throughout the island. Knossos is the only palace to be reoccupied.	Mainland palaces emerge, including at Tiryns, Mycenae, Thebes, and Pylos.	A ship carrying cargo from throughout the eastern Mediterranean sinks off Ulu Burun, in modern-day southwest Turkey.	Destruction of the Mycenaean palaces brings an end to the palace economies, although there is limited reoccupation at some sites.	Iron metallurgy gradually becomes the dominant technology for tools and weapons, taken as the end of the Bronze Age in Greece.

Knossos *c.* 7000 – *c.* 1375 BCE

Minoan palaces such as the one at Knossos were built around a central court, with complexes of rooms opening off it.

The Bronze Age site at Knossos on Crete is the largest and most significant of the Minoan palaces. In addition, Knossos enjoyed a long and frequently prosperous history both before and after the Minoan era. The first settlers arrived at Knossos *c.* 7000 BC, and established their homes on the site of what was later to become the Minoan palace. The area was inhabited until the fourteenth century BCE, when the palace was destroyed by fire. The surrounding area then flourished for another 2,000 years, although the palace was never reinhabited. In the late first century BCE, the Roman emperor Augustus (63 BCE–14 CE) established a colony, Colonia Julia Nobilis Cnossus, to the north of the palace site, which became one of the main Roman cities on Crete.

By the nineteenth century CE, Crete had been visited by many travelers and antiquarians, including the poet Edward Lear (1812–88). The first archaeological excavations were conducted by the aptly named Minos Kalokairinos (1843–1907), an antiquarian who lived in Heraklion ("Candia"). In 1878, he uncovered a section of the west part of the palace and produced a sketch of the throne room. An edict of the ruling Ottoman government forced Kalokairinos to abandon his work, but he continued to discuss his findings with other archaeologists, including Arthur Evans (1851–1941) in 1894. Kalokairinos spread knowledge of Knossos throughout Europe by donating to museums examples of the large Minoan storage jars known as pithoi, which he had excavated in the west storage magazines of the palace. Subsequently, several other archaeologists wished to continue investigations at Knossos, including Heinrich Schliemann (1822–90), American Consul in Greece W. J. Stillman (1828–1901), the French archaeologist André Joubin (1868–1944), and the British archaeologist John Myres (1869–1954), before Arthur Evans eventually purchased the land that included the site of the palace. **GM**

FOCAL POINTS

TRIPARTITE SHRINE

The shrine on the west side of the central court had two stone-lined sunken pits, which Evans named the "Temple Repositories" due to the religious nature of the finds. They included objects made from faience, particularly female figurines holding snakes, which have been dated to around the seventeenth century BCE.

RECONSTRUCTIONS

Following his excavations of Knossos in the early twentieth century, Evans commissioned substantial reconstructions of the palace superstructure. These additions, based on images of buildings in Minoan wall paintings, were intended to provide an impression of the extent and opulence of the Minoan structures.

ARCHAEOLOGIST PROFILE

1851–84

Arthur Evans was born in 1851 into a fairly prosperous family. He initially worked as a journalist in Illyria (modern-day Croatia), and on his return to England was offered the post of Keeper of the Ashmolean Museum in Oxford, which he held from 1884 until his resignation in 1908.

1885–1903

Evans first traveled to Crete in 1894, one of his first visits being to Knossos. The end of the Ottoman rule of Crete in 1899

allowed Evans to complete his purchase of the Kephala Hill, which included the site of the palace of Knossos. Evans's excavations began at precisely 11 a.m. on March 23, 1900, and the first artifacts were exhibited in London in 1903.

1904–41

Excavations in the Knossos area continued for the next three decades and made Evans famous for the rest of his life; he received a knighthood in 1911. Evans died in 1941, a few days after his ninetieth birthday.

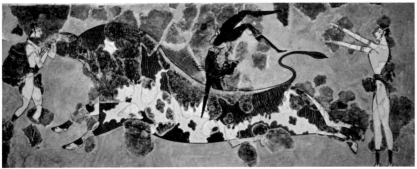

◄ The exciting and exhilarating —and no doubt extremely dangerous—Minoan activity of bull leaping may have taken place outside the palace, as the central court is too small. Wall paintings from Knossos show athletes balancing on the bull's back, waiting to be caught by their companions. Other evidence appears on seal-stones and figurines, in particular a group of fragmentary ivory statuettes from Knossos, interpreted as bull leapers.

Akrotiri *c.* 4500 – *c.* 1600/1500 BCE

The circumstances of the destruction of Akrotiri have enabled archaeologists to retrieve evidence that would not normally have survived, such as the use of wooden furniture. When cavities in the ash were located, plaster of Paris was poured into the voids to reveal the shapes of tables and beds, their form preserved even though the wood from which they were made had decomposed.

The archaeological site of Akrotiri is on the Aegean island of Thera (also known as Santorini), approximately 62 miles (100 km.) north of Crete. The island's location enabled it to benefit from Bronze Age trade routes in the Aegean, which meant Akrotiri attained a high level of wealth and culture. In particular, there is evidence of links with the Minoan society on Crete, namely some use of the Linear A script and some of the subjects depicted in wall paintings. However, although some themes, such as images of monkeys, are found on Crete, the majority appear to be unique to Thera.

A major volcanic eruption destroyed much of the island and buried the town of Akrotiri in a blanket of pumice and ash 66 feet (20 m.) deep, leading to its remarkable preservation. However, unlike the Roman sites of Pompeii and Herculaneum (see p. 302), no human remains were found, implying that the population was able to escape. Recent scientific studies have suggested that the volcanic eruption, conventionally dated to around 1500 BCE, may have occurred approximately a century earlier.

In the 1860s, the remains of a Late Bronze Age settlement were found on the nearby island of Therasia, during the quarrying of pozzolana (ash) for construction of the Suez Canal. An eruption of the Thera volcano in 1870 led to a visit by French geologist and volcanologist Ferdinand Fouqué (1828–1904), who identified remains on Thera similar to those on Therasia. A small-scale excavation was conducted, with further limited excavations taking place thirty years later. Greek archaeologist Spyridon Marinatos (1901–74) undertook surface exploration in the early 1960s, leading to major excavations from 1967. Christos Doumas (b. 1933) succeeded Marinatos as site director in 1974. **GM**

PAINTINGS

Wall paintings shed light on the appearance and activities of Akrotiri's inhabitants. Boys and girls are shown with partially shaven heads. Women of all ages are depicted wearing elaborate jewelry. Cosmetics, plausibly made from saffron and henna, were used to decorate lips, feet, fingernails, and in this instance, ears.

BUILDINGS

Marinatos chose as his excavation site Favatas, which had been the site of a small excavation by a French team in 1870. Marinatos's excavations revealed remarkable preservation of the buildings, some still standing up to two stories in height. Among the most notable features were the well-preserved wall paintings.

SHIP PROCESSION FRESCO

Wall paintings were found in many buildings in Akrotiri, both public and private. Some of the most important insight they provide is on the construction of ships in this period, information which has generally not survived elsewhere in the archaeological record.

Although a small number of shipwrecks dating to Akrotiri's peak have been found off the coasts of Crete, the Greek mainland, and southwestern Turkey, hull remains have proved elusive and the evidence is mainly the ships' cargoes. Accordingly, depictions of ships of this era provide invaluable evidence of the appearance and construction of ships both large and small.

The Ship Procession Fresco was found on one wall of an upper-story room in the building known as the West House. The composition, painted in miniature style, was 18 inches (45 cm.) high, and its entire length would have been 13 feet (3.9 m.). It shows a fleet of eight large and elaborately decorated ships, fitted with both oars and sails, accompanied by three smaller vessels, seemingly traveling between two ports. The passengers seated in the center of the larger ships are covered by an awning, their warrior status indicated by the helmets covered with plaques made from the tusks of wild boar. The highest ranking passenger on each vessel is depicted sitting in a cabin, or perhaps a litter or palanquin, at the stern of the ship, now known by the Homeric term *ikria*. The largest ship in the fleet, conventionally called the Admiral's Ship, was elaborately decorated with images of lions on its hull, garlands of flowers above the cabin, and a butterfly on its prow. A more violent aspect of maritime life was shown on the north wall of Room 5, where a fragmentary wall painting apparently shows a seashore battle, with defeated and drowning warriors.

Hisarlik *c.* 3000 BCE – 500 CE

The West Sanctuary at Hisarlik dates from the Greek city of Ilion (later Roman Ilium), founded *c.* 700 BCE. It is one of two sacred areas known at the site; the other is the Sanctuary of Athena.

✦ NAVIGATOR

The city of Troy, immortalized by Homer in the *Iliad*, has inspired countless writers and artists. Although the location has been disputed, Hisarlik in Turkey is usually identified as Homeric Troy. There were no visible traces of the city until Heinrich Schliemann excavated the mound of Hisarlik in the late nineteenth century. Excavations by Carl Blegen (1887–1971) in the 1930s clarified its occupation phases, and in the 1990s Manfred Korfmann (1942–2005) found that the city was larger than the mound itself.

Hisarlik was occupied for approximately 4,500 years, from *c.* 3000 BCE onward. The settlement that Schliemann found dates to around 2500–2300 BCE and was destroyed by a catastrophic fire. A city dating to the late thirteenth to early twelfth century BCE—the time of the supposed Trojan War—also suffered a disastrous fire, but it is uncertain whether there is any relation to the fabled sack of Troy. The legend of the Trojan War is based on an amalgamation of several ancient sources, most famously Homer's *Iliad*. Although aspects of the *Iliad* are anachronistic, the poem preserves some elements with a factual basis. The catalyst for the war was the elopement of the Trojan prince Paris and Helen, the wife of Menelaus, king of Sparta. Menelaus and his brother Agamemnon besieged Troy for nine years without success. The end of the siege came suddenly when the Greek forces, led by Odysseus, hid inside a wooden horse that the Trojans brought into the city. Caught unawares, Priam, king of Troy, was killed and his city laid to waste. **GM**

FOCAL POINTS

1 POSITION

Due to the silting of nearby rivers, the coastline is now almost 3 miles (5 km.) across the plain from the mound of Hisarlik. In the Bronze Age, the city was on the coast, when it commanded the strategic maritime route that led from the Aegean to the Black Sea.

2 WALLS

The spectacular remains of the walls recall Homer's description of Troy as "well-walled." Twenty-three sections of wall have been revealed, together with eleven city gates and a paved stone entrance ramp. This section in the West Sanctuary dates to c. 1300 BCE.

3 ALTARS

An enclosed sacred area, the West Sanctuary contains the well-preserved remains of two altars. The large altar dates from the Roman period, while the adjacent smaller altar was erected in the Hellenistic period on the foundations of a much earlier Archaic altar.

◄ Schliemann was keen to associate his discoveries with objects described in the Homeric epics. Accordingly, he linked finds of a highly distinctive type of cup with two handles with the *depas amphikypellon*, a two-handled cup mentioned by Homer. However, it is now known that this type of cup dates from around 2300 BCE, about 1,000 years earlier than the supposed date of the Trojan War.

ARCHAEOLOGIST PROFILE

1822–67

Heinrich Schliemann was born in Germany in 1822, the son of a pastor. His interest in the historical foundations of the Homeric poems began at the age of seven, after seeing a picture of Troy in flames in a history book. However, he did not pursue his interest in the ancient past until after achieving considerable success as a merchant. He retired from business in early middle age and spent several years traveling the world to study archaeology.

1868–70

Fired by his interest in Homer, Schliemann first visited the Ionian island of Ithaca in 1868 but did not succeed in his goal of finding the palace of Odysseus. From Ithaca, he traveled to the area of the Dardanelles in his search for Troy. The diplomat Frank Calvert (1828–1908), who had previously dug at the site of Hisarlik, persuaded Schliemann that Troy could be found through excavation of the mound there.

1871–79

Between 1871 and 1873, a massive team of workers employed by Schliemann dug trenches through the mound at Hisarlik, leading him to identify it as the site of Troy. He published his findings in *Trojanische Alterthümer* (*Troy and Its Remains*; 1874). Although some scholars were sceptical, his theories were widely accepted by the public. From 1874 onward, Schliemann also undertook excavations on the Greek mainland, beginning at the Bronze Age sites of Mycenae, where he discovered what he believed to be the tombs of Agamemnon and Clytemnestra. He published his finds in *Mykenä* (*Mycenae*; 1878).

1880–90

Schliemann excavated the site of the Treasury of Minyas at Orchomenos and the fortified site of Tiryns near Mycenae, and also carried out further excavations at Hisarlik. He died in Naples in December 1890.

Mycenae *c.* 1600 – 1100 BCE

Mycenae was immortalized in Homer's epic poem, the *Iliad*, as the home of Agamemnon, leader of the Achaean forces against the Trojans.

The archaeological site of Mycenae is around 1 mile (2 km.) from the modern Greek village bearing the same name, located in the northeast of the Peloponnese. The fortified citadel is built on a limestone outcrop. Although there had been occupation at Mycenae from the seventh millennium BCE onward, the archaeological remains that are visible today date from the sixteenth to thirteenth centuries BCE. These include two Grave Circles (funerary enclosures containing lavish burials), the famous heraldic Lion Gate, massive fortifications, and the remains of the palace. Further impressive evidence of engineering skill is an underground water cistern at the northeast of the citadel, protected by a secure entrance, which ensured that the inhabitants of Mycenae would have water in the event of siege. The archaeological remains extend outside the citadel, and much of the settlement lay on the southeastern slopes of the hill.

In 1874, Heinrich Schliemann (1822 – 90) conducted some trial excavations at Mycenae and in 1876 he continued work there on behalf of the Greek Archaeological Society. Using as a guide the writings of the Greek traveler Pausanias (*c.* 110 – 180 CE), who visited in the second century CE, Schliemann's excavations focused on the area inside the Lion Gate, where Pausanias suggested the legendary king Agamemnon and his companions were buried. Schliemann found burials inside what is now called Grave Circle A.

Archaeological research continues at Mycenae, with a particularly interesting discovery made in 2014 of a large piece of polished stone, identified by archaeologists as a fragment of a throne. It was the same type of stone as found on the decorated facades of *tholos* tombs at Mycenae and on the Lion Gate, the ceremonial entrance to the citadel. **GM**

◆ NAVIGATOR

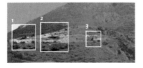

1 GRAVE CIRCLE A

Grave Circle A is a circular area, 90 feet (27.5 m.) in diameter, ringed by a low wall and containing six large graves in which nineteen people in total were buried. It was used from c. 1550 to 1500 BCE and then in c. 1250 BCE was enclosed within the citadel walls, suggesting it was revered.

2 CULT CENTER

The area known as the Cult Center—today protected by a modern roof—comprises five structures whose finds suggest they were used for religious purposes. In particular, the building known as The Temple contained terracotta snakes and figurines interpreted as deities and worshippers.

3 CITADEL WALLS

The Homeric epithet "well built Mycenae" is confirmed by the citadel walls, which extended for about 3,000 feet (900 m.). They were largely built in the style known as Cyclopean, derived from the belief that, the stones were so large that they must have been moved by the gigantic, one-eyed Cyclops.

MYCENAEAN *THOLOS* TOMBS

A type of tomb known as a *tholos* is found throughout Mycenaean Greece. The Treasury of Atreus at Mycenae, built c. 1250 BCE, is a well-preserved example, though it was already plundered when it was visited by Pausanias in the second century CE. It was once believed that such tombs were storehouses for valuables. Consisting of a round chamber (the *tholos*, from which this type of tomb is named) approached by an unroofed passage lined with dressed stone, the tomb is a remarkable feat of structural engineering. The chamber is constructed of thirty-three courses of dressed stone, fitted so that each course slightly overlaps the one above it, with the uppermost course being closed with a single block. The overlapping sections were then removed, so that the interior appears smooth and unbroken. The elaborate decoration of the tomb's exterior, now dispersed between several museums, suggests that the original appearance of the building must have been spectacular. No doubt the looted grave offerings would have been equally stunning.

HITTITES

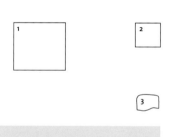

1

2

3

1 The Sphinx Gate at the Alaca Hüyük archaeological site in Alaca, Turkey, marked the entrance to the Hittite town.

2 Part of the Karabel relief near Izmir, Turkey. It depicts Tarkasnawa, the king of the Hittite vassal state of Mira, and dates to the thirteenth century BCE.

3 The clay tablet containing the Hittite version of the text of the Treaty of Qadesh (1259 BCE) was found at Boğazkale in 1906 and is now in the Ancient Orient Museum, Istanbul.

The Hittites (members of an ancient Indo-European people) initially settled in the area of Boğazkale, in central Anatolia, where they founded their capital Hattusa. From the start of the fourteenth century to the end of the twelfth century BCE, the Hittites dominated most of modern-day central and eastern Turkey, Syria, and the island of Cyprus.

The Hittite Empire was ruled by a Great King from their capital Hattusa and consisted of a number of client kingdoms that provided assistance to the ruler in terms of military and other support. One such kingdom was Mira, in western Turkey. A rock carving in Hittite style at Karabel (see image 2), inland from modern-day Izmir, was once considered as a marker of conquest erected by a Hittite ruler, although the translation of an associated inscription in Hittite hieroglyphic script reveals that it depicts a king of Mira.

The most spectacular Hittite archaeological remains are to be found at Hattusa (see p. 202) and nearby Alaca Hüyük. Excavations began at Alaca Hüyük in the 1930s and revealed a long history of occupation, including a Hittite town dating to the second millennium BCE. Archaeologists discovered a walled town with a formal gateway carved with sphinxes (see image 1). There were also several temples, residential areas, and an area for ironworking.

KEY EVENTS

c. 2000 BCE	c. 1650 BCE	c. 1595 BCE	c. 1400 BCE	c. 1350 BCE	c. 1340 BCE
The Hittites appear in Anatolia at the beginning of the second millennium.	Hattusilis I becomes the Hittite king and is considered to be the founder of the Hittite kingdom.	The Hittite army, led by Mursilis I (r. c. 1620–c. 1590 BCE), attacks and partly destroys the city of Babylon.	Tudhaliyas I becomes the Hittite king, a political change that signals the emergence of the Hittite New Kingdom.	Suppiluliumas I begins a reign that sees the northern areas of the empire secured and the Mitanni people of northern Mesopotamia under Hittite control.	The Hittite Empire has become one of the dominant powers of the Middle East alongside pharaonic Egypt.

Archaeological knowledge of the Hittites is supplemented by extensive documentary evidence. Two types of script were used: Hittite hieroglyphic and cuneiform (meaning wedge-shaped). The most important finds from Hattusa are the group of 5,000 clay tablets, broken into many fragments, inscribed with the cuneiform script. Many of these were found in 1906 close to one of the entrances to the Great Fortress. Up to this time, Nesite, the language used on the clay tablets, had not been deciphered, in part because there were insufficient texts for philologists to acquire a sufficient understanding to make decipherment possible. The extent of the archive at Hattusa meant there were sufficient texts to enable decipherment, which was successfully achieved by the Czech scholar Bedřich Hrozný (1879–1952) in 1915, working in Vienna. The tablets indicated that Boğazkale was ancient Hattusa, the Hittite capital, and have provided invaluable historical information on Hittite society and wider politics in the second millennium BCE, with references to other societies in the eastern Mediterranean.

A particularly informative tablet is a draft of the Sausgamuwa Treaty made in the thirteenth century BCE by the Hittite king Tudhaliyas IV (r. c. 1237–1209 BCE) and Sausgamuwa, king of Amurru, an area in modern-day Syria and Lebanon. Tudhaliyas listed the kings who he considered were his equals—those of Egypt, Babylon, Assyria, and Ahhiyawa, with the name Ahhiyawa crossed out in the draft. The location of Ahhiyawa is thought to refer to Mycenaean Greece (see p. 198) or the area adjoining the western coast of modern-day Turkey.

Another significant Hittite document is a peace treaty agreed in 1259 BCE by the Hittite king Hattusilis III (r. c. 1267–1237 BCE) and the Egyptian pharaoh, Ramesses II (c. 1303–1213 BCE), and known as the Treaty of Qadesh (see image 3). The treaty was drawn up between Hattusilis and Ramesses sixteen years after their armies clashed near Qadesh on the Orontes River in modern-day Syria, a battle in which both sides claimed victory. Two versions of the treaty were written, one in Hattusa, the other in Pi-Ramesses, the capital city of Ramesses II. The Hittite version was written in Akkadian, the common language of diplomacy, which was inscribed on a silver tablet and sent to Egypt, where it was translated into Egyptian. The reverse took place for the copy sent to Hattusa. Although the silver versions of the treaty have not survived, the text of the Egyptian version was carved on the walls of the temple at Karnak and the Ramesseum temple, and a copy of the Hittite text was discovered in the archives at Hattusa. The Treaty of Qadesh is commemorated with a copy placed above the Security Council Chamber of the United Nations in New York.

The Hittite kingdom came to an end c. 1200 BCE in the reign of Suppiluliumas II (c. 1207–1178 BCE), a son of Tudhaliyas IV. Hattusa and the other Hittite cities in Anatolia were abandoned, although the reasons and exact circumstances for the desertion remain a mystery. However, they were part of a wider series of destructions in the eastern Mediterranean region. **GM**

1312 BCE	Early 13th century BCE	c. 1274 BCE	1259 BCE	c. 1237 BCE	c. 1200 BCE
A solar eclipse is visible over Anatolia, recorded in a text by the Hittite king Mursilis II (r. c. 1346–c. 1320 BCE) and is known as Mursilis's Eclipse.	Muwatallis II (r. c. 1295–c. 1272 BCE) relocates the Hittite capital to Tarhuntassa in southern Anatolia. It moves back to Hattusa a few years later.	Muwatallis II, supported by a great number of vassal troops, wins the Battle of Qadesh against the young Egyptian pharaoh Ramesses II.	The Treaty of Qadesh between the Hittites and Egypt is agreed, the Hittite version preserved on a cuneiform tablet from Hattusa.	Tudhaliyas IV succeeds his father Hattusilis III as Hittite king. Carvings at the Yazilikaya sanctuary in Hattusa may honour Tudhaliyas in life or posthumously.	The Hittite kingdom comes to an end and Hittite cities in Anatolia are abandoned.

Hattusa *c.* 2500 – 1200 BCE

The archaeological site of Hattusa is in Çorum province, Turkey. The capital of the Hittite Empire, it is notable for its urban organization, the ornamentation of the Lion Gate, and rock art at Yazilikaya.

The archaeological site of Hattusa, the Hittite capital, is situated at an elevation over 3,100 feet (900 m.), south of the village of Boğazkale in central Turkey, approximately 124 miles (200 km.) east of Ankara. Hattusa has been the subject of long-term research by German archaeologists since the start of the twentieth century.

Occupying a favorable position at the head of a valley, occupation began at the site from the Early Bronze Age, probably *c.* 2500 BCE. In the late nineteenth to early eighteenth centuries BCE, Hattusa was part of a wide trade network and the location of a *karum*, an Assyrian merchant colony, albeit on a smaller scale than Kanesh (see p. 150). The city was at its height from *c.* 1400 to 1200 BCE, when the Hittite Empire fell, although the citadel survived and was reoccupied on a reduced scale until the middle of the first millennium BCE. The three main areas of this immense site of around 446 acres (180 ha.) are, from north to south, the Lower Town, the Büyükkale (Great Fortress), and the Upper Town. The city is surrounded by a series of gates and fortifications.

The reconstruction of a 213-foot (65 m.) section of the city wall and fortification towers has been undertaken in the northern part of Hattusa. The appearance of the towers is based on a fragment of a Hittite pottery vessel found at the site, now in the Museum of Anatolian Civilizations, Ankara. The fragment gives an impression of the appearance of Hittite buildings that have not survived in the archaeological record.

In 2011, one of the original sphinx sculptures, 8 feet (2.5 m.) tall, from the Yerkapi (Sphinx Gate) was returned to the museum in Boğazkale, having previously been on display in the Pergamon Museum, Berlin. **GM**

👁 FOCAL POINTS

CARVINGS

Situated 1 mile (2 km.) northeast of Hattusa, Yazilikaya is the most impressive Hittite religious complex. It consists of an outcrop of rock that forms two natural chambers, with figures carved in low relief on the rock walls. A narrow passage, guarded by carvings of winged demons with lion heads, leads to a chamber dominated by a large relief of a huge sword. Opposite is a group of twelve male deities carrying curved swords.

LION GATE

The Upper Town's fortification of a double wall with more than 100 towers are now in ruins. It had at least five gates, including the Aslanikapi (Lion Gate) in the southwest, the Yerkapi (Earth Gate, popularly known as the Sphinx Gate) in the south, and the Kralkapi (King's Gate, which shows a male deity) in the southeast. The Yerkapi, which still has some traces of its original sculpture, was built on an artificial bastion with an arched stone tunnel underneath.

HITTITE CAPITAL

The religious complex known as the Büyük Mabet, or Great Temple, is in the Lower Town in a walled area (1). Its ancillary buildings included storage rooms, adjacent to which is a complex of rooms that may have been living quarters. The Büyükkale, or Great Fortress (2), was a strategically positioned walled citadel. Most of the remains date from c. 1400 BCE, when there was much rebuilding, possibly including a residence for the Hittite rulers. There were also large administrative buildings, where important archives of clay tablets inscribed with the cuneiform script were found. The Upper Town (3) contains a group of temples and shrines, their plan of a ceremonial entrance, a central courtyard with colonnade, and an inner sanctuary being similar to the Great Temple.

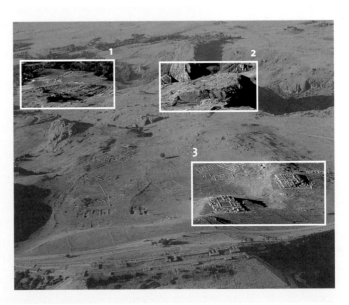

FIRST MESOAMERICAN CIVILIZATIONS

1 Located within modern-day Mexico City, the earliest construction stage of the 65-foot (20 m.) platform at Cuicuilco was built between 800 and 600 BCE. Its circular plan and carved stone obelisk display artistic canons distinct from those used by the Olmec and the Maya.

2 The first Olmec basalt portrait heads, such as this example, were carved at San Lorenzo. These personalized monuments provide solid evidence for the existence of powerful rulers by 1200 BCE. The tradition was continued at La Venta, Tres Zapotes, and La Cobata in the Gulf Coast region.

3 The spectacular mural scenes found in 2001 at San Bartolo, Guatemala, date between 200 and 100 BCE and are the earliest known Maya wall paintings. In this scene, a young king perforates his penis with a long, pointed awl to offer his blood to the gods.

Mesoamerican civilization emerged during the second millennium BCE in an area that extends south from Mexico's arid northwest into the humid jungles of Belize, Guatemala, El Salvador, and Honduras. Unlike the earliest Old World civilizations, it did not evolve in the valley of a great river that provided a natural communication route for the settlements along its banks. Indeed, Mesoamerica is the geographical opposite of those valleys surrounded by hills, since its rivers drain impressive volcanic sierras, with peaks over 16,400 feet (5,000 m.) that run through the center of the region. This altitudinal variation sharply divides the terrain into hundreds of ecological niches, from the plains and estuaries along its 6,215-mile (10,000 km.) coastline to its fertile mountain basins, perched at elevations above 6,560 feet (2,000 m.). The main challenge presented by this environmental mosaic with few navigable stretches of rivers was moving goods from one area to another without beasts of burden.

Yet diversity proved to be a key factor in fostering social complexity. Populations grew dramatically after 1300 BCE as the cultivation of corn, beans, and squash provided surpluses that could be invested in architecture, ceremonies, and material products. Population growth also spurred greater social inequality. Exotic goods acquired through long-distance exchange—jade, marine shells, cinnabar, cacao, iron-ore minerals, jaguar skins, and feathers—were used to highlight the prestige of society's more important members. These elites were people who had acquired wealth or knew how to invoke

KEY EVENTS

c. 12,000 BCE	7000 BCE	3400 BCE	3000 BCE	2500 BCE	1600 BCE
Hunter-gatherer populations enter Mesoamerica.	The first evidence of domesticated plants: maize, squash, and chili peppers.	Maize agriculture spreads throughout Mesoamerica as populations become more sedentary.	Domesticated dogs appear at Mesoamerican sites.	Permanent agricultural villages invest in wattle-and-daub structures and build underground storage facilities.	Pottery-making becomes common in Mesoamerican communities.

ancestral spirits and the forces of nature. Mesoamerica was never politically united, but its many ethnicities shared a cultural tradition comprising cosmological concepts and a sophisticated calendrical system that was sustained by trade, diplomatic relations, intermarriage, and conquest.

The earliest expression of complex society in Mesoamerica occurs along the Gulf and Pacific coasts of Mexico's transisthmian region. The inhabitants of San Lorenzo (see p. 206), La Venta, Laguna de los Cerros, Paso de la Amada, and Cantón Corralito communicated their ideas about the world using a shared art style and symbol set that is identified as Olmec. The corpus of this artistic production includes colossal stone portrait heads of rulers (see image 2), altarlike thrones, carved stelae, finely worked jade artifacts, and elegantly decorated pottery. Technical studies reveal that San Lorenzo was trading with highland communities for obsidian and iron-ore mirrors that were used as markers of privileged status. The practice of burying valuable artifacts, often caches of jade celts, as offerings was devised to consecrate the ground of the civic-ceremonial centers and convert natural territory into ritually active space.

After 900 BCE in the Maya area of southeastern Mexico, Guatemala, Belize, and Honduras, budding elites developed ways of expressing political power. Rulers at Ceibal, Cerros, Nakbé, Uaxactún, and Kaminaljuyú commissioned causeways, reservoirs, canals, and impressive architectural complexes, sometimes embellished with stucco reliefs expressing themes that tied themselves to the gods. Deep in the Guatemalan jungle at El Mirador, the Danta complex, 978 by 2,001 feet (298 by 610 m.) at its base and 230 feet (70 m.) high, is among the most impressive buildings of the ancient world. The early Maya established the tradition of burying their kings with offerings of jade, shell, and pottery in masonry tombs crowned by temples. Depictions of royal personages were carved on stelae, narrative scenes recording the sacrificial obligations of kings were painted on building interiors (see image 3), and by 300 BCE, scribes had begun to record history in hieroglyphic writing.

The highland basins of central Mexico also witnessed the material expressions of emerging inequality between 1100 and 900 BCE. Most of the evidence consists of elaborate ceramics and figurines, some using Olmec symbols, but shortly after 800 BCE, stone-faced platforms upon which public buildings were constructed appear at Chalcatzingo, Cuicuilco (see image 1), Tlalancaleca, and Xochitécatl. These sites, not yet true cities, produced stone sculpture or carved reliefs on natural outcrops, sometimes in the Olmec style but more often reflecting conventions that mark a divide between Mesoamerica's eastern and western subtraditions. Farther south, at San José Mogote in the Valley of Oaxaca, a carved stone slab dating to 600 BCE records the first evidence for the Zapotec writing and the ritual calendar. A century later, Monte Albán (see p. 208), which sits at the center of the Valley of Oaxaca, was founded as the first true city in the highlands. **PPN**

1400 BCE	800 BCE	600 BCE	500 BCE	300 BCE	100 BCE
The establishment of the first civic-ceremonial center at San Lorenzo in what is modern-day Veracruz, Mexico.	Public architecture appears throughout Mesoamerica.	The earliest evidence for Mesoamerica's dual-calendar system.	Establishment of early cities such as Monte Albán and the initial steps toward state formation.	Massive monumental architectural complexes are built in both highland and lowland Mesoamerica.	Large cities with populations of more than 10,000 appear in the central highlands.

San Lorenzo 1800 – 900 BCE

This statue of a ball player was placed facing east on a red sand and gravel floor, and then covered with a fill whose composition suggests it was obtained from older platforms that had been demolished.

 NAVIGATOR

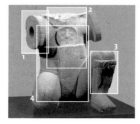

Located on a large natural island that rises 164 feet (50 m.) above the swampy floodplain of the lower Coatzacoalcos River drainage in southern Mexico, San Lorenzo existed in an unstable, though extremely rich, aquatic environment governed by the constantly changing riverine landscape. It was first occupied *c.* 1800 BCE and reached its greatest splendor between 1400 and 1000 BCE. During these centuries, the population of San Lorenzo fashioned their island home, leveling surfaces, filling ravines, and terracing slopes to create a capital that replicated one of the fundamental archetypes of their cosmology: the sacred mountain rising from the primordial waters of the underworld. The artificial plateau organized the settlement into ceremonial and administrative areas marked by stone sculpture, palaces and elite buildings at its center, while lower status groups were relegated to outlying areas.

Like all floodplains, the Coatzacoalcos drainage lacks stone. Large multi-ton natural boulders had to be dragged overland or floated down the rivers from a basalt flow in the volcanic Tuxtla Mountains 37 miles (60 km.) to the north so that San Lorenzo's craftsmen could sculpt them into the monuments that linked their community to the spirits of the otherworld and proclaimed the power of their rulers. Their statuary is famous for the colossal portrait heads, altarlike thrones, and life-size naturalistic figures. **PPN**

◉ FOCAL POINTS

1 DISK SOCKET

Sculpted in basalt, this half-kneeling ball player was mutilated prior to being buried between 1000 and 900 BCE as an offering at San Lorenzo. Disk sockets were carved on the figure's shoulders to attach arms, perhaps made of stone or wood. The ratchets incised on their surface show wear, suggesting that the arms could be maneuvered into different positions. Neither the head nor the arms have been recovered.

2 PECTORAL

The life-size figure wears a circular pectoral hanging from a band around his neck. The object's concave form indicates that it is a metallic mirror made from magnetite or ilmenite that had to be imported from the highlands. Similar mirrors were used by elite members of Olmec society, especially rulers. The six-pronged motif at its center may be an early symbol for fire or light. The uniforms players wore was often tied to themes of life and death.

3 LEG STRAP

The figure has a leg strap, or garter, below the left knee. It is not known what function this served. The garter consists of a braided cord from which hang two feathers attached by beads. Although the hot humid climate of Mexico's Gulf Coast does not favor the preservation of organic materials like feathers, these and other exotic items were highly prized, and indicators of privileged social status.

4 BELT

The figure wears his belt, perhaps made of thick leather, high around his ribs to protect him against blows from the large, hard rubber ball used in the Mesoamerican ball game. Likewise, the wide strap that passes between his legs would have served to protect his genitals from bruising by a flying ball. Ancient rubber was made from latex of the rubber tree, which is indigenous to the tropical areas of southern Mexico.

SCULPTED SCENES

Olmec monuments were strategically placed within San Lorenzo and its outlying communities to emphasize the political importance of certain families, or to create ritual scenes. Thrones and colossal stone heads commanded the patios of palaces to promote prestige and power, while other smaller sculptural elements appear to have provided theatrical backdrops for dramatizations of now-lost mythic tales. In 1987, three statues were found in place at the site of Azuzul, a satellite of San Lorenzo. Kneeling one behind the other before a larger seated feline figure, each of the two young men is attired in ceremonial garb. They wear symbolically incised rectangular pectorals on their chests, and the pleated flaps that cover their ears resemble those used by the rain deity. Each holds a bar on the ground in such a way that the viewer perceives they are about to rotate them into a vertical position. The composition may represent a ceremony designed to raise the "world tree," a cosmic axis whose roots penetrate the watery underworld and whose branches reach into the celestial realm. The ritual was devised to situate the fifth, vertical direction and open the access to these alternate levels of the universe.

Monte Albán *c.* 500 BCE – *c.* 700 CE

Monte Albán's Great Plaza was cut into the irregular surface of an impressive mountainous block at the center of the Valley of Oaxaca. The architectural endeavor took centuries to complete, but from the beginning it was designed to provide an extraordinary setting for civic and ceremonial activities with enough space for the entire population of the city.

✪ NAVIGATOR

Located on a mountain 1,312 feet (400 m.) high at the center of the Valley of Oaxaca in southern Mexico, Monte Albán was one of Mesoamerica's first great cities. In *c.* 500 BCE, this remote, unoccupied site may have been chosen by a political coalition for defensive reasons due to the increasing rivalry among the valley's chiefdoms, but like Olmec San Lorenzo (see p. 206), the center of the city was conceived from the beginning as a grand monumental enterprise designed to create a spectacular capital, replete with elegant palaces, dozens of temples, a ball court, and elaborate tombs. It endured for more than a millennium as the center of the Zapotec world.

Much of the early construction at Monte Albán involved earth moving, leveling, and filling the irregular mountaintop to create a huge plaza, oriented true north, measuring approximately 984 by 656 feet (300 by 200 m.). Natural rock outcrops were left along the borders and in the center of the plaza to serve as cores for the platforms upon which temples and palaces would be built. The city's layout placed the elite at the top and center, emphasizing their privileged relation to the gods and ancestors of the celestial realm.

The Zapotecs developed one of the earliest writing systems in the New World. They inscribed stone slabs in low relief to commemorate historical events and religious themes and set them into the facades of their buildings. The most famous of these are the so-called Danzantes (dancers) because of their contorted postures that provide the earliest evidence for the use of Mesoamerica's dual calendar. This chronological system, known as the Calendar Round, meshed a sacred cycle of 260 days with the 365-day solar year to create a fifty-two-year cycle, conceptually equivalent to a century. **PPN**

1 BALL COURT

Just off the southeast corner of the royal acropolis, Monte Albán's architects built an elegant ball court with an I-shaped plan and sloping interior walls. Several types of ball games were played in Mesoamerica and ball-playing was an important part of a ruler's ceremonial obligations.

2 SOUTH PLATFORM

The southern extreme of the Great Plaza is bounded by the South Platform. The two mounds on its summit are offset from its monumental central staircase. The base of the South Platform was faced with carved stones that display prisoners being brought before the ruler.

3 TEMPLES

The center of Monte Albán's Great Plaza is dominated by a composite building of three temples. An offering from the shrine of the central structure, Temple H, consisted of five ceramic jars inscribed with water glyphs, which suggests that water rituals were a primary theme of this complex.

ZAPOTEC WRITING

Although much of the Zapotec writing system has yet to be deciphered, from its inception around the middle of the first millennium BCE it appears to have been used to celebrate military prowess, first at San José Mogote and later at Monte Albán. Stelae 12 and 13 (500–400 BCE)—the earliest examples of writing at the hilltop city—were placed as the cornerstones of the first construction stage of Building L, a temple platform situated at the southwest corner of the site's main plaza. They are inscribed with vertical texts that contain dates, nouns, and verbs that seem to refer to the conquests of two rulers. The rest of Building L's facade was once embellished with row upon row of more than 300 stone slabs carved with captives who have been stripped naked and sacrificed. Many of the glyphs associated with these slain prisoners represent a date in the 260-day ritual calendar, and since in the Mesoamerican tradition a person was named for the day he or she was born, it is likely that these inscriptions provide the names of the victims.

▶

FIRST SOUTH AMERICAN CIVILIZATIONS

1 A painted relief mural of a human face with feline traits at Garagay, near Lima, Peru (*c.* 1200 BCE). The work shares many features related with the Chavín culture.

2 A relief sculpture of a warrior (*c.* 1600 BCE) at Cerro Sechín, northern Peru. The site, identified as an important area of the Casma/Sechin culture, was discovered in 1937.

3 A ceramic bottle in the shape of a feline head, found in the Jequetepeque Valley in northern Peru. Dated to between the fifteenth and ninth century BCE, it is a product of the Cupisnique culture, and was painted after the vessel was fired.

In pre-Hispanic South America, the term "civilization" refers to societies that produced aggregations of monumental buildings with some kind of recognizable architectural patterning. These settlements with an urban character were almost always linked to elaborate material cultures that might include stone sculptures and metal, ceramic, and textile artifacts. All of these are indicators of complex economies, political organizations, and ideologies.

In South America, most of these earliest civilizations are found in the modern state of Peru. That country's cultural predominance was first proposed in the archaeological literature of the 1950s, after Julian Steward (1902–72) defined the first centers of civilizations around the world. He argued that the Moche culture (*c.* 100 BCE–700 CE) of the north coast of Peru was among the earliest civilizations in the pre-Hispanic Andes. However, according to the definition of civilization stated above, the first ones in the Central Andes arose between the third and the first millennia BCE. Among others, they include the Caral, Sechín, Manchay, Cupisnique, and Chavín civilizations.

The civilization of Caral (2800–1800 BCE) is one of the earliest, and has been one of the most discussed by Andean specialists. Its discoverer, Ruth Shady (b. 1946), has compared Caral to other societies from around the world. She argues that Caral was the first Andean civilization, and the oldest in America. She believes that the city of Caral (see p. 212) was the capital of a pristine state in which the main forms of social cohesion were religion and the exchange of raw materials and artifacts. Subsequent research has indeed demonstrated

KEY EVENTS

c. 3000 BCE	*c.* 2600 BCE	2000 BCE	*c.* 1800 BCE	*c.* 1700 BCE	*c.* 1400 BCE
Several monumental buildings begin to be constructed in the Norte Chico region of northern Peru.	The first pyramidal buildings in Caral are built. Contemporary centers appear in the Supe valley.	Construction begins on the Sechín Alto site in the Casma valley.	Caral is abandoned by its builders. Pottery is first seen in La Florida, a temple of the Manchay culture.	U-shaped temples of the Manchay culture flourish in different valleys of the central coast of Peru.	The Cupisnique culture begins to build its main center of Huaca de los Reyes in the Moche valley.

that Caral was involved in an extensive economic and ritual network that included several communities on the coast and highlands.

Shelia and Thomas Pozorski argued that the political entity of Sechín Alto (c. 2000–1300 BCE) was developed in the rich archaeological valley of Casma, located on the north coast of Peru. Within this entity are the Sechín Alto architectural complex and the nearby sites of Pampa de las Llamas-Moxeque, Taukachi-Kon Kan, and Cerro Sechín. Together, these comprised an important concentration of buildings that, according to the Pozorskis, constituted the central capital of a state. Smaller buildings were organized around the monumental edifices of each of these sites. However, apart from sculptures in mud and stone located in some of the buildings (see image 2), the material culture is scarce, and no tombs have been found.

Contemporary with Sechín culture, during the second millennium BCE, an architectural tradition called the Manchay culture emerged on the central and north-central coast of Peru, between the Supe and Lurín valleys. It was characterized by the construction of large mud-and-stone buildings, erected to a U-shaped plan. In some cases, such as the site of Garagay in the Rímac valley in Lima, buildings were decorated with polychrome friezes and murals (see image 1). Also on the Peruvian north coast was the Cupisnique culture, which had among its main settlements the Caballo Muerto complex, located in the middle valley of Moche, near Trujillo city. This complex consisted of an extensive occupational area with monumental buildings; outstanding among these is Huaca de los Reyes, a U-shaped building decorated with friezes made of mud with anthropomorphic and feline motifs. Recent excavations in the archaeological site of Collud in the Lambayeque valley discovered a rectangular building decorated with polychrome friezes. The Cupisnique culture also developed its own distinctive ceramic tradition (see image 3).

However, among all these early, pre-Inca cultures in Peru, the Chavín culture most likely represents the first real civilization, given the monumentality of its constructions, especially in its homeland highland area. Chavín stone sculpture, used to decorate the walls of monuments, is equally impressive and suggests a complex organization of labor. The Chavín also produced exquisite pottery and sculpture, the quality and quantity of which were unlike that seen in earlier cultures. The culture's apogee in the Andean area began c. 800 BCE and extended up to 500 BCE; for its center it occupied the much older complex of Chavín de Huántar (1200–500 BCE; see p. 214). The impact of the Chavín culture was felt in different regions of the Andean world and several societies imitated or were influenced by its religion. Further, there is clear evidence that social groups deriving from the Manchay, Cupisnique, and Cajamarca cultures made contact at the Chavín de Huántar complex. After the collapse of Chavín culture, the Andean world generated new cults that preserved certain elements of Chavín culture that had found expression at Chavín de Huántar. **HT**

c. 1300 BCE	c. 1200 BCE	c. 1000 BCE	c. 800 BCE	c. 500 BCE	c. 200 BCE
The site of Sechín Alto begins to decline, but the coastal site of Las Haldas in the Casma valley becomes important.	The Chavín culture begins construction of monumental architecture at Chavín de Huántar.	Building of early monumental architecture in the Casma valley ends.	Chavín de Huántar reaches its apogee. The distinctive Janabarriu pottery of Chavín de Huántar appears and is imitated in different regions of the Andes.	Construction of monumental architecture in Chavín de Huántar ceases.	Societies with distinct regional identities flourish across the Andes.

Caral 3000 – 1800 BCE

Among the pyramidal buildings of Caral are architectural structures characterized by walls that enclose a central hearth with a ventilation duct. One such feature is the Altar of Sacred Fire, located in the Temple of the Amphitheater. At these altars, rituals would be performed with a small number of people around the central hearth.

The Norte Chico region on the north-central coast of Peru consists of a cluster of valleys formed by the Huaura, Supe, Pativilca, and Fortaleza rivers. About 70 miles (110 km.) north of Lima, the region is notable for containing a large accumulation of monumental archaeological sites, mostly built during the Late Pre-ceramic period (3000–1800 BCE). Of all the Norte Chico valleys, the Supe has received the most attention and archaeological investigation in the last two decades. Thanks to the work of the eminent Peruvian archaeologist Ruth Shady (b. 1946), the valley and especially its site of Caral have become well known. Caral is characterized by dense clusters of public buildings and is a key site in understanding the development of early societies.

Radiocarbon dating of Caral places it among the oldest expressions of monumental architecture in the central Andean region: buildings were constructed during the third millennium BCE. A series of platform structures built with stones and mud make up this settlement that, according to Shady, was probably the capital of an early state. The economic and political character of Caral society is currently much debated, but Caral and other settlements in the Norte Chico region are the product of a very early historical phenomenon in which a huge amount of labor was invested over several centuries.

The discovery at Caral of artifacts produced from exotic raw materials, some coming from areas as far away as the Amazon or the coast of present-day Ecuador, indicates that extensive exchange networks existed at that time. For example, spondylus shells at Caral are among resources also known to have been used in rituals at other distant early sites, such as Real Alto in present-day Ecuador. **HT**

HUMAN FIGURINE

About a hundred figurines made of unfired clay have been found within different architectural structures at Caral. They are anthropomorphic in character and are remarkable for the hairstyles and headdresses represented. Their function may have been related to propitiatory or fertility rituals.

SHICRA

Caral contains evidence of shicras, or bags made with cords of vegetable fiber, usually reeds. Shicras were used to transport and place the stones used at Caral and other Late Pre-ceramic sites. The use of shicras was common in much of the Norte Chico region and even extended to sites of the same period in northern Lima.

MONUMENTAL ARCHITECTURE IN THE NORTE CHICO REGION

The Great Temple at Caral is by no means the only large monument in the Norte Chico region. Indeed, the Supe valley alone contains many more settlements similar to Caral. Like the temple, they consist of pyramidal platforms with sunken circular courts. The buildings were all constructed in the same way, using stones and mud and employing shicra bags.

The well-known site of El Áspero, very close to the Peruvian coast and also built by the Caral culture, was scientifically excavated in the 1970s. More recent excavations by Ruth Shady's team confirm that there are architectural similarities with other sites farther up the Supe valley. This pattern supports Shady's hypothesis that a complex economic and political system existed in this valley. However, other sites in the valleys of the Norte Chico region that exhibit similar characteristics are of even greater antiquity than Caral itself. For example, at the sites of Bandurría, in the Huaura valley, and Caballete, in the Fortaleza valley, archaeologists obtained radiocarbon dates that precede the earliest dates of Caral by centuries. Yet, in addition, several of these valleys contain many sites contemporaneous with Caral.

Farther north, in the Casma valley, researchers have excavated buildings that share some architectural features with Caral but that are also several centuries earlier, having been begun c. 3500 BC. Clearly, more research is needed to establish an accurate timeline and explanation of the emergence of this great early phenomenon of monumental architecture in the valleys. Contradictions in the findings are currently generating a variety of hypotheses based on different economic, political, and ideological models of the cultures involved in the monuments' construction.

Chavín de Huántar 1200 – 500 BCE

Set in the main facade of the New Temple, the Black and White Portal is so called for its large cylindrical columns; the inner pair are made of black limestone, flanked by columns of white granite. On the column surfaces are carved winged anthropomorphic beings with features of falconlike birds.

Located at the upper end of the Conchucos valley in the northern highlands of Peru, in the Department of Ancash, the complex of Chavín de Huántar lies at an altitude of 10,350 feet (3150 m.) above sea level at the confluence of the Mosna and Wacheqsa rivers, two tributaries of the Marañón. Founded *c.* 1200 BCE, the site had a life of almost a millennium, and boasted a population of 3,000 inhabitants at its apogee. Impressive in its monumentality and antiquity, and above all its sculptural art in stone, it was investigated scientifically by Julio César Tello (1880 – 1947).

The complex's monumental area consists of a concentration of buildings made with stone and mud, among which stand large carved stone blocks. In addition, there are stone sculptures with complex designs inspired by animals such as felines, birds of prey and reptiles. Early investigators divided the site into the Old Temple and the New Temple, both of which are platform buildings that accumulated a great volume of stone, mud, and other archaeological remains over time. More recently, the architectural sequence of the construction phases has been detailed and dated more accurately. Outstanding features at Chavín de Huántar include the sunken circular plaza, the rectangular main square, the Black and White Portal, and galleries inside and below the buildings. A chamber inside the Old Temple contained the Lanzón, a statue of the central deity of the Chavín culture.

Chavín de Huántar was probably the center of a Pan-Andean religious cult whose leaders revealed "knowledge" about the natural and supernatural powers to elite visitors from far-ranging social groups. The acquisition of such knowledge was facilitated by the consumption of hallucinogenic plants that induced altered states of consciousness. **HT**

THE STELA RAIMONDI

Discovered by Italian scholar Antonio Raimondi (1826–90), this stone sculpture represents an anthropomorphic being with feline features and attributes related to snakes, holding a staff in each hand. In view of its morphology and iconography, it must have decorated an important wall of a main building in the site.

TELLO OBELISK

This replica of the obelisk discovered by Julio César Tello is over 8 feet (2.52 m.) high. The decorations on all four sides include a pair of complex zoomorphic beings, one male and one female, that have been related to the cayman. Many iconographic elements inspired by Andean plants and animals have been identified.

⏱ ARCHAEOLOGIST PROFILE

1880–1912

Julio César Tello was born in 1880 at Huarochirí in the highlands of the Department of Lima. In 1902, he entered the Faculty of Medicine of the National University of San Marcos in Lima. He graduated in 1908 with a thesis entitled "The Antiquity of Syphilis in Peru." In 1909, Tello obtained a scholarship to study anthropology at the University of Harvard, where he was trained by eminent intellectuals influenced by anthropologist Franz Uri Boas (1858–1942). He received his Master in Arts degree in 1911 and went on to travel through Europe in the years 1911 and 1912.

1913–30

Tello returned to Peru in 1913 and was appointed director of the archaeological section of Lima's National History Museum.

In 1919, he made an expedition to the Marañón river, where he conducted archaeological excavations at Chavín de Huántar. When Augusto Leguía was president of Peru, from 1919 to 1930, Tello developed a favorable political and academic platform from which to pursue his investigations. Between 1924 and 1930 he was the director of the Museum of Peruvian Archaeology.

1931–47

The Institute of Archaeological Investigations was created in 1931, and directed by Tello. Between 1942 and 1945, Tello carried out excavations at Pachacamac, an important archaeological site near Lima. From 1945, he directed Lima's National Museum of Archaeology, Anthropology and History until his death.

4 | The Iron Age and the Ancient World

1OOO BCE – 5OO CE

Iron technology was responsible for what can be regarded as the first industrial revolution, which transformed the productivity of labor. It also "democratized" war, putting cheap but effective weapons in the hands of ordinary citizens, thereby creating the basis for the city-state civilizations of Greece and Rome. Their empires had a huge impact on large swathes of the world, but many other regions—notably India and China—saw the flourishing of quite different civilizations.

THE AGE OF IRON

1 Iron sword and spearheads from the fifth century BCE.

2 A Roman bas-relief of the second century CE depicting blacksmiths at work.

3 Using iron for tools and weapons made quantities of bronze available for producing luxury objects. The bronze Vix krater dates to the late sixth century BCE.

Metallurgy has a long history. The first known objects made from native metals date to the ninth millennium BCE in Anatolia. Meteoric iron could be, and was, treated in the same ways as native metals. Iron ore smelting requires good control of the temperature and reduction conditions, and very high temperatures—above 2,800° F (1,540° C)—are needed to melt it. Achieving these was beyond the capabilities of the early metallurgists. Thus, the development of metallurgy in the Old World and the Americas concerned only other metals—gold, silver, copper, lead, and tin—around which a range of sophisticated technologies developed, practiced by experts and often managed by elites. The rarity of tin, required for making bronze, played a key part in determining the pattern of trade routes and the consequent expense restricted bronze use to important members of society.

In c. 1200 BCE, however, iron smelting began in West Asia. Iron ore needed to be reduced in a furnace at a high enough temperature to ensure that the slag melted and ran off, leaving the iron "bloom." A blown air supply, provided by bellows, enabled the fuel to burn. The resulting bloom was a mass of metallic iron still containing impurities from the fuel, which had to be driven out by forging (heating and hammering), leaving wrought iron, a soft, inferior metal that could not be hardened by heating. Carburization, however, transformed

KEY EVENTS

13th century BCE	12th century BCE	750 BCE	7th/6th century BCE	c. 500 BCE	500 BCE
The Hittite king Hattusilis III's letter to the Assyrian king Adad-nirari I discussing iron reflects the start of regular iron production in Anatolia.	A sideline of the copper industry in Cyprus is regular small-scale production of iron knives with ivory hilts attached with bronze rivets.	The Assyrian army uses iron helmets; those of the elite troops are inlaid with bronze decoration and there are simpler designs for ordinary soldiers.	Cast-iron production begins in the southern Chinese state of Wu, probably to eke out bronze supply for toolmaking.	Large-scale ironworking occurs at Meroë in the Sudan: slag and the remains of cylindrical furnaces attest to the scale of smelting operations.	The Nok of Nigeria begin ironworking, smelting iron ore at sites including Taruga, Samun Dukiya, and Do Dimi in cylindrical furnaces.

wrought iron into useful low-carbon steel by incorporating 0.5 to 1.5 percent carbon, generally by using charcoal as the smelting fuel. It was this development that made ironworking possible and worthwhile. Low-carbon steel was harder and stronger than bronze, and could take and keep an edge better; and its hardness could be varied by tempering. Skilled and nuanced ironworking developed thereafter—expert Celtic smiths, for example, produced swords with razor-sharp (hard but brittle) edges on softer, more elastic blades.

Once iron smelting and carburization had been developed, they spread rapidly, with iron becoming common in West Asia and Europe by *c.* 900 BCE. Ironworking also developed, perhaps independently, in sub-Saharan Africa in the later first millennium BCE and in India perhaps as early as 1300 BCE; and the technology was introduced into China by steppe nomads by the sixth century BCE. Ironworking was not, however, developed in the Americas.

The technology of smelting and working bloomery iron was relatively simple, requiring little specialist equipment: an easily constructed bowl furnace into which the iron and charcoal fuel are placed, and bellows to enable the temperature to be raised; tongs, hammer, and anvil to turn the bloom into usable wrought iron and work it into objects. Iron has the convenient property that pieces can be joined strongly by hammering them together (welding). The technology was therefore accessible to ordinary people with the necessary skills (see image 2) rather than being confined to specialists, stimulating the emergence of small-scale entrepreneurs, such as the itinerant smiths of Iron Age Europe. In addition, iron ores are abundant and ubiquitous. While some regions with substantial or high-quality ore sources became wealthy by trading in iron, most regions were able to obtain iron relatively locally and cheaply, altering the patterns of trade. Bronze supplies were now devoted to the production of luxury goods, such as fine jewelry, elite tableware (see image 3), and parade armor. Iron objects became common, metal tools, weapons (see image 1), and armor now within the reach of everyone. This had a considerable impact on the efficiency of many aspects of everyday life, such as agriculture, industry and construction, as well as warfare. Iron had advantages over bronze because it was harder, more durable, easy to repair, and easy to shape. It is thought that the advent of ironworking also had a democratizing effect, affecting social organization.

In China the path of development was different. While wrought iron was made there, the Chinese developed furnaces capable of achieving the temperature required to produce cast iron, using a powerful forced draft (blast furnace), something not achieved in the West until medieval times. This meant that they were able to mass-produce iron objects by casting in molds. Iron was produced on a large scale by elites, in large iron foundries. The development of ironworking, therefore, did not have the same social impact as elsewhere, although it enabled ordinary individuals to acquire metal tools. **JM**

c. 500 BCE	480–221 BCE	300 BCE	31 CE	1st century	1st millennium
The Chifumbaze complex in Africa starts ironworking, especially around Lake Victoria; sites such as Katuruka produce a type of steel.	China's increase in interstate warfare may be fueled by the mass-production of weaponry made possible by iron casting.	The Celts invent chain mail, made of interlocking, individually forged iron rings; a very labor-intensive and skilled activity.	Chinese prefect Du Shi introduces use of waterwheels to provide power for blowing machines (bellows) for blast furnaces.	Sri Lankans use horseshoe-shaped furnaces driven by induced draft, such as that at Dehigaha-ala-kanda near Sigiriya.	The Korean Kaya culture, in a region with high-quality iron ores, grows wealthy through smelting iron and producing tools and armor for export.

WEST ASIAN EMPIRES

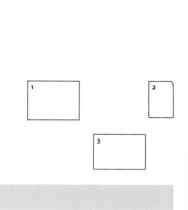

1 A clay cuneiform tablet with Babylonian astronomical text from Ashurbanipal's library at Nineveh. First excavated in the 1850s, it is the oldest surviving royal library in the world. The tablet records the daily motion of the planet Jupiter.

2 A stone relief dating from 716 to 713 BCE that was on the north wall of the palace of Assyrian king Sargon II at Dur Sharrukin. It shows a four-winged genie wearing richly patterned textiles with fringes and tassles. There was a prolific weaving industry in Assyria.

3 A stone relief from Ashurbanipal's palace at Nineveh. It shows an aqueduct and the terraced royal gardens of Sennacherib's Palace Without Rival at Nineveh, with its streams and exotic trees, probably the original of the Hanging Gardens attributed by the Greeks to Babylon.

During the twelfth century BCE, major climate changes brought widespread economic decline in eastern Mediterranean regions, with agricultural failure and famine, destructive migration, and the collapse of states, affecting the trade and stability of the Mesopotamian kingdoms farther east, including the rising state of Assyria. But by the late tenth century BCE, Assyria was recovering and expanding, particularly under Ashurnasirpal II (r. 883–859 BCE), who created a new capital at Kalhu (Nimrud, Iraq; see p. 222). Much of the Levant came under Assyrian rule, either as conquered kingdoms or as vassals paying tribute to gain Assyrian support against enemies. Ties were established between Assyria and Babylonia and maintained for nearly a century.

A late ninth-century BCE Assyrian decline saw revolts in the Levant, but Assyria regained its ascendancy under Tiglath-pileser III (r. 744–727 BCE). He created a professional army, supported by a communications network of roads, bridges, and royal messengers; reorganized the growing empire's administration into provinces; and deported huge numbers of defeated enemies to undermine opposition in their homelands and to undertake major projects such as the agricultural resettlement of underpopulated areas and the construction of the three great capital cities. The whole Levant came under Assyrian control under Tiglath-pileser and his successors, though there were frequent revolts (see p. 229), often incited by Egypt. These always ended in Assyrian victories, harsh reprisals, and the extraction of massive quantities of booty and tribute used to support and embellish the cities of Assyria,

KEY EVENTS

891 BCE	863 BCE	744 BCE	729 BCE	722 BCE	705 BCE
A treaty is agreed between Assyria and Babylonia, beginning an eighty-year peace between the two growing empires.	The Assyrian king Ashurnasirpal II inaugurates his new capital at Kalhu (Nimrud) with a ten-day banquet for 69,574 guests.	Tiglath-pileser III becomes Assyrian king, going on to expand the empire, create a professional army, and introduce an efficient administrative system.	Assyrian king Tiglath-pileser III, who supported Babylonia's legitimate rulers, defeats a Chaldaean usurper and takes the Babylonian throne.	Marduk-apla-iddina, a model king, unites the south to restore Babylonian independence, until finally defeated by Sargon II in 703 BCE.	Sargon II's death in battle and the loss of his body, indicating divine wrath, leads to abandonment of his new capital, Dur-Sharrukin (Khorsabad).

particularly the successive capitals Kalhu, Dur-Sharrukin (Khorsabad, Iraq), and Nineveh (see p. 224). Royal palaces and temples were decorated with paintings, sculptures, and reliefs. Their furnishings included textiles (see image 2), for which Mesopotamia had been famous for millennia, and fine objects, including glassware and ivories. Major works of hydraulic engineering were undertaken (see image 3) and some portions of Assyrian canals still survive in use today.

In 721 BCE, the Chaldaean sheikh Marduk-apla-iddina (d. c. 694 BCE) gained the Babylonian throne, opposing the Assyrians. War, interspersed with periods when Assyria ruled Babylonia, lasted until 648 BCE when the Assyrian king Ashurbanipal (r. 668–627 BCE) brought peace to the region. After his death, succession disputes undermined Assyria, which fell to the Babylonians and their allies the Medes in 612 BCE. The Babylonian empire, embracing all West Asia, prospered under Nebuchadnezzar II (c. 630–c. 562 BCE).

International trade flourished on a vast scale, contributing to the embellishment of Babylonia and its capital, Babylon (see p. 226) in modern Iraq. In 539 BCE, however, the rapidly expanding Persian Empire (see p. 258) conquered Babylonia. Despite the political change of control, Babylonian culture continued to flourish: the later Persian, Greek, and Roman societies of West Asia and its neighbors inherited a huge legacy from Mesopotamia that included advanced knowledge of astronomy, mathematics, medicine, military technology, pharmacology, and practical science, as well as a wealth of literature. For example, Babylonian astronomy (see image 1), though developed for the purpose of divination, encompassed a detailed knowledge of the movements and conjunctions of the sun, moon, stars, and planets, and their mathematics included positional notation and a forerunner of the concept of zero. **JM**

Nimrud 863–707 BCE and later

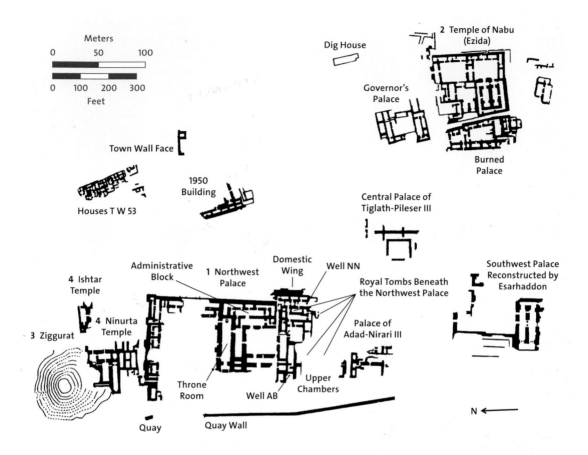

Meters
0   50   100

Feet
0   100   200   300

Dig House

2 Temple of Nabu (Ezida)

Governor's Palace

Burned Palace

Town Wall Face

1950 Building

Houses T W 53

Central Palace of Tiglath-Pileser III

Domestic Wing   Well NN

Administrative Block   1 Northwest Palace

Southwest Palace Reconstructed by Esarhaddon

4 Ishtar Temple

Royal Tombs Beneath the Northwest Palace

4 Ninurta Temple

Palace of Adad-Nirari III

3 Ziggurat

Throne Room   Well AB   Upper Chambers

Quay   Quay Wall

N ←

The citadel was surrounded by a wall, separating it from the rest of the city; on the western side this was part of the circuit wall of the city. Within this were successive kings' palaces, temples, and government buildings. Finds show that Nimrud was an important administrative and royal center long after the capital moved elsewhere after 707 BCE.

After its late second-millennium decline, the Assyrian Empire began to expand under Adad-nirari (r. 911–891 BCE) and his successors. Ashurnasirpal II founded a new capital for the growing empire, selecting the site of an existing administrative center strategically located on a tongue of land between the Tigris and the Great Zab. The construction of Kalhu (Nimrud, Iraq) took fifteen years. Ashurnasirpal inaugurated it in 863 BCE with a ten-day banquet for nearly 70,000 people: the food served included ten donkey-loads of shelled pistachios, 10,000 jars of beer, 14,000 sheep, and 10,000 gerbils. The city followed a standard plan, with a citadel accommodating palaces, administrative buildings, and temples, and a walled lower town. Nimrud's citadel occupied 49 acres (20 ha.) and the city 145 acres (360 ha.), while its surrounding wall was approximately 5 miles (7.5 km.) long. It remained the capital until 707 BCE.

Ashurnasirpal's successor, the energetic and successful Shalmaneser III (r. 858–824 BCE), built a separate palace complex, dubbed Fort Shalmaneser, in the southeast corner of the city. It included a magnificent palace, arsenal, parade ground, and treasury for the immense booty and tribute from conquered states. These were well excavated from 1949; the original citadel fared much worse, having been subjected to the plunderings and destruction wrought by nineteenth-century archaeologists, who focused on acquiring antiquities—especially relief carvings and inscribed clay tablets—for major sponsoring museums and other institutions, at the expense of knowledge of stratigraphy, context, and structural remains. Most recently, a fine Iraqi state team revealed the vaulted tombs of several Assyrian queens beneath the domestic quarters of the Northwest Palace. **JM**

FOCAL POINTS

1 NORTHWEST PALACE

This was the principal palace complex, built by Ashurnasirpal II. Stone panels with relief sculptures depicting the king's military and civic achievements decorated the walls of the courtyards and throne room. The entrance was flanked by colossal guardian sculptures of winged, man-headed lions and bulls. Beyond lay the *bitanu*, the domestic quarters of the palace; the administrative quarters were located in the northern part of the palace.

2 TEMPLE OF NABU

Nimrud's principal temple was dedicated to Nabu, son of the great god Marduk. Nabu was the god of writing and a particularly important deity in Assyria, where he was associated with Victory. Part of the temple's interior was laid out as a palace because it was intended for the private use of the god and his wife during important festivals. Treaties commissioned by King Esarhaddon (r. 680–669 BCE) were found here, guaranteeing his vassals would support his son Ashurbanipal's succession.

3 ZIGGURAT

Standing in the north of Nimrud, the ruins of a ziggurat dominated the citadel. It has been reported that the ziggurat was flattened in 2016 by extremists of ISIS using earth-moving equipment, along with other monuments at Nimrud. Before that event, the ziggurat's ashlar masonry survived only on its lowest stage; the rest consisted of its exposed mudbrick core alone.

4 NINURTA AND ISHTAR TEMPLES

Next to the ziggurat was a temple dedicated to the storm god Ninurta. Gypsum wall panel reliefs from that temple, held at the British Museum, London, show Ninurta with a thunderbolt in each hand, pursuing the winged monster Anzu. A temple to Ishtar, goddess of love and war, formed part of the same complex; its entrance was flanked by colossal stone sculptures of lions.

▲ After Kalhu ceased to be the capital, several of the palaces were used for storage. Large quantities of ivories were found here and in Fort Shalmaneser. This piece of furniture decoration shows a woman at a window; the sill is supported by palm columns.

NIMRUD QUEENS' TOMBS

Iraqi excavations from 1988 to 1990 unexpectedly uncovered four vaulted royal tombs beneath the floor of the Northwest Palace's domestic quarters. They contained terracotta or stone sarcophagi housing the royal dead, richly furnished with grave goods including magnificent jewelry made mainly of gold, often inlaid with gemstones, glass, or faience. These display exceptional skill in the goldsmith's craft, employing techniques such as granulation, cloisonné, and filigree to create crowns, necklaces, pendants, earrings, diadems, rings, and armlets with floral, figurative, and geometric designs. This gold diadem panel has a mosaic design of pale blue stone, carnelian, and gold, set in a lapis lazuli background; miniature pomegranates dangle from gold chains at its foot. Also accompanying the burials were vessels of terracotta, bronze, gold, silver, and rock crystal, and other priceless objects. One sarcophagus had two burials, identified by the inscribed objects buried with them as Yaba, wife of Tiglath-pileser III, and Atalia, queen of Sargon II. Another housed Mullissu-mukannishat-Ninua, who was Ashurnasirpal's wife.

Nineveh 707–612 BCE

Many reliefs in Assyrian palaces celebrate the king's successes in war or major achievements of civil engineering. A series in Ashurbanipal's palace depict the king's prowess hunting lions, a royal sport and duty since ancient times. The lions were kept specially in the royal park. These fine reliefs capture the drama of the confrontation between man and beast.

Nineveh was an ancient settlement in the Tigris valley, occupied since Neolithic times and, frequently, an important town in the region's long history. The Assyrian king Sargon II built himself a new capital, Dur-Sharrukin (Khorsabad, Iraq) in 713 to 707 BCE, but his ill-omened death in battle prompted his successor, Sennacherib, to abandon this city and transfer the capital to Nineveh. Nineveh remained the Assyrian capital until the empire fell in 612 BCE. Joint Iraqi-American excavations in 1987 to 1990 exposed dramatic evidence of the city's last hours: skeletons pierced by arrows and discarded weapons beneath the remains of a gateway destroyed by fire.

Nineveh was remembered in later ages and was a prize sought by early French and British archaeologists who began investigating Mesopotamia in the nineteenth century: both Khorsabad and Nimrud (ancient Kalhu) were mistakenly identified as Nineveh before British archaeologist Austen Henry Layard (1817–94) began his excavations in Kuyunjik mound in 1846. By the time of his second expedition from 1849 to 1851, advances in the decipherment of Akkadian cuneiform allowed inscribed material to be read and the mound identified as Nineveh's citadel, where Layard exposed magnificent reliefs (see p. 234) and sculptures of gigantic guardian figures within the palaces of Sennacherib and his grandson Ashurbanipal; he also recovered quantities of cuneiform tablets and other antiquities. The antiquity-hunting excavations were continued by others in the 1850s; a huge consignment of finds, dispatched toward the British Museum, was lost, along with other finds from the French excavations, when the transports were attacked on their way down the river. Work here continued during much of the period from 1870 to 1914; and further work was undertaken in the 1930s by British archaeologist Max Mallowan (1904–78), who revealed traces of the city's early history. Since the 1990s, Nineveh has suffered from looting and more recently from the violent attentions of ISIS. **JM**

RECONSTRUCTED SHAMASH GATE

When he moved the capital to Nineveh, Sennacherib constructed his Palace Without Rival on the northern citadel (Kuyunjik) as his royal residence and center of government and administration. A second citadel contained the arsenal. A massive wall with many well-fortified gates surrounded the city.

ASHURBANIPAL'S LIBRARY

Ashurbanipal employed scholars to search out and copy every extant literary work from his realms, amassing over 1,500 cuneiform texts. These included epic literature; historical works; scholarly compendia of astronomical, medical, pharmacological, and technological knowledge; religious works; dictionaries; and "wisdom literature."

HYDRAULIC ENGINEERING AND SENNACHERIB'S GARDENS

From early times the Mesopotamians had been masters of hydraulic engineering, employing irrigation for agriculture by the sixth millennium BCE and by the third constructing sophisticated networks of canals, with weirs, dams, and regulators, to irrigate their crops and control river flooding. The Assyrians brought this expertise to a new peak. Ashurnasirpal constructed the Patti-hegali canal from the Great Zab to water the area surrounding his new capital at Kalhu, creating orchards and gardens: its channel included a rock-cut tunnel. Sennacherib was even more ambitious: he constructed a canal that ran for more than 30 miles (50 km.) from Bavian in the Zagros Mountains to Nineveh. Its course included the Jerwan aqueduct, weirs, dams, and tunnels, and he used it to supply the city and furnish its surrounding lands with water for irrigation and created an artificial marsh, stocked with deer, wild boar, fish, and waterfowl, and gardens including a royal pleasure park. This was built on tiered terraces, with a pillared pavilion at the top and streams flowing through it, and was stocked with exotic trees and plants, including spices and cotton. To carry water to the gardens' summit, Sennacherib describes a device similar to the Archimedes screw but anticipating Archimedes (c. 287–c. 212 BCE) by centuries: probably a bronze spiral inside a bronze cylinder, whose rotation drew up the water from a reservoir to empty at a higher level. The British Assyriologist Stephanie Dalley (b. 1943) has argued convincingly that Sennacherib's park (see p. 221) was what the Greeks described as the Hanging Gardens, mistakenly locating these in Babylon (see p. 226), since they often confused Assyrians with Babylonians. Assyrian hydraulic engineering was not only used for benign purposes: when Sennacherib wreaked vengeance on Babylon for its repeated attempts to shake off the Assyrian yoke, he completed its sack by diverting a branch of the Euphrates to flood and devastate the city.

Babylon 612–539 BCE and later

The chief event of the Babylonian year was the twelve-day Akitu New Year festival, held at the spring equinox. A procession bore the statues of Marduk and other gods from Marduk's temple in the city's heart through the Ishtar Gate and along the Processional Way to the Akitu temple north of the city.

◆ NAVIGATOR

Colored by hostile Biblical descriptions, Babylon was portrayed as the epitome of decadence and oppression, though the Greeks attested to its magnificent cultural legacy. So when early archaeologists approached the city in the nineteenth century, it was with considerable interest. They were disappointed. Babylon was built mainly of mud brick, unspectacular and hard to detect. They abandoned Babylon and southern sites in favor of the splendors of the Assyrian north. Things changed when German archaeologist Robert Koldewey (1855–1925) began work here. His excavations between 1899 and 1917 exposed the city's layout and identified its royal palaces, massive city walls and gates, temples, and the Processional Way. This was the city refurbished and extended by the first Neo-Babylonian king, Nabopolassar (c. 658–605 BCE), and his son, Nebuchadnezzar II, who presided over the early days and finest flowering of the Neo-Babylonian Empire. Koldewey cut a deep sounding to investigate earlier periods but the high water table prevented him reaching the levels belonging to Babylon's first great king, Hammurabi (r. 1792–1750 BCE). The glazed bricks that made up the Ishtar Gate, Processional Way walls, and Nebuchadnezzar's throne-room facade were shipped to Berlin, where these were rebuilt and still stand in the Pergamon Museum (above). In the 1980s, Saddam Hussein (1937–2006) had a replica of the Ishtar Gate erected at Babylon and restored some of the city.

After the Babylonian Empire fell to Persia, Babylon retained its position as a major city for many centuries, under Persian, Hellenistic, and Seleucid rule, dwindling in importance under the Parthians, and was gradually abandoned in Sasanian times. **JM**

⊙ FOCAL POINTS

1 DIVINE SYMBOLS

The Ishtar Gate was the most potent symbol of Babylon's magnificence. It was decorated with bulls, representing the storm god Adad, and dragons (*mushussu*), the magically protective creature sacred to Babylon's patron god Marduk, which combined a lion's forelimbs, an eagle's legs for hindlimbs, horns, and a snake's head, body, and tail. Lions, sacred to the goddess Ishtar in her aspect as goddess of war, decorated the walls that flanked the Processional Way.

2 GLAZED BRICK DESIGNS

The Mesopotamians were skilled workers in vitreous materials. They made faience from the fifth millennium BCE; developed glass and were manufacturing it in quantity by 1600 BCE; and rapidly solved the technological problems involved in bonding glass to baked clay, enabling them to make glazed pottery, tiles and bricks. The designs built from glazed bricks decorating Babylon's Ishtar Gate and Processional Way are among their finest works.

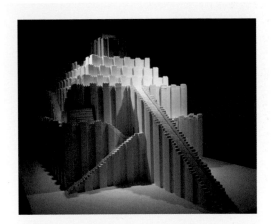

ETEMENANKI ZIGGURAT

Marduk was the principal Babylonian deity by the late second millennium BCE. His temple, Esagila, was at the city's heart; destroyed by the Assyrian king Sennacherib, it was rebuilt and embellished by Nebuchadnezzar II. Immediately to its north was the walled precinct containing the ziggurat Etemenanki, a probable inspiration for the biblical story of the Tower of Babel. It had seven tiers, each painted a different color. Built over the remains of Hammurabi's earlier ziggurat, it was founded by Nabopolassar, on divine instructions delivered in a dream, and completed by Nebuchadnezzar. The roof of the shrine on the uppermost level, accessed by an internal stair, may have been used for astronomical observation.

◄ West of the Ishtar Gate on the banks of the Euphrates lay the main palace complex; the southern palace was within the inner city, the northern palace outside, with gardens between them. This magnificent frieze of glazed bricks decorated the throne room in the southern palace—its thick baked brick walls were covered with wooden paneling, ornamented with precious metals, ivory, and gemstones.

IRON AGE WEST ASIA

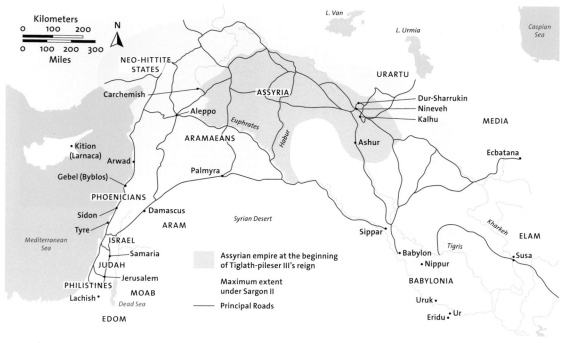

Kilometers
0 100 200

0 100 200 300
Miles

L. Van

L. Urmia

Caspian Sea

NEO-HITTITE STATES

Carchemish

ASSYRIA

URARTU

Dur-Sharrukin
Nineveh
Kalhu

Aleppo

Euphrates

MEDIA

ARAMAEANS

Habur

Ashur

Ecbatana

Kition (Larnaca)

Arwad

Palmyra

Gebel (Byblos)

PHOENICIANS

Sidon

Damascus

Syrian Desert

Kharkeh

ELAM

Tyre

ARAM

Sippar

ISRAEL

Mediterranean Sea

Samaria

Tigris

JUDAH

Jerusalem

Babylon
Nippur

Susa

PHILISTINES

MOAB

BABYLONIA

Lachish

Dead Sea

Uruk

EDOM

Eridu Ur

Assyrian empire at the beginning of Tiglath-pileser III's reign

Maximum extent under Sargon II

— Principal Roads

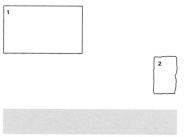

1 The Assyrian Empire grew in the eighth century BCE from a modest state in northern Iraq to dominate all West Asia.

2 An Aramean bas-relief of a dromedary and rider excavated in Syria at the site of Gozan (modern Tell Halaf), which was conquered by the Assyrians in the late ninth century BCE.

After the fall of the Hittite Empire in *c.* 1200 BCE, small independent city-states emerged in eastern Anatolia and northern Syria, often founding new towns and cities. Initially Carchemish was the most powerful. They continued to use the Hittite hieroglyphic script and Hittite styles of art and architecture, exemplified by the many relief sculptures with which they decorated their palaces. Interspersed with these Neo-Hittite states in northern Syria and spread over the regions to the east and south were other small states whose rulers had an Aramean tribal background: most powerful of these was Aram, with its capital at Damascus. By the late seventh century BCE, the Neo-Hittite states and many of their Aramean neighbors had been conquered by the Assyrians and Neo-Hittite culture died out.

Expansionist Assyrian kings from the late tenth to late ninth centuries BCE brought much of the Levant either under Assyrian rule or enticed or cowed into vassalage. A period of Assyrian retrenchment gave the states of western West Asia breathing space, but the accession of Tiglath-pileser III in 744 BCE saw the beginning of renewed Assyrian expansion, culminating under Esarhaddon (r. 680–669 BCE) in an empire that controlled all West Asia and part of Egypt. An Assyrian king's death was often seen as an opportunity for subject states

KEY EVENTS

c. 1000 BCE	*c.* 1000 BCE	9th century BCE	9th century BCE	887–856 BCE	853 BCE
Dromedaries, domesticated earlier for meat and milk, begin to be ridden, opening up the Syrian-Arabian desert for trade routes.	Twelve tribes of Israel are united under King David into the United Monarchy; this splits into the kingdoms of Israel and Judah in 931 BCE.	The Phoenician city-state of Tyre in Levant grows in power and establishes colonies to obtain raw materials, including Carthage.	The Phoenician alphabet (developed from the Canaanite alphabet) spreads through West Asia, reaching Greece by the eighth century BCE.	Ithobaal I of Tyre reigns. He takes control of Sidon and southern Phoenicia; this United Kingdom of Canaan endures until *c.* 700.	A coalition of Levant states, led by Aram-Damascus, and including Egyptians and Arabs, hold off the Assyrians at the Battle of Karkar.

to rebel. However, the Assyrians always regained the upper hand eventually and their vengeance was notorious, with leaders killed, cities sacked, and thousands deported to other parts of the empire (see p. 234).

The central coastal region was occupied by Phoenician city-states (see p. 230). Seafaring traders, the Phoenicians began to establish colonies through the southern Mediterranean, of which Carthage was the most important. Skilled in shipbuilding, navigation, naval warfare, civil engineering, and many crafts, they were often employed by other states. Their seaborne trade made them useful to the Assyrians, who treated them less harshly than other rebellious subject nations. Early users of the twenty-two-letter Canaanite alphabet that developed in the second millennium BCE, they helped to disseminate this writing system; it was also spread by Aramean deportees employed as clerks in the Assyrian Empire, rendering their Aramaic language, which became the lingua franca of West Asia under the Persian Empire, replacing Akkadian.

The Aramean states had strong links with Aramean pastoralist groups who exploited the desert fringes, frequently harrying their settled neighbors, such as the Babylonians. Pastoralism played an important part in the mixed economies of Transjordania's small kingdoms, along with agriculture, including the production of wine and olive oil. Israelites lived here and farther west, while on the southern coast and adjacent inland region were the five city-states of the Philistines, probably descendants of twelfth-century migrant settlers. In c. 1000 BCE, King David defeated the Philistines and united the twelve tribes of Israel into the United Monarchy, establishing its capital at Jerusalem (see p. 232), which he and his son Solomon fortified, expanded, and embellished. International trade flourished under Solomon, who worked closely with the Phoenicians. After his death, the United Monarchy split in 931 BCE into a northern kingdom, Israel, and a southern kingdom, Judah, between which there was often hostility.

In c. 1000 BCE, the use of the domestic camel (see image 2) for riding opened up the interior of the desert regions that lay between the Levant and Mesopotamia; and more importantly that of Arabia, where caravan trade began to develop along routes on the eastern side of the Yemeni mountains. This linked the incense producers of southwest Arabia with markets in West Asia and provided a lucrative livelihood for the camel-keeping Arab pastoralists who plied these routes. Southwest Arabia had a long history of sophisticated water-control systems for agriculture. In the first millennium, these were developed to a new level, supporting the emergence of states, particularly Sab'a (Sheba; see p. 236), famed for its trade contacts with Solomon. By the sixth century, Babylonia was heavily involved in the Arab caravan trade: the last king, Nabonidus, who reigned from 555 until 539 BCE, spent ten years in Tayma, an oasis from which Babylonia maintained its trade links with Arabia. His absence may have contributed to his state's fall to the Persians. **JM**

743 BCE	c. 685 BCE	599–96 BCE	587 BCE	572 BCE	539 BCE
The Assyrian victory over allied northern states at the Battle of Kummuh begins their conquest of northern Levant and domination of regions to the south.	King Sennacherib (r. 704–681 BCE) receives gifts from Karibilu, king of Saba' (probably Karib'il Watar under whose rule Saba' becomes dominant).	A Phoenician naval expedition sponsored by the Egyptian king Necho II (r. 610–595 BCE) sets out from the Red Sea and reputedly circumnavigates Africa.	Following an unsuccessful revolt and a siege, Jerusalem is sacked and Judah falls to Babylonians; 4,600 Judeans are deported to Babylonia.	The Babylonian sacking of Tyre after a thirteen-year siege undermines Phoenician participation in Mediterranean trade. Carthage becomes independent.	The Persian king Cyrus (c. 600–c. 530 BCE) conquers the Babylonian Empire; he allows the exiled Judeans to return home.

Phoenician Trading *c.* 1100 – *c.* 400 BCE

This relief, from the bronze Balawat Gates (*c.* 845 BCE), was commissioned by the Assyrian king Shalmaneser III and shows citizens of Tyre bringing tribute to him after his campaign in the region in 858 BCE. The Tyrians load their ships with the tribute and row from their island city to the mainland, where they join the procession of tribute bearers.

The widespread disruptions of the twelfth century BCE (see p. 220) saw the downfall of Ugarit (Ras Shamra) in Syria, one of the Levant's principal trading states, but soon other coastal city-states began to rise up and assert themselves. Known from this time as the Phoenicians—from the Greek *phoinix* (red), referencing the highly prized dye, Tyrian purple, that they extracted from murex marine mollusks—they were probably descendants of coastal Canaanites. They, however, identified themselves as citizens of separate independent city-states: these included Sidon and Arwad in Syria, and Gebel (Byblos) and Tyre in Lebanon; the latter, Tyre, was pre-eminent in the earlier first millennium BCE.

Since coastal agricultural land was limited, the Phoenicians obtained much of their grain, olive oil, and other necessities from their neighbors, trading their fine craft products and timber, particularly cedar, from the adjacent mountains. Phoenicians were often employed as craftspeople, pilots, or sailors by foreign powers, who also hired their ships. They established trade routes right through the Mediterranean, founding colonies from Kition (Larnaca) in Cyprus to Gadir (Cádiz) in Spain beyond the Straits of Gibraltar to obtain valued raw materials. Fine shipbuilders, seafarers, and navigators, the Phoenicians were in the forefront of naval design and maritime engineering.

The Assyrians brought most of the Phoenician city-states within their empire; Tyre remained independent but paid massive tribute and latterly operated under severe restrictions. Their Babylonian successors, however, sacked Tyre, effectively destroying the Phoenicians' role in Mediterranean trade. Phoenicians enjoyed renewed prosperity within the Persian Empire (see p. 258), particularly Sidon, but the international situation had changed irrevocably. Mediterranean sea trade was now being controlled by Greeks and Tyre's former colony, Carthage, was now a major power (see p. 284). **JM**

✦ NAVIGATOR

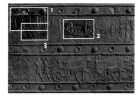

👁 FOCAL POINTS

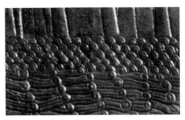

1 CITY OF TYRE

Tyre had defensive walls with towers. The lower town contained residential, industrial, and commercial quarters and the upper town had administrative buildings, temples, and elite housing. The temple to Melqart, with its twin pillars, dominated the city.

2 WATERCRAFT

These ships are *hippoi* (horses), small vessels for coastal or river transport. Another relief shows them carrying and towing timber. Bigger merchant ships propelled by sails undertook longer journeys at sea, carrying large cargoes.

3 ISLAND

Tyre enjoyed a defensible island location but its mainland territory was narrow. According to the Bible, when Hiram of Tyre (r. 971–939 BCE) did building work for King Solomon, he demanded twenty Galilean cities in his fee, giving Tyre farmland.

◄ The Phoenicians were famed craftspeople, using materials they imported and those they produced themselves, such as glass, faience, textiles, gold jewelry, and Tyrian purple dye. Their products, such as ivories and carved or mold-cast glass objects, were widely circulated in West Asia and beyond. The distinctive Phoenician art style was strongly influenced by Egypt, its motifs including sphinxes and lotus flowers. Metalwork, in copper, bronze, silver, and gold, included bowls with delicate hammered low-relief designs.

SAILORS AND COLONISTS

The Phoenicians sailed as far as the Atlantic to obtain new sources of metal ores and other materials, abandoning coast-hopping routes and making direct latitude crossings using the Pole Star for directional navigation. They established coastal trading colonies in Sicily, Sardinia, southern Spain, and north and northwest Africa. Colonization may have begun as early as 1110 BCE, the traditional date for Tyre's founding of Gadir (Cádiz) on the Spanish Atlantic coast. Archaeological evidence here dates to at least the eighth century. Gadir gave access to the metals of the Rio Tinto mines: copper, gold, and abundant silver. Colonies engaged in agriculture and industry.

Jerusalem Tenth – sixth centuries BCE

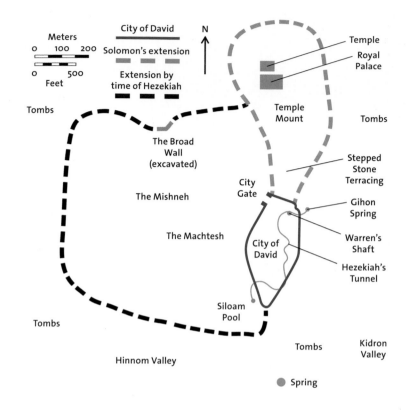

Meters
0   100   200
0   500
Feet

City of David
Solomon's extension
Extension by time of Hezekiah

N

Temple
Royal Palace

Temple Mount

Tombs

Tombs

The Broad Wall (excavated)

Stepped Stone Terracing

Gihon Spring

City Gate

The Mishneh

Warren's Shaft

The Machtesh

City of David

Hezekiah's Tunnel

Siloam Pool

Tombs

Tombs

Kidron Valley

Hinnom Valley

● Spring

Jerusalem was located on trade and communications routes. It commanded the fertile Kidron Valley, with a water supply from the Gihon Spring. Another spring, in the Hinnom Valley below the city, supplied water to irrigate fields. The city was built on a defensible ridge west of the Kidron Valley; by the 8th century, occupation had spread to the western hill.

According to the Bible, when David became king of the united tribes of Israel in the tenth century BCE, he selected for his capital a site in neutral territory. A small town, Jebus, already existed here: its Jebusite inhabitants were swiftly overcome by David's army, but remained in the city he then created. His son Solomon continued his building work, expanding the city within the fortifications from about 15 to 37 acres (6–15 ha.), taking in the higher upper part of the ridge. A royal palace was constructed here, and on the ridge's highest point the Temple. Work was then undertaken by the Phoenician king Hiram of Tyre, who reigned from 971 to 939 BCE. The Phoenicians supplied the required raw materials, cedar, and other timber from their own mountains and precious materials acquired through trade; renowned craftspeople in wood, ivory, and glass, they furnished the skills needed to construct and decorate the buildings.

After the kingdoms divided in 931 BCE, Jerusalem became the capital of Judah. When the Assyrians conquered Israel and destroyed its capital Samaria in 722 to 721 BCE, many of its inhabitants fled to Jerusalem, where King Hezekiah (r. 727–698 BCE) extended the city walls to defend the western area in which these refugees settled. When Hezekiah himself revolted against the Assyrians, he strengthened the city's defenses, constructing a tunnel from the external Gihon Spring to give the city a protected water supply: Jerusalem did not fall when Sennacherib (r. 704–681 BCE) besieged it in 701 BCE. It was, however, sacked by the Babylonians in 587 BCE. Some fifty years later, the Persian king Cyrus, having conquered the Babylonians, allowed Jerusalem's exiled citizens to return and rebuild.

Excavations in Jerusalem began in 1864 and many have taken place since then. These have exposed portions of the fortification walls, areas of housing, and aspects of the water supply; some burned remains, and many iron and bronze arrowheads, bear witness to the Babylonian sacking of the city. **JM**

SILOAM POOL

The Gihon Spring lay outside the city, but an undated early tunnel, Warren's Shaft, gave access to a natural shaft through which its waters could be drawn up 40 feet (12 m.). Hezekiah commissioned a rock-cut tunnel, 1,600 feet (500 m.) long and 6 feet (1.8 m.) high, with a channel that carried the waters of the spring to a reservoir, the Siloam Pool, within the city walls, a remarkable feat of engineering.

ARTIFICIAL HILLSIDE

Land on the ridge summit was increased, probably in the late second millennium BCE, by constructing artificial terraces on the northeast slope. Parallel and cross-walls were built and filled with rubble, creating the foundations for the stepped terraces, which were rebuilt by Solomon and reinforced by Hezekiah. Houses were built on them when the city expanded in the seventh century.

SOLOMON'S TEMPLE

Chief among the buildings that Solomon commissioned from Hiram, king of Tyre, was the Temple; it was destroyed by the Babylonians in 587 BCE. Though constructed under Solomon over a seven-year period, the Temple had been planned in detail by David. It was built to house the most sacred object in the worship of Jehovah, the Ark of the Covenant, a chest containing the Tablets of the Law. Set on a podium of ashlar masonry and built of limestone, it was a rectangular building 50 feet (15 m.) high. Its porch led into a hall from which steps led up to the Holy of Holies—an inner sanctum that measured 30 feet (9 m.) in each direction and that housed the Ark. It was roofed with cedar of Lebanon, which was also used to panel the interior; its doors were of olive wood. All within was coated in gold and decorated with gemstones and glass. A lower three-story building containing storerooms wrapped around the sides and rear: this served as the national treasury. In front of the Temple stood two pillars called Boaz and Yachin, their capitals decorated with copper. An eighth-century inscribed ivory pomegranate, perhaps from a priest's staff, is the only known surviving relic of the Temple. Situated on the Temple Mount, a sacred place, the Temple's possible remains cannot be excavated, so archaeologists are reliant on the Bible for information about it. Some of the features mentioned, such as the tripartite plan and associated cultic artifacts, are paralleled by excavated temples of this period. For example, the bases of a pair of freestanding pillars flank the entrance to the small Israelite shrine at Arad and similar pillars are known from earlier temples. Horned altars for burning incense have been found in a number of temples, including at Megiddo and Beersheba.

Siege of Lachish 701 BCE

Siege engines assisted the Assyrians to take walled cities. This relief shows bricks from Lachish's walls being gouged out by powerful spears mounted on wheeled rams of wood and leather. The defenders throw torches, hoping to ignite them, but the Assyrians constantly douse them in water to keep them damply fireproof.

⬦ NAVIGATOR

Between 1849 and 1851, British archaeologist Austen Henry Layard (1817–94) conducted excavations at the Assyrians' final capital, Nineveh, Iraq (see p. 224), funded by the British Museum. Tunneling along the line of its walls, he focused on exposing reliefs in the palace of Sennacherib (r. 704–681 BCE). An important sequence of reliefs running around one room narrated the king's siege of a rebellious city, labeled as 'Lakisu (Lachish): an exciting discovery, since the Siege of Lachish was already known from the Bible. When Sennacherib's predecessor, Sargon II, died in 705 BCE, a number of Assyria's vassal states, supported by Egypt, seized the opportunity to rebel—among these was Judah. Sennacherib mounted a punitive expedition in 701 BCE. Having driven back the Egyptian forces from the south coastal region, he turned inland and besieged Judah's second city, Lachish. Employing prisoners of war as builders, the Assyrians constructed a ramp so they could attack the weaker upper portion of the walls with their siege engines. As both biblical accounts and the reliefs narrate, Lachish's citizens put up a brave defense but the city fell to the might of Assyrian arms. The relief's centerpiece, visible from the room's main entrance on the opposite wall, shows Sennacherib seated on his throne surveying booty and captives paraded before him. Behind him is the Assyrian camp. This sequence, like other reliefs, served a propagandist purpose: emphasizing Assyrian might, and the terrible fate that awaited those who rebelled against their Assyrian rulers. **JM**

1 THE ASSYRIAN ARMY

The Assyrian army was a professional, highly competent force. In the first rank are the shock troops of the infantry, armed with spears and round shields. Behind them are massed the artillery, archers, and slingers hurling slingstones. All are protected by pointed iron helmets and iron-scale body armor.

2 VICTIMS OF DEFEAT

Lachish has begun to fall. Prisoners emerge from a city gate. They are beginning the long walk into exile. From Sennacherib's time onward, kings treated prisoners of war like other booty, distributing them as slaves. However, the leaders held responsible for the rebellion were executed, often after torture.

3 THE SPOILS OF WAR

A procession wends its way across the landscape: soldiers laden with booty, including furniture, and prisoners leading laden camels, donkeys, or bullock carts. Some carry their children; others are luckier and have a place on a cart. The captive Judaean men are distinctively dressed in caps with earflaps.

EXCAVATING TELL ED-DUWEIR

From 1973 to 1987, a team from Tel Aviv University led by Israeli archaeologist David Ussishkin (b. 1935) excavated the site of ancient Lachish at Tell ed-Duweir, Israel, revealing not only the remains of a large fortified city but also evidence of the siege itself. The city was built on a mound, surrounded by deep wadis on most sides but vulnerable to attack from the southwest, where an access road ran up to the city gate. The Assyrians built their siege ramp here: this was revealed in the excavation. It was constructed of boulders covered by a layer of pebbles set hard in mortar. An enormous quantity of discarded weaponry was found here, particularly at the breach the Assyrians made in the wall, including bone and iron arrowheads and slingstones. On the inner side of the wall, Ussishkin discovered a counter ramp hurriedly constructed by the defenders to protect the wall, but in vain.

Marib c. 700 BCE – 610 CE

A watercourse, the Wadi Dhana, flows down from the Yemeni mountains into Arabia's central desert, collecting run-off from mountain valleys fed by the monsoon rainfall. The ancient Marib Dam was constructed to break the torrent's force and divert its waters, irrigating an area of about 40 square miles (100 sq. km.).

✦ NAVIGATOR

Early farming settlements in southwest Arabia were established in the highland plateaux, cultivating hillside terraced fields, and in the lowlands around wadis and oases. Two annual monsoons brought heavy but short-lived rainfall, necessitating the early development of water-management techniques. Lowland settlement and interregional contact increased in the early first millennium BCE, when small states appeared in this area. These included centrally located Saba' (Sheba), which gained control of most of the region in the seventh century BCE. Three other major states—Hadramawt in the south, Qataban, and Ma'in farther north—had developed and broken away from Saba' by the late fourth century BCE. The early first millennium BCE also saw the development of a lucrative incense trade route linking southwest Arabia with West Asia. Sources there associate Saba' with Dedan, a north Arabian oasis and trading station.

The Sabean capital Marib (in modern Yemen), established in the oasis fed by the Wadi Dhana, was the largest city in southwest Arabia, its stone walls enclosing an area of about 300 acres (120 ha.). Its ruins were discovered in 1843 by French pharmacist Joseph Arnaud (1812–84), who copied many inscriptions. Though later expeditions investigated many sites, Marib was not excavated until the 1980s, by the German Archaeological Institute in Sana'a. Inscriptions refer to a royal palace in the city but this was not located. Beyond the city lay gardens and two temples dedicated to the Sabean national god, Almaqah: one, the Awwan Temple, whose courtyard has monolithic limestone pillars at its entrance, was excavated from 1951 to 1952 by a U.S. team. Marib's most impressive remains, 4 miles (7 km.) upstream from the city, are the ruins of the Marib Dam, built c. 700 BCE to break the torrential seasonal flow of the Wadi Dhana and divert its waters into irrigation channels and small reservoirs constructed across the surrounding land. **JM**

⦿ FOCAL POINTS

1 LANDSCAPE AND WATER MANAGEMENT

From the third millennium BCE, the people of this region erected small earthen dams across the Wadi Dhana, diverting its waters into networks of irrigation channels. Water management for agriculture had a long history in southwest Arabia, with hillside terracing being constructed as early as 3800 BCE and check-dams to slow flood waters by 4500 BCE.

2 CONSTRUCTION

Initially, the dam was built using walls of closely fitted limestone blocks with a rubble-filled interior. Later construction changed to a solid, highly waterproof stone and cement core bonded to an outer stone facing by stone cross-beams, whose ends protruded from the walls. The dam built up as silt raised the ground level, eventually became too high and difficult to maintain.

3 MARIB DAM

The silt deposited annually by the river constantly raised the level of the land, making it necessary to build dams ever higher upstream. To achieve greater permanence, in *c.* 700 BCE the small earthen dams were superseded by the Marib Dam, a stone barrage with sluices, 1,950 feet (600 m.) long. This survived in use until 610 CE, when it was abandoned.

◄ The consonant-only alphabetic script invented in second-millennium BCE Levant was rapidly adopted and modified to write southwest Arabia's South Semitic languages: inscriptions are known by the eighth century BCE. The South Arabian script had twenty-nine letters (more than the related twenty-two letter Phoenician script from which most later alphabets developed). Stone inscriptions abound in western Arabia, where by the mid first millennium BCE almost everyone was literate.

TRADE IN INCENSE

Incense was important in the ancient Middle East, for making medicines, aromatics and cosmetics, and to burn in religious ceremonies. Frankincense was especially esteemed: the Egyptians obtained it in the second millennium BCE by voyaging through the Red Sea to Punt (probably Eritrea). The development of camel riding by 1000 BCE transformed the trade, making it possible to travel north to south through the desert fringes east of Arabia's western mountains. This route created an overland link between the frankincense producers of southwest Arabia and consumers in West Asia, via the oases of northwest Arabia—Tayma, Duma and Dedan. Though Saba' and other states of southwest Arabia depended on agriculture, the incense trade contributed to their prosperity.

CLASSICAL GREECE

1 This bronze statue of a figure in a crested Corinthian helmet and a closely fitting cloak dates to 510–500 BCE and is thought to depict a Spartan warrior.

2 A Persian bronze conical helmet from the loot after the Battle of Marathon in 490 BCE. The Greeks added an inscription on the rim that dedicates the booty to the god Zeus.

3 The ruins of the *tholos*, once a circular building, in the agora beneath the northwest slope of the Acropolis in Athens, Greece.

The classical Greek world comprised a series of independent city-states, or poleis, with a shared Hellenic cultural identity. In the fifth century BCE there was domination by major cities such as Athens, Thebes in Boeotia, Corinth, and Sparta. The Greek world included the colonies that had been sent out from the eighth century BCE onward. By the fifth century BCE, there were Greek settlements around the shores of the Black Sea, in Cyrenaica (modern Libya), southern Italy and Sicily, the south of France, and parts of southern Spain. The Greek trading port, or *emporion*, of Naukratis in the Nile Delta continued to provide access to the riches to Egypt.

One of the key events was the invasion of the Greek mainland by a Persian army in 480 BCE. An attempt by a largely Spartan (see image 1) force to hinder their progress was destroyed at the mountain pass of Thermopylae. The Persian force reached Athens, destroyed the city and removed some of the sculptures back to Persia. An Athenian naval force defeated the Persian navy off the island of Salamis, close to Athens, and a combined Hellenic army crushed the Persian army at the Battle of Plataea. These victories were commemorated in the Greek world in monuments such as the tripod at Delphi, and the developing iconography in which barbarians—represented by centaurs, giants, and Amazons—were defeated by Greeks. Some Persian armor was dedicated in the sanctuary at Olympia (see image 2). More significantly, Athens (see p. 244)

(see p. 244)

KEY EVENTS

10th century BCE	9th century BCE	8th century BCE	776 BCE	490 BCE	480 BCE
Cult practice is first carried out at the Sanctuary of Zeus at Olympia.	The Spartan sanctuary of Artemis Orthia is established.	The first votive offerings to Apollo are carried out at Delphi.	The first Olympic Games is held.	The Athenians repulse the first Persian invasion of Greece at the Battle of Marathon.	The Greek mainland is invaded by a Persian army, resulting in the destruction of Athens.

became the head of the Delian League that developed into an empire. Members of the organization opted to pay Athens a tax rather than supply ships and men, and excavations on the Athenian Acropolis and the surrounding areas have found parts of these tribute lists cut onto colossal marble stelae.

Money from this tribute was used to enrich Athens, in particular the Athenian Acropolis. Excavations by the American School of Classical Studies at Athens have recovered significant remains of the democratic and legal heart of the city of Athens, the agora. Their work has recovered a series of structures such as the *bouleuterion*—where the boule, or council of Athens, met to make decisions—and the *tholos* (see image 3), where the tribe in charge of Athens for a certain month was based. Archaeological work in the area has recovered pottery marked with the two Greek letters "DE," indicating a public pottery.

Part of Athens's power came from its control of silver mines in its territory. Excavations by Greek and Belgian teams at Thorikos have explored some of the mines and the related facilities, including areas to process the ore. The work required large quantities of water; therefore, because this is an arid landscape, massive cisterns were constructed to ensure that sufficient water was provided.

The growing power of Athens was challenged by Sparta and Corinth in the Peloponnesian War that broke out in 431 BCE. This was recorded by the Athenian historian Thucydides (*c.* 460–*c.* 404 BCE). He made the point that the settlement of Sparta was relatively impoverished. British excavations at some of the sanctuaries at Sparta, such as that of Artemis Orthia, have demonstrated a limited number of significant buildings. One of the key engagements during this war was on the island of Sphacteria, near Pylos in the western Peloponnese, when an Athenian force managed to defeat the Spartans. Excavations in the Athenian agora have found a Spartan hoplite shield with an inscription indicating that it had been captured at Pylos.

One aspect of the cultural identity was the creation of Panhellenic games that were open to all Greek states. Three of the centers were located in the Peloponnese at Olympia, Nemea, and Isthmia, with the fourth at Delphi (see p. 242). These events continued into the Roman period, and the Roman emperor Nero (37–68 CE) even took part in the games at Olympia.

During the fifth and early fourth centuries BCE, there was a growing emphasis on planned cities, which probably influenced developments in the Greek colonies. Excavations in the port of Piraeus have found *horoi*, or boundary markers, that appear to have been used in the mid to late fifth century BCE to identify facilities such as the military port as well as what may have been a holding area for slaves. The Greek colony of Euesperides, near modern Benghazi, Libya, was excavated by a British team in the 1950s. This noted a planned set of housing as well as workshops for processing purple dye. At the end of the fifth century BCE, the city of Rhodes was created, combining earlier cities on the island. Aerial photography has identified parts of the street plan. **DG**

479 BCE	478 BCE	447 BCE	438 BCE	431–404 BCE	86 BCE
The Hellenic army defeats the Persian army at the Battle of Plataea.	The Delian League—a confederacy of ancient Greek states under the leadership of Athens—is founded.	Construction begins on the Sanctuary of Athena on the Acropolis in Athens.	Construction of the Parthenon is completed and the statue of Athena Parthenos is dedicated.	The Peloponnesian War is fought between Athens and Sparta. It ends with the capitulation of Athens after a blockade by the Spartans.	Delphi is plundered by the Roman general Sulla (138–79 BCE).

Olympia   Tenth century BCE – second century CE

Construction of the Temple of Zeus began in 470 BCE and finished in 457 BCE. In the sixth century CE, an earthquake damaged the temple, and its ruins, including sculptures, were preserved by silting and mud slides from the nearby Kladeos River. The temple housed a statue of Zeus by the sculptor Pheidias, placed in the temple c. 430 BCE.

There is evidence of cult practice at the Sanctuary of Zeus at Olympia in western Greece from about the tenth century BCE. The eighth century BCE saw an increase in cult activity, with 776 BCE being the traditional date of the start of the festival of Zeus, held every four years, and, accordingly, the first Olympic Games. The archaeological record indicates an increase in the number of offerings, although there is a lack of surviving architecture from this period.

The lists of victors are partly preserved in literary sources. Although the first victorious competitors are from the Peloponnese, by early seventh century BCE there are victors from the whole of the Greek world. Accordingly, it had become a true Panhellenic sanctuary. The earliest temple on the site was the Temple of Hera and Zeus, later with a dedication solely to Hera, which dates from the early sixth century BCE. By the middle of the fifth century BCE, the Temple of Zeus had been built, and a century later the Echo Stoa, also called the Stoa Poikile (Painted Stoa), and the temple to the Mother of the Gods, the Metroon, was built c. 300 BCE. All of these buildings were in the Altis, the sacred area of the sanctuary. However, there were other buildings outside the Altis, some of which, such as a *bouleuterion* (council house), were concerned with the administration of the sanctuary. The Leonidaion, built in the fourth century BCE, was a complex of rooms surrounded by a colonnade, used to accommodate distinguished visitors. There was also construction in the Roman period, most notably a large fountain on the northern edge of the Altis, originally decorated with statues. It was constructed by the wealthy orator and politician Herodes Atticus (101–177 CE) in the mid second century CE, indicating the continuing importance of Olympia into the Roman period. **GM**

STADIUM

The stadium was used for athletics events at the games. It dates to the fourth century BCE, and could accommodate up to 40,000 people, who would have sat on earth embankments. Umpires sat in a stone-built stand to the south of the stadium, 197 feet (60 m.) from the starting or finishing lines, which are still visible.

NIKE OF PAIONIOS

The statue of the goddess Nike is a rare, original, free-standing work from the classical period. An inscription on the base records that it was dedicated at Olympia by the Messenians (southwest Greece) and Naupactians (central Greece) after their victory against the Lacedaemonians from Sparta in the Archidamian War (431–421 BCE).

LEGACY OF THE ANCIENT OLYMPIC GAMES

Ancient Olympia has left an indelible legacy on the modern world, most notably through the modern Olympic Games, founded in 1896 by French historian Pierre de Frédy, Baron de Coubertin (1863–1937), taking inspiration from their ancient counterparts.

The lighting of the Olympic torch for both modern summer and winter games takes place in front of the Temple of Hera in the sanctuary at Olympia. Furthermore, the design of the obverse, or front side, of the medals awarded at the summer Olympic Games from 2004 onward depicts the Nike of Paionios alighting in the Panathenaic stadium in Athens. The Nike of Paionios was also the inspiration for the statue known as the Friedensengel (Angel of Peace) erected in Maximilian Park in the Munich suburb of Bogenhausen, unveiled in 1899. The statue commemorates the years of peace following the Franco-Prussian War (1870–71).

In the modern Olympic Games, a representative competitor, judge, and coach are chosen to take an oath to abide by the rules. In the ancient Olympics, competitors, family members, and trainers took an oath before a statue of Zeus Horkios (Zeus of the Oaths) in the council house at Olympia, undertaking not to cheat and not to take bribes. The organizers of the games, also took an oath not to take bribes and to make fair judgments. There is a reference to the breaking of an oath to Zeus in the scene on the east pediment of the Temple of Zeus at Olympia. The mythical characters Pelops and Oenomaus are shown taking an oath before Zeus. Oenomaus was killed during their chariot race as a result of Pelops having bribed Oenomaus's charioteer, whom he later killed to keep the secret. The retribution was a curse on Pelops and his descendants, including Atreus, Thyestes, and Agamemnon, whose tragedies are well attested in literary sources.

Delphi Eighth century BCE – second century CE

The Sanctuary of Apollo at Delphi is situated on the southwestern slope of Mount Parnassos in central Greece. Major excavation of the sanctuary took place between 1892 and 1903, undertaken by the French School at Athens.

✦ NAVIGATOR

The Sanctuary of Apollo at Delphi was a Panhellenic sanctuary serving the whole of the Greek world. Although there is limited evidence of cult in the Mycenaean period, the sanctuary flourished from the eighth century BCE, when votive offerings first appear and the Oracle was consulted. The first Pythian Games in honor of Apollo were held in the early sixth century BCE, by which time Delphi was a fully Panhellenic sanctuary. Several treasuries were constructed, small buildings dedicated by city-states throughout the Greek world. At this time, many non-Greek rulers also made dedications at Delphi, including King Croesus of Lydia (d. c. 546 BCE) in western Anatolia. Delphi was plundered by the Roman general Sulla (138–79 BCE) in 86 BCE, and the emperor Nero removed 500 statues in the mid first century CE. However, the emperor Domitian (51–96 CE) restored the Temple of Apollo; and the emperor Hadrian (76–138 CE), a great admirer of Greece, was a major benefactor. By the second century CE, Delphi received many visitors including Pausanias, whose detailed account provides information that would otherwise have been lost.

The Sacred Way leads from the sanctuary entrance to the Temple of Apollo, passing several treasuries. Above the temple is a theater, which was completed by King Eumenes II of Pergamon (d. c. 160 BCE) in the second century BCE. Up to 5,000 spectators in thirty-five rows of seats were able to attend musical contests. Higher up the hillside is the stadium, where the athletic competitions of the Pythian Games took place; the start and finish lines are still visible. The stadium could accommodate up to 6,500 spectators, with a separate area for officials on the north side. **GM**

FOCAL POINTS

1 TEMPLE OF APOLLO

The Temple of Apollo was reconstructed following an earthquake in 373 BCE, based on the plan of an earlier temple. Fragments of sculpture from the pediments of both temples include themes of Apollo's arrival in Delphi. Reputedly the Oracle of Delphi was consulted in the *adyton* of the temple.

2 TREASURY OF THE ATHENIANS

The Treasury of the Athenians probably dates to *c.* 480 BCE, though some would date it earlier. Its sculpted metopes depict the mythical exploits of Herakles and Theseus. Two musical compositions known as the Delphic Hymns to Apollo, written in the second century BCE, were inscribed on one wall.

3 KRATEROS MONUMENT

A large rectangular niche is all that remains of the monument of Krateros (c. 370–321 BCE), a Macedonian general. Erected in the fourth century BCE, it originally housed a bronze statue group showing Krateros saving the life of Alexander the Great (356–323 BCE) during a lion hunt.

CHRYSELEPHANTINE STATUES

Examples of gold and ivory chryselephantine statues are rare. The most complete archaeological evidence came from the Halos deposit at the Sanctuary of Apollo at Delphi. In 1939, archaeologists unearthed the remains of at least seven statues. They had been damaged by fire and then buried no later than 420 BCE, although the figures were older. The statues are of different sizes, the most famous being the heads of three statues, one male (above) and two female, about two-thirds life-size.

◀ The Sanctuary of Athena Pronaia, known colloquially as the Marmaria (Marbles), is situated to the east of the Sanctuary of Apollo. The significant buildings are the sixth-century BCE Temple of Athena and two treasuries, one built by the city of Massilia, modern-day Marseille in southern France. The most famous building is the fourth-century BCE circular structure, or *tholos*, whose function is unknown.

Athens and the Parthenon 447 – 438 BCE

All the surviving original sculpture from the Parthenon has been removed. Most of it is housed in the Acropolis Museum in Athens and the British Museum in London.

◆◈ NAVIGATOR

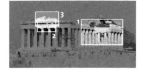

In 448 BCE, Pericles (c. 495–429 BCE), leader of the Athenian democracy, promoted the idea of rebuilding the sanctuary of Athena on the Acropolis, which had been destroyed by Persian invaders in 480 BCE. The sanctuary had not been rebuilt earlier, because the Athenians had undertaken to leave the site as a memorial. Pericles's aim was to enhance the prestige of Athens by building a sanctuary on a scale that no other Greek state could imitate.

Construction of the buildings began in 447 BCE and the sanctuary was rebuilt in less than fifty years, including the Erechtheum, the Temple of Athena Nike, and the monumental gateway known as the Propylaia. The Parthenon itself was begun in 447 BCE and dedicated in 438 BCE. It is known from inscriptional evidence that the sculpture was completed in 432 BCE. The architect of the Parthenon was Ictinus, assisted by Callicrates. Using marble from nearby Mount Pentelicus, they incorporated specific architectural refinements into their design, to enhance the appearance of the building when viewed from a distance. Among these were an upward curve of the temple platform and a slight swelling of the column centers as they decrease in diameter toward the top.

The Parthenon was built using a combination of columns sculpted in two architectural orders: Doric in the colonnade surrounding the cella (inner chamber) and Ionic in the chamber itself. The cella of the Parthenon is divided into two parts, which were not connected. It is thought that the original name of the west cella was the Parthenon, which translates as "room of the maidens." From the fourth century BCE onward, the whole temple was referred to as the Parthenon. **GM**

FOCAL POINTS

1 DAMAGE

The Parthenon suffered severe damage in 1687 when it was besieged by Venetian forces fighting against the Ottoman Empire during the Great Turkish War (1683–99). The Parthenon was being used by the Ottoman forces to store gunpowder, which was ignited by a Venetian mortar round.

2 SQUARE PANELS

The square panels displayed ninety-two metopes, carved in high relief, the originals now in museums. The four sides showed mythical combats: a Gigantomachy on the east, the Sack of Troy on the north, an Amazonamachy on the west, and a Centauromachy, the best preserved, on the south side.

3 PEDIMENT

Both pediments were once decorated with marble sculpture, the fragments of which are now in museums. The theme of the west pediment was the contest between Athena and Poseidon for the patronage of Attica, and the east pediment showed the birth of Athena.

STATUE OF ATHENA PARTHENOS

The Parthenon once held a statue of the goddess Athena by the renowned fifth-century BCE Athenian sculptor Pheidias. Although the statue no longer survives, it was described by the Roman writer Pliny (*c.* 61–*c.* 113 CE) and Greek geographer Pausanias (*c.* 110–*c.* 180 CE) as being approximately 38 feet (12 m.) tall, made from gold and ivory. Athena's skin was rendered by a veneer of ivory, and gold was added for her clothing, which also served as Athens' gold reserve and was removed between the late fourth and early third centuries BCE.

The detailed literary accounts enable copies of the Athena Parthenos statue to be identified. The most famous smaller version is a Roman copy, the Varvakeion statuette, named after the area where it was found in Athens and dating to between the second and third centuries CE. At approximately 3 feet (1 m.) high, the Varvakeion statuette gives a good impression of the appearance of the Athena Parthenos statue, but not the scale and grandeur of the original. The goddess is depicted standing erect, wearing a tunic reaching to her feet and a helmet. She holds a statue of Nike, goddess of victory, in her right hand and a spear in her left. A decorated shield lies at her feet and a serpent is nearby. Traces of red and yellow paint are preserved in many parts of the statue. The Varvakeion statuette is now in the National Archaeological Museum of Athens.

GREATER GREECE

1 A mosaic of Roman nobility at the house in Morgantina, Sicily.

2 A fourth-century BCE red-figure Attic krater, with scenes of the mythical Calydonian boar hunt and fight between centaurs, discovered at a necropolis in Spina, Italy.

The Greek colonial settlements in the western Mediterranean have long been the focus of archaeological study and excavation. These date from the early precolonial settlements on the island of Ischia in Italy to the major colonies such as Tarentum and Syracuse. Since the eighteenth century, travelers have described and investigated some of the temple remains associated with the colonies. Some of the most important were at Paestum (see p. 250) in southern Italy and at Akragas (modern Agrigento) in Sicily. The fifth-century temple of Olympian Zeus at Akragas included colossal architectural statues more than 25 feet (7.5 m.) high. The colony of Selinus (modern Selinunte) in Sicily also has a number of surviving temples (see p. 248). The Temple of Athena at Syracuse was incorporated into the later cathedral.

A strand of archaeological investigation has been to identify how colonies were established in southern Italy and Sicily. Excavations at Megara Hyblaea in eastern Sicily sought to confirm the sequences presented in the writings of the fifth-century BCE Athenian historian Thucydides. The archaeological work has constructed a sequence of chronologies based on pottery. Studies of excavated pottery from Gela and Selinunte, both in southern Sicily, have suggested caution over the use of historical sources to create a firm sequence.

KEY EVENTS

728 BCE	720 BCE	c. 600 BCE	Early 6th century BCE	Mid 6th century BCE	6th century BCE
Megara Hyblaea is established. It is excavated in 1949 by a French team trying to identify the start of the colonization of Sicily.	The colony of Sybaris is founded from Achaea in the northern Peloponnese and Troezen in the Argolid.	Paestum is founded. It is first excavated in 1907 by Italian archaeologist Vittorio Spinazzola (1863–1943).	The colony of Massilia is established. Excavations there in 1967–70 recover remains of the Greek and Roman harbor installations.	A Greek community is established at Morgantina on Sicily.	An extramural sanctuary is built at the mouth of the Sele river near to Paestum. It is uncovered by Italian excavations in the 1930s.

In Sicily one aspect of research has been the growing Hellenization of the local populations. This has been a theme of the work at Morgantina in the southeast part of the island. The earliest settlement has been dated to the tenth century BCE, but it seems that a Greek community was established there in the mid sixth century. Some of the private houses in the city were decorated with fine mosaics (see image 1). The city was destroyed by Rome in 212 BCE. A major hoard of early Hellenistic silver was looted from the city but has now been returned to the island; excavators have identified the pit from which the hoard was removed along with modern coins left by the looters. A large acrolithic statue, perhaps representing the female deity Aphrodite, seems to have been dedicated in one of the sanctuaries in the city.

The survey of Metapontum at the mouth of the Basento river in southern Italy has demonstrated the way that the land was divided up for the Greek colonists. The hinterland, or *chora*, was separated into areas that are likely to have been assigned to individual colonists. A number of rural farmsteads and communities have been identified, as well as a rural sanctuary decorated with painted terracotta architectural fittings. This survey work has begun to inform the discussions about the way that Greek colonies were to provide new areas of farmland for populations moving from the Greek heartlands.

The colony of Massilia (modern Marseille) was established in the early sixth century BCE by settlers from Phocaea. Excavations around the Old Port have recovered remains of the defenses. Ceramic transport amphorae made in the hinterland of the colony are found along the south coast of France and into Spain, as well as up the Rhône Valley. Massilia is likely to have been the entry point for the massive bronze wine krater found in the La Tène burial at Vix in northern France.

A Greek trading settlement was established at Spina at the mouth of the Po river. This gave Greek cities access to the northern part of the Adriatic. Excavations by Italian archaeologists have uncovered thousands of graves frequently furnished with Athenian figure-decorated pottery (see image 2). The earliest material appears to date from the late sixth century BCE. Spina is likely to have been an important gateway to Central Europe, and Greek material found in Hallstatt contexts in Austria and Germany may have arrived via this route.

Greek colonies are also found around the shores of the Black Sea and north Africa. The colony of Istria at the mouth of the Danube is thought to have been founded by the city of Miletus in western Anatolia in modern Turkey. Excavations have revealed pottery that can be dated to the mid seventh century BCE. Work in Georgia on the east side of the Black Sea is starting to reveal the extent of Greek interaction with local populations in their search for resources by the urban communities of the Greek world. One of the few areas of north Africa to be colonized was Cyrenaica in modern Libya. The sequence of settlement was described in detail by the historian Herodotus (*c.* 484–*c.* 430 BCE). **DG**

5th century BCE	480 BCE	409 BCE	c. 400 BCE	397 BCE	212 BCE
The Temple of Hera is built at Paestum.	Carthage is defeated at the Battle of Himera.	Selinus is sacked by the Carthaginians under Hannibal. it is finally abandoned in 250 BCE.	Paestum is taken over by the Lucanians.	Motya is sacked by Dionysius I of Syracuse (c. 430–367 BCE).	The city of Morgantina is destroyed by Rome.

Selinus Seventh century BCE

Temple C at Selinus (Sicily) dates to the early sixth century BCE. Some of the columns were formed by a single piece of quarried stone, whereas others consist of a number of stone blocks. The temple was decorated with reliefs depicting Artemis and Leto; Herakles; and Perseus slaying the Gorgon. Architectural terracottas were used for the upper part of the building.

From the eighth century BCE onward, a number of Greek city-states, or poleis, started to establish colonies in the western Mediterranean, especially in southern Italy and Sicily. A broad historical sequence was provided by the Athenian historian Thucydides as part of his discussion of the Athenian expedition to Sicily against the city of Syracuse in 415 BCE.

The colony of Selinus (modern Selinunte) was located on a promontory on the coast of southwest Sicily. It was a foundation of Megara Hyblaea, a colony of Megara established on the east coast of Sicily, traditionally in 728 BCE. The first-century BCE historian Diodorus Siculus suggested that Selinus was founded in 651 BCE, while Thucydides suggested 628 BCE. The archaeological evidence from the site suggests the earlier foundation date.

Selinus was an ally of Carthage against other Greek cities in the early part of the fifth century BCE. This was understandable, because its immediate neighbors to the west were the Phoenician settlements of Motya (see p. 286), Panormus, and ilybaeum. Carthage was defeated at the Battle of Himera in 480 BCE. Selinus was ranged against Segesta and her Athenian ally in the great expedition against Sicily in 415 BCE. The Carthaginians under Hannibal, son of Giskon, sacked Selinus in 409 BCE. It was finally abandoned in 250 BCE and the population moved to the city of Lilybaeum.

One of the characteristics of Selinus was its planned nature with a grid layout. This included the settlement on the acropolis as well as adjacent areas. These features became a key feature of colonies such as Euesperides in north Africa and new establishments such as Piraeus, the port of Athens, and the city of Rhodes. The acropolis area was surrounded by a wall. This grid pattern continued into the Carthaginian phase of the city, when the fortifications were strengthened. **DG/GM**

TERRACOTTA FIGURINE FROM THE SANCTUARY OF DEMETER MALOPHOROS

On the hill to the west of the acropolis was the Sanctuary of Demeter Malophoros. This was refurbished with a monumental square gateway c. 420 BCE. The temple was simpler than elsewhere in the city; it may date to the early sixth century. Excavations have recovered terracotta dedications showing the goddess Demeter.

TEMPLE OF HERA

The Temple of Hera (Temple E) dates from the mid fifth century BCE, and was constructed in the Doric style with six columns at the end. It was decorated with a series of metopes (carved panels) showing mythological scenes, such as Actaeon being attacked by the hounds unleashed by Artemis, and Herakles slaying an Amazon.

TEMPLES OF SELINUS

One of the striking features of the colony are the colossal temples constructed in the sixth century BCE, decorated with reliefs and architectural features in terracotta. Three temples stood on the eastern hill (Temples E, F, and G). Temple G was over 357 feet (109 m.) long, with eight columns across the front and seventeen along the sides. It appears that, due to its ambitious scale, the temple was never completed, and studies of the column capitals suggest that the western end may still have been under construction in the late fifth century BCE, nearly a century after the temple had been started. The interior may have been open with a free-standing temple at the center. Two rows of columns were inserted into the inner cella. Unfinished column drums have been identified in quarries to the west of Selinus. An inscription from the temple acknowledges the deities of Selinus for bringing a victory, and records the dedication of a gold object

weighing 60 talents (approximately 3,600 lb./1,560 kg.). It thus seems possible that the temple was funded from booty in an unspecified conflict on the island. The temple was completely wrecked by an earthquake.

Temple F, probably dating to the mid sixth century, has six columns across the front, with a second row behind. Unusually, the spaces between the exterior columns were filled with high panels. It was originally decorated with architectural terracottas, though these appear to have been replaced with ones in stone in the early fifth century BCE.

To the north of Temple C lay Temple D, probably dating to the late sixth century BCE. During the mid fifth century BCE, temples A and O were constructed on the acropolis. Temple A had a monumental stone altar with colonnades and stepped access. Interior stairways provided access to the roof.

Paestum Seventh – fifth centuries BCE

A major temple, likely dedicated to Hera, was constructed at Paestum, probably in the middle of the fifth century BCE. This may have been intended to replace the earlier temple of Hera. It was constructed in the Doric style with six columns across the front, and was 197 feet (60 m.) long.

The Greek colony of Poseidonia, more frequently known by its Latin name of Paestum, was located on the Bay of Salerno on the west coast of Italy to the south of Amalfi. It was founded from the colony of Sybaris in southern Italy c. 600 BCE. Sybaris itself had been founded c. 720 BCE from Achaea in the northern Peloponnese, and Troezen in the Argolid. The earliest imported Corinthian pottery from the surrounding cemeteries supports a date for the foundation in the late seventh century BCE. The city was surrounded by a wall consisting of limestone blocks, although its actual date is uncertain. Excavations have revealed the remains of the round council chamber, or *bouleuterion*, that may have been able to seat 1,200 individuals.

During the sixth century BCE a series of temples were constructed that continue to dominate the site. These are aligned in a way that suggests the colony had a grid layout of a form known from elsewhere in the Greek world. The earliest was the Temple of Hera, sometimes called the Basilica. Excavations have revealed remains of a limestone altar in front of the temple.

Another temple, dedicated to Athena, lay in the northern part of the city. It measured some 108 feet (33 m.) in length, and had six columns across the front. The interior porch had columns in the Ionic order. It appears to date to c. 500 BCE, based on its architectural style. The identification is confirmed by fifth- and fourth-century BCE representations of the goddess Athena that were found in an adjacent votive deposit. The sanctuary was used in the Roman period, and there is an inscribed piece of pottery with the name of the goddess Minerva, the Latin equivalent of Athena. **DG/GM**

TOMBA DEL TUFFATORE

One of the most spectacular finds is the Tomba del Tuffatore (Tomb of the Diver), which was discovered in 1968 and dates to *c.* 470 BCE. The roof panel depicts a naked diver plunging into the sea, and it has been suggested that the image is a metaphor for the passage between life and death. Inside the tomb, diners are portrayed reclining on couches, one of whom is playing the game of kottabos, in which participants flicked wine dregs at a target. Another panel shows a krater (a vessel for mixing wine and water) resting on a table.

TEMPLE OF HERA THE BASILICA

The earliest temple at Paestum was dedicated to Hera, consort of Zeus, and was constructed *c.* 550 BCE. This is usually known by the misleading name of the Basilica, so-called because in the eighteenth century it was mistakenly believed to be a Roman building and public meeting space. The temple was constructed in the Doric style, with nine columns across the short end, and was 178 feet (54.3 m.) in length. The central room, or cella, was divided in half by an unusual row of seven columns.

SANCTUARY AT FOCE DEL SELE

The town of Paestum was taken over by the Lucanians in *c.* 400 BCE, a period contemporary with the fall of other Greek colonies to the north, such as Cumae and Capua. Their presence is notable in the cemeteries where highly decorated wall paintings have been found. The period coincides with the development of the red-figured style of pottery known as Paestan. The decoration continued to draw on Greek mythological themes.

A Latin colony was established at the site in 273 BCE, followed by a further Roman colony in 71 CE. This settlement used a grid pattern to lay out the new elements, including a forum and a temple constructed in the Roman style on a raised podium. The area around Paestum remained isolated until the seventeenth century. In 1768, English engraver Thomas Major published *Ruins of Paestum otherwise Poseidonia in Magna Graecia*, containing some drawings by Italian engineer Count Felice

Gazzola (1698–1780). In 1784, all Gazzola's drawings were published and the site became known more widely, soon forming part of the Grand Tour. Excavations started in 1907 and continued throughout the twentieth century.

In 1934, a sanctuary was located 6 miles (9 km.) north of Paestum at Foce del Sele. It appears to be that described by the classical geographer Strabo (*c.* 64 BCE–*c.* 21 CE). The sanctuary contained a temple in the Doric order, with eight columns across the front, as well as a smaller structure, perhaps a treasury, which was decorated with metopes, or carved reliefs. They show the labors of the Greek hero Herakles. Another represents Sisyphos, who is depicted rolling a boulder up a slope with a winged demon to his rear. The structure has been dated by associated pottery to the second quarter of the sixth century BCE. The temple itself was decorated with reliefs showing a procession of young women.

IRON AGE ELITES IN EUROPE

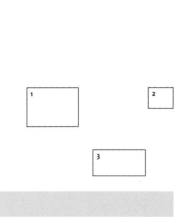

1 The handle of a bronze flagon found at Basse Yutz in Moselle, northeastern France in 1927. The wine jug dates to c. 450 BCE and is inlaid with coral and enamel in the form of an animal head. Such jugs would have been used at banquets by important figures.

2 The largest hall at the archaeological site of Gudme in central Denmark is 154 feet (47 m.) long. The hall was built c. 300 CE. The magnate at Gudme was perhaps a prince or king of a large area.

3 An aerial view of Maiden Castle in Dorset, England. It is a complex Iron Age hill fort. At its peak, the fort was densely populated and covered 116 acres (47 ha.). Finds from the site reveal that activities such as metalworking and textile production took place here.

The differences in access to status and wealth that emerged at the end of the third millennium BCE were amplified over the course of the second millennium. Techniques for the production of durable goods, specifically metals, were improved and refined. Transportation infrastructure, including wheeled vehicles and shipbuilding techniques, enabled commodities and the goods that were exchanged for them to be moved across the landscape. Individuals and communities amassed wealth and controlled key resources, and ensured that their riches and the status that came with them were passed down from one generation to the next.

Bronze (see image 1), made from copper and tin, continued to be important during the early centuries of the first millennium BCE. Moreover, iron use began. In addition to metal sources, salt became an important resource. One of the preservation techniques for meat and fish was salting. Coastal communities made salt by evaporating seawater, often using special ceramic pans. Inland, water from brine springs could be evaporated like seawater, but in some localities with complicated geological histories, vast deposits of rock salt left by ancient seas could be mined. Communities that controlled these salt deposits, such as at Hallstatt and Hallein in Austria (see p. 254), could accumulate considerable wealth.

Eventually, Iron Age chiefs in central Europe established contact with Greek trading colonies along the Mediterranean. The most important of these was at Massalia, modern Marseille, which was linked by the Rhône and its tributary

KEY EVENTS

c. 1000–800 BCE	c. 800–400 BCE	c. 650–530 BCE	c. 600 BCE	c. 530–480 BCE	c. 520–500 BCE
The transition from the Bronze Age to Iron Age across central and northern Europe.	Intensive salt mining takes place at Hallstatt in Austria.	A mud-brick wall is in use at the Heuneburg (see p. 256) in southwestern Germany.	Greeks establish a trading colony at Massalia (present-day Marseille), southern France.	Monumental buildings are erected at Mont Lassois in France.	Elite individuals are buried at Hochdorf in Germany and Vix in France.

the Saône to the headwaters of the Rhine, Danube, and Seine. Iron Age elites controlled the trade that sent agricultural products, furs, and probably slaves downstream to the Greeks, who in return provided the products of Greek workshops and wine. The luxury goods made by the Greeks were used in lavish displays, particularly in burials. Royal residences were characterized by large buildings, often surrounded by areas with workshops and farmsteads.

In northern France and southern Britain, fortified sites were built on high ground. Known as hill forts, they appear to have been the seats of local leaders and their retainers, but without the ostentatious displays of wealth that are seen in central Europe. The fortification systems of the hill forts are often complex in order to make attacking them as difficult as possible, since it appears that warfare was endemic among the small Iron Age political units. A classic example is Maiden Castle in Dorset, southwest England (see image 3).

A similar concentration of wealth based on imported luxury goods took place a millennium later, this time in southern Scandinavia. Here, the Iron Age accumulation of status and wealth was expressed in the emergence of magnates—powerful individuals whose riches derived from the products of the workshops that surrounded their opulent residences and farmsteads in the hinterlands. Excavated examples of the seats of Iron Age magnates include Gudme (see image 2) in Denmark and Uppåkra in Sweden. At both sites, hall-like buildings were apparently used for ceremonial purposes.

The Iron Age elites of temperate Europe were opportunists who took advantage of the demand by Mediterranean societies for the products of the fields, pastures, and forests of northern Europe and the British Isles, and transformed it into wealth. It is difficult to know the extent to which this wealth was translated into political authority. Perhaps some elites controlled trade, others were in charge of warfare, and still others had religious authority to mediate between the gods and people. Eventually, the singular power of the Iron Age elites was diluted by mercantile activity. **PB**

c. 500 BCE	c. 400 BCE–400 CE	c. 350–300 BCE	c. 200 BCE–400 CE	c. 201–300 CE	c. 300
A hill fort is established at Maiden Castle in Dorset, England, that expands over the next centuries.	Bog bodies are deposited in wetlands across northern Europe (see p. 314).	The Hjortspring boat is deposited in a Danish bog with war-booty sacrifices (see p. 316).	Irish royal sites function as ceremonial centers.	A large wooden building, possibly for use as a temple, is constructed at Uppåkra in southern Sweden.	About 500 people settle at Gudme in Demark. The settlement comprises a magnate's farm surrounded by nearly fifty smaller farms.

Hallstatt 800–400 BCE

The salt deposits under the mountain at Hallstatt consist of veins of nearly pure rock salt that run through a mixture of clay and salt. They were formed millions of years ago when a shallow sea basin evaporated, before the area was uplifted, folded, and shifted to form the Alps. Similar large salt deposits are known from other parts of Alpine central Europe. For example, those at Hallein, not far from Hallstatt, were also exploited during the Iron Age.

The modern town of Hallstatt, Austria, clings to the side of a long, deep lake at the foot of a mountain. High above the town, the mountain is split by what geologists call a hanging valley, known as the Salzbergtal, where the top of a massive salt deposit lies only a few feet below the surface. Salt mining began in the Salzbergtal in the Bronze Age and continues today. During the early part of the Iron Age, between 700 and 500 BCE, Hallstatt became one of the most remarkable localities in European prehistory, whose astonishing wealth was based on the extraction and export of salt.

Since medieval times, salt miners at Hallstatt have been finding traces of ancient activity. They came across timbers and objects of wood, leather, and cloth buried in a matrix of salt. The weight of the salt mountain had caused the shafts in which they were deposited originally to close up. By the eighteenth century, records indicate that miners recognized that these finds were prehistoric. In 1734, the body of a man was found preserved in the salt, still wearing his clothes and shoes—a prehistoric miner probably killed in a collapse. Although the body was very well preserved, it was buried in Hallstatt graveyard the next day, so he is not available for scientific study.

During the nineteenth century, the manager of the salt mines, Johann Georg Ramsauer (1795–1874), excavated the Early Iron Age cemetery. During these excavations, he found 980 burials. Since then, additional excavations have added to the number of graves that have been studied by archaeologists, which now totals more than 1,500. Archaeologists estimate that there were originally 5,000 to 6,000 graves in the valley, many of which have been destroyed or remain to be found. **PB**

ANCIENT MINING METHODS

The prehistoric miners followed the veins of salt by tunnelling into the mountainside. In order to avoid cave-ins, they shored up their shafts and side galleries with timbers. Bronze picks were used to cut away at the salt face. To facilitate this process, they first incised a vertical groove. Then, on each side, they cut two curving grooves to form a circular or heart-shaped outline. The two lobes of salt formed from this pattern of grooves were then broken off from the salt wall and carried out of the shaft.

SALT TRADE

Salt was in high demand throughout prehistoric Europe for conserving meat and fish. From Hallstatt, the salt was sent in all directions, and the returns on this trade flowed back into the mining community. Far from the mine, salt was exchanged for other commodities, but near the mine, much of the salt was exchanged for luxury goods. This led to the accumulation of tremendous wealth by the Iron Age inhabitants of Hallstatt, exemplified by the gold dagger with scabbard found in a Hallstatt tomb.

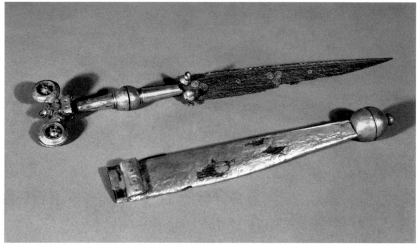

HALLSTATT CEMETERY

In the valley below the mine entrance, the Hallstatt community buried its dead between 800 and 400 BCE. Some of the graves contain cremated bones, while in others complete skeletons are found, usually oriented east to west. The analysis of the bones shows that Hallstatt was an ordinary Iron Age community, comprising family households. Even the children were engaged in physical labor so salt mining was probably a family activity.

The wealth of the Hallstatt miners was reflected in the objects found in the burials. These include bronze and iron weapons such as swords and daggers, bronze bowls and cauldrons, helmets and buckets, well-made pottery and glass vessels, and ornaments of metal, amber and glass. Cremation burials seem to have been preferred by the wealthier members of the community.

The other story of Hallstatt cemetery is the history of its excavation, undertaken by Ramsauer in 1846 to 1863. He engaged an artist to document the burials in watercolor renderings of each grave, showing the type of grave, position of the skeleton or cremated bones, and the grave offerings. Additional excavations were carried out for the remainder of the nineteenth and the first part of the twentieth centuries. During the past two decades, the Natural History Museum of Vienna has been systematically excavating additional burials using modern techniques. One discovery is that Ramsauer rarely recovered ceramic vessels due to their fragmentation by soil pressure. Recent excavations have been far more successful, revealing an additional richness to the Hallstatt grave inventories.

Heuneburg Sixth century BCE

In *c.* 650 BCE, much of the ramparts of the Heuneburg hill fort were reconstructed with sun-dried mud brick, an inappropriate material for the climate of central Europe, but which showed that the chief had contact with distant lands. The wall was destroyed in the late sixth century BCE and it was rebuilt using timber cribs filled with earth and stone.

The Iron Age chiefs who ruled southwestern Germany and eastern France made contact with traders in the Greek colony at Massalia (modern Marseille) in the sixth century BCE. The Rhône and Saône rivers formed a natural corridor between the upper reaches of the Rhine, Danube, and Seine rivers and the Mediterranean coast. A lively trade in the exchange of furs, hides, meats, and slaves for the products of Mediterranean workshops and wine ensued. These exotic goods were a source of wealth for the Iron Age elites in central Europe and markers of their power and prestige.

Hilltop settlements in west-central Europe, many of which had been the locations of settlement for several centuries already, became more elaborate. Several dozen of these "princely" seats are known, including those at the Heuneburg on the Danube and Mont Lassois on the Seine. Ramparts enclosed palatial dwellings as well as workshops in which raw materials obtained from the Mediterranean societies were worked into local forms. For example, coral was prized as an inlay for fibulae, the safety-pin garment clasp favored by Iron Age fashion.

The wealth made its way into burials of elite individuals under large mounds. One of the most spectacular is the burial at Hochdorf in southwest Germany, discovered in the late 1970s, in which the skeleton of a man lay on a bronze recliner accompanied by drinking equipment, a bronze cauldron from southern Italy, and a wooden ceremonial wagon. In 2015, a princely burial at Lavau in eastern France contained bronze bowls with handles shaped like feline heads. At first, the person in the Lavau tomb was thought to be a woman, but subsequent genetic analysis confirmed that it was a man. **PB**

SETTLEMENT

Investigations around the base of the hill on which the Heuneburg sits have revealed a fortified lower settlement covering nearly 50 acres (20 ha.) with houses and workshops. To get into this settlement, it was necessary to pass over a ditch on a bridge and then through a monumental gate. Wood from the bridge was dated to 590 BCE with tree rings. Outside this settlement were farmsteads surrounded by palisades. Thus the Heuneburg was the center of a vast industrial and agricultural landscape.

PRINCELY TOMBS

Alongside the hill forts in which the elite lived and their retainers worked, lavish burials are the other defining characteristic of the period between 600 and 400 BCE in west-central Europe. In many cases, these were looted already in ancient times, but occasionally an undisturbed one is found. Such was the case at sites like Vix and Lavau in France and Hochdorf in Germany, which have yielded immense quantities of luxury goods, including products of workshops in Italy.

THE LADY OF VIX AND HER KRATER

On the floodplain of the Seine in the village of Vix in the shadow of Mont Lassois in Burgundy, France, lie many sites contemporaneous with the settlement on the plateau above. These include a large rectangular ditched enclosure with fragments of limestone statues, and multiple burial mounds. One such mound is 125 feet (38 m.) in diameter. Its timber burial chamber was excavated in the early 1950s. As was the case at Hochdorf, it contained a four-wheeled wagon, although in this case the wheels had been removed from the chassis and placed against the wall. On the wagon's platform was the body of a woman wearing a large gold neck ring, whose terminals were decorated with miniature winged horses. She is known as the Lady of Vix.

The dominating feature of the burial chamber was an enormous bronze vessel called a krater. It was more than 5 feet (1.6 m.) tall, weighed nearly 460 pounds (208.6 kg.) and could hold 242 gallons (1,100 L.). It is almost certain that it was designed to hold wine mixed with water for ostentatious consumption, as this was how a krater would be used in the Greek world. Archaeologists can trace the Vix krater to a workshop in the Greek colony of Magna Graecia in southern Italy that was active c. 530 BCE. Also in the tomb were Attic black-figure drinking cups made c. 520 BCE, all of which places the Vix burial somewhere in the last quarter of the sixth century BCE. The astonishing thing is that someone in eastern France wanted the immense bronze vessel transported from southern Italy. This presumably involved a sea voyage, transport up the Rhône to its headwaters and then overland to the Seine—a distance of nearly 1,000 miles (1,600 km.). All this effort was to enable the elites of Mont Lassois to demonstrate to their retainers that they had access to the Greek workshops and vineyards.

PERSIAN EMPIRE

1 Cyrus II's propagandist autobiography, the Cyrus cylinder, includes an account of his conquest of Babylon.

2 The tomb of Cyrus II at Pasargadae, Iran.

3 A frieze of Persian archers from Darius's palace at Susa, Iran.

By the early seventh century BCE, the Assyrians knew of Medes to their east and, later in the century, of a Persian kingdom in Anshan, adjacent to Elam (in modern southwestern Iran). By this time the Medes had probably developed a considerable state, with its capital at Ecbatana. They attacked the failing Assyrian Empire in 614 BCE, and in alliance with the Babylonians destroyed its capital Nineveh in 612 BCE. The Medes then moved north, defeating Urartu (Armenia) and attacking Lydia, a kingdom controlling most of western Anatolia, with whom they signed a treaty in 585 BCE. Their next king, Astyages, probably spent much of his reign from 585 to 550 BCE extending the Median Empire into eastern Iran. By this time, according to the Greek historian Herodotus (c. 484–c. 425–30 BCE), the Persians were vassals of the Medes. Cyrus II (c. 600–c. 530 BCE), a descendant of the legendary ruler Achaemenes (hence, the Achaemenid dynasty), became Persian king in 559 BCE. In 550 BCE, he deposed Astyages, apparently supported by the Median army. He conquered Lydia in 547 BCE, the Greek cities of Asia Minor, and Babylon in 539 BCE (see image 1), and inherited the Babylonian Empire. He treated his conquests with tolerance and mercy, retaining former officials in post, and managed to win

KEY EVENTS

550 BCE	547 BCE	525 BCE	Late 6th century BCE	515 BCE	513 BCE
Cyrus II, king of Anshan, overthrows Astyages, king of the Medes, becoming ruler of the combined kingdom of Medes and Persians.	The capture of the Lydian capital Sardis by Persians ends forty-five years of competition between the Anatolian state of Lydia and the major Iranian powers.	Cambyses conquers Egypt but dies on the journey home. Darius I justifies his accession in an inscription carved on a rock at Behistun, Iran, in 519 BCE.	An exploratory expedition sponsored by Darius I goes from Asia Minor to Kabul, descends the Indus River and returns via the Red Sea.	Darius I founds the royal center at Persepolis, a symbolic representation of the empire. His successors Xerxes I and Artaxerxes I continue work there.	Darius I conquers Thrace and then extends the Persian Empire as far as the Indus River, bringing it to its greatest extent.

much support. He made the old Median capital Ecbatana his summer palace and built a new capital at Pasargadae. Excavations here have uncovered the remains of stone pillared halls, typical of Achaemenid architecture, set around a formal park, a feature that became a Persian tradition in later eras. Cyrus later extended the empire's boundaries to at least the Syr Darya River in Afghanistan; but in 530 BCE, he was killed fighting in central Asia (see image 2). The throne passed to his son Cambyses, who conquered Egypt in 525 BCE. After Cambyses died in 522 BCE, Darius I (550–486 BCE), a member of a minor branch of the Achaemenid family, seized the throne. Most of the empire rose against him, but he put down the rebellions within the year. He extended the empire to Thrace in the west and the Indus region in the east.

While his predecessors had been content to inherit the existing administrative organizations of their conquests, Darius I reorganized the empire into a single system, creating satrapies (provinces) administrated by governors who were relatives or close associates of the king. He introduced a system of regular provincial taxation or tribute, and undertook other reforms. In 515 BCE, he began work on a great royal center at Persepolis (see p. 262), continued by his successors; and built a winter palace at Susa (see image 3). To ensure speedy communications he established a road network, including a Royal Road linking Susa to Sardis (see p. 260), with way stations where horses could be changed. Darius I also completed a canal begun by the pharaoh Necho II (r. 610–595 BCE) linking the Nile to the Red Sea. It was probably in his reign that worship of Ahura Mazda was adopted as the state religion. Its ideology encouraged the Persian kings to promote and maintain harmony—organizing their subjects to ensure it—thereby keeping at bay the evils of disunity and disorder and accepting that to succeed in this their own behavior must be beyond reproach.

Darius I's attempt to conquer Greece in 490 BCE ended in defeat, as did the attempt ten years later by his son Xerxes I (c. 519–465 BCE), who quelled rebellions in Egypt and Babylonia. The Persian Empire had reached its greatest extent and was the largest the world had yet known. Violent succession disputes and rebellions, particularly in Asia Minor and Egypt, periodically shook the empire without threatening its stability. In 338 BCE, Artaxerxes III was murdered; from a subsequent round of further murders Darius III, a distant relative of the royal line, emerged in 335 BCE as king and began restoring the empire, but was cut short in his efforts by the arrival in 334 BCE of Alexander, king of Macedon (356–323 BCE), who swept through the empire, defeating Darius in three battles. After Darius was murdered, Alexander assumed the throne, continuing his conquest of the remaining provinces. Despite the change in ruler, the empire's efficient administrative system allowed it to continue to function. Alexander's successors carved it up between them, but many aspects of life continued with little change, the Hellenistic world (see p. 276) exploiting the cultural, economic, administrative, and political legacy of the Persians. **JM**

490 BCE	480 BCE	480 BCE	404–401 BCE	331 BCE	329 BCE
A Persian expedition against Greece for supporting the Greeks of Asia Minor in a revolt ends in the Athenians' surprising victory at Marathon.	For his Greek invasion, Xerxes I constructs a pontoon bridge across the Dardanelles and cuts a ship canal through the Athos peninsula.	Xerxes I attacks the Greek states. The Persians are again defeated, in a sea battle at Salamis and a land battle in 479 BCE at Plataea.	Cyrus the Younger (423–401 BCE), son of Darius II, rebels against his brother Artaxerxes II's assumption of the throne, but is defeated and killed at Cunaxa.	Alexander defeats Darius III at the Battle of Gaugamela. Darius escapes, but is murdered by Bessos, satrap of Bactria.	Alexander catches and executes Bessos, who has claimed the throne as Artaxerxes IV; Alexander controls Macedonia, Greece, and the Persian Empire.

Sardis Seventh century – 334 BCE (and later)

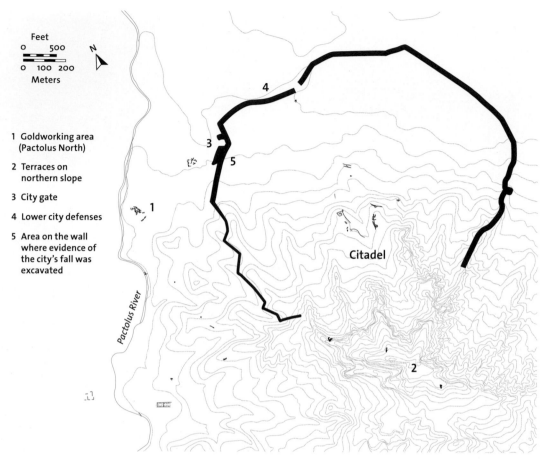

Feet
0   500

Meters
0   100   200

N

1 Goldworking area
   (Pactolus North)

2 Terraces on
   northern slope

3 City gate

4 Lower city defenses

5 Area on the wall
   where evidence of
   the city's fall was
   excavated

4

3

5

1

Citadel

2

Pactolus River

The citadel of the city of Sardis was perched on an almost impregnable high ridge; below it, the residential area of the lower city spread out over the north slopes. These were set on terraces linked by a stair and on the valley floor, extending well beyond the massive defensive wall. Excavations have revealed the defenses, houses, shrines, and industrial remains of the Lydian and Persian periods, which includes a gold refinery.

By the seventh century BCE, the powerful kingdom of Lydia had emerged in western Anatolia. Its capital, Sardis, was situated in an agriculturally productive landscape —on a key trade route linking the Aegean with West Asia—and it controlled the Pactolus river, a rich source of alluvial gold. During the mid-seventh-century BCE reign of Gyges, founder of the Mermnad dynasty, Lydia was attacked repeatedly by Cimmerians, steppe nomads who were threatening northern West Asia at this time. They were finally driven away by Gyges's great-grandson Alyattes, who began expanding eastward, thus coming into conflict with the Medes in 590 BCE. In 585 BCE they made a peace treaty, marrying Alyattes's daughter to Astyages, the Median king's son, who became king later that year. Alyattes's son Croesus further expanded the Lydian kingdom to encompass all of western Anatolia up to the Halys River. In 550 BCE, the Persian king Cyrus II overthrew Astyages. Believing his enemies weakened, Croesus consulted the Delphic oracle, which said that if he attacked the Persians a great empire would be destroyed: erroneously encouraged, he engaged the Persians at Pteria in c. 547 BCE. Neither side won and Croesus withdrew. Cyrus,however, pursued the king to Sardis and took the city after a short siege. Sardis flourished under both the Persians and their successors. It became the capital of a satrapy (province) under Persian rule, and the western terminus of the Royal Road, a key part of the road network that helped maintain the Persian administrative, military, and economic system. Sardis was the base of operations for Persian attempts to crush revolts by the Greek city-states of Asia Minor, and was itself burned down by these rebels in 498 BCE. Excavations by U.S. teams have taken place at Sardis since 1910 and are ongoing. **JM**

CITY DEFENSES

With a width of at least 60 feet (18 m.), and built of mud brick with a stone-boulder facing and external glacis, the city's walls were far more monumental than defense required and so were clearly intended to impress. Finds uncovered by the excavators included dramatic evidence of the city's sack by the Persians in 547 BCE, in the form of destruction debris from their demolition of the defenses, containing burned remains, and covering the bodies of soldiers who died defending the city.

COINAGE

Croesus is credited as being the inventor of coinage: stamped pieces of precious metal (electrum initially) whose value was guaranteed by the issuing authority. The idea of coinage spread rapidly in the Greek and Persian world, due to it being useful both economically and as a propaganda tool for the issuing state or ruler. In West Asia, however, where the use of weighed silver as currency was long established, coinage was adopted only after the Persian conquest.

GOLD REFINERY

To the north, outside the city wall, excavations uncovered the remains of an important and interesting industrial installation. Sardis was located on the Pactolus river, which carried considerable quantities of alluvial gold that could be recovered by panning. It has been suggested that the Lydian empire extracted the gold that had been eroding into the river over the ages. This was not pure gold, however, but electrum, a natural alloy of gold containing up to 40 percent silver and a little copper.

Evidence uncovered at Sardis Pactolus North revealed that the city's inhabitants had developed parting by cementation, the advanced technology required to refine the gold. The electrum was beaten into thin foil to maximize its surface area and placed in a closed container interleaved with brick dust and salt (sodium chloride): this pot was then heated over a long period at a temperature below the melting point of gold. The

salt and silver vaporized and formed silver chloride, which became mixed with the brick dust, leaving pure gold. The silver could be recovered by smelting the remaining mixture with lead to form a silver-lead amalgam. This was heated in cupels (bowl hearths) in a continuous blast of hot air to remove the impurities by cupellation (already an established technology in West Asia), separating the metals into a tiny ingot of pure silver and a slag of base metal oxides, predominantly lead chloride. Furnaces with fragments of electrum foil and tiny drips of gold as well as hundreds of cupels bear witness to the use of these techniques at Pactolus North. Lydia's wealth became legendary due to Croesus's generosity to shrines in Greece. For example, his offerings to the Delphic oracle included a gold statue 5 feet (1.5 m.) high, gold dishes, furniture decorated with gold and silver, and a huge quantity of gold ingots.

Persepolis 515 – 330 BCE

The royal center at Persepolis was built on a massive stone-faced terrace measuring 1,500 by 985 feet (455 by 300 m.). Darius I and his successors built palaces here: like the Apadana, these probably served as halls where gatherings were held. Magnificent relief carvings decorate many of the stairs, plinths, doorways, and gateways of the complex, depicting the king in his majesty and representatives of the peoples of the empire.

The royal center at Persepolis, 25 miles (40 km.) southwest of the Persian capital at Pasargadae, was founded by Darius I *c.* 515 BCE. Work here continued under his son Xerxes and grandson Artaxerxes I, and the main buildings were probably completed by 450 BCE, although several later kings added palaces. A huge terrace was constructed of stone and earth faced with limestone blocks; on this were built a number of official buildings, including a vast Apadana (audience chamber) and a treasury housing tribute from across the empire, including gold bracelets with animal terminals, silver amphorae and gold and silver beakers and bowls. A massive fortification wall surrounded the top of the terrace; access from the plain below was by a monumental double staircase, at the head of which was an imposing Gate of All Nations. Lesser buildings covered the plain.

The complex was designed by Darius as a symbol of his empire: many parts of the architecture, such as stairs, plinths, and door frames, were decorated with figures representing all his subject nations and their produce; materials sourced from throughout the empire were employed in its construction, as were craftspeople from many regions. Its monumentality emphasized the state's power; its stylistic and thematic uniformity combined with the diversity of the individuals and tribute depicted to create an impression of harmony, stability, order, and unity.

Alexander the Great captured Persepolis in 330 BCE and burned it down—some believe in a drunken orgy, others in revenge for the Persians' destruction of Athens 150 years earlier. Whatever the reason, the resultant debris served to cover and preserve the reliefs that decorate the center. Antiquarian interest led travelers to visit Persepolis by the seventeenth century, and later record its remains. In the 1930s, it was excavated by the Chicago Oriental Institute, and more recently by the Iranian Antiquity Service, while conservation work has been undertaken by a team from the Italian Institute for the Middle and Far East (ISMEO) in Rome. **JM**

◆ NAVIGATOR

FOCAL POINTS

1 TREASURY

Treasures received as tribute, including beautiful stone vessels, were stored here, more as an archive representing the wealth and diversity of the empire than a treasury in the financial sense.

2 APADANA

The central hall of the Apadana, where annual tribute from subject nations was formally presented, was flanked by porticoes with stone columns 66 feet (20 m.) high, bearing double bull's head capitals.

3 GATE OF ALL NATIONS

Persian art and architecture blended elements from nations of the empire. Like Assyrian palace entrances, the Gate of All Nations was flanked by sculptured figures of human-headed winged bulls.

4 HALL OF 100 COLUMNS

In this pillared hall, only the bases of the columns remain, along with the stone door jambs: these were decorated with reliefs showing the king enthroned, and the nations of the empire.

◄ Reliefs show tribute bearers from twenty-three nations, each identified by the offerings they bear, typical of their region's produce; their distinctive clothing; and their specialist weaponry. These include Scythians with pointed hats; Medes in baggy pants with bow case, axe and short sword; Bactrians in belted tunics, pleated pants, and high boots, leading a camel; Lydians in cloaks and beehive hats (seen here); and barefoot Indians in dhotis.

NAQSH-I RUSTAM

A number of royal tombs were carved into the hillside at Naqsh-i Rustam, 4 miles (6 km.) from Persepolis. Darius I's tomb is identified by an inscription; three others, uninscribed, probably housed Xerxes I, Artaxerxes I, and Darius II. All took the same form. A large cross-shaped area of cliff was removed to create a flat surface. In its center was carved a palace facade, with pillars supporting a roof of wooden beams. A central opening between the pillars led to the interior, where the bodies of the king and members of his immediate family were interred in rock-cut sarcophagi. Darius I's tomb also bore a scene showing the king and Ahura Mazda, the supreme god.

PARTHIANS AND SASANIANS

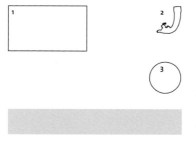

1. The ruined Taq-i Kisra is all that remains of the capital, Ctesiphon, 22 miles (35 km.) southeast of Baghdad, Iraq.

2. Ivory rhyton (ritual drinking horn) from Nisa, Turkmenistan (second century BCE).

3. Sasanian silver plate depicting a hunting scene from the tale of Bahram Gur and Azadeh (c. fifth century CE).

The Hellenistic Seleucid kingdom lost its eastern province of Parthia in c. 238 BCE to Iranian-speaking nomads from east of the Caspian in central Asia. Over the following century these nomads spread eastward into Bactria and westward through Iran to Mesopotamia. In 141 BCE their ruler, Mithridates I of Parthia (c. 195–132 BCE), was crowned in the Seleucid capital, Seleucia-on-the-Tigris. By 113 BCE his successor Mithridates II had advanced further west to establish the Parthian frontier at the Euphrates river, bringing it into competition with the expanding Romans. As Parthia was well situated to take advantage of the developing trade route through central Asia to China (see p. 268), its hostility to Rome spurred the latter's development of the sea route through the Red Sea and the Indian Ocean to western India, bypassing the established land route. Mutual hostility came to a head when a Roman army under Crassus invaded in 53 BCE and was utterly defeated at Carrhae in Syria. The Parthian use of cavalry archers gave them a military advantage over the Romans: they employed a strategy of faking a retreat, then turning in the saddle and firing a stream of arrows, the so-called "Parthian shot."

A see-saw of hostilities continued throughout the duration of the Parthian Empire, with a brief period of peace from 10 BCE, but by 58 CE hostilities had resumed. In 116 CE the emperor Trajan captured the Parthian capital, Ctesiphon;

KEY EVENTS

238 BCE	141 BCE	1st century BCE	53 BCE	116 CE	224
Iranian-speaking nomads from central Asia east of the Caspian, led by Arsaces, seize control of the Persian satrapy of Parthia in eastern Iran.	The Parthian ruler Mithridates I is crowned king at Seleucia-on-the-Tigris. Their winter capital at Ctesiphon is possibly established now.	Development of the form of the *iwan* exemplifies the replacement of Hellenistic cultural elements by Parthian traditional forms.	Political and commercial conflict between Parthia and Rome climaxes in a disastrous Roman defeat in the battle of Carrhae.	The Roman emperor Trajan captures Ctesiphon. Parthia, beset by enemies to the east and west and internally unsettled, begins to decline.	A rebellion by Ardashir in Persis results in the overthrow of the Parthian Arsacid dynasty and its replacement by the Sasanian dynasty.

though his further advance was a failure and he was forced to retreat, the Parthian regime was undermined and the empire declined from this time onward, suffering internal problems and external attacks.

The Parthian state had a loose feudal political structure, with powerful nobles directly answering to the king. One noble, Ardashir (180–242 CE), a local ruler in Persis (southwest Iran), gradually gained control over his neighbors: when in 224 CE he usurped a royal prerogative by founding a new city, Gur (see p. 266), the Parthian king Artabanus V attempted to punish him. Ardashir defeated the army sent against him, and killed Artabanus in single combat, becoming the empire's first Sasanian ruler. Ardashir reorganized the administration, centralizing power in his own hands and establishing a hierarchical organization. He systematized the coinage and established Zoroastrianism as the state religion, one of many ways in which the Sasanian monarchs consciously presented themselves as heirs to the Achaemenids.

Ardashir's successor, Shapur I, extended the empire, defeating the Romans, gaining control of Armenia and Georgia, and seizing territory in the east from the Kushan Empire: his empire now stretched from the Euphrates to the Indus and the Amu Darya. Competition and conflict with the Roman-Byzantine Empire continued throughout the Sasanian Empire, particularly over involvement in the lucrative Silk Road trade. In the fourth and fifth centuries CE, participants in this trade were also threatened by the Hephthalites, ferociously aggressive central Asian nomads to whom the Sasanians were forced to pay tribute. In the sixth century Khusrau I finally drove back the Hephthalites, but high taxation and a rigid class system, coupled with the endless conflict with the Roman-Byzantine Empire, weakened the Sasanian Empire so that it crumbled when attacked by the Arabs in the seventh century (see p.422).

Excavations at many sites have yielded fine examples of these empires' art and architecture. During the earlier Parthian period, there was considerable continuity of Hellenistic art and architecture, shown, for example, in fine ivory rhyta (drinking horns) decorated with animal heads (see image 2). By the late first century BCE, Parthian styles were beginning to emerge. Architectural features included the *iwan*, a vaulted hall with one end open onto a courtyard. This became a distinctive element of major Parthian buildings, and fine examples were built in the holy city of Hatra in northern Mesopotamia; its later elaboration under the Sasanians is exemplified by the magnificent sixth-century Taq-i Kisra *iwan* (see image 1) at Ctesiphon, the Parthian and Sasanian capital. Changing styles and cultural affiliations are also shown in coins. Sculptures and reliefs of Parthian monarchs in tunics and baggy pants attest to their nomad heritage. Sasanians also wear pants and are frequently portrayed wearing armor in their many rock reliefs and on their fine silver dishes, decorated with hunting scenes (see image 3). **JM**

240–272	490	531–578	562	614–628	637–651
Shapur I defeats three Roman emperors— Gordian III, Philip the Arab, and Valerian— conquers Armenia, and overruns the Kushan empire in the east.	A politico-religious movement resembling communism, led by the prophet Mazdak, produces internal upheaval in the Sasanian empire.	Khusrau Anushirvan reforms the Sasanian civil and military administration and revitalizes irrigation systems.	Rome and the Sasanians sign a fifty-year peace treaty, but in 572 the new emperor Justin II repudiates it, provoking further war.	Khusrau Parviz conquers Syria and Egypt but is defeated in 622 and 627 by the Eastern Roman emperor Heraclius; peace is signed in 628.	A Muslim army seizes Ctesiphon in 637. The young Sasanian king, Yazdgird III, flees. His assassination near Merv in 651 ends the dynasty.

Gur Third century CE

Like some earlier Parthian cities, Gur was laid out to a circular plan, symbolizing the world. Concentric streets lie within a perfect circle that is 1¼ miles (1.95 km.) in diameter. Around the city was a stamped clay rampart with gates corresponding to the main roads dividing it into quadrants; a 10-foot (3-m.) ditch and rampart encircled this.

◆ NAVIGATOR

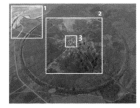

Ardashir Papakan (180–242 CE) was a local ruler in Persis (southwest Iran) who gained control of all southern Iran. His rebellious activities were ignored by his overlord, the Parthian king Artabanus V, until he founded a city. When Artabanus attacked Ardashir and was killed, Ardashir became the first king of the Sasanian dynasty.

Ardashir's city, named Ardashir Khurreh, or Gur (Light of Ardashir's Victory), lay in the Firuzabad river plain, below cliffs on which he built a fortress containing barracks and his palace, Qal'a-ye Dukhtar. The palace was accessed by stairs from the southwest and a monumental gateway. Its eastern portion contained the public area, including an *iwan* (a vaulted hall with one end open onto a courtyard) and a domed hall; residential quarters to the west comprised a courtyard surrounded by rooms. Ardashir later built a larger and more magnificent palace beside the river on the edge of the plain.

Ardashir dug irrigation canals and drained the originally swampy plain, converting it to farmland for growing cereals, fruit, and vegetables. In an adjacent valley, traces remain of an aqueduct commissioned by Ardashir to carry spring water from a tunnel cut into the mountains. Livestock were grazed on the surrounding wooded hills.

In the tenth century CE the city's name was changed to Perozabad, meaning "City of Victory." This later became Firuzabad, now the name of the modern city to its east. Archaeologists surveyed Gur in 1972, and excavated its two palaces between 1975 and 1978. Recently, excavations by an Iranian and German team led by Dieter Hoff have uncovered the remains of a bathhouse and several monumental buildings, including a Zoroastrian fire temple, as well as a royal cemetery. **JM**

1 IRRIGATION BY QANATS

Evaporation and salinization are problems with canal irrigation. To combat these, the people of Iran used qanats, skillfully planned underground canals invented by their Median or Urartu predecessors, to draw water from aquifers by gravity flow. Ventilation holes along a qanat's course allowed it to be cleaned and maintained.

2 INNER CITY OF GUR

The walled inner city, 1,500 feet (450 m.) in diameter, contained the official buildings and elite residences. The Takht-e Neshin, a substantial masonry building excavated in this area, is believed to have been a fire temple. An *iwan* on each of the temple's four sides surrounded a central room with a dome 46 feet (14 m.) in diameter.

3 TOWER

At the center of the city a tower, 100 feet (30 m.) high, marked the point from which twenty radial streets were laid out, dividing the city into sectors. Walls extending from these partitioned the whole surrounding landscape. The tower symbolized Ardashir at the center of his realm; as god's regent, his role was to protect the world.

▲ On the cliffs north of Gur, Ardashir commissioned relief sculptures to commemorate significant events. One shows his victory over Artabanus: the crown prince Shapur unseats the Parthian vizier while his father kills the Parthian king. Another depicts his investiture as king by the god Ahura Mazda, unusually portrayed in fully human form. A diadem is presented to the king, who is attended by three nobles, including Shapur.

THE SECOND PALACE AT GUR

Ardashir's second, unfortified royal palace contained a large *iwan* reception hall and three domed halls: here the king gave audience, enthroned in a niche on a high raised platform. Beyond was a large courtyard from which opened the many barrel-vaulted rooms of the palace's residential quarters. The arches of the *iwan* are echoed by arches over all the doorways and niches in the palace's internal walls. Decorative motifs, copied from the Persian palace at Persepolis (see p. 262), were executed in the plaster that covered the walls and ceilings. Residential rooms were also found in the palace's upper story, where passages and galleries ran around the three domes.

THE SILK ROAD

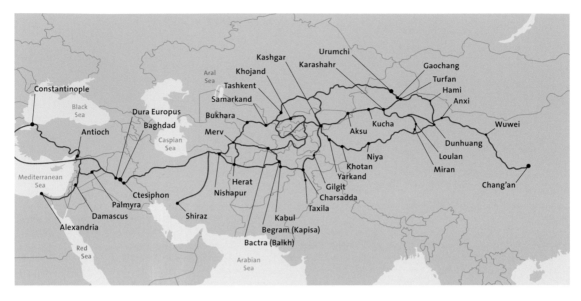

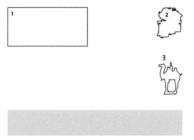

1 The overland network of the Silk Road.

2 A fragment of silk showing a fanged beast from Gaochang in Xinjiang, China, a stopping point on the Silk Road.

3 A *sancai* glazed tomb figure of a camel and rider created in the eighth century during the Tang dynasty.

From very early times, tenuous links have existed through central Asia from China to the West. The development of nomadic pastoralism in the steppe greatly facilitated West–East contacts, with mobile peoples providing a conduit for trade. The Chinese enjoyed an ambivalent relationship with these fluid tribal groups: they were a menace, constantly raiding Chinese territory; nevertheless they were the route by which China could obtain horses and Western goods in exchange for silk and grain. Alliances were created, with many a minor Chinese princess being sent as a bride to a nomad chief; and the Chinese built walls (see p. 364) to keep the nomads out.

In the second century BCE, one nomad confederacy, the Xiongnu, drove another, the Yuezhi, out of the eastern steppe; the Yuezhi retreated west, establishing themselves in Bactria, west of the Pamir mountains. The contemporary Chinese emperor Wudi (156–87 BCE) sought to make common cause against the troublesome Xiongnu, in 138 BCE sending an envoy, Zhang Qian (d. 114 BCE), to negotiate with the Yuezhi. Though his embassy failed, Zhang Qian returned to China and painted a glowing picture of the opportunities for profitable trade, particularly to acquire the famed Heavenly Horses of Ferghana. Wudi was convinced and sent a military expedition to establish the route. Despite horrendous losses of men crossing the desert wastes of the Takla Makan (Gobi Desert) region, a viable route was mapped out and outposts established to enable it to operate. Thus began the fabled Silk Road (see image 1), the connection through central Asia between China and the

KEY EVENTS

138–125 BCE	124 BCE	102 BCE	220 CE	6th century	565
Chinese envoy Zhang Qian is sent to secure an alliance with the Yuezhi. He fails but forges a trading link with the West that becomes the Silk Road.	Emperor Wudi sends an embassy to Parthian king Mithridates II, who reciprocates, establishing an alliance that enables trade to flow.	Emperor Wudi's army captures Khojand on the Syr Darya river, source of the Heavenly Horses; Chinese control of Tarim Basin is established.	Fall of the Han dynasty; in 224 the Parthian dynasty is overthrown; Rome loses eastern provinces; the Kushans collapse—undermining Silk Road trade.	Nestorian monks successfully smuggle silkworm cocoons to the West, hidden in a bamboo staff, breaking the Chinese monopoly of silk production.	Turkish nomads capture Silk Road cities of Samarkand, Bukhara, and Tashkent; Byzantines make alliance with them to trade.

countries of the West, South Asia, Persia, and the Mediterranean powers; countries connected since Persian times by trade routes. Soon Chinese silk was traveling west along the route, along with lacquerware, while horses from Ferghana, Roman gold and glassware, and Indian gemstones flowed east. A snapshot of the trade is provided by a first-century CE merchant's storehouse at Begram, Afghanistan, filled with goods in transit (see p. 272).

The Silk Road left the Chinese capital, Chang'an, and passed through the Gansu corridor to the Dunhuang oasis (see p. 274), where a trading city developed, one of many established by the Chinese or settled by traders—some traveling the whole route, the majority content to operate caravans along a single part (see image 3). From Dunhuang the road divided, one branch running north and the other south around the Tarim Basin that enclosed the Takla Makan Desert. The routes met again at Kashgar; from here a road ran south over the Karakoram Range of mountains into India, where it fed into Indian trade networks. Another route ran west over the high passes of the Pamirs, then divided, one route leading north across the Syr and Amu Darya rivers to Samarkand and Bukhara; the other going south through Bactra (Balkh) to join another route into India, passing through Taxila (see p. 354), or continuing west, where the routes met again at Merv (see p. 270), whence they ran to western cities. This network evolved rapidly and continued in use until the late 15th century, when the development of sea routes around Africa rendered the Silk Road obsolete. Thereafter many of its cities declined and were abandoned. Explorations and excavations, especially by Hungarian-British archaeologist Aurel Stein (1862–1943) in the early twentieth century, have uncovered many of its glories: not only the treasures of Dunhuang, but the remains of settlements where the dry desert conditions have preserved organic remains, including paintings, wooden houses, textiles (see image 2), and wooden tools; and most importantly manuscripts, which chart the Silk Road's history.

It was not only trade goods that passed along the road. In its early days, Buddhists and others carried their religions to China; by the third century, Chinese pilgrims returned, visiting holy places in India. The route also carried ideas, technological know-how, and plants, as well as diseases and hostile military expeditions. The Chinese took control of the eastern part of the network, establishing their Western Protectorates as far as the Pamirs, maintaining forts with conscript garrisons that policed the route and kept the nomads at bay. In some periods the Chinese lost control of the region, through internal decline or external force. The wealth of the caravan cities, their productive oasis agriculture, and their cosmopolitan culture contrasted with the extreme hardships and hazards of the route, such as freezing deserts and treacherous mountain passes, and being at the mercy of nature and hostile nomad neighbors—horrifically exemplified by Genghis Khan (1162–1227), who sacked many of the cities before devoting effort to promoting Silk Road trade. **JM**

629–645	630–640	711–713	751	1218	1271
Chinese Buddhist pilgrim Xuanzang (602–664) travels the northern route around Tarim Basin to India where he visits Buddhist holy places.	Tang Chinese emperor Taizong (599–649) wrests control of Tarim Basin from the Turks; by 649 Chinese control extends to the Pamirs.	The Arab commander Qutaiba ibn Muslim (d. 715), based in Merv, captures the cities of Bukhara, Samarkand and Ferghana, and sacks Kashgar.	Chinese defeat by Arabs at the Battle of Talas ends their control of central Asian Silk Road cities, now coming under Islamic supervision.	The murder of 450 Muslim merchants, including a Mongol envoy, sparks Genghis Khan's sack of Samarkand, beginning his conquest of Asia.	Explorer Marco Polo (c. 1254–1324) goes with his father and uncle on the Silk Road to the court of Kublai Khan (1215–94). He stays there for seventeen years.

Merv Sixth century BCE – mid sixteenth century CE

A mosque built by Abu Muslim after 748 CE beside the Majan canal became the center of a new Abbasid city (now Sultan Kala). In the eleventh to thirteenth century, this comprised 840 acres (340 ha.) within the city walls, with 519 acres (210 ha.) of walled suburbs to the north and south.

Merv's Achaemenid settlement (modern Erk Kala, Turkmenistan), whose walls still stand, became the citadel of Antiochia Margiana (modern Gyaur Kala). It was founded c. 290 BCE by the Seleucid king Antiochus I (324–261 BCE) as a base against the threat of nomad incursions. Merv, commanding the Margiana oasis, became a staging post on the Silk Road. Margiana supported the Sasanian revolt against Parthian rule in 224 CE (see p. 264), and Merv became a Sasanian military and administrative center and international trading hub. A cosmopolitan city, its inhabitants were mainly Zoroastrians but included Buddhists, Manicheans, and Nestorian Christians. Margiana's fertile lands were farmed by irrigation from the Murghab delta.

Merv fell to the Arabs in the seventh century, becoming a base from which Arab eastern conquests continued. It attracted Arab settlers, who were housed in a separate walled town, Shaim Kala. Merv helped overthrow the Ummayads, the Abbasid dynasty being proclaimed here in 748 by the commander Abu Muslim (d. 755), who subsequently built a new city, Marv al-Shahijan (Marv the Great; modern Sultan Kala). A major canal through the city provided a public water supply, with pipes leading to buildings and reservoirs. The original city became an industrial suburb, with pottery and metalworking workshops. Merv became an outstanding center of learning, with an observatory and major libraries, attracting important scholars. In the tenth century, Merv was one of the world's largest cities, its population perhaps 200,000.

In 1221, the Mongols invaded the region. They razed Merv, butchering its population, except for 400 craftsmen who were sent to work in the Mongol court. Evidence of the city's subsequent economic decline was excavated from 1992 to 2000. Excavations have occurred at Merv since 1890, including recent British and Turkmen investigations of the city's well-preserved defenses. Merv's cities are now an archaeological park. **JM**

✦ NAVIGATOR

1 CITY WALLS OF SULTAN KALA

The architecture of Merv was made of mud—sometimes baked brick, but often rammed packed earth; most of it was then protected with a mud plaster. Merv's cities and citadels were surrounded by walls, still standing to a considerable height: 7½ miles (12 km.) of walls surround the Islamic city of Sultan Kala, of which a portion is seen here.

2 MAUSOLEUM OF SULTAN AHMAD SANJAR

The city's twelfth-century ruler Sultan Sanjar (c. 1084–1157) was buried in a tomb in the city's center: a square structure, with painted wall plaster inside. Its dome was originally covered with turquoise tiles: reputedly the sight of sunlight glinting from this alerted travelers that they were within a day's camel journey of the city.

3 DECAY AND CONSERVATION

Rain, snow, sand-laden winds, and vegetation have eroded Merv's architecture over the centuries, and a rise in the water table due to the Karakum dam has increased the pace of deterioration. A project by University College London and Turkmen official bodies is experimenting with ways to record and conserve it.

▲ Four conical mud-brick icehouses survive south of the city. Built in the Seljuq and Timurid periods, these were used for storing ice cut in winter for use in summer. Wooden beams stretched across the interior may have been structural supports or used to suspend food to keep it chilled. This example, icehouse 1, is about 56 feet (17 m.) in diameter at its base and survives to 49 feet (15 m.) high.

GREAT KYZ KALA

Köshks (fortified palaces) were erected west of the city from the seventh century onward. These were elite extramural retreats surrounded by orchards and gardens; some have been excavated. Their design made them cool in summer and warm in winter. The Great Kyz Kala is the largest: it is two stories high, incorporating a rectangular platform. Its sides were corrugated, with a crenellated parapet. It was entered through an arched entrance in the upper story, approached by a stair or ramp. The platform had no entrance: its rooms were accessed via a stair from the north end of the upper floor and lit by windows at the corrugated wall's base. The upper story had a courtyard surrounded by rooms, roofed with barrel vaults or domes. The northern stair led also to the roof.

Begram First century CE

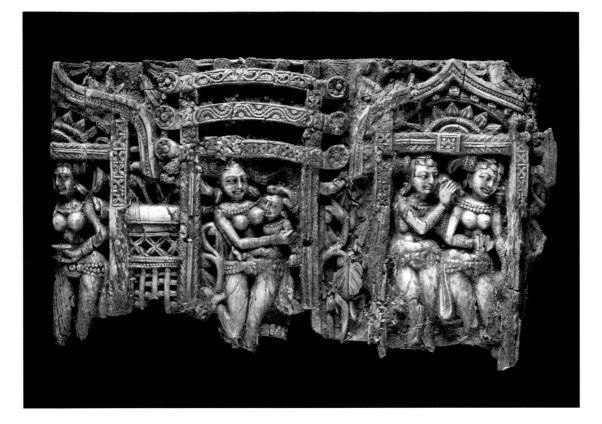

The treasures of Begram were carefully stacked by type. Both rooms contained ivory furniture decorations, glass vessels, pottery, and stone and bronze objects. Room 10 also stored ostrich eggshell vessels, and Room 13 contained poorly preserved Han Chinese lacquerware.

In the 1830s, British explorer Charles Masson (1800–53) discovered ancient coins at Begram, 50 miles (80 km.) north of Kabul, Afghanistan. The site continued to be plundered for coins in the following decades. Granted a thirty-year monopoly on archaeological work in Afghanistan from 1922, the French Archaeological Delegation selected Begram as a site to investigate. In 1936, they excavated inside the surviving fortification wall of New Royal City, uncovering a main street flanked by stores and workshops. Continuing in 1937, they discovered a supposed royal palace in an adjacent area. Here they found a storeroom (Room 10) blocked off with bricks: it contained a spectacular collection of objects, including Indian ivories and Roman glassware, dated by the excavators to between the first and fourth centuries CE. Further excavations in 1939 revealed another blocked room (Room 13): it contained similar material, with the addition of Chinese lacquerware. The rooms' walls were plastered and painted. French work at Begram continued in 1941 to 1942 and ended in 1946.

This Begram material was originally interpreted as a palace treasury accumulated over several centuries. However, recent work shows that it probably all dates to the first century CE. Furthermore, the objects are very varied, but stored systematically, by material and type. While some pieces were reasonably valuable, others were inexpensive in their day. It is now thought that they were the stock-in-trade of a merchant based at Begram, involved in the Silk Road trade network. Begram, possibly identifiable as ancient Kapisi—summer residence of the Kushan emperors—was strategically placed for trade: from here a route led south to Kabul and the Khyber Pass, the main route through the mountains into Gandhara, reaching Taxila (see p. 354) and from there heading south into India. Going north, a route led to Bactra (modern Balkh), joining the Silk Road east to China and west to the Roman Empire. **JM**

PAINTED GLASS BEAKERS

In the first century CE, Alexandria in Egypt was a major industrial and commercial center in the Roman Empire, famed for its glassware including painted glass beakers. These depict mythological stories such as the Rape of Europa, scenes from everyday life, wild animals such as leopards, and gladiators.

BRONZE WEIGHT

Small bronze busts, representing figures such as the god Mars, were probably cosmetic jars, and are fitted with a stopper. Later, however, loops were added for suspension and they were used as steelyard weights. These were trading equipment, reinforcing the probability that the Begram finds were a merchant's stored wares.

IVORIES, PLASTER MEDALLIONS, AND A NOVELTY BRONZE

Both storerooms at Begram contained many carved ivories, in poor condition, necessitating careful excavation—in situ reinforcement before lifting—and specialist conservation thereafter. A few pieces were sculpted in the round, the majority were low-relief panels, and all had decorated wooden furniture, long since decayed away: footstools in Room 10, chairs and couches in Room 13. Tiny copper nails, some still in place, attached the ivories to the wood.

The carvings are stylistically Indian. They show Indian themes: architecture such as palace balconies, stupa gateways, and horseshoe-arched shrine doorways; scantily clad figures often embracing; and animals and mythical creatures, interwoven with plant and geometric patterns.

Although the human figures range from indolent courtiers and lively musicians to stern guards and venturesome riders, almost all are female. A few pieces are carved in bone rather than ivory. These pieces were probably imported from the Ganges region, where such art was common in stone and terracotta—ivory rarely survives.

Many plaster medallions were stacked in Room 13. These depicted classical themes. One represents the infant winged Eros (Cupid) holding a butterfly; others show scenes, busts, and floral decoration. Rather than decorative objects in their own right, these were probably templates for disposable molds used to cast these decorations in bronze. If so, Begram may have been an industrial center as well as a trading hub.

A strange bronze object found has been called an aquarium. The bronze basin portrays the gorgon Medusa, covered by fish with movable tails, which were operated by wires and weights from below. A thick glass plate protected the surface, separated from it by a circular piece of wood. Another bronze plaque completed the object; it is not clear how it operated.

Dunhuang Fourth century CE onward

The Mogao Caves are carved into the cliffs above the Dachuan River near Dunhuang, China. They are filled with frescoes and hand-molded clay sculptures of gods and saints. The caves were founded in 366 CE and extended up until the fourteenth century.

The Mogao Caves, also known as the Caves of the Thousand Buddhas, are one of the world's largest and longest-used sites of Buddhist art. They are located 15 miles (25 km.) southeast of the oasis of Dunhuang in Gansu province on the edge of the Gobi Desert in western China, the ancient meeting point of the northern and southern routes and an important outpost of the ancient Silk Road. Constructed from the fourth century CE onward, more than 1,000 cells and cave sanctuaries with wall paintings and sculptures bear testimony to this flourishing center for Buddhist worship, teaching, and learning. Today, 492 caves are preserved, housing approximately 484,376 square feet (45,000 sq. m.) of murals and more than 2,000 painted sculptures.

From its beginnings to the Tang dynasty (618–907 CE), Dunhuang experienced a heyday and became a center of commerce, trading, and Buddhist belief. Under the patronage of Empress Wu Zetian (624–705 CE) a large number of caves and two large Buddha statues were constructed in Mogao. Paintings depicting the life of Buddha, as well as scenes of daily life, are of unmatched historical value. Most of the caves have paintings all over the walls and ceilings, with geometric or floral ornaments, as well as figurative images such as Buddha and Bodhisattvas. The scenes of everyday life are sometimes portrayed in minute detail. Cave 302 of the Sui dynasty (581–618 CE) depicts a camel pulling a cart along the Silk Road. In Cave 61, a landscape of Mount Wutai of the Song dynasty (960–1279 CE) is an early example of Chinese cartography showing roads, rivers, cities, and temples.

Dunhuang and the Mogao Caves were almost abandoned due to shifting trade routes from the Ming dynasty (1368–1644 CE) onward. After the discovery of the Library Cave in 1900, the site became a subject of scientific research. **MP**

NIRVANA CAVE

Cave 148, the Nirvana Cave, has a rectangular layout and dates from 705 to 781 CE in the Tang dynasty. The Thousand-Buddha motif of small, seated Buddhas—after which the caves are named—is painted on the ceiling. The cave houses the second largest reclining figure in the caves, a Buddha measuring 47 feet (14.5 m.) long made of stucco on a sandstone frame. More than seventy-two stucco statues of his followers, restored during the Qing dynasty (1644–1911 CE), surround him in mourning.

ARTISTIC STYLE

The unique artistic style of Dunhuang art mixes together the Han Chinese artistic tradition with styles assimilated from ancient Indian and Gandharan customs; and at a later stage an integration of the arts of the Turks or ancient Tibetans is also visible. This mural on the south wall in Cave 217 was created from 705 to 707 CE and it is thought to depict the *Sutra of the Supreme Sacrosanct Dharani from the Buddha's Summit* or a parable from the *Lotus Sutra*.

LIBRARY CAVE

Cave 17, or the Library Cave, has an area of approximately 84 square feet (7.8 sq. m.). It was built between 851 CE and 867 as a memorial chapel for a monk. In the middle of the eleventh century, the monks sealed the entrance by building a wall on which they painted a mural. In 1900, the caretaker of the cave complex, Daoist monk Wang Yuanlu (c. 1849–1931), rediscovered and opened it. The cave's precious treasures included more than 50,000 manuscripts, as well as prints, paintings, and ritual objects.

About 90 percent of the objects found were texts of religions important at the time, such as Buddhism, Daoism, Manicheism, Zoroastrianism, and Nestorianism. They also included the earliest complete printed book, the *Diamond Sutra* scroll (a Chinese translation from Sanksrit of the most famous Buddhist sutra) dated to 868 CE. The remaining 10 percent include a wide range of writings: official and private correspondence; Confucian classics; social and economic documents including sale contracts; loan and pawn shop documents; accounting ledgers; and calendars with subjects such as constellations, medicine, and weaving. The documents were written in Chinese, as well as Tibetan, Khotanese, Sanskrit, Uighur, Sogdian, Turkic, and Kuchean.

After the discovery, the Mogao Caves became a subject of curiosity. Many of the Library Cave's books and treasures were given away or sold, including to Hungarian-British archaeologist Aurel Stein and French sinologist Paul Pelliot (1878–1945). A small quantity of manuscripts were transported to Beijing in 1910, but many were lost. In 1994, the British Library set up the International Dunhuang Project to coordinate and collect scholarly work on the manuscripts and other material.

THE HELLENISTIC WORLD

The Hellenistic World started to form during the fourth century BCE with the rise of the Macedonian Empire and the reordering of the region that had been dominated by the Greek city-states. King Philip II of Macedonia (382–336 BCE) expanded into the rest of Greece, defeating alliances. One of his main palaces was at Vergina (see p. 280) in northern Greece.

The campaigns of Alexander the Great (356–323 BCE) against Persia were commemorated in a series of victory monuments. One of the most stunning is the Alexander mosaic (see image 1) from the House of the Faun at Pompeii, Italy. It represents the defeat of Darius III (d. 330 BCE) at the Battle of Issus (in modern Turkey) in 333 BCE. The mosaic shows Alexander charging at the head of his cavalry, and Darius fleeing from the battle on his chariot. Another, the Granicus monument, commemorates twenty-five of Alexander's companions killed in the Battle of the Granicus (in modern Turkey) and was erected at Dion in Macedonia. It was moved in 146 BCE, after the annexation of the province, and displayed in the Porticus Metelli at Rome. This complex, remodeled by Emperor Augustus (63 BCE–14 CE), was found in the Campus Martius near to the Tiber.

Alexander pressed as far as the Indus and remains of planned Greek cities have been identified at locations such as Taxila, Pakistan (see p. 354). Art from Gandhara, covering the region of modern Pakistan and Afghanistan, is thought to have been heavily influenced by the Hellenistic world. Alexander died at Babylon (in modern Iraq) and was buried in Egypt.

1 The Alexander mosaic (c. 100 BCE) is a Roman floor mosaic originally from the House of the Faun in Pompeii, Italy.

2 Detail from a mosaic depicting Alexander the Great during a lion hunt from the House of Dionysus in Pella, Greece, and dating to c. 320 BCE.

3 A marble wall block from the Temple of Athena Polias at Priene, Turkey. The inscription records the gift of funds from Alexander the Great to complete it.

KEY EVENTS

400 BCE	4th century BCE	4th–3rd century BCE	336 BCE	334 BCE	333 BCE
The Macedonian royal capital is established at Pella. Greek excavations led by Photios Petsas and C. Makaronas are carried out there in 1957–64.	Urban planning is carried out at Taxila, as revealed in excavations in 1913 by British archaeologist John Marshall (1876–1958).	Monumental tombs are constructed at Vergina.	King Philip II of Macedon is assassinated. Tomb II, at Vergina, discovered in 1977, is identified by some as his.	Twenty-five of Alexander's companions are killed at the Battle of the Granicus.	Alexander defeats Darius III at the Battle of Issus.

After the death of Alexander, the areas of his conquests were broken into kingdoms ruled by his former generals. The Seleucids built their city at Antioch in Syria. This was based on a grid pattern that had become popular in the Greek world from the mid fifth century BCE onward. Few traces of the Hellenistic city have been recovered. The Macedonian royal capital at Pella had been established in 400 BCE and was the birthplace of Philip II. This flourished in the third century BCE and was finally abandoned in 168 BCE as Macedonia was incorporated into the Roman Republic. Excavations have found remains of a number of elite houses, many decorated with pebble mosaics (see image 2).

One of the most spectacular royal cities was constructed at Pergamon in northwest Turkey. The Attalids had defeated the Gauls, who had occupied central Turkey, and they constructed a city that acknowledged the inspiration of Athens. The iconography of Pergamon that celebrated the defeat of its barbarian neighbors echoed that at Athens, where the defeated Persians were represented as giants, Trojans, or Amazons. The Attalids also became benefactors of the city of Athens. Their monumental double-layered stoa that flanked the east side of the agora, the political heart of the city of Athens, was a benefaction by Attalus II (220–138 BCE) in the mid second century BCE. A further stoa, a benefaction of his elder brother Eumenes II (d. c. 160 BCE), ran along the south side of the Athenian Acropolis adjacent to the Theater of Dionysus.

Egypt was controlled by the Ptolemies, and one of the most splendid Greek cities was built at Alexandria (see p. 278). Underwater investigations have revealed some of the elements surrounding the Pharos, or lighthouse. Remains of the Temple of Serapis and some of the cemeteries have also been recovered.

One of the best-explored planned cities dating to the Hellenistic period is at Priene in western Turkey. Excavations in the Temple of Athena Polias recovered the dedicatory inscription, dating to 334 to 330 BCE, that records the benefaction of Alexander the Great (see image 3). Public buildings such as the *bouleuterion*, or council chamber, reveal the political workings of the Hellenistic city.

During the third century BCE, the Ptolemies established naval bases in the Aegean. U.S. excavations at Koroni in Attica, Greece, have recovered one of the bases that was used against the Macedonian occupation of Athens. German work on the island of Thera (now Santorini) has recovered some of the inscriptions linked to the Ptolemaic garrison, including an altar dedicated by an officer who was in charge of the Ptolemaic possessions on Crete, Thera, and the Peloponnese. A British archaeological team has recorded the remains of the fortified Ptolemaic naval base on the Methana peninsula in the Peloponnese.

The Hellenistic kingdoms lasted into the Roman period. Antiochus I (c. 86–38 BCE), of Commagene in eastern Turkey, was the grandson of the Seleucid ruler Antiochus VIIII (242–187 BCE). He ruled Commagene from 69 BCE and became an ally of Rome. His mausoleum on Nemrut Dag in the Eastern Taurus mountains in Turkey indicates that he was considered divine. **DG**

332 BCE	323 BCE	3rd century BCE	168 BCE	1st century BCE	31 BCE
Alexander seizes Egypt from the Persian Empire.	Alexander dies at Babylon at the age of thirty-three.	The Ptolemies establish naval bases in the Aegean. In 1995 a number of Ptolemaic sculptures are recovered from the seabed at Alexandria.	Pella is abandoned as Macedonia is incorporated into the Roman Republic.	Cleopatra VII orders the construction of the Caesareum temple at Alexandria.	Octavian defeats Mark Antony at the Battle of Actium.

Alexandria Fourth century BCE

The Pharos, or lighthouse, constructed at the end of the harbor mole, was probably completed in the early third century BCE. The building can be visualized from ancient representations on coins and mosaics, such as this sixth-century CE example from Qasr Libya in Libya.

Alexandria lies to the west of the Nile Delta. It was one of a series of cities that carried its name because of an association with Alexander the Great. It became one of the major harbors of the ancient world, and it has been estimated that by the Roman period it had a population of over half a million people.

Alexander seized the province of Egypt from the Persian Empire in c. 332 BCE. After his death in 323 BCE, one of his generals, Ptolemy, took his body to Memphis, where it was buried. Ptolemy established the Greco-Macedonian ruling dynasty and made Alexandria the capital. He then brought Alexander's body to Alexandria, and Ptolemy IV Philopator (c. 238–205 BCE) created a dynastic burial. The location of this tomb has been the subject of a series of investigations, though its precise spot has not been identified.

The city was established along Greek lines and with a grid pattern. One of its most important cultural institutions was the library, containing, according to ancient reports, about half a million texts. Sadly these texts have been lost, although their popularity in the library allowed them to be copied and this helped some of them to be passed down to the present day. Another Ptolemaic institution was the Caesareum temple, constructed by Cleopatra VII (c. 69–30 BCE). This was constructed in honor of her lover Mark Antony (83–30 BCE). Such actions scandalized the people of Rome and were used to advantage by their opponent Octavian, later Emperor Augustus, who defeated them at the Battle of Actium in 31 BCE. The Caesareum was re-established by Augustus, who brought obelisks from Heliopolis to add to it in 14 CE. In the nineteenth century, one obelisk was removed to London, where it is displayed on the Embankment (and known as Cleopatra's Needle), and the other to New York, where it was placed in Central Park. **DG/GM**

COLUMN KNOWN AS POMPEY'S PILLAR

Adjacent to the Serapeion is a granite column removed from Heliopolis, bearing the cartouche of Thutmose III (d. 1426 BCE). An inscription says it was re-erected in 291 CE in honor of Emperor Diocletian (245–316 CE) after he took the city. The column is in a fifth-century mosaic from Sepphoris, Israel, depicting Alexandria.

SPHINX OF PTOLEMY XII AULETES

In 1998, a sphinx of Ptolemy XII Auletes (c. 112–51 BCE), father of Cleopatra VII, was raised from the seabed close to Alexandria by French archaeologist Franck Goddio (b. 1947). Over twenty-five sphinxes have been recovered from the sea off Fort Qaitbay. Some of them have inscriptions indicating they derive from Heliopolis.

FINDS FROM THE CITY OF ALEXANDRIA

Some of the most exciting discoveries have been made in the waters around Fort Qaitbay, constructed in the late fifteenth century. During the 1990s, French archaeologists recorded the finds of ancient sculpture on the seabed, including columns with the cartouche of Ramesses II (d. 1213 BCE), erected at Heliopolis and reused in the city in the Ptolemaic period. Other finds included obelisks belonging to Seti I (d. 1279 BCE).

One of the most spectacular finds was a colossal granite statue of a male figure, plausibly one of the Ptolemies, more than 15 feet (4.5 m.) high. A statue of Isis, 23 feet (7 m.) tall—perhaps over 39 feet (12 m.) with a headdress—was recovered from the same area in 1961. It appears that the two figures had been displayed next to each other, as a British underwater team had identified their bases. Other fragmentary colossal statues and their bases have been recovered in the same area.

One of the cults that Ptolemy I established at Alexandria was that of Serapis, which combined a cult from Sinope in northern Turkey with an Egyptian one. Sadly, the cult statue from the Serapeion by the fourth-century BCE Greek sculptor Bryaxis has not survived, being destroyed by Theophilus, Bishop of Alexandria (d. 412 CE) in 391 CE. It was described by ancient authors as being dark in color, and a second-century CE copy, in a dark marble, was recovered during British excavations in the gymnasium of the city of Salamis on Cyprus. A gold tablet with the cartouche of Ptolemy III (d. c. 221 BCE) and a text in Greek shows that the sanctuary was developed during the Ptolemaic period. The Serapeion was damaged during riots in the city in 116 CE, and as a result the emperor Hadrian (76–138 CE) arranged for the rebuilding of the sanctuary. His name was attached to the dedication of an Apis bull found in one of the subterranean galleries in the sanctuary.

Vergina Fourth–third centuries BCE

The facade of Tomb II at the site of Vergina, Greece. It has a series of columns surmounted by a painted set of metopes and triglyphs. Above them is a painted panel depicting a hunting scene.

The archaeological site of Vergina in northern Greece is the location of the ancient palace of the Macedonian royal family, where the mountains overlook the Aliákmon river. The area was occupied in the Iron Age and a series of mounds dating to 1000 to 700 BCE has been identified.

French archaeologist Léon Heuzey (1831–1922) discovered the site in 1855. Six years later, a team from the French School at Athens began excavations of the cemetery and the palace. In 1938, Constantine Rhomaios (1874–1966), from the University of Thessaloniki, began to investigate the palace and some of the elite tombs. Exploration of the Great Tumulus began in 1952 but it was not until 1977 that Tomb II—identified by some as containing the remains of King Philip II of Macedon—was found. Excavations have revealed the foundations of the palace in the foothills of Mount Paikon. The buildings lay on a terrace with views across the plain toward the river. The square complex was entered by a monumental gateway on the eastern side. This led to a large courtyard surrounded by a Doric colonnade. A covered walkway gave access to some dining rooms, identified by their offset doors, ranging in size from seven to thirty couches. The rooms on the north side overlooked a theater and the valley. A pair of dining rooms on the south side of the complex were accessed from a central porticoed room. It is likely that they were reserved for the king and his immediate associates. On the east side, adjacent to the gateway, was a circular structure, or *tholos*, perhaps a throne room. However an inscription to "Herakles of the ancestors" in the *tholos* suggests that it served as a cult room because the hero was regarded as the founder of the royal house. **DG/GM**

In 1977, when Greek archaeologist Manolis Andronikos (1919–92) entered Tomb II, he discovered a gold chest, or larnax, containing the remains of an individual, a couch, and silver plate. There was also a piece of textile dyed purple and decorated in gold, some bronze vessels, and a set of armor. Such grave goods suggested that the tomb was that of someone wealthy, and the starburst emblem on the lid of the larnax indicated that it belonged to a member of the Macedonian royal family.

THEATER

The theater was to the north, overlooked by the palace. The audience would have been seated facing the valley below. Excavations suggest that there were stone seats at the front, and other wooden tiers set against the bank. A skene building was set behind the semicircular orchestra. Historical sources place the assassination of King Philip II in the theater by his bodyguard while he was attending the wedding of his daughter Cleopatra to Alexander of Epirus (350–331 BCE).

MONUMENTAL TOMBS

Excavations revealed several monumental tombs dated to the fourth and third centuries BCE, often with a facade with Ionic columns with pediments.

The Bella Tumulus, to the west of the site, included stone-carved couches placing the deceased in a dining and drinking context. A painting above the door of the inner chamber may show the deceased.

The Great Tumulus, excavated by Manolis Andronikos, contained four tombs, two of which had not been looted. Tomb I was decorated with a painting showing Persephone driven to the underworld in the chariot of Hades. Tomb III was found undisturbed. It contained the remains of Alexander IV (323–c. 310 BCE), son of Alexander the Great and Roxane (c. 310 BCE). His cremated bones were contained in a silver hydria with a golden wreath. Tomb II was also found undisturbed. A study was made of the remains from the larnax in

its main chamber to attempt to identify the deceased. A suggestion based on facial reconstruction was that the individual was Philip II, King of Macedonia and father of Alexander the Great. The remains of a young woman placed in a second larnax have been linked to Cleopatra, the last of Philip II's seven wives. The identifications have been questioned, citing discrepancies between weight standards recorded on metal vessels from the tomb and the date of death of Philip II.

Another hypothesis is that the occupants of Tomb II are Philip III Arrhidaios (c. 359–317 BCE), a son of Philip II, along with his wife Adea Eurydike (d. 317 BCE). An additional proposal, based on skeletal remains, is that the unidentified male and female buried in Tomb I could be Philip II and Cleopatra. However, the identity of the occupants of Tombs I and II remains uncertain.

CARTHAGINIAN EMPIRE

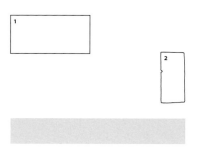

1 The archaeological site of Tharros on the Sinis Peninsula in Sardinia, Italy.

2 A gold-leaf Pyrgi Tablet with Phoenician text dating to the sixth century BCE.

The early levels excavated at sites such as Sabratha and Lepcis Magna in Libya have revealed imported Athenian pottery dating to the fifth and fourth centuries BCE. These finds may reflect Phoenician seasonal activity on the south side of the Gulf of Sirte to the west of the Greek colonial area of Cyrenaica. Oea (modern Tripoli) is also likely to have been a Phoenician settlement. These provided ports along the route to Carthage (see p. 284) from the eastern Mediterranean, avoiding mainland Greece and the Peloponnese.

Historical sources say that Carthage (in modern Tunisia) was settled from Tyre (in modern Lebanon) in the ninth century BCE, although this is not supported by archaeological evidence. It is most likely that it was in the eighth century, contemporary with the growth of Greek colonies in southern Italy and Sicily. The tension between the Phoenicians and the Greeks became apparent in the coalition between the Carthaginians and the Etruscans against the expansion of Greek colonies that led to the naval battle off Alalia, Corsica, in 535 BCE. This coalition is reflected in the gold plaques in Phoenician (see image 2) and Etruscan script and excavated at the sanctuary site of Pyrgi (modern Santa Severa, Lazio, Italy) in Etruria. A Carthaginian force was defeated at Himera in northern Sicily in 480 BCE, and booty from the battle may have been used to build one of the monumental temples at Selinunte in the south of the island.

see p. 284

KEY EVENTS

814 BCE	8th century BCE	8th century BCE	Late 8th century BCE	c. 700 BCE	7th century BCE
The Phoenician settlement at Carthage is founded (according to traditional dating). It is excavated in 1857 by Charles Ernest Beulé (1826–74).	Greek colonies in southern Italy and Sicily expand.	The Nora stone, found in 1773 at Nora in Sardinia, is inscribed.	The Phoenician settlement at Tharros is started. Excavations there in 1830 recover remains of the Phoenician cemeteries.	A Phoenician ship containing transport amphorae sinks near the island of Gozo, Malta. It is excavated by a French team in 2014.	Phoenician trading occurs in the Balearic Islands, as evidenced by fieldwork carried out on Ibiza in 1982–86.

Gelon (*c.* 540–478 BCE), tyrant of the cities of Gela and Syracuse, made the dedication of a tripod and a statue of Victory (Nike) at Delphi in Greece. It is thought this may be linked to dedications of Etruscan armor at Olympia in Greece by his successor, his younger brother Hieron (d. *c.* 467 BCE), and the Syracusans, perhaps associated with the Carthaginian and Etruscan alliance.

Carthage then became a hub for Phoenician activity in the western Mediterranean. From there, the Phoenicians settled the western part of Sicily with a city at Motya (see p. 286). This continued until the destruction of Motya by the Syracusans in the early fourth century BCE. The main center of Phoenician activity on the island became Lilybaeum (modern Marsala).

The spread of the Phoenicians across the western Mediterranean can be mapped by trading ports. The site of Tharros (see image 1) in western Sardinia indicates that the Phoenician settlement started in the late eighth century BCE. This earliest phase has been detected in the *tophet* (burial area) where children were buried. The cemetery attached to the settlement contained a quantity of important Greek material, including Athenian pottery. This suggests that some of the distribution of Athenian pottery in the western Mediterranean is the result of Phoenician rather than Greek activity. The Punic settlement at Tharros continued until *c.* 238 BCE. The Phoenician settlement of Nora in the south of the island was established by the eighth century BCE. Several stelae relating to its *tophet* have been recovered.

One of the key sites for Punic activity was Cádiz, Spain. This was traditionally settled in the twelfth century BCE, although the earliest archaeological material can be dated to the eighth century. The attraction is thought to be the silver mines in the Rio Tinto area that were exploited from that date. Mining activity is marked by the presence of Attic SOS amphorae, named after the lettering on the necks, which point to the possibility that trade in olive oil was a component.

There is a growing body of evidence of Phoenician shipping from underwater excavations. A wreck dating to *c.* 700 BCE from near Gozo, Malta, included a large number of transport amphorae as well as grinding stones. A comparable wreck was found on a reef at Bajo de la Campana near Cartagena, Spain. It included elephant tusks, tin, copper ingots, and unprocessed argentiferous ore.

Literary traditions hint at Carthaginian explorations along the Atlantic coast of west Africa. The Greek geographer Strabo (*c.* 64 BCE–*c.* 21 CE) recorded a tradition claiming there were 300 Phoenician settlements along this coast. There is some archaeological evidence of limited activities on the African coast down to the island of Mogador, Morocco, where potsherds with Punic graffiti have been discovered.

Carthage came into a series of conflicts with the Roman Republic as it expanded. The First Punic War (264–241 BCE) was fought to establish control over the Strait of Messina in Sicily. The Carthaginian Empire finally fell in 146 BCE after the destruction of Carthage in the Third Punic War (149–146 BCE). **DG**

7th century BCE	535 BCE	480 BCE	397 BCE	264–241 BCE	146 BCE
A Phoenician ship sinks at Bajo de la Campana, Spain. Excavation of the wreck in 2007–11 shows trade in metals and luxury items.	The Carthaginians and Estruscans fight as a coalition against the Greeks at the Battle of Alalia.	A Carthaginian force is defeated at the Battle of Himera in northern Sicily.	The city of Moyta is destroyed by the Syracusans.	The First Punic War is fought to establish control over the Strait of Messina in Sicily.	The destruction of Carthage brings an end to the Third Punic War and results in the fall of the Carthaginian Empire.

Carthage Ninth–second centuries BCE

A *tophet* burial ground was found in 1921 in the Salammbo district. Many of the burials were of infants and children, sometimes accompanied by small offerings and jewelry. The area seems to have been in use for much of the Punic occupation of the site. It also contained a number of dedications to the prominent deity of Carthage, Tanit.

The Phoenician settlement of Carthage in present-day Tunisia was traditionally founded in 814 BCE, a date corroborated by eighth-century BCE pottery. Carthage was located at a key point in the Mediterranean, opposite western Sicily, also with a Phoenician settlement at this time. The city provided a gateway to southern Spain, with its important sources of silver; to the west coast of Africa, where there is some archaeological evidence of Phoenician exploration; and to a string of Phoenician settlements along the north coast of Africa, Sardinia, and the Balearic islands. In 146 BCE, the Roman general Scipio Africanus the Younger (*c.* 185–129 BCE) sacked Carthage and then burned the city, and excavations found a thick layer of ash on the hill of St. Louis that could be dated by Italian black-glossed pottery of the mid second century BCE.

During the 1970s, there was an international effort to record the archaeological remains of the city, including the harbor facilities. Archaeologists confirmed that there were two harbors, as described by the writer Appian (fl. second century CE), now two silted lagoons. Excavations at the Admiralty Island area identified material from the Punic layers, including Athenian pottery dating to the fifth century BCE. Ship sheds used to dry-dock the naval fleet and other naval facilities were found. About 307,368 cubic yards (235,000 cu. m.) of earth was excavated to create the harbors, which had capacity for 200 ships. Archaeologists identified how the Roman colony reused the destroyed Punic facilities.

A U.S. team has investigated the Punic layers of the city, the citadel of Byrsa, whose focus was the hill of St. Louis and the site of a *tophet*. Evidence was found of the defensive walls of the Punic city, made of ashlar blocks with a rubble fill. **DG/GM**

ROMAN THEATER

The theater may originally date to the reign of Emperor Augustus (63 BCE–14 CE), although the widespread use of marble from the island of Proconnesus (now Marmara Island, Turkey), suggests that it was rebuilt in the late second century CE. It may have been reconstructed as part of an imperial benefaction received to assist with the rebuilding of part of the city destroyed by fire during the reign of Emperor Antoninus Pius (86–161 CE) in the late 140s CE.

ROMAN AMPHITHEATER

The amphitheater at Carthage was built on flat ground. One of the largest in the Roman Empire, it is estimated it had the capacity to seat 30,000 people. One of the finds is an inscription recording the donation of a set of games, including a four-day gladiatorial show and wild beast hunt, promised by a local magistrate. The amphitheater was probably constructed in the early second century CE, and subsequently restored during the reign of Emperor Marcus Aurelius (121–180 CE).

ROMAN CARTHAGE

After the destruction of Carthage in 146 BCE in the Third Punic War, the site was left unoccupied by the Romans. In 44 BCE, Julius Caesar (c. 100–44 BCE) decided that Carthage should be resettled due to its strategic location, although this was not effected until the reign of Augustus. He leveled the remains of the earlier Phoenician settlement, and rebuilt the city on a grid pattern. This city became an important center and was the focus for the province of Africa Proconsularis comprising modern Tunisia, northeast Algeria and part of west Libya. It was attacked by the Vandals in 439 CE, and Carthage fell to the Arabs in the late seventh century CE.

The Roman theater, excavated in 1904 and 1905 by Paul Gauckler, seated just over 11,000 people. Two colossal marble statues of Apollo and the hero Hercules may be linked to the establishment of the Pythian Games, under the protection of Apollo, during the reign of Septimius Severus (145–211 CE). A burned layer from the theater coincided with damage to many of the marble fittings, and this may have been sustained in the attack of 439 CE.

Excavations have revealed some of the buildings from Late Antiquity, including a vaulted building dating to c. 400 CE. A U.S. team discovered a sixth-century CE pilgrimage complex at the site of Bir Ftouha, including a baptistery and a basilica. A team from the University of Quebec identified a circular monument constructed on the Odeon Hill. This structure is 28 feet (8.4 m.) in diameter and appears to have been a memorial to a local dignitary. A basilica was constructed next to it. A further basilica, 281 feet (85.5 m.) in length, was excavated on the Byrsa. Another Canadian project has identified the walls in the vicinity of Teurf el-Sour that were built c. 425 CE to protect the city.

Motya Eighth–fourth centuries BCE

Excavations at the Motya site on the island of San Pantaleo in Sicily suggest that the rectangular cothon, or what was interpreted as an artificial harbour, was associated with a religious complex. From the sixth century BCE onward, the main cemetery for the settlement was on the mainland, which was accessed via a causeway.

The remains of the ancient city of Motya are located in western Sicily. The site lies on a small island of about 111 acres (45 ha.) in the middle of a lagoon, and the city was reached in antiquity by a narrow causeway. Motya was established in the eighth century BCE by the Phoenicians and became a buffer in the western part of the island between the Greek colonists and the Phoenicians who then dominated the western Mediterranean. It was a staging post for the interaction between Carthage and the island.

During the sixth and fifth centuries, Motya was in contact with the wider Greek world. Transport amphorae, probably containing wine and olive oil, were derived from the islands of Chios and Samos in the Aegean, as well as the Greek colony of Massalia (modern Marseille) at the mouth of the Rhône. Greek figure-decorated pottery from Corinth, dating to the sixth century BCE, has been recovered.

The Cappidazzu sanctuary at the northeast of the island lies within a wall that dates to the mid sixth century BCE. It contained a long building with side aisles, probably a temple, although the Phoenician deity has not been identified. A slab in front of this structure may have served as a base for three *betyls*, or sacred stones. The earliest structure in the sanctuary was associated with a well and dates to the second half of the seventh century BCE.

One of the most spectacular finds is the Motya Charioteer. It is a Greek victor's statue representing the winner of a chariot race and may have been displayed in the Cappidazzu sanctuary. There has been much debate regarding how a Greek statue was found in a Phoenician context. One hypothesis is that it formed part of the booty from one of the Greek colonies on Sicily and that the statue is a monument honoring the achievement of a local ruler. **DG/GM**

MOTYA CHARIOTEER

This marble statue of a charioteer may have been carved by a Greek sculptor. Stylistically it dates to *c.* 470 to 460 BCE— nearly contemporary with the bronze charioteer found at Delphi dedicated by a tyrant of Gela in Sicily. The statue was found in 1979 near a potter's workshop and may have been reused as part of a barricade erected during the Syracusan siege of 397 BCE.

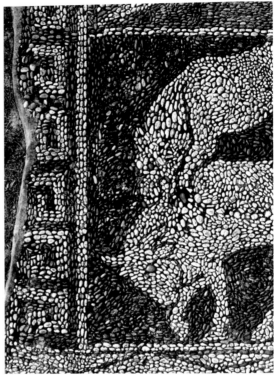

HOUSE OF THE MOSAICS

Motya was largely abandoned after the sack of 397 BCE. However, some structures indicate limited occupation. They include the House of the Mosaics, named after a black-and-white mosaic of river pebbles showing a lion attacking a bull within a decorative meander-design border. Recent excavations have identified Phoenician kilns from this period.

ISLAND LIFE

An area on the northwest side of the island contained a series of cremation burials in clay containers accompanied by clay figurines. They suggest that the area was in use from the seventh century BCE. Within this area were approximately 1,000 stone stelae, some dedicated to the Phoenician deity Baal Hammon. British archaeologists interpreted the area as a *tophet* where children were sacrificed, although this theory is now less certain.

An industrial area in use from the seventh century BCE was excavated near the north gate. The presence of mollusk shells, ovens, and clay-lined pits suggests that this was an area for extracting purple dye, which was highly prized in the ancient world.

A stone wall 1 mile (2 km.) long was built around the island, probably in the late sixth century BCE. Its north side cut across an existing cemetery with about 200 cremation burials, suggesting that earlier phases of

the settlement relied on maritime defenses. Some of the burials contained imported Corinthian pottery that relates the activities at Motya to what was happening elsewhere in Sicily. The fortifications were rebuilt with bastions in the late fifth century BCE. There were at least two gates, one on the north side with two towers adjacent to where the causeway joined the island. There is evidence of where the wheels of carts have worn away the road surface. The doors closing the gate had large bronze hinges, one of which was recovered in the excavations. A second gateway with two towers has been excavated on the south side.

The city was sacked by Dionysius I of Syracuse (*c.* 430–367 BCE) in 397 BCE. It has become a *terminus post quem* (the earliest possible dating) for a type of impressed decoration on Athenian black-glossed pottery that became widespread during the fourth century BCE.

ARCHAIC ITALY

1 An Etruscan hut ash-urn dating to the eighth century BCE that was found at the necropolis of Osteria, Vulci, in Lazio.

2 An arm-shaped ivory flabellum handle from the Barberini Tomb at Palestrina in Lazio, dating to the seventh century BCE.

The settlement of Greek colonies in southern Italy and Sicily came into contact with the indigenous Italian populations. This is particularly important for the area in Campania around the Bay of Naples. Excavations at Capua have been able to demonstrate the changing cultural influences. One of the key research questions has revolved around the interaction between the two groups. Greek settlers from Euboea had set up a trading point on the island of Ischia to handle the iron ore from the island of Elba; it was processed at Populonia in central Italy, and later moved to the Campania at Cumae.

Excavations in northern Italy have identified a recognizable Villanova culture that dates from the ninth century BCE. The term is applied to the settlements in the Po Valley as well as in Campania. Cemeteries contain cremation burials, some placed in biconical containers. Some graves of this period contain amber ornaments, indicating that central Italy was linked to a trading system that reached into northern Europe. From the ninth century BCE, there are examples of ceramic cremation urns made in the form of huts (see image 1) that were in use in the area of Latium (modern Lazio) in central-western Italy.

Growing contact with the eastern Mediterranean through the eighth century, prior to much of Greek colonization, is shown by an oriental phase. This may have been the result of contacts with Phoenicians. This period is reflected by the presence of exotic oriental material. The Regolini-Galassi Tomb at Cerveteri in Lazio (see p. 290) was cut into the tufa and placed under a large mound. There

KEY EVENTS

9th century BCE	9th century BCE	8th century BCE	7th century BCE	753 BCE	Late 7th century BCE
The Villanova culture in northern Italy begins.	The first cremation urns in the form of huts are in use in the area of Latium.	Contact between Italy and the eastern Mediterranean increases.	The Regolini-Galassi Tomb is constructed at Cerveteri in Lazio. It is discovered by archaeologists in 1836.	Rome is founded.	Oriental materials are featured in burials at Palestrina in Latium.

were several pieces of silver plate that appear to have been made in the eastern Mediterranean. Some of the pieces carry a short Etruscan inscription. In the seventh century BCE, some of the pottery produced in the southern part of Etruria appears to have been decorated by Greek potters using some of the oriental motifs. Equally rich burials with oriental material from the late seventh century BCE have been found at Palestrina in Latium. The Bernadini Tomb included a gilded silver bowl decorated with Egyptianizing scenes; its rim was decorated with serpentine attachments. Silver bowls from the Barberini Tomb, also at Palestrina, include motifs derived from both Egypt and Assyria, suggesting that they were made in the Phoenician area of the eastern Mediterranean and then transported to Italy. Finely carved Phoenician-style ivories (see image 2) may have been carved locally by eastern artisans. Cremation burials at Pontecagnano in Campania include a number of eastern materials, including silver plate. The character of the finds is similar to those found in Etruria, implying that there were broader regional cultural identities.

Archaeological excavations, as well as illicit activity, have explored many of the Etruscan cemeteries dating to the sixth and fifth centuries BCE. Tombs were cut into the tufa and the walls decorated with elaborate paintings. The Tomb of the Augurs at Tarquinia in Lazio, dating to the late sixth century BCE, shows two male figures wrestling against a pile of stacked bowls; this is thought to represent part of the funerary games. The tombs of Vulci in Lazio were notable for the large numbers of Athenian figure-decorated pottery that they contained; these were eagerly sought after by the major museums in Europe in the nineteenth century. One of the early nineteenth-century collectors spoke of the "truffles" found in the cemeteries. The theme of the banquet, or symposium, was picked up in some of the tomb decorations such as the Tomb of the Leopards at Tarquinia that dates to the early fifth century BCE. This shows the banqueters reclining on couches while being entertained by music.

Major temples have been explored in the sanctuary of Pyrgi (now Santa Severa) in Lazio, as well as at Tarquinia. Temples have been excavated at Gravisca, the port of Tarquinia, and a podium with a grand staircase has been found at Orvieto in Umbria. Etruscan temples were frequently decorated with architectural terracottas that were brightly colored.

While there has been much interest in the cemeteries of Etruria, there is a growing emphasis on the towns themselves. Marzabotto, near Bologna, was laid out with a grid system in the sixth century BCE. The port of Spina, on the Adriatic coast, is now seen as central to the interaction between northern Italy and central Europe. Rome, lying to the south of Etruria, was traditionally founded in 753 BCE. Excavations in the area of the later Roman Forum (see p. 294) have brought to light evidence for early activity in the city. In particular, a deposit near the later Temple of Concord included a group of sixth-century BCE material that appears to have been a votive deposit. **DG**

6th century BCE	6th century BCE	560–550 BCE	c. 510–500 BCE	c. 500 BCE	Early 5th century BCE
The Tomb of the Augurs at Tarquina in Lazio is decorated with a painting of two male figures wrestling.	The town of Marzabotto is constructed on a grid system.	The Boccanera terracotta plaques, showing sphinxes and mythological scenes, are placed in a tomb at the Banditaccia cemetery at Cervteri.	Architectural terracotta figures are used to decorate an Etruscan temple at Portonaccio near Veii, north of Rome. They are discovered in 1916.	Bilingual gold tablets containing a dedication in Etruscan and Phoenician are inscribed. They are discovered in 1964 at the sanctuary at Pyrgi.	The Tomb of the Leopards at Tarquinia is decorated with scenes of a banquet.

Etruscan Cerveteri Seventh–sixth centuries BCE

The uniquely decorated interior of the Tomb of the Reliefs in the Banditaccia necropolis (c. 325–300 BCE) at Cerveteri, Italy. The colorful stucco reliefs of objects such as pitchers and knives recall a domestic setting, while the representations of shields and helmets suggest the elite status of the deceased.

The Etruscans lived in an area that covers the modern regions of Tuscany, western Umbria, and northern Lazio. The town of Cerveteri, known to the Greeks as Agylla and to the Romans as Caere, lies 29 miles (46.5 km.) northwest of Rome near the coast. The occupation of Cerveteri can be traced to the Proto-Villanovan and Villanovan periods before the Etruscans. Archaeological attention has focused on the rock-cut tombs at the site of the ancient city. The Regolini-Galassi Tomb was discovered in 1836 and dates to the late seventh century BCE. It contained a number of items, many of gold and silver, which reflected contact with the eastern Mediterranean. Tombs dating to the sixth century BCE were decorated with large terracotta panels painted in polychrome. Some of the finest are the Boccanera plaques recovered from the Banditaccia necropolis and sold by German archaeologist Wolfgang Helbig (1839–1915) to the British Museum in 1889. These show processions of men and women moving in opposite directions. At the head is a scene thought to show the Judgment of Paris, part of the Trojan myth, depicting the Trojan prince alongside Hermes, the messenger of the gods.

The fourth-century BCE Tomb of the Reliefs is laid out like a dining room, with sculptures of couches and drinking vessels as well as reliefs of armor hanging on the walls. Among the items that have been identified is a game board of a type that is known from examples found at Etruscan tombs in the Po Valley.

It is thought that Cerveteri was a center for the production of black burnished pottery known as *bucchero*. This type of material was manufactured from the second quarter of the seventh century BCE. Figure-decorated pottery echoing imported Corinthian wares also started to be produced. In addition, it has been suggested that Cerveteri was a center for bronze-working from the seventh century BCE. **DG/GM**

BANDITACCIA CEMETERY

Many of the tombs replicate the style of Etruscan houses and provide the only surviving evidence of Etruscan residential architecture. The layout of the cemeteries, such as those at Banditaccia and Monte Abatone, present the ideal of a planned town with streets, neighborhoods, and small squares containing thousands of tombs that line the streets in regular patterns. There are tombs designed for inhumation burials, which contrasts with the earlier Villanovan practice of cremation.

SARCOPHAGUS OF THE SPOUSES

The Etruscan elite's adoption of the Greek culture of wine drinking and associated activities is seen in the late sixth-century BCE terracotta sarcophagus lid found at Banditaccia cemetery in 1845. Known as the Sarcophagus of the Spouses, it shows a married couple reclining on a couch and the wife resting on a cushion in the form of a wineskin. The concept of the deceased reclining at an eternal banquet continued into the late fifth century BCE on stone-cut sarcophagi from the same cemetery. In the second century, the deceased are often shown banqueting or sleeping on the lids of terracotta burial urns.

CONTACTS BETWEEN THE ETRUSCAN AND ANCIENT GREEK WORLD

Many of the tombs at Cerveteri contained Athenian black- and red-figure pottery to supply the dead with the objects needed for a symposium: kraters, or wine-mixing bowls; *oinochoai*, or jugs for pouring; and a range of drinking cups.

Cerveteri maintained strong links with the Greek world, dedicating a treasury in the Panhellenic sanctuary of Delphi. Excavations in Cerveteri have revealed remains of sanctuaries, including one dedicated to Uni, the equivalent of the Greek goddess Hera, and another to Hercle, equivalent to the Greek hero Herakles. The latter had dedications of Athenian pottery including a red-figured cup decorated by

Onesimos showing the sack of Troy. Sanctuaries and domestic houses appear to have been decorated with painted terracotta revetments attached to the roofs.

The harbor for Cerveteri was northwest at Pyrgi (now Santa Severa), where excavations have uncovered the remains of substantial temples. The mid-fifth-century BCE terracotta frieze of Temple A depicts the mythological scene of the Seven Against Thebes, which shows similarities with centaurs from the pediment of the Temple of Zeus at Olympia. Temple B was similar in form to Greek temples, though it too was decorated with architectural terracottas, in this case portraying the feats of Herakles.

IMPERIAL ROME

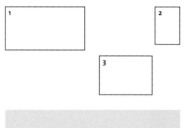

1 The Augustan image of civic religion on the carved scenes on the Ara Pacis was propaganda for Emperor Augustus.

2 The Great Cryptoporticus in the east wing of the Domus Aurea (64–68 CE) has frescoed walls and ceiling vaults.

3 Roman soldiers cross the Danube River using a pontoon bridge as they march to Dacia in one of the 155 scenes depicted on Trajan's Column.

Rome became an empire on the accession of Augustus (63 BCE–14 CE), the first emperor of Rome, in 27 BCE. By this time, the city had risen in importance, consolidating the overseas territory acquired from the third century BCE onward. Augustus created an efficient administration for the provinces, with some—for example, Egypt—being directly ruled by Augustus and others under the control of the Senate. He also resettled veterans of the recent civil wars in colonies around the empire. In addition, Augustus initiated the construction of impressive architectural monuments in the city of Rome, some of which were the result of the addition of the imperial cult to Roman religion. One of the monuments in Rome honoring Augustus was the Ara Pacis Augustae (Altar of Augustan Peace; see image 1), commissioned by the Senate in 13 BC and dedicated in 9 BCE.

As the city developed, so did types of housing. The emperor and members of the imperial court had lavish housing, with the most notorious being that of Nero (37–68 CE): Domus Aurea (Golden House; see image 2). Its most spectacular element was a rotating banqueting hall, described by the writer Suetonius (69–c. 135 CE). In 2009, archaeologists identified a circular room that they believe to have been the room described. More modest dwellings were the apartment blocks known as insulae. The best impression of this type of town life can be gained from the surviving insulae at Ostia (see p. 296).

KEY EVENTS

27 BCE	27–25 BCE	38 CE	64	80	117
Octavian is granted the title Imperator Caesar Divi Filius Augustus (Commander Caesar, son of the deified one). He becomes the first Roman emperor, Augustus.	Augustus's son-in-law, Marcus Vipsanius Agrippa (63–12 BCE), begins construction of the Pantheon. It is destroyed by fire in 80 CE.	The Aqua Claudia and Anio Novus aqueducts are constructed. The Porta Maggiore gate supports both aqueducts as they enter the city.	A great fire sweeps through Rome, causing severe destruction and damage. According to the historian Tacitus (56–c. 120), it began in the Circus Maximus.	The Colosseum is dedicated by the emperor Titus (39–81) and is marked by the first games held in the amphitheater.	Death of the emperor Trajan, during whose reign the Roman Empire had reached its greatest extent.

Leisure activities are also reflected in the archaeology of Imperial Rome. The Baths of Caracalla, built in the early third century CE during the reigns of Septimius Severus (c. 145–211 CE) and Caracalla (188–217 CE), covered about 62 acres (25 ha.). The complex comprised not only public bathing facilities, but also a library. It was decorated with sculptures, including the Farnese Hercules, an over-life-size statue of the mythic hero created in the early third century CE. The statue was rediscovered in 1546, when it was acquired by Cardinal Alessandro Farnese (1520–89 CE). In addition to the gladiatorial games and other activities held in the Colosseum (see p. 298), the Circus Maximus, used primarily for chariot racing, could accommodate 150,000 spectators. This area, which had a long history, was rebuilt in stone during the Imperial period.

The military victories of Imperial Rome are celebrated in monuments. Trajan's Column (see image 3) commemorated victories against the Dacians, a region in modern Romania. It is a single monument, 98 feet (30 m.) high, which was completed in 113 CE. A sculpted frieze winds around the column and relates the events of the campaign. A small chamber in the base of the column was designed to accommodate the ashes of Trajan (53–117 CE).

Rome's pre-eminence began to wane when Constantine I (c. 280–337 CE) refounded the city of Byzantium, renamed Constantinople, in 324 CE to serve as his capital (see p. 410). Although Rome remained capital of the western empire, its fortunes declined further, and in 476 CE the western empire is considered to have ended when Romulus Augustulus (r. 475–476 CE) was deposed. **GM**

118–128	203	271–275	315	360–380	410
The Pantheon is rebuilt by the emperor Hadrian (76–138), incorporating the original inscription naming M. Vipsanius Agrippa as its dedicator.	The Arch of Septimius Severus is built to commemorate the emperor's victories against the Parthians.	Political instability sees the construction of defensive walls around the city in the reign of the emperor Aurelian (c. 215–275).	Constantine I (Constantine the Great) dedicates a triumphal arch to commemorate his victory over Emperor Maxentius (d. 132).	The Temple of Saturn (see p. 294) is restored following a fire, largely reusing building material from earlier periods.	Rome is attacked by Visigoths led by their leader Alaric (c. 370–410). The events are recorded by the historian Zosimus.

Roman Forum   900 BCE – seventh century CE

The Roman Forum lies at the center of Rome. The archaeological remains comprise a rectangular space surrounded by the ruins of ancient temples and government buildings such as the Senate House, or Curia Julia, which faces the eastern side of the Arch of Septimius Severus and Temple of Saturn.

NAVIGATOR

The Roman Forum was constructed between the Palatine and Capitoline hills at the head of a marshy inlet of the Tiber river in Rome. By the fifth century BCE, the Forum had become the symbolic center of the Roman Republic. The present grouping of buildings was begun by Gaius Julius Caesar (c. 100–44 BCE) and developed by Emperor Augustus (63 BCE–14 CE) , including construction of the Temple of the Deified Julius Caesar, which was dedicated in 29 BCE. Destructive fires between 14 and 9 BCE led to the rebuilding of the Temple of Castor and Pollux and basilicas on the northern and southern sides of the Forum. Other buildings were added, including the Temple of Concordia Augusta, dedicated in 10 CE to replace an earlier temple. Other new buildings were limited to temples to deified emperors until the construction of the Arch of Septimius Severus in 203. A fire in 283 led to rebuilding by Emperor Diocletian (245–316), including the reconstruction of the Basilica Julia and the Senate House, the latter converted into a church in the seventh century. By this time, the population of Rome had decreased to less than 10,000, and there was a consequent decline in the upkeep of the Forum buildings. Some began to collapse, such as the former Temple of Concordia Augusta in 790. The ruinous state of some of the buildings was exacerbated in the fifteenth and sixteenth centuries by the reuse of stone for new building in Rome.

The Forum was not investigated archaeologically until the early nineteenth century, when trenches were sunk around the Arch of Septimius Severus and the Column of Phocas. Work to excavate the Forum began in the late nineteenth century and was completed by 1910. Scientific excavation of the area commenced in the 1980s. **GM**

◉ FOCAL POINTS

1 CORINTHIAN COLUMNS

Titus began the Temple of Vespasian and Titus after the death of Vespasian (79 CE) and Domitian completed it. The remaining architecture dates to between 80 and 85 CE. This comprises three Corinthian columns and part of the entablature, decorated with implements used in sacrifices.

2 IONIC COLUMNS

The Temple of Saturn is considered to be the first temple in the Forum, dedicated in 497 BCE. It housed the public treasury. An inscription indicates the building was restored after a fire, probably between 360 and 380 CE. The remains of the facade consist of eight Ionic columns.

3 ARCH

The Arch of Septimius Severus was built in 203 CE to commemorate his victories against the Parthians. Coins show a statue of him and his sons, Caracalla and Geta (189–217), in a chariot on top of the arch. Caracalla removed an inscription to Geta on the arch after murdering him.

▲ The single Corinthian column honours the Byzantine emperor Phocas (547–610). Its inscription says it was erected on August 1, 608. It is the latest honorific monument in the Forum.

SENATE HOUSE AND LAPIS NIGER

The Senate House was rebuilt in 283 CE on the foundations of an earlier building planned by Julius Caesar and completed by Augustus in 29 BCE. It originally had a facing of white marble up to its windows, above which was a coating of white stucco, of which traces remain. The original bronze doors were removed to the Church of St. John Lateran in 1660. The floor of red and green porphyry was laid in the fourth century in the *opus sectile* technique. In 630, the building was converted by Pope Honorius I (d. 638) into the Church of St. Hadrian, almost all traces of which were removed following restoration in 1935 to 1938. The dark paved area in front of the Senate House is known as the Lapis Niger (Black Rock). Excavations revealed that it overlies the remains of a group of earlier monuments, buried in the first century BCE, as well as a tufa wall erected *c.* 900 BCE, the earliest remains on the site. Among the monuments is a stone block dating from *c.* 570 to 550 BCE that bears an early Latin inscription. The exact meaning of the inscription is unclear, but it seems to place a curse on anyone who moves it. It is possible that it functioned as a boundary stone.

Ostia Antica Fourth century BCE – fourth century CE

A typical example of an insula is the House of Diana (c. 150), originally at least three stories high. Two of the sides of the building open onto separate streets and many of the rooms opening directly onto the streets were used as single-unit shops. The private dwellings were the inner rooms, lit by means of an open courtyard at the center of the building.

Ostia Antica served as the port of ancient Rome, and during Roman times was at the mouth of the Tiber. Alluvial silting led to its abandonment as a port, and it is now about 3 miles (5 km.) from the sea. Ostia's significance lies in its excellent preservation due to its abandonment, and the light it sheds on commercial activities— particularly the grain trade—and housing in the second and third centuries.

Ostia was one of the earliest Roman colonies, founded in the later fourth century BCE. Its initial role was to protect the trade outlet at the mouth of the Tiber against piracy, and at this time it was primarily a naval base rather than a commercial center. It flourished after the First Punic War (264–241 BCE) between Rome and Carthage, before Rome's main naval base was relocated to Misenum on the Bay of Naples. By the late 1st century BCE, the vast majority of Rome's imports arrived at Ostia, which accordingly led to a new port structure. However, the problem with silting led to new port facilities, and in 42 CE work began on a monumental harbor constructed to the north of Ostia known as Portus, near the modern-day village of Porto. By the second century, Portus had two harbor basins, which were connected to the Tiber by an artificial channel.

Many of the less wealthy inhabitants of Ostia lived in multi-occupation buildings known as insulae. Most were constructed of concrete faced with brick, and have several stories. Some insulae have good amenities, but are different in character from the luxurious and often ostentatious individual houses, such as those preserved at Pompeii (see p. 302). It was not until the later third and fourth centuries that the port declined and some individual insulae were converted into single-family homes. **GM**

The inscription on this mosaic, "NAVICVL ET NEGOTIANTES KARALITANI," indicates that this section of the Piazzale delle Corporazioni (Square of the Guilds or Corporations), the principal meeting point for traders at Ostia, was occupied by shippers and businessmen of Karalis (modern-day Cagliari) in Sardinia. The objects depicted either side of the ship are interpreted as corn measures, indicating that the ships sailing from Karalis brought grain to Ostia for storage, then onward transmission to Rome.

BATHS OF NEPTUNE

Some of the largest public buildings in Ostia were bath complexes. The Baths of Neptune were built during the reign of the emperor Hadrian (76–138) in the second century. One room, approximately 59 feet (18 m.) long and 34 feet (10.5 m.) wide, has a mosaic floor whose single scene is the god Neptune. He is depicted driving four seahorses, surrounded by imaginary sea creatures, typical of the marine designs favored in bathhouses.

COMMERCIAL LIFE AT OSTIA

Ostia's coastal location, with good harbor facilities at Portus, led to it becoming the focus for the supply of corn to Rome, just over 12 miles (20 km.) away. During the time of the republic, Rome was unable to provide sufficient grain to feed the populace, and imported grain via Ostia, initially from Sicily and Sardinia and later from Egypt.

Horrea (warehouses) stored grain prior to being shipped along the Tiber on barges. The Grandi Horrea were constructed in the first century and expanded in the second century, alongside the development of the artificial harbor at Portus, but had fallen out of use by the end of the fourth century. The storerooms were accessed directly from quays on the Tiber. Suspended floors protected the perishable contents of the rooms, likely to have been grain, from damp. It has been estimated the *horrea* would hold enough grain to feed 15,000 people for a year.

Commercial life in Ostia is also reflected in the mosaics of the Piazzale delle Corporazioni. Around a U-shaped colonnade there are more than sixty small rooms, most about 13 feet (4 m.) wide and 15 feet (4.5 m.) deep. Their floors are separate scenes made from black-and-white mosaic, most dating to the late second and third centuries, and often decorated with images that reflect the activities of those using the rooms. Commercial associations from throughout the ancient world are represented, including Alexandria, Carthage, Sabratha, Karalis, and Arelate, with north African cities being the most popular. It is not only the extent of the geographical area but the range of goods that is striking: corn, ivory, flax, and rope. Inscriptions concerning trade guilds at Ostia create a vivid impression of the activities that centered on Ostia and the town's harbor at Portus.

Colosseum *c.* 70 CE

The Colosseum could accommodate around 50,000 people. Spectators sat in different areas, strictly demarcated according to their rank in society. The elliptical arena was built over a system of passages and stairways known as the hypogeum.

⬡ NAVIGATOR

The Flavian Amphitheater, popularly known as the Colosseum, was begun during the reign of the emperor Vespasian in 69 to 79. It was dedicated in 80 by his successor Titus and was marked by the first games held in the Colosseum. It was the site of gladiatorial games and *venationes* (wild-animal hunts) that were favored entertainments in the first century. Spectators entered through a series of arched entrances, and recent cleaning of these has revealed traces of carved numbers, painted in red, which were intended to help direct spectators to their seats.

After the arena had fallen out of use, the Colosseum was used for private dwellings, stables, and workshops between the ninth and fourteenth centuries. An earthquake in 1349 weakened the structure of the building and made it too dangerous to use. In the fifteenth and sixteenth centuries, in common with other ancient buildings in Rome, the Colosseum was plundered for building stone. In the eighteenth century, the belief that the Colosseum was the site of the martyrdom of early Christians led Pope Benedict XIV (1675–1758) to forbid the removal of stone, stopping further destruction. Stations of the Cross were erected, although removed in the late nineteenth century. However, other Christian references remain, including a cross dedicated by Pope John Paul II (1920–2005).

The architecture of the Colosseum has influenced later buildings. Renaissance architects borrowed the hierarchy of the "assemblage of orders," the three different architectural orders seen on the exterior. A modern adaptation of the Colosseum's series of superimposed arcades is found on the Palazzo della Civiltà Italiana in Rome, designed in 1937 and known as the Colosseo Quadrato (Square Colosseum). **GM**

1 UPPER SECTION

There were 240 masts at the top of the Colosseum, which supported the *velarium*, a retractable cloth awning that protected spectators from the sun and rain. Roman sailors from the imperial fleet at Misenum operated the rigging of the *velarium*.

2 SEATING

The emperor and the priestesses of the goddess Vesta sat in boxes close to the arena, with senators also accommodated at this level. The equites sat in the next level up, followed by the plebeians. The poor, slaves, and women sat at the top.

3 HYPOGEUM

The hypogeum housed capstans to raise the cages containing the wild animals. There were also hydraulic mechanisms used to flood the arena for the *naumachiae* (mock sea battles), although these were apparently short-lived.

◄ The arches and vaults of the Colosseum were constructed from brick-faced Roman concrete, with the outer walls faced with travertine, a form of limestone. The Colosseum was designed with three superimposed stories of arcades, framed by engaged columns in the Doric (or Tuscan), Ionic, and Corinthian architectural orders. The highest level of the structure is pierced by a series of windows flanked by pilasters with Corinthian capitals.

AMPHITHEATER ACTIVITIES

A good visual source of information about the activities of Roman amphitheaters such as the Colosseum are mosaic floors, found across the Roman Empire. They provide images of human and animal combatants, as well as the musical accompaniment. The gladiators' costumes differ between the various regions of the empire. A diverse group of scenes appear on a mosaic floor from the Roman villa at Nennig, near Trier in Germany, dating from *c.* 225 to 250. Panels show pairs of gladiators, some overseen by a referee, and hunters attacking animals, as well as a water-organ and horn being played in the arena. It is likely that this type of mosaic decoration was used by the owner of the villa to demonstrate his interest in the amphitheater and may have commemorated a real event.

ROMAN ITALY

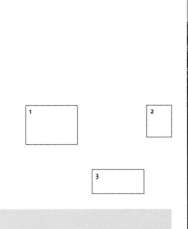

1 The remains of the once flourishing Roman port of Cosa in southwestern Tuscany have provided valuable insights into Roman harbor construction and trade in the Mediterranean.

2 The Arch of Trajan in Benevento, southern Italy. The Roman triumphal arch was erected in honor of Emperor Trajan across the Via Appia (Appian Way), at the point where it enters the city.

3 The remains of the hull of one of the two ships recovered from Lake Nemi in Lazio. The ships may have been made to emulate the royal barges used by the Ptolemies in Egypt.

During the Republic, Rome expanded its territory. Tarentum (modern Taranto), a Greek colony in southern Italy, was taken by Rome in 272 BCE. The city of Syracuse was captured in 211 BCE and the island of Sicily was formed into a province. Booty from these cities was taken to Rome and displayed on the Capitolium or in the Roman Forum.

The port of Cosa (see image 1), in Etruria in modern Tuscany, has mapped the development of the town from the establishment of a Latin colony in 273 BCE through to the medieval period. Part of the ongoing project included a survey of the harbor and its facilities. This included the discovery of a major fish farm with tanks and processing areas, suggesting it was a center for producing *garum*, a fish sauce that was exported in transport amphorae. The hinterland was used for growing grapes. Garum and Cosan wine were exported in amphorae made near Cosa. Many are stamped with "Ses" or "Sest" and appear to be linked to the Sestii family, who are known to have had estates around Cosa in the late Roman Republic. These stamped amphorae are found widely distributed in the western Mediterranean. A villa has been excavated at Settefinestre in Tuscany as part of a wider survey of Cosa and its territory, the Ager Cosanus. This was a luxury house with facilities for processing olives and grapes from the estate.

Knowledge of Roman urban life has been enriched by the excavation of the Roman cities of Pompeii and Herculaneum (see p. 302) that were destroyed and buried by the eruption of Vesuvius in 79 CE. Private houses provide some of the

(see p. 302)

KEY EVENTS

4th century BCE	273 BCE	272 BCE	211 BCE	2nd century BCE	80 BCE
Ostia is founded. The first excavations there were opened by Giuseppe Petrini, on behalf of Pope Pius VII (1742–1823).	A Latin colony is established at the Tuscan port of Cosa.	The Greek colony of Tarentum in southern Italy is taken by Rome.	The city of Syracuse is captured by Rome and the island of Sicily is formed into a province.	The Villa of Mysteries is constructed just outside Pompeii.	Pompeii becomes a Roman colony.

best-preserved examples of Roman frescoes as well as mosaics. Herculaneum is particularly important, because the excavators have been able to recover organic materials that were carbonized by the high temperatures of the pyroclastic flows that swept through the cities.

Excavations at Lake Nemi, close to Rome, recovered the remains of two large wooden vessels (see image 3) constructed for the emperor Caligula (12 – 41 CE), and described by the historian Suetonius (69 – c. 122 CE). They were 230 feet by 66 feet (70 by 20 m.) and 240 by 79 feet (73 by 24 m.) and were equipped with mosaic floors and other luxury items to turn them into floating palaces. Portus (near modern Porto) at the mouth of the Tiber river is one of the most ancient harbours in the Mediterranean and has been the subject of a series of excavations and geophysical surveys.

The Roman port of Pisa was identified during redevelopment in the city. Sixteen ships were found dating from the first century BCE to the fourth century CE, some of which were freighters. One contained a cargo of amphorae; some with whole olives rather than oil. The packing for the amphorae came from the Bay of Naples, suggesting the home base for the vessel.

One of the great imperial monuments from Italy was the Arch of Trajan (see image 2) at Beneventum (modern Benevento, Campania) that was erected in 114 CE. It was built to greet the emperor as he returned from his campaigns against Parthia before he crossed Italy on the Via Appia (Appian Way); however, the emperor died in 117 CE and never saw the structure. Other imperial villas include Hadrian's Villa at Tivoli in the hills outside Rome (see p. 304).

The Roman villa at Piazza Armerina, in southern Sicily, contained more than forty rooms. Many were decorated with splendid mosaics that may have been the work of craftsmen based in north Africa. The villa in its final form dates to the fourth century CE, although it has not been possible to identify the owner with any certainty. However, the depiction of games in the Circus Maximus at Rome hint at someone of senatorial rank. **DG**

Pompeii and Herculaneum 79 CE

The Capitolium temple was constructed in the mid second century BCE and rebuilt *c.* 80 BCE, marking Pompeii's change in status to a Roman colony. It was dedicated to three deities: Jupiter, Juno, and Minerva. Set on a high podium, the temple provided an impressive focal point at the north of the forum, which was the social heart of the town.

P ompeii and Herculaneum were small towns close to the Bay of Naples, thriving until they and other settlements in the area were engulfed in 79 CE by the eruption of the volcano Vesuvius. Their significance lies in the preservation of entire towns at a precise moment in time, giving knowledge of the commercial, political, and domestic life of their inhabitants.

From 80 BCE, when Pompeii became a Roman colony, developing prosperity led to new building, including an amphitheater built in 70 BCE, which could hold up to 15,000 spectators. Some reconstruction in the town was necessary following an earthquake in 62 CE, a precursor of the eruption seventeen years later.

Domestic life is reflected in the houses found at Pompeii and Herculaneum. The largest are the single-story dwellings known as atrium houses, constructed from *c.* 220 BCE. The atrium, a hall surrounded by rooms, was the area closest to the street. It served as an interface between the outside world and the home, and was used to reflect the owner's wealth and status, as well as for everyday activities such as storage. Approximately a third of houses in Pompeii had a garden surrounded by a colonnade. There is evidence of the layout of the gardens, as well as the plants and trees grown. The *triclinium* (dining room) was often placed facing the garden. Dining rooms may have taken the form of the stone bases of the couches used by diners, as depicted in wall paintings. However, this type of house required a lot of space, and at Pompeii there are remains indicating the addition of galleries and upper stories, and the rooms adjacent to the main entrance being converted into single-roomed shops leading directly off the street. **GM**

VILLA OF THE MYSTERIES

The Villa of the Mysteries, just outside the walls of Pompeii, was built in the second century BCE and discovered in 1909. The villa covered approximately 40,000 square feet (3,716 sq. m.) and had at least sixty rooms, many of which have wall paintings. The most striking, and the one after which this villa is named, is in the dining room. It is decorated with more than twenty life-size figures against a red background. The theme is generally considered to be a female initiation rite into the cult of Dionysus, the god of wine and religious ecstasy.

VESUVIUS

The House of the Centenary in Pompeii was discovered in 1879 and is thought to have had a wealthy owner. This detail from a fresco at the house features a representation of Vesuvius, before it lost its top in the eruption. The long-dormant volcano erupted in 79 CE following a series of small earthquakes. It discharged an ash cloud 18 miles (30 km.) high, whose collapse led to a series of pyroclastic surges, avalanches of superheated ash and gas racing down the slopes of Vesuvius at speeds estimated of up to 98 feet per second (30 m./s).

HERCULANEUM AND PRESERVATION

Herculaneum was originally situated on the shoreline of the Bay of Naples, and was a wealthier town than Pompeii. Unlike its neighbor, Herculaneum was engulfed by a thick layer of pumice up to 65 feet (20 m.) deep, making excavation more difficult.

At Pompeii the presence of victims of the eruption was indicated by cavities in the ash, whereas excavations at Herculaneum in the 1980s found approximately 300 skeletons. The bodies found in the two ancient towns account for only 10 percent of their estimated populations. One-third of Pompeii and two-thirds of Herculaneum are still not excavated and it is possible that many bodies have yet to be uncovered in and around the towns.

Many objects at Herculaneum were carbonized by the extreme heat. This removed the moisture from them and so prevented decay. A feature of Herculaneum is well-preserved carbonized wood. Recent archaeological work has revealed a complete wooden roof, with beams up to 23 feet (7 m.) long.

Herculaneum's Villa of the Papyri, excavated between 1750 and 1765, contained eighty sculptures and a library of papyrus scrolls, the latter giving the villa its popular name. Approximately 1,800 papyri were recovered, with recently developed techniques being employed to read the texts without unrolling the scrolls. Most of the texts were written by the Epicurean philosopher Philodemus of Gadara (c. 110–c. 35 BCE).

Hadrian's Villa 118 – 134 CE

Soon after taking power, the emperor Hadrian began work on a magnificent new country residence at modern-day Tivoli in Lazio. It covers a vast area of 296 acres (120 ha.) and is the largest villa known from the Roman world.

Hadrian's Villa is a large, landscaped, architectural complex of more than thirty separate buildings, considered to be the high point in architectural opulence of the Roman Empire. Construction was started by Emperor Hadrian (76–138) shortly after his accession in 117 CE and was substantially completed in less than twenty years. The villa is in Tibur, now Tivoli, 17 miles (28 km.) east of Rome. Hadrian was not the first wealthy Roman to favor Tibur, which was popular as a summer resort. Those who stayed there included Emperor Augustus (63 BCE–14 CE) and the poets Horace (65–8 BCE) and Catullus (c. 84–c. 54 BCE). However, the most grandiose residence was Hadrian's Villa.

The architecture and decoration of some of the buildings added by Hadrian may reflect places he had visited during his travels around the Roman Empire. Although Hadrian's biography, included in the *Historia Augusta* (*Augustan History*) written two centuries later, names some of the buildings, including the Canopus and the Academy, definite associations with actual buildings are unknown.

Below the villa was a network of underground passageways. The principal roadway extends about 1 mile (1.6 km.) from north to south and is 10 feet (3 m.) wide. Other evidence of those who served the emperor may be found in the Hospitalia, thought to have accommodated high-ranking villa staff, and the Cento Camerelle (Hundred Chambers), which consisted of four stories of rooms, similar to insulae in Rome and Ostia (see p. 296).

A recent discovery is an area interpreted as honoring Hadrian's lover, the Greek youth Antinoüs (c. 110–130 CE). Fragments of sculpture in Egyptian style were found here, and the original decoration may have included the obelisk now in the Pincio gardens in Rome. **GM**

◆ NAVIGATOR

👁 FOCAL POINTS

1 SERAPEUM

The semi-domed structure at the southern end of the lake is named the Serapeum after the sacred area dedicated to the Greco-Egyptian god Serapis. It is believed to have served as an outdoor *triclinium* (dining room). There is a reflecting pool between the two buildings that flank the dining area.

2 SCULPTURES

The lake has colonnades along its length, decorated with statues. They include modern-day copies of the Roman sculptures that were based on the Caryatids, figures of young women from the Erechtheion on the Athenian Acropolis which date to the fifth century BCE.

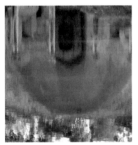

3 LAKE

The Canopus artificial lake is 390 feet (119 m.) long and 59 feet (18 m.) wide. Canopus was an ancient Egyptian town near modern-day Alexandria. It lay at the mouth of the Canopic branch of the Nile, and it is thought that the lake may be a symbolic representation of this waterway.

▲ The Teatro Marittimo (Maritime Theater) is one of the earliest parts of the villa, indicated by bricks dated to 117 CE. It is a private apartment with its own bathing suite on a circular island, separated by a canal surrounded by a colonnaded enclosure.

AFTER HADRIAN

The villa remained in use after Hadrian's death, being used by the second century emperors Antoninus Pius (86–161) and Marcus Aurelius (121–180), and by Diocletian (245–316) in the third century. Constantine (c. 280–337) did not favor the villa, and it fell into ruin. The land on which Hadrian's Villa stood had been split between a number of owners, one of whom was Giuseppe Alessandro Furietti (1685–1764), who bought the rights to excavate part of the villa. Among his finds was this small mosaic panel, now in the Capitoline Museums, Rome. Made from small tesserae, the scene shows doves drinking from a bowl. Opinion is divided on whether it is a Hellenistic original of the second century BCE by the mosaicist Sosus, or a copy. Other notable finds are the stone sculptures of a young and an old centaur, also now in the Capitoline Museums.

ANCIENT JEWS

1

2

1 The ruins of the high-level Roman aqueduct at Caesarea Maritima on the Mediterranean coast of Israel, south of Haifa. The aqueduct originates about 5 miles (7.5 km.) northeast of Caesarea.

2 A detail from a mosaic at the House of the Nile Festival at Sepphoris in Galilee. It includes an image of the Nilometer that was used to measure the height of the flood waters.

Jerusalem has been the focus of a series of excavations (see p. 232). It is a city that has been occupied for millennia and is overlain by culturally sensitive structures. At the heart of the city lay the temple, the focus for the Jewish people, which was begun by King Herod the Great (73–4 BCE) in c. 20 BCE. The temple was destroyed in 70 CE by the Roman army that sacked the city. The sacred candelabrum is shown in one of the reliefs on the Arch of Titus, dating to the first century CE, in the Roman Forum. The ashlar walls surrounding the temple platform are prominent along the west side and incorporate the Wailing Wall. Excavations at the foot of the temple platform have revealed blocks that were toppled onto the stone pavement during the destruction of the city. The Temple Mount is occupied by the Al-Aqsa Mosque. Excavations in the western part of the city have found remains of Jewish houses of the first century CE that include features such as baths for ritual cleansing. However, there are elements of Roman architectural and decorative influence, suggesting that the Jewish elite were acquiring non-Jewish customs.

Herod built one of his palaces at Herodium to the south of Jerusalem. This was described by the Jewish historian Flavius Josephus (c. 37–100 CE). Excavations have revealed the remains of a theater, indicating that Herod had acquired a taste for classical plays. A bathhouse complex was constructed along Roman lines with a range of heated rooms but also included a *mikvah*, or stepped basin, where washing according to Jewish custom could be carried out. Herod chose to be buried at the site of Herodium.

KEY EVENTS

c. 300 BCE–c. 200 CE	2nd century BCE	1st century BCE	37–4 BCE	c. 20 BCE	c. 30 CE
The Dead Sea Scrolls are written. They were discovered in caves on the edge of the Judean Desert in 1947.	Jerusalem is resettled after being sacked by the Babylonians in 586 BCE.	The town of Sepphoris in Galilee is built. U.S. excavations under Leroy Waterman (1875–1972) uncovered its remains in 1930.	King Herod the Great reigns over Judea.	Herod orders the construction of a temple at the center of Jerusalem.	Pontius Pilate orders the crucifixion of Jesus.

Herod's most impressive palace was at Masada, overlooking the Dead Sea (see p. 310). The complex on the steep cliffs reflected his taste for Roman culture. His Winter Palace was constructed at Jericho, close to the Wadi Qelt that cuts through the Judean Desert. It was a strategic location, close to the road up to Jerusalem. The palace made use of the water supply from the Wadi Qelt and, as in many royal palaces, there are a number of ritual basins. The palace contained dining rooms that were built in the Roman style.

To the south of Jericho and on the western side of the Dead Sea are the remains of a Jewish religious community at Qumran (see p. 308). The site is significant because of the association with the finds of the Dead Sea scrolls in a series of caves in the neighboring cliffs.

The formal Romanization of Judea was marked by the construction of a city at Caesarea Maritima on the coast. This had been developed by Herod, and an artificial jetty was built during the first century CE to protect shipping on a coast that had little natural protection. The city had no abundant natural water supply and had to be supplied by an aqueduct (see image 1). Caesarea became the base of the Roman administration and excavations have found a Latin inscription recording the dedication of a temple linked to the imperial cult and Emperor Tiberius (42 BCE–37 CE) by the Roman governor Pontius Pilate (d. c. 36 CE), who ordered the crucifixion of Jesus (c. 4 BCE–c. 30 CE) outside Jerusalem.

The town of Sepphoris in Galilee was built in the late first century BCE. This included a theater, dating to the late first century BCE and probably capable of seating about 4,500 people, suggesting that classical plays were part of the cultural taste of the population. One of the mosaics in the House of the Nile Festival represented scenes from the Nile (see image 2) and includes a personification of Egypt as a woman. The house dates to the fifth century CE.

One of the most impressive Roman cities that has been excavated is Scythopolis at Bet She'an in the Jordan Valley. It developed during the reign of the emperor Hadrian (76–138 CE). The colonnaded streets have been reconstructed after they were toppled by an earthquake in Late Antiquity. The theater seated 7,000 people and was built in the late second century.

Jerusalem was re-established under Hadrian as Aelia Capitolina and became the headquarters of the Tenth Legion, based in the southwestern corner of the city. The present Damascus Gate through the city walls contains part of the fortifications built at this time. Remains of one of the colonnaded streets with shops behind have been recovered during recent excavations. In Late Antiquity some of the sites associated with the life of Jesus were monumentalized. In particular, the Church of the Holy Sepulchre was constructed in 330 to commemorate the site of his crucifixion and the tomb where he was buried. Remains of Jewish tombs dating to the first century CE can be seen under the church, suggesting it was outside the walled area of the city of Jerusalem. **DG**

66–70	70	1st century	132–135	Late 2nd century	330
The First Jewish Revolt against Roman rule in Judea takes place.	The Roman army sacks the city of Jerusalem, resulting in the destruction of Herod's temple.	Jewish houses with features such as baths for ritual cleansing are built in Jerusalem.	The Second Jewish Revolt against Roman rule in Judea occurs.	A theater seating 7,000 people is built at the Roman city of Scythopolis at Bet She'an in the Jordan Valley.	The Church of the Holy Sepulchre is constructed in Jerusalem to commemorate the site of Jesus's crucifixion.

Qumran Eighth century BCE – second century CE

One of the features of the community at Qumran was the scriptorium where the scrolls were written. It contained tables coated with plaster that were used for preparing the scrolls. Inkwells were also recovered. An adjacent room appears to have been equipped with cupboards and may have served as a library.

The archaeological site of Qumran lies on the edge of the Judean Desert and on the western shore of the Dead Sea to the south of Jericho. In 1947, Bedouin shepherd boys exploring the caves in the foothills discovered a series of scrolls that had been hidden there. These became known as the Dead Sea Scrolls.

One of the first containers to be opened from Cave 1 contained three texts; one by the Jewish prophet Isaiah; another, a commentary on a text of the minor prophet Habbakuk; and the third concerned the Community Rule of a Jewish group who were using the prophetic texts to structure their lifestyle. The scrolls passed through the hands of a dealer in Bethlehem before being sold to Athanasius Yeshue Samuel (1907–95), the Metropolitan of Jerusalem of the Syrian Orthodox Church, and to Israeli archaeologist Eleazar Sukenik (1889–1953) on behalf of the Hebrew University of Jerusalem.

The cave where the scrolls had been found formed part of Jordan, and were explored by a team led by Roland de Vaux from the Jordanian Department of Antiquities and the Ecole Biblique in Jerusalem. They located fragments of seven scrolls in Cave 1. Another thirty-three fragmentary scrolls were discovered by Bedouin in Cave 2. Several thousand scroll fragments were found in nearby caves, including a text of the Book of Samuel. It is likely that 530 scrolls were represented, some written in Greek as well as Hebrew and Aramaic. Other nearby sites included a scroll of the Septuagint (Greek) version of the Exodus. Cave 11 was unearthed by Bedouin in 1956. One of the texts found there was the Temple Scroll. The Dead Sea Scrolls from the various sites date from the third century BCE to the second century CE. **DG/GM**

FOCAL POINTS

ISAIAH SCROLL

The Isaiah Scroll is one of the seven Dead Sea Scrolls that were first recovered in 1947. It contains all of the Hebrew version of the biblical book of Isaiah, a document that was seen in the first century as anticipating the future arrival of the Messiah to redeem the Jewish people. Such anticipation was met with concern by the Roman authorities. Further scrolls were discovered in the same cave, including a second text of Isaiah, as well as the War Scroll and the Thanksgiving Scroll.

COPPER SCROLL

A systematic search of the caves in the vicinity of Cave 2 recovered the so-called Copper Scroll (inscribed on copper sheets), and fourteen other fragmentary scrolls in Cave 3. Most of the Dead Sea Scrolls are written on parchment, with a few written on papyrus; the Copper Scroll is unique because it is etched on metal. It is also unusual because it records a series of sixty-three hoards of gold and silver that had been hidden away in the area of the Dead Sea and the vicinity of Jerusalem.

SETTLEMENT AT QUMRAN

It was evident that the scrolls were linked to a nearby community and a research excavation was initiated to explore the site. The location had already been identified by French archaeologist Charles Clermont-Ganneau (1846–1923), and may have been Secacah, which is mentioned in biblical texts. The settlement was excavated by Roland de Vaux between 1951 and 1956. The earliest settlement can be traced to the eighth century BCE. The fortified settlement seems to have been destroyed in c. 586 BCE, when Jerusalem was sacked by the Babylonians. The site was resettled during the second century BCE, and severely damaged in an earthquake of 31 BCE.

One of the features of the site was the *mikvah*, or ritual baths. These allowed the purification of members of the community who were able to immerse themselves in water that had been collected from the run-off in the nearby wadi. There was clear division so that those entering the bathing area did not come into contact with those who had been purified. Some of these baths were located in the vicinity of the refectory, and this may confirm the suggestion by Jewish historian Flavius Josephus that purification was carried out before eating.

The cemetery contained some 1,000 graves that were oriented north to south. Studies have suggested that this may reflect a population of approximately 200 for the community. This figure is supported by the pottery recovered from the refectory, a building about 72 feet (22 m.) long.

The site was abandoned in 68 CE during the First Jewish Revolt (66–70 CE) against Roman rule in Judaea. It then became the location of a small Roman garrison that continued into the Hadrianic period and the Second Jewish Revolt (132–135 CE) against Rome.

Masada First century BCE

General Flavius Silva with the Tenth Roman Legion encircled Masada with a series of forts and proceeded to construct a siege ramp from the western side. This work was protected by the establishment of locations for siege artillery that could provide covering fire against the defenders. Some of the wood used in this ramp is still preserved.

Masada is located on top of a rocky outcrop in the Southern District of Israel overlooking the Dead Sea. It served as a palace for Jewish rulers from the second century BCE, as well as the tragic setting for the Jewish garrison. Herod the Great developed the site between 36 and 30 BCE. His other major building works included the great palace complex at Jericho to the north of the Dead Sea and the construction of the new temple in Jerusalem. Masada was the site of the Herodian Winter Palace. The architectural style was unashamedly Roman with Corinthian capitals and frescoes, some of which evoked the use of precious marbles. This style is echoed in some of the first-century CE elite houses that have been excavated in Jerusalem and is in contrast with the stance adopted by various Jewish religious groups, who placed a growing emphasis on their Jewish identity and purity. Masons' marks on some of the column drums associated with these structures indicate that Jewish stonemasons had been involved with the work. A second palace was identified on the western site of the acropolis containing mosaic floors, and a bathhouse. Like the northern palace, the walls were decorated with Roman-style architectural frescoes.

The site was excavated by Israeli archaeologist Yigael Yadin (1917–84) from 1963 to 1965 on behalf of the Hebrew University of Jerusalem, the Israel Exploration Society, and Israel's Department of Antiquities. The work was supported by a large international team of volunteers. There was a logistical challenge to get water and supplies to the top of the fortress, and support was provided by the Israeli army. A stairway was placed at the top of the Roman siege ramp so that the excavators could enter from the west. **DG/GM**

HEROD'S WINTER PALACE

The Herodian Winter Palace used a series of terraces overlooking the valley and beyond to the hills of Moab (in modern Jordan). The middle terrace contained a circular building that may have originally included columns. This was connected to the upper part of the fortress by a hidden staircase. The upper terrace included rooms decorated with Roman-style mosaics.

APODYTERIUM IN BATHHOUSE, PALACE COMPLEX

The palace complex included a Roman-style bathhouse that reflects the cultural changes that were taking place in the royal family. The complex included a caldarium, or hot room, on a raised hypocaust used for underfloor heating. The walls were decorated with architectural wall paintings. In a late phase, a small ritual bath had been inserted into the apodyterium, or changing room.

ROMAN SIEGE OF MASADA

Masada contained space for the garrison as well as cisterns, features that are reminiscent of the great Hellenistic palace site of the Attalids on the acropolis at Pergamum, Turkey. Adjacent to the bathhouses was a complex that seems to have served as a store for the palace and its community. The Jewish historian Flavius Josephus discusses this complex, suggesting that there was enough military equipment for a force of 10,000 men.

Masada became one of the last strongholds in the First Jewish Revolt that erupted in 66 CE. Excavations have found a series of clay storage jars, some inscribed in Hebrew script. Coins associated with this period carry the message "For the freedom of Zion." Further coin hoards of the period of the revolt were found in the courtyard building to the south of the storerooms. A number of biblical texts on scrolls were found during the excavations, including the book of Leviticus.

The Roman garrison of Masada was captured by the Jewish rebel Menahem. The Romans sacked the city of Jerusalem in 70 CE, and then turned to those garrisons elsewhere in the region. The Jewish group at Masada was led by Eleazar ben Jair. Josephus described the Roman siege of Masada and the suicide pact for the last defenders as they realized that the Roman forces were about to break into the fortress. It is reported that 960 took their own lives, ending the siege in 73 CE. Few bodies have been discovered (see p. 518), though one skeleton near the bathhouse was found near plates from scaled armor. Nearby was the body of a woman whose braided hair had been preserved.

The site was subsequently garrisoned by Roman troops, and there is evidence of a Christian community here in the fifth and sixth centuries. This included a Byzantine church decorated with a mosaic floor.

CELTS

1 Bibracte in Burgundy, France, is a Gaulish oppidum. It was the capital of the Aedui tribe and an important hill fort.

2 The Broighter Collar's motifs are classic La Tène: sinuous, vegetal tendrils looping along the lengths of the two hinged tubes that make up the torc.

3 The royal site of Navan Fort in County Armagh, Northern Ireland, consists of a circular bank and ditch, 774 feet (236 m.) in diameter, which encloses a mound.

The first mention of the Celts comes from the Greek writer Herodotus (c. 484 – c. 430 BCE). He wrote that the Danube river arose in the land of the Keltoi, the most western people in Europe. Subsequent authors, such as the Greek philosopher Poseidonius (c. 135 – c. 51 BCE) and Roman ruler Julius Caesar (c. 100 – 44 BCE), added more information to the characterization of Celtic peoples, including the Gauls (see p. 318) who lived on the territory of modern France. The Celts were defined as an ethnic group, although the name was an ethnonym imposed by others in order to make sense of the patchwork of prehistoric societies that inhabited western Europe.

Various peoples known through archaeology have been called Celts, starting with the Iron Age elites of central and western Europe (see p. 252). A more secure association is with the later Iron Age peoples of Atlantic Europe. They had a distinctive material culture and decorative style, but also left a legacy in the form of Celtic languages, the descendants of which are known today as Irish, Scots Gaelic, Welsh, and Breton.

Archaeologically, an important marker of Celtic society is the La Tène art style, named after the discovery, in 1859, of a deposit of decorated metalwork in a drainage ditch near Lake Neuchâtel in Switzerland. Similar metalwork had been found in northern Italy, attributed by Roman authors to Celts who crossed the Alps c. 400 BCE. The La Tène art style that arose in the fifth century BCE represents the borrowing of elements from classical Mediterranean motifs by craftsmen in west-central Europe and transforming them into novel patterns.

KEY EVENTS

c. 450 BCE	c. 350 BCE–500 CE	c. 300 BCE	c. 300–200 BCE	c. 200 BCE–400 CE	c. 200 BCE
The La Tène art style begins in central Europe.	In northern Europe, the victors of battles commence the practice of depositing the weapons and boats of their defeated rivals in bogs.	The La Tène style spreads to the British Isles and develops its insular variant.	The Clonycavan and Oldcroghan men are killed in Ireland.	Irish royal sites function as ceremonial centers.	The first oppida is established in central and western Europe.

These are abstract, flowing, and curvilinear, often evoking comparison to vegetation and vines. Animals sometimes appear as fantastic beasts, while humans are usually depicted as stylized heads. Metal objects such as shields were the favored media for La Tène art. The spread of its motifs followed the trade in wine that linked the barbarians of central and western Europe with Mediterranean civilizations. By c. 300 BCE, the La Tène style had spread to the British Isles, where metalsmiths took it to new levels of abstraction and beauty. One spectacular example was the gold neck ring, or torc, found in a deposit at Broighter, northern Ireland, in 1896. The Broighter Collar (see image 2) dates to the first century BCE and is made from sheet gold, on which a design was engraved and then brought into relief by hammering the background.

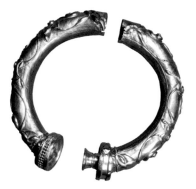

Although Celtic polities are often called tribes, they were complex chiefdoms or even nascent kingdoms. The spiritual and ceremonial lives of the Celts are an important dimension of their culture, about which archaeology and written texts provide information. Caesar mentioned Druids who were in charge of religious and ceremonial matters. Their status appears to have been outside political authority, suggesting that there were multiple paths to high social standing. The practice of ritual killing and the deposition of corpses in bogs occurred across northern Europe (see p. 316); it was not confined to the Celtic world. Nonetheless, the bog bodies of the British Isles, such as Lindow Man in Britain and Clonycavan Man and Oldcroghan Man in Ireland, reflect ceremonial behavior that some believe involved the institution of kingship (see p. 314).

In central and western Europe, especially in France, societies identified with the Celts built fortified centers called oppida, which are described in detail by Caesar. A typical oppidum (see image 1) has a strong wall of stone laced with timber that encloses an immense area. The length of the wall meant that it was effectively impossible to defend against attacks at multiple points, so it was more for show than for protection. Within the walls were residential precincts, industrial zones, and ceremonial buildings. The combination of multiple functions at a single site has led some archaeologists to argue that oppida had an urban character.

Different evidence of social complexity during the Iron Age is found in Ireland, where several hilltop locations have been demarcated with banks and ditches, within which are often traces of round timber ceremonial structures. These were different from the oppida, in that they lack evidence for dwelling and industrial activity. Known as royal sites, the most important are found at Navan Fort (see image 3), Tara, Rathcroghan, and Dún Ailinne. It is not clear that they were the seats of kings, as has been attributed to them in myth. Nonetheless, activities that reinforced social differences, such as feasting, took place at them. One of the most remarkable finds at Navan Fort was the skull of a Barbary ape (*Macaca sylvanus*), native to northwest Africa, indicating that even this remote corner of Europe had distant connections. **PB**

c. 100–1 BCE	58 BCE	2 BCE–119 CE	43 CE	476	*c.* 800
The decorated gold objects in the Broighter Hoard are produced in northern Ireland.	Julius Caesar invades Gaul.	Lindow Man is killed in England.	The Roman conquest of Britain begins.	The conventional date for the collapse of the Roman Empire in the West.	The Book of Kells is produced, probably in Scotland. Its rich decoration is a descendant of the prehistoric art motifs seen on metalwork.

Bog Bodies Fourth century BCE – early centuries CE

In 1950, peat diggers found the body of a man in a bog near Silkeborg, Denmark. Tollund Man had been strangled, and the rope was still tied around his neck. In 1952, about 11 miles (18 km.) from Tollund at Grauballe, another body was discovered. Grauballe Man had not been strangled. Instead, his throat had been cut from ear to ear.

Across much of northern Europe, from Russia to Ireland, lakes formed in hollows left behind by the retreating ice sheets. Over time, the lakes became choked with vegetation, which decayed, leaving deposits of peat. The peat bogs provided ideal environments for the preservation of organic materials. As the peat accumulated, it sealed ancient finds in an oxygen-free environment where microorganisms that cause decay could not live.

Starting in the eighteenth century, peasants cutting peat for fuel began to find human bodies. By the end of the nineteenth century, it came to be recognized that these bodies were very old, dating to prehistoric times. Yet often they were reburied in soil and quickly decayed. In the early twentieth century, however, archaeologists realized that they were an important aspect of prehistoric life in northern Europe.

After World War II, two developments spurred scientific and popular interest in the bog bodies. First, difficult economic conditions led to increased use of peat for heating and cooking. Second, peat diggers knew to contact the authorities if they came across any trace of a body, and archaeologists usually arrived quickly on the scene. During the early 1950s, this led to the recovery of several important Danish bog bodies in relatively good condition, such as Tollund Man and Grauballe Man, dating to the fourth and third centuries BCE respectively. By the 1960s, the use of peat for fuel declined, but then demand for peat surged again, for suburban gardens. This meant, however, that peat was now mined with large machines that scrape the surfaces of the bogs layer by layer. As a result, bog bodies found in recent decades are usually fragmentary; whatever is left after the mechanical peat digger has passed.

Most bog bodies are dated by carbon-14 to the last four centuries BCE and the first several centuries CE. Almost all of these individuals were killed violently. They provide one of the most arresting aspects of Iron Age life across northern Europe. **PB**

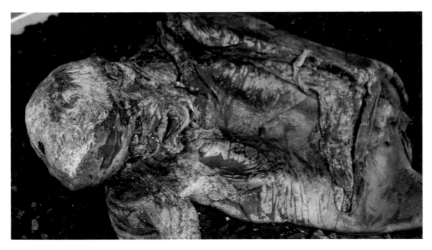

LINDOW MAN

In 1984, Lindow Moss near Manchester, England, was being scraped for peat. On a conveyor belt, a human foot appeared, and more body parts were found in the bog. Thus Lindow Man saw the light of day for the first time since about the first century CE, when he was strangled and struck on the head. His throat was also slit. What was left of him indicated he was about twenty-five years old and stood 5 feet 6 inches (170 cm.) tall, wearing nothing but a beard, mustache, and a strip of fox fur around one arm.

CLONYCAVAN MAN

A few months apart in 2003, two major finds were made in the central Irish boglands. Oldcroghan Man was 6 feet 6 inches (200 cm.) tall. His smooth hands indicated that he did not do manual labor. Clonycavan Man was short, 5 feet 2 inches (160 cm.) tall. He had elaborately styled hair, using pine-resin gel traced to Spain or southern France. Their deaths occurred during the fourth or third century BCE. Clonycavan Man was killed by multiple blows, including one to the chest with a sharp object.

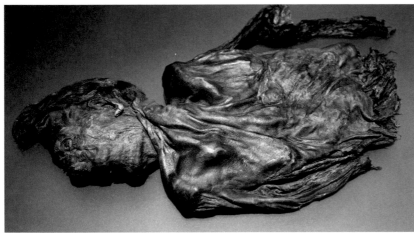

HOW ARE BOG BODIES PRESERVED?

Waterlogged peats contain very little oxygen. The microorganisms that cause organic material to decay cannot live in such an environment, which is what causes bogs to accumulate as new layers of vegetation die but cannot decompose. Moreover, most bogs are acidic, which also keeps the number of microorganisms down. For many years, these were believed to be the two key factors in the preservation of the bog bodies; but they do not account for the surprising detail that the bog bodies provide, down to the beard stubble on Tollund Man, the gelled hair of Clonycavan Man, and the manicured fingernails of Oldcroghan Man.

Recent studies have shown, however, that the chemistry of the bog does more than inhibit decomposition. It acts upon the corpse submerged in the bog to change it chemically. Sphagnum moss is the main plant component of peat bogs. As it decays, it produces a chemical—sphagnan. When sphagnan comes into contact with a corpse, it does several things.

First, it removes calcium from the body, which gives any bacteria that can survive in the low-oxygen, acidic bog water even less to feed on. As a result, many bog bodies have few, if any, bones left. At the same time, sphagnan binds nitrogen, denying even more food to bacteria.

Second, sphagnan is a natural tanning agent that preserves the skin, hair, nails, and internal organs of the bog bodies, as well as any clothing or other objects (such as the rope used to strangle Tollund Man) made from wool or hide. Thus, the skin of the bog bodies looks leathery because it really has become a kind of leather, but their contorted poses are because of the decalcification of their bones.

Scandinavian War-booty Sacrifices *c.* 350 BCE – 500 CE

A reconstruction of the Hjortspring boat in the National Museum of Denmark in Copenhagen. The boat was 62 feet (19 m.) long and 6 feet (2 m.) wide. It was built from a bottom plank and two long spars on each side, which were extended to form prows. Planks of lime wood formed the sides, joined by ten crossbeams that provided seats for rowers.

Bog bodies were not the only sacrifices found in the wetlands of northern Europe. Starting in the final centuries BCE and especially in the first centuries CE, the victors of clashes between raiding parties deposited the weapons and boats of their defeated rivals in bogs. These deposits are known as war-booty sacrifices. More than 300 war-booty sacrifices are known from Denmark alone, with more from Sweden and Norway. They often contain hundreds of weapons, and occasionally body armor and other equipment. In several cases, whole boats have been found.

One of the earliest war-booty sacrifices is the boat found on the island of Als in Denmark at a locality called Hjortspring. Although discovered in the nineteenth century, it was not until the 1920s that excavations revealed an immense quantity of weapons, many of which were broken, along with the fragments of the boat. Excavations in the 1980s recovered other parts of the boat, which could be radiocarbon dated to 350 to 300 BCE, making Hjortspring the earliest war-booty sacrifice from Denmark.

Danish archaeologist Klavs Randsborg (b. 1944) has calculated that the number of spears and swords at Hjortspring would have been the equipment of a force of about eighty warriors. Most carried shields and two spears, while a group wore chain mail and carried swords. The assumption is that the boat and the weapons belonged to a defeated war party that arrived by water, and that the victors sacrificed these objects to deities.

Sacrificing war booty continued into the first centuries CE. At this time, barbarians from outside the imperial frontiers served in the Roman army, and the raiding parties of the north acquired weapons from Roman workshops or copies made along the frontier. **PB**

👁 FOCAL POINTS

HJORTSPRING WEAPONS

Most weapons in the Hjortspring deposit were spears between 4 and 8 inches (10–20 cm.) long with spearheads of bone or iron. Some had broken-off shafts made of ash in the sockets. Two of the eleven swords had been deliberately bent. Preserved in the waterlogged deposits were oval or rectangular wooden shields. Rust marks of many small iron rings suggest the presence of chain mail, the earliest known from Europe.

WEAPON FINDS AT NYDAM

There are several war-booty sacrifices at the Nydam bog in southern Denmark. Most of the weapons are spears, but about a third of the warriors carried swords based on Roman designs. Several longbows made of yew and hazel were found, representing a new weapon system in Scandinavian Iron Age warfare. A fibula, or ornamental safety pin, is similar to those worn by Roman officers but is probably a copy made in northern Europe.

ILLERUP ÅDAL

The first archaeological discoveries were made at the river valley of Illerup Ådal in eastern Jutland (Cimbrian Peninsula) in 1950, during some drainage work. The area was subsequently excavated from 1950 to 1956, and again in 1975 to 1985.

A series of offerings were found that date from the third to the fifth centuries CE. The largest is known as Illerup Ådal A, with more than 350 shields, 366 lances, 410 spears, more than 100 swords, eleven sets of riding gear, and many other items dating to c. 210 CE. Unlike Nydam, however, no boats or archery equipment were found at Illerup. The weapons had been systematically destroyed—swords were broken across and shields smashed—and were then thrown into the ancient lake either from boats or from the shore.

Skeletons of four horses, presumably belonging to the defeated army, bear traces of injuries that appear to have been inflicted ritually, by several individuals with different weapons attacking them simultaneously. Strontium isotope ratios indicate that they came from Denmark or southern Sweden.

By this time, Roman items had reached the northern areas far beyond the imperial frontier. Two hundred Roman silver coins issued by the emperors Nero (37–68 CE) through to Commodus (161–192 CE), the most recent from 187/188 CE, were found in clumps, suggesting that they had been in small pouches. In the barbarian societies, Roman coins were possibly acquired as payment for their services, but served more as status symbols.

Metallurgical techniques seen in many of the swords discovered indicate that they were made in Roman workshops. Some Roman sword blades have makers' marks and inlaid images of Roman gods and goddesses, although the hilts could have been added locally by Scandinavian craftworkers.

Alesia 100 BCE – 400 CE

A monument to the Celtic god Ucuetis at the archaeological site of Alesia at Alise-Sainte-Reine in Burgundy, France.

Alesia holds a symbolic place in French history as the location of the final stand by the Gallic leader Vercingetorix (d. 46 BCE) against the might of Rome. The final conquest of Gaul by Julius Caesar, the Gallic Wars that took place between 58 and 52 BCE are documented by Caesar in his *Commentarii de Bello Gallico* (*Commentaries on the Gallic War*; 58 – 49 BCE). Caesar recorded his struggle against Vercingetorix, who by 52 BCE had become the leader of all the indigenous tribes from the river Seine in the north to the river Garonne in the southwest. Caesar wrote that this culminated in a battle at Alesia, the capital of the Mandubii tribe, an oppidum (the word used by Caesar to describe hill forts) where Vercingetorix and his troops had taken refuge.

Despite its historical importance, the actual location of Alesia was not known, and in 1864 the Emperor Napoleon III (1808 – 73) issued an official decree that Alesia was situated on Mont-Auxois, near Alise-Sainte-Reine, a town in the Burgundy region of France, whose name Alise is similar to Alesia. However, controversy surrounds the identification of Mont-Auxois as Alesia; some scholars have observed that the geographical description of Alesia given by Caesar in his *Commentaries* does not correspond to Alise-Sainte-Reine.

Other evidence of the period of the Gallic Wars can be found close to the oppidum of Liercourt-Erondelle in northern France. Aerial photography suggests an enclosure with a ditch near the oppidum, and the area has also produced Iron Age pottery and coins. It is unclear, however, whether those guarding the hill fort were Roman or Gallic. Although other enclosures in this region, identified as camps, are sometimes associated with Caesar's Gallic Wars, they are likely to be later in date. **GM**

⊙ FOCAL POINTS

ROMAN FORTIFICATIONS

A section of the Roman fortifications that would have surrounded the hill fort has been reconstructed at the MuséoParc Alésia in Alise-Sainte-Reine, which opened in 2012. The reconstructions are based on the account by Caesar and the excavations commissioned by Napoleon III from 1861 to 1865.

STATUE OF VERCINGETORIX

The presumed battle site is overlooked by a statue of Vercingetorix, commissioned in 1864 by Napoleon III from the sculptor Aimé Millet (1819–91) and the architect Eugène Viollet-le-Duc (1814–79). The sheet-copper statue stands more than 21 feet (6.5 m.) high and dominates the landscape.

BIBRACTE

Vercingetorix was made leader of the indigenous Gallic tribes at the oppidum of Bibracte on Mont Beauvray in Burgundy. Founded in the second century BCE, Bibracte was capital of the Aedui tribe and, at its height, had an estimated population of between 5,000 and 10,000 inhabitants. The Aedui were treated favorably by the Romans and, accordingly, had contact with the Roman world before the conquest of this part of Gaul in 52 BCE, helped by its strategic position on an important trading route along the rivers Loire and Saône. This is apparent from the discovery of amphorae imported from Italy, which would have contained wine. The status of Bibracte meant that it was left unscathed after the Roman victory at Alesia, and Caesar wrote *Commentaries on the Gallic War* at Bibracte. The foundation of Augustodunum (Autun) in *c.* 15 BCE led to the gradual abandonment of Bibracte, because the need for the protection given by its location on Mont Beauvray became unnecessary.

The first excavations at Bibracte were funded by Napoleon III and conducted by French archaeologist Jacques-Gabriel Bulliot (1817–1902) from 1867 and continued by his nephew, Joseph Déchelette (1862–1914), from 1897. On Déchelette's death in 1914, archaeological work ceased at Bibracte. However, a major multinational research project began in 1984.

Modern-day visitors to the archaeological park at Bibracte can see public buildings, houses, workshops, and fortification walls from the Gallo-Roman town, extending over an area of 494 acres (200 ha.). The reconstructed fortifications extend 3 miles (5 km.) around the Gallo-Roman site and, with their main gateway, were constructed in the first century CE. An earlier fortification, still covered and preserved beneath the forest, was built in the second century BCE when Bibracte was founded, and extends 4 miles (7 km.) around the site.

THE ROMAN ARMY AND FRONTIERS

1 The remains of Milecastle 39 on Hadrian's Wall, northeast England.

2 A bronze head (c. 27–25 BCE) of Emperor Augustus found in Meroë, Sudan.

3 Roman gold coins unearthed during excavations at Kalkriese, Germany, in 2016.

As the Roman Empire expanded, it was secured by the Roman army that consisted of two major groups: the legions formed by Roman citizens, and auxiliary units that were drawn from the range of communities from across the empire. Roman legionary bases, forts, and marching camps are part of the rich archaeological legacy of such activity as well as military equipment from a range of sites.

In Britain, the movements of the Roman army as part of the invasion can be detected at a number of sites. The Iron Age hill forts at Hod Hill and Maiden Castle in Dorset were the subject of assaults. British archaeologist Mortimer Wheeler (1890–1976) identified skeletons with Roman artillery bolts still embedded. Veterans from these early campaigns were settled in newly established colonies at former bases such as Colchester (see p. 330). Some of the names and military units are recorded on the military funerary stelae.

In a militarized province such as Britain, the three legionary fortresses were the main bases: Caerleon in south Wales, Chester on the River Dee, and York in the east. These were located to protect against any uprisings in Wales or northern England. The fortress at Inchtuthil in Perthshire was built as part of the campaign of Gnaeus Julius Agricola (40–93 CE) into Scotland.

KEY EVENTS

137 BCE	134–133 BCE	77–84 BCE	c. 25 BCE	9 CE	43
Numantia in Spain (see p. 322) is captured and lost by an army led by Gaius Hostilius.	The second siege of Numantia is undertaken by Scipio Africanus the Younger.	Gnaeus Julius Agricola conquers Wales, northern England, and parts of Scotland.	A bronze head of Emperor Augustus is taken on a raid of Roman Egypt's southern borders by a Kushite army.	Three Roman legions are massacred at the Battle of Teutoburg Forest in Germania.	The Roman invasion of Britain begins.

One of the most impressive fixed frontiers was constructed in northern England during the reign of the emperor Hadrian (76–138 CE). This ran for 80 Roman miles or 73 miles (117.5 km.) long from Wallsend on the north banks of the river Tyne (to the east of modern Newcastle upon Tyne) to Bowness on the Solway estuary. The frontier as originally conceived consisted of a stone-built or turf wall (see image 1) that may have served as an observation platform looking north. Building stones show that the wall was built by military engineers drawn from the three legions based in Britain. This was strengthened by fortlets every mile, with two turrets during the intervening space. Originally the main garrisons were held along the military road, the Stanegate, that ran to the south. However, a decision was made to move these onto the line of the wall itself. Excavations at forts such as Chesters and Housesteads have revealed remains of the earlier structures that preceded the forts. To the north of the wall was a broad ditch. In some places, work had to be abandoned due to the rock formations; in the central section the ditch was never constructed, as the wall was constructed along the Whin Sill ridge.

Under the reign of Hadrian's successor, Antoninus Pius (86–161 CE), the Roman frontier was moved northward and Hadrian's Wall was abandoned temporarily. A new turf wall was constructed for 37 miles (60 km.) from Bo'ness on the Firth of Forth in the east to Old Kilpatrick on the River Clyde in the west. This was strengthened by a series of small forts. Excavations at Rough Castle show that the fort was defended by a series of pits originally containing sharpened stakes and known as *lilies*, because they resemble the flowers in a macabre description of what would happen if an attacker was impaled.

The Rhine and Danube frontiers were protected by wooden palisades and ditches that run for more than 310 miles (500 km.). These were built in the second century CE to protect the empire from tribes to the east. Rome had been wary of Germania since losing a number of legions under Publius Quinctilius Varus (d. 9 CE) in the Teutoburg Forest during the reign of Augustus (63 BCE–14 CE) in AD 9. Investigations in the region of Kalkriese by a British army officer identified a large number of military finds that seem to be linked to the disaster. All the coins (see image 3) appear to have been minted prior to 9 CE.

One of the most detailed sets of Roman forts have been identified on the edge of the Nubian Desert. These were constructed to defend Egypt from raids to the south. Excavations in a Nubian temple recovered a bronze head of Emperor Augustus (see image 2), likely seized during a Nubian raid on Egypt.

From the third century onward the Roman Empire was under growing pressure from invasion. The North Sea coast of Britannia, as well as corresponding coastal areas in Continental Europe, were defended by new bases. In Britain a series of stone-walled bases were constructed from Brancaster in north Norfolk to Portchester on the Solent. The massive towers at Burgh Castle show that the fort was protected by artillery. **DG**

43	73	85	122	142	2nd century
Colchester in England (see p. 330) is taken over by the Romans.	The Romans lay siege to Masada in the Judean Desert, bringing and end to the First Jewish Revolt.	Roman occupation begins at Vindolanda in northern England (see p. 324).	Emperor Hadrian orders the construction of Hadrian's Wall in northern England.	Antoninus Pius orders construction of the short-lived Antonine Wall, after the Roman frontier is moved north into Scotland.	Wooden palisades and ditches are built along the Rhine and Danube frontiers to protect the empire from tribes to the east.

Numantia Fourth century BCE – fourth century CE

After the defeat by Rome in 133 BCE, the architecture of the typical Celtiberian rectangular houses changed and a more complex plan, with additional rooms, was adopted. Some houses were built in a Romanized style. One example has Tuscan columns forming a portico. This courtyard was linked to the living areas by stone staircases.

Numantia, in Spain, was a major city of the Arevaci, an indigenous pre-Roman group of people. It lies near the modern town of Garray in the Upper Douro Valley. The earliest occupation of the site has been dated to the Bronze Age. A Celtiberian settlement developed from the fourth century BCE. After a lengthy siege, the city was taken by the Romans. A town named Numantia was established on the site by the reign of Augustus, and this continued to be occupied until the fourth century CE. Some of the housing and remains of the walls have been excavated.

German historian and archaeologist Adolf Schulten (1870–1960) and members of the German Archaeological Institute conducted excavations at Numantia between 1905 and 1912. Renewed scientific excavation of the Celtiberian town began in 1990, and the Celtiberian cemetery was discovered in 1993.

The settlement at Numantia covered an area of about 20 acres (8 ha.) and was protected by a series of earthworks. Some of the buildings were laid out in a grid pattern, with some of the houses backing onto the ramparts. One feature of Numantia was stone cisterns sunk into the ground, circular or square in shape. In addition to those found in private houses, others were for communal use, often situated at crossroads in the city. Another type was situated in the courtyard of a private house and consisted of a flight of stone steps descending into the cistern. Some of the streets had drains, covered with stone slabs, and were laid out to allow the waste water to flow outside the city.

There are several examples of Roman bathhouses in the city, including one that is now partly beneath an unfinished commemorative monument begun in 1842. It was intended to foster a Spanish national identity by drawing on the story of the Celtiberians' defiance to external Roman power as a symbol of resistance. **DG/GM**

QUERNS

Archaeologists have learned more regarding the diet of the inhabitants of Numantia by analysis of the residues found on some of the many querns discovered at the site. Analysis revealed traces of wheat, barley, and acorns, all of which were ground to produce flour. Other analyses of querns identified coarsely ground malt, a key element of beer production. Celtiberians in the Spanish highlands drank a type of beer made from fermented grain, *caelia*, as opposed to wine.

CELTIBERIAN HOUSE AND WALL

A typical Celtiberian house, based on a rectangular plan divided into three rooms, has been reconstructed at Numantia. The rooms had separate functions. Usually, one was devoted to domestic industry, such as textile working and food preparation. Another room would be a living area with a fireplace and benches to sleep on. The third room would be used for storing food and tools. Adjacent to the house, a section of the wall of the Celtiberian settlement has been reconstructed. Elsewhere on the site is a reconstruction of a house from the Roman period.

SIEGE OF NUMANTIA

Numantia became the focus of Roman attention. It was captured and lost by an army led by Gaius Hostilius Mancinus in 137 BCE. This led to a second siege from 134 to 133 BCE by Scipio Africanus the Younger (*c.* 185–129 BCE), which entailed the construction of a series of camps around the town, linked by an extended stone siege wall, 10 feet (3 m.) high, running for 6 miles (9 km.). It was strengthened by towers at intervals and a protective ditch.

Adolf Schulten was intrigued by the account of the siege of Numantia recorded by the historian Appian in *The Spanish Wars* (*c.* 165 CE). Excavations were conducted on the site in the early twentieth century by German and Spanish teams. They identified the internal features of the forts, including their administrative headquarters and barracks. Schulten tried to identify the sequences of sieges of Numantia preceding that of Scipio. His analysis of the barracks has been used to clarify the organization of Rome's field armies during this period of the republic. Excavations suggested that the besiegers built low walls around their tents to protect them during the winter. A reassessment of the coin finds from the site by archaeologists from the University of Exeter and from Spain suggests an alternative reading. They indicate that the original siege works consisted of two major camps for the army, and that the circumvallation was supported by seven forts and two fortlets. This matches the number of forts described by Appian.

Vindolanda First – fifth centuries CE

A large pre-Hadrianic bathhouse, built of brick and tile, has been identified outside the walls of Vindolanda. The brick pillars supported the floor of the bathhouse and allowed hot air to circulate beneath the caldarium (hot room) and tepidarium (warm room). The fragmentary nature of the building is the result of the removal of building materials when the bathhouse was demolished in the second century CE.

The Roman fort of Vindolanda lies at Chesterholm, near Bardon Mill in Northumberland, England. The garrison was established on the Roman road known as the Stanegate that ran across the northern Pennines, which predated the building of Hadrian's Wall.

The most recent archaeological evidence indicates that the earliest Roman occupation at Vindolanda dates to around 85 CE, toward the end of the campaigns in Scotland of the Roman provincial governor Gnaeus Julius Agricola that culminated in the victory of Mons Graupius. A thin wooden writing tablet—one of many preserved because of the waterlogged conditions at Vindolanda—suggests that at this time the unit based at the fort was the First Cohort of Tungrians, from northern Gaul, under the command of Julius Verecundus. The unit strength was given as 752, including six centurions. However, the document also indicates that large numbers were absent, including a group of 337, perhaps with two centurions, at Coria—probably the Roman base at Corbridge located farther east, where Dere Street crossed the river Tyne.

During the 90s CE, the fort was enlarged, perhaps enclosing up to 10 acres (4 ha.). Wooden writing tablets recovered from this layer suggest that Iulius Verecundus continued in his command of the First Cohort of Tungrians. The fort was rebuilt around 97 CE, with evidence of the praetorium, its main administrative building, having been found. Part of the garrison archive indicates that by around 100 CE the commander was Flavius Cerialis, commander of the Ninth Cohort of Batavians, also from northern Gaul. In addition, the Third Cohort of Batavians formed part of the garrison at this time and transferred to the Danube in 104 CE in preparation for Trajan's campaigns against Dacia, celebrated on Trajan's Column in Rome. Around 105 CE, the fort was abandoned and a concerted effort made to destroy the garrison archive in a series of fires. **DG/GM**

VINDOLANDA 291

The waterlogged nature of the site has preserved organic material, including leather shoes and part of the garrison archive. Approximately 1,000 documents written on thin wooden tablets provide information about the strength of the garrison and its deployment. Personal letters include Vindolanda 291, an invitation to Sulpicia Lepidina, wife of Flavius Cerialis, to the birthday party of Claudia Severa, wife of Aelius Brocchus, commander of a nearby fort.

HOUSES

The local civilian settlement (vicus) outside the fort was established in the 160s CE, contemporary with the rebuilt fort. In addition to shops, dwellings, and workshops, the vicus also contained a series of houses, suggesting that some soldiers from the garrison lived there with their families. One well-constructed masonry building has an unusual layout with rooms arranged around a narrow courtyard. Once thought to be an inn for travelers, it is now identified as the house of the garrison commander in the early third century CE.

VINDOLANDA IN THE SECOND CENTURY CE AND LATER

There was a garrison at Vindolanda in the early 2nd century CE, and a barrack block from this period has been excavated. A wooden tablet suggests that the soldiers, apparently commanded by Oppius Niger, were the First Cohort of Tungrians. An inscription found near the east gate of the fort records the death of the centurion commanding the unit, Cornelius Victor from Pannonia in modern-day central Europe. Another tablet from this period indicates the presence of Roman legionaries, plausibly posted temporarily, suggesting that Vindolanda served as a base in preparation for the construction of Hadrian's Wall. A large wooden structure dating from around 120 CE may have been part of the accommodation provided for the emperor Hadrian during his visit.

A new fort was constructed at Vindolanda around 163 CE, indicated by a very fragmentary dedicatory inscription that appears to name Sextus Calpurnius Agricola, governor of the province of Britannia from c. 163 CE to around 166. This fort was damaged in what may have been uprisings at the end of the second century, and it was refurbished in the early third century. A further fort was constructed in the early fourth century; this was damaged during incursions in 367. Vindolanda was subsequently reoccupied, but then finally abandoned at the start of the fifth century.

In the 1930s, the estate at Chesterholm, which includes the archaeological site, was purchased by British archaeologist Eric Birley. Excavations by Birley, and subsequently by his sons Robin and Anthony, have provided valuable information about civilian life on the northern frontier of the Roman Empire. The settlement continues to be excavated by the Vindolanda Trust as part of an ongoing research project, including a replica of a section of Hadrian's Wall.

THE ROMAN WEST

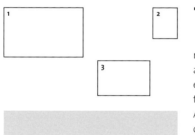

1 The Casa dos Repuxos at the Conimbriga site in Condeixa-a-Velha, Portugal.

2 The Roman amphitheater at Caerleon, Wales, was built c. 90 CE.

3 The Mausoleum of the Julii at Saint-Remy, France.

The Roman West is considered to be the areas of Hispania (Spain and Portugal), Gallia or Gaul (France and parts of neighboring countries) and Britannia (England and Wales). The Iberian provinces, with their rich agricultural and mineral resources, especially gold and silver mines, were among the first to become Roman outside the Italian peninsula. During the early first century, the political importance of Hispania grew. Evidence of the Roman presence in Hispania is most apparent in larger centers such as Augusta Emerita (Mérida) with a theater, circus, amphitheater, and bridge over the Guadiana river. Evidence of Roman occupation is also to be found in smaller locations, such as Medinaceli in northwest Spain, which has a Roman triumphal arch, and the Roman towns of Mirobriga and Conimbriga (Condeixa-a-Velha) in Portugal. Conimbriga's remains include an amphitheater and houses such as the Casa dos Repuxos (House of Fountains; see image 1), with mosaics dating to the second century and water fountains in its garden.

The Roman conquest of Gallia began in the second century BCE and continued until the Gallic Wars (58–52 BCE). There is plentiful evidence of the effect of Roman influence in modern-day towns in southern France such as Nîmes (see p. 328),

KEY EVENTS

206 BCE	197 BCE	133 BCE	52 BCE	16–13 BCE	43 CE
The Iberian peninsula becomes Roman after the defeat of the Carthaginians.	The provinces of Hispania Ulterior and Hispania Citerior are created.	The end of the siege of the Celtiberian settlement of Numantia by Roman forces. Most surviving inhabitants commit suicide (see p. 322).	The final conquest of Gaul by Gaius Julius Caesar (c. 100–44 BCE) culminates in the battle at Alesia (see p. 318).	Hispania Ulterior divides into Lusitania (Portugal and part of western Spain) and Baetica (Andalusia). Hispania Citerior becomes Tarraconensis.	Roman forces invade Britain. The traditional landing place is Rutupiae (Richborough in Kent, England).

Saint-Rémy, Arles, and Orange. An example of the Romanization of the local inhabitants is found at Saint-Rémy, where the Mausoleum of the Julii (30–20 BCE; see image 3) was erected close to the triumphal arch alongside the main road into what was then the town of Glanum.

Rome's acquisition of the western provinces of Spain and Gallia Narbonensis (Languedoc and Provence) led to the first period of contact with Britain. The latter had one of the few western sources of tin, which led to a trade route. The acquisition of the northern coast of Gallia aided the Roman conquest of Britain. In 43 CE, the emperor Claudius (10 BCE–54 CE) assembled four legions close to Gesoriacum (Boulogne-sur-Mer) to invade Britain. Once the invasion was secure, he led the army to Camulodunum (Colchester; see p. 330). From there, Roman legions moved throughout England, into Wales and toward the Scottish lowlands. Commercial activity followed soon after the military conquest, seen through imports of pottery from southern Gallia. By the end of the first century CE, there were three permanent legionary fortresses at Isca (Caerleon), Deva (Chester), and Eboracum (York). In addition, Hadrian's Wall was constructed (see p. 320). Colonies were founded in the province at Colchester, Gloucester, Lincoln, and York, and towns developed in places such as Londinium (London) and Verulamium (St. Albans). There are significant archaeological finds from all these sites, ranging from structures such as amphitheaters (see image 2) to domestic items, such as hairpins.

Roman influence in the western provinces gradually declined, and between 400 and 420 CE the Western Roman Empire lost Britannia and most of Hispania and Gallia. The Western Empire was formally dissolved in 476 CE. **GM**

c. 60	c. 122–130	c. 260	306	404	476
Boudicca (d. c. 60 CE), queen of the Iceni tribe, leads an uprising against the Roman forces at Camulodunum (Colchester).	Emperor Hadrian (76–138 CE) builds a wall across the northern border of Britannia between the river Tyne and the Solway Firth.	The Gallic Empire is established by the rebel emperor Postumus (d. 268 CE) but retaken by Aurelian (c. 215–275 CE), fourteen years later.	Constantine I (c. 280–337 CE) is proclaimed Roman emperor at Eboracum (York) in northern Britain following the death of his father.	The outlawing of gladiatorial games sees amphitheaters fall out of use, although some, such as that at Nîmes, are reused for other purposes.	The Western Roman Empire is formally dissolved. The former provinces are occupied by groups including the Suebi and Visigoths.

Nîmes Second century BCE – fourth century CE

The Maison Carrée was much admired by the U.S. president Thomas Jefferson (1743–1826) and influenced his design for the State Capitol building in Richmond, Virginia.

◆ NAVIGATOR

There is a wealth of sites with archaeological remains from the Roman period in the south of France, including the city of Nîmes and its nearby aqueduct bridge of Pont-du-Gard. Nîmes, known in antiquity as Nemausus, was the capital of the local Volcae Arecomici tribe before its conquest by the Romans and incorporation into the province of Gallia Narbonensis in the second century BCE. The town further developed in the reign of the emperor Augustus (27 BCE–14 CE), and was honored with the name Colonia Augusta Nemausus. The town was fortified during his reign, although the only remains are the Porte d'Auguste, which was one of the main gates to the town, and the Tour Magne, which stands on Mont Cavalier, the highest point of the city. Although the construction of the Tour Magne dates from the Roman period, it incorporates the remains of an earlier Iron Age monumental tower.

The Maison Carrée (Square House), a name first applied to the building in 1560, stood in what would originally have been the Roman forum in Nîmes, of which no other buildings remain. Dating to the Augustan era, the Maison Carrée was a temple whose exceptional preservation is the result of subsequent reuse for a variety of functions. The temple was dedicated as an example of the imperial cult to Gaius Caesar (20 BCE–4 CE) and Lucius Caesar (17 BCE–2 CE), who Augustus had intended to be his heirs. They were the sons of Marcus Vipsanius Agrippa (c. 63–12 BCE), appointed governor of Transalpine Gaul in 39 or 38 BCE by Augustus when he was still known as Octavian. **GM**

👁 FOCAL POINTS

1 ROMAN STYLE

The temple is typically Roman in architectural form, with a staircase at the front and the whole building on a high podium. Built from local limestone, it would originally have had porticoes on three sides, now no longer present. Temples in this style are relatively rare in Roman Gaul.

2 DEDICATORY INSCRIPTION

Two lines of small holes on the facade of the Maison Carrée indicate the position of the dedicatory inscription made in individual letters, probably made from bronze, but now no longer present. The temple was dedicated to Gaius and Lucius Caesar, establishing a date of *c.* 1 CE for its construction.

3 COLUMNS

The columns of the Maison Carrée are in the Corinthian order, the most elaborate of the Greco-Roman architectural orders, decorated with stylized acanthus leaves and scrolls. The capitals are carved in three different styles, suggesting that three separate teams of artisans were employed.

▲ The amphitheater at Nîmes (first century) held 24,000 spectators. Although it fell out of use after the outlawing of gladiatorial games in 404 CE, a village subsequently developed inside the amphitheater, which by the eighteenth century had about 700 inhabitants. It was demolished in the nineteenth century.

PONT-DU-GARD

An essential element of Roman towns was the provision of a good water supply. Roman Nîmes was served by an aqueduct whose remains are well preserved. Built in the first century BCE, it carried water for 31 miles (50 km.) from the town of Uzès, at the source of the river Eure, to Nîmes. The route involves a combination of masonry structures, channels and tunnels to maintain a gradual falling gradient. The most famous structure is the aqueduct bridge now known as the Pont-du-Gard, which crosses the river Gardon. At its highest point it is 161 feet (49 m.) above the river, making the Pont-du-Gard the highest surviving bridge in the Roman world.

Roman Colchester 43 – fourth century CE

The Fenwick Hoard comprises jewellery and coins dating to the 1st century CE, which was buried in a silver box below the floor of a house destroyed by fire. The hoard is archaeologically significant because it was found under the Boudiccan destruction debris, and it is thought it was buried for safekeeping during the early stages of the revolt.

Colchester, known to the Romans as Camulodunum, was already an important settlement in the late pre-Roman Iron Age. Situated in southeast England, it was a stronghold of the Trinovantes, one of the indigenous tribes. The settlement was one of the first the Romans took over in 43 CE, and by 49 it had become a colony and the first capital of a new Roman province named Britannia. Public buildings were constructed, the largest of which was the Temple of Claudius, dedicated after the emperor's death in 54, when he was deified. The temple was destroyed during the Boudiccan Rebellion of c. 60. Archaeological evidence to support the rebellion was found in 2014, with the discovery of the so-called Fenwick Treasure, a hoard of jewelry and coins dating to the Roman Republic and early Empire. The same excavation revealed human remains dating from this period.

After the rebellion, archaeology suggests that Camulodunum was quickly rebuilt. In 2016, archaeologists reported the discovery of a structure believed to have been the arcade of the rebuilt Temple of Claudius. It consisted of a large central arch flanked by twenty-eight smaller arches. Sections of the smaller arches were first discovered in 1954, but the extent of the structure was not revealed until full development of the site. Another recent discovery has been the remains of a second-century circus, the only one as yet identified in Britain. It has been estimated that the circus, which was used for chariot racing, would have accommodated 8,000 people.

Gosbecks, a few miles to the southwest of the city center, was the focus for pre-Roman settlement, which continued after the conquest. Excavations and aerial photography have revealed a temple complex and a Roman theater seating up to 5,000 people.

Archaeological evidence of the political upheaval in the western provinces during the late third century is demonstrated by the deposition of coin hoards, one of which was found in Colchester in 2011. Archaeologists discovered more than 1,000 coins dating between 251 and 271, issued in the reigns of nine different emperors. **GM**

BALKERNE GATE

Camulodunum was surrounded by a defensive wall of about 2 miles (3 km.). Significant remains of the wall are still standing, with one section incorporating part of the second-century Balkerne Gate. This was the main entrance to the town from Londinium (London), and is the only remaining Roman gateway in the wall.

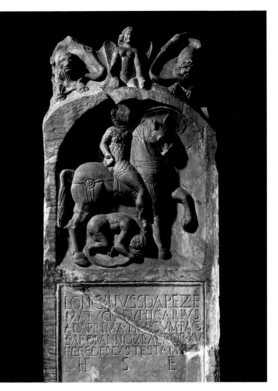

ROMAN GRAVESTONE

Workmen found this tombstone of auxiliary cavalryman Longinus Sdapeze in Colchester in 1928. The inscription says he was born in Sardica—now Sofia, Bulgaria—and that he died aged forty after fifteen years of service to the Roman army. The bas-relief shows him on horseback trampling on an Iron Age Briton.

THE BOUDICCAN REBELLION

The Boudiccan Rebellion is described by the historian Tacitus (56–c. 120) in the *Annales* (*Annals*; 118 CE), although it should be noted that this is written from the perspective of the victorious Romans. Tacitus recorded that on the death of Prasutagus (c. 10 CE–c. 60), the king of the Iceni, a client kingdom in East Anglia, the imperial procurator Decianus Catus ordered that the kingdom of the Iceni should be annexed. The refusal to accept Boudicca, the widow of Prasutagus, and her daughters as his heirs, and their subsequent humiliation, led to the rebellion. Taking advantage of the absence of the provincial governor Suetonius Paulinus, who was campaigning in north Wales, the Iceni and the neighboring Trinovantes, revolted.

Boudicca led her supporters to Camulodunum, where they stormed the town. The inhabitants knew that Boudicca and her rebel army were marching toward them, but were not evacuated. The surviving inhabitants retreated to the Temple of Claudius.

After a two-day siege, Boudicca and her forces burned and destroyed the temple. The attack on the town has left a layer of debris under the center of Colchester. The layer consists of the stumps of the burned clay walls of buildings that lie under the broken and collapsed fragments of clay from the upper parts of the walls.

Tacitus records that Boudicca's supporters also attacked Londinium (London) and Verulamium (St. Albans), although archaeological evidence does not support extensive destructions of the settlements.

On hearing of the revolt, Tacitus wrote that Suetonius returned from Wales along the road now known as Watling Street—the Roman road from north Wales and central England to London and the southeast. There he met Boudicca's forces. Little is known of the battle, although its location is thought to have been somewhere along Watling Street.

THE ROMAN EAST

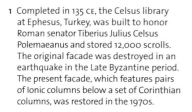

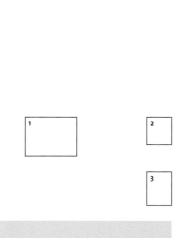

1 Completed in 135 CE, the Celsus library at Ephesus, Turkey, was built to honor Roman senator Tiberius Julius Celsus Polemaeanus and stored 12,000 scrolls. The original facade was destroyed in an earthquake in the Late Byzantine period. The present facade, which features pairs of Ionic columns below a set of Corinthian columns, was restored in the 1970s.

2 The temple of Asclepius at Pergamon (modern Turkey) consisted of a round cella and portico adjoining the main open space of the sanctuary. It was a gift of the Roman senator L. Cuspius Pactumeius Rufinus, a contemporary of the emperor Hadrian (76–138 CE).

3 The columns of the Temple of Jupiter at Baalbeck, Lebanon, stood 66 feet (20 m.) high. One of the stones that was intended to be used in the podium of the temple has long been known (Hajjar al-Hibla) in the nearby quarry.

Rome acquired a series of Hellenistic kingdoms in the eastern Mediterranean. The acquisition of Macedonia following the battle of Pydna in 168 BCE established the province of Macedonia, which controlled the main road, the Via Egnatia, linking Rome with the Adriatic ports and therefore its eastern provinces in Anatolia. Macedonia became the battleground in the civil war that followed the assassination of Julius Caesar (100–44 BCE). After the defeat of Brutus and Cassius by a force under Mark Antony and Octavian at the battle of Philippi in 42 BCE, a Roman colony was founded and this became the leasing city of the province. French excavations have revealed the public buildings in the forum area as well as the theater. A series of Late Byzantine churches have also been recovered.

The province of Achaea covered much of mainland Greece, including the Peloponnese. Cities such as Athens retained their Greek identity, although a temple of Rome and Augustus was placed on the Acropolis to the east of the Parthenon (and on the site of an earlier Attalid dedication). A new colony was established by Julius Caesar at Corinth in 44 BCE, shortly before his death, on the site of the classical city that had been destroyed in 146 BCE. Excavations by the American School of Classical Studies at Athens have focused on the area of the Roman forum. Imperial portraits were recovered from the basilica. A small piazza by the theater had an inlaid bronze inscription (although the bronze lettering has been lost) showing that it was the benefaction of Erastus, a member of the local elite who had been elected aedile, in fulfillment of his

KEY EVENTS

c. 350 BCE	168 BCE	1st century BCE	44 BCE	44 BCE	42 BCE
A Roman theater is constructed at Corinth with an inscription to Erastus, its benefactor.	Macedonia is acquired by the Romans following the battle of Pydna.	Palmyra in Syria (see p. 334) becomes part of the Roman Empire.	Julius Caesar establishes a new colony at Corinth in Greece.	Julius Caesar is assassinated.	Brutus and Cassius are defeated by a force under Mark Antony and Octavian at the battle of Philippi.

election promises. Careful study of the classical temple constructed in the sixth century BCE shows that it had been adapted in the Roman period to conform to Roman cult practices. Corinth controlled the narrow Isthmus of Corinth. Parts of the two artificial harbors at Cenchreae on the Saronikós Gulf and Lechaeum on the Gulf of Corinth have been excavated. These allowed the transfer of cargo between ships from the eastern Mediterranean and avoided the dangerous passage around the southern Peloponnese.

The site of the Roman colony of Antioch (modern Antakya in Turkey) has been the subject of a series of British and American excavations. One of the most complex inscriptions recovered from the site was a bilingual (Latin and Greek) copy of the *Res Gestae* of the emperor Augustus (63 BCE–14 CE) placed in the temple associated with the imperial cult. This narrative record of his achievements was originally erected outside his mausoleum in Rome, but copies are known from several locations in the Greek east, including one at the temple of Roma and Augustus in Ancyra (modern Ankara). British excavations in the extramural sanctuary of Men Askaenos recovered hundreds of dedications to this male Anatolian deity, who was associated with the Roman female deity Luna. There was a small stadium associated with the sanctuary and a sequence of dedications recall the series of games that were established in the second century.

The city of Ephesus was the subject of investigations to locate the colossal Temple of Artemis known as the Artemision. Parts of the temple were located and acquired by the British Museum. Austrian archaeologists have been working in the city for over a century. One of the most dominant features is the theater cut into the side of the hillside and facing the road from the harbor (although the coast is now some distance from the site). A series of gymnasia that included lecture halls have been recovered from the site. One of the more unusual buildings was the library of Celsus (see image 1), which also contained the mausoleum of the benefactor. A sanctuary containing a double temple linked to the imperial cult was recovered from the upper agora.

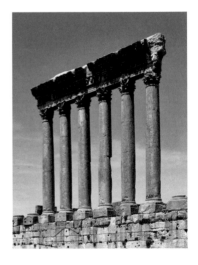

Work at Aphrodisias in western Turkey has recovered a major complex of the imperial cult. Constructed by the Julio-Claudian emperors, it was decorated with a series of reliefs, including a panel showing the emperor Claudius (10 BCE–54 CE) subduing the personification of Britannia. Studies have also been made on the stadium that can be linked to a series of games known from inscriptions.

At Pergamon—the birthplace of Galen, one of the most celebrated physicians of the ancient world, who served in the court of the emperor Marcus Aurelius (121–80 CE)—there was a major sanctuary of the healing god Asclepius (see image 2). This unusual building may have been a deliberate evocation of the Pantheon at Rome. Another of the most imposing sanctuaries in the Roman east was the Temple of Jupiter (see image 3) at Baalbeck (ancient Heliopolis) in the Bekaa Valley, in what was the Roman province of Syria. **DG**

25 BCE	Late 1st century BCE	c. 14 CE	129	135	262
The Romans take direct control of Antioch. It is turned into a colony soon afterward by Augustus, who names it Caesarea Antiochia.	Aphrodisias in western Turkey comes under the personal protection of Augustus.	Augustus writes his *Res Gestae*, summarizing the military and financial resources of the empire and his political testament.	Galen is born at Pergamon, site of a shrine of the healing god, Asclepius. Galen's influence on medical theory lasted until the seventeenth century.	The library of Celsus at Ephesus in Turkey is completed. It was excavated and reconstructed by Austrian archaeologists in 1970–78.	The Temple of Artemis at Ephesus is destroyed by invading Goths. It was excavated by David Hogarth in 1904–05 on behalf of the British Museum.

Palmyra First – sixth centuries CE

A monumental gateway was positioned on the west side of the Temple of Bel, although not centrally, giving this classical building an unusual appearance. The square sanctuary, or *temenos*, was surrounded by a wall, with a colonnade of Corinthian columns on the inside and Corinthian pilasters on the outside.

Palmyra is in eastern Syria and was a key location on the road linking the Mediterranean with Mesopotamia and specifically Dura on the Euphrates river. It emerged as a trading center after the breakup of the Hellenistic kingdoms in the east, although excavations have revealed activity dating to the Neolithic period.

The settlement of Tadmor (as Palmyra was originally known) was unsuccessfully raided by Mark Antony (83–30 BCE) in 41 BCE. The Parthians who occupied this part of Syria were defeated in 38 BCE. The territory of Palmyra was delineated in 11 to 12 CE by Creticus Silanus, Roman governor of the province of Syria. The city became part of the Roman Empire under Tiberius (42 BCE–37 CE) and established Roman-style institutions. Several inscriptions from the city show links with the Julio-Claudian family, especially Germanicus (c. 16 BCE–19 CE).

Western visitors rediscovered Palmyra in the seventeenth century. In 1691, Dutch artist G. Hofstede van Essen (1693–1702) prepared a panorama of the city. British explorers Robert Wood and James Dawkins visited the site in 1751 and published an account of their discovery in 1753. The published drawings of the city helped to inspire Neoclassicism, especially in England, where the Grand Tour encouraged an interest in the classical world. Palmyra was investigated by a German team under Theodor Wiegand (1864–1936) in the years preceding World War I. In 2015, the site suffered damage during the Syrian Civil War. The Temple of Bel, the Temple of Baal Shamin, and other structures were destroyed by explosives. Khaled al-Asaad (1934–2015), the local archaeologist responsible for the remains, was executed by the militant group ISIS. **DG/GM**

TEMPLE OF BAAL SHAMIN

The new construction that followed the visit of the emperor Hadrian (76–138 CE) included the Temple of Baal Shamin, dedicated in 139 CE in the northern part of the city. The sanctuary is thought to have been established by 23 CE, a date provided by an inscription from the surrounding colonnade. The extremist group ISIS destroyed the temple in 2015. It was overlooked by the castle Qalat Ibn Maan.

BURIAL TOWER OF ELAHBEL

The burial tower of one of the local elite, Elahbel, built in 103 CE, was also destroyed by ISIS in 2015. This monumental tomb reflects Elahbel's benefaction of the temple of Nebo in the city. The temple was constructed in the Roman style with a low podium and Corinthian columns. The structure was placed inside a courtyard that was accessed from the south side of the grand colonnaded street that cut through the city.

ROMAN PALMYRA

Roman control led to several building projects, including the Temple of Bel, dedicated in 32 CE, in the southeast part of the city. Although the focus of worship was a Syrian deity, the architectural style was Roman. Access to the sanctuary was via a monumental stepped propylea that contained several gates. The building was reused in the early twelfth century as a fortress.

Palmyra was one of the cities visited by the emperor Hadrian in 129 CE, and was subsequently awarded the epithet "Hadriana." The theater, likely to have been constructed in the second century CE, had a stage building decorated with Corinthian columns.

In 267 CE, Zenobia (d. 274 CE) assumed power in Palmyra, but the city was retaken by the Romans in 272 CE. Diocletian (245–316 CE) created a fortified garrison in the city in 300 CE with a Temple for the Standards. Also from this period was a bathhouse constructed by Sosianus Hierocles, the governor of Syria. The city was represented by Bishop Marinos in the Council of Nicaea in 325 CE. It continued to function as a recognizably classical city until the middle of the sixth century CE.

A characteristic of Palmyra were towers containing burials. Spaces for the dead were closed with panels decorated with portrait heads, important for showing the fashionable hairstyles and jewelry of the elite. The dead were identified by short inscriptions. External sculptures, such as on the tomb of Kithoth, son of Thaimarsu, show the deceased reclining on a couch surrounded by members of his family. Further types of tombs were cut underground with narrow chambers where the bodies were placed. The second-century CE Hypogeum of the Three Brothers—named after the inscription naming Male, Saadai, and Naamain—was laid out in a T-shape with sixty-five narrow recesses from the four main chambers for the bodies.

ROMAN AFRICA

1 The Arch of Trajan at the Timgad archaeological site near Batna, Algeria.

2 Praetorium at the ruin of Lambaesis, near modern Tazoult, Algeria.

3 The amphitheater at Sabratha, Libya, which dates to the second century CE.

The north African provinces of the Roman Empire west of Egypt contain some of the most impressive preserved urban landscapes. From east to west the provinces were Cyrenaica, Tripolitania, Africa Proconsularis, Numidia, Mauretania Caesariensis, and Mauretania Tingitana. The Roman cities that developed in this region were founded either on the site of settlements that had been established by Punic traders, or at local regional centers.

The main center in Cyrenaica was the city of Cyrene (modern Libya), which was founded as a Greek colony in the late seventh century BCE. It developed as a Ptolemaic city and was incorporated into the Empire in 96 BCE. Following a Jewish uprising in 115 to 117 CE, the city was damaged, and it was rebuilt with the support of the emperor Hadrian (76–138 CE). The Greek character of the city changed with the replacement of Roman architecture—temples like that of Asclepius in the agora, for example—that were placed on raised podia. At the turn of the third century there was a move, found elsewhere in the Empire, of adding more porticoes to the streets and in the main public spaces.

In Tripolitania there have been major excavations at Sabratha. The city was rebuilt in the late first century CE following a major earthquake. It gained a more Roman feel with the addition of a forum. This included the creation of the

KEY EVENTS

218–201 BCE	c. 150 BCE	146 BCE	c. 146 BCE	96 BCE	1st century CE
The Second Punic War results in Roman hegemony over the western Mediterranean.	Dougga is incorporated into the Numidian kingdom.	The Third Punic War ends with the destruction of Carthage by Rome.	A mausoleum at Dougga is dedicated to Ateban. The inscription is removed in 1842 by Thomas Reade, who gives it to the British Museum in 1852.	The Greek colony of Cyrene is incorporated into the Roman Empire.	The city of Sabratha in Tripolitania is rebuilt following a major earthquake.

Capitolium that was built using marble imported from western Anatolia. There were major sanctuaries of Egyptian deities, including Serapis and Isis. During the second century, the city gained the status of a municipium. In this period a temple to the imperial cult was constructed initially for the worship of Marcus Aurelius (121–180) and his co-ruler Lucius Verus (130–169). A key structure was a late second-century amphitheater that could seat about 10,000 people (see image 3). A major theater for about 5,000 people was built during the early third century. This included a raised stage decorated with architectural reliefs. The city was damaged by two major earthquakes in the fourth century and some of the architectural elements were used to construct a defensive wall.

The city of Lepcis Magna (see p. 340) had a Roman architectural feel. The forum area was dominated by three temples on raised podia for Rome and Augustus, Hercules, and Bacchus. The character of the city was transformed in the early third century by a series of benefactions from the emperor Septimius Severus (c. 145–211), who was born there. The third city of Tripolitania was Oea (modern Tripoli); remains include an archway dating to 163–164.

Dougga (see p. 338), in Africa Proconsularis, has been an important source of Latin inscriptions showing how local families supported their community and promoted Roman values and cultures. The city remains include temples dating to the late second and early third centuries. The growth of such cities, with their demand for water by cultural institutions such as bathhouses, meant that water supply was crucial in the region. A 31-mile (50 km.) long aqueduct supplied Roman Carthage and remains of the raised section near Uthina have survived.

A Roman legionary base was established at Lambaesis (see image 2) during the reign of the emperor Trajan (53–117). This was garrisoned by the Third Augustan Legion. This base supported a network of forts garrisoned by auxiliary troops to the south of the Aurès Mountains and on the desert frontier. An inscription from Agneb dating to 174 indicates a Roman military presence well to the south of the province. These lines of forts were extended in the late second century during the reign of Septimius Severus, probably during the governorship of Anicius Faustus. Some may have held units of 100 men, and were probably intended to deter raiding parties. Epigraphic evidence suggests that these forts were supported by the construction of free-standing towers.

Legionary veterans from Lambaesis were settled at Timgad (Thamugadi), which was founded in 100 CE. The colony was designed on a grid pattern within a rectangular area. This initial area was expanded in the late second century, and included the construction of a theater and a public market. Septimius Severus built a monumental arch on the road from Lambaesis (see image 1). One of the more unusual buildings in the colony was a library identified by a Latin inscription that showed it was the benefaction of Marcus Julius Quintianus Flavius Rogatianus. It included a large semicircular room at the heart of the complex, as well as a series of small reading rooms. **DG**

1st century	100	115	2nd century	2nd century	3rd century
Lepcis Magna becomes a colony with full rights of Roman citizenship.	The emperor Trajan creates the military colony of Timgad in Algeria.	A Jewish uprising against emperor Trajan begins in Cyrene.	Septimius Severus extends the line of Roman forts at Lambaesis.	An large amphitheater with seating for around 10,000 people is built at Sabratha.	Lepcis Magna receives a series of benefactions from the emperor Septimius Severus.

Dougga Second century BCE – fifth century CE

The theater at Dougga in Tunisia, complete with its skene building at the back of the stage, has survived. The audience was protected from the sun by a huge awning that stretched across the auditorium. It is estimated that it would have held about 3,500 people. An inscription shows that it was constructed in c. 168 CE.

The Roman colony of Colonia Licinia Septimia Aurelia Alexandriana Thuggensis, now Dougga, is in modern-day Tunisia. It lies 62 miles (100 km.) to the southwest of Tunis at a height of more than 1,640 feet (500 m.).

Burials dating to the second millennium BCE have been discovered in the deepest levels of the town. It is thought that the interior of Tunisia was settled by west Phoenicians from the fourth century BCE. The earliest historical mention of the town, then called Tokai, dates to 307 BCE during the campaign of Agathocles of Syracuse (361–289 BCE) in Sicily. Settlements dated to the third and second centuries BCE have been identified in the southern part of the town, immediately above the prehistoric levels. One room contained a number of storage amphorae. Another house with courtyard was discovered under a Roman house. Elsewhere an elaborate oven, apparently used for baking, was found. Some of these layers seem to have continued in use until the Roman period.

After the defeat of Carthage by Rome in the Second Punic War (218–201 BCE), the Numidians expanded into Punic territory, with Dougga incorporated into the Numidian kingdom by c. 150 BCE, leading to further development. Excavations by a German–Tunisian team in the southern part of Dougga have revealed evidence of housing from the Numidian settlement. Pottery from Numidian levels contained transport amphorae that was produced around Carthage from the third century BCE and that ceased production just before its destruction in the mid second century. However, there were a number of late second-century BCE Italian wine amphorae as well as Italian Campana black-glossed wares, common from the second century BCE onward, indicating trade with Italy. Stratified bronze coins include three minted in Rome in 157 or 156 BCE. This evidence shows that Dougga flourished after Rome's destruction of Carthage in 146 BCE and the creation of the province of Africa. **DG/GM**

TOMB OF ATEBAN

A tomb dating to c. 146 BCE is associated with Ateban, who was either a Numidian ruler or the builder of the tomb, recorded in an inscription written in Numidian and Punic. The high podium is surmounted by pilasters, and the whole surmounted by a small pyramid. The tomb was decorated with a relief showing a chariot.

CAPITOLIUM TEMPLE

The main temple in a colony was the Capitolium, where the Roman gods Jupiter, Juno, and Minerva were worshipped. The Capitolium at Dougga was built in 166 to 167 CE, during the joint emperorship of Marcus Aurelius (121–180 CE) and Lucius Verus (136–169 CE). It was constructed in the Roman style with a raised podium.

DOUGGA IN THE ROMAN PERIOD

Rome's conquest of Dougga led to an influx of Roman settlers who remained separate from the indigenous population. Stratified pottery finds suggest the street plan was expanded during the late first century and amphorae indicate regular contact with Italy and Spain.

The colony developed during the second century. An inscription shows that an aqueduct was dedicated during the reign of Commodus (161–192 CE). The Piazza of the Winds open area constructed during his reign was a benefaction of a local citizen, Quintus Pacuvius. A carving showed the directions of the twelve winds, each designated by its Latin name. Private houses of this period were decorated with mosaics.

In 205, the emperor Septimius Severus (c. 145–211) gave the community the status of a municipium (municipality). The well-preserved Temple of Juno Caelestis was built by the emperor Alexander Severus (209–235 CE). Twenty years later Dougga was granted the full status of a *colonia* (colony). Many of the sculptural finds and mosaics from the site are in the Bardo Museum in Tunis.

Much of the study of Dougga has concentrated on the wealth of inscriptions, probably in excess of 2,000, which help to demonstrate how benefactions worked in a Roman colonial setting. Recent work by French archaeologists has identified about one hundred sites around Dougga linked to olive cultivation. It is likely that Dougga was important for the supply of grain to Rome. The local elite, so prominent in the epigraphic record, probably made their wealth from these agricultural riches.

Dougga fell to the Vandals in 439, although finds of transport amphorae indicate it retained contact with the wider Mediterranean world. The city became part of the Byzantine Empire in 533, and then was subject to the Arab conquest of 698.

Lepcis Magna First century CE

Emperor Septimius Severus came from Lepcis. After he became emperor in 193 CE, he visited the town in 202 CE or 203 and donated several buildings, including a forum, colonnaded streets, and a civic basilica with forty granite columns imported from Aswan, Egypt. One of his monuments was a four-way arch with a frieze depicting him and his family.

Lepcis Magna in Tripolitania, modern Libya, is believed to have been established by the Phoenicians at the mouth of the Wadi Labdah. It is located 62 miles (100 km.) southeast of Tripoli on the Mediterranean coast. Some inscriptions use the form "Leptis," which is how the city is sometimes known; and Magna, reflecting its size, is thought to have been added in the first century CE. Italian excavations revealed Phoenician graves, with a small amount of imported Athenian black-glossed pottery dating to the fifth and fourth centuries BCE. This was one of a series of harbors along the north African coast linking the Phoenician-controlled western Mediterranean with the east. Excavations under the old forum suggest occupation from the third century BCE.

The town was attacked unsuccessfully by local tribe, the Garamantes, in 69 CE. It gained the status of a municipality under the Flavian emperors at the end of the first century BCE, and then became a colony with full rights of citizenship under the emperor Trajan (53–117 CE) with the title "Colonia Ulpia Traiana Augusta Fidelis Lepcis Magna."

In the late seventeenth century, the French consul in Tripoli removed marble from the site for building projects in France, such as Versailles. In 1816, the British consul in Tripoli removed a large number of architectural features to build a Roman temple at Virginia Water in Windsor Great Park, England. The city started to be excavated from the 1920s during the Italian occupation of Libya. In 1943, as the British forces pushed back the Axis Forces in north Africa, archaeologists John Bryan Ward-Perkins (1912–81) and Mortimer Wheeler (1890–1976), both serving in the British Army, intervened to protect the site; Ward-Perkins was subsequently charged with protecting important archaeological and cultural monuments as Allied forces pressed into Italy. Ward-Perkins went on to become a director of the British School at Rome. He continued to maintain a strong interest in the site, and the School has been active in its recording and preservation. **DG/GM**

◉ FOCAL POINTS

MARKET

The market was donated to the city in 9 to 8 BCE by a member of the local Libyphoenician elite, Annobal Tapapius Rufus. Its two circular buildings were each surrounded by octagonal colonnades. People could buy and sell food in the shade. The benefactor's bilingual inscription was placed above the main entrance on the east side of the market. The complex, which contained other benefactions from the colonial magistrates, was rebuilt during the reign of Septimius Severus.

THEATER

As well as donating a market to the city, Annobal Tapapius Rufus, bestowed a theater, dated by an inscription to 1 to 2 CE, making it the earliest in Roman Africa. Parts of the skene building, decorated with Corinthian columns, have survived. Five flights of steps divided the stands into six segments. A temple to the deified emperors situated behind the theater was built in 43 CE by Iddibal Tapapius, his name suggesting his family were part of the pre-Roman Punic community.

LIFE IN LEPCIS MAGNA

Lepcis Magna grew in the first half of the first century CE, dated by an honorific dedication by C. Gavius Macer of 29 to 30 CE. There are two distinct grids containing long rectangular blocks, or insulae, for the housing. Some of the earliest planned areas may date to the second century BCE.

An amphitheater was added to Lepcis Magna in 56 CE, with seating for about 15,000 people. Another amenity for the city was a hippodrome. At the heart of the city lay the forum, which was developed from the mid first century CE. This was surrounded by the administrative and legal buildings, such as the basilica on the northern side. On the south side was a temple dedicated to Rome and Augustus (63 BCE–14 CE).

A major baths complex, decorated with imported marbles, near to the old forum was donated to the city in 126 to 127 CE, during the reign of the emperor Hadrian (76–138 CE). The complex contained marble copies of Greek bronze statues, such as the Diadumenus (430 BCE) by the Greek sculptor Polyclitus. The Hunting Baths to the northwest of the town are some of the best preserved in the Roman Empire. They are thought to have been constructed during the second century CE. The surrounding sand dunes had covered the complex, allowing the vaulted roof to be preserved. The name is derived from the painted ceilings showing hunting scenes.

The city became an important source of olive-oil production from at least the first century BCE onward. The harbor was protected by a stepped jetty to ease the transfer of cargo. There are remains of a pharos, or lighthouse, to help guide the ships along the shore. A number of warehouses were constructed in the vicinity. Much of this development took place in the reign of Septimius Severus.

THE NABATEANS

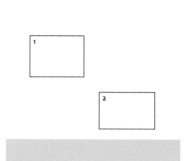

1 Aerial photograph of the ruins at Avdat in the Negev Desert, Israel. After Petra, Avdat was the most important Nabatean city on the incense trade route. The city was established in the third century BCE.

2 Ruins of the South Baths at Bosra in Syria. After the city became the capital of the Roman province of Arabia in 106 CE, it acquired many Roman attributes including baths (one of three in the town) to provide for the legion stationed on its outskirts.

The Nabateans occupied the desert lands between Syria and the frontiers of Egypt. The historian Hieronymus of Cardia, who served with Antigonus Monopthalmus (382–301 BCE) in Syria in the late third century BCE, recorded that the Nabateans indulged in banditry. He emphasized that they were part of the trade route that brought frankincense, myrrh, and spices from the area known as Arabia Felix to the Mediterranean. The Elder Pliny, who was killed in the eruption of Vesuvius in 79 CE, described in his *Natural History* the route taken by frankincense to the port of Gaza. He used the difficulty of the route to explain the excessively high prices demanded in the Roman world. Inscriptions and papyri from Petra (see p. 344) show that the Nabateans spoke a form of Aramaic, a fact hinted at in historical texts mentioning their use of "Syrian letters." Epigraphy also provides details of the king lists for the Nabateans that stretched from Aretas I in 170 BCE to Rabbel II, who died in 106 CE.

One of the resources that they controlled was bitumen, probably from the Dead Sea. Ancient sources recorded that this was used for the mummification process in Egypt. An attempt by Demetrios Poliorcetes (337–283 BCE) to control the supply in the early third century BCE met with disaster. Historical Jewish texts from the second century BCE suggest that local tribes other than the Nabateans were involved in raids on the caravans passing through the territories.

Archaeological evidence from sites such as Avdat (see image 1), on the edge of the Negev Desert in southern Israel, suggests that the Nabateans were largely nomadic in the first century BCE. However, during the first century CE,

KEY EVENTS

312 BCE	312 BCE	170 BCE	25 BCE	1st century CE	106
The existence of Petra is first recorded.	The Nabateans are attacked by Antigonus Monopthalmus.	Aretas becomes the first king of the Nabateans.	Aelius Geallus leads a Roman expedition against the Sabaeans and Nabateans.	The Nabateans begin to settle after leading a largely nomadic existence.	The last king of the Nabateans, Rabbel II, dies.

perhaps as late as 70 CE, they started to settle, and this required the management of water resources by building dams in the wadis. Fieldwork has identified a sharp rise in Late Nabatean settlements in this part of the Negev. Petra in Jordan was a key link in the trade route. To the west lay the centers of Avdat and Halutza on the route to Gaza. Petra seems to have been a well-established center of the Nabateans. In 312 BCE, Antigonus Monopthalmus attacked them when they gathered at "the rock," likely to be identified as Petra. The retreating Greek force was intercepted and the Nabateans dispersed into the desert. An inscription gives the name of the city as Raqmu.

After the conquest of Egypt, Rome started to move against the Sabaeans and the Nabateans with an expedition under Aelius Gallus in 25 BCE. Ports within the province of Egypt began to develop maritime routes that connected the Roman world directly with India and Sri Lanka, thus bypassing the Nabateans. The province of Arabia was created in 106 CE, and epigraphic evidence shows that the first governor was Claudius Severus. A legionary base for the Third Cyrenaica Legion was created at Bostra (modern Bosra) in Syria (see image 2). A papyrus letter written in March 107, from one of the soldiers to his father in the Nile Delta, indicates a familiarity with Petra, eight days' march to the south. Bostra was connected to Petra and the Gulf of Aqaba by a Roman road that inscriptions indicate was being put in place by 111 CE. A unit from Bostra was located at Petra, and a fort was located to the south at Humayma. Petra itself seems to have become the metropolis for this new province, as recorded in the inscription from the arch in the city. Nabatean inscriptions from near Avdat indicate that a new chronology or era was instituted from this incorporation of the province. **DG**

106	111	4th century	551	1812	1958–61
Emperor Trajan creates the province of Arabia, with Bostra as its capital.	A Roman road from Bostra to Petra and the Gulf of Aqaba is constructed.	A series of Christian churches is constructed at Petra.	Petra is struck by a major earthquake. It is abandoned at the end of the sixth century.	Swiss traveler John L. Burckhardt (1784–1817) records the remains of Petra in Jordan and publicizes them in his posthumous *Travels in Arabia* (1829).	Excavations at Avdat in the Negev Desert reveal the Nabatean settlement, religious centers, and the late antique fort guarding the desert route.

Petra Fourth century BCE – seventh century CE

The Roman theater at Petra, Jordan. Cut into the side of the gorge, it could seat 4,000 spectators. Traces of earlier structures, almost certainly linked to a roadway and cut into the rock face, can be seen at the top of the auditorium. The theater was equipped with a building decorated with columns, which would have obscured it from the outside.

Petra, on the east side of the Jordan river, was a key city of the Nabateans. First recorded in 312 BCE, it rests on the caravan route from Gaza on the Mediterranean coast, across the Jordan Valley, and thence south to Aqaba, east to Kuwait, and southeast into Arabia. There were developing trade links with India in the early empire, and cities such as Petra would have been critical for these extended routes.

Petra came into contact with Rome during the Republican period under Pompey the Great (106–48 BCE), who claimed a victory over Arabia. Petra became part of the Roman Empire in 106 CE with the formation of the new province of Arabia. A triumphal arch was constructed in honor of the emperor Trajan, and an inscription from the Small Temple in the heart of the city carries an honorific text for Trajan dated between 106 and 114.

From the fourth century onward, a series of Christian churches were constructed, one of the earliest dating after the earthquake of 363, and an early Nabatean tomb converted to a church in the mid fifth century. Three Byzantine churches have been excavated by the American School of Oriental Research. The so-called Blue Chapel reused blue columns from an earlier Nabatean building. A library attached to one of the churches, which contained about 140 papyrus scrolls written in Greek, was destroyed by fire in the early seventh century. The tombs cut into the rock faces take a number of forms. The Obelisk Tomb, whose entrance is flanked by four obelisks, had a square chamber with five spaces for bodies. The tomb is adjacent to the Bab el-Siq Triclinium, laid out in the form of a classical dining room. Petra was struck by a major earthquake in 551 and abandoned at the end of the sixth century. The ruins came to the attention of the West when Swiss geographer Johann Ludwig Burckhardt (1784–1817) came across them in 1812. **DG/GM**

KHAZNAH

Petra is accessed via a narrow gorge, the Siq. At the entrance to the site is the Khaznah (Treasury), with an imposing two-story classical facade with Corinthian columns cut into the rock face. A series of chambers lie behind the facade, and it is thought the Khaznah may have served as a temple of the deity Manathu.

QASR AL-BINT TEMPLE

The Qasr al-Bint Temple, perhaps dedicated to the god Dusares, is thought to belong to the late first-century BCE Nabatean period. It was approached via a flight of steps, and was faced by four columns, flanked by the projecting walls of the temple. Behind the portico was the main cella, followed by three chambers.

THE ARCHITECTURE OF PETRA

Petra had a colonnaded street, a feature of many Roman cities in the eastern part of the empire, which excavations in the 1950s dated to the early second century CE. On the south side of the colonnade were areas designated as markets, though one may have served as the civic forum. At the eastern end of the colonnade lay a nympheum fed by the water supply that ran through the Siq.

Recent survey work at Petra has concentrated on the collection of water from nearby wadis and its redistribution around the city via a series of channels and clay pipes. Flash floods are likely to have been a threat in antiquity, just as they are today. A cistern under the sanctuary associated with the Great Temple would have contained approximately 85,788 gallons (390,000 L.) of water.

At the west end of the colonnaded street was the Great Temple, accessed via steps and a gateway. The sanctuary covers 81,375 square feet (7,560 sq. m.), and

parts of its decoration date to the first century CE. Architecturally the temple appears to be Nabatean, perhaps dedicated to Manathu, although some of the pilasters reflect the Corinthian style of architecture. The lower part of the sanctuary was surrounded by 156 columns with capitals decorated with Asian elephants. Recent studies have shown that the temple was decorated in bright colors. Opposite the temple was the royal palace and a complex structure interpreted as the upper and lower gymnasia.

The colonnaded street ends at the gate to the temenos, or sacred precinct, decorated with columns suggesting an early second-century CE date. The structure may have taken the form of a large triumphal arch with three passageways. The temenos contained an inscription referring to the Nabatean king Aretas IV, who reigned from 8 BCE to 40 CE, indicating that it was likely to date to the Nabatean period.

AFRICAN IRON AGE CIVILIZATIONS

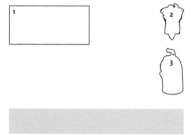

1 The rulers of the Kingdom of Kush (Sudan) were buried at Meroe beneath small, narrow pyramids, ranging from approximately 20 to 98 feet (6–30 m.) in height.

2 An intricate bronze ceremonial object from the ninth century CE, found in Igbo-Ukwu, Nigeria, held in the collection of the National Museum, Lagos.

3 A modeled terracotta head (c. 500 CE) from Lydenburg, South Africa, housed in the University of Cape Town collections.

The Iron Age in Africa broadly covers the period from the first appearance of iron-working technologies in the first millennium BCE until historical times. Given this long duration and the vast areas it covers, it is a catch-all name for quite different societies, with diverse subsistence strategies, in various environments. Unlike in Europe, there is no preceding Copper or Bronze Age in Africa outside Egypt and parts of North Africa, although early copper-working is known from several sites in Mauritania and Niger, dating from around the ninth century BCE.

The availability of iron for tools, which would have hugely facilitated clearing land for agriculture, is linked to the spread of agriculturalists and the growth of sedentary societies. These range from small villages, typical of the sub-Saharan African Early Iron Age, to the large urban centers and kingdoms that developed as a result of settled living. Examples include Aksum, Ethiopia (see p. 350), during the first millennium CE and, in the south, Great Zimbabwe (see p. 476) in the second millennium CE.

The origins of African metallurgy are unclear and much debated. The big question is whether ironworking technology diffused into and across Africa via the Mediterranean or was independently invented in Africa. Iron artifacts are one source of evidence, but some might have been made from meteoric iron or traded. Clues to the actual manufacture of iron include finds of slag (the waste product of smelting) and furnace remains (including tuyères, the clay pipes through which air is pumped into furnaces).

KEY EVENTS

c. 3300 BCE	c. 2000–1200 BCE	c. 900–800 BCE	c. 700–500 BCE	c. 600–500 BCE	c. 300–100 BCE
Iron from meteors is used to make beads in ancient Egypt.	The invention and development of iron-smelting technology in Asia Minor.	Early evidence for African copper smelting, from Mauritania and Niger.	Early ironworking at the ancient city of Meroe in Sudan.	Evidence for early iron smelting by the Nok culture at Taruga in Nigeria.	Early evidence for iron use and smelting at Djenné-Jeno in Mali.

Some evidence for the Phoenicians introducing iron-smelting to north Africa comes from the site of Carthage, in present-day Tunisia. Meroe (see image 1), capital of the Nubian kingdom of Kush, on the east bank of the Nile (in present-day Sudan), was formerly considered as a center from which iron technology may have spread throughout Africa. Ironworking had begun there by the seventh or sixth centuries BCE. Huge slag heaps suggest the scale of the industry there by the end of the first millennium BCE, before the city fell to the kingdom of Aksum in c. 330 CE.

In sub-Saharan Africa, some of the most important finds come from Taruga, in Nigeria, where ironworking associated with the Nok culture (see p. 348) is securely dated to c. 600 BCE. Early dates of c. 2000 and 1500 BCE have been proposed for finds in Niger and the Central African Republic respectively, but the dating has been challenged. Djenné-Jeno in Mali has also yielded relatively early dates of third to second centuries BCE.

Sites of early iron-using groups in eastern and southern Africa appear remarkably similar over a wide area. These village sites show evidence of stock-keeping, cultivation of crops such as sorghum and millet, and metallurgy. They are assigned to the Chifumbaze culture, thought to represent peoples speaking languages belonging to the Bantu language family spreading through the eastern regions of Africa, from Kenya to South Africa. This rapid dispersal of large numbers of people between the second and fourth centuries CE may account for their relative homogeneity.

Most of these groups also made distinctive pottery. Ceramic studies have been central in Iron Age research. It is assumed that distinctive pottery styles, designs, and motifs represent and so help to map past linguistic and social groups in the landscape. Pottery studies have also been used to trace genealogies and relationships among groups. For example, Urewe and Kwale ware, from Kenya and environs, may somehow be ancestral to pottery styles found far to the south. Terracotta heads from Lydenburg, South Africa (see image 3), dating to the mid first millennium CE, are examples of early Iron Age artworks in the subcontinent. Other celebrated artworks come from Igbo-Ukwu in Nigeria, where highly sophisticated cast-bronze sculptures (see image 2) were made, perhaps from the ninth century CE onward.

The impact of iron was economic, social, and cultural. Ironmaking and iron artifacts were ritually important and imbued with symbolism. Because indigenous iron smelting has persisted into the present in some areas, ethnoarchaeological studies have provided glimpses into their significance. For example, traditional clay smelting furnaces were often equated with female bodies and decorated with female physical attributes.

Although debates continue about the origins of iron-working, the technology was a key element in new ways of living that had consequences as diverse as population growth and the organization of labor. **AS**

c. 100 BCE–0	c. 100 CE	c. 100–200	c. 200–500	c. 500–600	c. 800–1000
The first use of iron in the Lake Victoria area, east Africa, is associated with the Urewe group.	Founding of the great early Iron Age trading center of Aksum, in the Ethiopian highlands.	The rapid southward dispersal from southern Kenya/Tanzania of peoples whose sites are assigned to the Chifumbaze culture.	Chifumbaze sites, of a subtype named the Matola tradition, appear in the subcontinent, as far south as the South African coast.	Production of the Lydenburg heads, unusual and early terracotta sculptures in subcontinental Africa.	Sophisticated bronze-working at the west African site of Igbo-Ukwu, Nigeria.

Nok Culture 500 BCE – 200 CE

Many Nok culture artifacts have been found either on the surface of the landscape or in alluvial deposits. Alluvial sediments are laid down by water, and so the finds are not necessarily in their original context. Important Nok sites are Taruga, Samun Dukiya, and Katsina-Ala, where artifacts were found in situ. Because these are non-alluvial sites, their dating is far more secure.

The village of Nok lies in the center of Nigeria, on the Jos plateau. Tin mining in the early twentieth century unearthed fragments of sophisticated terracotta sculptures. British archaeologist Bernard Fagg (1915–87) was the first professional researcher to investigate these remains, and his work led to the recognition of an early, and previously unknown, West African civilization. It had developed by at least the mid-sixth century BCE, and perhaps earlier.

Excavations to determine the context of the terracotta figures established that the people of the Nok culture were both the earliest makers of such artworks and perhaps the earliest known manufacturers of iron in sub-Saharan Africa. Iron smelting at the site of Taruga, where a number of furnaces were excavated, is dated to the 4th century BCE. These early dates, comparable to the earliest in North Africa, and the distinctive local design of the furnaces have fueled the idea that African iron-working technology was an independent invention, rather than a technology that diffused through the continent from North Africa and environs. The fact that the clay used for all the terracotta artworks is mineralogically very similar suggests a common source of materials, and perhaps even a centralized ceramic industry practiced by highly skilled artisans. If so, it may be a very early example of craft specialization in a socially stratified African society.

By c. 200 CE the Nok culture was on the wane. One explanation is that it had grown to the point at which people were over-exploiting natural resources, including wood to fuel the furnaces for iron-working. Ongoing research seeks to clarify the Nok culture's origins, decline, and relationship, if any, to later local art traditions such as that of Ife. **AS**

JEMAA HEAD

In 1944 Fagg was brought a ceramic head—similar in style to the terracottas found around the village of Nok—to examine. It had apparently been stuck on a pole and used as part of a scarecrow, in the nearby village of Jemaa. This piece, which has been dated to c. 500 BCE, clearly shows the characteristic coarse-grained clay.

REGIONAL DIFFERENCES

The Nok terracottas share stylistic features, such as elaborate hairstyles and physical proportions. Despite these common elements, some regional differences and sub-styles seem to have existed. For example, heads showing marked elongation are of a style typical of the finds made at Katsina-Ala, southeast of Nok.

TERRACOTTA FIGURES

The Nok terracotta figures, which range from about 4 inches (10 cm.) to nearly life-size, are icons of African art. Most depict human subjects, both male and female, in a range of postures (such as sitting, standing, or kneeling). The figures are hollow and were built up initially like pots, using the coil technique. Many were sculpted subtractively, which may indicate that their manufacture had its origins in a preceding tradition of carving from wood. A slip was then applied and the figures were burnished to create a smooth finish before firing.

Stylistically, the figures share a number of common features, although their variations suggest the hand and vision of individual makers. The head is large compared to the body, and some pieces have finely sculpted detail, including jewelry and elaborate hairstyles. The distinctive eyes are triangle-like, with the pupil represented by a pierced indentation. Some figures may depict diseased individuals.

The function (or functions) of these remarkable works of art remains unknown. Among the possibilities are that they were images of ancestors, ritual objects or charms against misfortune, grave markers, or architectural decorations. Recent excavations at one Nok culture site indicate that some figurines were buried in pits in organic containers, possibly baskets.

The importance of the Nok figures in art history is immense. Although most pieces are fragmented, intact works have been found, and these have a high value in the international art market. This has led to both looting from Nigerian museums and the circulation of forgeries. Ceramics can be dated by thermoluminescence dating, in which ceramics are heated to release trapped radiation. Measuring this allows an estimate of the time that has elapsed since the piece was fired. The method can be used both to establish the age of genuine pieces and to identify fakes.

Aksum First – seventh centuries CE

The ruins of the ancient city of Aksum are found close to Ethiopia's northern border. The city's most renowned surviving monuments are a group of memorial obelisks, or stelae.

Aksum (or Axum) was one of the great African kingdoms of the first millennium CE, its prosperity based largely on trade. In its heyday it covered areas of northern Ethiopia and Eritrea, extending to parts of Egypt, Sudan, and southern Arabia. The kingdom's chief settlement, also named Aksum, was a key center in trading networks that reached as far as Rome and southern India, via its chief port, Adulis, on the Red Sea.

The origins of Aksum are not entirely clear, but pre-Aksumite sites in the late first millennium BCE tell of Iron Age peoples whose culture already showed signs of Arabian contact and influence. The Aksumite kingdom thrived from the first to seventh centuries CE, exporting ivory and other animal products such as hides, as well as salt and slaves. Imports from Arabia, India, and the Mediterranean region included copper and bronze goods, glass, spices, and silks. Its growing military strength allowed it to extend its territories, both in Africa and Arabia. Along with Egypt and Meroë, it was one of the few African kingdoms with a written language.

Only about two percent of Aksum has been archaeologically investigated. Its most famous remains are its enormous stone stelae, or obelisks, some marking graves and tombs. The Aksumites minted gold, silver, and copper coinage. Prosperity and power went hand in hand. Conquests included that of its trading rival, the Nubian city of Meroë, c. 320. Under King Ezana, the ruler from c. 330 to 356, Aksum began to adopt Christianity.

Aksum's decline was probably a slow shrinking as Arabian and Persian traders in the Red Sea became more dominant. Over-exploitation of natural resources and irregular rainfall may have contributed, and the capital was abandoned in the early seventh century. **AS**

UNDERGROUND TOMBS

Some tombs of high-status individuals have been explored and documented. As in Egypt, most have been plundered, from antiquity through to more recent times; nevertheless, archaeologists have found a wealth of artifacts in situ. The Tomb of the False Door is thought to date to between the late fourth and early fifth century. Its carved door is an architectural illusion and is identical to that on the Obelisk of Aksum, a stela repatriated from Rome.

COINAGE

Aksum began minting its own coins in *c.* 270, most likely for its international trading operations. Coins bore inscriptions in Greek and later in Ge'ez, the indigenous Ethiopian language. Pre-Christian coins carried images of the symbolically important crescent moon. This was later replaced by Christian images and epithets. Because the coins carry the names of Aksumite kings, they have provided useful historical information.

STELAE

Aksum is known for its stone stelae. Hundreds of small, undecorated examples come from an area of non-elite burials, the Gudit Field, but the most celebrated are seven massive ornamental specimens in the Stelae Park, dating to the fourth century. One, known as the Obelisk of Axum, was taken to Rome by Italian armed forces in the 1930s but repatriated and re-erected in Aksum in 2008.

The stelae were carved from single blocks of nepheline syenite rock from a quarry about 4 miles (6 km.) away. Their size and the degree of detail were linked to social status, with some of the largest and most elaborate examples being associated with the underground tombs of Aksum's highest nobility.

The largest, the fallen Great Stela of Aksum, has been described as one of the largest monolithic structures ever attempted in the ancient world.

It would have been over 108 feet (33 m.) tall and weighed approximately 690 tons (700 tonnes). The undecorated base that would have been inserted in the ground is about 10 feet (3 m.) long. It may have fallen immediately, because this was insufficient to anchor a structure of such massive weight and height.

The decorated stelae were carved to resemble multistory palaces. Although Aksumite buildings probably did not exceed two or three stories, the carved details seem to represent elements of local architecture. Features include elaborately carved false doors, windows, and beams. Some have the Greek two-handled wine cup, or kylix, carved on a stone base plate. The motif may relate to ritual offerings. Holes drilled into the apex indicate that something, perhaps a metal plaque, was once affixed there.

SOUTH ASIA—FROM CITIES TO EMPIRE

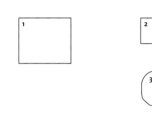

1 A c. 150 BCE rock-cut, Buddhist shrine (chaitya) at Bhaja in Pune, Maharashtra. The open horseshoe-arch entrance is a distinctive architectural feature.

2 The Mahapali Refectory in the northern ruins of Anuradhapura, Sri Lanka. The city was founded in the fifth century BCE. There were several refectories, or dining rooms; monks who were entitled to eat there were issued with wooden ration tickets.

3 A punch-marked coin of the Mauryan Empire. These bore five punched symbols—including a sun and a six-armed sign—continuing the practice of the earlier Magadhan kingdom.

During the second and early first millennia BCE, farming cultures flourished in the Indian subcontinent, and in some regions towns developed. Excavations at one Ganges valley settlement, Kausambi, revealed a vast mud-brick rampart. By the sixth century BCE, kingdoms were emerging in the Ganges valley and adjacent regions, their prosperity based on agriculture and trade. Fortifications have been discovered in settlements such as Rajagriha (Rajgir), capital of the centrally located kingdom of Magadha. Coinage, silver bars, or disks punched with symbols of the issuing kingdom (see image 3) began in the fifth century in both the northwest and the central Ganges valley, rapidly becoming widespread. Sometime after 530 BCE, when the Achaemenids annexed the northwest (see p. 258), the Brahmi and Kharoshthi scripts developed in India. This was a time of religious reformation, when new religions grew out of Hinduism, notably Jainism and Buddhism, inspired respectively by Mahavira (d. 527 BCE) and Gautama Buddha (563–483 BCE). From these sprang monastic orders that, over the centuries, benefited from royal and private lay patronage to accumulate land and wealth for the benefit of the community.

The kingdoms and states of the Ganges valley and neighboring regions fought for power and land, the more successful gradually swallowing the others. Magadha, its capital now moved to Pataliputra (see p. 356), became increasingly

KEY EVENTS

6th century BCE	563–483 BCE	326 BCE	305–303 BCE	303 BCE	3rd century BCE
Rival Mahajanapadas (major states) emerge in the Ganges valley: Magadha, Kosala, Kashi, and the Vrijji republic become the most powerful.	Buddha, born prince Gautama, renounces his princely life, gains enlightenment at Bodh Gaya. Devoting his life to preaching, he dies at Kusinagara aged eighty.	Alexander the Great (356–323 BCE) invades Sindh (modern Pakistan). Chandragupta proposes an alliance with him to attack the Nandas of Magadha.	Chandragupta, now ruler of both Magadha and most of the north and central regions, defeats Alexander's successor, Seleucus Nicator (358–281 BCE).	Greek historian and envoy Megasthenes resides at Pataliputra, where he records observations of the Mauryan court in his Indica, now lost.	First secure evidence of Brahmi and Kharoshthi scripts, probably developed earlier; both derive ultimately from the alphabetic scripts of the Levant.

powerful, defeating its rivals, until Chandragupta (d. *c.* 297 BCE), founder of the Mauryan dynasty, gained control of most of north India in the late third century, with his son Bindusara and grandson Ashoka (r. 272–232 BCE) continuing Magadha's conquests. After conquering Kalinga in 261 BCE, with huge loss of life, however, Ashoka experienced a change of heart: possibly converting to Buddhism, he devoted his reign to promoting peace and the well-being of his subjects, publicly avowing his benign intentions in edicts inscribed on rocks and pillars in every region of his empire. Trade was increasingly important, with Magadha enjoying a strategic location. The river network linked to the Bay of Bengal and the western Indian Ocean, where seaborne trade propelled by monsoon winds was developing, reaching its height some time later when the Romans became involved. Gandhara in the northwest, now part of the Mauryan Empire, linked with overland routes to east and west, particularly through the city of Taxila (see p. 354). When the Mauryan Empire declined, not long after Ashoka's death, Bactrian Greek kingdoms seized control of Gandhara and other Mauryan possessions in the northwest. Many were later overwhelmed by groups moving in from neighboring regions: Sakas (Scythians) from the western steppe, the Parthians, and finally the Kushans by the first century CE.

Sakas also penetrated south into western India, where they encountered the Satavahanas, who created an empire controlling the Deccan and adjacent regions in the first century BCE and early centuries CE; whereas farther east in the Ganges valley, the Mauryas had been succeeded by the Shungas. While their state was smaller, the Shunga Empire rivaled the Mauryans in their patronage of the arts. The Satavahanas were equally liberal; wealthy patrons sponsored the building of monuments, temples, and monasteries, many carved into the soft laterite rock of the Deccan. Fine sculpture and architecture are seen in Buddhist monuments such as the Great Stupa at Sanchi (see p. 358).

In Sri Lanka's capital, Anuradhapura (see image 2), to which Buddhism had been introduced by Ashoka, a different style of art and architecture developed. Here water-control technology, supplying both irrigation for farming and tanks (pools and reservoirs) for domestic water and bathing, began by 300 BCE and was highly developed by the early centuries CE, with sophisticated systems of canals, dams, and reservoirs. South India and other parts of the subcontinent also developed irrigation, increasing agricultural productivity. South India benefited from seaborne trade with Southeast Asia, a source of gold, tin, and spices.

In the first century CE, the Kushans advanced south, gaining control of the Ganges region as far as Pataliputra. Their hold was relatively short-lived, and by the fourth century a new Indian dynasty, the Guptas, ushered in another era of artistic flowering and economic prosperity in the region. The subcontinent saw many dynasties gain power and encourage cultural florescence: none, however, rivaled the Mauryan Empire in geographical extent, centralized power, or mercantile and agricultural prosperity. **JM**

272–232 BCE	250 BCE	50 CE	1st–2nd centuries	115–140	460
The reign of the greatest Mauryan emperor, Ashoka. He controls most of the subcontinent, bringing peace, prosperity, and religious harmony.	Third Buddhist Council is held at Pataliputra under Ashoka, who sends out evangelical Buddhist missions, including his son Mahinda to Sri Lanka.	Tradition says St. Thomas works as a carpenter for Saka king Gondophernes at Taxila; he later travels to South India, where he introduces Christianity.	Buddhist cave temples and monasteries are carved into laterite hills at Bedsa, Bhaja, Karle, Nasik, and other localities in the Deccan.	The reign of Kaniska, the greatest Kushan king, across an empire from Amu Darya to Gujarat and central Ganges. He proves himself a great patron of Buddhism.	White Huns (Hephthalites) sack Taxila, rampage south, and destroy the Gupta Empire in *c.* 467. They depart, leaving destruction and chaos.

Taxila Sixth century BCE – 460 CE

Taxila's second city, Sirkap, was laid out in a grid plan following Greek notions of planning. A wide main street ran through the city center from the north gate toward the citadel. Smaller streets opening from it at right angles divided the city into blocks: many contained substantial private houses, often with a stupa shrine.

As a major participant in international trade and frequently changing hands politically, the great city of Taxila (in modern Pakistan) was open to influences from many directions. Culturally rich, Buddhist texts record it as the seat of a university. It lay in a fertile basin served by two streams, which brought it agricultural wealth.

British archaeologist John Marshall selected Taxila for major excavations in the 1920s. In the Bhir Mound he uncovered the remains of a city probably founded under the Achaemenids, although its early material reflects cultural links with the developing Ganges cities. Most of the remains here belonged to the Mauryan period: Marshall exposed four main streets and many narrow lanes, with houses of various sizes. A pillared hall was probably a shrine; finds from a small nearby building included mold-made terracotta votive figures, probably for sale to worshippers.

The Bhir Mound saw a short-lived occupation by Bactrian Greeks, who soon moved farther into the valley, founding Taxila's second city, Sirkap, in the second century BCE. This was occupied continuously into the second century CE, maintaining its original Indo-Greek checkerboard layout throughout. A citadel, walled off from the lower town, occupied the city's southern portion. Sirkap was briefly occupied by the Kushans in the mid first century CE, before they established a new city, Sirsukh, in the valley's north. Poorly preserved, little of Sirsukh was excavated.

Throughout its history, Taxila was a major trade center, located at the crossroads of two major routes. One, the Silk Road, ran west through Iran to the empires of the Mediterranean, and east through the central Asian oasis cities to China. The other linked Taxila with the Ganges cities to the south and into the wide-ranging land and sea networks of which they were a part. Finds from Taxila bear witness to this trade: they include bronze sculptures from Alexandria and classical silver vessels. **JM**

GANDHARAN ART

The remarkable Gandharan art style developed in the Taxila region: it blended the realism of Greek sculpture with the symbolism of indigenous Indian iconography from Buddhism and traditional folk religion. Its fine works include statues of the Buddha and relief sculptures decorating stupa plinths, which often show lively scenes of contemporary daily life, packed with detail, inspired by Buddhist history. In this particular example, the Buddha is shown meeting with a group of devotees.

DHARMARAJIKA STUPA

Many Buddhist monasteries and shrines were established in the tranquility of the valley, often sponsored by pious kings or lay patrons such as rich merchants. These included the Dharmarajika stupa, a large complex probably founded by Ashoka. Here, a large decorated central stupa was surrounded by smaller stupas, chapels, an apsidal temple, and monastic buildings. Skeletons discovered here belonged to unfortunate monks and nuns slaughtered by the White Huns (Hephthalites) in 460 CE.

CITIES OF TAXILA

Taxila's prosperity probably began in the sixth century BCE, when the region was annexed by the Persian Empire, connecting into its extensive trade network. By the time that Alexander the Great conquered the Persians, this region was a patchwork of small independent states. In 326 BCE the king of Taxila—his capital a small city on the Bhir Mound—made common cause with Alexander, who was, however, prevented by mutiny from advancing further into India. Alexander's death in 323 BCE coincided with the rise in India of Chandragupta Maurya, who seized the throne of Magadha and began conquering neighboring states. By the time that Seleucus Nicator had gained control of Alexander's eastern possessions, Chandragupta was unassailable: Seleucus's attack on the northwest ended in his defeat at Chandragupta's hands. The Mauryans remodeled the Bhir Mound city, with regular straight streets containing houses, stores, and shrines.

In 189 BCE, the northwest fell to Greeks who had made small kingdoms in Bactria and soon built a new city at Taxila, Sirkap. Despite being fought over by rival Indo-Greek dynasties, and successively passing to central Asian Sakas (Scythians) in the early first century BCE and Parthians around 19 CE, Taxila prospered. Sirkap became a great city, its streets filled with people of many nations and religions, worshipping at its Jain and Buddhist shrines and at the Zoroastrian fire temple at Jandial in the valley.

The city fell to the Kushans in the first century CE, but Indo-Greek culture still flourished. The Kushans became Buddhist converts and patrons, who built many shrines and monasteries and a new fortified city, Sirsukh. In 460 CE, however, attacks by a new wave of central Asian nomads, the ferocious White Huns (Hephthalites), are vividly evidenced by skeletons found in streets, houses, and shrines—this spelled the end for the city.

Pataliputra *c.* 400 BCE – 500 CE

Ruins of a palace at Pataliputra. D. B. Spooner's excavations at Kumrahar in Pataliputra revealed the ruins of a palace: a wooden substructure on which was constructed a pillared hall (110 by 140 feet/34 by 43 m.). Its chunar sandstone pillars, arranged in eight rows of ten, had the high polish distinctive of the Mauryan period. Only the pillar bases (and one broken pillar) have survived, set at intervals of 16 feet (5 m.); they probably originally stood around 30 feet (10 m.) high.

In 1783, English geographer James Rennell (1742–1830) correctly identified the Mauryan capital Pataliputra with modern Patna. British archaeologist Alexander Cunningham (1814–93) inspected the area in the mid nineteenth century and concluded that the Ganges had eroded away most of the ancient city. However, L. A. Waddell (1854–1938) of the Indian Medical Service explored it in 1892: taking the accounts of early Chinese pilgrims as his guide, he identified visible traces of all the Ashokan palaces, monasteries, and other major buildings they described. Waddell perceptively identified the Kumrahar locality as a palace: excavations here in 1895 exposed traces of a pillared hall.

Around 400 BCE, wooden ramparts were built to fortify a village, Pataligrama, situated at an important Ganges ferry crossing. It enjoyed a prime strategic location, protected all around by rivers. The waterways were important trade highways, the Ganges linking the northwest to the port of Tamralipti (Tamluk) in the Bay of Bengal and the Son connecting with the Deccan and the west. The transfer of the Magadhan capital from Rajagriha (Rajgir) to Pataliputra decades later reflects the rising importance of commerce and a shift from land to river transport.

From 1912 to 1913, U.S. archaeologist D. B. Spooner (1879–1925) uncovered a Mauryan pillared hall at Kumrahar; his excavations, sponsored by the Parsi industrialist Ratan Tata, employed 1,300 laborers. Later, a substantial section of wooden rampart was excavated in the Bulandibagh locality. Small excavations and chance discoveries have revealed other minor sections of wooden city wall, Mauryan sculptures, architectural elements, and objects, including a sculpture of a female attendant with a fly-whisk from Didarganj and fine terracotta figurines of elaborately dressed women. Pataliputra was, in its day, one of Asia's greatest cities. Given its importance, it has attracted remarkably little investigation. **JM**

FORTIFICATIONS

The city of Pataliputra was entirely surrounded by a moat and a wooden palisade, with 570 towers and 64 gates, according to accounts by Megasthenes (*c.* 350–*c.* 290 BCE), a Greek scholar and envoy to the Mauryan court. Excavations in the Bulandibagh locality revealed details of these ramparts, preserved by waterlogging: two lines of timber planks, surviving to 16 feet (5 m.) high, 12 feet (3.75 m.) apart, originally with an earthen fill or a hollow passage between them, and floored with squared cross-timbers.

PATALIPUTRA CAPITAL

The free flow of ideas between India and the West, known since Achaemenid times, increased during the Mauryan period. Pataliputra's architecture demonstrates considerable Achaemenid influence in general layout, for example the pillared hall; in materials, with stone replacing wood in free-standing architecture; and in decorative detail. This Persepolitan capital exemplifies the adoption of Achaemenid and Hellenistic motifs such as palmettes, rosettes, interlocking spirals, lotus petals, and a bead-and-reel band.

HISTORICAL SOURCES AND PATALIPUTRA

In its heyday, Pataliputra was visited by Megasthenes, envoy of the Seleucid king Seleucus Nicator. He wrote an account of his observations both of the city and of life at the Mauryan court. Although this has not survived, many passages from Megasthenes' text are quoted by other classical authors whose works are extant. Megasthenes describes many palaces at Pataliputra with gilded pillars and extensive grounds housing tame peacocks and large ornamental fishponds. He says that the royal palace was built entirely of wood but was nevertheless beautiful and resplendent. He mentions also the cosmopolitan nature of the capital city, thronged with foreigners including Greeks.

Pataliputra was the capital of the great Chandragupta Maurya, who carved out the Mauryan Empire, uniting most of the subcontinent. Chandragupta was assisted by his first minister, Kautilya, who wrote a manual on governance, the *Artha-shastra* (which has similarities to Machiavelli's *The Prince* of 1513 CE). Kautilya's work included advice not only on managing the king's subjects and his kingdom's external relations, but also on the layout of cities and on settlement organization and hierarchy. Elements of Pataliputra's architecture illustrate the practical application of his advice, such as the city's moat, and the gap between Kautilya's theories and reality: for example, the wooden fortification walls surrounding Pataliputra, since Kautilya advised against using wood for this purpose, advocating that ramparts be constructed of earth faced with brick or stone. It is clear from the *Artha-shastra* that urban planning was important by Mauryan times.

Sanchi Third century BCE – fifth century CE

The stupas at Sanchi follow the standard form. The stupa itself consists of a square drum carrying a hemispherical dome surmounted by a small square railing containing a pole with three stone disks representing an umbrella, symbolizing protection. A massive stone railing surrounds the stupa, undecorated here, though many stupas are decorated.

⬡ NAVIGATOR

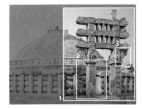

In Buddhist and other Indian religious traditions, stupas were sacred funerary monuments that covered reliquaries containing the cremated remains of a saint. The Mauryan emperor Ashoka, who may have been a Buddhist convert, probably built the first stupa at Sanchi in the third century BCE. The site was located on a quiet secluded hilltop, 5½ miles (9 km.) from the important city of Vidisha, home of Ashoka's queen. From the mid second century BCE, under the Shunga dynasty, wealthy merchants and other Buddhist supporters from the city showed their piety by sponsoring further work on the monument. The stupa was encased in stone and enlarged, railings were erected and two smaller stupas were built. In the first century CE, under the Satavahana dynasty, gateways were added to the original stupa (known as the Great Stupa). Other buildings were also erected at the site, including temples and monasteries. Over the centuries, Sanchi saw further episodes of creativity, interspersed with long periods of neglect.

The site was eventually deserted, but it began to attract antiquarian attention in the early nineteenth century. This brought a series of investigations, ranging from the Archaeological Survey of India's limited excavations in 1851 to vandalism and treasure-seeking, which caused considerable damage to the monuments. The site was rescued by British archaeologist John Marshall (1876–1958), who between 1912 and 1919 excavated buried portions, cleared the vegetation and debris, and repaired and restored the monuments, turning the site into an attractive archaeological garden, complete with small museum. Since then Sanchi has remained one of the crowning glories of Indian art and architecture. **JM**

◉ FOCAL POINTS

1 EAST GATEWAY (TORANA)

Four gateways, or toranas, mark the entrances. Like many early Indian architectural elements, the toranas are a translation into stone of much earlier simpler wooden originals. The gateway decorations combine Buddhist stories and themes with folk art, while the pillar capitals are an Indian development from Achaemenid and Greek forms.

2 DECORATION

The pillar uprights and crossbars are decorated with scenes from the life of Buddha and from his former incarnations. The people in these scenes are dressed in the style of the first century CE, when the carvings were executed, and they engage in activities that give a fascinating insight into life in this period, particularly in courtly circles.

3 YAKSHI (FEMALE SPIRIT)

Elements from folk art and religion appear in the carvings, including half-bird, half-human creatures. This figure, a yakshi (or benevolent female spirit associated with fertility and abundance), is a *vrksadevata* (tree spirit), shown here with a mango tree. Her arms and legs are covered with bangles, universally worn by Indian ladies since Indus times.

STUPAS AND THE BUDDHA

Traditionally, Buddha was born a prince in the sixth century BCE and grew up isolated from earthly woes. One day, however, he witnessed sights that revealed the full range of human suffering. He renounced the world and sought enlightenment, eventually achieving it. He spent the rest of his life traveling in order to preach. When he died, kings who had adopted his teaching fought for ownership of his corporeal remains: eventually they divided them into eight parts, over which they erected stupas in their respective kingdoms. These became places of veneration, where people performed pradakshina (circumambulation). Miniature stupas were also a focus of worship in Buddhist temples until it became acceptable to depict the Buddha in human form as a statue.

◄ In the early days of Buddhism, it was forbidden to show the Buddha in human form. In scenes from his life, Buddha was therefore represented by symbols such as an umbrella (a royal symbol) when he was still a prince, his footprints, as well as a throne, the Mahabodhi tree under which he gained enlightenment, a dharmachakra (the Wheel of the Law), symbolizing his first sermon, and a stupa, symbolizing his death.

THE CHINESE EMPIRE

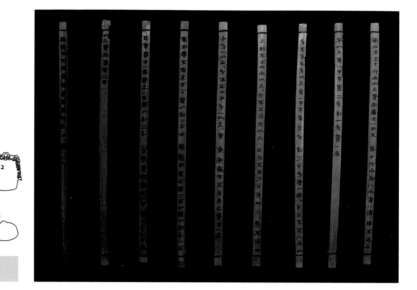

1 Bamboo slips with Qin legal texts from an official's burial at Shuihudi found in 1975. The Qin did not have a legal code in the sense of a set of laws enacted at one time. The body of statutes comprised the commands of current and previous rulers.

2 A bronze *bo* bell that belonged to Duke Wu of Qin (d. 678 BCE), excavated at Taigongmiao in Baoji, Shaanxi province, in 1978. *Bo* bells are large-scale percussion instruments that were played at court rituals and feasts.

3 An iron counterweight from a Qin dynasty steelyard, unearthed in 1986 in Baofeng, Henan province. Engraved on it is a forty-character imperial edict about unifying weights and measures in Qin times.

In 771 BCE, during the Zhou dynasty (1045–256 BCE), an invasion of northern barbarians drove the Zhou rulers eastward. The state of Qin became responsible for guarding the western frontiers. Gradually moving eastward and occupying the original Zhou territory, Qin brought about the disintegration of the Zhou clan and rose to become one of the most powerful states during the Warring States period (475–221 BCE). Excavations of bronze and lacquer objects testify to the highly developed material culture of the Qin (see image 2).

In 256 BCE, the Zhou dynasty came to an end, leaving half a dozen smaller states fighting for predominance. Thanks to clever battle tactics, the organization of an effective defense, and the successful formation of a resistant army, the Qin were finally victorious over all the other states.

In 221 BCE, King Zheng of Qin (259–210 BCE), by then ruling "All under Heaven," proclaimed himself Qin Shihuangdi (First Emperor of Qin) and ascended the throne. The empire was the biggest that China had ever seen. It probably comprised more than 1 million square miles (2.6 million sq. km.), and stretched from the Sichuan Basin in the west to the Yellow Sea in the east and from the Ordos region in the north to the lowlands south of the Yangtze river. It was divided into thirty-six commanderies.

The First Emperor set up a sophisticated legal system. Qin legal documents on 1,150 bamboo slips were found in the grave of a local official at Shuihudi, Yunmeng, in present-day Hubei province, including statutes and case records (see image 1). The emperor wanted to impose uniformity in all aspects of life,

KEY EVENTS

256 BCE	c. 246 BCE	221 BCE	221 BCE	220 BCE	220 BCE
The Qin state destroys the last remnants of the Zhou ruling clan and ends the Zhou dynasty.	Prince Ying Zheng of Qin ascends to the throne at the age of thirteen.	King Zheng defeats the smaller kingdoms of the Warring States period and claims the "Mandate of Heaven" to rule China as its first emperor.	The First Emperor, Qin Shihuangdi, adopts Legalism as the state philosophy and bans all other schools of thought.	Qin Shihuangdi creates a unitary state by imposing centralized administration. He starts to standardize the writing script, weights, and measures.	Work starts on constructing highways to connect the capital city of Xianyang in all directions with the administrative center.

introducing several reforms: currency, weights, and measures were standardized, and a uniform system of writing was established. Excavations in the Qin palace in Xianyang, today's Shaanxi province, brought to light bronze weights and bushels (see image 3). Cast on them were the names of the workmen who were in charge of casting the bronze and manufacturing the products. The unit of weight or the content of the bushel and sometimes the year were added, evidence of the harmonization of the differing standards and the beginning of serial production in imperial or state workshops.

After Qin's victory over its rivals, China became an agrarian state. In the heartland of the empire the extremely fertile loess soil brought high harvest yields. Some problems arose with the water supply, requiring the further development of a water system. Architect Li Shu was ordered to build a canal for grain transport. Measuring more than 22 miles (35.4 km.) long, the Lingqu Canal in Xing'an county, Guangxi province, connects the Xiang and Li rivers and joins the Yangtze basin and Pearl river basin.

One of the most influential projects was the construction of a system of highways (*chidao*), connecting the Qin capital of Xianyang with the Qin-governed territory. According to historical records, Qin created the highway system in 220 BCE, including at least five highways leading from Xianyang into the surrounding mountains. It was important to facilitate the transportation of men, commodities, and information.

Simultaneously, Xianyang saw a great deal of construction activity. Surrounded by mountain ranges and in an area of rich soil, Xianyang was a walled city and already home to many palaces before the unification. Qin Shihuangdi decided that the city limits had become too small, and in 221 and 212 BCE he ordered the construction of new palaces and the extension of old buildings. Palace No. 1 has been thoroughly investigated. A rammed earth platform served as a foundation for the two-story building, and is still visible today. It was probably part of a huge palace compound. Roof and floor tiles, gilded door hinges and colored fragments of interior murals have been discovered.

The ideology of the new state incorporated elements of Legalism, Daoism, and Confucianism, philosophical theories that had been established in the fifth to third centuries BCE. Officials identified more and more with Confucian learning, which emphasized ambition, honesty, and loyalty as well as filial piety. But Legalism gained power over the ruling clan. The major representatives of this philosophy were not interested in cosmology or personal ethics, but in establishing effective institutional structures, proposing political solutions to disorder in the state, and also in centralizing and accumulating power.

Through a series of revolts and rebel alliances, the Qin imperial house was overthrown in 206 BCE, when rebel forces captured the capital of Xianyang. The short-lived but powerful Qin dynasty thus came to an end. **MP**

c. 220 BCE	214 BCE	213 BCE	210 BCE	210 BCE	207 BCE
The construction of the Great Wall of China (see p. 364) is initiated. The older single walls of the Warring States period are unified and new sections erected.	Qin Shihuangdi sends troops to expand the southern territories. Construction begins on the Lingqu Canal for grain transport.	To prevent the growth of subversive thought, Chancellor Li Si (c. 280–208 BCE) orders the burning of all philosophy, poetry, and history books.	In a move to suppress intellectual dissent, Li orders 460 philosophers to be buried alive.	Qin Shihuangdi dies and finds his last resting place in his huge tomb, guarded by 8,000 terracotta warriors (see p. 362).	The Qin dynasty disintegrates. The army of rebel leader Xiang Yu's (232–202 BCE) defeats the Qin army and founds the Han dynasty.

Terracotta Army Third century BCE

The terracotta warriors are lined up in corridors separated by rammed earth walls, as if preparing themselves for a battle in either the military camp, the field headquarters, or even on a battlefield. UNESCO declared the Qin tomb complex a UNESCO World Heritage site in 1987.

One of the most spectacular excavations that changed the archaeology world was the discovery of the Terracotta Army. It was long known that the pyramid-shaped hill close to the small village of Lintong, in the vicinity of Xi'an, in China's Shaanxi province, contained the tomb of Qin Shihuangdi, the First Emperor. In the 1930s and 1940s, the first artifacts came to light, and in 1961 the area was declared a National Cultural Monument. In 1974, when digging for a well, farmers came upon red fired bricks and life-size human clay figures. This discovery led to a large-scale excavation of the necropolis of the tomb of the First Emperor, with work still continuing today.

The total area of the necropolis of the First Emperor has been estimated at 21.6 square miles (56 sq. km.). Located 1 mile (1.5 km.) east of the tomb are the three pits containing the Terracotta Army and a fourth empty pit. Farther to the north, an artificial underground lake had been created, with bronze water birds and terracotta musicians. The area under archaeological survey also includes the production site for the terracotta soldiers and the cemetery for the workers, who died while constructing the vast complex.

The Terracotta Army comprises different branches of the armed forces, together with chariots and horses, as well as their weapons. To date, the number of terracotta soldiers is more than 8,000, with 130 chariots, 520 horses, and 150 cavalry horses, but some are still buried in the pits. The life-size figures vary in height, uniform, and hairstyle in accordance with rank. They were made in a serial system of manufacture like an assembly line, using loess clay from the surrounding area. Molds were used for the individual elements of the sculptures, such as legs, arms, heads, and bodies. **MP**

CONSTRUCTING THE FIGURES

The craftsmen used the coiling and slab-building techniques for the figures. They started with a base plate and feet, then built up the legs. The torso was attached to the legs, and then the arms and head were inserted. The clay pieces had to be dry enough to fit together, but moist enough to enable adhesion.

LOOTING AND ARSON

During the excavation it was found that most of the warriors had been destroyed, because only 200 years after the burial the tomb was looted and burned. Much of the weaponry was robbed, leaving behind the unarmed troops, and most of the paintwork on the archers, charioteers, generals, grooms, and horses had faded away.

SECRET BEHIND THE TOMB

Chinese historian Sima Qian (c. 145–c. 87 BCE) described the First Emperor's tomb in his history of China *Shiji* (*Records of the Grand Historian*), written c. 85 BCE.

He wrote: "In the ninth month, the First Emperor was interred at Mount Li. When the First Emperor first came to the throne, the digging and preparation work began at Mount Li. Later, when he had unified his empire, 700,000 men were sent there from all over his empire. They dug through three layers of groundwater, and poured in bronze for the outer coffin. Palaces and scenic towers for a hundred officials were constructed, and the tomb was filled with rare artifacts and wonderful treasure. Craftsmen were ordered to make crossbows and arrows primed to shoot at anyone who enters the tomb. Mercury was used to simulate the hundred rivers, the Yangtze and the Yellow river, and the great sea, and set to flow mechanically. Above were representations of the heavenly constellations; below, the features of the land. Candles were made from the fat of 'man-fish,' which is calculated to burn and not extinguish for a long time. . . .

"After the burial, it was suggested that it would be a serious breach if the craftsmen who constructed the mechanical devices and knew of its treasures were to divulge those secrets. Therefore after the funeral ceremonies had been completed and the treasures hidden away, the inner passageway was blocked, and the outer gate lowered, immediately trapping all the workers and craftsmen inside. No one could escape. Trees and vegetation were then planted on the tomb mound so that it resembles a hill."

Tests on the soil of the tomb mound have shown unusually high concentrations of mercury. There are no plans to excavate the complex at present for fear that the exposure might damage the buried treasures and architectural structures.

The Great Wall *c.* 220 BCE – seventeenth century CE

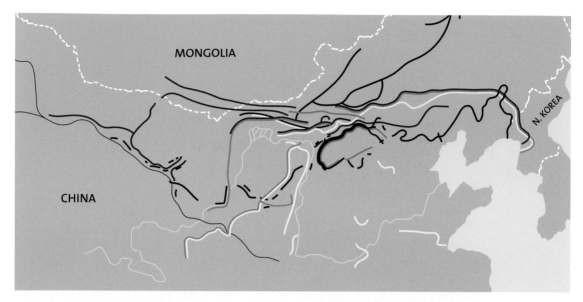

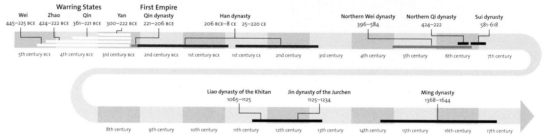

Warring States				First Empire								
Wei	Zhao	Qin	Yan	Qin dynasty	Han dynasty			Northern Wei dynasty	Northern Qi dynasty	Sui dynasty
445–225 BCE	424–222 BCE	361–221 BCE	300–222 BCE	221–206 BCE	206 BCE–8 CE 25–220 CE			396–584	424–222	581–618

5th century BCE 4th century BCE 3rd century BCE 2nd century BCE 1st century BCE 1st century CE 2nd century 3rd century 4th century 5th century 6th century 7th century

Liao dynasty of the Khitan
1065–1125

Jin dynasty of the Jurchen
1125–1234

Ming dynasty
1368–1644

8th century 9th century 10th century 11th century 12th century 13th century 14th century 15th century 16th century 17th century

It took several dynasties and a millennium to build the Great Wall of China. It is the world's longest man-made structure.

The greatest monument ever built, the Great Wall of China is also emblematic of the extreme centralization of the Chinese imperial state, but is testimony, too, to the severe military threat represented by the northern nomads from the Eurasian steppe. Built along an east–west line across the northern borders of China, the Great Wall is a fortification that acted as a protection against the northern invaders. It stretches from the Lop Lake in the west to Dandong in the east. Within the construction, watchtowers with signal fires, troop barracks, and garrison stations were erected.

Three dynasties were mainly responsible for the construction of the Great Wall: the Qin (221–207 BCE), the Han (206 BCE–220 CE), and the Ming (1368–1644 CE). In the Qin era, soldiers, farmers, and convicts were used as laborers. Local materials were used in construction, such as stones from the mountains in the uplands and rammed earth in the lowlands. To build the rammed-earth walls, a temporary frame made of wooden planks was used as a mold for the desired shape and dimension of a wall section, then a damp mixture of sand, gravel, and clay was poured in layers of 3 to 6 inches (7–15 cm.) and compacted to around 50 percent of its original height. After drying out, the planks of the frame were raised and the process repeated. Some parts of the landscape did not allow continuous building of the wall, so natural barriers such as mountain ridges were used to link parts of the structure. The Ming dynastic wall used bricks and stones, and was much stronger. It comprised more than 25,000 watchtowers and helped to defend the empire against the Manchu invasion *c.* 1600. However, the Manchu crossed the wall in 1644 and founded the last Chinese Empire, the Qing dynasty (1644–1911 CE). **MP**

LENGTH

The best-preserved parts of the Great Wall were constructed from the fourteenth to the seventeenth centuries, during the Ming dynasty. After a four-year period of archaeological survey and investigation, the total length of the wall was revealed in 2012. The accurate length is 13,170.69 miles (21,196.18 km.).

WATCHTOWER

The Jinshanling section of the wall lies 77 miles (125 km.) northeast of Beijing and was constructed during the Ming dynasty. It has sixty-seven watchtowers, including the Large Jinshan Tower, 36 feet (11 m.) high. The two-story stone tower has narrow windows on all four sides and the top floor served as a storehouse.

RECORDS OF THE GRAND HISTORIAN

The Great Wall is traditionally known to the Chinese as the *Wan li Chang cheng* (Ten-Thousand-Mile-Long Wall). The term appeared for the first time in *Shiji* (*Records of the Grand Historian*; *c.* 85 BCE), written by China's first scientific historian, Sima Qian. As the official court historian for the Han dynasty, Sima Qian developed a definitive history of China using pioneering methods of reconstructing the past through primary sources.

Sima Qian wrote: "Qin having completed his unification of the empire [in 221 BCE], dispatched Meng Tian [a general who died leading campaigns to the Xiongnu tribes in the north and constructing the Great Wall] to lead a force of 300,000 men and advanced north, expelling the Rong and Di [barbarians] in the North and making them depart from the region south of the Yellow river. He built a long wall [*Chang cheng*] following the contours of the land and utilizing the narrow defiles to set up frontier posts. It started at Lintao [south of Lanzhou, in Gansu province] and extended to Liaodong [peninsula in northeast China] extending for a distance of over 10,000 li. Crossing the Yellow river, it followed the Yang mountains, twisting and turning as it proceeded to the north."

The Great Wall is mentioned only briefly by Sima Qian probably because the Qin-dynastic construction was not a completely new project, and the existing walls were connected and extended. The earliest part was built in the fifth century in the state of Qi (today's Shandong province) as a rampart to protect the agro-pastoralist communities against the nomadic groups from the north, when China was divided into a number of individual kingdoms during the Warring States period, so-called because of the long struggle among several rival dynasties for power. As well as protecting China from outside aggressors, the Great Wall also helped preserve its culture.

JAPAN'S YAYOI AND KOFUN PERIODS

1

2

3

1 Reconstructions of a raised-floor storehouse and a surface dwelling were built at the Toro site in Shizuoka Prefecture after twelve dwellings were excavated by archaeologists.

2 This *sueki* ceramic fruit bowl from the Kofun period was likely fired in an *anagama* kiln, half-buried in the ground.

3 Known as a *dōtaku*, this bronze ceremonial bell originates from the Yayoi period. It is decorated with a grid design and on the sides has pairs of small projecting disks with a spiral relief pattern.

With its origins in the fourth century BCE, the Yayoi culture was Japan's first rice-farming and metal-using culture, gradually replacing the hunting and gathering lifestyle that had existed for many thousands of years. The culture appeared on the island of Kyūshū and spread northeastwards toward Honshu, concentrating in five major regions: northwest Kyūshū, Setouchi, Kansai, Kantō, and Tōhoku.

As the Yayoi population increased, it developed a more stratified and complex society. Food production of rice became stable and could sustain larger populations, which meant that settlements became fixed. Most of the Yayoi people lived an agrarian lifestyle and settled in villages with thatched houses. Yayoi villages also had raised-floor buildings (see image 1), which were most likely rice storehouses and also predecessors of modern Shinto shrine architecture. Rice paddies were divided into smaller fields. Wooden fencing marked off the large fields, some of which covered more than 4,300 square feet (400 sq. m.). Judging from implements found in the area, cultivation was accomplished using stone reapers, wooden rakes, and hoes. Yayoi burial grounds were located not far from the villages. The most common burial type was a small trench in the middle and an enclosed square ditch covered by low mounds, a precursor of the later Kofun mound tombs.

The Yayoi period (*c.* 300 BCE–*c.* 250 CE) saw the beginning of bronze and iron casting—introduced from the Asian mainland—and ceremonial bronze weapons, swords, spears, and halberds were produced. Bronze ceremonial bells

KEY EVENTS

c. 300 BCE	*c.* 300–200 BCE	*c.* 300–100 BCE	*c.* 200 BCE	1st century CE	57
Wet rice agriculture, probably from Korea, emerges in the Japanese archipelago. The first paddy fields can be traced to around this time.	Yayoi potters produce complex forms of pottery vessels with fine clay, fired at a high temperature.	Bronze and iron implements are imported from the Asian mainland, initiating genuine metal manufacturing.	Square burial mounds surrounded by ditches are built for the first time; they are precursors of the later kofun tombs.	The Yayoi settle in Toro, south of Tokyo, and establish rice paddies. Later, archaeologists excavate thirty paddies and 1,210 feet (370 m.) of waterways.	The date of the earliest written mention of Japan, in the Chinese *The Book of the Later Han Dynasty*.

were decorated with geometric patterns, such as hatched lines, triangles, and spirals (see image 3). On some examples, domesticated animals and scenes of daily life were depicted. Excavations have also yielded bronze mirrors and coins that bear similarities to Chinese Han dynasty (206 BCE–221 CE) bronzes. By the first century CE, iron agricultural tools and weapons were being used. Furthermore, with the acquisition of knowledge about textiles, clothing made great progress compared with the preceding Jomon period (14,000–300 BCE). The cloth was woven on primitive looms, using vegetable fibers.

The Kofun period (250–552 BCE) is characterized by the construction of large tumuli, or tomb mounds, for the members of the ruling class. These tombs are the most important source for understanding the social and political organization and the material culture of the Kofun period. Ranging in area from 37 to 79 acres (15–32 ha.), there are approximately 30,000 known Kofun mounds. In terms of shape, there are several types, including circular (*empun*), square (*hofun*), and keyhole-shaped (*zenpō-kōen-fun*; see p. 368). The last type is peculiar to Japan. While most circular and square mounds are relatively small, at less than 164 feet (50 m.) in diameter, keyhole-shaped mounds can be very large, sometimes exceeding 1,312 feet (400 m.) in length. Funerary goods discovered in the early tombs, mainly of ceremonial use, included iron weapons and armor, thereby indicating that the individuals buried there bore considerable religious and military influence. Archaeologists have also excavated mirrors, earrings, bracelets, equestrian gear, crowns, shoes, terracotta figures, and personal ornaments made from precious beads, as well as worked gold and copper.

Massive quantities of small and large—sometimes nearly life-size—hollow earthenware funerary objects, known as *haniwa* (clay cylinder), were placed on top of Kofun tombs. The earliest *haniwa*, dating from *c.* 250 to *c.* 450 CE, were simple creations and most were cylindrical. Later *haniwa* were made in numerous different forms, such as horses, chickens, birds, fans, fish, houses, weapons, shields, sunshades, pillows, and men and women. These haniwa display the contemporary clothing, hairstyles, farming tools, and architecture of the era, and are therefore important as a historical archive of the Kofun period. Another significant contribution to the material culture of the Kofun was *sueki* (offering ware pottery). The technique was introduced to Japan from Korea in the middle of the fifth century. *Sueki* is usually made of blue-gray clay and fired at a very high temperature, between 2,012 and 2,192 degrees Fahrenheit (1,100–1,200°C), in a reduction atmosphere. The products were generally made on the wheel and usually served the function of everyday utensils (see image 2) and ceremonial vessels.

More exchange occurred between Japan and the continent of Asia late in the Kofun period. Buddhism was introduced from Korea, probably in 538, exposing Japan to a new body of religious doctrine. **MP**

150–250	270–300	391	471	538	540
The confederations of chiefdoms form into political bodies, indicating that Japan is developing into a more organized state.	The first large keyhole-shaped mound tombs are built for elite members of society.	Japan conquers the Korean peninsula, defeating the Baekje and Silla kingdoms (see p. 462), and wages war against Goguryeo.	The Inariyama sword bears an inscription of 115 characters, confirming that the person buried in the tomb is the influential warrior Wowake.	Buddhism is introduced officially into Japan, offering moral and intellectual benefits.	The first register of immigrants is made. They mainly come from the Korean peninsula; most intend to stay and integrate with society.

Daisenryō Kofun Fifth century CE

Daisenryō Kofun has been designated a sacred religious ground and it is forbidden for anyone to access it. The main part of the tomb has remained untouched for more than 1,000 years.

◆ NAVIGATOR

Kofun, which means "ancient grave," were mainly constructed between the early third century and the early sixth century CE, during the period that was named after the tombs. They were built in various forms. The most common type, the *zenpō-kōen-fun*, is shaped like a keyhole with one square end and one circular end when viewed from above. The largest keyhole-shaped tomb in Japan is Daisenryō Kofun, located in the city of Sakai in Osaka Prefecture. It is believed to be the tomb of Emperor Nintoku, the sixteenth emperor of the Kofun period, and it was built in the middle of the fifth century. The circular mound is 816 feet (249 m.) in diameter and 115 feet (35 m.) high; and the adjoining front mound is 1,000 feet (305 m.) wide and 108 feet (33 m.) high. Daisenryō Kofun covers 79 acres (32 ha.), measuring a total length of 1,594 feet (486 m.). Consequently, it is twice as long as the base of the renowned Great Pyramid in Giza, which makes it one of the world's biggest tombs.

The tumulus is surrounded by three moats, the soil from which was used to build the mound itself. When it was constructed, the Kofun's three-tiered slopes were covered with stone and grass, with vast quantities of small terracotta *haniwa* figures lining each terrace. Platforms for religious ceremonies were also integrated, built on either side of the tomb at its narrowest point. When a great storm ravaged the city of Sakai in 1872, during the Meiji period (1868–1912), the Nintoku tomb suffered severe damage. Archaeologists who entered the outer portion of the tumulus discovered armor, helmets, glass bowls, plates, and clay jars, as well as terracotta *haniwa* figures in the shape of dogs and horses. Many of these artifacts are exhibited now in the Sakai Museum, Osaka. **MP**

1 CONSTRUCTION

The amount of earth used to construct the tomb is estimated as being equivalent to 270,000 10-ton trucks. And the scale of the tomb is also surprising; it took nearly sixteen years to complete, assuming a team of 2,000 people working on it each day.

2 SUBORDINATE TOMBS

Daisenryō is surrounded by a total of twelve subordinate tombs, both large and small, some of which lie directly across the street within the bounds of Daisen Park. There were probably more than 15,000 *haniwa* figures placed on top of these tomb mounds.

▲ This sixth-century hollow earthenware *haniwa* head displays the oval eyes, slit mouth and triangular nose typical of this type of tomb figure.

ETA FUNAYAMA TUMULUS

Kofun tombs existed in large numbers in the south of the Japanese archipelago. One of the most impressive was the Eta Funayama Tumulus, which dates to the late fifth to early sixth centuries. It was a keyhole-shaped burial mound 203 feet (62 m.) long at the center of a cluster of mounds in Kumamoto Prefecture, Kyūshū.

As early as 1873, excavation took place and a set of exquisite burial goods was found in the sarcophagus-style stone burial chamber, which was situated in the round portion of the mound. Swords (one with an inscription inlaid in silver), armor, weapons, a gilt-bronze headdress, gilt-bronze shoes, gold earrings, jewels and other ornaments, six bronze mirrors, and ceramic utensils came to light. Some of the magnificent gold and gilt-bronze ornaments are thought to have been imported from the Korean peninsula, testifying to the fact that exchange and relations between the Japanese archipelago and the Korean peninsula were flourishing at this time.

THREE KINGDOMS PERIOD, KOREA

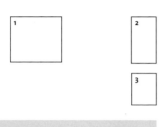

1 Discovered in the complex of Goguryeo Tombs, Anak, the fourth-century tomb of Dong Shou is decorated with a series of murals. In the scene depicted here, a noblewoman is attended by her serving maids.

2 This sixth-century gilt bronze incense burner from the Baekje kingdom was excavated from an ancient Buddhist temple site in Chungcheongnam-do.

3 Simpler in appearance than other Silla gold crowns, this example—excavated from the Geumnyeongchong Tomb in Gyeongju—has a pair of antler-shaped ornaments and a decorated band but lacks jade beads.

In the Korean peninsula, the transition from the Bronze Age to the Early Iron Age began in c. 300 BCE, and archaeological evidence shows a direct relationship with China at this time. Iron culture was absorbed, and from c. 100 BCE almost all tools were made of iron. New pottery technologies were also adopted from China. The so-called Proto Three Kingdoms period (1–300 CE) refers to the primordial state of the Three Kingdoms period (300–668 CE). At this time, the Chinese Lelang commandery occupied the Pyongyang area and served as an economic and cultural passage from China to Japan. Brick chamber and stone mound tombs or wooden coffin tombs were predominant, filled with a variety of burial goods, including bone or stone tools and ornaments, beads, and the first lacquered artifacts. During the Three Kingdoms period, the Korean peninsula was actually divided into four ruling bodies: Goguryeo in the north, Baekje in the southwest, Silla in the southeast, and the Gaya confederacy in south-central Korea.

Goguryeo (37 BCE–668 CE) was the first and the largest of the three kingdoms, spanning the northern territories of southern Manchuria, the southern Russian Maritime province, and the northern and central parts of the Korean peninsula. It absorbed neighboring polities over time and became a sizeable kingdom. In 372 CE, Goguryeo adopted Buddhism and announced a code of laws in an effort

KEY EVENTS

4th century BCE	c. 300 BCE	108 BCE	1st century CE	3rd century	313
The first states are formed on the Korean peninsula.	Iron technology is introduced into Korea from China. Iron is then produced locally in the southern part of the peninsula by the second century BCE.	The Han dynasty (206 BCE–220 CE) establishes the Lelang commandery, bringing Chinese burial customs to northern Korea.	The potter's wheel and kiln firing are introduced into Korea from China. This leads to a large variety of ceramics being produced.	Hard, high-fired gray stoneware replaces the soft, low-fired earthenware of earlier periods.	Goguryeo seizes the territory of the Lelang commandery, bringing to an end more than 400 years of Chinese authority.

to establish a proper ruling system. The art of construction is represented in fortresses, temples, and tombs. The most impressive are tombs with mural paintings, such as those found in the Complex of Goguryeo Tombs in Anak, near Pyongyang (see image 1), and in Ji'an, China. Metallic art also flourished in Goguryeo, and among the best-known items are ancient plated crown ornaments, earrings, shoes, and belt pendants.

Founded in the area of the Han River (present-day Seoul), the Baekje kingdom (18 BCE–660 CE) reached its peak in the fourth century. It adopted foreign culture from China and influenced the Asuka culture in the Nara region of Japan. The largest earthen fortress was Pungnap in the Han River basin, with roof tiles and ceramics, such as celadons, imported from China. The most impressive tomb was that of King Muryeong (462–523 CE), which lay untouched in the Gongju area for more than 1,400 years. An epitaph recording the personal history of the deceased was discovered, along with 2,900 burial goods, the majority of which were imports from China. Evidence of high-quality sixth-century metalwork is provided by a heavily ornamented gilt bronze incense burner, with a dragon stand and phoenix lid (see image 2).

Silla (57 BCE–676 CE) emerged from Saro in Gyeongju and developed into a strong kingdom after adopting codified laws and Buddhism from China. Archaeologically, Silla is represented by golden crowns and wooden chamber tombs with stone mounds. Gold and iron mines were exploited within the kingdom, exemplified by crowns with either tree- or antler-shaped ornamentations on their frames (see image 3). In addition, they were decorated with comma-shaped jades or spangles and were probably used in ritual or royal ceremonies. Golden belts, earrings, necklets, shoes, and exquisite pottery vessels were placed in the richly furnished tombs. The overall shapes and manufacturing techniques of a few Silla objects, such as glass cups, decorated swords, and bead necklaces with inlaid ornaments, are similar to artifacts excavated in regions of the Mediterranean and Western Asia.

The Gaya confederacy (42–562 CE) was located in the lower reaches of the Naktong River valley. Gaya was a center for exchange and it developed gradually on the basis of rich iron ore and intensive trade networks. Iron ingots excavated from Gaya tombs were not only used as raw material for tools but also as money. Gaya experienced several wars and manufactured a variety of weapons, such as swords, spears, arrows, axes, and dagger axes. Armor and harnesses for horses reflect the typical Gaya style over time. The distinctive pottery is a refined gray-blue hard stoneware, made in climbing kilns, and reddish-brown earthenware for daily use. Large quantities of pottery were placed in Gaya tombs: for example at Daeseong-dong in graves dating from the mid fourth to early fifth centuries. In 532 and 562 CE, Silla conquered the Gaya states. The Silla culture was greatly affected by the absorption of Gaya, such as in its tomb pottery, and sometimes it is not easy to distinguish between the two. **MP**

357	408	5th–6th century	500–514	535	648
The Anak Tomb No. 3 is built. Laid out like a palace, it is probably the oldest Goguryeo-type tomb with wall paintings.	The earliest type of landscape painting in Korea is painted on the walls of the Deokheung–ri tomb, Goguryeo.	Cheonmachong (the Tomb of the Heavenly Horse) and Hwangnam Daechong (the Big Double Tomb) are built for the Silla royal family.	During his reign, Silla king Chijung introduces ploughing by oxen and builds irrigation works.	The Silla kingdom adopts Buddhism as the state religion.	Silla establishes an alliance with the Chinese Tang dynasty (618–907).

STEPPE NOMADS

1 The Pazyryk carpet is from the burial mound of a member of the Scythian elite at the Pazyryk Valley in the Altai Mountains, Siberia. It dates to the fifth to fourth centuries BCE and is the world's oldest known woven carpet. The border depicts men on horses and men leading horses.

2 A wooden deer with leather antlers from the Pazyryk burial mounds. One of at least six such figures, it would have originally been covered in gold.

The Eurasian steppe grasslands extend from Moldova in southeastern Europe east through Ukraine, southern Russia, Kazakhstan, Xinjiang, and Mongolia. In its western part, the steppe runs along the northern edges of the Black Sea and the Caspian Sea. Its central part largely comprises Kazakhstan, while in the east the Xinjiang and Mongol steppe is a high, dry plateau. In prehistoric times, the Eurasian steppe was the home of nomadic peoples known as pastoralists, who kept grazing animals like sheep and cattle and moved with them in search of fresh pastures. Pastoralists grew few, if any, crops, and had dwellings and equipment that could be easily transported.

Domestic plants and animals came to the edge of the western steppe from the Middle East in c. 6000 BCE, but they did not extend further north of the Black Sea for at least a millennium. By this point, it became clear that the potential of the steppe grasslands for cultivation using Neolithic methods was limited. Hunter-gatherer societies persisted in many areas, eventually adopting domestic livestock with little evidence of cultivation, while agriculture took root in areas outside the grasslands. Just north of the steppe in southern Ukraine, settlements of the Trypillia culture (see image 2) sprang up just after 4000 BCE.

KEY EVENTS

c. 6000 BCE	c. 4000–3500 BCE	c. 3500 BCE	c. 3300–2500 BCE	c. 3000 BCE	c. 2100–1800 BCE
Domestic plants and animals arrive at the western edge of steppes in southeastern Europe.	Wheeled vehicles are invented, probably in central or southeastern Europe.	Horses are first herded and milked in northern Kazakhstan.	The Yamnaya culture establishes the basic mobility and herd-management pattern of steppe nomads.	Yamnaya migrations are believed to introduce Indo-European languages to eastern and central Europe.	Chariots and multiple horses are used in high-status burials of the Bronze Age Sintashta culture.

During the first half of the fourth millennium BCE, changes can be observed in the structure of and artifacts from settlements in northern Kazakhstan, with some sites having dozens of houses. The most significant change involved horses, which at sites like Botai constitute almost the entire animal bone sample. Horses were a prominent wild species throughout the steppe, but the concentration on them in large village sites signaled a transformation of their relationship with people. It seems that the Botai horses were herded. Their teeth show evidence of having been bitted, while pottery contains residues of equine milk lipids, indicating the consumption of mare's milk. The practice of herding, milking, and eating horses spread across the steppe.

Wheeled vehicles emerge in the archaeological record during the first half of the fourth millennium BCE. Preserved wheels are found in waterlogged deposits in central Europe, and representations of four-wheeled wagons, on pottery or as models, appear in southeast Europe around the same time. Cattle appear to have been the providers of power for the earliest wheeled vehicles in Europe. In c. 3300 BCE, the Yamnaya culture emerged in the western steppe and persisted for about a millennium. Yamnaya communities combined the use of wheeled vehicles and horse riding. With wheeled vehicles, they could transport their food, tents, and other possessions, while on horseback they could manage their herds. This form of nomadic pastoralism spread across the steppe.

The impact of the emergence of nomadic pastoralism was widespread. Studies of ancient DNA have revealed the reach of steppe cultures far into Europe. Connected with this westward movement was the dispersal of Indo-European languages, which can be traced to the steppe nomads particularly through words for "wheel." At the dawn of the Bronze Age, high-status burials of the Sintashta culture in Kazakhstan contain chariots, an innovation for mobility and warfare. At the same time, isotope studies indicate that there was variability in the diet, including cultivated plants like millet.

The elites in steppe society accumulated wealth through their livestock holdings and via trading contacts with other societies. Around the Black Sea, pastoral nomads encountered Greek merchants in c. 600 BCE and became known to history as Scythians (see p. 374), while in the east they engaged with the Chinese dynastic civilizations of the first millennium BCE. The wealth of the eastern pastoralists has become known through the frozen tombs at Pazyryk and Ukok in Siberia, where water seeped into timber chambers and froze, preserving the contents that include textiles (see image 1) and horses.

It was from this area on the Chinese border that the Huns emerged several centuries later and migrated across Eurasia. These horseriding pastoralists penetrated far into Europe under their leader Attila (d. 453), causing havoc in the margins of the disintegrating Roman Empire and penetrating its borders. A combined force of Visigoths and Romans defeated the Huns in a battle near Châlons, France, in 451 CE, and they retreated back toward the east. **PB**

c. 600 BCE	c. 500–400 BCE	c. 400–200 BCE	c. 300 BCE	c. 370 CE	451
Nomads of south Russia and Ukrainian steppes encounter Greek traders, and enter history as the Scythians.	A twenty-five-year-old woman is buried in a timber coffin on the Ukok plateau. Outside the chamber were six horses, each killed by a blow to the head.	The Pazyryk frozen tombs are constructed in the Altai Mountains, Siberia.	The Ryzhanovka kurgan (burial mound) is built over the grave of a Scythian chief in the Ukraine.	Bands of Hun warriors penetrate into eastern Europe.	A combined force of Romans and Visigoths defeat the Huns at Châlons, France.

Scythian Tombs Seventh – third centuries BCE

This silver bowl with gold-plate ornament from the Gaymanova burial mound in the Zaporozhye region shows two burly, bearded Scythian warriors reclining against boulders, in a moment of relaxation, apparently having a conversation. They are wearing fur-trimmed, belted leather tunics with jewelry around their necks.

Along the northern coast of the Black Sea, Greeks from the Aegean coast of Anatolia established colonies at the mouths of the rivers that flowed south from the steppe of Ukraine and southern Russia. Beginning in the seventh century BCE, dozens of colonies were set up, but some of the best known are Olbia, Chersonesos, and Panticapaion. In many cases, they developed into substantial urban centers, with temples, monumental buildings, and cemeteries. The purpose of these colonies was to obtain resources, such as timber, grain, fur, and slaves, that were in demand in the Greek city-states. This trade brought Greek civilization into contact with the nomadic peoples of the steppe.

Over the next several centuries, these colonies flourished and the local societies became known as the Scythians through the writing of authors such as Herodotus (c. 484–c. 430 BCE) and Strabo (c. 64 BCE–c. 21 CE). Generally, the Scythians had cordial relations with the Greeks, which gave them opportunities for accumulating wealth. Evidence for this wealth appears in the tombs of the Scythian elites, which provide insight into their reciprocal relationship with the Greeks as well as the values of their society. The Scythians had a particular appetite for the products of Greek workshops, both in the Greek homeland and in the Black Sea colonies. These workshops produced finely crafted objects in gold and silver on which Scythian themes were interpreted by Greek artisans. Wild, even mythical, animals and fighting warriors are two common decorative themes, although some motifs reflect the peaceful everyday life of the pastoral nomads.

Later, during the fourth century BCE, some of the Scythians in contact with the Greeks appear to have abandoned the nomadic life and established settlements themselves. At Elizavetovka at the mouth of the Don river, a Scythian center of craft production and trade was fortified with ramparts and ditches. **PB**

SCYTHIAN TOMBS ON THE STEPPES

Scythian burial mounds, known as kurgans, dot the steppe of southern Russia and Ukraine, although some have eroded or been ploughed away. A ditch around the perimeter of some mounds may have marked the area of feasting for the burial ceremony. The knowledge that kurgans contain lavish burial offerings of gold and silver has made them a prime target for looters over the past two millennia. Enough have survived, however, to provide evidence of the world of the Scythian elite.

INSIDE A SCYTHIAN TOMB

A typical Scythian tomb had a burial shaft that reached a depth of 30 to 50 feet (10–15 m.) into the firm loess soil of the steppe. At the base of the shaft, the sides were widened to form a burial chamber that was usually reinforced with timber shoring. Alcoves were sometimes dug into the sides of the chamber. The dead Scythian, along with the bodies of retainers accompanying their master in death, and the grave offerings were placed in the chamber. Earth and rocks were poured down the shaft to seal the tomb.

TOLSTAYA MOGILA

In 1971, archaeologists excavated a large Scythian kurgan at Tolstaya Mogila in southern Ukraine. The main grave, containing the body of a Scythian chieftain, about fifty years of age, had been looted in antiquity. However, the robbers, in their haste, missed two key artifacts: a sword in a gold scabbard and a gold chest ornament called a "pectoral," which would have been worn hanging from the neck. They also missed a secondary burial shaft that contained the remains of five people, including a young woman and infant with rich grave offerings, a young man with a bow, another young woman with food, and an adult man with a wagon and several horses. These people are believed to have been servants of the chieftain in the main chamber. Traces of feasting, including the remains of thirty-five horses and fourteen wild pigs, were found in the ditch surrounding the kurgan.

Archaeologists believe that the Tolstaya Mogila pectoral was made in a Greek workshop, probably as a custom order from a Scythian chief. It comprises many individually cast 24-carat gold figures and ornamental details soldered onto a gold plate, 12 inches (30 cm.) at its widest point. The piece would have required detailed planning and composition prior to its execution. It is divided into three horizontal tiers. The top tier depicts everyday activities, including a child milking a sheep and two men making a shirt, along with horses, cattle, and sheep; the middle tier has vegetal designs. The bottom tier shows mythical beasts such as griffins, which suggests a cosmological significance. Today, the pectoral is housed in the State Hermitage Museum in St. Petersburg; it is perhaps the most iconic Scythian artifact discovered to date.

COLONIZATION OF THE PACIFIC

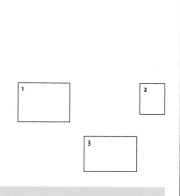

1 This reconstructed stamped Lapita pot has a typical geometric design, although stylized faces also occur. The Teouma site in Vanuatu shows that one use for these highly decorated pots was as burial containers.

2 The *Hokulea*, seen here sailing off the island of Oahu, Hawaii, is a full-scale replica of a *wa'a kaulua*, a Polynesian double-hulled voyaging canoe.

3 The tiki statues at Hiva Oa island, the second largest island of the Marquesas Islands, are some of the largest ancient tiki statues in French Polynesia.

The Pacific Ocean covers about one-third of Earth's surface. Culturally, the region is diverse, and it is usually divided into Melanesia, Micronesia, and Polynesia. Biogeographically, the many thousands of remote islands of the Pacific range from tropical to temperate, and from large volcanic islands to small limestone and coral islands, as well as tiny atolls. Consequently, the colonization of the Pacific required great feats of voyaging by skilled navigators.

Modern humans had reached the continent of Sahul by 50,000 years ago. Evidence from the cave sites of Buang Merabak and Matenkupkum on New Ireland and open sites at Yombon on New Britain shows that the islands of the Bismarck Archipelago were reached at about the same time. Kilu Cave in the Solomons has evidence dating from *c.* 27,000 BCE, whereas Manus Island was reached by *c.* 20,000 BCE. It is clear that this first phase of colonization of Australasia and near Oceania involved planned voyaging by competent seafarers.

The Lapita cultural complex first appeared in the Western Pacific in *c.* 1500 BCE and dispersed rapidly throughout near and remote Oceania as far as Tonga and Samoa, a distance of more than 1,865 miles (3,000 km.). Lapita is best known for its distinctive, highly decorated pottery. The stamped designs (see image 1) are very similar over the whole region, presumably reflecting shared symbolic meaning. Other distinctive material culture items found in Lapita sites include shell ornaments, polished stone adzes, shell fish hooks, files, bone awls, and tattooing needles. Most Lapita sites are coastal, and sometimes houses were built on piles over the water. Marine resources, including fish, turtles, and

KEY EVENTS

Before 50,000 BCE	40–35,000 BCE	26,000 BCE	c. 20,000 BCE	c. 7000 BCE	1450 BCE
The Australia–New Guinea continent of Sahul is colonized.	Caves at Buang Merabak and Matenkupkum are occupied, as is a site at Yombon in the Bismarck Archipelago.	The Kilu Cave site on Buka Island is occupied. It provides the oldest evidence of occupation in the Solomon Islands.	The first settlement on Manus Island involves a total sea crossing of 124 miles (200 km.).	Agricultural systems in the New Guinea Highlands are established. They provide the earliest evidence of these practices.	Settlement occurs on the Marianas Islands when voyagers arrive from Luzon in the Philippines.

shellfish, played an important role in the Lapita diet. The Lapita colonists brought domestic animals (pigs, dogs, and chickens) with them, and cultivated a mix of crops from both Southeast Asia and New Guinea. Stable isotope analysis of bones from the cemetery at Teouma in Vanuatu suggests that, at least early on, the colonists relied heavily on marine resources and domestic animals, and that establishing productive crops may have taken some time. Linguistic evidence suggests that Lapita colonists originally came from Southeast Asia, most probably from Taiwan, and genetic evidence from Teouma confirms a Southeast Asian origin for the early colonists.

Polynesian culture emerged about 3,000 years ago in West Polynesia. Both Hawaii and the Marquesas Islands (see image 3) were reached by 900 to 1000 CE, and Polynesian navigators reached South America by 1000, returning with new plants including kumara (sweet potato). New Zealand, the last major land mass to be occupied, was settled permanently by c. 1200.

The last millennium in the Pacific saw great diversification in social and political organization. Complex stratified societies emerged in several areas, based on intensive agricultural production. Monumental architecture is a feature of many areas, the best known of which is Easter Island (see p. 378). Pacific colonization undoubtedly involved purposeful exploration, by people with sophisticated navigation skills and canoe-building technology. Computer simulations and experimental voyaging in replica canoes (see image 2) demonstrate how these first explorers used prevailing winds and currents to travel safely and return. The double-hulled outrigger canoe was probably the key innovation that made such exploration possible. **CB**

1500 BCE	1350–950 BCE	1160–800 BCE	900–1000 CE	1200	1500
The Lapita cultural complex first appears in the Western Pacific.	The Lapita colonists spread into the Pacific as far as Tonga and Samoa.	The Teouma cemetery exists on Efate Island, Vanuatu. Today it is the oldest known cemetery within the Pacific Islands.	The Polynesian settlement of Hawaii, the Marquesas Islands, and Rapa Nui (Easter Island) occurs, although the last may have been earlier.	The permanent Maori settlement of New Zealand is established.	Fortified settlements known as *pa* appear in New Zealand (see p. 380).

Easter Island Early centuries CE

The volcanic island of Rapa Nui is the remotest outcrop of permanently inhabited land on the planet, located 2,328 miles (3,747 km.) from South America and 1,398 miles (2,250 km.) from Pitcairn Island. Roughly triangular in shape, it covers 66 square miles (171 sq. km.).

✦ NAVIGATOR

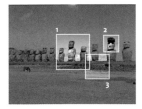

Rapa Nui was first settled by Polynesians, probably from the Marquesas Islands, but debate still continues as to when. Archaeological and linguistic evidence points to the early centuries CE, since the islanders' form of Polynesian was very archaic. Dozens of people colonized the island, bringing with them crops, chickens, and rats (dogs and pigs, central to Polynesian life, do not seem to have survived the journey). The island must have remained isolated from the world until Europeans arrived in 1722; otherwise, the language would not have remained archaic, and pigs and dogs would certainly have been imported. Environmental studies have shown that the island was originally covered by a thick forest of palm trees and was home to a wide range of birds. The Polynesian settlers, in adapting the island to their needs, gradually removed the forest cover and also wiped out or drove away most of the birds. These settlers developed one of the most extraordinary Stone Age cultures, best known for its hundreds of stone platforms and statues; yet it also produced wonderful wooden figurines, the richest rock art in the Pacific, boat-shaped houses of stone and thatch, and a unique script known as rongorongo, comprising rows of glyphs incised on pieces of wood. The islanders had a royal clan, which provided the hereditary chiefs. They seem to have lived peacefully for perhaps 1,000 years, with communities cooperating with each other in the transport and erection of statues. But then something happened that caused radical changes; evidence suggests that it was drastic deforestation and perhaps a rising population. Conflicts arose, weapons were mass-produced, and statues were toppled. The Europeans would eventually bring catastrophe to the island and almost wipe out its inhabitants. **PGB**

👁 FOCAL POINTS

1 STATUES

About 1,000 stone statues, or *moai*, were carved by the islanders over a period of perhaps 500 years from 1000 to 1500 CE. All variations on a theme, they represent ancestors who were venerated rather than worshipped. Many were erected on *ahu* (platforms), with their backs to the ocean.

2 PUKAO

Only statues on *ahu* were given eye sockets (for detachable eyes of white coral) and also headdresses, or *pukao*, made of cylinders of red scoria. These were doubtless rolled from the quarry at Puna Pau and then raised to crown the *moai*, probably by being dragged up sloping beams of wood.

3 AHU

There are at least 313 *ahu*, placed parallel to the shore. They comprise a rubble core faced with masonry without mortar and range in size from quite small to more than 490 feet (150 m.) in length, as here at Ahu Tongariki. The landward side has a ramp paved with lines of beach boulders.

▲ Most of the *moai* were carved out of soft tuff at the volcanic crater of Rano Raraku using stone picks known as *toki*. Many were left unfinished and are still attached to the bedrock.

BIRDMAN RACE

A novel democratic method was adopted for choosing a chief, along with a new religion focused on fertility and first fruits. Each candidate selected a young man to represent him in the contest. Every spring, in September, people gathered at the cliff-top ceremonial village of Orongo, and on the day of the race the competitors had to descend the 985-foot (300 m.) cliff, swim 1.2 miles (2 km.) out to the islet of Motu Nui and wait there for a sooty tern to lay an egg. The egg then had to be brought back across the ocean, up the cliff and handed intact to the competitor's master. The winning master then became birdman (chief) for the year.

Pa in New Zealand 1500 CE

Pa defenses made use of natural features of the landscape. Volcanic cones were often fortified and there are many such sites in the Auckland area, including Maungakiekie. The entrance to the *pa* is often an inconspicuous narrow gap in the defensive bank and ditch.

Perhaps the most distinctive sites in New Zealand are the fortified settlements, or *pa*. There are thousands of these sites, most of them in the North Island. Commonly, they take advantage of topography and are located in naturally defensible locations with a strategic outlook, such as hilltops, headlands, or spurs. Complex fortifications include palisades, banks, and ditches. Natural slopes were also modified to make them steeper. Many *pa* resemble the hill forts of Iron Age Britain. However, some were also built in swamps or on artificial islands in lakes.

Pa first appear in *c.* 1500, probably as a result of increasing population and competition for resources, and they were still in use at the time of British settlement in the nineteenth century. At that time, many *pa* were refortified to adapt to fighting with guns and artillery. They were built by family groups or clans as defensive retreats in time of conflict. However, they also commonly functioned as focal points for many aspects of community life, including craft production, and as centers of power and ceremony.

There are many different types of *pa*, ranging from small fortified homesteads to large settlements with complex defenses. Within the defenses, terraces, and platforms were constructed for houses and industry. Storage pits for *kumara*, or sweet potato, are also common features. At sites that have been excavated, it is clear that some *pa* have very complex histories of building and use. They were not usually lived in continuously. Depending on the season, people spent a considerable amount of time away from the *pa*, fishing, hunting, or tending gardens. They may indeed have spent most of their time in *kainga*, or undefended settlements, only retreating to the *pa* in times of conflict. **CB**

⊚ FOCAL POINTS

Storage pits known as *rua* are common features in *pa*. Certain crops, such as *kumara*, or sweet potato, could only be grown in summer on the North Island, and so Maori developed ways to store tubers over the winter as food and also as seed stock. There were several different types of storage pit within the *pa*. Some were dug directly into banks of earth, whereas others were dug into the ground and a roof was built over the top. They were designed to protect the tubers from destructive insects, rats, and mold. In addition, the *rua* protected the stacks of tubers from the rain, and some were fitted with internal drains.

WEAPONS

Warfare was common in Maori society and highly ritualized. Often fighting occurred over land or resources, but might also involve *mana* (prestige) or *utu* (revenge or retribution for insults or injuries). Weapons included fighting staffs, spears and clubs. Wood, stone, and whalebone were all used to make weapons. *Mere pounamu* (greenstone clubs) were symbols of authority and highly prized. *Pounamu* (greenstone) is found only in the South Island and traded throughout New Zealand. Peace agreements often involved the exchange of weapons made of *pounamu*, symbolizing permanence.

FIRST SETTLERS

New Zealand, the last major land mass to be occupied by humans, is quite different from the other Pacific Islands. For example, it is considerably bigger and its climate ranges from subtropical in the north to cold temperate in the south. New Zealand was permanently settled by 1200 but probably already was known and visited by 1000. The first settlers do not seem to have brought pigs or chickens with them, but encountered rich animal resources on the island, such as marine mammals, fish, shellfish, and birds, including eleven species of the giant flightless moa.

Hunting and gathering was a key element of the economy for the original settlers, particularly in the south, where tropical crops such as taro and sweet potato could not be grown. In addition to providing a source of meat, moa were important because their skins and feathers were used for clothing and their bones were carved into fish hooks and jewelry. They were easy prey as they had no natural predators and the once abundant species were quickly hunted to extinction.

5 | The Medieval World
500–1600 CE

The modern world was formed in the crucible of medieval Europe. The distinctive character of European feudalism, the division of the continent into warring states, the role of towns and commercial farming, and a host of other factors created the space for the emergence of an enterprising "middling sort" that pioneered a new kind of capitalist economic system. Other parts of the world remained relatively conservative, though capable of extraordinary cultural achievements.

SOUTH AMERICAN CIVILIZATIONS

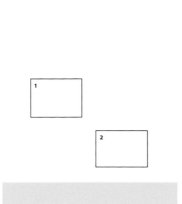

1 The site of Chan Chan near Trujillo in northwestern Peru. The Chimú built their main citadels at Chan Chan using thick mud that was poured elaborately to form walls.

2 The Gate of the Sun from Tiwanaku in Bolivia. It has forty-eight winged effigies carved on to the lintel, all of which look toward the central motif of a personage with face surrounded by lines, possibly sun rays.

The most important prehistoric civilizations of South America developed between the first and fifteenth centuries CE. These are societies such as the Moche, Nazca, Tiwanaku, Wari (see p. 390), Chimú, and Inca. They were located in the high Andes mountains and in the river valleys that flow into the Pacific watershed in the central and south-central Andean region that corresponds to modern Peru and Bolivia.

The Moche has long been considered the true first state in the pre-Hispanic Andes, and developed between the first and ninth centuries. Its people built a coastal state along the dry northern Peruvian desert. While there is debate about political and economic structure, there is no doubt that the Moche developed a territorial and ideological unity throughout the rich northern valleys along the coast. The world-famous burials of the Moche elite that contain enormous quantities of grave goods are evidence for a highly stratified society in which wealth was amassed for elaborate monuments and ceremonies.

Contemporary with the Moche, the settlement of Cahuachi emerged as the capital of the Nazca polity on the southern coast of Peru between the second and sixth centuries. It concentrated its power by a series of ritual and religious practices of which the Nazca Lines geoglyphs formed an important part.

Tiwanaku, located in the Bolivian altiplano in the high Lake Titicaca basin, was the most important political and religious ceremonial center in the south-central Andes between the sixth and eleventh centuries. This planned, urban capital spread over 2 square miles (5 sq. km.) and was home to at least

KEY EVENTS

c. 100 CE	c. 200	c. 300	c. 550	c. 750	c. 850
Construction begins on the Huaca de la Luna (Temple of the Moon) in the Moche River valley in present-day Peru.	The Lord of Sipán (see p. 388) rules in Huaca Rajada-Sipán in Peru. He is a powerful leader of Moche society.	Cahuachi, in Peru, reaches its apogee as the capital of the Nazca.	A climatic shift starts on the north coast, causing a crisis. Human sacrifices are made in Plaza 3 of the Huaca de la Luna.	The Wari Empire commences expansion outside the Ayacucho region in Peru.	The inhabitants of the Huacas de Moche (see p. 386) start to abandon the settlement.

50,000 people. The civic core included massive stone-faced pyramids and palaces (see image 2). Surrounding the core were adobe buildings that housed the artisan and commoner classes. Tiwanaku established colonies as far south as Moquegua in southern Peru and in the coastal valleys of northern Chile.

Contemporary with Tiwanaku was the culture of the Wari, the first Andean empire. Its capital, Huari, controlled the territory throughout the south-central highlands of Peru. Wari developed important political and religious practices from earlier societies, like Pukara and Nazca, but also shared organizational features with the Tiwanaku.

One of the last great states, which competed with the Incas during its expansion on the coast of Peru, was the Chimú. It developed between the eleventh and fifteenth centuries. Its capital, the city of Chan Chan (see image 1) was built at the mouth of the Moche Valley and sprawled across 14 square miles (36 sq. km.). Chan Chan contained palaces, cemeteries, and reservoirs. A large cluster of workshops and households is still evident between the citadels.

The Incas were the last great civilization of the pre-Hispanic Andes. They conquered areas that span the present territories of Colombia, Ecuador, Peru, Bolivia, Chile, and Argentina. Their cities were large concentrations of buildings built in carved stone in the highlands, but of mud adobe on the coast. Inca cities were characterized by large plazas and buildings that housed the main institutions of the state. The Inca Empire was integrated by an elaborate road system. Cuzco, housing 125,000 people, served as its capital and was one of the most elegant cities at the time of the arrival of the Spaniards in 1533. **HT**

c. 900	c. 1000	c. 1100	c. 1450	c. 1470	1532
The Wari Empire begins to lose power in the Andean territory.	The builders of Tiwanaku in present-day Bolivia start to desert the city.	The first citadels are built in Chan Chan, Peru.	Inca Emperor Pachacuti (r. 1438–71) rebuilds much of the city of Cuzco in Peru.	The Inca Empire conquers the central and northern coast of Peru. The Incas conquer the Chimú.	The Spaniards arrive in Cajamarca in northern Peru. They capture the last free reigning Inca emperor, Atahualpa (c. 1502–33).

Huacas de Moche *c.* 100 – 850 CE

This high-relief mural at Huaca de la Luna's Plaza 1 has yet to be deciphered. However, various motifs and figures appear to represent human warriors and fishermen, and animals including a serpent, two foxes, two buzzards, a monkey, and an iguana.

The Huacas de Moche are located on the north coast of Peru in the lower Moche River valley on the outskirts of the city of Trujillo in the region of La Libertad. They are one of the most important architectural complexes of Moche society. The archaeological area, which includes the two main buildings, Huaca del Sol (Temple of the Sun) and Huaca de la Luna (Temple of the Moon), covers approximately 740 acres (300 ha.). The settlement occupied an extensive area at the western base of Cerro Blanco on the south margin of the Moche River valley and it may have had 10,000 inhabitants at its apogee. Its imposing architecture and the treasure found in its graves made it a target for looting since early colonial times. German archaeologist Max Uhle (1856–1944) investigated the site in the late nineteenth century.

The Huacas de Moche were constructed using a huge quantity of rectangular adobe mud bricks that formed monumental platforms. Indeed, Huaca del Sol is one of the largest adobe structures in the pre-Hispanic Americas. The overlapping of construction phases and remodeling of the structures over time gave the buildings their final stepped appearance. In addition, a vast urban area developed between the two large stepped platforms. At present, there is a consensus among experts in the field that the Moche society comprised at least two major regions: Northern Moche and Southern Moche. The Huacas de Moche belonged to the region of the Southern Moche and are viewed as the capital of this political entity. A series of enclosures and plazas characterize the Huaca de la Luna, and its multicolored murals depict scenes related to a religious cult and the Moche political structure. Human sacrifices and burials have also been found in the settlement, but without the kind of opulent artifacts found at the tombs of the Lords of Sipán (see p. 388). **HT**

HUACA DEL SOL

Huaca del Sol is the most imposing building and one of the most voluminous architectural works of South America. It is estimated that originally it would have been 1,132 feet (345 m.) long by 525 feet (160 m.) wide at its base, with a height of more than 130 feet (40 m.). Huaca del Sol was built with mud adobe over a series of architectural phases that gradually increased its volume. Investigations have found evidence that shows its importance as a political and administrative building.

URBAN SECTOR

In the flat area between Huaca del Sol and Huaca de la Luna, a series of architectural complexes has been discovered that coexisted with the main buildings. These would be the urban sectors where permanent inhabitants of the city lived and worked, principally specialist craftsmen who offered their skills to the Moche elite. Archaeologists have unearthed storage spaces on the wide plain, as well as workshops where ceramics, textiles, and metal and stone artifacts were produced.

MURALS AT HUACA DE LA LUNA

Huaca de la Luna is the second building in architectural volume at the archaeological site. The main platform of Huaca de la Luna is approximately 950 feet (290 m.) long by 690 feet (210 m.) wide at its base, with a height of 65 feet (20 m.). Moche iconography is depicted in this building using high-relief murals. Likewise, evidence of human sacrifice has been discovered, reinforcing the religious character of the structure.

Among the greatest attractions of Huaca de la Luna are its polychrome murals. More than 64,583 square feet (6,000 sq. m.) of reliefs have been uncovered. These extraordinary and well-preserved painted sculptural friezes are one of the great discoveries of Moche archaeology, especially since there are no written texts associated with the Moche culture to help explain their beliefs and customs. The motifs of animals, plants, and fantastical characters seen in the murals suggest that the Moche were able to express themselves using a complex visual language. The intricate murals decorate surfaces of the adobe walls. Their three-dimensional designs were created using mud to make high reliefs. The figures and the areas between them were then painted in bright colors—mainly red, yellow, white, and black.

There are several friezes that stand out through their sheer size, particularly those that decorate the front walls that face the main plaza (Plaza 1). There is a possible series of personages at different levels, according to their hierarchy. Other murals in more private architectural spaces also reveal a complex Moche cosmovision: for example, the western wall of the Corner Room. Friezes in the interior of the Huaca de la Luna were found with more repetitive decorations, such as those that describe heads of an anthropomorphic being with feline features within diamond-shaped designs.

The Lords of Sipán *c. 200 – 600*

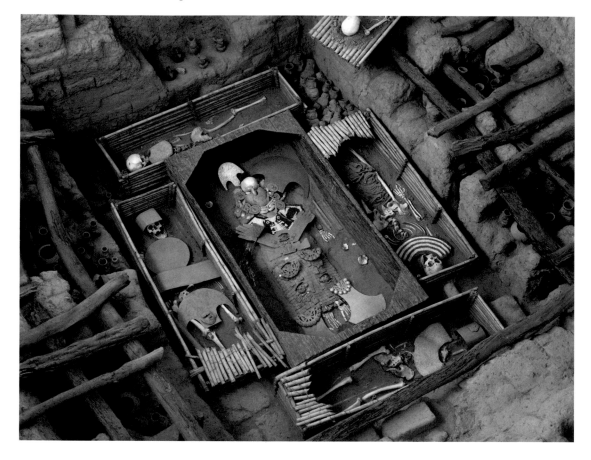

This reconstruction of the excavated tomb of the Lord of Sipán shows his remains in a coffin at the center. The elite leader was found adorned in gold, silver, and copper jewelry and ornaments. The noble was aged between thirty-five and forty-five at the time of his death, and is known to have ruled the Lambayeque Valley in the late third century.

◆ NAVIGATOR

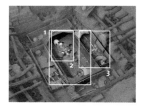

In the valley of Lambayeque, on the north coast of Peru, is Huaca Rajada-Sipán, a construction made with mud adobe. In 1987, as a result of a series of fights between local looters, the existence of a rich tomb on a platform connected to the main building was revealed. Walter Alva and his team stopped the looting, and in the course of archaeological excavation they discovered the intact tomb of a member of the local Moche elite, who has become known as the Lord of Sipán.

The tomb of the Lord of Sipán was one of the most important in the pyramid. But others followed, most notably those of the Old Lord of Sipán and what is thought to be a Moche priest. Inside the funerary platform built of adobe, a rectangular chamber was fitted with roofs supported by wooden beams. The funerary platform grew in volume by superimposing new construction phases that included burial chambers. The main occupant of each tomb was a male who had been placed inside a wooden coffin, accompanied by a large number of sumptuous objects of metal, mainly of gold, silver, and copper. The most extraordinary objects found were headdresses, nose rings, pectorals, scepters, ear ornaments, and backflaps. In addition, other artifacts made of clay, wood and seashells constituted a rich cluster of grave goods. Likewise, in many cases the main subject was accompanied by the sacrifice of women and men of lower status. There were also sacrifices of dogs and camelids. The principal personages were the rulers who occupied the highest hierarchy within Moche society in this region. Their military and religious attire, along with their grave goods, indicate that these subjects possessed the actual and ideological power in the society. According to Moche iconography, the Lords of Sipán established intimate relations with supernatural beings and forces. **HT**

1 SKELETONS

Physical anthropological studies indicate that these individuals reached an average height of 5 feet 2 inches (1.6 m.), and they enjoyed a better diet than the rest of the population. DNA evidence reveals that although the Lord of Sipán and the Old Lord of Sipán were separated by about four generations, they shared the same DNA. This indicates that there was a lineage of rulers.

2 SYMBOLS OF POWER

Moche rulers symbolized their authority using objects, mainly made from precious metals. The scepters found in the tombs of Sipán bear designs related to the main personage. The headdresses of semilunar form also signify the power of the elite Moche. Finally, there is a *sui generis* metal artefact, the backflap, which would have been suspended from a belt around the waist.

3 HUMAN SACRIFICES

The burial of individuals in the tombs of Sipán indicates that human sacrifices occurred to accompany the leaders of Moche society on their journey to the afterlife. Two males with amputated feet were buried by the long sides of the coffin at the center. The discovery of clothes and artifacts related to these victims identifies them as warriors.

▲ This Moche ceramic depicts a priest sacrificing two animals, a repeated theme in Moche iconography. Initially such figures were thought to be mythological beings. But the similarity between their distinguishing attributes and the grave goods found in tombs proved that the figures depict real people and events.

🕐 ARCHAEOLOGIST PROFILE

1951–76

Peruvian archaeologist Walter Alva was born in Contumazá, Cajamarca. He studied archaeology at the National University of Trujillo. In 1975 and 1976, he served as supervisor of Archaeological Monuments of the Region of Lambayeque.

1977–93

Alva was appointed director of the Brüning Archaeological Museum in Lambayeque in 1977. He carried out research at different archaeological sites, such as Salinas de Chao (1977), Morro de Etén (1979), and Purulén (1983). In 1987, Alva, together with his team, including Susana Meneses (1943–2002) and Luis Chero (b. 1958), discovered the Lord of Sipán. In

1988, they discovered the tomb of the Priest and in 1989 that of the Old Lord of Sipán. A year later, the Peruvian government awarded him the Orden El Sol del Perú (Order of the Sun of Peru) for distinguished service. In 1993, Alva and Christopher B. Donnan (b. 1940) published a book on the findings at Sipán.

1994–PRESENT

In 2002, the Royal Tombs of Sipán Museum was inaugurated in the city of Lambayeque. Alva is still the director of the museum today. He carried out archaeological research at sites such as Huaca Ventarrón and Collud-Zarpán in 2007. He also continues to investigate archaeological sites in Cajamarca in Peru's northern highlands.

Huari *c.* 500 – 1000

The Robles Moqo vessels are characteristically decorated with designs related to an anthropomorphic being very similar to that of the main character depicted on the Gate of the Sun megalithic sculpture at Tiwanaku. They have been found, broken and buried in pits as offerings, in Huari, Conchopata, Pacheco, and other Wari-related sites.

Huari was the capital city of the Wari Empire, one of the earliest empires in the pre-Hispanic Andes that developed between the sixth and eleventh centuries. Huari is located in the southern highlands of Peru, about 16 miles (25 km.) from the city of Huamanga in Ayacucho region. Huari extends for 618 acres (250 ha.) on a plateau 8,858 feet (2,700 m.) above sea level. It is an extensive human settlement of urban character, comprising rectangular buildings made of stone and mud. At its height it may have had a population of 40,000 people. There are several sectors in the site, such as Moraduchayuq, Cheqo Wasi, and Vegachayoq Moqo, which had different economic, political, and religious functions, especially related to elites. The presence of palaces, temples, mausoleums, and cemeteries has been established. In addition, there are a number of non-elite structures. Likewise, ceramics workshops have been recognized, such as the one that would have produced the Robles Moqo ceramic style. In addition, some sectors have been embellished with anthropomorphic sculptures made with volcanic rock.

Huari was the capital of an extensive empire that spread to the northern highlands in Cajamarca and to the south near Cuzco. On the Peruvian coast and middle valleys, the imperial presence is less evident, but there are areas with Wari occupations, such as El Castillo de Huarmey to the north and Cerro Baúl in the south. Wari influence can be detected on the northern coast in late Moche sites such as San José de Moro. The Wari Empire coexisted with the Tiwanaku state, although their relationship is not clear. The Wari assimilated Tiwanaku elements, mainly religious, which materialized in architecture, stone sculpture, ceramics, textiles, wood, and metallurgy. **HT**

◉ FOCAL POINTS

D-SHAPED TEMPLE

The most important and extraordinary ritual structures of the Huari site are the D-shaped temples. They have also been found in other provincial centers of the Wari Empire. Recent excavation at the site discovered that inside one of the D-shaped temples was a column of stone that could have served to calculate the passage of time by observing the shadows projected by the sun. The ritual burial of human heads and camelids was evident inside another of the temples.

WARI TEXTILES

This Wari poncho is made from wool and cotton. Wari textiles, generally made from camelid fiber, represent some of the finest craftsmanship in Andean prehistory. Fragments have been found in parts of the Andes where the Wari had control or influence. The discovery of spindles and weaving tools support the idea of Wari workshops and cloth tribute for the state. The textiles have various designs and contain iconography related to the main figure on the Gate of the Sun at Tiwanaku.

WARI: THE FIRST ANDEAN EMPIRE

One of the most spectacular discoveries concerning the Wari Empire was made in 2012 by a team led by Polish archaeologists at the site of El Castillo de Huarmey. Located in a valley on the northern coast of Peru, this Wari provincial capital included a complex funerary building, or mausoleum, that was found intact by the archaeologists. They excavated the remains of fifty-eight aristocratic women accompanied by human sacrifices and 1,300 grave goods of high quality, such as fancy vessels, textiles, earspools, necklaces, and weapons.

One of the main explanations of the sociopolitical nature of Wari was raised by Peruvian archaeologist Luis Guillermo Lumbreras (b. 1936) in the late 1970s. He claimed that Wari could have been a militaristic empire. This proposal generated an important debate on the way in which the expansive Andean societies spread. In the absence of intensive studies in Wari sites, the imperial proposal was left aside to propose other scenarios, where economics and religion would have played an important role in the dispersal of artifacts and architectural features similar to those of Huari.

However, in light of the latest discoveries, especially those from El Castillo de Huarmey and Espíritu Pampa near Cuzco, it has been established that the Wari state effectively controlled certain regions politically. Thus, architectural complexes like Viracochapampa or Pikillacta were imperial administrative centers that controlled areas important for the Wari elites.

In the southern area, between the highlands and coast, one Wari site that has been intensively investigated is Cerro Baúl, which is a classic example of a political, economic, and religious enclave. Even the explanation of its nature is complex because it coexisted in the same valley with Tiwanaku settlements.

MESOAMERICAN CIVILIZATION

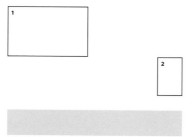

There are many opinions about what constitutes a civilization, but most scholars would agree that monumental architecture is its most constant and obvious manifestation. Mesoamerica first witnessed the construction of massive building projects at a few sites as early as the second millennium BCE, but after 100 CE the time and labor invested in huge temple platforms, elegant palaces, and elaborate public works increased exponentially as cities grew up in both the highlands and lowlands. Between 100 and 900, ethnically and linguistically diverse states transformed Mesoamerica into a dynamic world system, separated by geography yet interconnected by a shared symbol system, long-distance trade, marriage alliances, diplomacy, and warfare.

Certainly there were powerful leaders prior to this time, but the first millennium CE saw the clear emergence of dynastic kings. The earliest evidence of them comes from Maya sites, such as Tikal in Guatemala, where historical texts record the foundation of royal lineages c. 100. However, the institution of divine kingship may be even older, since the insignia commonly used by later rulers to mark their regal status can be found in much earlier burials or displayed in murals and building facades. These include the headdress of the

1 The Pyramid of the Niches at El Tajín in Veracruz, Mexico, has six tiers embellished with elegant flying cornices and 365 niches referencing the solar year.

2 The graceful Temple of the Sun at the Maya site of Palenque, Mexico, projects the ideology of divine kingship.

KEY EVENTS

100 BCE–200 CE	c. 50 CE	c. 100	c. 150	200	378–500
Zapotec Monte Albán initiates its political expansion beyond the Valley of Oaxaca in southern Mexico.	The huge eruption of the Popocatépetl volcano causes major demographic changes in Mexico's central highlands.	The first dynastic kings are documented in the Maya area.	The construction of the ceremonial core at Teotihuacan, Mexico, begins.	Teotihuacan accelerates its imperial expansion.	Teotihuacan penetrates Maya dynasties.

royal deity Hu'unal, the monarch's belt with masks and jade plaques, and the throne scaffolding required for the coronation ceremony. By the end of the fourth century, many sites began to erect stelae and altars to record the major events in the lives of their kings.

The first millennium, usually referred to as the Classic period, can be divided into two parts. The earlier, dating between 100 and 600, was dominated by Teotihuacan (see p. 394) in Mexico, while the later, 600 to 900, originated in the midst of Teotihuacan's political collapse and included both the flowering and the fall of the Maya kingdoms in the southern jungles. Teotihuacan was a political enterprise that began to expand beyond the confines of the Basin of Mexico during the second century; and by the late fourth century, Maya inscriptions record the arrival of its representatives, accompanied by military personnel, at sites such as La Sufricaya in Belize and El Perú in Guatemala.

The imperial aspirations of Teotihuacan extended to Monte Albán (see p. 208) in Oaxaca, the settlements along the Gulf Coast and into the arid regions of the northwest. Its merchants traded for exotic raw materials—shell, mica, greenstone, feathers, and cotton—that were given added value in the city's many domestic workshops, while the Teotihuacan architectural and ceramic styles were liberally copied throughout Mesoamerica. Between 550 and 600, the political structure of the city began to fray and, in a violent struggle from which the empire never recovered, many temples and palaces were sacked and burned. However, Teotihuacan's demise opened the door for other cities and kingdoms to embark upon their own expansionist initiatives. This led to a surge in propagandistic building programs, and a related flowering of the arts, in addition to increased warfare among now freely competing states like Palenque, Yaxchilán, and Dos Pilas in the Maya area, and Cacaxtla (see p. 398), Cantona, and Xochicalco in the central highlands. Built on a smaller scale than Teotihuacan's overpowering pyramids, the Temple of the Sun at Palenque (see image 2) celebrates divine kingship. Its interior shrine contains a finely carved panel that records the ancestry of Kan B'alam II, who ruled from 684 to 702. Its roof was once decorated with stucco images of the king and supernatural beings. El Tajín (see image 1) developed its own Late Classic architectural style in the tropical lowlands of Veracruz. The steps of the Pyramid of the Niches are framed by sloping bands with mosaic step-frets and recalls the hieroglyphic staircase at the Maya city of Copán (see p. 396) in Honduras.

As Teotihuacan's supremacy faded, its image was incorporated into Mesoamerica's collective memory as a golden past, and over the succeeding centuries there would be numerous attempts to revive its fame and glory. Nonetheless, its downfall led to the collapse of dynastic regimes all over Mesoamerica between 800 and 900. In their wake, a new world order, based on ideological revitalization and innovative ways of governing, emerged in the Yucatán Peninsula and the central highlands of Mexico. **PPN**

c. 600	600–1100	c. 750	c. 770	c. 800	830–910
The Teotihuacan state collapses.	El Tajín, in Veracruz, rises and becomes the most important center in northeast Mesoamerica after the fall of the Teotihuacan Empire.	Colored murals are painted in Maya style at Cacaxtla in modern-day Tlaxcala, Mexico.	The largest-known Maya palace is built at Cancuén in present-day Guatemala.	Monte Albán is abandoned.	Political systems in the southern Maya lowlands collapse.

Teotihuacan 100 BCE – 600 CE

Rising 141 feet (43 m.) high at the northern end of the Street of the Dead, Teotihuacan's Pyramid of the Moon is second in size to the Pyramid of the Sun (in the foreground). Completed in the fifth century at the height of the city's prominence, its final stage encases six previous buildings and highly symbolic dedicatory offerings, including sacrificed humans and animals.

Located 30 miles (50 km.) northeast of modern Mexico City, Teotihuacan was Mesoamerica's leading city for more than 500 years. With a peak population of 125,000 spread over 8 square miles (20 sq. km.), by 500 CE it was the sixth largest city in the world. Like many early urban centres, Teotihuacan was a community of immigrants. Some were attracted by economic opportunities, but others were refugees who arrived in the aftermath of a catastrophic eruption of Popocatépetl volcano c. 50. During the next century, Teotihuacan's leaders established a civic-ceremonial centre in a space consecrated by multiple buried offerings, including sacrificed humans, animals of prey, rain-god effigy vessels, and multi-ton greenstone orthostats (upright slabs).

The urban layout centers on the Street of the Dead, an axis 3 miles (5 km.) long and oriented 15.5 degrees east of north. Major monuments, such as the Sun and Moon pyramids, the Great Compound, and the 4,305 square-foot (400 sq. m.) Ciudadela with its Temple of the Feathered Serpent, which was dedicated with mass human sacrifice, line the avenue's northern section. Residential areas, organized into more than 2,000 multifamily masonry apartment compounds, spread out in an orthogonal layout that indicates a high degree of centralized planning. High-status residences were located near the ceremonial areas, while lower-class housing was relegated to the outskirts of the city.

Evidence for contact with the Maya area appears occasionally in the city's mural art, but the jadeite pectorals, ear ornaments, and bone chemistry of the three individuals placed in a fourth-century dedicatory offering in the Pyramid of the Moon tie the governing elite of Teotihuacan to the rulers of certain Maya kingdoms. **PPN**

TEMPLE OF THE FEATHERED SERPENT

The Temple of the Feathered Serpent lies at the city center. Its seven tiers were once decorated on all four sides with sculptures of feathered rattlesnakes that bear the headdress of the Primordial Crocodile. Situated over a tunnel laden with offerings, as many as 200 captives were sacrificed to consecrate the temple.

MURAL

Many of Teotihuacan's murals depict rituals. This looted fragment shows an individual wearing an animal headdress. The speech-scroll shows he is chanting as he spills his blood in a sacrificial rite. The woven mat in front of him holds the two spiny points of maguey cactus leaves used to draw his blood.

A NEW WAY OF LIVING

Hierarchically organized into neighborhoods, ethnic enclaves, and districts, Teotihuacan's apartment compounds represent a new urban lifestyle. Most were built between 200 and 300, after earlier structures were razed to open space for them, but over time they were often significantly remodeled. The more elegant walled residences were constructed according to a predetermined design, but occasionally several small compounds would be integrated into a single large grouping.

The apartment compounds vary in size: the smallest cover approximately 9,690 square feet (900 sq. m.), while the largest have over 86,000 square feet (8,000 sq. m.) of construction. Although there is no standard format, most are centered on a ritual courtyard with a miniature temple-shrine for offerings. Living quarters consist of rooms with porticoes set on low platforms around a small patio with an impluvium that drained run-off from the flat roofs and served as a light source for the windowless structures. The apartments were connected by passageways that opened into light wells, where cooking and other domestic chores took place. All the compounds had subfloor drains that directed rainwater into open canals in the narrow streets. Stylized murals decorated the walls of high-status homes.

Many neighborhoods were involved in craft activity. Inhabitants produced obsidian blades and projectile points, textiles, carved shell, featherwork, stucco and pottery from raw materials imported from all over Mesoamerica to create finished articles for export to distant centers.

Ethnic enclaves from Oaxaca, the Gulf Coast, and Michoacán have been identified among Teotihuacan's apartment compounds. As opposed to the other immigrants in the city, these groups chose to maintain their ethnic identity over many generations, rather than entirely embrace the social norms of Teotihuacan.

Copán 400 – 800

Located at the base of the city's main temple, the four sides of Altar Q record sixteen kings of Copán's dynasty. Here, Yax K'uk Mo', the foreign lineage founder who took office in 426—perhaps in the faraway city of Teotihuacan—hands the royal insignia to Yax Pasaj Chan Yoaat, who, in 776, commissioned the carving to validate his right to the throne.

Spanish explorer Diego García de Palacio (1540 – 95) discovered the ruins of the ancient Maya city of Copán in 1570. Explorers John Stephens (1805 – 52) and Frederick Catherwood (1799 – 1854) rediscovered them in 1839, and Stephens introduced Copán to the outside world in his travel log *Incidents of Travel in Central America, Chiapas and Yucatan* in 1841. Since then, research has produced one of the most complete records of an ancient Maya polity. The extensive archaeological explorations and the large number of hieroglyphs inscribed on buildings, stairways, stelae, and altars have allowed scholars to cross-check the historical texts with data obtained from excavations.

Located in western Honduras, Copán was the capital of an important Maya kingdom between 426 and 822. A magnificent hieroglyphic stairway that records Copán's dynastic history leads to its Acropolis, a massive complex of temples and royal tombs that dominates its civic-ceremonial core. To the north of the acropolis lies a small yet stunning ball court and the Great Plaza, where extraordinary high-relief portrait stelae of Copán's kings stand; to the south are the remains of the royal palace.

The founder of Copán's dynasty, Yax K'uk Mo' (d. 437), is described as a Lord of the West, the title held by overlords who claimed legitimacy from the highland Mexican city of Teotihuacan. Isotopic analysis of his skeleton, found inside a Teotihuacan-style platform buried within the acropolis, demonstrates he was a foreigner—perhaps from Tikal to the west, where earlier, in 378, Teotihuacan had penetrated the dynastic line. He and his descendants used Teotihuacan motifs in their dress and on their monuments to solidify this connection. To validate further his claim to Copán's throne, Yax K'uk Mo' married a local woman, possibly of royal blood. Copán's decline began in the eighth century, when the nobility increasingly challenged the king's power by engaging in rituals and using emblems that had previously been reserved for the dynast alone. The last king, Ukit Took (r. c. 822 – 30), left his monuments unfinished as the kingdom unraveled. **PPN**

✦ NAVIGATOR

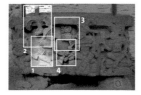

1 SHIELD

The skeleton of Yax K'uk Mo' had a severe unhealed fracture of the right forearm, a parry wound that he perhaps suffered during battle. The broken ulna formed a false joint, making it unstable. The small square shield might be a prosthetic device that allowed the ruler to regain limited use of his arm. Notably, on Altar Q the ruler uses his left arm to pass the scepter.

2 YAX K'UK MO' HEADDRESS

This shows the western face of Altar Q. Although Yax K'uk Mo's goggle-eyed mask is identified with Teotihuacan's Storm God, isotopic analysis of his bones and teeth show that he was not from that central Mexican city. Unlike the other fifteen rulers on Altar Q, each posed upon his name glyph, Yax K'uk Mo', which translates as First Quetzal Macaw, wears his name—a quetzal with macaw markings—in his headdress.

3 DATE

Written in hieroglyphs using the Maya system of recording time, July 2, 763 marks the accession of Yax Pasaj Chan Yoaat (Rising Sun) to the throne. He commissioned few monuments but he built many structures on the acropolis, including the last stage of Temple 16, which was dedicated to Yax K'uk Mo'. Altar Q was placed at the foot of this building.

4 SCEPTER

The scepter that Yax K'uk Mo' hands to Yax Pasaj Chan Yoaat (d. c. 810) is a symbol of royal authority validating his claim to the throne, yet its nature is unclear. Some identify it as a flaming dart or torch that represents the passing of the sacred fire of dynasty from one ruler to the next. Curiously, it does not represent the K'awiil scepter that the lineage founder received when named king.

FREDERICK CATHERWOOD

When John Lloyd Stephens was commissioned U.S. ambassador to Central America in 1839, he embarked on a journey through the Maya lowlands with his British draftsman, Frederick Catherwood. Copán was the first archaeological site they explored, and here Catherwood began to record the baroque sculpture with the help of his *camera lucida*. His accurate illustration of Stela H was one of twenty-five hand-colored lithographs published by Catherwood in 1844 in *Views of Ancient Monuments in Central America, Chiapas and Yucatán*.

Dedicated in 730, Stela H was carved in the high-relief style of Copán's later years. It was once thought to be the image of a woman because of the long jaguar-skin skirt covered with a netting of jade beads that the figure wears, but scholars now identify this striking sculpture as Copán's thirteenth ruler, Waxaklaju'n U B'aah K'awiil (d. 738), costumed as the Maize God. He is depicted in a headdress with the leaves and ears of the plant. During his reign, from 695 until 738, he sponsored significant sculptural programs and building projects, and is remembered as one of the kingdom's greatest sovereigns. His fortunes came to an end when he was captured and beheaded by a vassal lord from the neighboring site of Quirigua.

Cacaxtla 600 – 950

The Battle Mural of Cacaxtla embellishes the palace's main courtyard. It presents in vivid detail a series of naked captives, who still wear their bird headdresses and clutch their shields as the victorious jaguar warriors cut out their hearts. The center of this detail shows the defeated captain piercing his cheek with a spear as he submits to his fate.

 **NAVIGATOR**

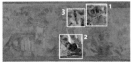

With the demise of Teotihuacan's imperial system, numerous small statelets, with populations of approximately 10,000, emerged to vie for power in Mesoamerica's central highlands. Cacaxtla, located 62 miles (100 km.) southeast of Teotihuacan in Mexico's Puebla-Tlaxcala Valley, was one of these, and its defensive hilltop position reflects the conflicted geopolitics of the post-Teotihuacan era.

Cacaxtla's acropolis, a mound 82 feet (25 m.) high measuring 656 by 361 feet (200 by 110 m.) at its base, was raised over the ruins of earlier occupations by the newly arrived Olmeca-Xicalanca in the seventh century. This royal compound formed the core of the city's civic-ceremonial activity. Its southern extreme, which was probably the ruler's residence, consists of rooms on either side of a corridor leading into an open court delimited by elongated structures with multiple doorways and, on the west, a temple. The central section contains a courtyard, bounded by elegant porticoed buildings with resplendent murals, while at the northern end there is a high mound with sunken court. Grain storage bins were kept within the palace confines, perhaps to store tribute payments.

Cacaxtla is known for its extraordinary murals. These were executed in a Maya style foreign to Mexico's highlands, leading some scholars to argue for a Maya presence there in the late eighth century. Curiously, however, excavations have produced few artifacts imported from Maya cities and, aside from the paintings, the Maya connection is weak. The simplest explanation for the exotic murals is that they were painted by artists trained in the Maya tradition, either commissioned by royal authorities or captured during a battle like the one depicted in the main courtyard. **PPN**

1 WARRIOR

The victorious captain menaces his opponent with a dart inserted in his spear-thrower. In front of his face is a symbol associated with sacred warfare and beyond that a glyph that provides his name, Three Deer Antler. Four bloody hearts that he has taken from his sacrificed captives hang from his belt.

2 GLYPHS

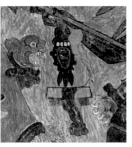

Two glyphs hang below the warrior's hand. The lower one perhaps names the soldier while the upper one—consisting of a quadripartite disk (signifying something of great value), a set of teeth (alluding to the verb "to take") and a bloody heart—might be read as "I take your heart."

3 BLOOD

Heart sacrifice is often alluded to but rarely shown in Mesoamerican art. Hearts skewered on knives are paraded, but the sacrificial act seldom appears. Here the battered individual's entrails spill from the gash made under his ribs by the warrior standing over him to remove the organ.

JOURNEY OF FOUR DOG

Not all of Cacaxtla's murals display the gory violence of warfare. An alternate theme was executed in a corridor used prior to the Battle Mural. This painting was modified as new building programs were implemented, the last of which required adapting the mural to a newly emplaced staircase. The final format shows an aged figure named Four Dog outfitted to personify the Maya merchant god. He carries a staff and is dressed in jaguar skins—including a helmet, boots, and gloves—and jade jewelry. He stands upon a feathered serpent that ascends the stairs. The scene is framed by a band containing aquatic animals, indicating an underworld association.

Behind Four Dog rests a large backpack containing various high-value goods: jars of exotic liquids, pigments or incense, a basket, textiles, feathers, a wide-brimmed hat topped with an animal effigy, and a huge turtle carapace. In front of the figure is a cacao tree and beyond that are two maize plants that sprout human heads.

MAYA

1 The painting on this drinking vessel (c. 750–850) shows warriors escorting a bound captive to be presented before their king. The prisoner has been stripped of his clothing. Behind him stands a soldier with his hafted stone ax poised for the decapitation.

2 This relief (c. 785) shows a provincial lord, or *sajal*, of Laxtunich genuflecting before his liege, Itzamnaaj B'ahlam III of Yaxchilán, as he presents three bound captives in 783. The king is seated upon a throne carved with his names and titles in a room within the royal palace, as indicated by the curtains at the top.

3 Yaxchilán Lintel 25 (c. 725) commemorates Lady K'ab'al Xook performing a bloodletting ritual to honor her husband's accession to the throne in 681. Paper strips stained with her blood were burned in the bowl on the floor to conjure a figure, wearing a Teotihuacan storm-god mask.

At the peak of their great civilization, the Maya occupied a diverse territory covering 125,097 square miles (324,000 sq. km.) that included the hot dry plains of the Yucatan Peninsula, the dense rain forests of the Petén, and the valleys of the volcanic Guatemalan highlands. They spoke more than thirty languages and dialects that are as similar to one another as are the European Romance languages, indicating their common origin. Signs of cultural complexity, specifically the monumental architecture that materializes political power, emerge around the middle of the first millennium BCE at sites like Nakbé in northern Guatemala, and shortly thereafter, during the Late Preclassic (300 BCE–200 CE), large settlements with truly impressive building complexes, elaborate burials, stone sculpture, and hieroglyphic texts begin to appear throughout the region. These early civic-ceremonial centers coincide with the emergence of kingship as the defining political institution of Maya society.

The first centuries of the Classic period (200–900) witnessed the rise of many cities and minor centers, the spread of high culture and hieroglyphic writing (see p. 402), and the founding of dynasties. Toward the latter part of the fourth century, inscriptions, murals, and carved stelae provide evidence that the empire of Teotihuacan (see p. 394) in Mexico's central highlands became an important player in Maya politics. In 378, the Teotihuacan-backed warlord Ochk'in K'awiil Siyaj K'ahk' (West-Lightning-Fire-Is-Born) and his men

KEY EVENTS

3114 BCE	2500 BCE	600–400 BCE	300 BCE	1st century CE	378
The mythological creation of the Maya world.	Sedentary agricultural life takes hold.	Monumental architecture and carved stone monuments appear.	The earliest known Maya writing is employed at San Bartolo in Guatemala.	The initial royal dynasties are founded.	Teotihuacan establishes its influence at Tikal.

deposed the ruler of the great city of Tikal, and over the next four decades new Teotihuacan-affiliated dynasties were established at Copán (see p. 396), Uaxactún, Río Azul, Palenque, and other sites. From the takeover until Tikal's defeat by Caracol in 562, Teotihuacan helped shape the geopolitics of the Maya world, and it may be no accident that Tikal's misfortunes coincide with the political collapse of Teotihuacan.

The decipherment of Maya hieroglyphic writing has transformed the archaeology of this region into a historically-based field of inquiry. The texts inscribed on monuments, temples, and tombs detail dated events that allow researchers to reconstruct the histories of many royal families (see image 3). These records narrate the rise of Calakmul, center of the Snake dynasty, as the new power in the wake of Tikal's conquest, a position it would hold until its own defeat in 695.

The texts and monuments dating to the latter part of the Classic period reflect the sustained and bitter rivalries among Maya dynasties, battle after battle in which captives were taken to be sacrificed, as rulers vied for vassals and tribute. Kings are often depicted on carved stelae and lintels (see image 2), standing triumphantly upon or in front of their soon-to-be sacrificed captives; combat and victorious celebration are also the themes of Bonampak's unparalleled murals; and even the more delicate art of vase painting (see image 1), at which Maya artists excelled, reveals the constant martial leitmotif. The decipherment of the Maya's words tells a story of powerful competitive kings, shifting alliances, glorious victories and crushing defeats.

One of archaeology's great mysteries has to do with the collapse of the Classic Maya political system. During the ninth century, in the midst of constant warfare, city after city ceased to erect commemorative monuments and few new building programs were initiated. The last dated monument was dedicated at Toniná in 909, and after that most of the southern tropical forest cities were abandoned.

Stress related to growing tribute demands to sustain elaborate ceremonial spectacles, economic competition from neighboring areas, the interruption of trade along the river systems, disease, internal factionalism, and the mounting power of the nobility have been proposed as explanations for the decline of the southern Maya dynasties. Some scholars hold that royal power was eroded by the ecological damage caused by the mismanagement of the fragile rain forest environment, as jungle was cleared to feed growing populations, while others argue that a prolonged drought exacerbated existing problems, creating a downward spiral from which there was no return. The mystery of the Maya demise, however, is that the region never recovered its former importance. In contrast, in the northern Yucatan Peninsula, Classic Maya centers like Uxmal and Kabah, which survived into the tenth century, witnessed the rise of a challenging new ideology at Chichén Itzá. **PPN**

378–436	830–910	850–1150	1220–1440	1502	1524–1697
Teotihuacan-affiliated dynasties are founded at many sites.	The southern Maya centers collapse.	The rise of the Toltec-Maya state at Chichén Itzá.	The Mayapan confederacy replaces Chichén Itzá as the center of power.	Italian explorer Christopher Columbus (1451–1506) encounters a Maya trading canoe off the coast of Honduras.	The Spanish Conquest of the Maya brings with it conflict and disease.

Maya Glyphs *c.* 300 BCE – *c.* 1600 CE

Commissioned in 667 by Ruler 2, Piedras Negras Panel 2 depicts an earlier king, Ah Cauac Ah k'in, with his son behind him, as he receives vassals from Yaxchilan, Bonampak, and Lacanha. The surrounding text describes this as a "war helmet ceremony" that took place in 510.

For the Maya, the sixteenth century was a calamitous time. Christopher Columbus (1451–1506) made the first contact with them in 1502, and in the following decades successive expeditions introduced foreign diseases, which led to the demise of up to 90 percent of the native population. The Spanish missionaries, who arrived in the 1520s, proceeded to burn all of the native books and cult items they could find in order to root out pagan practices. Thus, disease and religion brought literate Maya culture to an end.

Luckily, one Spanish monk, Diego de Landa (1524–79), wrote a treatise on Maya culture, which included an "alphabet." Four hundred years later, in 1952, Russian scholar Yuri Knorozov (1922–99) showed that this alphabet was actually a syllabary, an observation that paved the way for the decipherment of one of the most beautiful systems of visual language ever devised. Shortly afterward, as Tatiana Proskouriakoff (1909–85) plotted stylistic changes in the sculpture of Piedras Negras, Guatemala, she found a patterning of glyphs and dates that seemed to reflect events in the human life cycle; correlating these data, she was then able to identify the signs for birth, enthronement, capture, and death, and so demonstrate that the ancient inscriptions dealt mainly with royal life histories.

More recently, scholars have shown that Maya writing was developed in the first millennium BCE by members of the Greater Ch'olan language family. Half of its 800 symbols have been deciphered, and many others are at least partially understood. Like early Sumerian cuneiform, Maya script consists of signs for words and signs for syllables (which are phonetic), and allows for a complete rendition of the spoken language. As part of their artistic endeavor, skilled noble scribes developed numerous variants of these signs, creating a dazzling calligraphy to register the deeds of their rulers and conjure their gods. **PPN**

CHOCOLATE-DRINKING VESSEL

The glyphs around the rim identify this as Chuy-ti Chan's chocolate-drinking vessel; his father, an eighth-century ruler of the Ik' kingdom, sits on the throne. Chemical analysis of the ceramic paste shows that the vase was made in another kingdom, suggesting that it was a gift crafted specially for the king's son.

A MAYA REVIVAL

Deciphering the Maya script took 150 years of intermittent work. After the initial recognition of the bar-and-dot counting system by Constantine Rafinesque (1783–1840) in 1832, it was not until 1960 that Tatiana Proskouriakoff established the historical nature of the inscriptions. By the end of the twentieth century the decipherment of the forgotten script began to reopen the doors to an ancient past.

After being silenced for 500 years by the imposition of Hispanic culture, Maya history is now finally being returned to the Maya. Spurred by the desire of epigrapher Linda Schele (1942–98) to return the hieroglyphs to modern Maya communities, MAM (Maya for Ancient Mayan) was founded to bring scholars together in international conferences and to transfer their work to the six million living Maya so that they would have first-hand access to the words of their forefathers. The organization sponsors workshops taught by the Maya themselves in their own languages in Mexico and Guatemala.

DRESDEN CODEX

The Dresden Codex is one of three (or four) native books that survived the evangelization process. Copied from earlier texts during the thirteenth century, it enabled Ernst Förstermann (1822–1906) to determine the initial date of the Maya calendar as August 11, 3114 BCE. The codex deals with gods, divination, and astronomy.

NORTH AMERICAN ARCHAEOLOGY

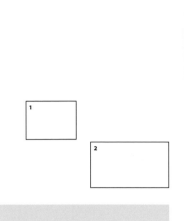

1 Head-Smashed-In Buffalo Jump was in use from *c*. 5500 BCE to the Historic period. Bison were herded from natural gathering basins into stone drive lanes and then stampeded over the cliff. At the base of the cliff, the animals were butchered and then moved to base camps located away from the kill site itself.

2 Serpent Mound is an effigy mound that is about 1,300 feet (396 m.) long and 1 to 3 feet (0.3–0.9 m.) high. It may represent a snake eating an egg. Recent radiocarbon dating places the construction of this mound to *c*. 300 BCE.

The earliest evidence for humans in the New World stretches back almost 20,000 years (see p. 40). Surer evidence exists for human occupation at the end of the Pleistocene (*c*. 10,000 BCE), when early hunter-gatherers hunted large game (megafauna) such as the mammoth, mastodon, and giant bison. Their archaeological remains comprise kill sites where the animals were killed and butchered. These hunters left behind skeletons and also beautifully worked projectile points, of which Clovis and Folsom are the best examples.

As the overall climate of the continent warmed, the megafauna became extinct and bison evolved into smaller species. In some parts of the continent, the hunting of bison continued as the mainstay of Native American culture. In states such as Colorado, Montana, and Wyoming, and the Canadian provinces of Alberta and Saskatchewan, Native Americans developed the technique of herding hundreds of the animals into specially constructed corrals or driving them over cliffs. These "catastrophic kills" show a high level of community planning and organization. A very good example of this is the Head-Smashed-In Buffalo Jump (see image 1), located in southern Alberta.

Elsewhere on the continent, the warming climate initiated the Archaic Period (approximately 8000–2000 BCE; see p. 70). Hunters and gatherers relied on a wider range of animals and plants and they also developed new technologies. Toward the end of the Archaic period Native Americans began the domestication of plants. This allowed them to become more sedentary and over time villages emerged, and then, in two regions in particular, what could

KEY EVENTS

18,000 BCE	10,000 BCE	8000 BCE	5500 BCE	3000 BCE	2200 BCE
Early evidence of humans is laid down in the New World at Pedra Furada, Brazil.	The Pleistocene ends as the great glaciers retreat northward and global warming conditions lead to the Holocene.	The Archaic period begins. Later, a gradual change occurs from a nomadic lifestyle to a more sedentary one.	Bison are first herded over the 30-foot (9 m.) cliff at Head-Smashed-In Buffalo Jump, Alberta, Canada.	The domestication of plants begins (animals are not domesticated, with the exception of dogs and, in the southwest, turkeys).	The migration into the High Arctic from Alaska takes place. Arctic peoples focus on the exploitation of terrestrial and marine resources.

legitimately be called towns. Interestingly, these two regions were dissimilar environmentally. The dry deserts of the southwestern United States (Arizona, New Mexico, and the southern parts of Colorado and Utah; see p. 408) saw the development of great pueblos made of stone and timber, and the creation of complex water control systems. These ancient peoples also made exquisite pottery. In the second area, located along the southeastern seaboard and up along the Mississippi River, farmers lived in small villages. Along the banks of the Illinois and Ohio rivers, Woodland peoples (1000 BCE to 1000 CE) built earthen mounds in a variety of shapes and for a variety of functions. Conical grave mounds were often organized into distinct cemeteries. Other structures were so-called "effigy mounds," such as Serpent Mound (see image 2) in Ohio. The culmination of these processes is seen in the Mississippian culture.

Native American cultures were changed radically when European colonization occurred. The earliest evidence of this is the few Viking settlements along the coastline of northeast North America (see p. 432). Europeans brought with them the scourge of smallpox and economic, cultural, and religious oppression, from which the tribes of the continent have still not fully recovered. The Battle of the Little Big Horn (see p. 512) was the best-known example of Native American resistance to American annexation of their land. **PD**

c. 300 BCE	800 CE	800	1000	16th century	1876
The Serpent Mound is constructed near Peebles, Ohio. The snake depicted is open-mouthed with its tail closely coiled.	Complex societies begin to appear in the southwestern United States.	The Mississippian culture develops. It becomes a highly stratified society reliant on a vast trading network and intensive farming (see p. 406).	The Viking settlement of northeastern North America is established at L'Anse aux Meadows, Newfoundland.	European colonization by Spanish, French, and English explorers is in full force. The Spanish move into North America from their colonies in Mexico.	The Battle of the Little Big Horn takes place. It is the last major victory by Plains Indians over the U.S. Cavalry.

Cahokia 800 – 1550

The largest of the Cahokia mounds is Monks Mound. This earthen platform mound, with a footprint of 15 acres (6 ha.), rises almost 100 feet (30 m.) over the surrounding landscape. It was topped by a wooden structure that may have been a chieftain's house, a religious building, or a combination. The mound may have taken 200 years to complete.

The Mississippian-culture site of Cahokia is the largest pre-Columbian settlement in North America. It is located east of modern-day St. Louis, close to the confluence of the Missouri and Mississippi rivers. Cahokia comprises a wooden stockade 2 miles (3 km.) long and a large central plaza, satellite plazas, and communal buildings, and numerous earthen mounds. Platform mounds are flat-topped and pyramidical, and were topped by wooden buildings. Other mounds contained burials and are both conical and trapezoidal in shape. The so-called Mound 72 was the final resting place for an important male in his forties. He was interred with grave goods, including a cache of arrowheads, and more than 200 skeletons were found buried in the mound.

West of Cahokia, archaeologists have located a series of postholes arranged into five circles. The site has been dubbed Woodhenge. One of the circles, comprising forty-eight posts, was reconstructed in 1985 with a diameter of 400 feet (122 m.). The posts clearly had astronomical and calendrical significance, marking solstices and equinoxes.

Cahokia was occupied between 800 and 1400. It relied on the intensive cultivation of maize, beans, and squash, which may have supported a maximum population of 20,000. Specialized craftsmen working in clay, wood, copper, shell, and stone made tobacco pipes, effigies, masks, headdresses and weapons, both functional and symbolic, to name just a few. Cahokia was the center of a far-flung trade network extending from the Gulf of Mexico to Hudson Bay, and from the eastern seaboard to the Great Plains. Owing to its early date, some archaeologists have suggested that Cahokia was the model for all subsequent Mississippian centers. **PD**

AMERICAN BOTTOM

Cahokia was organized around a central plaza surrounded by platform mounds and burial mounds. This photograph clearly shows the fertility of this area, known as the American Bottom. Unfortunately, modern development continues to encroach on the site's integrity.

KELLER FIGURINE

The variety of objects found in Mississippian sites includes wood, shell, and copper, and well-preserved textiles, baskets, and feathers. Many of them were part of religious rituals. This object, known as the Keller figurine, was made of flint clay, locally available in the Cahokia area. It depicts a woman engaged in a corn ceremony.

CIVILIZATION DEBATE

The Mississippian culture lasted from approximately 800 to 1550 and is found in a huge section of the southeastern United States extending as far east as Florida and as far west as Oklahoma, with large population centers located in the rich river plains of the Mississippi and its tributaries. As is to be expected, given the vastness of its reach, the Mississippian culture exhibits much geographical and cultural variation.

Scholars dispute the precise political organization that underpinned Cahokian and Mississippian society. All scholars recognize that society was ranked, meaning it had some form of social classes, because the organization needed to build such huge structures would have necessitated some degree of ranking. Moreover, the disparity in the type of graves and grave goods found in Mississippian burials also points to a social hierarchy. However, there is disagreement over the intensity of this ranking and whether it was

permanent or fluid; the basis of this ranking and whether it was economic, religious, or both; and the degree to which Cahokia and other Mississippian polities were themselves hierarchically ranked.

Mississippian sites, especially Cahokia, have been the subject of the debate regarding whether they are a civilization or not. For archaeologists, especially those working in the Old World, the term "civilization" constitutes a stage of human society with a number of variable criteria, such as cities, class ranking, professional standing army, writing, and so on. North American archaeologists have been less concerned to determine whether a prehistoric society is civilized or not. What is less controversial is that Cahokia and other large Mississippian sites were urban centers with large populations and a clearly delineated social ranking that was economic, political, and religious in nature.

Chaco Canyon 850 – 1250

An overview of Chaco Canyon, with Pueblo del Arroyo Great House in the foreground. Although the arroyo ran only seasonally, the villagers were able to harness the water that flooded off the canyon top during the spring rainy season through a series of complex dams and ditches that fed the fields along the canyon floor.

In the high desert of northern New Mexico, Chaco Canyon was the centre of a cluster of Ancestral Pueblo villages that flourished between 850 and 1250. Archaeologists have discovered a series of villages of varying size along a 12-mile (19 km.) section of the canyon. The thirteen villages, sometimes called "Great Houses," typically comprise a number of interconnected rooms (residential and storage), and circular religious structures, or kivas, arranged around central plazas. Satellite imagery has revealed that Chaco Canyon was the hub of a network of ancient roads totalling approximately 400 miles (650 km.) that connected the canyon to outlying Chacoan sites. These roads were very straight, not deviating from their paths to avoid natural obstacles. There is evidence at Chaco of trade objects that came from contemporary Mesoamerican (see p. 392) cultures, such as copper bells and macaw skeletons. The consensus of archaeological opinion is that Chaco Canyon was occupied permanently, perhaps as a regional, even international, trade center. However, some scholars have suggested that it was occupied only periodically for pan-regional religious gatherings.

The Ancestral Pueblo Tradition (formerly called the Anasazi Tradition) is one of three contemporary traditions of the southwestern United States: the Ancestral Pueblo, centered on the Four Corners region where the states of Colorado, Utah, Arizona, and New Mexico converge; the Hohokam Tradition, found in the Sonoran Desert of south-central Arizona; and the Mogollon, located in southern New Mexico and extending into northern Mexico. The three traditions emerged from the preceding Desert Archaic as separate entities about 2,000 years ago and lasted at least until c. 1450. **PD**

PUEBLO BONITO

Pueblo Bonito is the largest of the Great Houses. It contained at least 300 individual rooms, and thirty-two kivas. Many of the structures, made from carefully shaped stone masonry, may have stood four or five storeys high. The building techniques were so good that many of Bonito's walls still stand.

CHACO POTTERY

Chaco potters followed the ceramic tradition of the northern southwest but developed their own style. They made objects such as storage containers for food and water, cooking vessels, ladles and rattles. This pitcher was recovered from Pueblo Bonito. The paint was made from plant dyes and applied with a yucca brush.

ARCHAEOLOGY IN THE SOUTHWESTERN UNITED STATES

The American Southwest has probably the longest tradition of archaeological exploration on the continent. At the end of the nineteenth century, museums— especially on the eastern seaboard—were hungry for objects to fill their display cases, and reports of the impressive pottery and turquoise objects that were being discovered attracted early antiquarians. The uncontrolled digging of "Indian curios," for private profit increased.

Sites like Chaco Canyon and Mesa Verde (located in southwest Colorado and boasting almost 5,000 Ancestral Puebloan sites, 600 of which are cliff dwellings) were excavated for their treasures, sometimes by unscrupulous pot hunters who sold their loot to private collectors in the United States and abroad. The damage done to sites at Mesa Verde forced the U.S. government to pass the Federal Antiquities Act of 1906, which provided some degree of protection for archaeological sites.

The excellent preservation of archaeological sites and artifacts that resulted from the region's aridity meant that southwestern archaeologists were at the forefront of the developing discipline of archaeology. In the early part of the twentieth century, stratigraphic excavation (see p. 530) was applied to southwestern sites long before many other areas of the United States. In addition, southwestern archaeologists led by Alfred V. Kidder (1885–1963) were among the first on the continent to develop the organization of artifacts by stylistic change through time, which allowed archaeologists much better control in dating sites.

Finally, dendrochronology, or tree-ring dating (see p. 532), was first developed in the southwest, the result of the extensive use of timber in building construction. For the first time on the continent, archaeologists had a technique for assigning absolute calendrical dates to their sites.

BYZANTIUM

1   The Hippodrome of Constantinople in Istanbul. The circus was the sporting and social center of Constantinople, the capital of the Byzantine Empire.

2   Emperor Theodosius I removed the Obelisk of Thutmose III from Karnak, Egypt and erected it on the racing track at the Hippodrome. The sculptures on the base of the obelisk show Theodosius I and his family watching a chariot race.

3   The Roman emperor Constantine I decorated his capital with artworks from across the empire. The Tripod of Plataia, now known as the Serpent Column, lies on the Hippodrome.

The city of Byzantium, later known as Constantinople, and then Istanbul, was founded as a Greek colony in the seventh century BCE. The city was situated on the western side of the narrow straits of the Hellespont; with a natural harbor known as the Golden Horn, Byzantium was in a strategic location, with access to the Aegean and the Black Seas.

Byzantium was sacked c. 195 CE as a result of its opposition to the Roman emperor Septimius Severus (145–211), but its importance made it impossible to ignore and Severus began its restoration shortly afterward. The city was refounded by the Roman emperor Constantine (c. 280–337) in 324 to serve as the new capital of the Roman Empire. It was officially inaugurated in 330, when it was renamed Constantinople. The city became the center of the Byzantine Empire, being particularly prosperous from the time of Justinian I (483–565), who reigned from 527 to 565. This was a time of conquest, with Byzantine power extending into modern-day Italy, North Africa, and Spain. Constantinople became a center of learning and fine architecture, to the extent that Procopius (c. 490–c. 560), court historian of Justinian, recorded in his work *On Buildings* (c. 558) that it was home to magnificent palaces and public buildings, of which almost nothing now remains.

A rare survival from an earlier era is the Hippodrome (see image 1), built by Severus in 203 and subsequently enlarged by Constantine. At 1,476 feet (450 m.) long it is estimated to have held up to 100,000 people. Constantinople was famous for chariot racing in the Hippodrome, with fierce rivalry between

KEY EVENTS

7th century BCE	203 CE	324	330	395	413
Byzantium is founded as a Greek colony in what is now the Old Town of Istanbul.	Construction of the Hippodrome, an area used for chariot racing, begins on the orders of the Roman emperor Septimius Severus.	Byzantium is refounded with the name Constantinople by the Roman emperor Constantine to serve as the new capital of the Roman Empire.	Constantinople is officially inaugurated. The new name means "the city of Constantine."	Theodosius I, the last emperor to rule over both eastern and western Roman empires, dies.	Theodosius II (401–450) commissions the first phase of construction of new city walls (see p. 412) to replace those built by Constantine.

the opposing supporters of different factions. Although the factions had originated as trade guilds in the Roman period, by the Byzantine era they had developed associations with political and religious views. An exception to the rivalry was in 532, when members of the Blue and Green factions joined to protest against the Emperor Justinian in the Nika (Victory) Riots. After much destruction, Justinian, with the support of his empress, Theodora (c. 500–548), ordered their suppression and more than 30,000 were killed in the Hippodrome. Unsurprisingly, chariot racing was subsequently banned for years following the riots. As well as chariot racing, the Hippodrome would have been used for ceremonies connected with the imperial court, a practice that continued into the Ottoman period. The Hippodrome was initially excavated in 1950 and 1951, and subsequent clearances for building in the 1980s and 1990s have revealed other architectural elements, most notably the curved end of the racing track, several rows of seats, and some columns.

There are two major monuments on the *spina* (central section) of the Hippodrome which were already several centuries old when installed. In the center is a bronze column in the form of twisted serpents (see image 3). This was originally part of a victory monument dedicated at the Panhellenic sanctuary of Delphi in central Greece. It commemorates the defeat of the Persians at the Battle of Plataia in 479 BCE by the Greek city states whose names were inscribed on the coils of the serpents. The Greek writer Thucydides (c. 460–c. 404 BCE), writing in the second half of the fifth century BCE, recorded that a golden tripod originally stood on the column. This is no longer present, nor are the heads of the serpents. The bronze column was taken to Byzantium when the city was refounded by Constantine as Constantinople. The other monument, the upper section of an Egyptian obelisk, originally commemorated the campaigns of the Egyptian ruler Thutmose III, who reigned from 1479 to 1425 BCE. The more recent images on the base (see image 2), which include Theodosius I (347–395) and his family watching a chariot race, commemorate the erection of the obelisk in Constantinople by Theodosius, and are an excellent example of Byzantine relief sculpture.

The city continued to thrive until it was plundered during the Fourth Crusade in 1204. The damage included the destruction and looting of the church of Hagia Sophia (see p. 414) dating to the sixth century, and the removal from the Hippodrome of a bronze statue of four horses, originally drawing a chariot. The horses, which date to the second or third century, were taken to Venice and placed on the facade of St. Mark's Basilica.

During the next 200 years, the Byzantine Empire contracted. In 1453 the city's walls were breached by the forces of the Ottoman ruler Mehmet II (1432–81), later known as Mehmet the Conqueror. The city was captured by the Ottomans after a siege on May 29, 1453, marking the formal end of the Roman and Byzantine empires. **GM**

527	532	726	9th century	1204	1453
Justinian I becomes emperor. During his reign, the Byzantine Empire expands and Constantinople becomes a center of learning.	Protesters from the Green and Blue chariot-racing factions destroy many buildings in the Nika Riots, including the church of Hagia Sophia.	The Iconoclastic period begins when Leo III (c. 675–741) issues an edict against representational art, which remains in force until 843.	Over the next three centuries, the walls of the rebuilt church of Hagia Sophia are decorated with magnificent mosaics.	The city of Constantinople is ransacked by soldiers of the Fourth Crusade on the way to Jerusalem.	The Byzantine Empire formally comes to an end on May 29 when Constantinople is captured by the forces of the Ottoman ruler Mehmet II.

Theodosian Walls Fifth century

The Theodosian Walls have been partially reconstructed. They still follow the gradient of the land. There were ninety-six towers, ten main gates, and several postern gates. This shows the outer wall and the wall of the moat, with a tower of the inner wall in the background.

Among the most stunning ancient monuments of Istanbul are the huge walls built by Theodosius II, who was Eastern Roman Emperor from 408 to 450. UNESCO recognized their significance in 1985, when the main city walls, referred to as the Land Walls, and their surroundings were included in the four historic areas of Istanbul to be inscribed as a World Heritage Site.

The Theodosian Walls were not the first city walls; ancient authors including Dio Cassius (c. 150–235) refer to the walls of Byzantium in Greek times. In the early third century the Roman emperor Septimius Severus, as part of his rebuilding of the city, doubled the size of the walled area. Constantine from c. 325 had new walls constructed 2 miles (3 km.) west of the Severan walls, which he had demolished.

The Theodosian Walls extended the area of the city. The walls stretch approximately 4 miles (7 km.) from the upper section of the Golden Horn to the shores of the Sea of Marmara. The first phase of construction, the main inner curtain wall and its towers, was completed in 413. However, an earthquake in 447 led to a reconstruction of part of the wall and its towers, which, according to literary sources, was undertaken in only sixty days. A second wall and moat were erected in front of the original wall, creating three lines of defense for the city, forming a barrier 230 feet (70 m.) thick.

The appearance of the walls has changed since the fifth century, with modifications being undertaken in the seventh and twelfth centuries. In addition, in the fifteenth century Mehmet II incorporated the city's main gate, part of the walls, and four of its towers into the fortress of Yedikule (Seven Towers). **GM**

BANDS OF BRICK

The inner wall was constructed with a core filled with mortar made of lime and crushed bricks. This was faced with limestone and included seven to eleven bands of brick, 16 inches (40 cm.) thick. As well as their decorative effect, the brick bands also served to strengthen the wall.

PERIBOLOS

The peribolos is a terrace that separates the main inner wall from the lower outer wall and is still visible on parts of the Theodosian Walls that have been renovated. The peribolos was between 50 to 64 feet (15–20 m.) wide and could accommodate soldiers to defend the outer wall.

GOLDEN GATES OF CONSTANTINOPLE

The two most famous gates of Constantinople both had the name Golden Gate, one set into the Constantinian Wall, the other into the Theodosian Walls. The name is found in a literary source written in 425, which names the gate in the Constantinian Wall as the Porta Aurea. This gate was destroyed in an earthquake in 1509 and the only surviving information about it is a description written in the fifteenth century.

The existing marble gate, set into the inner city wall, was probably erected by Theodosius II, being planned as part of the Theodosian Walls. Some scholars favor the view that the gate is earlier than the Theodosian Walls and was erected in the reign of Theodosius I and, accordingly, would have been a free-standing triumphal arch with three arched openings.

Literary accounts indicate that the inner gate supported a sculpture of a chariot drawn by two, or possibly four, elephants. The central arch of the gate has lines of small holes which indicate the position of two texts made from individual letters, likely to have been made from bronze, but now no longer present. The inscriptions were in Latin, which until the late fifth century remained the normal language of Roman imperial monuments, although the inscriptions on the Golden Gate could not have been read by most of the inhabitants of Constantinople, who would have spoken Greek.

When Mehmet II built the Yedikule fortress, the outer section of the Golden Gate became redundant and was sealed up, although it remains partly preserved. The columns, capitals, and bases which have been added to the gate are not from an original structure and have been reused. Fragments of some of the sculptures, including one depicting Victory, which decorated the gate have been recovered and are in Istanbul Archaeological Museum.

Hagia Sophia Sixth century

Restoration of Hagia Sophia's interior took place between 1847 and 1849 under the direction of Swiss-Italian architects Gaspare (1809–83) and Giuseppe Fossati (1822–91). At this time, medallions bearing the names of Allah, Muhammad (570–632), and the first four caliphs were suspended on the interior columns.

Hagia Sophia was the third church on this site in the city of Constantinople, now Istanbul. The second church was destroyed in the Nika Riots of 532, and the construction of the present building was begun immediately after by Emperor Justinian I, being completed in 537. The architects were Anthemius of Tralles (c. 474–c. 533) and Isidore of Miletus, who constructed a building so impressive that until the fifteenth century it was reputed to have been the largest known enclosed space. The building was damaged on several occasions over the centuries by a series of earthquakes. Twenty years after its completion the original central dome collapsed, to be replaced by a modified one, which necessitated the support of additional buttresses. The top of the present dome is 180 feet (55 m.) from ground level, and measures approximately 105 feet (32 m.) from north to south and 101 feet (31 m.) from east to west. Hagia Sophia was ransacked in 1204 by soldiers of the Fourth Crusade, who destroyed the altar. Following the capture of the city in 1453 by Ottoman ruler Mehmet II, the building became a mosque. Additions to the interior include the *mihrab* (niche pointing in the direction of Mecca) and *minbar* (pulpit). The building functioned as a mosque until 1932, after which time it was converted into a museum by President Kemal Atatürk (1881–1938), opening in 1935. Modifications at this time included the exposure of Byzantine wall mosaics.

An intriguing feature of Hagia Sophia is an inscription carved in the ninth century into the marble barrier in the south gallery. The runic inscription gives the names of two Vikings called Halvdan and Are. It is possible that Halvdan and Are were mercenaries, or even serving as bodyguards to the Byzantine emperor. **GM**

⟪◉⟫ FOCAL POINTS

MINARETS

The four minarets rise to a height of 197 feet (60 m.) and were added gradually to Hagia Sophia after it became a mosque. The earliest dates to the late fifteenth century or early sixteenth century; the other three were added over the next 100 years. The pressure of the main dome necessitated both the internal support of half-domes, and the gradual addition of twenty-four external buttresses during the Byzantine and Ottoman periods.

OMPHALION

The Omphalion is the name given to an *opus sectile* mosaic 18 feet (5.5 m.) square in the middle of the southeastern quarter of the space under the dome. A central disk of gray granite is surrounded by smaller disks of stones including red and green porphyry and pink granite, the whole inside a border of green marble. The use of the mosaic, probably laid in the ninth century, is unknown, although it may be where emperors were crowned.

BYZANTINE MOSAICS

Hagia Sophia is noted for the fine examples of Byzantine mosaics from different eras. The mosaics were made from small pieces of glass—either colored or covered with gold and silver leaf—with mother of pearl.

The earliest mosaics, either plain gold or abstract designs, date from the time of the Iconoclastic emperors, between 726 and 843.

The figured mosaics date from after this era, with perhaps the earliest being in the apse of the church; it depicts the Virgin and Child. There are a number of well-executed examples found in the south gallery of Hagia Sophia. Some depict members of the imperial court, such as the mosaic showing the emperor Constantine IX Monomachus (c. 980–1055) and the empress Zoë (c. 978–1050), who ruled in her own right with her sister Theodora (c. 981–1056) before her marriage. Another mosaic, dated to 1118, depicts the Virgin and Child between the emperor

John II Comnenus (1087–1143) and the empress Irene (1088–1134), with an image of their young son, Alexius (1106–42), added later.

Perhaps the best known mosaic from Hagia Sophia shows a composition known as a Deisis showing Christ, the Virgin, and St. John the Baptist, dating to the thirteenth century.

Not all the mosaics are complete today; in particular, only three of the original seven figures of Patriarchs on the western tympanum, the area below the dome, are in good condition.

A particularly fine mosaic in Hagia Sophia is in the vestibule. It shows the Virgin and Child flanked by the emperors Justinian I and Constantine I, and is dated to between 975 and 1000. Both emperors are depicted making offerings to the Virgin—Justinian gives a model of the church of Hagia Sophia and Constantine a model of the city of Constantinople.

GERMANIC BARBARIANS

W hen the Roman armies overran Gaul in the last century BCE, they established two provinces on the west bank of the Rhine river—in today's Netherlands, Belgium, and eastern France—that they called Germania Inferior and Germania Superior. To the east of the Rhine lay a large territory that Romans called Germania Magna. Although the Romans may have entertained hopes of establishing new provinces across the Rhine, their expeditions into the area resulted in failure.

For several centuries, the Romans and the Germanic barbarians coexisted across a tense but porous Imperial frontier. A lively trade emerged in the products of Roman workshops that were desired by the barbarians, and in agricultural and forest products such as grain, meat, and furs that the barbarians could supply to the Romans. By the fourth century CE, the barbarians had become organized into tribal political units. Many of them had served in the Roman military and then returned home, bringing their knowledge of weapons and tactics with them. They also brought the Roman coins with which they had been paid (see image 3), and the barbarian elites sought these not for their face value but as markers of prestige. Within the Imperial frontiers, Roman authority broke down. Groups of barbarians took advantage of local political vacuums and began to move into Roman territories.

1 A reconstructed Anglo-Saxon village at West Stow in Suffolk, England.

2 Gold and garnet sword hilts and scabbards from the grave furnishings of the Frankish king Childeric I.

3 A sixth-century gold bracteate based on a Byzantine coin from a Norwegian hoard.

KEY EVENTS

58 BCE	9 CE	43	166–180	c. 200	410
Gaius Julius Caesar (c. 100–44 BCE) invades Gaul.	German tribes defeat Roman general Publius Quinctilius Varus's legions at the Battle of the Teutoburg Forest in northwest Germany. He kills himself.	The Romans invade Britain.	The Germanic barbarians and Romans fight along the Danube frontier in the Marcomannic Wars.	A war-booty sacrifice is made at Illerup Adal in East Jutland, Denmark.	The Visigoths sack Rome.

Historians characterize the fourth to the seventh centuries as the Migration period during which large movements of populations occurred. These have been described by chroniclers, often writing a century or more after the movements are believed to have occurred. Archaeologists often find such migrations difficult to document. Migrating peoples left few traces of abrupt cultural change in the archaeological record. Instead, it seems that groups of barbarians joined their brethren who had settled in the Roman frontier, many of whom had adopted Roman customs and the Latin language, while being sufficiently disruptive to be discussed as intrusive aliens by later chroniclers.

The Goths arrived from the east and crossed the Roman frontier along the lower Danube. Some archaeologists believe that they can be traced to northern Poland during the second century before they moved southeast to the area north of the Black Sea before turning to the west. During the fourth century they became divided into two separate branches. The Ostrogoths remained in southeastern Europe, while the Visigoths moved farther west and sacked Rome. Many of them settled within the Roman territories. When the Huns from central Asia entered central Europe and fought their way into eastern France, a combined force of Romans and Visigoths stopped them.

Many other barbarian groups originated directly from Germania Magna. These include the Vandals, who were pushed out of central Europe into the Roman territories and eventually went to Spain and even North Africa, and the Alemanni, who clashed with the Romans along their frontier in southern Germany during the third and fourth centuries. During the fourth century the Franks crossed into Belgium and northern France and settled down. As Roman authority declined, Frankish kings became more prominent. Among them was Childeric I (d. 482), who was buried at Tournai, Belgium. Workmen discovered his grave (see image 2) in 1653. It reveals much about the Frankish royal succession, since his tomb would have been arranged by his son, Clovis (c. 466–511). Multiple horse burials were found nearby, echoing practices found centuries earlier on the steppes. The eighty-nine Roman gold coins found with him were from the reigns of highly regarded emperors covering centuries. Three hundred gold bees decorated the cloak in which Childeric was buried. The Merovingian royal dynasty that emerged with Childeric and continued for several centuries is seen as the foundation of French national identity.

In eastern England, migrants from Germania Magna arrived during the fifth century. This was portrayed by later chroniclers as having been a deluge of immigrants who overwhelmed native Romano-British communities, but again archaeology does not support this. Instead, the Anglo-Saxons appear to have arrived as small groups who lived side by side with native communities with little disruption (see image 1). Eventually, they came to occupy the upper strata of society, so that during the sixth and seventh centuries there were a number of Anglo-Saxon kingdoms throughout eastern England. **PB**

451	476	481	c. 625	793	2009
The Romans and Visigoths defeat an army of Huns led by Attila (d. 453) in France, which retreats eastward.	The end of the Roman Empire in the west. The Germanic leader Odoacer (c. 433–493) overthrows Romulus (r. 475–476) and then rules Rome.	Childeric is buried at Tournai wearing a signet ring bearing an inscription. He is interred with 300 Roman coins covering five centuries.	An Anglo-Saxon king, possibly Raedwald (r. c. 599–c. 625), is buried at Sutton Hoo, near Woodbridge in East Anglia, England (see p. 420).	Vikings raid the Christian monastery on the island of Lindisfarne off the northeast coast of England, signaling the start of the Viking Age.	The Staffordshire Hoard of seventh-century Anglo-Saxon objects is discovered in a field in Hammerwich, Staffordshire, England (see p. 418).

Staffordshire Hoard   c. 550 – 670

Objects from the Staffordshire Hoard. Discovered buried beneath a farmer's field in Staffordshire, England, it is the largest hoard of Anglo-Saxon gold ever found.

◆ NAVIGATOR

The Staffordshire Hoard is the name given to a large group of Anglo-Saxon objects discovered in 2009 in a field in Hammerwich, Staffordshire, England, by a metal detectorist. In 2012, the same field yielded almost ninety additional objects. The hoard contains more than 4,000 objects made from gold, silver, and copper alloy, and decorated with materials such as garnets. The style of the objects suggests that most were made in England between c. 550 to 670, with the majority dating from the seventh century, although the reason for burying them is unknown. The hoard contained just over 11 pounds (5 kg.) of gold and just over 3 pounds (1.4 kg.) of silver. Scientific analysis of various gold objects indicates that in many cases the original artisans knew how to treat the upper surfaces to make the gold more pure and accordingly appear more golden.

A very rare find was a helmet, only the fifth Anglo-Saxon helmet to be discovered in England, which had seemingly been dismantled prior to being buried. Archaeologists have identified about 1,500 thin pieces of silver, some gilded, many less than ⅜ inch (10 mm.) across, from the helmet. The designs include real and imaginary animals and birds, together with warriors, some of whom themselves wear helmets. Helmet bands, ear pieces, most of the cap, and the crest from the helmet have been found among the hoard.

Many of the items from the hoard had been removed from the objects they decorated before they were buried. These include one made of thick sheet gold, which shows two eagles facing each other and holding a fish vertically between them. Although the piece's function is not definitely known, it is likely that it was a mount from a shield. **GM**

◉ FOCAL POINTS

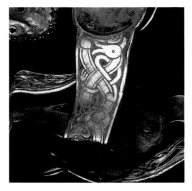

1 FOLDED CROSS

A large gold cross is thought to have been folded to save space within the hoard before it was buried. Such a large cross may have been used in processions, on an altar or to decorate the front of a bible. A reconstructed replica of this cross was presented to Pope Benedict XVI on his visit to the United Kingdom in 2010.

2 SWORD FITTINGS

Many objects were parts of swords: pommel caps, upper and lower hilt guards, and hilt collars. Over seventy pommel caps were found, made from gold and silver. Many were decorated with inlaid garnets, glass, or rock crystal. There were several pyramid-shaped objects, originally from straps holding the sword in its scabbard.

3 INSCRIBED BAND

A band of gilt silver bears a biblical inscription in Latin. The text, which differs slightly on either side, is: "Rise up, O Lord, and may thy enemies be dispersed and those who hate thee be driven from thy face" (Numbers 10:35). Rivet holes suggest it was originally attached to another object, perhaps a reliquary or a bible.

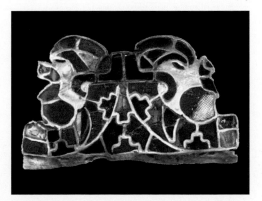

▲ Three pieces from the hoard were identified as belonging together, although the purpose of the object is unknown. One is a stud with a piece of multicolored glass, the largest piece of glass in the hoard. It slots into a cylinder decorated with garnets, which in turn fits a base plate ornamented with garnets and gold plates with animal designs.

CLOISONNÉ TECHNIQUE

Many of the gold objects from the Staffordshire Hoard were ornamented with garnets, and sometimes glass, using the decorative technique now known as *cloisonné*, from the French word *cloison*, meaning "cell." A pattern of small cells was first fabricated using thin gold strips. A paste made from beeswax was put at the bottom of each cell, supporting a piece of textured gold foil below a thin piece of garnet, both of which had been cut to the shape of the cell. Because many of the objects are damaged, it is possible to see the backing foils where garnets have been dislodged, such as on the right of the sword mount. The purpose of the gold foil was to reflect light and make the object flash. In addition to the *cloisonné* technique, some large garnets were mounted, such as on the cross.

Sutton Hoo Seventh century

An imprint of the buried ship under Mound 1 was found during excavations in 1939. The boat was 14 feet (4.5. m.) across at its widest point, and 5 feet (1.5 m.) deep. Its sides were constructed using the clinker technique with nine overlapping planks, probably of oak, riveted together. The sides were reinforced with twenty-six interior frames.

In 1938, landowner Edith Pretty (1883–1942) engaged a local archaeologist, Basil Brown (1888–1977), to investigate a group of barrows on her estate along the Deben river near the North Sea coast of eastern England. Although the first mounds that Brown and his helpers dug at Sutton Hoo had been robbed in antiquity, they found enough to establish that they dated to the Anglo-Saxon period in the second half of the first millennium, and covered cremation burials. Brown focused his attention on a single large mound, designated Mound 1, during his work the following year. In it, they found rows of iron rivets in the trench. Brown concluded that he had uncovered a buried boat whose planks had decayed, leaving the rivets embedded in the soil. He followed the outline of the boat, which reached 89 feet (27 m.) long, and then followed the rows of rivets down to the bottom. Archaeologist Charles W. Phillips (1901–85) of the University of Cambridge took charge of the excavations of the central burial chamber in 1939. With war looming over Europe, excavation of the central burial chamber began on July 13 and continued for seventeen days. The burial deposit contained 263 artifacts, including textiles and wooden, bronze, iron, silver, and gold items.

Archaeologists returned to Sutton Hoo in 1965 to 1971 and in 1983 to 1992 to finish the excavation of Mound 1 and excavate other mounds. They established that Sutton Hoo was a cemetery for the Anglo-Saxon elite and determined the sequence in which the mounds were built. In c. 600, cremations in bronze bowls were placed under mounds 33 to 50 feet (10–15 m.) in diameter. Next, a young man was buried in a wooden coffin c. 610, along with weapons, a bronze cauldron, and a backpack containing lamb chops. His horse lay nearby under the same mound. Two ship burials were constructed c. 625, including the Mound 1. Burials continued through the remainder of the seventh century. **PB**

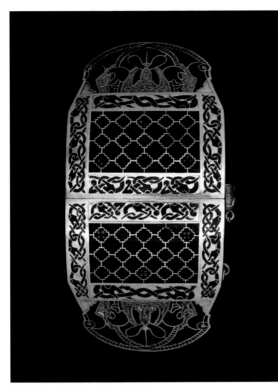

SHOULDER CLASP

The burial chamber in Mound 1 contained precious objects including a gold shoulder clasp inlaid with garnet cloisonné and glass. The garnets come from western Asia and are underlaid with gold foil. The clasp has loops for attaching it to a garment. The central panel is bordered with designs of interlacing beasts.

HELMET RECONSTRUCTION

Armour in the burial under Mound 1 included an iconic iron helmet that has been reconstructed. Probably modeled on late Roman parade helmets, it is covered with copper panels with warrior motifs. Its face guard depicts a flying creature with wings spread over the eyebrows and its body extending down over the nose.

WHO WAS BURIED AT SUTTON HOO?

Shortly after the discovery of the sumptuous burial at Sutton Hoo in 1939, historian H. Munro Chadwick (1870–1947) hypothesized that the grave in the ship under Mound 1 was that of Raedwald, king of East Anglia from c. 599 to c. 625. Raedwald is known from the account of the Venerable Bede (c. 672–735), writing a century later. He had accepted Christianity and used this connection to his advantage, but then abandoned it. The identification of Sutton Hoo with Raedwald has persisted in scholarly circles, although it is far from certain. It is clear that the person buried in the Sutton Hoo ship was a member of the high-born Anglo-Saxon elite, and almost certainly a king, but exactly who remains equivocal.

The burial under Mound 1 at Sutton Hoo displays interesting Scandinavian connections, taken as reflecting interaction across the North Sea. Burial in a ship is a Scandinavian practice, seen in roughly contemporaneous chieftains' graves at Vendel and Valsgärde near Stockholm. The similarity of the helmet from Sutton Hoo to one from Valsgärde is striking. The historian Alex Woolf (b. 1963) has argued that the central Swedish graves and the one at Sutton Hoo were both connected to emergent kingdoms in southern Scandinavia during the early seventh century.

The elites who organized the cemetery at Sutton Hoo were almost certainly pagans who resisted efforts at Christianization, and the overtly pagan character of the burial rites is interpreted as a reaction to missionaries dispatched from the Merovingian Empire. The Scandinavian character of the boat and weapons has been taken to signal the declaration of an ideological alliance with pagan Scandinavia against the Christianity coming from continental Europe. However, the presence in the Sutton Hoo burial of coins and other artifacts with continental connections complicates this interpretation.

ARABS

I n 613 a new religion, Islam, began to develop in Mecca, through the teachings of the prophet Muhammad. In 622 he and his followers fled to Medina: this event, the Hegira, marks the beginning of the Muslim era. The religion spread rapidly within Arabia and by 633 Muslim armies were overrunning Iraq and Syria. In 636 they decisively defeated the Sasanians at Qadisiya, capturing their capital Ctesiphon (Iraq) in 637 and conquering their empire by 642. The Muslim forces also seized Cairo (see p. 424), Egypt, and much of North Africa, reaching Spain by 711; the following year they conquered Sindh and western central Asia up to the Syr Darya river. By this time a Muslim state had been established and in 661 Mu'awiya, emir of Syria, declared himself Fifth Caliph, founding the Ummayad caliphate.

Later, in 750, disaffection in the eastern region culminated in a revolt that overthrew the Ummayads and created the Abbasid caliphate. Around the same time, Arab expansion beyond the Amu Darya had clashed with the Tang Chinese, Tibetans, and Turghiz. In 751, on the border of present-day Kazakhstan and Kyrgyzstan, the Battle of Talas, though won by the Arabs, set a limit to their further expansion and defined the spheres of influence of powers in the region.

1 A fountain and inner courtyard of the only surviving Abbasid palace in Baghdad, Iraq. It was erected under Caliph Al-Naser Ledinillah (1179–1225).

2 An earthenware dish decorated with blue underglaze, dating from the ninth century (Abbasid period).

KEY EVENTS

622	632	661	from 751	756	762
Enduring hostility in his native city, Mecca, the prophet Muhammad, his family, and followers flee to Medina (the Hegira).	The prophet Muhammad dies; the caliphate under Abu Bakr starts, succeeded by Umar in 634 and then Uthman in 644.	Ali, Muhammad's son-in-law and fourth caliph, is murdered. A growing schism leads to the Ummayad caliphate and the Sunni and Shi'ite sects.	The Arabs learn papermaking technology from Chinese captured at the Battle of Talas; a paper mill is set up at Baghdad.	Ummayad emir Abd al-Rahman I (731–788) breaks away from the Abbasid caliphate and founds the independent emirate of Cordoba in Spain.	Baghdad is founded by Caliph al-Mansur (c. 714–775) as capital of the new Abbasid Empire; by 814 Baghdad is probably the world's largest city.

Under the Abbasids the Islamic world enjoyed peace and stability. They founded a new capital at Baghdad in 766; this shifted to Samarra (see p. 426) in 836 but reverted back to Baghdad in 892. Baghdad was a renowned center of culture and learning, particularly under the famous caliph Harun al-Rashid (763/4–809). Arab scholars accumulated knowledge of the cultural, scientific, and technological achievements of their predecessors, including the Greeks and Romans, and built on these foundations to make their own advances in mathematics, medicine, astronomy, architecture, and many other fields. The Abbasids built palaces and mosques in every city, including Baghdad (see image 1); some of them were remarkable architectural achievements.

This period saw the peak of Silk Road trade (see p. 268), in which the Arabs participated. Trade flourished in many directions, including from North Africa across the Sahara to the developing cities of the West African savanna. Arab merchants engaged significantly in maritime trade, taking advantage of the monsoon winds and sailing down the Red Sea or the Gulf, through the Indian Ocean to East Africa, India, and, by the early ninth century, to Indonesia and China. By 900 Arab merchants were establishing trading colonies on the East African coast, obtaining gold and other metals, ivory, and slaves in return for manufactured goods. Exports from the Islamic world often reflected their technological sophistication and expertise, and included textiles, glassware, carved wood, metalwork, arms, and pottery vessels such as fine glazed wares (see image 2). Produce, notably sugar and spices, was also exported from the Arab world. By the 10th century, Arab traders were operating in southern Russia and trading with the Vikings. Trade also flourished with Europe, despite simmering conflict with the neighboring Byzantine Empire.

The initial unity of the Abbasid caliphate did not last; new dynasties were seizing control of outlying regions and establishing their own states. Notable among these were the Fatimids, who seized Egypt in 969, briefly also controlling Palestine and Syria and ruling until 1171. In the mid-ninth century the caliphate lost its power to the Buyid dynasty, which conquered Baghdad in 945; the caliphate thereafter exercised only spiritual power. The eleventh century saw the rise of the Seljuk Turks, originally from central Asia, who converted to Islam in 970. By 1037 they had begun to expand across Iran, driving out the Buyids by 1055 and taking Baghdad, and by 1092 controlling the region from Anatolia to the western Silk Road cities. Subsequently different groups, with a variety of ethnic and cultural backgrounds, took control of smaller or larger regions of the Islamic world. As a whole this continued, with a Muslim empire established in India in 1175, and Muslim converts as far afield as Indonesia and the Philippines. A major blow to Islamic culture was dealt by the Mongol invasion in the thirteenth century, but their conversion to Islam and rapid assimilation made this only a temporary setback. **JM**

786–809	9th century	921–22	1037	1095–99	1258
Abbasid industry, commerce, culture, prosperity, and patronage of the arts and sciences reach their zenith under Caliph Harun al-Rashid.	Known as the "Belitung wreck," an Arab dhow is lost in Indonesian waters with a cargo of Chinese porcelain and other precious goods. It is discovered in 1998.	Arab explorer and envoy Ibn Fadlan records impressions as he travels in Russia; he witnesses a Viking chief's ship cremation.	The Seljuks, originally Turkic central Asian nomads, invade Persia. In 1055 they sack Baghdad and found their empire.	Responding to Byzantine pleas for help against the Seljuks, the First Crusade sacks Constantinople and captures Jerusalem.	Mongols led by Hulagu sack Baghdad and kill the caliph, ending the Abbasid caliphate; Genghis Khan dies and so the Mongols do not follow up the conquest.

Coptic and Islamic Cairo Fourth century

The Hanging Church of Sitt Mariam is situated above a gatehouse of the Roman fortress in Babylon-in-Cairo. The church was probably built during the patriarchate of Isaac (690–92), on the site of an earlier church. It became the seat of the Coptic Patriarch in 1047.

Babylon-in Cairo, or Old Cairo, is situated 3 miles (5 km.) to the south of modern Cairo. The origins of the settlement are obscure, with the classical writers Diodorus Siculus and Strabo convinced that it was founded by Babylonian prisoners brought to Egypt by King "Sesostris" (Ramesses II, who reigned 1279–1213 BCE). Another tradition holds that the Persians built a fort at the site during the sixth century BCE. What is known is that the Romans built a fort and stationed a garrison here. Today Babylon preserves many important Christian buildings, as well as a wealth of antiquities housed in the Coptic Museum, which is built on the site of the Roman fortress.

The fourth-century Church of Saints Sergius and Bacchus is dedicated to two soldier-martyrs killed by Emperor Maximian (c. 250–310). It is the original model for the earliest Egyptian-Byzantine churches used by the Copts. Local tradition claims that its crypt provided refuge for the Holy Family during their period of exile in Egypt. Nearby is the Ben Ezra Synagogue, which, again according to local tradition, is located on the spot where the infant Moses was found by the pharaoh's daughter. The Greek Orthodox Church of St. George is a round church situated on top of a round Roman tower. Although it traces its origins to the tenth century, the current church is a recreation following a fire in 1904.

In 640, General Amr ibn al-As (d. 663) conquered Egypt and in 641, after a seven-month siege, Babylon surrendered. Amr left Babylon intact, building a Muslim capital, Al-Fustat, to the south. Amr's city was founded as a military headquarters, so that Egypt could become a base for the Arab campaigns against Byzantium and for the conquest of North Africa. It included Africa's first mosque, the Mosque of Amr. Al-Fustat grew into a major port, but in 1168 was burned to prevent it from falling into Crusader hands. **JT**

👁 FOCAL POINTS

ST. CATHERINE'S MONASTERY, SINAI

The Copts believed that it might sometimes be appropriate to withdraw from the world in search of spiritual values. At first, holy men retreated to the deserts where they lived as hermits in caves. Gradually, the more famous hermits started to attract followers. This led to the development of monasteries with enclosed communities. St. Catherine's Monastery, constructed between 548 and 565, is believed to have been built at the site where Moses saw the burning bush.

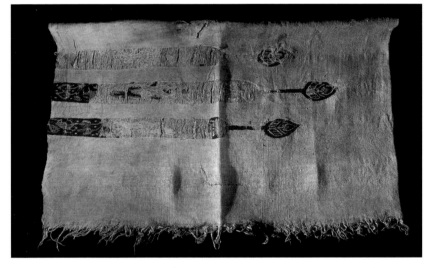

TEXTILES

Egypt's warm, dry climate has ensured the survival of many post-Pharaonic textiles dating to Coptic and Islamic times. Made of wool and linen, they include religious vestments, burial garments and wrappings, everyday clothing, and household furnishings. They provide colorful evidence of a distinctive folk art, and preserve a category of organic materials that does not usually survive in the ancient world. This fragment of linen and wool, with richly colored embroidered bands, is an example of a Coptic textile dating to the sixth century.

COPTIC

Egypt's Christians are known as Copts. The name is derived from the Greek word *Aigyptios*, meaning Egyptian. Following the Arab invasion, *Aigyptios* mutated into *qibt*. The word "Copt" was first used in Europe in the sixteenth century to distinguish the Christian Egyptians from the Muslim majority. Historically Egypt's Copts spoke a direct descendant of the ancient Egyptian language. By the third century, Coptic had became a medium for the translation of biblical texts so that they could be read by the Egyptian population. Other important works in Coptic included the writings of St. Anthony (*c.* 251–356) who, as Egypt's first Christian hermit, lived in a small cave in the Eastern Desert. Since Coptic has a limited vocabulary, the religious texts included many Greek words. Coptic manuscripts began to arrive in Europe from the seventeenth century, and this enabled scholars to study the language. Following

the Arab invasion, Coptic became an essentially dead language, confined to the church liturgy. Arabic was now the official language and script of Egypt.

The dynastic Egyptians wrote their language using hieroglyphic, hieratic, or demotic scripts. None of these scripts included vowels; it was assumed that the reader knew where the vowel would occur in the words. The Coptic script did include vowels. It employed the Greek alphabet plus seven signs borrowed from the demotic script, which had to be used for Egyptian sounds not represented in the Greek alphabet. The fact that elements of the ancient Egyptian language persisted in the Coptic texts helped scholars to understand the pronunciation of words written in hieroglyphic, hieratic, and demotic scripts. Coptic provided a vital link in the decipherment of hieroglyphs.

Abbasid Samarra 836–892

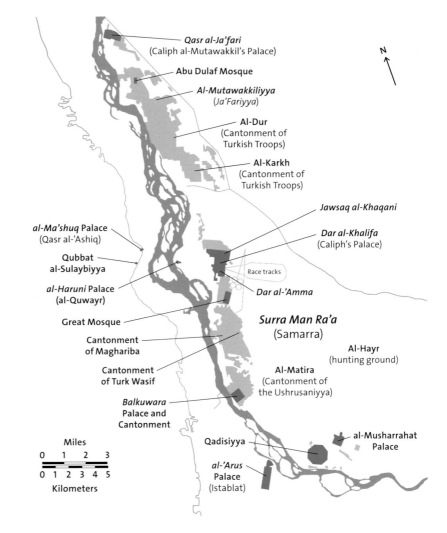

Qasr al-Ja'fari
(Caliph al-Mutawakkil's Palace)

Abu Dulaf Mosque

Al-Mutawakkiliyya
(Ja'Fariyya)

Al-Dur
(Cantonment of
Turkish Troops)

Al-Karkh
(Cantonment of
Turkish Troops)

Jawsaq al-Khaqani

Dar al-Khalifa
(Caliph's Palace)

al-Ma'shuq Palace
(Qasr al-'Ashiq)

Qubbat
al-Sulaybiyya

al-Haruni Palace
(al-Quwayr)

Race tracks

Dar al-'Amma

Great Mosque

Surra Man Ra'a
(Samarra)

Al-Hayr
(hunting ground)

Cantonment
of Maghariba

Cantonment
of Turk Wasif

Al-Matira
(Cantonment of
the Ushrusaniyya)

Balkuwara
Palace and
Cantonment

al-Musharrahat
Palace

Qadisiyya

al-'Arus
Palace
(Istablat)

Miles
0   1   2   3

0 1 2 3 4 5
Kilometers

Samarra's buildings, stretching
25 miles (40 km.) along the
eastern bank of the Tigris
river, were not protected
by a common fortification,
although city walls surrounded
individual settlement areas.
The octagonal pavilion Qubbat
al-Sulaybiyya was built on the
opposite, western side of the
river in 862 and 863.

Disturbed by conflict between his Turkish troops and the citizens of Baghdad, Abbasid caliph al-Mu'tasim (796–842) decided to found a new capital further north at Samarra, near Qadisiyya, the uncompleted city of Caliph Harun al-Rashid. Here he built a palace surrounded by military cantonments. Abbasid Samarra reached its greatest extent under Caliph al-Mutawakkil (822–61), who constructed twenty palaces, including Balkuwarra. In 859 he also built a new city, Ja'fariyya, siting his royal palace, Qasr al-Ja'fari, at the northern end. Mutawakkil also constructed a congregational mosque, Abu Dulaf: this had a spiral minaret similar to that of the Great Mosque, built by Mutawakkil in his original city a decade earlier.

After 870 Samarra was gradually abandoned, and the capital was moved back to Baghdad in 892. However, Samarra became a center of pilgrimage from the tenth century, and in modern times it has again grown into a major city. Samarra's early remains were extensively excavated in 1911 and 1913 by Ernst Herzfeld (1879–1948). Iraq's Directorate of Antiquities has conducted excavations and conservation work here since 1936. Derek Kennet (b. 1962) undertook extensive survey work and limited excavation here in 1983 to 1989. Samarra has suffered badly in Iraq's recent conflicts: in 2006 and 2007 deliberate bombing damaged the dome of the al-Askari shrine and destroyed its minarets. **JM**

GREAT MOSQUE OF AL-MUTAWAKKIL

In 849 to 852, Caliph al-Mutawakkil constructed a Grand Mosque, the largest in the Islamic world. Only its outer wall and minaret now survive, the latter 170 feet (52 m.) high and accessed by a spiral staircase. The mosque's prayer hall had seventeen aisles; covered porticoes in its outer enclosure provided additional space for worshippers at Friday prayers. Remains of marble columns, glass mosaic decorations, and glass wall panels attest to its original magnificence.

QASR AL-'ASHIQ—THE BELOVED PALACE

Samarra's last caliph, al-Mu'tamid, built a palace, al-Ma'shuq (the Beloved), now known as Qasr al-'Ashiq, on the opposite side of the Tigris c. 877–882. Excavated in the 1960s, it has been extensively restored. The large palace had an *iwan* and domed chamber, and a central courtyard surrounded by a complex of chambers. The palace was frequently remodeled during its long occupation, which continued after Samarra was abandoned as the capital.

AL-MU'TASIM'S CITY

The city that Caliph al-Mu'tasim founded at Samarra was officially named Surra Man Ra'a: "He who sees it is delighted." The location was well known for its game, providing good hunting, but was poor in resources to support a settlement. According to the Abbasid historian al-Ya'qubi (d. 897), Caliph al-Mu'tasim employed architects to survey the area for the new city. The plan, laid out in 836, detailed the locations of nobles' palaces, residential areas for administrative staff, and cantonment housing for various army units and ordinary people (mainly conscript laborers). There was a mosque with separate markets for different types of merchandise around it. In the city center was Dar al-Khalifa, a 310-acre (125 ha.) palace complex, set in grounds that included ancillary buildings such as stables, barracks, and accommodation for palace staff; a large formal garden; probably other gardens, pavilions, and sunken basins originally holding pools; a polo ground

with accommodation for spectators; and the starting line of a racecourse. The palace itself had two parts. In the south was the Dar al-'Amma, the public area of the palace, 600 by 660 feet (180 by 200 m.) in extent: this included the great triple *iwan* where the caliph gave audiences on Mondays and Thursdays; domed throne halls decorated with carved marble; and other public offices. On the eastern side of the building lay an enormous courtyard ("the esplanade"), 610 by 1,128 feet (186 by 344 m.) in extent. The private part of the palace, al-Jawsaq al-Khaqani, occupied the northern area, surrounded by a defensive wall. This had a reception hall block and residential quarters. Excavations in one part, the harem, uncovered a domed room with painted wall decoration. The palace is lavishly decorated with geometric designs molded in stucco. Glazed tiles, painted wooden beams, and glass mosaic work have also been found.

VIKINGS

1 A Viking silver pendant retrieved from a grave at the Birka archaeological site on the island of Björkö in Lake Mälaren, Sweden. The site is home to the largest Viking Age grave field in Sweden.

2 A seventh-century Viking bridle mount found at one of the boat graves at Vendel, Uppland, in eastern Sweden.

3 The impressive rune stone at Rök is considered to be the earliest example of written literature in Sweden.

P opular accounts of the Vikings (also called Norse, Norsemen, and in eastern Europe, Varangians) often focus on their reputation for bloodthirsty mayhem and pillage. The beginning of the Viking Age is marked by the sack of the monastery at Lindisfarne in England by Scandinavian raiders in 793. Vikings from the maritime traditions of Norway and Denmark embarked on adventures during the eighth, ninth, and tenth centuries that brought them to Britain, Ireland, France, and even into the Mediterranean.

Viking society developed from earlier Iron Age societies in southern Scandinavia. Fuelled by war booty and pay to mercenaries who had served in Roman armies, the competitive acquisition of wealth by elite magnates was already underway. Local craftwork produced exquisite jewelry and ornate weapons. Some examples of these can be seen in the Vendel (see image 2) and Valsgärde burials near Uppsala in Sweden.

Yet pillage and slaughter on foreign shores is only one aspect of the Viking experience during the second half of the first millennium. The Viking heartland includes Sweden, Denmark, and the coast of Norway, and their traces are still visible across the landscape. These include burial mounds, rune stones and settlement sites. The word "Viking" is thought to be derived from the Swedish *vik* meaning a bay or harbor, which reflects their participation in maritime commerce. Continuing a tradition seen from the early centuries of the first millennium, much of their attention was focused on the development of emporia for conducting this trade.

KEY EVENTS

c. 750	793	841	845	862	c. 870
The Vikings set up a trading emporium at Birka in Sweden.	Vikings attack and sack the monastery at the island of Lindisfarne, Northumbria, England.	A Viking naval encampment is established at Dublin, Ireland.	The Vikings sack Paris, France.	Vikings, led by Rurik (d. 879), take charge at Novgorod (see p. 440) in Russia.	Viking settlement in Iceland begins.

Birka is located on Lake Mälaren, about 20 miles (30 km.) west of Stockholm. During the mid 700s, a trading center emerged at Birka and flourished for approximately 200 years. Trading connections reached as far as Kiev and Constantinople to bring silver (see image 1), gold and glass to Birka in exchange for iron and especially furs. Thousands of paw bones from squirrels, foxes, and martens have been found, the result of furs being prepared for export. At Birka, craftworkers made bone combs, iron goods, and textiles, supported by farms in an agricultural hinterland. At its peak, about 700 to 1,000 people lived at Birka. Many are buried in the cemetery that surrounds the settlement.

To facilitate commerce, Vikings mastered shipbuilding, drawing on techniques developed over the previous two millennia in northern Europe. Roskilde Fjord, west of Copenhagen in Denmark, has a narrow passage to the sea. In an attempt to block this passage during a conflict, several Viking ships were sunk across it (see p. 434). One of them was a cargo vessel designed to carry a heavy load across the open ocean. The importance the Vikings attached to ships is seen in their use in the burials of their kings, as at Oseberg and Gokstad in Norway.

The elite strata of Viking society possessed a degree of literacy. The letters of their alphabet are runes, which appear most often on large upright stones across the Scandinavian landscape. Rune stones were typically erected to memorialize an event or a person. One of the most famous is at Rök, Sweden. It stands 5 feet (1.5 m.) high and has about 280 runes on the front and 450 on the back (see image 3). It was placed by a man called Varin during the ninth century to commemorate his dead son, but the text also contains mythical and epic allusions. Other Viking stones provide their message in pictures, not runes. Many such picture stones are found on the island of Gotland in the Baltic Sea.

A recurring theme on rune stones is the death of someone during an expedition either in the west or in the east. Vikings made their way from the Baltic into the river systems of Russia, and forged a trading route south to Constantinople. Along the way, many stayed to establish trading posts, such as those at Staraya Ladoga and Novgorod, and played leading roles in the formation of early towns. In the west, Vikings were even more active. In addition to their raiding and plundering, they established kingdoms such as the one in Northumbria with York (see p. 430) as its capital and founded towns like Dublin and Limerick. Eventually, their travels took them across the North Atlantic, made possible by their seaworthy boat designs. They settled in Iceland c. 870, where they established farms. A century later, they discovered Greenland, thus beginning several centuries of Scandinavian settlement. Some of the Greenland Vikings reached the eastern coast of North America, founding at least one settlement at L'Anse aux Meadows in Newfoundland (see p. 432).

The true Viking Age is considered to have ended in the eleventh century. This was when many Scandinavians adopted Christianity, and political unification under central royal authority absorbed the competing kingdoms. **PB**

c. 890	c. 960	c. 985	1042	1960	1994
Timber is cut for a ship that is used for the burial of a king ten years later at Gokstad in Vestfold, Norway.	Harald Bluetooth (c. 910–c. 987), king of Denmark and Norway, converts to Christianity.	The first Viking settlement in Greenland is founded.	A Viking longboat, found in Roskilde Fjord in Denmark in 1962, is built in Dublin.	A Viking settlement at L'Anse aux Meadows in Newfoundland, Canada, is discovered.	Bluetooth wireless communication protocol is invented, named after King Harald I, known as Bluetooth.

York Ninth – tenth centuries

Underneath the Viking settlement at York is clay subsoil, which prevents drainage. The result is that the Viking refuse became waterlogged and, in this environment, the lack of oxygen prevented decay. Organic materials, including wood, textiles, leather and even human excrement, are preserved superbly.

The city of York, located on the Ouse river in northeastern England, lies on two millennia of archaeological deposits. Beginning as the Roman fortress of Eboracum, it developed into the Anglo-Saxon trading center of Eoforwic, and by the seventh century it was the seat of the kings of Northumbria. Yet the archaeology of York is better known for the years between 866 and 954 when it was the Viking center of Jorvik.

In 866, an army of Danish Vikings marched north from East Anglia and captured York. Renaming the town Jorvik, they built it up into the capital of the kingdom they established in Northumbria. They strengthened the Roman ramparts and established new streets, several of which converged on a new bridge on the Ouse. Along these streets they built houses and workshops on long narrow plots. The dwellings, with their gable ends facing the street, were at the front of the plot, while the area behind was used for craft production and other commercial activities.

There was constant warfare between the Vikings in Northumbria and the English kings, culminating in the defeat of the last Viking king of Jorvik, Erik Bloodaxe (c. 885–954), in 954. Many Vikings did not leave and the century that followed was still influenced by Scandinavian culture. During this period, the population of York was said to be 30,000, and when the Domesday Book was compiled in 1086, York was second only to London in size.

Much of the knowledge of Viking York comes from excavations between 1976 and 1981 in Coppergate. Within an area of about 11,000 square feet (1,000 sq. m.), archaeologists excavated Viking layers up to 30 feet (9 m.) deep, built up of household and workshop refuse, animal and human waste, and the remains of houses and workshops. **PB**

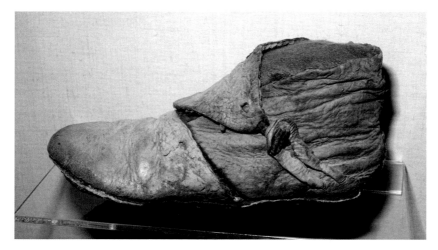

CRAFTS

Archaeologists found evidence of many industrial processes and craft activities within the workshops excavated. In addition to pottery production, Viking craftworkers made wooden cups. One workshop appears to have belonged to a blacksmith who made knives and keys. Other workshops specialized in working copper, silver, and gold. Amber was made into jewelry. There is evidence for weaving and leatherworking, including shoemaking. Bone and antler were carved into combs.

TRADE

Materials found in Coppergate came from great distances. This is not surprising, given that the Vikings had wide-ranging connections. Thus, walrus ivory from Greenland, amber from the Baltic, and silk from Asia arrived in the workshops. Wine was obtained from the Rhineland. Even a cowrie shell came to Jorvik from the Red Sea. Other raw materials, such as iron ore and antler, were sourced from nearby. Iron coin dies, used in the striking of coins, were found in an area used for metalworking.

DIET AND DISEASE

The superb preservation of organic remains in the Viking deposits at Coppergate yielded information about the inhabitants' diet and living conditions. Five tons of animal bones were recovered from this relatively small area. These were mainly from cattle, with some sheep and pigs. Compared with other periods of occupation at York, fowl—mainly chickens and geese—were more abundant in Viking and Anglo-Scandinavian times, which is corroborated by the quantities of eggshell found in the waterlogged deposits. Fish was an important component of the diet, particularly eel and herring. Wheat, oats, and barley were staple crops, along with fruits like blackberries and nuts such as walnuts.

The people of Jorvik lived in close quarters in their tightly packed houses. Refuse was discarded in the back yards, in which a mixture of food refuse including offal, decaying plants, industrial waste, old building materials, ashes, and human and animal excrement accumulated. Among the finds at Coppergate are coprolites, preserved human and animal feces. One specimen, the 7-inch (19.5 cm.) long Lloyds Bank coprolite, indicated that its producer subsisted largely on meat and bread, but it also contained hundreds of eggs of intestinal worms.

The living conditions were foul and squalid. Areas used for weaving contained evidence of sheep lice, while the floors of many buildings had traces of human fleas and lice. The primary function of the many bone and antler combs was to remove lice from hair. Puparia of house flies indicate that there must have been a continuous buzzing in the air as the insects were drawn to the fetid conditions. The conditions in Jorvik were widely known and in one Icelandic saga the town is referred to as the "dank demesne."

Vikings in North America Tenth century

A recreation of a Norse sod longhouse at L'Anse aux Meadows on Newfoundland, Canada. The large houses excavated at the site used building techniques similar to those used in Norway during the same period, including a wooden structure covered with turf from the peat bog, a pointed roof, and thick peat partitions on the sod floors.

The Vikings rank among the greatest voyagers of all time, roving and rampaging through north, central and eastern Europe between the eighth and eleventh centuries. But it was not just to the east and south that they looked. Their sagas also tell of a rich land to the west of their homeland, one that was finally visited by explorer Leif Eriksson (c. 970–c. 1020), son of Erik the Red (950–c. 1003), founder of the first European settlement on Greenland in c. 985.

It has long been believed that this land, called Vinland, was somewhere on the coast of northeast North America, but apart from the sagas there was no other proof that the Vikings had landed on the continent until 1960 when Norwegians Helge (1899–2001) and Anne Stine (1918–97) Ingstad excavated a site at L'Anse aux Meadows on the northern tip of Newfoundland. Parks Canada undertook more excavations in the 1970s. Together, the two expeditions uncovered the remains of eight longhouses made of wood and sod, ancillary buildings, a smithy, and a charcoal kiln. The site is very different from what indigenous peoples would have left behind and is likely Viking in origin. Artifacts such as a bronze cloak-fastening pin, a spindle whorl, and iron rivets are identical to objects from contemporary sites in Iceland and Greenland in c. 1000. Archaeological evidence suggests that the site served as a base for repairing longships before they sailed south and west into the Gulf of St. Lawrence. It appears that it was occupied for just a few decades, because archaeologists did not find storage barns, stables, or burials, all indicative of extended occupation. It is not known why the site was abandoned, but possibly the climate made cultivation impossible, or its isolation made the settlement unsafe. **PD**

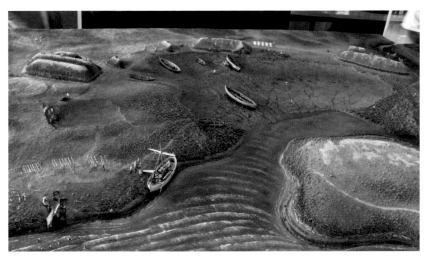

L'ANSE AUX MEADOWS MODEL

Archaeologists did not find standing structures: the longhouses had been reduced to their sod foundations, appearing as bumps in the landscape. After excavation the site was reburied. The remains of the buildings have been protected by inert material and sodded over. This model at the museum at L'Anse aux Meadows shows what the Norse camp would have looked like: a small community that was built a short distance inland on a narrow gravel terrace by a water-logged peat bog, close to a stream.

POINT ROSEE, NEWFOUNDLAND

In 2015, satellite imagery revealed the possible existence of another Viking site, Point Rosee, at the extreme southern tip of Newfoundland, about 300 miles (483 km.) south of L'Anse aux Meadows. The site comprises a shallow pit that is surrounded by small rocks. The fire pit held almost 30 pounds (13.5 kg.) of iron slag—a sign of metallurgy not associated with native people of the region. Norse travelers are the likely candidates for leaving traces of this technology. A definitive interpretation of this site awaits further investigations.

VIKING SAGAS AND VINLAND

The early accounts of Viking discoveries, including their discovery of North America, come from the Viking sagas. These are ancient Norse stories told by word of mouth for many years and then later written down for future generations to read. The earliest written version of the sagas dates to the twelfth century.

According to the sagas, in *c.* 960 Erik the Red's family were banished from his homeland in Norway. After arriving in Iceland where he was again banished (for murder), he went to Greenland in *c.* 985, where he established the first Norse settlements.

The second of the three sons of Erik the Red, Leif Eriksson, continued his father's wanderlust. Believing the rumors of a rich and forested land where winters were mild, wild grapes were to be had in abundance and wheat grew, he sailed west to a place called Vinland. The name itself is shrouded in uncertainty. Perhaps the Vikings made a substitute for fermented wine from juice made from the wild berries found in the area. The exact location of Vinland is still not determined; different scholars place it as far north as Newfoundland and as far south as the coast of Maine.

Tracing the origins of the Vikings in North America became a mini industry in the nineteenth century, and led to some fanciful interpretations of various buildings. The Newport Tower in Rhode Island was touted as a Viking structure. However, radiocarbon dating shows it was built in the late seventeenth century.

Roskilde Ships   Eleventh century

The Skuldelev 5, now at the Viking Ship Museum in Roskilde, is one of the warships once used for blocking Roskilde Fjord. Although classified as a longship, it was small for this class, only about 56 feet (17 m.) long and able to carry about thirty men. Skuldelev 5 was built c. 1030 and shows evidence of numerous repairs.

In c. 1070, the Viking communities living in the northern part of the island of Zealand in Denmark evidently feared an attack from the sea. Roskilde Fjord, entered from the northern coast of Zealand, provided a direct route into the interior of the island, and if a seaborne army could penetrate the length of the fjord, there could be disastrous consequences. The fjord becomes narrow and shallow at Skuldelev, and so the people living around the waterway decided to fill a number of ships with stones and sink them in the narrows to block the channel and deny the enemy access.

For nearly 900 years, the ships lay at the bottom of the fjord until they were discovered in the late 1950s and excavated in 1962. Five Viking ships were found and excavated from the bottom of the fjord. They provide a sample of the various types of ships used by the Vikings during the eleventh century, as well as a detailed glimpse of the shipbuilding techniques that evolved in northern Europe during the previous two millennia.

The Skuldelev ships were built using the clinker, or lapstrake, technique. The oldest known clinker boat is the Danish Nydam Boat from c. 310 (see p. 317), and the type was also seen in the ghost boat in the grave at Sutton Hoo (see p. 420) in England. Long planks, or strakes, are overlapped to form the hull and attached to internal frames. They are riveted together where they overlap and the seams caulked with moss and pitch. A clinker ship is lighter than one in which the planks are butted seam-to-seam, due to the ability to use lighter planks and less caulk. Also, clinker boats can flex in rough seas without breaking up—a great advantage for Vikings venturing out on the open ocean. **PB**

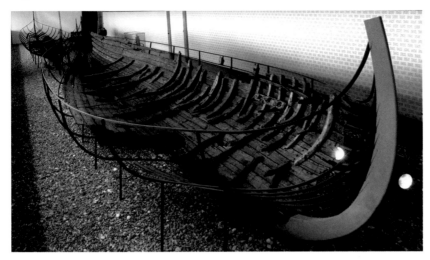

SKULDELEV 1

The Skuldelev 1 Viking ship is a large ocean-going cargo vessel built at Sognefjord in western Norway in c. 1030. It was repaired between 1060 and 1070, suggesting that it was in use over several decades. Sixty percent of the original ship has been preserved. Skuldelev 1 was about 52 feet (16 m.) long and 16 feet (4.8 m.) wide. The ship was constructed of pine planks and later repaired with oak and linden wood. With a crew of six to eight, it was capable of sailing in the Baltic Sea and the North Sea, as well as in the North Atlantic Ocean.

SKULDELEV 6

Neither a true cargo ship nor a warship, Skuldelev 6 is the smallest of the five vessels. It was built of pine, birch, and oak in western Norway, and was 37 feet (11.2 m.) in length and only 8 feet (2.5 m.) wide. At some point, the sides were raised with an additional plank. It is likely that Skuldelev 6 was originally built in c. 1030 for use as a fishing boat, only to be later converted into a small coastal transport. Two reconstructions have been built by the Viking Ship Museum: *Kraka Fyr* in 1998 and *Skjoldungen* in 2010.

DUBLIN LONGSHIP

One of the five Skuldelev ships was much longer than the others, and it was originally thought to be two ships, labeled Skuldelev 2 and Skuldelev 4. It was subsequently discovered that these were really one longship, so the label Skuldelev 4 was retired. Skuldelev 2 is a long seagoing vessel, originally about 100 feet (30 m.) long and 13 feet (4 m.) wide. It is thought to have had a crew of seventy to eighty men, of whom at least sixty were rowers. Fully equipped, Skuldelev 2 is estimated to have weighed 28 tons (26 tonnes). Unfortunately, only about 25 percent of the original ship was preserved underwater.

Skuldelev 2 was built c. 1042 somewhere near Dublin, the town that the Vikings had established on the River Liffey during the ninth century. It is made of Irish oak believed to have come from the Wicklow mountains. The ship was meant to carry a war party across the open ocean at high speed, up to 17 knots (31.5 km./h) when under sail. Yet its draft was sufficiently shallow to allow it to navigate into bays and to be pulled up on beaches. Skuldelev 2 is the kind of Viking ship that is celebrated in verse and sagas, probably used by a chief or war leader.

In 2000, work began at the Viking Ship Museum on a replica of Skuldelev 2, named the *Sea Stallion from Glendalough*; it was launched in 2004. Twenty oak trees were required to supply the timber for the hull, and other species—ash, pine, and willow—for the other fittings, oars, and shields. More than 8,000 iron rivets were needed to fasten the strakes. In 2007 the *Sea Stallion* was sailed from Roskilde to Dublin.

MEDIEVAL TOWNS

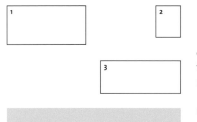

1 Archaeologists excavating an almost completely preserved wooden cellar from the twelfth century in Lübeck, Germany, in 2013.

2 Excavating a wattle-lined square pit that served as a well in the 12th to thirteenth century at Guildhall Yard, London, during the 1992 to 1998 dig.

3 A medieval town depicted in the *Liber Chronicarum* (*Book of Chronicles*, 1493) showing defenses, a planned street system, and houses of urban type.

It was the widespread destruction left in the wake of World War II that formed the catalyst for the development of the archaeological investigation of medieval towns (see image 3) across Europe, and for the recording of what remained of their historic buildings. Some historic cores had been flattened, while others were severely damaged; almost all faced substantial redevelopment, which would often radically alter historic town plans.

The rate of urban redevelopment varied enormously, not only across Europe, but also within different parts of individual countries, and even within the towns themselves. In most countries there was no national register of significant historic buildings to check what had been lost, and what should be saved. So setting these up was often a priority, and was already underway by the late 1940s. Some of the earliest urban excavations began in the early 1950s, as in London and Norwich (see p. 438), on bomb-damaged sites. The Society for Medieval Archaeology was established in 1957, and proved to be a catalyst for urban excavations—first in Britain and then in other parts of Europe.

Early excavations were interested in trying to establish the origins and growth of a particular settlement, while historical geographers were interested in the study of its layout and street-plan. Architectural historians were interested in the study and classification of building types, and their development. The need to be able to classify and date the finds generated by these excavations, and to establish typologies for them, became apparent as so much of these periods had not been studied before.

KEY EVENTS

1947	1951	1950s	1951–62	1961	1973–74
The Roman and Medieval London Excavation Council is founded to excavate bomb-damaged sites within the City of London.	Excavations start at St. Benedict's Gate in Norwich, England.	Early excavations begin in London, Canterbury, York, Bristol, Exeter, and Plymouth. There are similar developments in Hamburg and Bruges.	Excavations at Novgorod, Russia, reveal the medieval city's trading links. They are also shown by the Troitsky digs that begin in 1973 (see p. 440).	Major multiperiod excavations start in Winchester by Martin (b. 1937) and Birthe Kjølbye (b. 1941–2010) Biddle and are quickly copied elsewhere.	The excavation of Wood Quay in Dublin reveals the city's Viking origins, as well as its medieval remains.

The pace of redevelopment—and thus of urban archaeology—began to increase during the 1960s. In Winchester, England, this led to a massive program of excavations and the development of a new approach to open-area excavation that proved so successful that it was adopted in many other towns. By the late 1960s, archaeological investigations were taking place in historic towns in several northern European countries. As economic recovery in Europe continued during the 1970s and 1980s, so the pressures for redevelopment gained momentum and more excavations took place.

The period since 1980 has seen major developments in the systems of recording excavations, such as that developed by the Museum of London (see image 2); in the use of computers both on- and off-site; of more systematic environmental sampling; and of the involvement of conservators in the process. Urban excavation was always more complex and more expensive than most other fields of archaeology, and, because of the volume of data generated, took longer to bring to publication—in many cases taking years. By the late 1980s, archaeologists had begun to turn to developers to pay for this work.

In the early 1990s, the German city of Lübeck (see image 1) initiated a series of groundbreaking conferences that took a more systematic approach toward the study of medieval towns. These examined the evidence for trade, domestic buildings, infrastructure, crafts and industry, lifestyle and luxury, fortifications, monasteries and religious houses, and childhood and recreation; in certain towns, one could also add the evidence for waterfronts and harbors, while all towns also sit within a much wider hinterground, with which there will be strong links. This thematic approach is multidisciplinary, and leads to an informative understanding of the role and dynamics of that settlement. **DE**

1976–81	1990	1990s	1992	1995–2015	2009–14
The Coppergate excavation in York investigates part of Viking Jorvik. This highlights York's Scandinavian heritage.	Changes to English planning laws mean developer-funding becomes the norm. Archaeological mitigation strategies are introduced.	The German reunification process leads to substantial redevelopment in historic towns in the former East Germany.	English Heritage launches its strategy for the management of the archaeology of historic towns.	The Lübeck Colloquiums on Urban Archaeology in the Hanseatic Region look at thematic approaches to the investigation and study of towns.	One of the most extensive archaeological excavations in Europe takes place at the Gründungsviertel, Lübeck.

Norwich Eighth – eighteenth centuries

A motte-and-bailey castle was established in Norwich soon after the Norman Conquest in 1066 and was built by 1075. A large area of the Anglo-Scandinavian borough was cleared to construct it. Excavation revealed there were two successive earthen mounds topped by a stone keep. The castle mound is the largest motte in England.

The English city of Norwich in East Anglia developed on either side of a crossing of the Wensum river. It is surrounded by a rich agricultural hinterland. This city has a wealth of surviving historic buildings and excellent documentation. Excavation began in 1948, increased dramatically after 1971, and continues to this day.

Several Middle Saxon settlements developed within the future town during the eighth and ninth centuries, as shown by place names and finds; the most successful of these was Northwic. Danish occupation of this area c. 870 to 917 is evidenced by an early tenth-century, D-shaped enclosure on the north bank; contemporary activity has also been identified at several sites on the south bank. Following the defeat of the Danes in 917, Norwich grew in importance and boasted a mint by 935. In 1066 there were between twenty-five and forty churches here. Excavation has identified at least twenty buildings and numerous burials and finds of this Anglo-Scandinavian period.

With the advent of the Normans, a castle was built over the site of ninety-eight Saxon tenements, and a new French borough laid out to the west; a major cathedral precinct was established on the eastern side of the city in 1094. By the 1140s, there was expansion north of the river, burgeoning crafts and industries (including cloth finishing), and a growing population. The city walls were built between c. 1280 and 1340. By the latter date there were four friaries and nearly seventy churches here. The city suffered badly in the Black Death, but gradually recovered.

In 1507, a major fire swept through much of the city; the remains of several burned houses have been excavated at Pottergate. When the cloth industry began to decline, the city invited Huguenot refugees in 1565 to revive its fortunes; they became known as the "Strangers." Finds of Low Countries assemblages attest their presence here in the later sixteenth and seventeenth centuries. From c. 1660 to 1730 Norwich was England's second largest city in terms of wealth; its cultural heritage from this period is outstanding. **DE**

THE FIRE OF 1507

Most of the houses had timber superstructures, and were closely packed. A fire on March 25, 1507, is said to have destroyed 40 percent of the city, and this layout must have helped the fire to spread quickly. In Pottergate a row of buildings was excavated in 1974, and was found to have deep, brick-lined cellars, which were filled with all the items that had collapsed into the cellars when the floors above gave way. This is a time capsule of early sixteenth-century households. Elm Hill is Norwich's most famous medieval street and looks much the way it did when it was rebuilt after the fire.

MEDIEVAL STONE BUILDINGS

There is a dearth of good freestone in this area, so most buildings were made of timber, cob, or clay. The use of stone was exceptional, and was mostly reserved for higher-status buildings such as the Cathedral that was begun in 1096, or for details such as door and window surrounds. However, careful survey and research has identified eighteen medieval stone buildings. The most famous of these is the Music House of c. 1140 but in the 1980s another twelfth-century stone building was excavated at St. Martin-at-Palace Plain.

EXCAVATION AT ALMS LANE

An excavation at Alms Lane in 1976 exposed part of the tenth-century ditch belonging to the Danish fortified enclosure on the north bank. This large ditch stayed open until the late eleventh century, when it was infilled with rubbish including leatherwork debris. In the next two centuries the area was peripheral, and was used for industries such as ironworking and quarrying.

A brewery and a smithy occupied this block from c. 1275 to 1350. In c. 1375 the site was cleared and these industries were replaced with housing. These late medieval houses were single-storied, two-roomed, clay-walled, and thatched. The impact of the fire of 1507 led to the rebuilding of Alms Lane by c. 1520, with two-storied buildings set on flint and brick rubble wall footings, tiled roofs, and permanent hearths and chimneys. In the later sixteenth century, the site was home to Huguenots, while by c. 1650 at least seven families were crowded onto this site. The "Strangers" were invited to Norwich to teach the locals how to make cloth of superior quality and by 1579 there were about 6,000 Strangers in the city, mostly living in the poorer areas north of the river. By c. 1720, the buildings had become much higher, more complex, and more densely packed to cope with the rising population.

Novgorod Tenth century

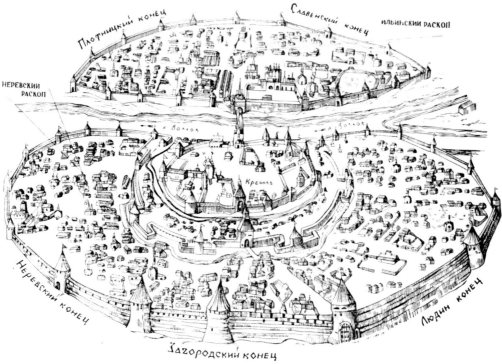

НЕРЕВСКИЙ РАСКОП

ПЛОТНИЦКИЙ КОНЕЦ

СЛАВЕНСКИЙ КОНЕЦ

ИЛЬИНСКИЙ РАСКОП

р. ВОЛХОВ

КРЕМЛЬ

НЕРЕВСКИЙ КОНЕЦ

ЛЮДИН КОНЕЦ

ЗАГОРОДСКИЙ КОНЕЦ

During Viking and medieval times, Novgorod was defined by a network of winding streets paved with timbers. When the timbers became waterlogged, extra layers of logs were placed on top of the wet timbers, to make a new, dry pavement. At one location, archaeologists found twenty-eight street levels, dated by tree rings between 953 and 1462.

Today a city with more than 200,000 inhabitants, located on the Volkhov river about 93 miles (150 km.) south of St. Petersburg, Novgorod (sometimes called Veliky Novgorod) has been occupied continuously since the tenth century, making it one of the oldest towns in Russia. As is the case at York (see p. 430) in England, clay soil beneath Novgorod prevents water from draining away, so layers of organic debris have built up over the last eleven centuries, reaching 20 feet (6 m.) in places. As a result, wood, leather, and other organic remains have been superbly preserved. After early archaeological investigations in the 1920s, excavations have taken place at Novgorod continuously for the last sixty years.

During the eighth and ninth centuries, Viking merchants from Scandinavia began to trade with native Slavic communities along the Volkhov. In doing so, they established fortified trading strongholds, such as Rurikovo Gorodische, which lies about 8 miles (13 km.) upstream from Novgorod. Amulets, carvings, and other Scandinavian-style artifacts discovered indicate a Viking presence there. In the middle of the ninth century, the Viking prince Rurik (d. 879) was invited to come to restore order during a period of internecine conflict. By the early part of the tenth century, the focus of settlement had shifted downstream to Novgorod, which grew into a large town made wealthy through trade. Its population was a mixture of Slavs and Vikings, who intermarried. The Scandinavians did not colonize the Novgorod region, but the high-ranking citizens were often of Viking descent, even if they eventually adopted Slavic names.

During the next several centuries, medieval Novgorod flourished. Its workshops produced craft goods, wealth from long-distance trade accumulated with its merchants, and it had strong ties to Scandinavia. At the same time, it played a major role in the establishment of Kiev and the nascent Russian state. By the end of the fifteenth century, however, Novgorod was eclipsed in power and wealth by Moscow. **PB**

HOUSES AND WORKSHOPS

The streets of Novgorod were lined with fenced compounds that enclosed a house and its storage huts, workshops, and stables arranged around a courtyard. Most compounds were about 50 by 100 feet (15 by 30 m.), but a few were up to three times that size, presumably residences of the elite. The houses were built in a log-cabin style, primarily of pine and spruce. Some were two, possibly three, stories tall, with plank floors. Different parts of the town seem to have specialized in specific crafts.

COMMERCIAL CENTER

Novgorod was part of a vast trading network that extended from northwestern Europe to Byzantium. Wine, incense, spices, nuts, exotic woods, and cloth passed through Novgorod creating wealth. Products of the Russian forests were traded to Viking mercantile centers like Birka in Sweden and Visby on Gotland. The latter had a special association with Novgorod, particularly with regard to the trade in wax, fueled by the demand for candles in Catholic churches throughout Europe.

BIRCH-BARK MANUSCRIPTS

The waterlogged deposits at Novgorod preserved a remarkable category of artifact: pieces of birch bark with writing on them. First noticed during excavations in 1951, hundreds have been found in deposits that date between the middle of the 11th century and the early fifteenth century. Since only a small fraction of Novgorod has been excavated, it is estimated that thousands more lie buried beneath the modern city. Known as *beresty* in Russian, the birch-bark manuscripts provide a remarkable glimpse of life in medieval Novgorod during its peak years as a commercial and cultural center.

Beresty were made by boiling pieces of birch bark collected in the surrounding forests. Boiling removed the rough outer layers, allowing the soft inner layers to be inscribed with a stylus made from bone or metal. No ink was used. Most were written in a local early Slavic dialect, Old Novgorodian, which has provided insights into the formation of modern east Slavic languages, although at least one that dates to the thirteenth century was written in an archaic Finnic language.

The topics of the birch bark texts are generally household, business, legal, and governmental matters. Some are love letters. During the thirteenth century, a boy aged six or seven, Onfim, wrote what appear to be homework exercises involving writing the alphabet and religious passages, as well as pictures of knights, horses, and beasts.

The *beresty*, as well as many finds of the styli used to inscribe them, indicate a high level of literacy among the inhabitants of medieval Novgorod. Given its commercial character, however, it would be necessary to document transactions and household activities, so writing was an important business skill that was cultivated by the inhabitants of the town.

MEDIEVAL WARFARE

1 Built by the Hospitaller Order of Saint John of Jerusalem, Krak des Chevaliers near Homs, Syria, is one of the best-preserved Crusader castles.

2 In this detail from the Bayeux Tapestry (1066–77), Saxon troops confront Norman cavalryman armed with lances.

3 Offa's Dyke was built on the orders of Offa, king of Mercia from 757 to 796.

Knowledge of medieval warfare—its tactics, weaponry, warships, and fortifications—comes from a broad range of sources, including medieval histories and literature, tapestries, tombs, sculpture, and archaeology. The last encompasses not only the results of fieldwork on battlefield sites, but also the investigation of fortifications and shipwrecks, and discoveries of weaponry and armor on cemetery and settlement sites.

The fall of Rome in 410 left a power vacuum, and many of the tribes who fought to seize large parts of the former empire—the Huns and the Visigoths, for example—are known from archaeology, which falls into two broad categories: weaponry and fighting equipment, and fortifications. Thanks to the excavation of cemetery sites and the documentation of casual finds, there is a substantial amount of evidence for the range of arms and body protection that was in use in many of these societies for much of the early medieval period (c. 410–c. 1050). During the fifth and sixth centuries, the best surviving evidence for fortifications comes from western and northern Britain, where numerous hill forts and promontory sites were occupied and/or refurbished—South Cadbury, Tintagel, and Dunadd, for example—and from Ireland, where numerous ring forts and crannogs attest to turbulent times. Viking raids began in the seventh century and continued to the ninth century, to be followed by

KEY EVENTS

413–439	1066	1066	1139	1260	c. 1314
Theodosius II builds new land defenses around Constantinople. Two tiers of great walls are erected across the peninsula for some 4 miles (6.4 km.).	At the Battle of Fulford (now in York), the Norse defeat the Saxon army. An extensive metal-detecting survey later reveals evidence of early metalworking.	At the Battle of Hastings, the Normans defeat the Saxon army and go on to conquer England. In the wake of the conquest, castles appear in England.	Pope Innocent II issues an edict against the use of crossbows.	Explosive hand-cannon are reputedly used by the Mamluks against the Mongols (see p. 444) at the Battle of Ain Jalut (Galilee).	Cannon arrive in Flanders. It is likely that they are also used in sieges at Metz in 1324 and at Algeciras in 1342–44.

invasion and settlement. In response to these and comparable threats from the Moors and the Magyars, as well as the subsequent decline of Carolingian power, numerous sites of refuge appeared across Europe, at Logne in Belgium, for example. Some palaces and monasteries began to be defended, more lordly residences were fortified, and the first defenses were erected around towns, including Norwich and South Cadbury. Linear earthworks such as Offa's Dyke along the Anglo-Welsh border (see image 3) and the Danevirke across the neck of Jutland, occasionally defined the boundaries of a state. The Vikings themselves built longphorts (enclosures) to protect their ships, ramparts around their towns—at Hedeby and Dublin, for example—and geometrical fortresses, including the Trelleborg at Fyrkat, to house their garrisons.

At the end of the early medieval period, the first castles begin to appear in northwest Europe, but it was not until the high and later medieval period (c. 1050–1550), and the successful invasion of England by the Normans in 1066 (see image 2), that castles were introduced into Britain. The following half-century saw increasing developments in the use of heavy cavalry and armor, and also the replacement of timber ramparts around towns with new stone walls. The lessons learned from the Crusades (1095–1216) at sites such as Krak des Chevaliers in Syria (see image 1) radically affected the design of castles and town walls; the following centuries saw both become ever more sophisticated—with more use of rounded towers, stronger gatehouses and barbicans, and sometimes multiple circuits—reaching their apogee perhaps at Carcassonne, France, or in Edwardian castles such as Beaumaris, Wales. In addition, the Crusades prompted the formation of the military orders, which developed their own distinctive fortifications, including the Teutonic Knights' strongholds at Marienburg, Poland, and Cēsis, Latvia. Archaeological excavations have taken place at numerous castle sites all over Europe, ranging from investigations of earthwork sites, such as Hen Domen in Powys, Wales, to large masonry structures such as Sandal Castle in West Yorkshire.

The late Middle Ages saw the construction of tower houses in Europe. This period also witnessed the development of the crossbow, improvements in the design of armor and the introduction of artillery. The traditional bow evolved into the longbow, which was used to devastating effect in many battles during the Hundred Years War—most notably at Agincourt (1415).

Toward the later part of the medieval period, changes occurred in the design of defenses both to incorporate cannon and to try to defend against the use of artillery by an enemy: town walls were lowered, strengthened with earthen ramparts, and protected by diamond-shaped bastions. By the late fifteenth century, cannon began to appear on ships. At the beginning of the sixteenth century, continued improvements in artillery, coupled with an often-tumultuous political climate, led to states building bastioned artillery forts in key positions as part of their national defense. **DE**

1346	1361	1443	1461	1513	1545
English troops under Edward III at the Battle of Crécy deploy between three and five cannon; they are also used at the siege of Calais in the same year.	The Battle of Visby is fought between an invading Danish royal army and a local Gutnish army. Five mass graves are dug outside the city walls.	The siege of Castle Kolno (Silesia) takes place. Archaeological investigation has since enabled the plotting of arms and weapons used in the siege.	At the Battle of Towton, the Yorkists defeat a larger Lancastrian army. The extent of the battle has since been plotted by metal-detecting.	The Battle of Flodden involves 40,000 English and Scottish troops. Three round shot and a few lead bullets are found in an archaeological survey.	The *Mary Rose* sinks in the Solent while going to war. The excavated remains give a unique insight into Tudor weapons and equipment.

The Mongols 1206 – c. 1369

The Mongols were nomads but Genghis realized that his empire needed a fixed center. He selected Khara Khorum, where his successor Ögödei constructed the Mongol capital. Kublai Khan later shifted the capital to Dadu (Beijing). A few buildings and artifacts survive, including stone tortoises that marked the city's boundaries.

In 1206, the Mongol chieftain Temujin (1162 – 1227) was proclaimed universal ruler, or Genghis (Chingis) Khan, by the united Mongol tribes. Genghis was a remarkable politician and military leader; having defeated rival Mongol tribes, he bound them together by the social and legal code that he instituted, which imposed a strict discipline but reformed abuses, helped the poor, and operated a meritocracy. Genghis organized the tribes into a formidable military machine that first defeated their enemy neighbors — Tibet, the Khara Khitai nomads, and Jin China — before rapidly moving on to conquer the Silk Road cities, eastern Persia, the Caucasus, and southern Russia.

By Genghis's death, the Mongols controlled an empire stretching right across central Asia to the Caspian Sea; under his sons and grandsons, the Mongol empire spread to control China, most of West Asia, Tibet, and Korea. The Mongols conquered their opponents with savage ruthlessness, but following that they brought peace, stability, and prosperity to the surviving inhabitants of their subject lands. Genghis promoted trade and craft activities, upon which the traditionally nomadic Mongols depended for the objects they used; he also practiced religious tolerance and encouraged literacy.

Despite growing tensions over the succession to supreme authority in the Mongol Empire, which by 1294 had in practice split into four separate khanates, Genghis's successors pursued his policies. Among their achievements: they built roads with regular way-stations and operated a swift postal service along them; patronized the arts, sciences, and education; made effective use of their subjects' skills, whether as administrators, experts in military technology, architects, or craftsmen; and encouraged trade that carried ideas, plants, technologies, and religions as well as goods throughout Asia and beyond. Unfortunately, the traders also carried disease: the Black Death. Beginning in China, it spread along the Silk Road into Europe in the mid fourteenth century, killing millions. **JM**

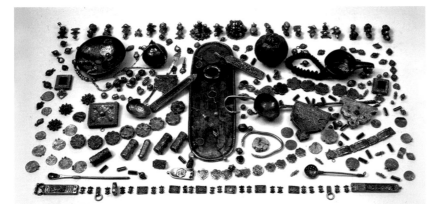

MONGOL HOARD

Genghis's grandson Batu, leading the Mongol army that later became known as the Golden Horde, conquered the southern Russian principalities by 1240. The Golden Horde dominated the region, receiving tribute, but declined after 1369. Their archaeological remains have been found in the northern Caucasus and along the Volga river. This late fourteenth-century hoard of objects, some of them gold, is from Simferopol in the Crimea.

KUBLAI KHAN'S INVASION FLEET

In 1281 Kublai Khan (1215–94), Genghis's grandson and Mongol ruler and emperor of China, sent a huge invasion fleet against Japan, where it met fierce resistance. In addition, a terrible storm (known to the Japanese as a "divine wind") sank many of Kublai's ships near Takashima island. The discovery of a Mongol commander's seal off Takashima led to underwater excavations in the vicinity from 1991; these revealed ship timbers, Mongol military equipment, including ceramic projectile bombs, and other material from Kublai's fleet.

WARFARE ON HORSEBACK

Trained from childhood to ride and hunt from horseback, Mongols made lightning raids and easily shook off pursuit; their mobility also aided reconnaissance. As nomads, they traveled light, and both they and their hardy steppe horses were able to campaign in winter. They shared these features with other nomad groups, but it was Genghis Khan's military genius that transformed Mongol warriors into disciplined, world-conquering soldiers.

Conscripting men aged fourteen to sixty, Genghis organized them in units of ten, 100, 1,000, and 10,000, each commanded by one man elected from the unit by the others. The men were lightly armored, wearing conical helmets and scale cuirasses; their horses were also armored. Traveling with up to five horses each, Mongols regularly changed mounts so as not to tire one, enhancing their travel speed. Discipline was absolute, and the troops drilled to execute precise maneuvers, following signals given with flaming arrows, drums, or banners. Using the composite bow, they killed men and horses en masse with clouds of arrows, and they often won against vastly superior numbers; lances were used to pick off individuals. Hand-to-hand fighting was avoided to minimize Mongol casualties. Tactics such as the feigned retreat played a major part in their success, along with advanced planning and flexibility in combat.

The Mongols let it be known that opposition was punishable by death: if a city failed to surrender immediately, its entire population would be massacred. Consequently, many cities surrendered without a fight. The Mongols also acquired military technology from their enemies, including Persian siege equipment and Chinese fire bombs, as well as enlisting specialist military personnel from conquered regions.

THE OTTOMANS

1 Panel of Iznik polychrome tiles at Atik Valide Mosque (1583).

2 Excavations at the tomb of Suleiman in Szigetvar, Hungary.

3 The Selimiye Mosque, completed in 1574 at Edirne, northwest Turkey.

The thirteenth century saw a weakening of the leading eastern Mediterranean powers: the Byzantine empire was damaged when the Fourth Crusade sacked Constantinople in 1204, and the Seljuks were defeated by the Mongols in 1243. By 1299, the embryo Ottoman state, a petty principality on the Seljuk-Byzantine border in northwest Anatolia, had begun to exploit the political vacuum and expand under its ruler Osman I (c. 1258—1326). Osman and his successors portrayed their conquests as a holy war, extending the territories within the Dar al-Islam (Islamic World). By 1354 the Ottomans had taken Gallipoli, on the European side of the Bosphorus, and by 1361 captured Adrianople, making it their new capital and renaming it Edirne.

Constantinople and Europe were weakened in the desperate aftermath of the Black Death, which had swept through from 1347. The Ottomans gained control of the Balkans and the independent petty states of Anatolia by 1400, and were ruling an empire stretching from the Danube to the Euphrates. After a setback at the hands of Tamerlane in 1402, they regained their lost territories by 1451, when Mehmet II (1432—81) acceded to the throne. Mehmet the Conqueror extended the empire to the borders of Hungary in the north, around most of the Black Sea coastal regions, and across the remaining portion

KEY EVENTS

1281	1341–50	1389	1402	1453	1460s
Ertoghrul, the first known ruler of a small state around Sogut on the Seljuk-Byzantine border, is succeeded by his son Osman, the first Ottoman sultan.	Bubonic plague, the "Black Death," originating in China, spreads through Asia and Europe via trade routes and kills up to half the population.	Decisive defeat of Serbians and Bosnians at the Battle of Kosovo gives the Ottomans control of much of the Balkans; Bulgaria is gained in 1393.	Tamerlane defeats the Ottomans at the Battle of Ankara but dies in 1405; principalities in the Balkans and Anatolia are lost but reconquered by 1451.	Constantinople falls to the Ottomans, ending the Byzantine Empire; the Ottomans preserve the city and it becomes their magnificent new capital, Istanbul.	Mehmet II begins construction of the lavishly decorated Topkapi Sarai, the Ottoman sultan's palace in Istanbul.

of Anatolia; he effectively destroyed the Byzantine Empire (see p. 410). His capture of Constantinople (Istanbul) in 1453 gave the Ottomans complete command of the Bosphorus, the key control point on the sea trade route linking Europe with Asia via the Black Sea and Mediterranean. The Venetians and Genoese were the main operators of this trade, but Mehmet's capture of the Genoese trading post of Kaffa in the Crimea in 1475 gained him control over the trading network's eastern leg. The Venetians and Genoese (themselves rivals) were now obliged to negotiate with or fight the Ottomans to maintain their trade. The Ottomans defeated the Venetians at sea in 1499; their developing naval forces remained a major threat to Europe's Mediterranean powers until 1571, when the Ottoman navy was defeated at Lepanto. Meanwhile, Muslim domination of the southern Mediterranean basin and disruptions to trans-Asian trade prompted other Europeans, notably the Portuguese, to seek sea routes to East Asia by sailing around Africa.

Mehmet's successors, Bayezid II and Selim I, came into conflict with the Persian Safavid Empire. Victory over the Safavids at Çaldiran in 1514 and the annexation of the border emirate of Dhu'l-Qadr brought the Ottomans into hostile contact with the Mamluk Empire, which they also defeated by 1517, when Selim took Cairo and gained control of Syria, western Arabia, and Egypt.

Selim's successor, Suleiman the Magnificent (r. 1520–66), renewed Ottoman expansion in eastern Europe, defeating Hungary at the Battle of Mohacs in 1526 and reaching the gates of Vienna in 1529, though his siege of the city failed. Suleiman died while besieging the Hungarian town of Szigetvar. His body was taken back to Istanbul for burial, but his heart and intestines were buried at Szigetvar. The tomb containing them was found in 2015 (see image 2).

By the sixteenth century the Ottoman Empire was a mature state, famed for its well-disciplined army and advanced firearms, including siege cannons; the magnificence of its architecture and patronage of the arts; its efficient bureaucracy; and its focus on education and charity, which included public soup kitchens, hospitals, and caravanserais. Among its most famous citizens was the great architect Mimar Sinan (1491–1588), who was responsible for more than 300 buildings. These included caravanserais, *madrassas*, bathhouses, and tombs, as well as civil engineering projects such as bridges, but his finest works were mosques. In the Selimiye Mosque (see image 3) at Edirne, one of the finest creations of Islamic architecture, he surpassed the enormous span of the dome of Hagia Sophia (see p. 414). Many mosques of this period were decorated with fine tiles (see image 1) from the town of Iznik.

Under Mehmet IV (1648–87) the Ottomans again expanded but the tide now turned, and between 1699 and 1795 they were pushed back by Austria, Poland, and Russia, while Egypt revolted in 1798 and broke away. Despite reforms the Ottoman Empire lost impetus through the nineteenth century, and the Western powers seized control of its territories after World War I. **JM**

1514	1520–66	1568–74	1571	1609–16	1683
Conflict with the Persian Shi'ite Safavid empire, supported by Ottoman religious dissidents, ends in Ottoman victory at the Battle of Çaldiran.	Suleiman the Magnificent reigns; a great patron of law, literature, and the arts, he extends the Ottoman Empire and creates a navy.	The Selimiye Mosque in Edirne is built by the great architect Sinan; its dome is wider and deeper than that of Hagia Sophia.	The Ottoman fleet is defeated by the Holy League in the Battle of Lepanto, off western Greece. It loses 20,000 men to the opponent fleet's losses of 7,500.	The Blue Mosque (see p. 448) is commissioned by Ahmet I. It is designed and built by Sinan's pupil, Sedefkar Mehmet Agha (d. 1617).	An Ottoman siege of Vienna is broken by Jan III Sobieski of Poland. In 1684 the Holy League begins to drive the Ottoman forces out of the Balkans.

The Blue Mosque 1609 – 1616

Inside the Blue Mosque, four massive piers support a central dome and four semi-domes; other semi-domes surround these, carried on buttresses; single domes sit in each of the four corners. The design creates a vast open hall, filled with natural light reflecting off the beautiful blue-glazed tiles. The donated carpets covering the floor are replaced regularly.

From 1603 the Ottomans fought an ill-fated war against Safavid Persia that they eventually lost in 1618, forfeiting most of their territory in the Caucasus region. To bolster national pride in the face of adversity, Sultan Ahmet I (1590 – 1617) commissioned a mosque, the Sultan Ahmet Mosque, now popularly known as the Blue Mosque because of the many blue tiles of its interior. He selected an imposing location, adjacent to Hagia Sophia, on the site of the former Byzantine emperors' palace, but attracted criticism by paying for the mosque's construction out of Treasury funds: such projects were generally undertaken in celebration of victories and financed from booty.

Sultan Ahmet's architect was an Albanian, Sedefkar Mehmet Agha. Although he was a gifted and favored pupil and assistant of the great architect Sinan (d. 1588), Mehmet succeeded him as Royal Architect only in 1606. He worked on the design and construction of the Blue Mosque from 1609 to 1616. Following in Sinan's footsteps, he based his design on the spacious domed architecture exemplified by Hagia Sophia (see p. 414), but modified to meet the different spatial requirements of Islamic sacred architecture.

In keeping with classical mosque design, the Blue Mosque has a precinct defined by a stone wall pierced by gates on three sides. Within this, the mosque and its integral courtyard occupy the central space. The gate toward the precinct's north corner led to the *madrasa* (theological school). Adjoining the mosque on its east side was a royal kiosk; a ramp allowed the sultan to enter on his horse. Inside were a loggia overlooking the Bosphorus, two rooms and access to the royal lodge inside the mosque, and a screened platform supported on marble columns and furnished with an elaborate *mihrab*. **JM**

◆ NAVIGATOR

1 MIHRAB AND MINBAR

The central feature of all mosques is the *mihrab*, an arched niche that shows the faithful the direction of Mecca. To the right is the *minbar*, the pulpit from which the imam delivers his sermon at Friday prayers. At the Blue Mosque both are made of richly decorated carved marble.

2 WINDOWS

The interior is lit by more than 200 windows, set in three tiers around the walls and around the base of the domes. The original stained glass was a gift to Sultan Ahmet from the Venetians, masters of glass making since medieval times, but most has been replaced with inferior modern glass.

3 IZNIK TILES

More than 20,000 Iznik tiles decorate the mosque. Iznik glazed ceramics, originally inspired by Chinese porcelain, began in the late fifteenth century with blue and white floral designs. Other colors were gradually added, but blue always predominated, as in the Blue Mosque.

▲ The Blue Mosque is unusual for having six minarets: the four at the corners of the mosque have three balconies each; the remaining two at the far corners of the courtyard each have two balconies. All the balconies are supported by stalactite corbels.

INNER COURTYARD

The Blue Mosque is approached through a marble-paved courtyard with a domed arcade of marble and porphyry columns around three sides and the mosque's portico along the fourth. The dome over the mosque's entrance bears a marble panel with a Koranic inscription. An elaborately carved fountain stands in the courtyard's center. A gallery outside shades faucets for the faithful to perform ablutions before praying.

INDIA AND SRI LANKA

Hinduism grew in importance in India in the later first millennium CE; Buddhism waned, though it continued in Sri Lanka to the present day. Northern India was politically fragmented, its more important dynasties including Rajput principalities in Rajasthan and Gujarat, operating from fortresses and encouraging trade and industry, and the Palas in Bihar and Bengal. Great kingdoms dominated southern India: the Chalukyas in the Deccan, and farther south the Pallavas and Pandyas, succeeded in the ninth century by the Cholas; these kingdoms were leaders in Indian Ocean trade, and their engagement with emerging kingdoms in Southeast Asia was reflected in the spread of Buddhist and later Hindu religion and architecture. Kings and wealthy citizens were major patrons of religious art and architecture, also donating land and workers to temple service. The temples funded land improvement, provided education, and sponsored trade.

Temples are the principal architectural remains. Rock-cut architecture declined as free-standing temples began to be constructed, characterized by a shrine surmounted by an elaborately decorated tower, whose form differed by region: a spire in the north, a curved tower in the east, and a tiered tower in the south. Temples were generally built within an enclosure; in the south these had tiered tower gateways (*gopuras*; see image 2) and the shrine was often

1 Old Delhi's Friday Mosque, Jama Masjid Mosque (1644–56), was built by Mughal emperor Shah Jahan (1592–1666).

2 One of the four *gopuras* of the Hindu Bhakthavatsaleswarar Temple at Tirukalukundram in Tamil Nadu, India.

3 The Gulbarga Fort (fourteenth century) was the headquarters of the Bahmani Sultanate in Gulbarga, Karnataka, India.

KEY EVENTS

8th century	1000–1025	1206	1336	1398	1509–30
The magnificent Kailasanatha Temple at Ellora becomes the last, spectacular example of Hindu rock-cut architecture.	Mahmud (971–1030) of Ghazana, Afghanistan, makes seventeen raids deep into India, and embellishes his city of Ghazana with the booty he acquires.	Qutb ud-Din Aibak establishes the Sultanate of Delhi. It is extended from Sindh and the Punjab to Bihar and Bengal by Iltutmish (d. 1236).	Vijayanagara city is founded in Karnataka, and a Hindu empire is created in order to repel Muslim sultans pressing in from the Deccan.	Tamerlane invades India and sacks Delhi, completing the disintegration of the failing Delhi Sultanate; its rump is conquered by the Lodis in 1451.	Krishnadevaraya, greatest ruler of Vijayanagara Empire, reigns; he increases the centralization of power, and is a great patron of temple construction.

preceded by a pillared hall (*mandapa*). Exuberant carvings, replete with meaning, cover the exterior and interior surfaces of many temples.

Pallava temples began to include a temple tank (pool or reservoir), a feature that became common in southern temple architecture. This in part reflects the authorities' responsibility to provide and maintain irrigation works for agriculture in southern India and to an even greater extent in Sri Lanka. Irrigation works continued to develop during the first millennium CE: tanks were ubiquitous and Sri Lankans built long canals and impressive dams as well.

The north was often invaded by steppe nomads or by settled neighbors from Persia and Afghanistan: from the eighth century onward the majority were Muslim. As part of Islam's initial spread, Sindh was briefly conquered by the Arabs in 712. In 1175 Muhammad of Gur (1149–1206) invaded India, and his successors founded and expanded the Sultanate of Delhi. Muhammad Tughluq, who seized power in 1320, briefly extended the sultanate far into the south, but it was already disintegrating when Tamerlane sacked Delhi in 1398.

In 1345 the ferocious Bahman Shah (1291–1358) seized control in the Deccan; his realm, centered at Gulbarga (see image 3), later broke up into five separate sultanates. Their southward expansion was prevented by the rise from 1336 of the Vijayanagara Empire (see p. 452), set on protecting Hinduism. At its height, around 1500, the dynasty of Vijayanagara kings controlled the southern third of the subcontinent, ruling as overlords and spiritual leaders of the southern kingdoms and chiefdoms that they conquered. Highly militarized, they kept at bay the Muslim forces to their north, adopting firearms and cannons, modernizing their cavalry (horses and elephants), and recruiting Muslim soldiers to their standing army. The empire was overthrown by a coalition of the Deccan sultans in 1565, but it left a legacy of improved agriculture; increased trade; revitalized temple construction; established towns with innovative secular architecture; and complex social institutions.

In 1526 Babur (1483–1530) conquered the Sultanate of Delhi, founding the Mughal dynasty, and defeated a confederacy of Rajput princes in 1527. Babur promoted Islamic culture and intellectual achievements in his new kingdom, harnessing the wealth it derived from irrigation agriculture, industry, and trade. His successors went on to create a huge and well-integrated empire that became famed for its patronage of art, architecture (see image 1), and intellectual life, backed, however, by overwhelming military force. Despite overall Muslim suzerainty, many areas remained under Hindu rule and the majority of the population continued to be Hindu in religious affiliation. Muslims took positions of authority in the Mughal administration and army, but found converts mainly among the lowest members of the caste hierarchy. Hindu states continued to control Sindh and Punjab, including the Rajputs and Mahrattas. The Mughal Empire declined after Aurangzeb (1618–1707) died, and gradually broke up into smaller states under rulers of various religions. **JM**

1526	1565	1570	1632–54	1639	1658–1707
Tamerlane's great-grandson Babur, originally from Ferghana in central Asia, defeats the Lodis at Panipat and founds the Mughal dynasty.	Vijayanagara is defeated at the Battle of Talikot by Muslim sultans of Deccan, who loot the city for six months; the city is abandoned.	Fatehpur Sikri (see p. 454) is founded as the Mughal capital. It is occupied until 1585, when Akbar (1542–1605) makes Lahore his base.	Mughal emperor Shah Jahan constructs the Taj Mahal gardens and mausoleum at Agra to commemorate his beloved wife, Mumtaz-i Mahal.	Shah Jahan (1592–1666) moves the Mughal capital to Delhi. In his new city, Shajahanabad, he builds the Red Fort and Jama Masjid Mosque.	Mughal emperor Aurangzeb reigns. He induces suffering and unrest among his Hindu subjects by imposing greater Islamic orthodoxy.

Vijayanagara 1336 – 1565

The Vitthala Temple at Vijayanagara, built by Krishnadevaraya in the 16th century, comprises a rectangular enclosure with gateways, the main shrine at its centre and subsidiary shrines and other buildings arranged in the remaining space. The central shrine was dedicated to Vitthala, an incarnation of Vishnu.

Vijayanagara—the name means City of Victory—was the capital of a Hindu empire that sprang up in southern India to counter Muslim forces that were overrunnning India; it succeeded in stemming the Islamic southward advance for more than two centuries. According to tradition, in c. 1336 two brothers, Harihara and Bukka, experienced soldiers serving a Muslim regional ruler as local governors, were persuaded to lead a crusade to defend the Hindu gods against Muslim rule. At its height, the empire they created was one of India's greatest states, controlling southern India and keeping at bay the sultanates to its north. Although constant warfare was a drain on the state's resources, its leaders' promotion of international trade and construction of irrigation works made the state productive and prosperous.

The city occupied 10 square miles (26 sq. km.) and was surrounded by seven concentric walls, the outer three containing agricultural land. The Royal Center at its heart, with a very extensive residential area to its east, was separated by a hill and irrigated land from the Sacred Center, which spread out along the south bank of the Tungabhadra river. Magnificent avenues approached the major temples, some flanked by stone arcades, public buildings and the stores and houses of wealthy merchants. A network of roads ran through the city, many paved with stone. Vijayanagara became one of the largest cities in the world, visited by foreigners who recorded their impressions of its magnificence. It was simultaneously a ceremonial and religious center, in which the king's role was pivotal; the state's administrative capital; a major commercial center; and a powerful military base.

The Vijayanagara Empire reached its peak under Krishnadevaraya (r. 1509–30). But in 1565 the Muslim sultanates defeated the Vijayanagara army at Talikota, in northern Karnataka, and sacked the city, plundering it for six months. Consequently the city was completely abandoned. However, in the early twentieth century the central part, Hampi, was investigated and partly excavated. Since the 1970s, extensive excavation, detailed recording, and restoration work have taken place here. **JM**

✦ NAVIGATOR

1 MANDAPA AND VIMANA

The main shrine is in two parts. The *mandapa* (pillared hall) has outer piers surrounded by slender columns; those inside are carved as rearing *yalis* (horned lions). Its stairs are flanked by elephant and *yali* balustrades; horses and their attendants decorate a frieze around its base. The *mandapa* leads into the *vimana* (main shrine), whose inner shrine has a pillared antechamber.

2 RATHA

In religious festivals, images of the gods are taken in procession in *rathas* (temple carts). From the twelfth century onward, South Indian temple complexes sometimes included a shrine in the form of a *ratha*, translated into stone. This example once bore a brick and plaster superstructure. The *ratha* housed an image of Garuda, the part-bird, part-human mount of Vishnu.

3 DRAMATIC SURROUNDINGS

Vijayanagara lies in the valley of the great Tungabhadra river, among granite cliffs and hills, in a region prone to volcanic activity. The forces of nature have created an extraordinary landscape strewn with massive boulders, some precariously balanced one on another, as if by a giant's hand. The city's intricately detailed architecture is skillfully threaded through this, to breathtaking effect.

4 GOPURA

Three *gopuras* (monumental gateways), on the north, east and south sides, give access to the Vitthala precinct. Their base is built of granite, the upper portion of brick and plaster, rising in receding tiers and elaborately decorated. *Gopuras* are a characteristic feature of the Vijayanagara architectural style, which continued to inform southern temple design long after the empire fell.

▲ Central to the city and its road network is the Hazara Rama (Ramachandra) Temple, the main royal shrine. Reliefs on the temple and its enclosure walls show scenes from the life of Rama, hero of the epic poem "Ramayana" and an important deity here.

THE ROYAL CENTER

The Royal Center at Vijayanagara includes many palaces, and sixty temples and other structures, grouped in adjacent compounds bounded by granite walls. East of the central Hazara Rama temple lie public and ceremonial buildings, with royal and elite residential buildings to its west. Buildings to its south include a hundred-pillared audience hall and a magnificent stepwell, supplied by an efficient network of water channels and aqueducts. The Queen's Bath (a water pavilion for royal bathing) features a central basin surrounded by an arcaded corridor with balconies. To the northeast is an enormous block of elephant stables featuring eleven massive domes, and the exquisite Lotus Mahal pavilion, a blend of Hindu and Muslim architectural traditions.

Fatehpur Sikri 1570–85

The Diwan-i-Khas at Fatehpur Sikri is a large hall. In its center is an extraordinary monolithic pillar with multiple brackets supporting a circular railed platform from which galleries run out to join the gallery around the wall: here the audience sat while discussions took place below. The Diwan-i-Am nearby, for public audiences, is a pavilion building with a small raised chamber on its west side where the emperor sat.

M ughal architecture was an impressive synthesis of elements from Islamic, Turkic, Persian, and Hindu architecture. Pillared halls, gateways, domes and an abundance of decoration were popular elements. It achieved a high level of harmony under Akbar (1542–1605), exemplified by the buildings at Fatehpur Sikri, and its greatest flowering under Shah Jahan (1592–1666), for example in his palace at Lal Qila (Red Fort) in Shahjahanabad (Delhi). Mughal architecture declined under later emperors.

Fatehpur Sikri was built by Akbar in 1571–72, using locally available red sandstone, but abandoned in 1585. The whole walled inner city is a palace, its separate components laid out geometrically. Its buildings include both massive imposing solid structures and light airy pavilions. Official buildings lay on the eastern side of the complex, private quarters on the west. The palatial elements of the Red Fort, begun in 1638, were enclosed within its massive fortification walls, also constructed as individual buildings, interlinked and separated by formal gardens. The buildings are of red sandstone, embellished with the finest materials, including marble and precious stones.

Mughal palaces had a number of elements. They included the Diwan-i-Am, an audience hall in which public business was conducted, and the Diwan-i-Khas, the private audience hall, where the emperor listened to discussions. There were also private residential buildings, and separate quarters—the *zenana*—housed the ladies of the royal household. Other parts of the palace could include a treasury; administrative offices; an arsenal; baths; accommodation for courtiers, guards, and palace staff; and stables. These elements were arranged as separate buildings, often interlinked, frequently set among gardens. **JM**

THE PANCH MAHAL

Fatehpur Sikri boasted a great variety of palatial structures, including the Ankh Michauli, or treasury; the adjacent "Astrologer's Seat," a small kiosk; and the Panch Mahal, a building with five tiers of pillared halls of diminishing length. Originally, there were screens between the pillars, which allowed royal ladies to walk there to enjoy the view over the Anoop Talao pool below, a place of recreation where concerts took place. Service facilities were mainly clustered in the lower part of the site.

ZENANA

Several *zenana* buildings were constructed at Fatehpur Sikri. The largest, Jodha Bai's palace, housed the royal ladies. Its large central courtyard was surrounded by rooms with decorated pillars and balconies; it was roofed with turquoise tiles. A smaller palace, Haramsara, accommodated lesser court ladies. The buildings were connected by a covered passage, allowing the ladies to move between them unobserved. Another smaller *zenana*, Mariam-uz-Zamani's palace, is situated nearby.

MUGHAL GARDENS

The memoirs of the first Mughal emperor, Babur (r. 1526–1530), record how keenly he missed the gardens of his home in central Asia. He thus created gardens in India, introducing the *char bagh*, a formal garden quartered by two intersecting waterways, symbolizing the rivers of paradise. The elements of the ideal Mughal garden included running water, pools reflecting the sky, fruit and shade trees, flowers, birds, grass, and pleasant breezes. Fatehpur Sikri has the first gardens incorporated into a Mughal palace, including one north of Jodha Bai's palace, a paved terraced garden on two levels. Like the *char bagh*, terraces became a frequent feature of Mughal gardens. Regular garden construction began with Akbar, who created many pleasure gardens in his capital at Lahore. Later Mughal royalty also took a keen interest in gardens. Two were created by the wife and daughter-in-law of Jahangir (1569–1627) on the river bank at Agra, arranged in tiers, with a *char bagh* at the top of the landward side. Jahangir's son, Shah Jahan, elaborated the form of the *char bagh* in the gardens that are the setting for the Taj Mahal, the tomb of his beloved wife.

Under Shah Jahan, gardens became an integrated feature of palace design, symbolizing paradise on earth. Their plantings were enhanced by the setting of buildings among them, blurring the distinction between structure and landscape. The whole palace at the Red Fort was designed as a garden, with pavilions and halls set on terraces. Its architecture mirrored garden form, particularly in the largest of the gardens, the Hayat Bakhsh. Columns were shaped like cypress trees; water channels ran within the buildings; and decorative flowers and plants made of marble and precious stones turned ceilings and walls into a virtual flower garden.

EAST ASIA

1 An aerial view of Hōryū Temple in Ikaruga, Nara Prefecture, Japan.

2 A Goryeo celadon (greenware) kettle in the form of a mythical dragon-turtle.

3 The floating red torii gate of Itsukushima Shrine stands in the Seto inland sea.

East Asia encompasses modern China, Japan, and Korea, which share a wealth of cultural material. From the sixth to the fifteenth centuries, regional trade networks in East Asia and long-distance trade routes to the Eurasian hemisphere aided the diffusion and exchange of technology and culture between East and West. These routes were the communication highways of the ancient world. New inventions (paper, compass, waterwheels), religious beliefs and social customs, as well as goods and raw materials (silk, porcelain, lacquer), were transmitted by people moving from one place to another.

In China the period from the Tang dynasty (618–907) to the Ming dynasty (1368–1644)—most of the medieval period—is sometimes referred to as the golden age, or classical age, and it remains unsurpassed for ceramics and architecture. Indeed, archaeology provides a vivid picture of social, economic, and cultural developments during this period. For example, Tang cities and tombs and Song dynasty (960–1279) palaces and royal gardens have been excavated. Six wooden ships dating from the Yuan dynasty (1271–1368) show the emergence of maritime trade, and the accompanying finds included bronze, ironware, and pottery together with 370 pieces of Cizhou porcelain. The ceramic industry enjoyed a new heyday from the Song dynasty onward. Both

KEY EVENTS

552	605	7th century	8th century	10th century	1085
Two Persian monks smuggle silkworms back from China to the Eastern Roman Empire, thus enabling silk production in Europe and Asia Minor.	The Zhaozhou bridge across the Xiao river is finished. Constructed by Li Chun during the Sui dynasty (581–618), it spans more than 123 feet (37.5 m.).	The adoption of Buddhism gives rise to cremation burial, more popular in the Unified Silla period of Korea than in the Yamato period of Japan.	The Hōryū Temple in Nara Prefecture is built. It includes the oldest wooden construction in Japan.	The huge palace complex of Manwoldae at the base of Mount Songak in North Korea is constructed during the Goryeo dynasty.	The first copper coins are produced in China.

court and private porcelain kilns, including the so-called Five Famous Kilns—Ru, Guan, Ge, Ding, and Jun—became household names.

The only fully excavated mausoleum of a Ming dynasty emperor was the Dingling Mausoleum, the tomb of the dynasty's first emperor, Zhu Yijun (1563–1620). Construction took more than six years, and the tomb has yielded 3,000 cultural relics, such as gold and silver vessels, and blue and white porcelain. Economics also developed rapidly during the Ming dynasty. The population boom that began in the Song dynasty accelerated, until China's population grew from 80 or 90 million to 150 million in three centuries.

Medieval Japan is marked by the beginning of the Asuka period (552–645). During this time, the imperial Yamato dynasty was established, along with the beginning of recorded Japanese history. The Yamato established power via a Chinese-based bureaucracy based on Confucianism and encouraged the spread of Buddhism, found throughout China. Construction of Buddhist temples occurred in cities and the countryside. Later Japan also displayed an orientation toward the traditional Shinto faith and Zen Buddhism, beginning in 1191.

In the centuries between the demise of the Heian civilization in the late 12th century and the reunification of Japan in the early seventeenth century under the Tokugawa shoguns, towns were built in many parts of the country. In addition to the new center of government at Kamakura, there appeared trading centres such as Sakai near Osaka, castle towns such as Ichijōdani, and towns associated with major religious centers. The archaeology of the medieval period has focused much of its effort on religious centers, cities, and castles. The Shintō Itsukushima Shrine, with its red torii gate (see image 3), has proved to be the earliest shrine building, dating from the sixth century, and approximately forty-eight Buddhist monuments have been documented in the Hōryū-ji area, in Nara Prefecture (see image 1). Several date from the late seventh or early eighth century, making them some of the oldest surviving wooden buildings in the world. Porcelain and pottery have also been also studied through archaeology, such as at the excavation site of the Tengudani Old Kiln in Arita, the birthplace and early production center of Arita porcelain.

The Goryeo dynasty (918–1392) was a high point in the history and culture of Korea. By the beginning of the tenth century, woodblock printing had developed to such a degree that the entire Buddhist scriptures were engraved in print. Korean "white hammered paper" was renowned in the East Asian hemisphere. Tombs and temples were constructed and are testimony to the great architectural achievements in Korea. Most of the Goryeo royal tombs are in the vicinity of Gaeseong, in North Korea. The mausoleum of Kongmin, who reigned from 1352 to 1374, is the best preserved, with a stone chamber and wall paintings. The most important metal objects of the period were Buddhist bronze temple bells and incense burners; celadon is the most renowned ceramic ware, discovered during tomb excavations (see image 2). **MP**

12th–13th century	1271–95	1271–1368	13th century	1400	1405
Celadon production and the invention of versatile metal printing are key cultural achievements of the Goryeo dynasty.	Niccolò (1230–94) and Maffeo (1230–1309) Polo make a second visit to China, accompanied by Niccolò's son Marco (1254–1324), who writes about their journey.	The Yuan dynasty capital of Dadu (now the city of Beijing) is built.	Silk Road trade reaches its height during the Pax Mongolica, a time of relative peace in Asia during widespread unification under the Mongol Empire.	The Golden and Silver Pavilions are built in Kyoto, Japan.	Zheng He (c. 1371–1433) leads the great maritime expeditions traversing the South China Sea and Indian Ocean to reach the east coast of Africa.

THE TANG DYNASTY

1 Vairocana Buddha is the central figure of Fengxian Temple at Longmen Grottoes.

2 An embroidered silk banner, found in the Buddhist cave temples of Dunhuang.

3 A gold-plated receptacle, discovered under the pagoda of the Famensi Temple.

After 300 years of division and fragmentation following the collapse of the Han dynasty in 220, China was once again unified under the Sui dynasty (581–618), which was replaced by the flourishing Tang dynasty (618–907). Successful diplomatic relations, international trade activities, cultural prosperity, and what is sometimes described as a "cosmopolitan style" made Tang China one of the greatest empires in the medieval world. Chang'an, its center and capital, saw merchants, clerics, and envoys arrive from India, the Arabian hemisphere, Korea, and Japan. In addition, architecture enjoyed a heyday in the construction of wooden halls, palaces, and temples, most of which were destroyed but whose style can be seen in Korean and Japanese temples. The Great Hall of Nanchan Temple, built in 782, is the only timber building that still exists. New architectural ideas were brought to China by Buddhist monks who erected monasteries and pagodas. From the Tang dynasty onward, brick and stone architecture gradually became more common.

Buddhist grottoes such as the Longmen Grottoes, Henan province (see image 1), are among the finest examples of Buddhist art. There are as many as 100,000 statues within the 1,400 caves, ranging from 1 inch (25 mm.) to

KEY EVENTS

618	630	663	683	7th–8th century	704
The reign of Gaozu, the first emperor of the Tang dynasty, begins.	Japan sends a first mission to the Tang and establishes formal relations.	Daming Palace in Chang'an is completed; it serves as the royal residence for more than 220 years.	Empress Wu Zetian, the only female monarch of the Tang, begins her reign.	The Bo people living in central China build cliff-burial chambers; 131 hanging coffins are found in 2015 outside Moping, Zigui county, Hubei province.	The Buddhist Giant Wild Goose Pagoda, located in southern Xi'an, Shaanxi province, is rebuilt.

57 feet (17 m.) in height. The Famensi Temple, located 75 miles (110 km.) west of Chang'an, is renowned for the discovery of a crypt lying untouched beneath the pagoda. Built in 874, the site is rare because of the perfect match between the archaeological data and historical events of Buddhism during the Tang. After a period of heavy rainfall, the pagoda of the temple collapsed, revealing three successive stone chambers, the innermost located beneath the core of the foundations. Sealed within a stone casket were 400 pieces of gold, silver, foreign glass, ceramics, and tea utensils—some of the finest relics of the Tang dynasty (see image 3). Most important was a set of reliquaries, each containing what is supposed to be a "finger bone" of Buddha, notoriously described by the poet Han Yu (768–824) in 819.

Chang'an was built on a square grid system, which divided the city into smaller areas for marketplaces, manufacturing areas, temple districts, administrative buildings, and the imperial palace in the north. Throughout the entire city, there were more than one hundred Buddhist monasteries, forty-one Daoist abbeys, two official temples, seven churches of foreign religions, and six graveyards. In 1999 archaeologists excavated the ruined round altar, where the emperor made sacrifices to Heaven. Situated in the east of the southern suburbs, it was built during the Sui period and abandoned at the end of the Tang. It is therefore older than the Temple of Heaven in Beijing. The round altar was constructed of rammed earth and layers of white plaster with four tiers of circular platforms, each measuring about 6 feet 6 inches (2 m.) in height and having on the periphery twelve flights of ascending steps, used for sacrificial ceremonies. Tang tombs (see p. 460) often contained tri-colored ceramic models of central Asian figures such as warriors, court ladies, horse riders and camels either with camel leaders and musicians or loaded with commodities.

The Silk Route trade flourished during the Tang dynasty, and caravans brought luxury and everyday goods from East to West through the Eurasian hemisphere. Horses were imported from Karashar and Kucha, glass goblets from Byzantium, jade from Khotan, medicines from Kashmir and India, crystals and agate from Samarkand, and cotton from Turfan. In exchange, textiles, tea, paper, and ceramics were export goods. Silk also remained a major item of trade. The finest silks were used for women's clothing and delicate paintings (see image 2). In addition, China engaged in thriving maritime trade and in large-scale production for overseas export. In 1998 the discovery of the so-called Belitung shipwreck, a silt-preserved shipwrecked Arabian dhow sailboat, in the Gaspar Strait, brought to light 63,000 pieces of Tang ceramics, silver, and gold. Foreign trade also brought new technologies to China, many of which facilitated the improved administration of the Tang, namely astronomy (for the state calendar), agronomy, hydraulic engineering, and traffic (for taxes, food, and commodities). **MP**

c. 710	747	*c.* 845	858	868	904
Liu Zhiji writes the *Shitong*, or *Historical Perspectives*, the first comprehensive work on historical criticism in any language.	Water-powered fan wheels that function like air conditioning are used to cool a hall in the Imperial Palace, Chang'an.	Under Emperor Wuzong, Buddhism is repressed and thousands of monasteries are destroyed.	The Grand Canal floods massively and inundates much land in the northern part of China.	*Diamond Sutra*, found at Dunhuang Buddhist cave, is the oldest full-length book printed at regular size and completed with illustrations.	The reign of Ai, the last Tang dynasty emperor, begins. He is assassinated by warlord Zhu Quanzong at the age of fifteen.

Tang Imperial Tombs   609 – 918

Qianling is the last resting place of the third emperor Gaozong, who reigned from 649 to 683, and his wife, Empress Wu Zetian, who followed him onto the throne. She ruled from 690 to 705 and was the only governing female empress. After Gaozong's death, she despatched geomancers to choose an appropriate tomb site on the Guanzhong plain, and they selected Mount Liang, at a height of 3,507 feet (1,069 m.) above sea level.

The great mausoleums of the Tang dynasty emperors were centered in the area near the capital of Chang'an and scattered across the Guanzhong plain. This area is known as China's Valley of the Kings, because it is not only the location of the mausoleums of emperors of both the Western Han (206 BCE–9 CE) and Tang dynasties, but also of hundreds of satellite tombs belonging to members of the imperial families, as well as leading civilian and military officials. The two largest Tang mausoleums are Zhaoling and Qianling. Zhaoling belongs to the second Tang emperor, known as Taizong. He ruled from 626 to 649 and oversaw one of China's greatest periods of cultural and political accomplishment. Zhaoling has the largest burial grounds among the royal tombs in China and the world. Satellite tombs of members of the royal family and officials accompany the mausoleum, and although some of these have been opened, the main tombs still await excavation.

The surface structures of these imperial tombs included monumental gates, a long spirit way lined with stone statuary, a large enclosed mortuary garden, memorial halls, chapels, lodges, shrines, and imperial quarters. At Qianling the burial ground comprised a complex of underground chambers, reached by descending diagonal ramps. Frescoes were added to the walls and tops of the passage, archway, corridor, and chambers, where images of maidservants, officials of various ranks, horse grooms and horses, soldiers, officials, and tomb guardian beasts reflect court life. Two frescoes—called "Painting of Polo Game" and "Paintings of Envoy and Guests"—depict cultural exchanges between China and regions to the west along the Silk Road. **MP**

👁 FOCAL POINTS

SANCAI HORSE

This standing horse has been decorated with the so-called three-color glaze technique known as *sancai*. The most common colors were brown, green, and cream-white, and they were often blended into one another to give a unique effect. Typically, *sancai* figures were produced as burial goods.

TOMB OF PRINCESS YONGTAI

Seventeen of the Tang imperial mausoleums at Chang'an were robbed during the late Tang and Five Dynasties period (907–960). Only a few have been excavated, such as the tomb of Princess Yongtai. Many fine wall paintings were discovered, including a series of sixteen maids of honor on the walls of the front chamber.

STONE SCULPTURES AT QIANLING

The spirit way (*shendao*) is an avenue or walkway connecting a tomb complex built for members of the nobility and the imperial family with its outermost boundary. Traditionally, a *shendao* began at the southern wall of the tomb and ran directly southward to the complex's southern outer edge. At Qianling mausoleum, the *shendao* is more than 0.6 mile (1 km.) in length. Lined up on either side of the avenue are stone sculptures of both fabulous beasts and recognizable animals, including winged horses, lions, and ostriches—from historical records, it is known that the khan of the Western Turks presented the ostrich (previously unknown in China) to the court in 620 CE, and another was sent from India in 650. Also present among the *shendao* sculptures are statues of a guard of honor and numerous officials, as well as horses standing with their grooms.

The monumental sculptures of humans standing on the *shendao* and elsewhere at Qianling reflect the cosmopolitanism of the Tang dynasty and offer evidence of the extent to which the emissaries of the Tang court were in touch with their counterparts in Western Asia. In one sanctuary within the complex stands a large retinue of stone figures representing the actual ambassadors and foreign envoys from more than sixty countries who attended the funeral of Emperor Gaozong. The heads of these figures were sculpted in the men's likenesses and, being more valuable than the plain and uniformly sculpted bodies, were hacked off and carried away by tomb raiders who plundered the burials during the mid and late Ming dynasty (1368–1644).

Not all of the sculptures at Qianling represent living creatures. Among those on the *shendao* are sets of octagonal stone pillars intended to deter evil spirits; three steles also exist, including one of a much later date, erected by the Qianlong Emperor (r. 1735–96).

THE UNIFIED SILLA KINGDOM

1 Cheomseongdae Royal Observatory in Gyeongju is 29 feet (9 m.) high. It was used twenty-four hours a day, all year round, by state astronomers who observed and recorded celestial phenomena.

2 The Sakyamuni Buddha at Bulguksa Temple is seated on a lotus pedestal. It is facing out to sea and holds one of its hands in bhumisparsa mudra, the earth-touching position.

The South Korean kingdom of the Unified Silla brought together the cultures of three earlier kingdoms, after having defeated Baekje, Goguryeo, and Gaya (see p. 370). It was also under the influence of Tang China and central Asia, absorbing their foreign traditions and cultural achievements. Diplomatic relations with the Tang emperors led to successful economical and artistic exchange, in which luxury goods, books, and works of art were imported from China, and Korean students traveled to China to study Buddhism or Confucianism. By the seventh century, Buddhism was the dominant religion in Silla, practiced by the monarch, aristocrats, and common people. Silla also had maritime contacts with Japan and the Arabian hemisphere.

Unified Silla had strong kings and local administration. Gyeongju became the capital city and developed into a cosmopolitan city modeled on Chang'an, the Chinese capital. New temples and palaces were built, as well as centers for scientific studies. Under Queen Seondeok, who reigned from 632 to 647, the Cheomseongdae Royal Observatory (see image 1) was constructed. This bottle-shaped astronomical tower has twenty-seven courses of stone blocks, and it is the oldest existing observatory in East Asia.

KEY EVENTS

668	674	682	7th century	c. 750	751
After defeating Baekje, Goguryeo, and Gaya, Silla rules alone as the Unified Silla.	King Munmu (626–681) begins the construction of an artificial pond, now known as Anapji, and garden, close to the old palace site.	The National Confucian Academy is established, and scholarship in mathematics, historiography, and astronomy flourishes.	Zen Buddhism is introduced to Korea from China.	The *Pure Light Dharani Sutra* is created; it is the oldest known woodblock print in the world.	Work begins at the Bulguksa Temple site, and the Seokgatap stone pagoda is built.

According to historical records, King Munmu, who reigned from 661 to 681, began the construction of an artificial pond now called Anapji (Lake of Wild Geese and Ducks) near the Weolseong Palace (Moon Palace) in Gyeongju in 674 (see p. 464). Excavations of the area around the pond—the original name of which was Wolji (Moon Pond)—have brought to light tiles, Buddhist images, and pottery, metal, and lacquer vessels. A pine boat, almost 19 feet (6 m.) long, was discovered on the shore. The palace area, where state banquets were held and foreign guests received, has been partly reconstructed around the pond.

Although Silla was the last Korean kingdom to accept Buddhism, it immediately adopted it as a state religion, which strengthened national identity in Unified Silla. More than sixty Buddhist temples were constructed around Gyeongju, most of which were destroyed during the Mongol invasion. Bulguksa Temple, on the slopes of Mount Toham, was considered a masterpiece of Buddhist architecture. It was built between 751 and 774, based on the plan of ancient Indian cave temples. It comprises a rectangular antechamber and a domed main chamber that contains a seated Sakyamuni Buddha (see image 2), the Buddha of the Enlightenment. Forty-one figures, including bodhisattvas, disciples, and guardian deities are located in the vicinity of the Buddha. In the temple's restored state, there are two pagodas and several halls, with the Hall of Great Enlightenment being the main building in the temple complex. Bulguksa Temple has been added to the UNESCO World Heritage list, together with the Buddhist cave temple at Seokguram in the same area.

Large amounts of metal were needed to cast the bells for another of Gyeongju's Buddhist temples, Hwangryong, which was completed in the seventh century. This nine-story structure was built entirely of wood with no iron nails. It was the tallest building in East Asia, reaching a height of 262 feet (80 m.), and the tallest wooden structure in the world at the time of its completion.

However, perhaps the most exquisite examples of metalwork are the so-called *sarira*, or reliquaries, which usually hold small remains of the historical Buddha and Buddhist texts. They comprise several layers of gilt-bronze containers and an innermost container sometimes made of glass. The glass excavated from Silla temples and tombs provides evidence of trade with Western Asia. Late Roman, Sasanian, and Syrian glass has been found, and also vessels made locally, using high lead composition glass. Discoveries of crucibles and clay molds for glass making provide clear evidence for this local production.

Pottery in the Unified Silla period was densely decorated. Due to a change in burial practice under Buddhism, jars were produced for burying funerary ashes and these often bore stamped motifs of lotus flowers. Unglazed and glazed wares—with no great change in use since the former kingdoms—were manufactured in large quantities. Figurines of horses, oxen, dancers, officials, foreigners, zodiac figures, soldiers, and servants were found in tombs and are evidence of contact with Tang China and beyond. **MP**

774	788	790	8th–9th century	8th–9th century	935
The Buddhist cave temple at Seokguram, east of Gyeongju, is completed.	An examination for state administrators based on Confucianism is introduced.	The Bulguksa Temple complex, representing the land of Buddha, is completed.	Intensive relationships are established with Tang China, leading to widespread Chinese cultural influence on Korea.	Contact with Japan and the realms of the Silk Road flourishes.	The last king of the Unified Silla, King Gyeongsun (897–978), surrenders to King Wang Geon (877–943), the founder of the Goryeo kingdom.

Anapji Seventh century

Anapji pond and its reconstructed buildings form part of the royal palace site of Silla in South Korea. The artificial pond had five buildings, 4,363 feet long (1,330 m), along its shore, located to command full views of the pond.

Anapji is situated in Gyeongju, Gyeongsangbuk province, South Korea, and is part of the old Wolseong palace complex and historic garden area of the Unified Silla dynasty. During archaeological surveys and excavations the pond was drained in 1972, revealing thousands of Silla artifacts. Many of these were restored and relocated to the Gyeongju National Museum.

The original name of the pond was Wolji (Moon Pond). The thirtieth King of Silla, Munmu, started the construction of the artificial pond and pleasure garden. After the defeat of the Unified Silla the area was deserted and the pond became known as Anapji meaning Lake of Wild Geese and Ducks. Historical records first mention the pond in the *Samguk Sagi* (*Chronicle of the Three Kingdoms*) in 1145: "An artificial pond was dug in the palace grounds, and a mountain was made in the pond. Flowers and plants were planted, and rare birds and animals were raised in the mountain."

At this time Anapji served as a resort garden with rare plants and animals. To impress Tang dynasty (618–907) Chinese envoys, miniaturizations of the twelve famous peaks of China's Wu mountains were terraced around the lake. Palace buildings and pavilions were erected, such as the Imhajeon (Ocean-facing Hall). All of the pavilions have now vanished, but some of the original foundation stones are still visible by the lakeside.

Excavations in the silt layers of the area around the pond, brought to light 30,000 ancient artifacts. They included 5,798 tiles, 1,748 vessels, 1,132 wooden objects, 843 metal objects, 694 iron objects, 434 animal bones, 86 wooden plates, and 62 stone artifacts. One very rare find was a boat, almost 19 feet (6 m.) long, made of pine planks, which was discovered on the shore of the pond. A large number of Buddhist relics were also found, including gilt-bronze standing Buddha images and small bodhisattva plaques that were probably used as altarpieces. **MP**

ROYAL PALACE

The Ocean-facing Hall is presumed to be the main structure of the East Palace used by the Crown Prince. The 'Ocean' is presumed to be the pond. It was built west of the mountain with twelve peaks, copying the Wu mountains in China, and was used as a banquet and reception pavilion until the fall of the Unified Silla period. It could seat more than 1,000 people, and was a venue for court diplomacy and entertainment. Records of the events held in the hall are given in the *Chronicle of the Three Kingdoms*:

697	King Hyoso (32nd king) held a party for his subjects.
786	Storms destroyed Imhae and Inwha Gate.
804, 847, and 867	Imhae Hall was repaired.
860	King Honan (47th king) convened a meeting.
881	King Heongang (49th king) held a party. He played *geomungo* zither and sang.
931	King Daejo, the founder king of the Goryeo dynasty, was invited to Imhae Hall and a party was given in his honour by King Gyeongsun (last King of Silla).

DRAINAGE

Gyeongju took shape under King Munmu. The city was located on a broad plain and constructing the artificial pond helped the drainage of the site. A refined drainage system was employed to cope with changes in rainfall.

ROOF TILE

The tiles found have 300 pattern styles. Some have inscriptions with the manufacturing date of 680. Green-glazed specimens with dragon designs were used on roof edges to ward off evil spirits.

ASUKA TO NARA PERIOD

1 The Asuka-dera Temple in Nara Prefecture on southern Honshu is one of the oldest Buddhist temples in Japan.

2 The miniature Tamamushi Shrine at the Hōryū Temple in Nara Prefecture is made from wood, metal, and lacquer. It is decorated with paintings depicting various aspects of Buddhist cosmology.

3 The Asuka Bijin (Beautiful Women) mural from the Takamatsuzuka Tomb in Asuka village, Nara Prefecture.

The Asuka period (552–645) is regarded as Japan's first historical period. Asuka is the name of an area near the city of Nara, and the former residence of the emperors. In this period, significant social, political, and cultural transformations took place. This was mainly due to the introduction of Buddhism as a religious system, which partly replaced Shinto beliefs.

Buddhism was spreading out from India, through the Silk Routes via China, and was already 1,000 years old when it arrived in Japan. As it was assimilated into various cultures, it underwent changes in its iconography and artistic styles. It also brought innovations from the areas it had passed through: the Chinese written language, the standardization of weights, and the minting of coins. In addition, the idea of a historical record came from the mainland and spread throughout the Japanese archipelago. Because of Buddhism's influence Emperor Tenmu (c. 631–686) enacted a law in 675 to prohibit the use of livestock and the consumption of some wild animals such as monkeys.

As Buddhism was in its heyday, so Buddhist temples started to be built, such as the Asuka-dera Temple (see image 1) dating to 606, with its large seated gilt-bronze image of the Shakyamuni Buddha. An industry in Buddhist art also began and Buddhist temples were decorated with religious paintings. A rare example of Asuka period painting is seen on the panels and doors of the Tamamushi Shrine (see image 2) at the Hōryū Temple complex.

KEY EVENTS

538	6th century	600–59	601–07	604	708
The Japanese capital is located in Asuka, on the plains near Nara.	Buddhism is introduced in Japan.	Japan sends envoys to Tang dynasty (618–907) China	Prince Shōtoku builds the Buddhist Hōryū Temple in Ikaruga, Nara Prefecture.	Prince Regent Taishi Shōtoku (574–662) introduces the Seventeen Article Constitution, based on Confucian political and ethical ideals.	Construction of the new capital city of Nara begins.

In 741, Emperor Shōmu (701–756) issued an edict to build temples in the capital and in the countryside. The Tōdai Temple (Great Eastern Temple) with its Shōsō-in Repository (see p. 468) was constructed in 743. It was one of the Seven Great Temples in the city of Nara, and its Daibutsu-den (Great Buddha Hall) houses the world's largest Buddha. Forty-eight lacquered cinnabar pillars, 5 feet (1.5 m.) in diameter and 98 feet (30 m.) tall, support the blue-tiled roof of the hall. According to records, more than 2,600,000 people were involved in its construction, contributing rice, wood, metal, cloth, or labor. The original complex comprised pagodas, which were among the tallest buildings of the time. Destroyed by earthquakes, the pagodas were rebuilt several times. Archaeological surveys and excavations at the complex have brought to light charcoal, clay bricks, and fragments of copper and bronze, connected with the construction of the Great Buddha. Most of the temple treasures were long gone, but two swords found in 1907 underneath the Buddha's knee have been classified as donations by Shōmu's wife, Empress Kōmyō (701–760).

Politically, China and Korea set the example for a bureaucratic government with a central administration. This system was dominated by the imperial court, which reigned over subordinate clan chieftains. Numerous official missions of envoys, priests, and students were sent to China in the seventh century. From 600 to 659, Japan sent diplomatic emissaries to China and Korea. This exchange had an influence on Japan's funerary culture. Tombs in this period differ from their predecessors. The Takamatsuzuka Tomb, dating to the end of the seventh or beginning of the eighth century, was excavated in the early 1970s at Akusa village in Nara Prefecture. The stone chamber with an adjacent passageway is covered by an earthen mound. It holds a sarcophagus that opens to the south. The walls inside the tomb are coated with plaster. Colored murals on the walls and ceiling (see image 3) show courtiers in clothing typical of the Korean Goguryeo Kingdom (37 BCE–668 CE), as well as the White Tiger, Vermillion Bird, Azure Dragon, and Black Tortoise constellations.

Every imperial dynasty before the eighth century manifested its claim on power by building a capital city, along with an imperial palace. In the Nara period (710–784) the capital was located at Heijō-kyō, the present-day city of Nara. It was modeled after the Chinese Tang capital Chang'an, but without surrounding walls. Merchants, traders, and envoys from China, Korea, and India introduced foreign cultures and ideas through the Silk Road, turning the city into the first international capital and urban center of Japan. The population grew to 200,000, with 10,000 people working as government officials.

The Nara period also saw a tremendous amount of cultural development. The oldest written historical and mythical sources, the *Kojiki* (*Records of Ancient Matters*, 712) and especially the *Nihon shoki* (*Chronicles of Japan*, 720) have proved to be an important tool for historians and archaeologists, because they constitute the most complete extant historical record of ancient Japan. **MP**

708	712–720	734	743	784	794
The first Japanese coin is minted.	The first national histories of Japan are compiled.	The assemblage of hollow-core, dry lacquer Buddhist sculptures is completed at Kōfuku Temple, one of the Seven Great Temples in Nara.	Emperor Shōmu founds the Tōdai Temple in Nara with the world's largest bronze Buddha statue.	The Japanese capital moves to Nagaoka.	The Heian period begins; it lasts until 1185.

Shōsō-in Repository c. 743

The Shōsō-in Repository lies within the Tōdai-ji Temple complex, once one of the powerful Seven Great Temples in the city of Nara, Japan. Shōsō-in is located to the northwest of the Daibutsuden (Great Buddha Hall), which houses the world's largest bronze statue of the Buddha Vairocana, known in Japanese as Daibutsu.

The Shōsō-in Repository was originally built to serve as an ordinary storehouse within the Tōdai-ji Temple complex, but from the middle of the Nara period (710–94) it has been dedicated to the storage of treasures. The majority of the Shōsō-in treasures are considered to date from the eighth century. They have a unique historic attribution and provenance, and range from works of art and crafts to sutras, documents, and manuscripts. Most of the artifacts housed at Shōsō-in were produced locally, but also to be found there are imported objects from China and Korea, as well as more distant countries such as India, Iran, Greece, Roman Italy, and Egypt. For this reason, the Shōsō-in Repository has been dubbed "the end of the Silk Road."

In the year 756, Empress Kōmyō (701–760) offered the Great Buddha of Tōdai-ji more than 600 objects in memory of her recently deceased husband, Emperor Shōmu (701–56). The empress repeated her offering to the Buddha five times. In the Heian period (794–1185), a large number of objects, consisting of treasures, documents, and instruments used for Buddhist services, were transferred to the Tōdai-ji Temple.

The Shōsō-in Repository is constructed of Japanese cypress (*hinoki*) and has a hipped roof covered with traditional tiles. It is 108 feet (33 m.) long and 31 feet (9.4 m.) wide and has an overall height of 46 feet (14 m.). The floor is raised 9 feet (2.7 m.) above the ground, and its foundation of natural stone protects against moisture and dampness. Shōsō-in's exact construction dates are unconfirmed, but work definitely would have been finished by 759, when lists made of bequested items stored there reached completion.

The number of treasures still preserved at Shōsō-in exceeds 9,000 items. They range from artifacts deriving from Nara social and cultural life to gifts and donations from abroad: manuscripts, ritual implements, stationery, paintings, textiles, musical instruments, sports uniforms, arms and armor, garments and accessories, artisan tools, incense burners, and medical items. The objects are of many different materials, including metal, wood, lacquer, tortoiseshell, horn, ceramic, glass, and silk. **MP**

⦿ FOCAL POINTS

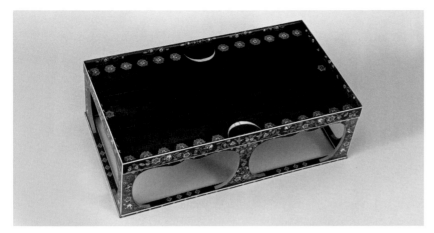

SUGOROKU BOARD GAME

Sugoroku, which literally means "double six," is a Japanese board game. It was introduced to Japan from China in the sixth century and the rules are similar to those of Western backgammon. The Shōsō-in houses eight sugoroku boards made using the marquetry technique, with ivory, antler, boxwood, ebony wood, and bamboo inlay. Also included in the Shōsō-in collection are six ivory dice and eighty-five sugoroku pieces made from rock crystal, amber, and glass.

DECORATED BRONZE MIRROR

Also housed at Shōsō-in is this cast-bronze mirror, or Hei Raden Hai no Hakkaku Kyo, whose back is a rare example of decoration with mother-of-pearl inlay, practised in China and Korea by the eighth century. Other materials typically used were *yakō*-shell (green snail), amber with painted color underneath, red sandalwood, ivory, and malachite. This design features the hosoge, a mythical flower that combines aspects of peony, lotus, and other flowers.

LISTED FOR ETERNITY

Whereas the majority of the ancient artifacts now housed at the Shōsō-in Repository were excavated from tombs or settlements, the Shōsō-in artifacts were collected. This means that they were in excellent condition when they were first stored in Shōsō-in Repository, and they have been preserved in a suitable environment and climate. Although many of the items were made in Japan, the style and decoration of the majority of the treasures is typical of the Chinese Tang dynasty. Indeed, the Shōsō-in objects constitute the greatest collection of Tang-style artifacts in the world.

The objects have been registered accurately on a series of lists according to their acquisition. The first one is known as the List of Rare Treasures of the State (*Kokka chinpō chō*), and it states the purpose and the contents of the offerings made by Empress Kōmyō. Of particular note within the Shōsō-in Repository are the numerous musical instruments. The quantity

and variety of different string, wind, and percussion instruments provide a considerable insight into musical traditions during the Nara period. Significantly, the collection comprises a seven-stringed zither, a four-stringed lute, various flutes, mouth organs, harps, panpipes, metallophones, and a range of drums. The five-stringed, short-necked biwa lute (*Gogen biwa*) is particularly noteworthy because it is the only surviving example of its kind. It was made out of sandalwood and spectacularly decorated with a camel rider in mother-of-pearl inlay.

Since the beginning of the Meij era (1868–1912), the Shōsō-in treasures have been under the management of the central government of the imperial household. Usually they are inaccessible to the general public, and the annual Shōsō-in exhibition only displays up to seventy objects for a short period of several weeks.

SOUTHEAST ASIA

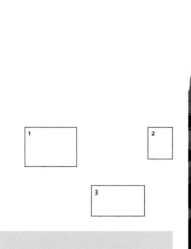

1 A seated Buddha on the upper terrace of Borobudur Temple, Java, is surrounded by small stupas.

2 These ancient ceramic bowls are from a Chinese shipwreck found in the Java Sea, Indonesia.

3 Part of the Angkor complex in Cambodia, Bayon Temple is renowned for its extraordinary bas-relief scenes and numerous apsara (angelic dancer) statues.

Between approximately 150 BCE and 150 CE, most of Southeast Asia was influenced by the more mature cultures of its neighbors to the north and west. At the same time, international trade was expanding rapidly. For the first time, Indonesian outrigger canoes were able to travel as far as the East African coast; Indian glass beads were traded to Bali and the mainland states; and Cambodia was a center of trade with China and the Roman Empire. Chinese mirrors and Roman glass have even been excavated from this area.

By the sixth century CE, Indian political, cosmological, and religious influence on the mainland was significant. Kingdoms in Thailand were keen to adopt Indian ideas, and the first Sanskrit inscriptions were found on the islands of eastern Kalimantan and western Java. Indian styles, mainly of religious art, also spread through Southeast Asia, developing local characteristics and new forms. By the following century, Chinese and other Buddhist scholars had arrived in Palembang in southern Sumatra to study Buddhist doctrine and to copy manuscripts. During the eighth century, temple and court complexes of surpassing grandeur were constructed in Myanmar, mainly at Pagan. One of the finest examples is the Borobudur Temple, which was built in central Java. It was constructed in three tiers: a pyramidal base with five concentric square terraces, the trunk of a cone with three circular platforms, and at the top, a monumental stupa. The walls and balustrades were decorated with fine low reliefs, and around the circular platforms, seventy-two openwork stupas with Buddhas were constructed (see image 1). Between 850 and 875, a major Hindu

KEY EVENTS

c. 1–200 CE	c. 100–500	1st–6th century	7th–12th century	775–830	790
Numerous glass beads of Indian manufacture found throughout the mainland attest to the growing trade between India and Southeast Asia at this time.	The most striking complex of prehistoric large stone monuments in Indonesia is found around Pageralam in Sumatra.	Oc Eo is the commercial center of the Funan kingdom (present-day south Vietnam and Cambodia), involved in maritime trade.	The Cham towers in Nha Trang, Vietnam, are built.	The Buddhist shrine of Borobudur is constructed in Java.	King Jayavarman is the founder of the Khmer kingdom in Cambodia.

temple group was constructed at Prambanan, also in central Java, thus indicating the coexistence of the two religions. Khmer kings started to build temples with a central stylized phallus as an object of worship, the *lingam* of the Hindu god Shiva. An unfinished temple relief on the outer wall in the splendid Buddhist temple of Bayon at Angkor Thom (see p. 472) includes this Hindu symbol in a scene with apsaras (see image 3). Bayon was the last state temple to be built in Angkor, and it has 216 gigantic faces on its temple towers.

From the sixth to the tenth centuries, large-scale settlements flourished in Thailand, most likely as part of international trade routes linking South and Southeast Asia. The exact nature of these towns and their relationships remains unclear. Chinese influence, too, was due to trade networks, which employed Southeast Asian shipping to carry mainly silks westward via the Maritime Silk Road. Around the sixth century, merchants began sailing to Srivijaya, and goods were shipped directly to this Sumatran port. The limits of navigation technology and the prevailing wind direction during parts of the year made it difficult for the ships of the time to proceed directly from the Indian Ocean to the South China Sea. The small city-state of Srivijaya developed into an important center for the expansion of Buddhism, but its wealth and influence faded when changes in nautical technology in the tenth century enabled Chinese and Indian merchants to ship cargo directly between their countries. The shipwreck of Koh Sdach, found in the Kiri Sakor district, southwest Cambodia, connects Cambodia to maritime trade routes in the gulf of Thailand and mainland Southeast Asia. Cooking pots, storage jars with four loop handles, basins, bottles, *kendi* (drinking vessels), dishes, plates, mortars, porcelain, and celadon bowls were found (see image 2). Preliminary analysis of the ceramics indicates that they could originate from two kilns in Thailand. **MP**

Angkor Wat and Angkor Thom Twelfth century

Angkor is one of the most important archaeological sites in Southeast Asia. It is located in the vicinity of Siem Reap, about 150 miles (240 km.) northwest of the present Cambodian capital of Phnom Phen, and stretches more than 155 square miles (400 sq. km.), including the surrounding forests and the remains of the capitals of the Khmer empire, Angkor Wat and Angkor Thom.

The word "Angkor" derives from a Sanskrit term meaning "the holy city." However, Angkor was not a city in the normal sense, but rather a bustling place, with temples, monuments, reservoirs, and irrigation systems, that expanded over the centuries. Its impressive monuments, large water reservoirs, and a sophisticated irrigation system built according to several different ancient urban plans testify to an exceptional civilization with a high level of social order. Temples such as Angkor Wat and Bayon at Angkor Thom are fine examples of the most sophisticated Khmer architecture.

Angkor Wat is the largest religious monument in the world, covering 402 acres (163 ha.). Construction as a Hindu temple began under King Suryavarman II, who reigned from 1113 to c. 1150, but the building was gradually transformed into a Buddhist temple by the end of the twelfth century. It is a combination of a temple mountain and a later plan of concentric galleries, built of sandstone joined by natural resins or slaked lime. Situated on the northwest shore of the Tonlé Sap lake, which provided water for irrigation, Angkor Wat had an elaborate system of canals and moats, dominated by two huge reservoirs (barays). Inner and outer galleries and a temple with three galleries and central tower were decorated with Buddhist and Hindu reliefs.

Angkor Thom includes the ruins of the Bayon Temple and many other temples, but few residential structures. It was built by Jayavarman VII, who ruled from 1181 to c. 1206 or 1220, and covers an area of more than 2,224 acres (900 ha.). The greatest complex, the Bayon Temple, is renowned for its fifty-four towers, each covered with huge faces of an Avalokiteshvara, the bodhisattva of compassion. **MP**

BAS-RELIEFS

Remarkable bas-reliefs depicting scenes of daily life and historical events are situated below the Buddha faces on the towers of the Bayon Temple. The one shown here (detail) is located in the southern part of the eastern gallery and it portrays a Khmer army on the march into battle. Armed with javelins and shields, the soldiers are traveling on foot, but they are led by cavaliers riding bareback and officers with bows or javelins mounted on elephants. The military procession is accompanied by musicians and a dancing figure beating a gong. Covered carts containing army provisions complete the line.

SACKING OF ANGKOR

By the beginning of the ninth century, Jayavarman II had unified the regional chiefdoms of Chenla into the powerful Khmer Empire. In the late ninth century, Yasovarmon I, who reigned from 889 to 910, moved the capital to Angkor, which remained the center of this powerful state until 1431, when it was sacked and looted by Siamese troops. After the collapse of Angkor, its inhabitants largely abandoned the area, leaving reconstruction and maintenance works unfulfilled. It was not until the nineteenth century that archaeologists began a restoration process.

RECENT DISCOVERIES

In 2012 and 2015 archaeologists discovered numerous previously undocumented medieval cities not far from the ancient temple city of Angkor Wat. To examine their find, they used airborne laser-scanning technology, an advanced geospatial technique for archaeological mapping of cities that are hidden under vegetation. The investigation area covered a total of 734 square miles (1,901 sq. km.) and revealed a number of large cities, probably densely populated, under the tropical forest floor. Archaeologists assume that some of these cities, dated roughly to the twelfth century, rival the size of Cambodia's present-day capital, Phnom Penh. The survey also uncovered the sophisticated structure of the city complexes, including water and irrigation systems built hundreds of years earlier than was previously assumed.

The findings will shed new light on how the ancient Khmer cities developed and grew to the size of mega-cities, dominating the southern part of Cambodia and finally declining during the fifteenth century.

AFRICAN STATE FORMATION

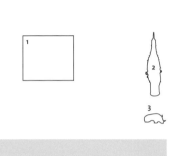

1 Reconstruction of a burial chamber at one of the Igbo-Ukwu sites. It depicts a high-status individual who was buried with five of his attendants.

2 A cast bronze, probably of a queen mother named Idia. Benin bronze sculptures were made using the lost wax casting technique.

3 The Mapungubwe golden rhinoceros was made between *c*. 1220 and *c*. 1290. Excavations in the 1930s revealed twenty-seven graves. Three contained gold artifacts, grave goods that were associated with high status persons of the ruling elite.

In Africa, ancient Egypt is the quintessential popular example of a "great civilization," but the prosperous and highly developed cultures, settlements, and cities of the rest of the continent are less recognized. Among the earliest are the Nok culture (Nigeria, see p. 348), Meroe and Aksum (northeast Africa, see p. 350) and Djenné-Jeno (Mali). From the late first millennium onward, numerous other notable kingdoms, city-states, and empires flourished.

Archaeologists have long been interested in the evolution of social organization, the classic sequence being band—tribe—chiefdom—state. Traditionally, traits signaling complexity included agriculture, metallurgy, writing, urbanization, craft specialization, and a division of labor, class stratification, and centralized political power. All these are relevant when considering the trajectories of African precolonial societies, but not all can be explained in terms of this "package" of features. For example, most were preliterate and not all were top-down hierarchies or "states" in the conventional sense. Power was derived from a variety of resources (such as cattle, land, and trade), differently distributed and variously wielded.

Inevitably, interpreting the evidence can be difficult. At Igbo-Ukwu in eastern Nigeria, the burial complex of a high status person (see image 1) has been dated to around the end of the first millennium. Among the rich grave goods were hundreds of cast bronze pieces of extraordinary proficiency and hundreds of thousands of trade beads. Analogies with the medieval Igbo kingdom of Nri, in the same area, suggest that the grave may be that of a priest-king from a non-hierarchical society.

Kingdoms and empires of the first millennium, including the empires of Ghana (Mali and Mauritania) and Kanem (Chad and environs), were succeeded by many more across the continent in the following millennium. The Songhai Empire (late fifteenth century–1591) was one of the largest African polities ever, covering nearly 580,00 square miles (1.5 million sq. km.) of West Africa and the Sahel at its zenith. The Nigerian center of Ife, founded in the mid 1st millennium, is celebrated for its bronze, terracotta, and stone sculptures, made between the thirteenth and sixteenth centuries. Variability among these polities, even when they coexisted in similar conditions and had similar economies, has led researchers away from ideas about unilinear socioeconomic evolution and turned attention to diversity in their internal social dynamics.

In southern Africa, three states were prominent through the second millennium: Mapungubwe (1220–90), where the excavation of a hilltop graveyard site has provided evidence of early goldsmithing (see image 3), Great Zimbabwe (1100–1450, see p.476), and Khami (1450–1830). Recent research at Mapela, Zimbabwe, suggests that, instead of single states dominant at one time, more than one kingdom may have coexisted.

Monumental architecture has been another traditional hallmark of advanced development in the Western narrative of great civilizations. This partly explains the attention given to sites such as Great Zimbabwe, but other equally impressive structures also existed. The Benin Empire, which emerged in c. 1200, is known for its skilled bronze artworks (see image 2). Less well known are the walls of its capital city, which are not well preserved. A network of moats and ramparts made from earth, 9,940 miles (16,000 km.) long, defended the city and enclosed an area of 2,510 square miles (6,500 sq. km.). The Walls of Benin have been hailed as the planet's largest archaeological structure.

By the fifteenth century, Africa was traversed by trade networks that eventually stretched around the globe. The presence of oriental trade beads in many African sites is one indicator of the extent of these intercontinental contacts. Numerous traders and travelers, including Islamic writers and, later, Europeans left written records of the cities they visited. Ultimately though, European contact was often destructive, leading to conquest, colonialism, and the destruction of centuries-old centers and cultures. The brutal trans-Atlantic trade in African slaves, especially from West Africa to the New World, was initiated by the Portuguese in the early sixteenth century. Benin City, recognized by early Portuguese writers as prosperous, well-planned, and well-governed, was looted and razed by the British in 1897. Archaeology has played a key role in highlighting the sophisticated cultures of the African past. **AS**

12th–13th century	c. 1200–1400	c. 1220	Early 16th century	1591	1897
Ethiopia's Christian ruler commissions a series of rock-cut monolithic churches (see p. 480) for his vision of a "New Jerusalem."	The tradition of high-quality bronze and terracotta sculptures attains new heights in works from the Yoruban city of Ife, Nigeria.	The rise of Mapungubwe, an early southern African urban center where the ruling elite live on top of an easily defended hilltop.	The trans-Atlantic trade in slaves begins, with African slaves transported to Portuguese and Spanish colonies in the New World.	The defeat of the Songhai Empire by Moroccan forces at the Battle of Tondibi leads to the decline of trans-Saharan trade.	A punitive expedition by British troops leads to the razing of Benin City and the looting of its artworks, the world-famous Benin bronzes.

Great Zimbabwe   Eleventh – fifteenth centuries

The sinuous, mortarless walls of Great Zimbabwe's Great Enclosure, 36 feet (11 m.) high, are its most spectacular feature. Despite their height, they were probably not designed for defensive purposes. A prominent feature of the complex is the Conical Tower. Its distinctive form may refer to the shape of grain bins.

The site of Great Zimbabwe is famous both for its impressive ruins of drystone wall buildings and for the debates that have raged about the mystery of its origins. Even today, the myth clings on that it was built by a foreign race of superior culture and skills. However, archaeology has clearly shown that it was the center of a wholly indigenous kingdom, of the ancestors of the present-day Shona people. The Shona word *dzimbabwe* translates as "stone house."

Great Zimbabwe lies in southeastern Zimbabwe about 19 miles (30 km.) southeast of Masvingo. It is the largest of several hundred stone-walled settlements in the region attributed to the Zimbabwe culture, and the largest such structure in sub-Saharan Africa. The site extends over approximately 1,977 acres (800 ha.). Occupation probably began in the eleventh century CE, on a hilltop adjacent to the stone-walled Great Enclosure, which dates to the fourteenth century. Structures and floors made of *daga* (earth and mud brick) also existed but, inevitably, these have not been preserved as well.

The dates and sequences of different occupation areas within the site are still being researched and refined. Interpretations of their functions also diverge, but many believe that the Hill Ruins were—at least initially—the residence of the elite. It was here that eight carved soapstone birds, believed to be emblems of royal status, were found.

Over the next three centuries, Great Zimbabwe grew into a prosperous state. Subsistence was based on cattle and agricultural crops. It was important as a node in the cross- and later intercontinental trade networks of the era, evidenced by finds of glass and ceramics from Persia and China, and coins from the island of Kilwa Kisiwani, off the Tanzanian coast. The principal exports were probably gold and ivory. European traders visited the city in the sixteenth century, although by this time it had been in decline for fifty years or more.

Reasons for that decline are debated, but probably included deforestation and environmental degradation, after centuries of supporting a population of perhaps 10,000 people. Declining trade and exhaustion of the gold mines are other possible factors. **AS**

👁 FOCAL POINTS

CHEVRON PATTERN

Part of the Great Enclosure's outer wall is ornamented with a chevron pattern that may have been symbolically significant. The sophisticated decorative stonework tradition was continued and further elaborated at Khami, 185 miles (300 km.) to the west, a center that arose after Great Zimbabwe's decline.

ZIMBABWE BIRDS

The carved birds found on the hilltop site at Great Zimbabwe are made from soapstone, and once stood on pedestals. Although referred to as birds, and despite their eaglelike features, they are not simply naturalistic representations of known avian species and some display humanlike elements.

🕐 ARCHAEOLOGIST PROFILE

1888–1928

Born in London, UK, Gertrude Caton-Thompson became interested in archaeology after visiting Egypt in 1906 and 1911 and, in 1915, excavations at a French Paleolithic site. In 1921 she studied Egyptology at University College London, under Flinders Petrie and Margaret Murray, and later enrolled at Cambridge University. Early fieldwork included excavations at Abydos, in Egypt, and in Malta, followed by pioneering scientific work on predynastic Egyptian cemeteries at El-Badari and the settlement of El-Hammamiyah. From 1925, she and Elinor Gardner extensively surveyed Neolithic sites in the Faiyum.

1929–85

In 1929, Caton-Thompson reported conclusively on Great Zimbabwe's indigenous origins. Returning to Egypt, she surveyed and excavated at Kharga Oasis (1930–33). In 1937, she initiated the first systematic excavation at the site of Huraydha, the Yemen. Though World War II ended her fieldwork, Caton-Thompson continued to work and publish, including a memoir. She died aged ninety-seven, in 1985.

MYTHS OF GREAT ZIMBABWE

Ever since Portuguese travelers first visited Great Zimbabwe in the early sixteenth century, the site has been subject to fanciful interpretations about its origins. The German geographer Karl Mauch (1837–75), who visited in 1871, enthusiastically promoted a link to King Solomon and the Queen of Sheba; Theodore Bent (1852–97) attributed it to Phoenicians or Arabs.

David Randall-McIver conducted the first properly scientific investigations in 1905–06. His excavations were limited, but he concluded that the city was medieval, not ancient, and identified its associated artifacts as the work of local Bantu-speaking peoples. More rigorous investigations by Gertrude Caton-Thompson in 1929 led her to affirm an indigenous origin. Her work decisively dismissed the racist colonial myth of exotic foreigners, and the notion that unsophisticated local peoples lacked the ability to create such impressive structures.

Kilwa Kisiwani Eleventh – sixteenth centuries

The ruins of Kilwa Kisiwani have been damaged by encroaching vegetation and coastal erosion and were placed on the UNESCO List of World Heritage in Danger in 2004. After a restoration program, the site was removed from the list in 2014. The restoration has helped to promote the island as a heritage tourism destination.

The island of Kilwa Kisiwani, close to the southern Tanzanian coast, was home to East Africa's most important medieval city-state. The settlement dates back to the eighth to ninth century, but reached its zenith in the second millennium, under the Islamic Kilwa sultanate.

Kilwa was known from sixteenth-century documents, such as the *Kilwa Chronicle*, a history of its Shirazi dynasty rulers. Archaeological investigations, begun in the 1950s by British archaeologist Neville Chittick (1924–84), have provided additional information on economy, material culture, daily life, and social relations. The island's prosperity and power were based on its important role in intercontinental trade between Africa and Asia, including the Arabian peninsula and China. Along with the ruined stone-built town of Songo Mnara, located on a neighboring island, Kilwa has yielded important insights into the development of Swahili culture and early Islamic architecture in East Africa.

Kilwa's wealth is attested to by the fact that it minted its own coins from the eleventh to fourteenth centuries. A coin bearing the mark of the Kilwa sultanate was found at Great Zimbabwe (see p. 476). Kilwa's rulers gained control of the important trade in African gold, shipped out via the key Mozambican port of Sofala, in the late twelfth century. In return for this key commodity, goods such as porcelain, glass, jewelry, and textiles were imported from India and China. The impressive buildings for which Kilwa is famous include the Great Mosque and the palace of Husuni Kubwa. Blocks of local coral were quarried for these large structures.

Kilwa's fortunes apparently declined in the late fourteenth century, but subsequently temporarily revived. However, the city, then home to perhaps 5,000 people, was conquered and plundered by the Portuguese in 1505. **AS**

HUSUNI KUBWA

Even though it was only briefly occupied and was abandoned before construction was finished, the fourteenth-century clifftop palace, Husuni Kubwa, was one of the most splendid residences in medieval Africa. The flamboyant palace was built for Sultan al-Hasan ibn Sulaiman, who ruled the island from 1310 until 1333. The 2-acre (0.8 ha.) site comprised residential quarters with about one hundred rooms, private and commercial court areas, a pavilion, and an octagonal swimming pool. Some areas were decorated with carved coral panels in designs unique in the region.

CERAMICS

Excavations at Kilwa have unearthed locally made, unglazed pottery, used by ordinary people for domestic purposes, as well as imported wares. Remains of ceramics and glass from as far afield as the Gulf and China are testament to Kilwa's extensive intercontinental trade networks. Exotic wares have been found in the coastal towns, but not in the rural interior. Fine objects, including Chinese celadon-glazed pieces and Persian faience, were probably the exclusive property of the elite and signifiers of their wealth and social status.

GREAT MOSQUE

Perhaps the most celebrated structure at Kilwa is the Great Mosque, which was the largest mosque in sub-Saharan Africa until the sixteenth century, and is the oldest standing mosque in the East African region. Some of the foundations date to the tenth century, although most of the main structure was constructed in two later phases.

The Northern Prayer Hall dates to the eleventh to twelfth century and comprised sixteen roofed bays. Supporting pillars carved from single blocks of coral were later replaced by timber.

Sultan al-Hasan ibn Sulaiman, who also built the vast palace of Husuni Kubwa, extended the older mosque in the fourteenth century. This created an extra thirty bays, sundry additional rooms, and an open court area that was enclosed in the fifteenth century. One of the rooms was once capped by the Great Dome, which was decorated with coral panels. It is thought to have been the first true dome on Africa's east coast and stood for nearly half a century. The Moroccan traveler Ibn Battuta (1304–c. 1368) remarked upon the splendor of the dome after he visited Kilwa in 1331.

Lalibela Twelfth – thirteenth centuries

Ethiopia has hundreds of rock-hewn churches, of which Lalibela is the country's most architecturally and historically important. Biete Medhani Alem (House of the Savior of the World) is thought to be the largest church of its kind in the world. Its local significance is as a living sacred place, central to the spiritual lives of Ethiopian Orthodox Christians today.

The small town of Lalibela is known for its eleven medieval churches, sculpted from the volcanic rock of northern Ethiopia's Lasta Mountains. It is named after Lalibela, a king of Ethiopia's Zagwe dynasty, who ruled from c. 1181 to 1221. During his reign, Saladin, the sultan of Egypt, conquered Palestine, including the holy city of Jerusalem on which the site of Lalibela was partly modeled. According to tradition, construction of the Ethiopian churches was inspired by Lalibela experiencing a vision of a "new Jerusalem" for pilgrims and worshippers in his own land. The site includes a canalized stream, the Yordanos, named for the symbolically significant Jordan river of the Bible.

Although not securely dated, the rock-cut churches of Lalibela were built over several centuries, with two probably once part of a seventh-century fort and palace. They are grouped into two main clusters—northern and eastern. Below ground lies a labyrinth of tunnels that connect the different structures, as well as ceremonial passageways, tombs, and storerooms. Some of the churches are monolithic structures, hewn so that they are completely detached from the cliff face. Perhaps the best-known church, Biete Ghiorgis (House of St. George), lies to the west, separate but connected to the other buildings by deep trenches. The architectural influences are diverse, but design details derived from the buildings of the great first-millennium Ethiopian kingdom of Aksum are common (see p. 350). Interiors feature carved pillars, arches, and vaulted ceilings, typically decorated with geometric designs. Biete Mariam (House of Mary) is adorned with unique painted designs, whereas Biete Golgotha Mikael (House of Golgotha Mikael) features low-relief sculptures of human figures. **AS**

YEMREHANNA KRISTOS

Located on a hill 12 miles (19 km.) north of Lalibela is Yemrehanna (or Imraha) Kristos church. It was built inside a natural cavern using alternate layers of timbered beams and plastered stone. Another remarkable Aksumite-style church commissioned by Zagwe dynasty kings, it predates the Lalibela churches by perhaps a century. Yemrehanna Kristos is notable for its striking facade, carved latticed windows, and elaborate paneled ceiling with geometric designs. Although laser scanning has revealed some structural cracks, its location inside a large cave has greatly aided its preservation.

AKSUMITE ARCHITECTURE

The design details of some of the Lalibela churches, such as Biete Amanuel (House of Emmanuel), replicate the style of Aksumite architecture. They include faux wooden window beam ends and door frames that refer to the great monumental stelae of Aksum. The facade is carved to recall the building technique of layering horizontal beams with stone and mortar. Invoking Aksum, as a symbol of strength and prosperity, may have been a strategy designed to legitimize the Zagwe dynasty's rule and associate it with the Ethiopian state's vast power in the first millennium.

BIETE GYORGIS

Biete Gyorgis, named after St. George, the patron saint of Ethiopia, is one of four monolithic rock-hewn churches at Lalibela, excavated from the soft pink volcanic rock. Legend has it that it was commissioned after St. George himself reproached King Lalibela for not building him a "house," and that the saint personally supervised its construction. The church measures 39 by 39 by 42 feet (12 by 12 by 13 m) and stands within a deep trench. Chambers and niches excavated into the walls of the surrounding trench house the remains of ancient religious figures, while some are inhabited by present-day Ethiopian Orthodox priests.

One of the church's most notable features is its cruciform floor plan, with the Greek cross motif also adorning the external roof. Other design elements include blind windows and references to the Aksumite architectural style. Biete Gyorgis is perhaps the most visually striking of Lalibela's churches, and certainly the best preserved.

Timbuktu Fourteenth – sixteenth centuries

Timbuktu held more than half a million ancient manuscripts in Arabic and local African languages. They date from the thirteenth century until the colonial era. Until recently, most were held in scores of private libraries. At risk of decay, and recently targeted by Islamist fundamentalists, thousands of manuscripts have since been exported for conservation and digitization.

Trade across the Sahara desert probably began in the early first millennium, but it took off after the introduction of the camel as a pack animal. Flourishing from the seventh to the eleventh centuries, the trans-Saharan trade was centered on gold, which was exchanged for salt from North Africa. In addition to the economic importance of cross-continental commerce, it aided the spread of Islam across large swathes of Africa during the second millennium.

Timbuktu, in present-day Mali, was one of many centers that thrived on the trans-Saharan trade. Strategically located on the edge of the desert, near the Niger river, it was originally settled in the mid-first millennium. It had become an important center of trade, culture, and Islamic learning by the 1500s. At this time, the city was home to perhaps 100,000 residents. Like other contemporary centers, it was also involved in the slave trade, with millions of sub-Saharan Africans trafficked along the trade routes. Early travelers' reports, such as that of Leo Africanus in the sixteenth century, described Timbuktu in medieval Europe as an exotic but remote city of great wealth. It became part of the Malian Empire in 1324 and was absorbed into the Songhai Empire in *c.* 1469. In 1591 it was taken by a Moroccan force, signaling the beginning of its subsequent decline.

The historical significance of Timbuktu as an Islamic center, and its old mosques and mausoleums, led to it gaining World Heritage Site status in 1988. In 2012 Timbuktu made global headlines after Islamic fundamentalists destroyed many ancient buildings, including fourteen of its sixteen mausoleums, some dating back to the thirteenth century. Fortunately, they have since been restored. **AS**

MOSQUES

Three mosques were at the center of Islamic scholarship in Timbuktu. Sankore (*c.* 1325–1433) was designed by architect Abu Ishaq al-Sahili, with a wooden frame within its mud walls; Djinguereber (*c.* 1327) was commissioned by Emperor Musa I of the Malian Empire; and Sidi Yahia (*c.* 1400) was built by Sheikh El-Mokhtar Hamalla and named after its first imam. In addition to religious learning, the three mosques offered the study of medicine, astronomy, and physics, among a variety of other subjects, to thousands of scholars. No trace remains today of a fourteenth-century palace known as the Madugu, also thought to have been built by Emperor Musa I.

SALT TRADE

Invaluable as a preservative, salt was a vital commodity. It was sometimes used as currency and was also a lucrative source of tax revenue for the rulers of several African kingdoms. In the fifth century BCE, Greek historian Herodotus mentioned a 450-mile (724 km.) "salt road" running between a remote salt mine at Taoudenni in northern Mali across the desert to Timbuktu. Trade in large slabs of quarried salt, weighing approximately 66 pounds (30 kg.), continues at Taoudenni today.

TRANS-SAHARAN TRADE

For perhaps a thousand years, the Sahara desert was criss-crossed by trade routes that connected the Mediterranean region with the subcontinent, reaching from eastern African states and kingdoms to western kingdoms and the Atlantic coast. Exotic goods discovered in many sub-Saharan African sites may once have been transported across the desert by camel caravans. Direct evidence of the trade is rare, although a French archaeologist in Mauritania in 1965 made a remarkable and evocative discovery: the remains of a camel caravan's cargo, perhaps abandoned or looted on the journey south. Comprising approximately 2,000 brass rods and large quantities of cowrie shells, it has been dated to the early twelfth century. Knowledge of trans-Saharan trade has changed ways of looking at the African past. Growing awareness of the importance and impact of the trade challenged existing myths of African cultural and technological backwardness, supposedly arising from the isolation of the "dark continent" from civilized Europe. In fact, via Saharan trade networks, sub-Saharan Africa was connected, directly and indirectly, to the Mediterranean region and beyond for many centuries, with extensive contact and mutual influence, particularly during the second millennium.

TOLTECS AND AZTECS

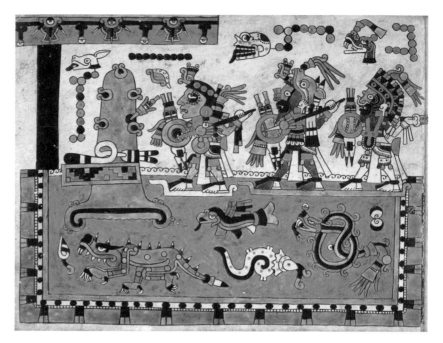

1 The Codex Zouche-Nuttall narrates the pilgrimage of the Mixtec Lord Eight Deer (1063–1115) and the Toltec Lord Four Jaguar.

2 The Toltec warrior columns at Tula depict soldiers of the Feathered Serpent wearing his insignia on their sandals.

3 Polychrome ceramics like this bowl from Cholula, Puebla, use elements of the Mixteca-Puebla stylistic tradition.

During the five centuries prior to the Spanish Conquest of the Aztecs in 1521, the great civilizations of the Classic period (200–900) were supplanted by smaller city-states that often formed alliances and confederations in order to promote their commercial interests and defend their territories. Gone was the emphasis on the authoritarianism of divine kingship; instead, mercantile interests began to flourish as a lively system of maritime trade developed to deal not only in prestige items but also in bulk goods, such as the high-quality salt produced along the shores of the Yucatán Peninsula. Cacao beans, which previously had been reserved for making a chocolate beverage consumed by elites, were now being adopted as a medium of exchange to facilitate burgeoning commercial transactions. These new trading networks were rapidly integrating Mesoamerica into a world system as the area experienced a vibrant wave of globalization.

The Postclassic period (900–1521) can be divided into three parts. The earliest, from 900 to 1150, witnessed the rise of Tula (see image 2), Chichén Itzá (see p. 486), and the Toltec civilization, while the Middle Postclassic period (1150–1350) saw the collapse of the Toltec system and ensuing migrations from the northern frontier of Mesoamerica into the central valleys where, according to both legend and archaeology, these new arrivals founded their own

KEY EVENTS

600	600–700	600–900	900–1150	1150–1250	1325
The Teotihuacan imperial system collapses.	Metallurgy technology from Ecuador is introduced and adopted to create ornaments and jewelry.	There is political ferment as the Classic period civilizations collapse.	The Toltec world order rises at Tula and Chichén Itzá.	Great migrations from the north into Mexico's central valleys occur.	The Mexica capital is founded at Tenochtitlan.

city-states. The final stage, from 1350 to 1521, was a time of empire building. In 1428, the Mexica of Tenochtitlan (see p. 488), the Acolhua of Texcoco, and the Tepanec of Tlacopan, themselves migrants from the northwest who had settled in the Basin of Mexico many generations earlier, joined together to forge the Aztec Empire and expand their influence over the highlands and into the tropical lowlands. To the west of the Basin of Mexico, in the modern state of Michoacán, the Tarascan people put together their own empire. They were fierce rivals of the Aztecs and fought a number of wars with them.

The Toltec cultural system transformed Mesoamerica in fundamental ways. It represented a revitalization movement, with martial and religious overtones, that spread rapidly throughout central Mexico and into the Maya area. It was, perhaps, a cult based on the mythico-historic figure of Ce Acatl Topiltzin Quetzalcóatl, the Feathered Serpent, and a desire to resurrect the golden past of Teotihuacan after several centuries of hegemonic struggles. Indeed, there is reason to believe that the original Toltec capital was Teotihuacan (see p. 394) itself. Sketchy legendary histories that were written down after the Spanish arrival indicate that numerous Postclassic statelets claimed Toltec ancestry, but whether or not they belonged to a Toltec Empire is a matter of scholarly debate.

Although many of the newly founded Postclassic city-states were ruled by kings, a few of the remaining native books, such as the Codex Zouche-Nuttall of the Mixtec region (see image 1), narrate instances of political intrigue as illegitimate offspring or celebrated warriors schemed to usurp power. The proliferation of rival polities and the shifting nature of their alliances coincided with increases in the crafting of sophisticated art objects that were used as gifts among noble families, since their members were involved in negotiations that required elaborate ceremonies to affirm strategic political coalitions.

Mesoamerica's increasing integration during the Postclassic is reflected in its shared iconography, often referred to as the Mixteca-Puebla Tradition, that stylistically harks back to the Classic art of Teotihuacan. The rich symbolism of this colorful artistic expression was used to create ritual almanacs and books that recorded genealogical histories; the murals that embellished the walls of temples and palaces; and the pottery (see image 3) used for feasts and offerings. It was also the basis for the powerful Aztec style.

The final centuries of the Postclassic saw the rise of two hegemonic empires. However, the Aztec capital of Tenochtitlan, now Mexico City, and the Tarascan seat in Tzintzuntzan, were very different cities. At the time of the Spanish Conquest, Tenochtitlan had a population of 100,000 while Tzintzuntzan's was barely 35,000. Yet the Tarascans offered vigorous resistance to Aztec incursions into their realm and in 1478 they soundly defeated the Aztecs on the battlefield. Eventually both sides established forts along their shared border, although, as archaeological analysis has shown, this did not stop Tarascan bronze and obsidian from entering Aztec territory. **PPN**

1376	1428	1440–69	1478	1502	1521
The first Mexica ruler, Acamapichtli (d. 1395), takes the throne.	Three city-states unite to form the Aztec Empire after winning the war of independence against their Azcapotzalco overlords.	The initial expansion of the Aztec Empire under Montezuma I (c. 1398–1469).	Aztec armies suffer a devastating defeat by Tarascan armies.	On his fourth voyage to the New World, explorer Christopher Columbus (1451–1506) encounters a Maya maritime trading canoe off Honduras.	A coalition of Spanish and Indian armies under Hernán Cortés (1485–1547) conquers the Aztec capital of Tenochtitlan.

Chichén Itzá 800 – 1050

Built at the end of the Classic period in the traditionally ornate Maya style of the northern Yucatán Peninsula, the entire facade of the east wing of the complex known as the Nunnery is faced with mosaic masks of the long-nosed rain god Chaak. Its doorway, made in the image of the earth monster's maw, evokes the entrance to the otherworld.

Recent studies indicate that Chichén Itzá emerged as a notable center during the eighth century, and that its authority grew steadily as the great Maya cities of the southern jungles declined. Between 800 and 1050, the city developed into a major economic power, covering more than 6 square miles (16 sq. km.) as it took control of the flourishing maritime trade in sea salt from its north coast ports at Isla Cerritos and Elam. Its long-distance mercantile networks, reinforced by military might, brought in obsidian, copper bells, and turquoise from the northwest and gold from southern Central America. Many of these items, along with sacrificed humans, were thrown into the Sacred Well as ceremonial offerings.

Archaeology, legend, and history all contribute to current understanding of Mesoamerica's Early Postclassic period, and yet the data from these different sources do not fit neatly into a single narrative. For more than a century, scholarly discourse has centered on the architectural and iconographic similarities between Chichén Itzá and the contemporary central Mexican city of Tula. But who influenced whom? Does Chichén Itzá articulate the dogma of a regional Maya revival, or does it materialize an invasive foreign ideology? Perhaps both, since the site clearly represents a reworking of Maya tradition into a new more flexible system that could respond to the shifting geopolitics of its time.

Chichén Itzá's political structure was unlike that of the Classic cities to the south. There, inscriptions identify kings as "divine lords," while at Chichén there is little evidence for dynastic rulership. Some suggest that the polity was governed by a council formed from the center's leading lineages and led by a principal spokesman. The imagery carved and painted on Chichén Itzá's buildings signals this rejection of dynasty in favor of oligarchy; most significantly, it focuses on groups of warriors rather than royal persons standing over bound captives. **PPN**

FOCAL POINTS

TEMPLE OF THE WARRIORS

Rain god masks grace the hybrid Maya-Toltec style buildings, such as the Temple of the Warriors. New Toltec hallmarks include the feathered serpent columns, whose upturned tails supported the wooden lintel that once spanned the entry, the militaristic chacmool altar centered in front of them, and the rows of pillars carved with an individual Toltec warrior on each side at the base of the platform. Inside, the temple walls were decorated with murals depicting the conquest of a Maya settlement by foreign invaders.

EL CASTILLO

Chichén Itzá's most famous structure is El Castillo, a 78-foot (24 m.) high Toltec-style platform that encases two earlier versions. Like Teotihuacan's Pyramid of the Sun, El Castillo has calendrical connotations. Each of its four staircases, which are framed by descending plumed serpents, has ninety-one steps and when added to the final dais of the temple above they total 365, the number of days in the solar year.

QUETZALCOATL

One of the most important, yet enigmatic, figures of Mesoamerica's ancient sagas is Ce Acatl Topiltzin Quetzalcoatl (literally meaning One Reed, Our Prince Feathered Serpent). He appears in the legendary histories of the Toltec cities of Tula and Cholula as well as in those of the Maya area. The highland sources relate that he was chosen to be the high priest and king of Tula in the tenth century. Since other "Quetzalcoatls" appear in later times, many scholars assume that Quetzalcoatl was his formal title, not his name. After years of successful rule and the promulgation of new doctrines, including a ban on human sacrifice, he was driven from Tula by a rival faction. He fled southeast to Cholula where he left four disciples to impart his creed at a temple dedicated to the deity Nine Wind Quetzalcoatl, and then departed for Tlapallan on the Gulf Coast. He was never heard from again. However, Maya histories continue the story. They speak of a military captain named Kukulcán (the Yucatec Maya word for feathered serpent) who, in 987, led an army of Toltec warriors to conquer northern Yucatán, including Chichén Itzá. This fabled military intrusion, which might be the subject of the many battle scenes that embellish Chichén Itzá's buildings, has often been used to explain the city's hybrid architectural style and foreign iconography. Others interpret these combat scenes as encounters between Chichén Itzá and its local enemies. The murals and bas-relief panels at the site include individuals dressed as Toltec soldiers: they wear the mosaic pill-box helmets and stylized butterfly pectorals, and they carry the atlatls, or spearthrowers, used by highland warriors since the time of Teotihuacan. Their leaders, encased in sun disks or surrounded by an undulating plumed serpent, direct them in battle as they lay siege to villages.

Tenochtitlan 1325 – 1521

Using the stone from Tenochtitlan's civic ceremonial buildings, the conquering Spaniards raised their own capital, Mexico City, directly on top of the ruined seat of Aztec imperial might. Since 1900, successive projects of urban archaeology have gradually uncovered the lower walls of the Great Temple's seven major construction stages and recovered scores of ancient monuments and offerings from beneath the modern streets.

When Hernán Cortés (1485–1547) anchored his ships off Veracruz in April 1519, he learned of a great empire whose seat, Tenochtitlan, was located in the highland Basin of Mexico to the northwest. Seven months later, he reached the capital and found one of the largest and most resplendent cities of the sixteenth century. Founded in 1325 on an island in Lake Texcoco, Tenochtitlan, and its sister city Tlatelolco, formed a dense urban sprawl of reclaimed land criss-crossed by canals, an American Venice covering 5.4 square miles (14 sq. km.) with more than 100,000 people. The city was designed according to Mesoamerican cosmology. It was divided into four quadrants, representing the four world directions, and at its center—the site of the vertical fifth direction that connected the three levels of the universe—was the ritual precinct, from which raised causeways stretched out to the mainland. This walled plaza had four gates and included the Great Temple, shrines for minor gods, buildings for the eagle and jaguar military orders, a skull rack to exhibit the heads of captured and sacrificed warriors, and a ballcourt. Directly outside the walls were the palaces of the empire's successive rulers.

The Aztec Empire was an alliance forged among the three major cities of the Basin of Mexico—Tenochtitlan of the Mexica, Tlacopan of the Tepanecs, and Texcoco of the Acolhua—after they won their war of independence from the overlord Tezozomoc in 1428. Led by Tenochtitlan, the alliance first extended its political control into the highly productive *chinampas* (artificial islands) of the freshwater lakes in the southern basin, and then expanded its hegemony into the lowlands and coastal areas to secure a steady stream of tribute and captives for Tenochtitlan's sacrificial altars. **PPN**

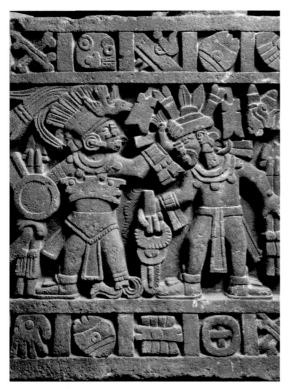

MOCTEZUMA'S STONE

Moctezuma's Stone is carved with cartouches showing the conquests of Emperor Moctezuma Ilhuicamina (c. 1398–1469). He wears the vertical feather headdress, triangular hip skirt, and stylized butterfly pectoral of a Toltec warrior; he grasps his opponent by the forelock in a standardized gesture of conquest.

COYOLXAUHQUI STONE

The Coyolxauhqui Stone was discovered by chance in 1978 in front of the Great Temple. The sculpture and the temple were designed to architecturally materialize the Mexica myth in which their patron god, Huitzilopochtli, kills his sister, Coyolxauhqui, because she and her 400 brothers have plotted against him and his mother.

IN SEARCH OF THE GREAT TEMPLE

Exploration of the Mexica's main temple has always been constrained by the post-Conquest city that was built over Tenochtitlan's ruins after its surrender in 1521. For centuries, it was known only from descriptions provided by the conquistadors. Although they exaggeratedly described the Great Temple as taller than the bell tower of Seville's cathedral, Cortés's map correctly shows a platform with twin west-facing towers. Major imperial monuments were recovered during the renovations of Mexico City's main square in 1790–92, including the Coatlicue statue and the Sun Stone, or Aztec Calendar. These finds ushered in a period of intense scholarship, relic collecting, and in 1825, the founding of Mexico's first national museum.

Archaeological excavations date back to 1900, when Leopoldo Batres (1852–1926) recovered materials exposed along a sewer line trench that cut through the Great Temple. During the succeeding decades, the number of finds in and around the ritual precinct increased as Mexico City modernized its infrastructure and built a subway system, but it was not until the Coyolxauhqui Stone was found that extensive explorations began to reveal the majesty of the pre-Hispanic civic-ceremonial center.

In each of its seven superimposed construction stages, the Great Temple was a single west-facing platform with two parallel staircases, one leading to the Temple of Tlaloc, the rain deity, and the other to the Temple of Huitzilopochtli, the Mexica's solar war god. Both sides were designed to evoke the myths associated with these two divinities, the Mountain of Sustenance presided over by the rain god on the north side and the Serpent Mountain where Huitzilopochtli was born on the south. More than 125 offerings, with thousands of items from all over Mesoamerica, were arranged according to cosmological symbolism in sub-floor stone boxes placed around the building.

THE INCA

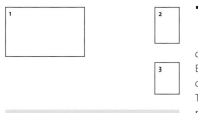

1. The Acllahuasi at Pachacamac was a type of convent for young women.

2. An illustration of an Inca leader by Felipe Guamán Poma de Ayala (c. 1535–c. 1616).

3. The Koricancha in Cuzco was dedicated to the sun god Inti.

The Incas were the last complex society of the pre-colonial Andes and they built an empire unrivaled in world history. Its territories extended over the entire coastal and highland Andean region, as well as into parts of the Amazon forest, reaching areas of modern Colombia, Ecuador, Peru, Bolivia, Argentina, and Chile. The imperial capital was in highland Cuzco, one of the richest and most sophisticated cities of ancient America (see p. 492). This city housed a large and diverse population and was the center of the main political and religious institutions. The Inca Empire was integrated with its provinces and far-flung administrative centers by the royal road of the Incas known in Quechua (commonly considered the original language of the Inca) as Qhapaq Ñan, meaning main or beautiful road. This great network of roads was also a fundamental element in its political economy and the construction of its sacred landscape.

The Incas expanded from the Cuzco valley at the beginning of the fifteenth century. Their empire was divided politically into four quarters (*suyus*) and in its entirety was called Tawantinsuyu, or Land of the Four Quarters. Each quarter took its name from the most important societies conquered in that region:

KEY EVENTS

c. 1000	c. 1200	c. 1400	c. 1450	c. 1470	1492
The process of intensive settlement of Cuzco begins.	The Inca state emerges as the Incas control the Cuzco area.	The Incas start their expansion outside the region of Cuzco.	Continued expansion extends through the Lake Titicaca basin. The construction of Machu Picchu begins (see p. 494).	The Incas conquer the major part of the coastal region of present-day Peru.	Christopher Columbus arrives in America. He lands on the island of San Salvador.

Collasuyu, Chinchaysuyu, Contisuyu, and Antisuyu. Relations between the Cuzco Inca elites (see image 3) and the dominated local elites were varied, with differing levels of integration and control. This generated a rich diversity of economic and political links and strategies that are still being studied today. However, it seems that although the two main strategies were political negotiation and relatively peaceful incorporation, as witnessed in the Chincha kingdom, at the opposite end of the scale were the invasion and subjugation of territories by military force.

Like every state, the Inca Empire instituted a series of official social practices that were embodied in architecture. Among the main institutions that can be recognized in the first instance is the official religion, which focused on the worship of the sun. In fact, according to ethnohistorical sources, the most elegant, well-constructed, and renowned buildings of the Inca Empire were temples of the sun (see image 3). The most important ones were in Cuzco, Isla del Sol on Lake Titicaca, and Pachacamac on the central coast of Peru. In addition, there were numerous minor temples of the sun throughout the Inca territory. The architecture of the Incas, especially in the highlands, was related to the adequacy of their buildings in the landscape and its relations with the observations of the sun, moon, and stars in the firmament. Huánuco Pampa, Pumpu, Vilcashuamán, and Tomebamba, among others in the highlands, are good examples of the construction of cities and the transformation and articulation of these with the sacred landscapes. In the coastal areas, sites such as Pachacamac (see image 1) stand out. In this case, articulated pre-Inca cults were incorporated into the Inca ones. These cities served many economic, political, and religious purposes, including the hosting of large numbers of local peoples at great festivals.

The material culture of the Incas is distinctive and recognized especially in textiles and ceramics. Fine fabrics were used as status symbols and used geometric iconographic designs known as *tocapus*. Furthermore, certain ceramics were employed in the main rituals related to the cult of the divinities and to the same Inca elite. Among the most iconic Inca ceramic forms are the cups (*keros*) and jars (*urpus* or Inca aryballos) in which the corn beer (*chicha*) was stored and served.

When the Spaniards arrived in 1532, the Inca Empire was in a political crisis caused by the war between two factions, one led by Huáscar (1491–1533) and the other by his brother Atahualpa (c. 1502–33). After a series of confrontations, Huáscar, who was the natural successor to the throne of the Inca in Cuzco, was finally defeated by Atahualpa. When Francisco Pizarro (c. 1475–1541) and his troops arrived in the Inca city of Cajamarca, Atahualpa was resting from his campaigns against his brother and was possibly planning his coronation in Cuzco. Atahualpa was captured by Pizarro in the plaza of Cajamarca and was held until he was finally tried and sentenced to death by the Spaniards. **HT**

1519	1524	1526	1530	1532	1533
Panama City is founded by Spaniard Pedro Arias Dávila (1440–1531).	Francisco Pizarro's first expedition leaves Panama City.	A raft crewed by natives from Tumbes is captured by Spaniard Bartolomé Ruiz (1482–1532) during an exploratory travel to the south.	Pizarro's third expedition commences. The goal is to reach and conquer the Inca Empire.	Atahualpa defeats Huáscar and kills him. The Spaniards capture Atahualpa in the Cajamarca plaza.	The Spaniards arrive in the Inca capital, Cuzco.

Cuzco c. 1000 – 1533

Cuzco is the archaeological capital of South America and one of the main tourist destinations in Peru. UNESCO declared the city a World Heritage site in 1983.

Built at the confluence of three rivers in the Huatanay river basin in the southern highlands of Peru, Cuzco was the ancient capital of the Inca Empire. It was a high-altitude city, located 11,155 feet (3,400 m.) above sea level. In its heyday during the Inca period, Cuzco and its surrounding areas housed up to 100,000 inhabitants, and the elegance and richness of its architecture made it one of the most sophisticated cities in pre-Hispanic South America.

Although Cuzco was reoccupied by the Spaniards during the colonial period, and many of its original buildings have undergone significant modifications, it is still possible to recognize the Inca urban footprint and to experience some of the principal buildings. The main plaza of Cuzco was the central hub of the city, and the well-known Temple of the Sun, or Koricancha, was an important religious center especially related to the observation of the sun. Other great buildings of the city were the ancient palaces of the Inca state rulers and official institutions such as the Acllahuasi, or the house occupied by the women chosen for the cult of the sun. In addition, Sacsahuamán was an important architectural complex located on a high hill in the extreme northwest of the city. The complex is made up of massive buildings and carved rock outcrops and features huge walls made of gigantic blocks of stone. Today, the esplanades at Sacsahuamán are used for the annual performance of the religious ceremony Inti Raymi during the June solstice. The urban spaces near the city were occupied by different architectural clusters and sacred sites or *huacas*. These buildings created a political and sacred landscape that was very important to Inca conceptions of their king in relation to the world. **HT**

TWELVE-ANGLED STONE

The twelve-angled stone is an extraordinary example of Inca stonework in Cuzco. It is a polygonal stone block that was part of the walls of one of the main Inca palaces of the city, possibly the Palace of Inca Roca. The well-preserved wall is located in the modern street called Hatun Rumiyoc. Elsewhere, a long and elegant wall on Loreto Street is one of the finest Inca architectural works to have survived. According to historical sources, this was one of the outer walls of the Acllahuasi, the house of the women chosen for the worship of the sun.

MAIN PLAZA

The central plaza comprised a large open space divided into two areas: Haucaypata and Cusipata. The main roads departed from this center toward the four parts, or *suyus*, that composed the empire. Important rituals and political performances related to Inca statecraft were performed in this plaza. It was the center or *axis mundi* of the Incas and it was there that the terraced platform or *ushnu* was located. This elevated structure was the place from which the key state rituals were directed. Around it were the important buildings of Inca religion and politics.

KORICANCHA

According to the early Spanish chronicler Bernabé Cobo (1582–1657), the main temples dedicated to the worship of the sun during Inca times were located on the Isla del Sol on Lake Titicaca; in Pachacamac on the central coast of Peru; and in Cuzco, the Koricancha. The last was considered to be the most important temple of the sun in the Inca Empire. In addition to its significance as a temple, the Koricancha is the center of a series of radiating lines, or *ceques*, that linked this building with a large number of sacred sites, or *huacas*, across the Cuzco landscape. From there, the existence of alignments related to the observation of the movement of the sun and other stars has also been recognized.

There are several accounts of the Koricancha that describe a huge amount of gold that covered its walls. In one chamber was a large gold sun disk that reflected sunlight to illuminate the temple. Other documents reported that there were life-size plants and animals of gold and silver. In addition, this temple contained a gold statue of Inti encrusted with jewels. Due to its wealth and its ideological importance, the Koricancha was one of the first buildings to be looted and then used to house a Catholic church; the Dominican religious order then appropriated the temple. In this way, it became a symbol of the ideological conquest by Western culture of the indigenous society.

Machu Picchu *c.* 1450 – 1533

At the top of a pyramidal terraced rock formation, the Intihuatana stone was sculpted from a large rock. This singular feature dominates the high part of one of the most important sectors of the site. It was a shrine or main *huaca* of Machu Picchu, which commanded an important view of the key sacred mountains of the region, and it was used to make astronomical observations.

Located in the Urubamba Valley, 50 miles (80 km.) northwest of the city of Cuzco, on a route that leads to the tropical forest, Machu Picchu is the best known Inca city in the world. It was built on the top of a mountain at about 7,975 feet (2,430 m.) above sea level and covers an area of around 12 acres (5 ha.). The city was probably founded around the mid-fifteenth century.

Machu Picchu has all the classic architectural components of an Inca city: plazas, temples, palaces, astronomical observatories, elite and servant residences, and storage rooms. In addition, there are unique buildings such as the Temple of the Sun. The site may have been one of the royal estates of the most renowned emperor: Pachacuti Inca Yupanqui. Some scholars suggest that this was also where he built his mausoleum.

The construction of Machu Picchu in such a rugged area of high rainfall and vegetation required that the Inca architects stabilize the terrain. In order to achieve this, they built terraces or platforms. A series of buildings with large blocks of stone, mainly extracted from a neighboring quarry, was also constructed on the leveled surface of the existing plain areas. The design of the city highlights the use of rocky outcrops, some of which were carved to imitate certain natural forms of the surrounding landscape.

Although known since colonial and republican times, Machu Picchu only became world famous when the U.S. historian Hiram Bingham (1875–1956) featured it in his articles in *National Geographic* magazine. Since then, the city has been the source of numerous archaeological and political debates with relevance for the Peruvian state and society. In addition, Machu Picchu is at present the main tourist attraction of Peru. **HT**

◉ FOCAL POINTS

TEMPLE OF THE SUN

This temple has a semicircular wall that was built to enclose the upper part of the rock outcrop where it is located. The windows allow observations and measurements of the movement of the sun, and one window lets in sunlight during the June solstice, thus illuminating the carved rock inside. Below the Temple of the Sun, at the base of the rock outcrop, there is a modified cave. It features large trapezoidal niches and carved walls. In the entrance, the stone was sculpted to create a stepped form. Even from inside the so-called mausoleum, it is possible to see mountain peaks.

TEMPLE OF THE THREE WINDOWS

Machu Picchu is an architectural wonder that articulates buildings within a stark and extraordinary natural landscape. This is exemplified by the Temple of the Three Windows, a structure is located in the Sacred Plaza. The three windows built into the walls of this unique architectural construction allow an excellent view of the mountains and the Urubamba river to the east of Machu Picchu. The open part of the building, to the west, faces the Pumasillo mountain. Excavations in this area produced fragments of ceramic vessels that were broken as a part of rituals.

◷ ARCHAEOLOGIST PROFILE

1875–1909

Hiram Bingham was born in Honolulu, Hawaii. He graduated from Yale University in 1898, and subsequently earned an M.A. at the University of California, Berkeley, in 1901. He received his Ph.D in history at Harvard in 1905. The same year, Bingham traveled to South America, visiting Venezuela and Colombia. In 1908 he journeyed from Buenos Aires, Argentina, to Lima, Peru, following the old route of Spanish commerce. A year later, he became a member of the faculty of history at Yale University.

1910–21

Sponsored by Yale University, Bingham made an expedition to Peru, specifically to Cuzco, in 1911. His goal was to find Vilcabamba, the last zone of resistance of the Incas during the Spanish Conquest. During this exploration, he discovered Machu Picchu and other sites of interest. Inspired by his finds, he soon returned to Peru and carried out archaeological investigations in Machu Picchu. In 1913, he published his first article on the site in *National Geographic* magazine.

1922–56

Bingham entered politics in 1922 when he was elected lieutenant governor of Connecticut. In 1924 he was elected to the Senate of the United States. Although he served in a series of political positions, he also returned to Machu Picchu in 1948 to inaugurate the road that now leads tourists to the site. Bingham died at his home in Washington, D.C.

6 | The Modern World
1600 CE—PRESENT

This chapter looks at the development of modern capitalism, including voyages of exploration, growing maritime power, the creation of overseas colonies, the rise of modern cities, industrial technology, and modern warfare. It ends with an assessment of the issues facing the field of archaeology today, from its relationship with indigenous peoples to the question of how to prevent damage to sites that are visited by thousands of tourists.

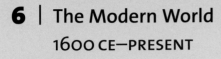

Ironbridge
p. 508

Shakespeare's Theaters
p. 504

Battle of the Little Bighorn
p. 512

The *Geldermalsen*
p. 500

SHIPWRECKS

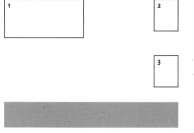

1 Domestic artifacts recovered from the
Mary Rose, including a wooden drinking
vessel, bowls and utensils, as well as a
leather flagon.

2 Gold coins from the wreck of the Armada
galleass *La Girona*, now in the Ulster
Museum, Belfast, UK.

3 The *Vasa* has been reconstructed and
restored using original timbers and parts.
It is on public display in Sweden.

Shipwrecks are a particular type of archaeological site because they represent a single deposition of material remains, usually accidental. Accordingly, they provide a record of objects that were in use at a single point in time. In addition, the underwater conditions may preserve items made from organic material that do not normally survive on land sites. In some cases, the timber hulls of ships, which are among the most complex objects made by pre-industrial societies, may endure.

Shipwrecks from periods with limited written records, such as the Aegean Bronze Age shipwreck found off Ulu Burun in Turkey (see p. 152), can provide invaluable evidence of ancient economies. However, shipwrecks from later historical periods can also represent types of activity not recorded historically, yielding valuable information on maritime and social affairs, and enabling study of physical evidence from the wrecks against a documentary background, one source complementing the other. Ships such as the *Mary Rose*, *La Girona*, *La Trinidad Valencera*, the *Vasa*, and the *Geldermalsen* (see p. 500) illustrate this.

The wrecks of ships from the Spanish Armada of 1588, found off the coasts of northern Britain and Ireland, include *La Girona*, a galleass (partly rowed galleon), which sank off the coast of County Antrim, Northern Ireland. *La Girona* carried personal items, including coins (see image 2) and fine examples of sixteenth-century jewelry, most notably a salamander-shaped pendant made from gold decorated with rubies. Spanish Armada wrecks also give evidence of more mundane items, including a distinctive type of small, globular pottery known as "olive jars," apparently used to carry the fleet's ration of olive oil. A study of the olive jars has provided information about the origin and production of this type of pottery, an area about which there is scant mention in literary sources. In addition, Armada wrecks give an insight into the accessibility of luxury goods. For example, sherds of blue and white Chinese porcelain were found on the wreck of *La Trinidad Valencera*, which sank in Kinnagoe Bay, County Donegal, Ireland. The porcelain can be identified as early imports that had come to Spain from China via the Philippines and Mexico. This unexpected find indicates that such items were among the accouterments of wealth.

Shipwrecks from the Baltic Sea have proved particularly rewarding for archaeologists. The low saline content of the waters of the Baltic has helped deter the wood-boring bivalve commonly known as the shipworm, which attacks submerged wooden hulls elsewhere. However, in recent years a rise in water temperature has increased the presence of the shipworm in the Baltic, potentially threatening shipwrecks that are still under water. An example is the remarkably well-preserved *Vasa*, a Swedish warship that sank in 1628 (see image 3). The *Vasa* was rediscovered in 1956, lying upright and virtually intact at a depth of 108 feet (33 m.) in Stockholm harbor; she was raised in 1961. After a major restoration program, which lasted about twenty years, the ship is now displayed to the public in a specially constructed and climate-controlled building. In addition to the hull, which has provided invaluable information regarding early seventeenth-century shipbuilding, elaborate wooden carvings that decorated the ship had been preserved in the harbor's soft mud. The ship's fittings also survived, including organic materials such as the sails, sail twine, and lengths of rope. Other finds inside the *Vasa* have provided information on life aboard a seventeenth-century Swedish warship. For example, one wooden chest contained a hat and clothes, still folded. The excellent preservation of wood has also given an insight into leisure activities on board the *Vasa*, with items ranging from a makeshift game board cut into a barrel lid to a well-crafted folding game board with carved counters, the latter found in the officers' stores.

The wreck of the English warship the *Mary Rose*, which sank in 1545, was rediscovered in 1967 and excavated and raised between 1979 and 1982. It is another excellent example of a historic shipwreck that has supplied information not available elsewhere. Although the "Anthony Roll," a visual record of ships presented to Henry VIII (1491–1547), includes an approximate depiction of the *Mary Rose*, excavation of the ship has provided numerous technical details previously unrecorded, together with objects that have no historical record, thereby giving a unique archaeological perspective into shipboard life in Tudor England. In particular, domestic finds show a difference in status between officers and other crew, the presence of the former indicated by objects such as fine china tableware and the remains of books, whereas the latter used wooden tableware (see image 1). **GM**

1920	1943	1961	1971	1982	1986
Two brothers are refused permission to salvage ships in Stockholm harbor to obtain dark timbers, popular for Art Deco furniture.	A prototype aqualung is tested. It incorporates a demand regulator, making extended underwater exploration possible.	The *Vasa* is raised and breaks the surface of Stockholm harbor. The well-preserved ship is soon able to float unaided and is towed into dry dock.	The wreck of *La Trinidad Valencera*, a Venetian merchantman commandeered to join the Armada, is found in Kinnigoe Bay.	The hull of the *Mary Rose* is raised and moved to a dry dock in Portsmouth, close to where it was built originally.	The wreck of the *Geldermalsen* is discovered off one of the islands of the Lingga Archipelago, Indonesia, by a British salvage operator.

The *Geldermalsen* 1746–1752

Ceramics from the *Geldermalsen* are raised from the shipwreck and brought to shore.

Built in 1746, the *Geldermalsen* was a spiegel-retour ship of the Dutch East India Company. Its measurements were very impressive: 42 feet wide and 150 feet long (12 by 42 m.) with a capacity of 1,150 tons. In August 1748 this great merchant ship left on its maiden voyage to the Indies. For the next three years, it sailed to different ports along the maritime Silk Road, loading and unloading its precious commodities. In July 1751 the *Geldermalsen* was given a new captain and crew, and was stocked up with water and fresh provisions. In addition, it was armed with iron and bronze cannons, rifles and pistols, hand grenades, broadswords, pikes, and 3,000 pounds (1,120 kg.) of gunpowder. The hull was fully loaded: besides a cargo of valuable tea, it was also carrying gold ingots and a large quantity of porcelain, stored in the lower decks as ballast. When passing the 55th latitude in the South China Sea, the ship collided with a reef and sank.

More than two centuries later, in 1984, Michael Hatcher (b. 1940)—a world-renowned salvage diver, adventurous explorer and treasure hunter—and his crew discovered the shipwreck of the *Geldermalsen*, with the majority of its load undamaged. Although the wooden cargo boxes holding the tea-leaves had already rotted, the tea itself had formed a thick protective layer like a soft bed underneath and above the porcelain and gold. Unfortunately, attention focused on the valuable cargo—later sold by British auction house Christie's—and although much of the ship's structure had survived intact, it was destroyed during the salvage operation. This caused outrage among archaeologists because the opportunity to investigate and document an eighteenth-century ship and the artifacts on board had been lost forever. **MP**

FOCAL POINTS

SPIEGEL-RETOUR SHIPS

Spiegel-retour ships were destined primarily for shipping goods between the home country and Asia. They looked like warships, but the dimensions of the hull were generous and specially adapted. For the transportation of valuable commodities—silk, porcelain, gold, and spices, for example—the hull was larger and with a stern shaped as a flat square or round plane. The cargo of the *Geldermalsen* included 147 gold ingots, shaped into bars and "shoes," and stamped with Chinese characters. At 20 to 22 carats, the gold was extremely pure.

PORCELAIN

The *Geldermalsen* was carrying nearly 150,000 ceramic pieces, and 203 chests were recovered during the salvage operation. The blue and white Chinese porcelain was intended to be sold on the European market, where it would have been used as everyday tableware. The design, known as the boatman pattern, inspired the willow pattern that was popular in the United Kingdom from the late eighteenth century. Among the pieces of porcelain were 171 dinner services, 63,623 tea cups and saucers, 578 tea pots, 14,315 flat dinner plates, 606 vomit pots, and 25,921 slop bowls.

MARITIME SILK ROAD

The Maritime Silk Road originated in the Han dynasty (206 BCE–220 CE). It was opened by Emperor Wu (156–87 BCE) and provided access to the Roman Empire via India. This was the first ocean route and earliest major maritime trading in the world. During the Tang dynasty (618–907 CE), ships sailed from Guangzhou (Canton), the starting point of the most important routes of the Maritime Silk Road. Countries throughout Southeast Asia, South Asia, West Asia, and even Europe dispatched emissaries to China to establish diplomatic relations, but more importantly to engage in trade, especially silk.

With enhancements in navigation technology, the accumulation of seafaring experience, the advantages of lower transportation costs, and the increased quantity of freight in marine trading, the Maritime Silk Road became the major passage for communication and trading between the East and the West after the Song (960–1279) and Yuan (1279–1368) dynasties. It was also a means for cultural exchange. Once established, the Maritime Silk Road was used increasingly throughout the Ming (1368–1644) and Qing dynasties (1644–1911).

EARLY MODERN LIFE

1 This engraving from c. 1830 by A. McClatchie after a drawing by T. H. Shepherd depicts a steam-powered barge on Regent's Canal, London, passing in front of a large gasworks. The canal opened in 1820.

2 Majolica was popular in the sixteenth century. This majolica pilgrim bottle from Urbino, Italy, is highly ornate and would have been used as a decanter or as decoration.

The five and a half centuries since the invention of printing in the mid fifteenth century saw enormous change, which affected almost every aspect of life. This period witnessed the development of major overseas trades in commodities, such as furs, spices, tobacco, sugar, tea, cocoa, coffee, and cotton—not to mention the invidious trades in slaves and opium—and several European countries established first trading posts and companies and then colonies over much of the world. It is also the era in which antiquarianism, museums, archaeology, and ethnography developed. Printing enabled literacy to spread across wider sections of society and new scientific discoveries to be disseminated quickly. It led to more rapid developments in the field of map making, which in turn sparked European interest in exploring more of the globe. Improvements in ship design and scientific instruments contributed to the success of some early voyages, and the potentially rich rewards were a huge incentive. The importation of exotic raw materials also led to the development of European industries to process them: for example, sugar and cocoa needed refineries, whereas cotton was made into finished textiles.

In the countryside, improved methods of agriculture led to estate reorganization, which often meant depopulation and migration to the towns, and advances in breeding animals increased meat production and quality. During the sixteenth and seventeenth centuries, the emergence of a gentry class initiated the building of new manor houses and lordly residences; these were accompanied by formal gardens and deer parks. By the eighteenth

KEY EVENTS

c. 1535–c. 1555	1538–46	1622	1628	1629	1644–46
Acton Court, Gloucestershire, transforms from a medieval manor house into a Tudor gentry home.	Nonsuch Palace, Surrey, is built for Henry VIII. It is mostly demolished in the eighteenth century. Later excavations uncover outstanding finds.	Martin's Hundred, Williamsburg, Virginia, is seized by Native Americans. Excavations reveal numerous graves and personal possessions.	Built for the king of Sweden, the *Vasa* capsizes and sinks on its maiden voyage.	The *Batavia* is wrecked off Western Australia. Excavation yields a rich assemblage of artifacts, including military and navigation equipment.	Civil War defenses are erected to defend the town of Newark in Nottinghamshire, U.K.

century, the land around many country houses was being emparked, and an interest developed in reshaping the landscape to give a less formal appearance.

Technological developments in industrial processes sparked an Industrial Revolution in England during the eighteenth and nineteenth centuries, which greatly boosted the production of both machinery and finished goods. These booming industries needed large workforces, which led to major movements in population and to the rapid development of burgeoning new towns—a process that was copied elsewhere. In turn, the mass production of factory-made products began to meet the demand for cheap goods from these urban populations. The new middle classes provided a market for higher status goods, such as table glass, pewter, and majolica (see image 2) in the sixteenth and seventeenth centuries, and silver, porcelain, and high-grade factory-made earthenwares at later dates. Quality furniture, fabrics, and textiles were popular throughout most periods. In the towns, architect-designed houses came into vogue, while new types of buildings, such as theaters (see p. 504), assembly rooms, libraries, museums, and public baths, appeared to meet leisure needs.

Industrial growth necessitated improvements in transport, both for the import of raw materials and the distribution of finished goods. Existing roads and bridges were improved or rebuilt, and new purpose-built roads were constructed. Ferries were often replaced with bridges. Canals were built to expedite the movement of goods and enjoyed a heyday during the seventeenth and eighteenth centuries in the United Kingdom (see image 1). However, the construction of the Suez and Panama Canals in the later nineteenth century shows how necessary these waterways were even at much later dates. The development of the railroads in the United Kingdom in the mid nineteenth century was revolutionary, not only for goods, but also for the development of tourism. A boom in railroad construction spread quickly to other countries, and by the start of the twentieth century rail networks were in use across much of the world. The development of manned flight in the early twentieth century was equally revolutionary in its impact, both in military and civil aviation: airfields and their associated infrastructure spread to many countries, while seaplanes greatly eased access to remote island communities. Ship design also improved markedly during this period, which saw the formation of the first permanent navies. To cope with the construction, repair, and maintenance of these vessels, specialist dockyards and shipbuilding yards developed.

The Dutch had always been faced with the challenge of living in a low-lying area prone to inundation. Consequently, they became skilled at draining and reclaiming land. From the early seventeenth century onward, they took this expertise to other countries, such as England, to reclaim poorly drained marshland.

European archaeologists were slow to study this period of early modern life, and the lead in developing artifact studies was often taken by colleagues in the New World, notably in the United States and Canada. **DE**

1692	c. 1720	1729	1813	1830	1914
Port Royal, Jamaica, is destroyed by an earthquake and tsunami. Its well-preserved remains are known as the city that sank.	West Whelpington, Northumberland, U.K., is deserted when all the tenants are evicted. It is now one of the largest village excavations undertaken in Britain.	Christ Church, Spitalfields, London, opens. Excavations have since examined about 1,000 burials from inside the vaults.	Two schooners are lost on Lake Ontario. Their well-preserved remains are later found by remote-sensing equipment.	Port Arthur, Tasmania, is founded and quickly becomes Tasmania's largest prison until 1877.	Striking miners are attacked at Ludlow, Colorado. Excavations of the tent colony have since revealed their living conditions.

Shakespeare's Theaters Sixteenth–seventeenth centuries

THE "GLOBE" THEATRE, SOUTHWARK (WITH THE "ROSE" THEATRE IN THE DISTANCE), IN 1613.

Built in 1599, the first Globe burned down in 1613 and was rebuilt a year later; it was pulled down in 1644. Excavation in 1989 showed that it had been polygonal. The work exposed a small segment of its inner and outer walls on the northeastern side; this included the base of a possible external stair turret. Two phases were apparent. In the earlier phase, the outer gallery wall had chalk-and-timber foundations. The second phase had brick foundation courses set on top of the earlier remains. The great bulk of this theater is now overlain by standing buildings.

In the Middle Ages, plays were performed by strolling players. The first permanent theater in England (the Red Lion) opened in 1567, but its use was short-lived. The fear of plague being spread by crowds prompted a ban in 1575 on the performance of plays within the city walls of London. This led to theaters being established just outside the walls in either Shoreditch or Southwark. The first such venue opened in 1576, and it was followed by eleven more theaters during the next thirty-five years. Eight of these were built north of the Thames: the Theatre (1576), the Curtain (1577), Blackfriars (1599), the Fortune (1600), the Red Bull (1604), Whitefriars (1608), the Phoenix (a.k.a. the Cockpit, 1616–17), and Salisbury Court (1629). Another four lay south of the river: the Rose (1587), the Swan (1595), the Globe (1599), and the Hope (1613–14). William Shakespeare (1564–1616) was associated with many of the earlier of these.

The sites of the Rose, the Globe, the Theatre, the Hope, and the Curtain have been subject to archaeological investigation. Most of the theaters appear to have been polygonal in shape, with a stage projecting into a large central open yard; this would have been surrounded by a three-storied lath-and-timber superstructure containing the galleries. Parts of the inner and outer wall footings for these superstructures have been found at all of the excavated sites. These theaters held up to 3,000 spectators, most standing in the central yard areas. The earliest floor surfaces at the Rose were of mortar, but the second phase was floored with compacted earth, cinder, and cracked hazelnut shells. At the Curtain, one of the entrances had been resurfaced with a compacted layer of sheep knucklebones; elsewhere the yard was surfaced with gravel. Finds included wall tiles, pottery bird whistles, broken ceramic money-boxes, a purse-frame, coins and tokens, clay pipes, a bone hair comb, and a metal fork, which was possibly a prop; food remains included shellfish, nuts, and fruit. **DE**

 FOCAL POINTS

THE ROSE

Built in 1587, the Rose was enlarged by about 20 percent, probably in 1592; it was closed in 1605 and demolished shortly after. Excavation in 1988–89 exposed parts of the theater and revealed two phases. The first was a small polygon measuring about 72 feet (22 m.) across. In phase two, the outer wall was relocated 8 feet (2.5 m.) farther out, and the old trapezoidal stage was replaced with a heavier and more substantial structure.

THE THEATRE

English actor and businessman James Burbage built the Theatre in Shoreditch in 1576. It was the first successful public playhouse in England, but was demolished in 1598. The polygonal structure had three tiers of galleries and a covered stage. Excavation in 2008 revealed a small segment of the northeastern arc of its outer wall, whereas an earlier geophysical survey identified a curving anomaly representing a parallel inner wall. The preservation was shown to be very good.

THE HOPE

Built in Bankside, Southwark, by Philip Henslowe and Jacob Meade for Lady Elizabeth's Men, the Hope opened in 1613–14. The theater also functioned as a Bear Garden, where the profitable sport of bear-baiting took place. It had two external staircases that led to "the heavens" for the spectators. It was necessary for the stage to be removable for the animal fights. The theater closed in 1619, and the building was pulled down in 1656. Some remains of the Hope were uncovered in 1999.

THE CURTAIN

Opened in 1577, the Curtain was threatened with demolition in 1600, but continued to exist until 1628—latterly hosting prize-fighting—when it vanished from the historical record. Excavations in 2012 and 2016 show that this was a rectangular building. In places, it reused the walls of earlier buildings, but its back section was newly built. Sections of the brick inner wall still survive up to 5 feet (1.5 m.) high; both the yard floor and the lower floor of the gallery are preserved largely intact.

A CATALOGVE
of the feuerall Comedies, Histories, and Tragedies contained in this Volume.

COMEDIES,

The Tempest.	Folio 1.
The two Gentlemen of Verona.	20
The Merry Wiues of Windsor.	38
Measure for Measure.	61
The Comedy of Errours.	85
Much adoo about Nothing.	101
Loues Labour lost.	122
Midsommer Nights Dreame.	145
The Merchant of Venice.	163
As you Like it.	185
The Taming of the Shrew.	208
All is well, that Ends well.	230
Twelfe-Night, or what you will.	255
The Winters Tale.	304

HISTORIES.

The Life and Death of King John.	Fol. 1.
The Life & death of Richard the second.	23
The First part of King Henry the fourth.	46
The Second part of K. Henry the fourth.	74
The Life of King Henry the Fift.	69
The First part of King Henry the Sixt.	96
The Second part of King Hen. the Sixt.	120
The Third part of King Henry the Sixt.	147
The Life & Death of Richard the Third.	173
The Life of King Henry the Eight.	205

TRAGEDIES.

The Tragedy of Coriolanus.	Fol. 1.
Titus Andronicus.	31
Romeo and Juliet.	53
Timon of Athens.	80
The Life and death of Julius Cæsar.	109
The Tragedy of Macbeth.	131
The Tragedy of Hamlet.	152
King Lear.	283
Othello, the Moore of Venice.	310
Anthony and Cleopater.	346
Cymbeline King of Britaine.	369

THE PLAYS

A number of early theaters were associated with Shakespeare, either as an actor or as a playwright. For example, the Rose was the first purpose-built playhouse to stage a Shakespeare play—*Henry VI, Part 1* in 1592. The Lord Chamberlain's Men, one of whom was Shakespeare, played at the Theatre from 1594 to 1597. Thirteen of Shakespeare's plays were written while he was based at the Theatre, and it is likely that they premiered there. They are *Henry VI* parts 2 and 3, *Richard III*, *The Comedy of Errors*, *Titus Andronicus*, *Love's Labour's Lost*, *The Two Gentlemen of Verona*, *The Taming of the Shrew*, *Romeo and Juliet*, *A Midsummer Night's Dream*, *Richard II*, *King John*, and *The Merchant of Venice*. In 1599 Shakespeare wrote *Henry V* while based at the Curtain.

Half of the construction cost of the Globe was met by the Lord Chamberlain's Men, including Shakespeare. It staged the first performances of *Hamlet*, *Othello*, *King Lear*, and *Macbeth*. The Prologue in *Henry V*—famously referring to "the wooden O"—was probably added to the play after Shakespeare's company moved there.

INDUSTRIAL ARCHAEOLOGY

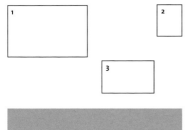

1 At Boott Cotton Mills Museum in Lowell National Historical Park, the weave room contains looms running at full speed.

2 One of the highlights of a visit to Big Pit National Coal Museum in South Wales is an underground tour of the mine.

3 The open-air museum at Hagen, Germany, demonstrates crafts, trades, and tools such as the trip hammers seen here.

ndustrial archaeology can be broadly defined as the archaeological study of the relatively recent industrial past through the physical remains of that activity. It is a branch of archaeology that is relatively specialized and has much in common with the study of the history of technology; there are overlaps with several other disciplines, including engineering, architectural history, and the museum world. Its study encompasses the various industrial buildings, machinery, technology, artifacts, sites, and landscapes, and their associated infrastructure that make up the industrial heritage.

The term "industrial archaeology" came to prominence in the mid 1950s, when substantial efforts were made to record parts of an industrial past that were fast disappearing. However, its origins lie several decades earlier. In 1918 the Sheffield Trades Technical Societies in the United Kingdom were formed to create a permanent record of the city's manufacturing and industrial history. This was followed two years later by the Newcomen Society, which was dedicated to the study of engineering and technology. In 1925 the world's first industrial museum opened at Slater Mill, Pawtucket, Rhode Island, which had been the site of a textile mill in 1793. During the late 1920s and early 1930s, the remains of early tin mining on Dartmoor were investigated and recorded, and in the 1940s Arthur Raistrick (1896–1991) began recording the evidence for

KEY EVENTS

1899	1935	1948	1959	1963	1964
The Bavarian Railway Museum opens in Nuremberg. It sets the model for later transport museums, such as the National Railway Museum, York.	The Cornish Engines Preservation Committee is formed by a small group of individuals. It is later renamed the Trevithick Society.	Excavations begin at Saugus Iron Works. The foundations of its major buildings and blast furnace are uncovered. About 5,000 artifacts are found.	The Council for British Archaeology forms an industrial archaeology research committee to campaign for the subject.	*Industrial Archaeology: An Introduction* is published by Kenneth Hudson (1916–99). It is one of the first books on the subject.	*The Journal of Industrial Archaeology* is founded. Kenneth Hudson is the first editor.

early lead mining in the Yorkshire Dales, U.K. In Germany, two open-air museums devoted to crafts and technology were founded in 1960, including the well-known site at Hagen (see image 3). In the United States, extensive excavations at the Saugus Iron Works in Massachusetts began in the late 1940s and led to the reconstruction of that works as a National Historic Site in the 1950s. The National Record of Industrial Monuments was created in 1965, followed in 1969 by the Historic American Engineering Record.

Early work in industrial archaeology tended to concentrate on recording the remains of old heavy engineering—mills and ironworks, for example—and extractive industries, such as coal (see image 2), metal ores, and stone quarries, which were felt to be at risk from redevelopment. However, as the discipline developed, its scope broadened to take in ancillary sites and their infrastructure. Areas of research now include the processing of agricultural products (milling, malting, brewing, distilling, and land drainage, for example); the structures associated with power for industry (water power, steam power, wind power, and animal power); communications (roads, rivers and canals, railroads, and air transport); and housing the workforce. Industries include manufacturing, which incorporates engineering works, car manufacture, aircraft production, glass, leather, and textiles (see image 1), and also the utilities: gas, electric, water, and sewage disposal. As a result, numerous industrial complexes and landscapes have now been designated as UNESCO World Heritage sites.

Since the 1980s, the pressures of redevelopment—particularly on brownfield sites in urban areas—have led to a steady growth in the archaeological investigation and recording of former industrial sites. Furthermore, the application of scientific techniques to such work is producing real dividends. **DE**

1967–68	1972	1978	1986	1999	2000
The New England textile mills survey is the first large-scale, industrial recording project for the Historic American Buildings Survey.	*Industrial Archaeology: An Historical Survey* by Arthur Raistrick is published.	Lowell National Historical Park is created, incorporating historic textile manufacturing sites around the city of Lowell, Massachusetts.	Ironbridge Gorge in Shropshire, U.K. (see p. 508), is designated a UNESCO World Heritage site.	The European Route of Industrial Heritage is established. It includes some of the most important industrial heritage sites in thirteen countries.	Blaenavon Industrial Landscape in South Wales becomes a World Heritage site. It includes Blaenavon Ironworks and Big Pit.

INDUSTRIAL ARCHAEOLOGY 507

Ironbridge *c.* 1500 – *c.* 1900

Coal outcropped on the hillsides of the gorge and could be dug both from adits driven into the hills and from shallow pits. After the Dissolution of the Monasteries (1536), coal mining, particularly on the south side of the gorge, expanded significantly. Consequently, by 1700 the population had more than doubled. The boom in coal allowed other trades to develop, such as blacksmithing and coopering.

The small town of Ironbridge is set within a gorge on the Severn River in Shropshire, United Kingdom. It lies at the southern end of the East Shropshire coalfield, and the river provided a direct outlet to the ports of Gloucester and Bristol. Deposits of coal, ironstone, clay, and limestone all lay close to the surface and so were easy to exploit at an early date. The town developed alongside of, and took its name from, a well-known cast-iron bridge that was built across the river between 1777 and 1781, but industrial development was already well established here by that date.

Coal mining had developed significantly in the area during Tudor and Stuart times, and there was already a sizeable community within the gorge. Iron smelting and clay working had also begun during these periods, but it was the perfection of the process of smelting iron with coke by Abraham Darby (1678—1717) at Coalbrookdale between 1709 and 1715— which allowed iron to be produced far more cheaply—that was to revolutionize the iron industry. The use of coke, rather than charcoal, also led to a vast increase in the amount of iron that could be produced. Consequently, iron production here enjoyed a massive expansion, and by the end of the eighteenth century the area had become one of the most technologically advanced in the world. A new planned town was built at Coalport by William Reynolds (1758—1803) during the 1790s, at the junction of the Severn with the Shropshire Canal. The town was associated with a new china works, a pottery, brick works, rope works, a timber yard, and two chain works.

When the iron industry began to decline in the nineteenth century, other industries developed to take its place. The manufacture of pottery, bricks, roof tiles, decorative tiles, and clay tobacco pipes flourished, for example. Manufacturers exploited the local clays and used first the Severn river, and then the new railroads, to export their products far and wide. In 1986 Ironbridge was designated a UNESCO World Heritage site. **DE**

IRON BRIDGE

This bridge replaced a ferry crossing and was built by Abraham Darby III (1750–91) between 1777 and 1781. It was initially a financial loss, but its construction allowed a town to develop on its north side. The single-span, cast-iron bridge is 99 feet (30.2 m.) long, and was designed by Thomas Farnolls Pritchard (1723–77); it has stone abutments at either end. From its official opening in 1781, it was run by the Madeley Turnpike Trust, whose brick tollhouse still stands on the road to the south.

IRON SMELTING AND SMITHING

A bloomery existed here in 1536, and the first blast furnace was built at Willey in c. 1618. By 1715 Abraham Darby had pioneered the use of air furnaces and coke to make iron; this, together with sand molding, led to the mass production of cast iron. Iron output greatly increased in the 1750s and 1760s. In the 1770s the use of blowing engines enabled forges to be built away from the river. The late eighteenth century saw the heyday of the local iron industry, making cannon and cast cylinders.

THE SUCCESS OF IRONBRIDGE

The Severn is one of the United Kingdom's greatest rivers and it empties into the Bristol Channel. Consequently, it provided a natural outlet for the manufactured goods produced in this area, which could then be shipped worldwide via the ports of Gloucester and Bristol. Conversely, raw materials (such as lead ore, or alternative sources of coal or iron ore) could be brought by river transport to Ironbridge.

The flow of the river through the gorge was always strong, and this made it ideal for powering waterwheels. In addition, many of the industries that were developed in the region used substantial quantities of water in their various production stages. This is particularly true of the fired-clay industries, but is also the case with many of the finishing stages associated with metal working. For these reasons, it is little surprise that many of the early production sites were located close to the river. The development of steam pumping engines from the later eighteenth century onward allowed new sites to be established farther away from the river.

In the mid nineteenth century, the advent of the railroad network provided a new means of transporting raw materials and finished products to and from the gorge. However, it also enabled visitors to come to the area in greater numbers, which significantly boosted the local economy. As industry began to decline, tourism gradually proved to be a welcome replacement. It was the interest generated by these visitors that eventually provided the impetus for the establishment of the Ironbridge Gorge Museum Trust in 1967. In turn, the work of this independent educational charity greatly assisted the designation of Ironbridge as a World Heritage site.

CONFLICT ARCHAEOLOGY

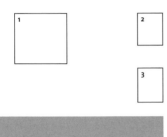

1 This iron face mask of a Roman cavalry helmet was excavated from the site of the Battle of the Teutoburg Forest, Kalkriese, Germany.

2 Many of the skulls found in a mass grave at Talheim, Germany, show evidence of blunt force trauma, as seen here.

3 In Europe, mass graves are relatively rare between 1300 and 1850 because soldiers were usually buried where they fell. At the site at Wittstock, archaeologists have been able to assess the skeletons and establish details about the soldiers' general health as well as how they died.

The archaeology of ancient or historical conflicts covers far more than the physical site(s) of a conflict—whether civil or military. It concerns the application of archaeological techniques to the study of all aspects of the encounter, including the victims and all of the detritus left behind. Historians have long studied military tactics and individual battles, and the first antiquarian observations about the spread of artifacts across a battlefield were made by Edward FitzGerald (1809–83) at Naseby, United Kingdom, in the mid nineteenth century. Occasional archaeological investigations of parts of battlefields began as early as 1905, at Visby in Gotland, but the systematic application of archaeological methods to the investigation of conflicts is a relatively recent development, beginning perhaps in the 1970s and early 1980s.

Although historians often refer to a battlefield, the term can be misleading in that some battles are known to have been protracted affairs that ranged over a considerable area and involved a number of separate episodes: for example, the Battle of Visby (1361) took place over several days in at least three different locations. Hence, one of the challenges facing the archaeologist is to locate the actual scenes of conflict. A variety of techniques are used, but the

KEY EVENTS

9 CE	c. 235	1628	1636	1642	1643
At the Battle of the Teutoburg Forest, Germanic tribes destroy three Roman legions. Military equipment is later found at the site.	The Battle at the Harzhorn takes place between Germanic tribes and Roman troops. About 1,500 artifacts are later discovered.	The Siege of Stralsund takes place. Excavation in 2010 uncovers a communications trench containing two skeletons with traumatic injuries.	A Swedish allied army defeats a combined Imperial-Saxon army at Wittstock. A mass grave containing eighty-eight skeletons is excavated in 2007.	Cavalry action at Edgehill produces a thin scatter of small caliber bullets, while the infantry action yields a denser scatter of larger caliber bullets.	The Royalist garrison is besieged in a fortified manor house at Grafton Regis, U.K. A detailed metal detector survey later plots the finds.

most common scenario is a combination of the following: desk-based assessments, earthwork surveys, geophysical surveys, metal detector surveys, and field walking. As with any form of archaeological investigation, the recording needs to be systematic and detailed throughout these processes, and appropriate arrangements must be made for the archiving of the site records and the curation of the finds, including any human remains.

Our knowledge of conflict in the prehistoric era comes almost entirely from archaeology. Some of the earliest evidence yet recorded is represented by Neolithic skeletons in a mass grave at Talheim, Germany (see image 2), killed using stone axes in *c.* 5000 BCE. Other examples of Neolithic and Chalcolithic violence include Ötzi the Iceman (see p. 546) and three skeletons, shot with flint arrowheads, interred in the Wayland's Smithy long barrow in Oxfordshire, United Kingdom, in *c.* 3610 to 3550 BCE. In the Late Bronze Age and Iron Age, the building of hill forts indicated more war-turbulent times, and occasional skeletal finds confirm this: at Hod Hill in Dorset, United Kingdom, a skeleton — shot by a Roman ballista bolt in the storming of that hill fort in *c.* 45 CE — was found in excavations. The Battle of the Teutoburg Forest, where the Roman general Varus lost three legions in 9 CE, has long been known from classical accounts, but its site was located initially by a metal detectorist at Kalkriese, near Osnabrück, Germany. Subsequent investigations revealed that the Romans had been ambushed in a long defile in the forests; excavation resulted in the recovery of more than 5,500 Roman objects (see image 1).

Historical accounts of battles are often partial and not always detailed. Archaeology can help to identify where actual conflicts took place and to throw light on the lives and equipment of the common soldier. It may show where certain types of weapons, such as artillery, were used, while the study of skeletal remains can reveal what kind of weapons inflicted which wounds, and how those weapons were used, for example at Visby, Towton, or Wittstock. In the seventeenth century, large-scale conflicts raged across Europe during the Thirty Years' War, while in the United Kingdom there were three civil wars. Archaeologically, one of the best-recorded conflicts is the Battle of Wittstock, in 1636. Meticulous work at this site in Brandenburg, Germany, enabled a reconstruction of the fighting tactics used and established where in Europe the various soldiers came from, as well as identifying five discrete layers of burials within the mass graves (see image 3). In other cases, the detailed plotting of bullets and cannon shot across a battlefield can help to identify where individual actions took place, and which parts of an army were in action there, for example at the English Civil War battle of Edgehill in Warwickshire.

More recent conflicts have been the subject of forensic archaeology — examining evidence for genocide in the Balkans and locating the bodies of people abducted, murdered, and secretly buried by paramilitary groups during the Irish Troubles. **DE**

1643–46	1644	1685	1746	1876	1914
The Royalist garrison is besieged several times at Boarstall in Buckinghamshire, U.K. A metal detector survey later plots the spread of bullets.	Parliamentarians defeat the Royalists at Marston Moor in North Yorkshire, U.K. Attempts are later made to plot metal-detected finds with varying success.	The Battle of Sedgemoor is fought. A desk-based assessment and metal detector survey have since enabled reconstruction of troop deployments.	The Battle of Culloden takes place in the Highlands. Earthwork burial mounds are formed.	The U.S. cavalry suffers heavy losses against a large force of Lakota, Cheyenne, and Arapaho at the Battle of the Little Bighorn (see p. 512) in Montana.	A German trench is dug at Bixschoote near Ypres, Belgium, and abandoned the following year. Nearby original French slit trenches are located.

Battle of the Little Bighorn 1876

This detail from *Custer's Last Stand* (1899) by Edgar Samuel Paxson (1852–1919) shows Custer standing in a beige uniform with a red kerchief. Paxson arrived in Montana in 1877, a year after the battle, and spent years doing research for his painting, including interviews with Indians who had been in the battle.

On June 25, 1876, on the banks of the Little Bighorn river that cuts through the grasslands of Montana, Lieutenant Colonel George Armstrong Custer (1839–76) rode into the annals of U.S. history. Brigadier General Alfred Terry (1827–90) ordered him to capture a large force of Cheyenne, Lakota, and Arapaho encamped along the banks of the Bighorn and to bring them and their families back to their reservation—a mission, according to the myth, approached by Custer with characteristic hubris. Distrusting the advice of his Crow scouts who told him he was about to meet a huge Indian encampment, Custer pressed on with his plan to attack and then take the survivors back to their reservation. Unfortunately, he had driven his men too hard. His 600 cavalrymen were fatigued even before the battle started, and most of them were undertrained and under-equipped. Custer decided to split his forces into three battalions led by himself, Major Marcus Reno (1834–89) and Captain Frederick Benteen (1834–98). Custer and Reno made a two-prong attack, either directly at the camp or in a sweep to prevent the women and children from escaping. Custer's own battalion of 210 cavalrymen was wiped out, the remnants of whom—the myth insists—clustered round the general until they fell to the Indian onslaught. No cavalrymen under Custer's direct command lived to say what happened. Reno and Benteen's units took heavy casualties and were either too distant from the battle or preoccupied with saving their own lives to notice.

In 1983, a grassfire swept the battlefield and surrounding area, allowing archaeologists to conduct a ground survey and excavations. After years of analysis of the artifacts and human remains, archaeologists and forensic anthropologists doubted the tale. **PD**

HUMAN VERTEBRA WITH METAL ARROWHEAD
Archaeologists recovered the skeletal remains of more than thirty troopers. Forensic anthropologists were able to reconstruct what the men looked like while alive and describe their last moments. One soldier had been shot in the chest with a repeating rifle, shot in the head with a pistol, and then had his skull smashed. To make sure he would be recognized in the afterlife as having been killed in battle, his chest had been slashed and arrows shot into him.

VIDEO SUPERIMPOSITION TECHNIQUE
Archaeologists found a bone assemblage along with European-style, non-regulation clothing including a rubber button such as those found on ponchos. The face bones indicated he was part white and part Indian. The only racially mixed individual to have been killed under Custer's command is scout Mitch Boyer (1837–76). Video superimposition was used to overlay a photograph of him on the bone. The fit was excellent and it is likely that the remains are his.

ARCHAEOLOGY EXPLODES THE MYTH

After the fire at the site of the battle, archaeologists investigated it over several years. They found 5,000 artifacts and much new data. By combining crime-lab methods with spatial patterning and artifact analysis, they verified cavalry positions and defined previously unknown Indian fighting areas.

Hundreds of spent cartridges, bullets, bits of military clothing and guns, and even metal arrowheads were recovered during the excavations of the battlefield. All firearms leave unique markings on the bullets fired from them. A careful ground survey of the battlefield using metal detectors to locate spent cartridges, followed by forensic analysis of the cartridges' unique markings, allowed archaeologists to map out the movements of the cavalryman and the Indian—or at least his rifle—across the battlefield.

Among their findings is that the hill where Custer made his famous last stand is marked by a heavy concentration of spent cartridges, but it is unclear whether Custer was one of the last of his men to fall, or even whether it was the site of a last stand at all.

Although the cavalry attacked the Indian encampment as a cohesive and well-ordered fighting unit, panic quickly set in among the troops and their discipline evaporated. It is now clear that Custer's force was wiped out piece by piece, cut down by sniping Indians whose repeating rifles were superior to the cavalrymen's single-shot carbines. It is unlikely that there was any hand-to-hand fighting. The final part of the battle is thought not to have taken place on Last Stand Hill as paintings and the myth suggest, but in a ravine, where soldiers were hunted down and killed.

INDIGENOUS ARCHAEOLOGY

1

2

1 Cliff Palace at Mesa Verde National Park, Colorado, was constructed using mainly sandstone, mortar, and wooden beams. It is the largest cliff dwelling in North America.

2 There is an abundance of Aboriginal rock art in the Kimberley region of Australia, a reflection of its cultural and artistic development. Studies are ongoing to date the artworks but it is possible that they are the oldest so far discovered in the world.

In the post-colonial world, archaeology has had a turbulent relationship with indigenous peoples. Within the settler societies of North America and Australasia, indigenous peoples were displaced and marginalized by European colonization and formed disempowered minorities within those nation states. Consequently, debates over the treatment of human remains, the ownership of cultural heritage, and interpretations of the past are common.

In the late nineteenth century, archaeology emerged as a sub-discipline of anthropology, the study of contemporary peoples. Much early archaeological research was intended to provide a temporal dimension to anthropological studies. An example is in the American Southwest, where archaeologists were able to show an unbroken link between sites such as those at Mesa Verde in Colorado (see image 1) and Pueblo tribes such as the Hopi and Zuni. Unfortunately, indigenous peoples—with justification—came to distrust the motives of archaeologists, in many cases feeling that scholars were using indigenous cultures merely as analogies to explain their own interpretations of the past. This distrust was enhanced by the attitude of many archaeologists, who believed that their discipline was the only way to learn of indigenous peoples' pasts, discounting the tribes' own oral histories as unreliable and sometimes fictitious. Even today, a common complaint is that archaeologists try to answer questions about the past that are of little interest to tribal members.

However, since the 1960s, as indigenous peoples have fought to gain a political voice and exercise more control over their own destinies, so too have

KEY EVENTS

1788	1889	1894	1906	1967	1968–74
The First Fleet arrives in Botany Bay, to the south of Sydney Harbor, and the colony of New South Wales is established.	Jesse Walter Fewkes (1850–1930) takes over the Hemenway Southwestern Archaeological Expedition in the American Southwest.	Cyrus Thomas (1825–1910) proves that the mounds of the midwest United States were constructed by the ancestors of modern Native American tribes.	The United States Congress enacts the Antiquities Act to set aside public lands in response to intensive looting of Native American sites.	Australian people vote in a referendum to recognize Aboriginal people in the constitution.	The discovery of Mungo Lady and Mungo Man establish that Aboriginal people occupied Australia for at least 40,000 years.

they become more involved in the practice of archaeology, in particular how archaeologists should treat indigenous human remains in the course of excavations, and more generally, which interpretation of the past should take precedence: scientific archaeology or indigenous history. A compromise was reached in 1990 when the United States Congress passed the Native American Graves Protection and Repatriation Act (NAGPRA), which established mechanisms not only for determining the ethnicity of human remains and objects on federal or tribal lands, as well as those archived in museums and universities, but also for returning the material to the appropriate tribe. As of yet Canada does not have a federal equivalent of NAGPRA. Rather, each province has its own set of procedures for dealing with these issues.

In Australia, nineteenth-century ideas about cultural evolution focused interest on Aboriginal people as representatives of early stages of prehistory— "living fossils"—who, unlike Europeans, had failed to develop and change. At best, their material culture and way of life could provide insights into the European Paleolithic or Mesolithic. Aboriginal people were famously characterized as "unchanging people in an unchanging land" and, until the development of radiocarbon dating in the 1950s, investigation of their past through archaeology was generally thought to be pointless. These ideas about social evolution contributed to broader social attitudes concerning the rights of Aboriginal people through the nineteenth and twentieth centuries, and their legacy continues to color relationships between Aboriginal people and archaeologists in Australia in a negative way.

The demonstration that Aboriginal people had occupied Australia for more than a few thousand years stimulated interest in Australian archaeology in the 1960s and 1970s, just at a time when Aboriginal people were increasingly fighting for political recognition and land rights. On the one hand, significant archaeological discoveries, such as the world's oldest cremation at Lake Mungo, lent weight in the public arena to Aboriginal claims to land, based on long association. On the other, there was increasing tension between Aboriginal groups and archaeologists over interpretation of the past and the control of research. At the same time, increasing development pressures led to a new wave of legislation protecting Aboriginal sites (see image 2), which gave a greater voice to Aboriginal people. As in North America, the treatment of human remains was at the center of much conflict, particularly because of the legacy of unscrupulous collecting practices that dispersed Aboriginal remains to museum collections around the world.

Since the 1980s, Australian archaeologists have been active in developing codes of ethics acknowledging the rights of Aboriginal people to control their own heritage. Active partnerships between Aboriginal groups and archaeologists at a grass-roots level have done much to break down barriers and have led to new research and new discoveries. **PD/CB**

1979	1985	1990	1992	1996	2015
The Archaeological Resources Protection Act is enacted by the U.S. Congress to protect archaeological sites and resources on public and Indian land.	Ayers Rock is handed back to the Anangu people, and the traditional name Uluru is restored.	NAGPRA is enacted by the U.S. Congress, giving tribes the legal right to reclaim ancestral burials, sacred objects, and other objects of cultural patrimony.	The High Court of Australia overturns *terra nullius* and establishes the existence of native title rights to land.	The Umatilla tribe and archaeologists begin a fierce legal battle over whether a 9,000-year-old skeleton is Native American.	The remains of Mungo Man are finally returned to the care of the Muthi Muthi, Ngiyampaa and Paakantji/Barkindji people.

ARCHAEOLOGY AND TOURISM

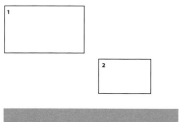

1 *Interior of the Basilica of St. Paul Outside the Walls in Rome* (c. 1750) by Giovanni Paolo Panini, whose work focused on scenes of Rome.

2 The Roman forum at Pompeii, destroyed by Mount Vesuvius (background), is a major tourist destination, attracting 2.5 million visitors each year.

People have always been fascinated by the remains of the past, especially the monuments of ancient civilizations. Ancient Greek travelers, for example, recorded tours to Egyptian monuments, and Pausanias's second-century visits to ancient Greek sites resulted in one of the first archaeological travelogues. In the eighteenth century, the Grand Tour introduced wealthy young European males to the antiquities of Italy and Greece (see image 1).

Today, archaeology is an important element of world tourism, with many countries pitching their archaeological past as a selling point. Organized trips take travelers from Easter Island (the colossal statues) to Cambodia (Angkor Wat); from New Mexico (Chaco Canyon) to England (Hadrian's Wall). In some places, tourists are allowed to participate in archaeological excavations, thereby assisting investigations that all too often are short of funding. However, there are advantages and disadvantages to the close relationship between archaeology and tourism. Anything that allows the public to better appreciate the past and the importance of archaeological resources is positive, and the interest has prompted some governments to take more care of historic sites, in some cases saving them from destruction. Unfortunately, the more popular archaeological sites become, the greater the threat to their existence. One of the best-known examples of this is the site of Pompeii in southern Italy. Preserved in the ash of Mount Vesuvius's eruption of 79 CE, the site is one of Italy's premier tourist attractions (see image 2), but the daily wear and tear is causing a continual problem. Similarly, at the renowned French cave of Lascaux, the effects of pollution from the site's visitors forced its closure in 1963. Today, tourists must visit an accurate reconstruction of the cave, which is itself a popular attraction.

As archaeological sites have attracted more and more tourists, archaeologists have turned their attention to what specifically is being revealed about the past, and whether this has any influence on the public's understanding of the present. Tourists enjoy visiting monumental sites such as the pyramids of Egypt more than, say, a visually unimpressive site. Yet some archaeologists would contend that emphasizing only the remains of the elite of an ancient civilization suggests inadvertently that the elite are all that is important. And that may have an impact on how visitors think about their own society. Also, different narratives about the past are possible, depending on what is emphasized and what is not, what is left in and what is left out. Until recently, archaeologists, who came mainly from the middle classes of Europe and the Americas, tended to construct a narrative that was of importance and interest to them. But indigenous peoples all over the world, as they increasingly regain some modicum of economic and political power after centuries of colonial abuse, now rightly argue that they should have a much greater say in how archaeological sites are treated; whether they should even be open to the general public; and what narratives of their past should be told. **PD**

ARCHAEOLOGY AND POLITICS

1

2

1 Nazi Minister Bernhard Rust (1883–1945; center) with archaeologists in Athens in 1937 when the German excavations at Olympia were resumed.

2 The lower terrace of the Northern Palace at Masada, Israel. The fortress was successfully besieged by a Roman army.

Despite the protestations of some archaeologists who believe that archaeology can be a pure and objective science of the human past, there can be little doubt that since its inception archaeology has had—and continues to have—an intimate relationship with contemporary political trends. The results of such a relationship have been beneficial but also sometimes troubling for archaeology and society.

Within the context of using archaeology to advance nationalist goals, there are good and bad examples. In the nineteenth century the prevailing opinion of Native Americans was that they were savages and needed to be educated to become more "American." When antiquarians began to study the earthen mounds of the midwest and the great platforms of the Mississippian culture, popular opinion, bolstered by "expert" testimony, concluded that Native Americans were incapable of building them. Their real builders were, to name a few suggestions, the Aztecs, the Phoenicians, even the Welsh. It was only archaeological research conducted at the end of the nineteenth century that ended such speculation and showed that the ancestors of contemporary tribes had built the mounds—something the tribes themselves had never doubted.

KEY EVENTS

1750	1848	1894	1912	1924	1929
De origine Germanorum by Johann Georg von Eckhart (1664–1730) discusses the origins of the German people.	*Ancient Monuments of the Mississippi Valley* is published. It veers away from assigning an aboriginal origin to the sites.	Archaeological techniques prove the ancestors of modern Native American tribes constructed the mounds of the midwestern United States.	*Die deutsche Vorgeschichte (German Prehistory)* by Gustaf Kossinna's (1858–1931) sets in motion the use of the past for Nazi political purposes.	Joseph Stalin (1879–1953) controls the Soviet Union and forces archaeologists to follow Marxist theory in the interpretation of their data.	Excavations by Gertrude Caton-Thompson (1889–1985) show that Great Zimbabwe was made by ancestors of the modern Shona Tribe.

More recently, after Israel became an independent country, state ideology spread the Myth of Masada (see p. 310), whereby in 73 CE Jewish defenders of the clifftop fortress of Masada (see image 2) committed suicide or killed each other, rather than fall victim to capture and execution by the besieging Roman army. This myth fitted well with the notion of a small state, Israel, surrounded by enemies and fighting valiantly. However, as Israel became more secure in defending itself, so the myth became questioned. Archaeologists and historians showed that there was no evidence of a mass suicide, and that other elements of the siege account by Jewish historian Flavius Josephus (c. 37–100) were false.

The worst example of archaeology being co-opted by the state occurred in Nazi Germany. The regime was fixated with declaring the German people as Aryans and the ancient and true occupants of Europe (see image 1). Nazi archaeologists and historians were directed to twist and falsify their findings to fit this interpretation. Examples include scratching the Nazi swastika on the base of prehistoric pots to demonstrate the antiquity of Nazism. Archaeologists were put in a horrible position—they knew the consequences of their disobeying such directives, although some willingly acquiesced.

Archaeology is also involved in internal political struggles, such as feminism, indigenous rights, and class issues. Feminist scholars have castigated the language of traditional archaeology. For example, postwar archaeological textbooks still referred to "The Origins of Man." It is argued that such terminology sends a message that females were of little importance. It has also been argued that the emphasis on artifacts such as projectile points prioritizes male activities over female ones. Engendered or gendered archaeology has provided an antidote to the traditional male domination of the field.

The relationship between archaeology and indigenous peoples has often been troubled (see p. 514). Archaeologists historically did not seem interested in the voices of indigenous peoples. Only in the past thirty years have these voices been encouraged as an integral part of the archaeological project. Class issues are also becoming more important in archaeological investigation.

Archaeology is increasingly reliant on rescue archaeology. Archaeological consulting firms are hired by government entities or companies to ensure that no important archaeological resources are destroyed. Archaeological consultants must work to a deadline and stay within budgetary constraints. Although most archaeologists are ethical and loyal to their subject, there is concern that the integrity of archaeological studies should not be compromised by outside factors, and that employee salaries and benefits are commensurate with the expertise needed to be an archaeologist. In addition, archaeologists use their own projects to elucidate past social and economic inequality and the impact of these on current society. **PD**

1930s	1939	1960s	1962	1984	1990
The Nazi regime co-opts archaeology and history to attempt to prove the antiquity and supremacy of the Aryan race.	Appointed professor of archaeology at the University of Cambridge, Dorothy Garrod (1892–1968), is the first woman to hold this position.	The rise of rescue archaeology to help protect archaeological sites from the impact of modern development.	Lewis Binford (1931–2011) begins to publish a number of papers under the rubric of New Archaeology in a quest to make archaeology a science.	The publication of *Archaeology and the Study of Gender* leads to the rise of a feminist or gendered archaeology.	The U.S. Congress enacts the Native American Graves Protection Act, giving tribes the legal right to reclaim ancestral burials and sacred objects.

7 | How Archaeology Works

The practice of archaeology has changed greatly since the first antiquarians carried out excavations in the eighteenth century, and it continues to evolve as new technology enables research to be conducted with ever greater precision and detail. From how we date the past to how we excavate, and from the use of lasers to "see beneath the earth" to DNA analysis of human skeletons, this chapter covers archaeology's major movements, breakthroughs, and theories.

THEORY AND PRACTICE

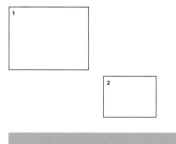

1 In 1784 Thomas Jefferson led the stratigraphic excavation of an Native American burial mound on his land in Virginia. He is known as a founding father of archaeology.

2 Art students drawing in the British Museum in London in c. 1857. In the nineteenth century classical sculptures dominated the museum's antiquities display.

n the eighteenth century, archaeology was not a distinct discipline, but its birth was close. All over Europe, antiquarians, primarily interested in the artifacts for their own sake rather than as sources of information on the past, dug into burial mounds and other visible remnants of a remote past. In a similar vein, Thomas Jefferson (1743–1826) excavated ancient Native American mounds on his Monticello estate in Virginia (see image 1).

Today, despite the development of numerous high-tech tools at their disposal, archaeologists still rely on survey or excavation to uncover the artifacts and sites that form the backbone of their study. Archaeological survey involves a reconnaissance of the ground looking for evidence of the past. This allows archaeologists to get a sense of what ancient remains are in an area. It is also cheaper than excavation, which is the physical digging up of a site. An archaeologist can opt to take a small area of a site and dig as deeply as necessary to find its earliest components and acquire the timespan of the site's use. Alternatively, an archaeologist can excavate a large horizontal swathe of the site, thereby gaining information on prehistoric activities, such as the food they ate. In practice, archaeologists combine both approaches.

Since World War II, the discipline has seen the emergence of remote-sensing technologies. Magnetometer or resistivity surveys can identify underground anomalies and provide a remarkably accurate picture of what is there, so the archaeologist can maximize efforts in the most productive areas of the site.

In the nineteenth century, museums were the prime repositories of the findings of archaeological expeditions, but curators were most interested in specimens that were visually attractive for public display (see image 2). This attitude has been superseded. Today it is estimated that for every week spent in the field, four weeks are spent in the laboratory where archaeologists curate and analyze artifacts. No artifact is ever discarded, because future researchers may discover knowledge in things that today may appear insignificant.

As the practice of archaeology has evolved, so too have the underlying principles that govern the questions archaeologists ask and the methods by which answers are given. Until the end of World War II, the primary concern of archaeology was to try to explain what the artifact was used for, who made it, where else similar artifacts could be found, and when was it made. But in the 1940s radiocarbon dating allowed archaeologists to give an absolute, calendrical date to any carbon-based object such as bone or wood. One atypical antecedent was the technique of tree-ring dating used on sites in the American Southwest. This breakthrough, and many other absolute dating techniques that followed, allowed archaeologists more time and freed up resources to investigate how people lived in the past and why they behaved as they did.

One response to these two questions was to try to understand past peoples' behavior in terms of their relationship to the environment: what did they eat, were they nomadic or sedentary, and so on. In the 1960s, there developed an influential sub-discipline—initially called the New Archaeology (now processual archaeology)—that promulgated archaeology as a science. This was resisted in many parts of the world by those who believed that archaeology owed its greatest allegiance not to the natural sciences but to history. Out of this resistance came a reaction that is sometimes called post-processual archaeology, although the term has fallen into disuse. Many archaeologists recognized that understanding the past is influenced by contemporary factors, such as political ideologies, or the concerns of indigenous groups over the treatment of their ancestors' skeletal remains and artifacts. This has led to archaeology being thrust into the contemporary political spotlight. **PD**

SURVEY

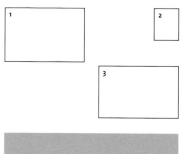

1 The layout of all the main buildings of this medieval monastery can be clearly seen in pasture from the air. The remains of its stone walls and column bases are quite well-defined, even though they are now covered with soil and vegetation.

2 Archaeologists measure soil resistivity with a ground tester at Saskatchewan, Canada. The survey data will be plotted onto a grid that covers the site area.

3 An archaeologist uses a magnetometer to survey the sub-surface in the ruins of Marib, Yemen, where the Queen of Sheba is said to have ruled.

Although certain historic buildings and monuments are still upstanding, many more are now either partially or completely hidden from view. Consequently, a major challenge facing archaeologists is how best to locate and identify these sites, plot their extents, and record their remains. Fortunately, there is a wide range of survey techniques to assist in these tasks, many of which are relatively inexpensive and non-destructive.

Research through old records and the study of early maps, photographs, and engravings can provide a rich trawl of information. References to unusual features or finds in antiquarian works or old newspapers have prompted archaeologists to look for specific sites; for example, villas have been relocated from descriptions of previous discoveries of mosaics. Similarly, the sites of forgotten medieval settlements have been rediscovered using early maps. This kind of systematic search is called a desk-based assessment. It is often combined with aerial photographic analysis. Both color and black-and-white photography are routinely employed, occasionally augmented with infra-red film and thermal-imaging equipment. Three main types of site have benefited from aerial photography (see image 1): cropmarks, soilmarks, and earthworks.

Cropmarks can be identified when deep features cut into the subsoil retain water and produce vegetation that is lusher or ripens more quickly; crops growing over a stone wall are more likely to be stunted. Soilmarks show as discolorations in freshly ploughed fields and betray the presence of sites that have been leveled. Consequently, the ditches around a prehistoric barrow may show as darker (soil-filled) rings around a pale (chalk) mound. Sites that have not been ploughed often survive as earthworks: prominent banks and ditches. Walls or house platforms are often represented by low banks or mounds, ditches by depressions. Their scale ranges from a few inches in height to the mounds of Norman castles. Earthwork surveys are produced by making a detailed record of the variations in height over a site. Most modern surveys are made with the use of an EDM (electronic distance measuring machine) or GPS (global positioning by satellite) equipment such as at Caracol in Belize (see p. 528).

Many more sites lie buried beneath arable farmland. Here, some may be revealed by the careful plotting of artifacts recorded during gridded field walking. Another way of plotting specific types of artifact clusters is the use of a metal-detecting survey. Both techniques may indicate the presence of former settlements or funerary sites lying just beneath the surface.

Geophysical surveys are very informative and they are used widely on rural sites such as at Stonehenge, United Kingdom (see p. 526). However, they identify geological anomalies as well as archaeological features, and so the real skill lies in being able to interpret the data. Two major types are employed: resistivity (see image 2) and magnetometer (see image 3). With resistivity surveys, an electrical current is passed through the soil and the variations in the resistance to that current are measured and recorded. As the resistance levels within the subsoil are closely related to its moisture content, any dry rocky features such as wall foundations will give a high resistance reading; clay-filled pits and ditches, because they retain water much better, will give a low response. Magnetometer surveys rely on the presence of weakly magnetized iron oxides in the soil. They were first used to detect fired-clay structures: this is because the magnetic particles in fired clay structures are aligned with the direction of the magnetic field at the time that they were allowed to cool (thermoremanence). On marine sites, magnetometer surveys are often used with side-sweeping sonar scans to map underwater anomalies. **DE**

Hidden Landscapes Project: Stonehenge

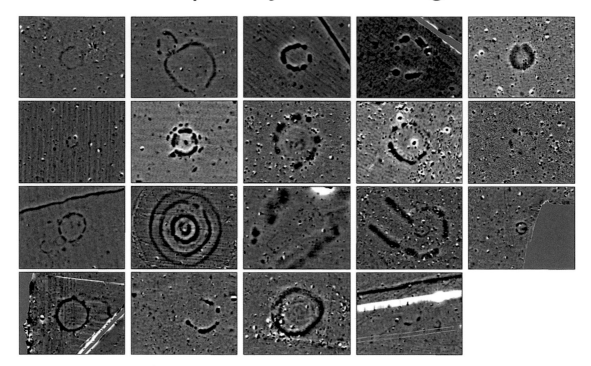

Magnetic data images of newly discovered monuments around Stonehenge in Wiltshire, England reveal a complex ceremonial landscape that consisted of timber and stone henges, and other ditched features. The combination of non-invasive geophysical research and excavations will reveal new dimensions to this landscape in the years to come.

The megalithic monument at Stonehenge on the Salisbury Plain in southern England has been studied by antiquarians and archaeologists for centuries (see p. 130). For a long time, investigations focused on the immense standing stones that form the most recent incarnation of the monument, and became increasingly professional as the twentieth century progressed. Excavations during the 1950s, most notably by Richard Atkinson (1920–94), enabled the general delineation of the construction phases to be assessed, and recovered charcoal to provide the first radiocarbon dates.

Yet it was apparent that Stonehenge was situated at the center of a complicated monumental landscape, and that to understand Stonehenge it was necessary to understand its surroundings. Since the beginning of the nineteenth century, the Bronze Age burial mounds, or barrows, surrounding Stonehenge had been targets for diggers like William Cunnington (1754–1810), and traces of ancient constructions in the flat land surfaces around Stonehenge could be observed from the ground and eventually from the air. One such feature is the Avenue, an earthwork 2 miles (3 km.) long, consisting of parallel banks that bound a flat corridor 40 feet (12 m.) wide running between Stonehenge and the Avon river. Another is the Cursus, so named because of its imagined resemblance to a Roman racetrack. The Cursus lies just north of Stonehenge and consists of a long and narrow earthwork enclosure 2 miles (3 km.) long, and between 330 and 490 feet (100–150 m.) wide. Its construction predates that of Stonehenge by several centuries.

Over the last two decades, there has been a burst of archaeological activity at Stonehenge by several different research teams. High-precision radiocarbon dating, isotopic analysis, and especially geophysical methods of archaeological prospection have been used alongside more traditional techniques. Given the scrutiny attached to anything related to Stonehenge, the standards of data collection and analysis are extremely high. The result has been a series of new findings about Stonehenge itself, the identification of new settlements perhaps associated with visitors to Stonehenge, and the discovery of an immense hidden landscape in which traces of ceremonial monuments made of timber can be seen beneath the surface. **PB**

◉ FOCAL POINTS

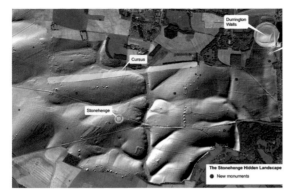

NEW MONUMENTS AROUND STONEHENGE

The Stonehenge Hidden Landscapes Project is a collaboration between the University of Birmingham and the Ludwig Boltzmann Institute for Archaeological Prospection and Virtual Archaeology. It uses modern techniques of geophysical prospection to study the landscape around Stonehenge. Some of its most important findings since 2011 have been the discovery of seventeen ritual monuments, made mainly from timber, that date from the second half of the third millennium BCE, when Stonehenge had attained the form seen today. Another important discovery was the outline of an earthen long barrow from the first part of the fourth millennium BCE. This mortuary structure, now invisible on the surface, was built shortly after the introduction of agriculture to Britain.

METHODS OF GEOPHYSICAL PROSPECTION

Archaeologists have looked beneath the surface using magnetometers coupled with high-performance computing and Global Positioning Systems. Signals from them can be processed to eliminate noise from small metal objects and can be fixed in space with accuracy. Ground-penetrating radar can detect other subsoil anomalies. The data from these two methods can be merged by computer to produce detailed maps of subsoil features.

PITS ON THE CURSUS

Several gaps were found in the bank that defines the Cursus, which would have enabled people to enter its interior without climbing over it. Geophysical surveys revealed a pit in the eastern end about 36 feet (11 m.) across and of unknown depth. It was aligned along the Heel Stone at Stonehenge and the rising sun on the summer solstice. At the other end was a similar pit aligned with the setting sun on the summer solstice. These elements of the landscape were integrated with the main megalithic construction at Stonehenge.

A PROCESSIONAL ROUTE?

The discovery of additional monuments and other features surrounding Stonehenge has posed new questions. How did people move about this landscape? Archaeologist Vince Gaffney (b. 1958) has proposed that the Avenue and the Cursus guided people across the terrain from monument to monument. The destination of such processions would have been Stonehenge. His theory has yet to be validated, but it is an example of how the new data have invigorated archaeological thinking about the site.

DURRINGTON WALLS

Durrington Walls lies near the west bank of the Avon river, about 2 miles (3 km.) northeast of Stonehenge. During the 1960s, a large henge monument built of concentric circles of timber posts was found here during road construction. The alignments of this monument and the Avenue also indicated celestial orientation.

Excavations starting in 2004 revealed a settlement covering 42 acres (17 ha.), with houses measuring 16 feet (5 m.) on each side and associated refuse deposits. The timber houses at Durrington Walls have similar sizes and layouts to the stone houses built at Skara Brae in Orkney (see p. 116) about the same time. Was there a direct cultural link across the length of the British Isles to account for this similarity?

The 80,000 animal bones from Durrington Walls came mainly from pigs and cattle, in a ratio of nine pigs to one cow. Such a ratio is unusual among contemporaneous animal-bone samples. Most of the pigs were killed aged either nine or fifteen months, and hence in the midwinter or the early summer, assuming they were born the previous spring. Strontium-isotope ratios (see p. 542) indicate that some of the cattle were brought from other parts of Britain. The settlement traces at Durrington Walls are interpreted as having been short-term habitations associated with feasting.

Lidar Landscape Recording: Caracol

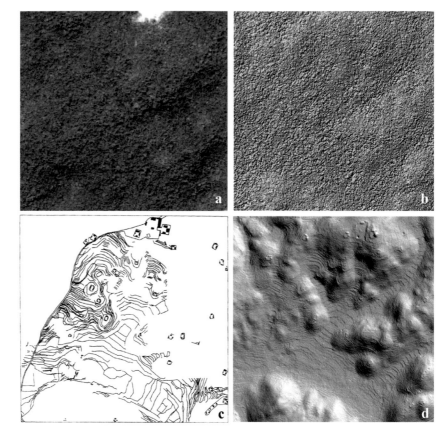

In the lidar-generated canopy surface model (top left and right), the dense jungle vegetation obscures the underlying structures. In the lidar hill-shaded bare earth image (bottom right) the vegetation layer has been removed to expose the topography, revealing the irregular landscape dotted with buildings and cloaked in agricultural terraces.

Archaeological survey in the Maya lowlands of Central America has changed radically from what it was during the twentieth century. Then, fieldworkers had to cut transects through dense jungle foliage with machetes to obtain a sample of buildings and artifacts that could be used to estimate site size and occupation density. The introduction of laser-based remote-sensing technology, commonly known as lidar (light detection and ranging), is providing researchers with a 3D view of everything on the ground surface, not only topography and vegetation, but also buildings large and small, caves, reservoirs, roads, agricultural terracing, and even the openings of underground storage pits and the scars of looted tombs.

Under the direction of Arlen (b. 1953) and Diane (b. 1953) Chase, the first large-scale use of airborne lidar in Mesoamerica took place in 2009 at Caracol, a Maya city in the Maya mountains of western Belize that peaked between 550 and 900 CE. In just nine hours of laser-on time, 4.28 billion points were documented using pulses of light to create a point cloud (a set of data points in a 3D coordinate system) of 77 square miles (200 sq. km.), a huge increase from the 9 square miles (23 sq. km.) of the site that were surveyed between 1983 and 2003 using traditional on-foot inspections. Indeed, not only did the lidar data cover a much larger territory than the field survey, but it also identified structures that previous work had missed. Most importantly, it showed Caracol to be a low-density urban settlement of more than 100,000 inhabitants that spread out over at least 62 square miles (160 sq. km.) in a pattern of dispersed nodes of public architecture connected by roads. In addition, the lidar imagery clearly identified residential groups scattered throughout vast swaths of agricultural terraces that were constructed to provide food for the city's expanding population. **PPN**

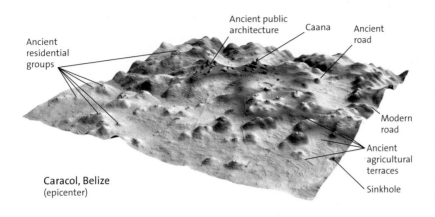

Ancient public architecture

Caana

Ancient road

Ancient residential groups

Modern road

Ancient agricultural terraces

Sinkhole

Caracol, Belize
(epicenter)

THREE-DIMENSIONAL IMAGES

Because of variations in the height of objects on the ground, lidar can be used to show their contours. Lidar generated an image showing Caracol's epicenter surrounded by residential compounds nestled on high ground among thousands of agricultural terraces that undulate over the rolling terrain. It revealed roads leading out from the monumental Caana complex at the site's center to plaza groups with public architecture, from which secondary roads led off to high-status residential areas.

CAANA

The Caana (sky-place) architectural complex lies at the epicentre of the city and dominates the site. When the Chases arrived in 1985, it was still covered by dense jungle. It was modified several times during the sixth and seventh centuries until it reached a height of almost 164 feet (50 m.) above the plaza floor to the south. While the many rooms on its two main tiers may have served residential and administrative purposes, the three pyramids that crown its summit are temples.

EXPANDING THE SURVEY

The Caracol lidar survey proved so effective in producing detailed spatial information in a densely forested environment that several archaeological projects joined together in 2013 to expand the coverage to 408 square miles (1,057 sq. km.) to the north of Caracol. For the first time, archaeologists working in the southern Maya jungles can look forward to having full coverage of surface remains. Although sites identified with lidar need to be ground inspected in order to establish their chronological placement, archaeologists can portray the terrain, agricultural systems, reservoirs, buildings, and roads of entire regions. This large-scale view of settlement patterning is essential for generating explanations of how ancient societies were organized.

In the past, understanding of Maya sociopolitical organization was based on fairly limited spatial data. The 2013 Belize lidar survey, in conjunction with more than a century of excavation, has revealed that as populations expanded during the Late Preclassic period (300 BCE–200 CE), different groups were establishing settlements in a regular manner over the landscape. As Caracol grew dramatically after 550 CE, those sites located between 3 and 5 miles (5–8 km.) from the city center were absorbed by the advancing urban sprawl. Archaeologists discovered that, at the same time, new building complexes were springing up in the suburban zone around the epicenter, probably to serve the mounting administrative and commercial needs of Caracol's growing population. The Belize lidar surveys revealed that Maya urbanism was different from the dense population concentrations that characterize the cities of the Mesoamerican highlands, and more similar to the patterns found in other tropical regions, like Angkor, the ancient Khmer capital of Cambodia.

EXCAVATION

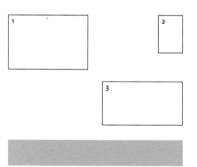

There are several techniques that can be used to investigate an archaeological site and determine its physical limits, but excavation is by far the most informative, establishing the nature, development, and chronological range of a site. Although the origins of archaeological excavation lie in the eighteenth and nineteenth centuries, it was only during the early twentieth century that archaeological techniques began to be organized in a systematic fashion and that standards were adopted widely across the profession.

Excavation is a costly, time-consuming process, which needs to be well planned. It is invariably destructive, and the larger the excavation, the greater the damage. Consequently, the decisions about which parts of a site should be investigated, how much of the site should be sampled, and how best to excavate it are key to the success of any project; other considerations include the sampling strategies for recovering artifacts and environmental evidence. Best practice is to try to leave untouched as much of the site as possible.

Any excavation consists of three major phases: preparation and planning; on-site works; and post-excavation stages. On-site works—the physical investigation of a site or group of sites—are familiar to the public because the excavation often takes place in plain view. However, the other two elements are equally important, and it is often only in the post-excavation stages that the final dating and interpretation of a site become clear.

A site consists of a series of deposits, features, and structures, representing the end products of natural and artificial processes: the record and analysis of their inter-relationships enable our understanding of how a site evolved. Because many sites evolved over several centuries, complex sequences of stratigraphy may be present (particularly in towns). By applying methodical

1 A grid of square excavation trenches is established at Denisova Cave, Siberia, Russia, leaving balks in between. It provides sections at regular intervals, a finite area from which finds can be recovered and a series of routes along which the spoil can be removed.

2 The archaeological excavation at Petriplatz, Berlin, revealed a huge cemetery and 3,700 skeletons.

3 Excavation in progress on the Forum Boarium—the central cattle market— in Rome.

techniques to the investigation and recording of these sequences, the history of the site is gradually revealed. The first stage is to establish an accurate planning grid (see image 1) over the site and to mark out the excavated area. Modern overburden is then removed (usually by machine) to the first obvious change in subsoil, and the surface is cleaned. Cleaning is essential to see any relationships between contexts clearly and to establish which features came first, and what was their extent and nature. Relationships are demonstrated by cutting vertical sections through a series of deposits, in carefully selected places: this determines the order in which deposits will be removed (beginning with the latest and working back). Detailed written, drawn, and photographic records are made of all features and sections, with relative survey levels taken throughout. All finds are recorded by context and the more important ones plotted three-dimensionally.

The great bulk of excavation work is still carried out by hand (see image 2). Digital instruments are used for accurately establishing survey grids and levels, while computers are utilized on-site to record details of contexts and finds. On some large projects, a combination of rectified photography and computerized survey and recording is used to create a digital, three-dimensional record of the excavation. Open area excavation requires a high level of recording and confidence and is best suited to professionals. A single large area is opened up (see image 3) and no permanent balks are left in position; rather, temporary sections are placed where they may be most useful and they are removed in stages as the excavation proceeds. Project teams include not only excavators, but also finds staff, environmental specialists, and conservators. Strategies are put in place to cover how much of a site will be sampled, which types of context should be targeted, what sizes of samples should be taken, and how best to collect and process these. Similarly, conservators will advise on how to excavate delicate or fragile items. In some cases, a large block of soil encasing a complex context may be cut out and taken intact to a laboratory, where it can be excavated under controlled conditions. **DE**

DATING THE PAST

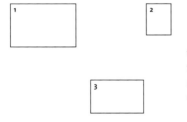

1 Dendochronology or tree-ring dating works best for hardwoods such as oak but can also be used for softwoods such as Douglas fir, seen here.

2 Evidence of human presence at Sierra de Atapuerca, Spain, has been registered at different stratigraphic levels.

3 The accelerator mass spectrometer at the Oxford Radiocarbon Accelerator Unit, United Kingdom, is used to determine dates of samples of organic material. Only a very small sample size is needed; consequently, the technique is particularly good for expensive or rare materials.

Establishing the date ranges of archaeological sites and artifacts is fundamental to our understanding of their significance. Two broad categories of techniques exist: relative dating and absolute dating. Using the former, a site can be dated by studying either the type of structures and finds that are present (typology and association) or the inter-relationships of the various contexts that were recorded (stratigraphy; see image 2). Most excavations are dated by a combination of these approaches.

Few structures or objects are inscribed with a precise date (exceptions are coins and gravestones, for example), but many have distinctive characteristics that mean they can be placed in an approximate date range. Archaeologists classify sites, structures, and objects into hierarchical systems to look for repetitive patterns. A type is a group of individual structures or items that share distinctive traits; arranging types into an assumed order of development can create a model chronology. A typological sequence might assume either progressive improvement or degeneration within a particular series.

Dating by association is based on the principle that when two or more types of objects are found together in a sealed context (a grave, for example), they were probably deposited simultaneously. From this, it can be inferred that they may have been in use and even manufactured at the same time.

In general, the further one goes down a stratified sequence, the earlier the date of deposition. Unfortunately, this can be complicated by later disturbance (stone robbing, for example), so the archaeologist needs to determine how a context was formed and what happened to it subsequently. By arranging the contexts into a relative sequence and then dating any one of them, a relative chronology (see p. 534) can be established. Where a context is firmly sealed beneath a known dated horizon (the construction levels of a dated building, for example), the latter provides it with a latest possible date. Conversely, where it lies above a firmly dated horizon, an earliest possible date can be established.

Absolute chronology (see p. 536) generally provides a more precise date than relative dating and encompasses a variety of techniques. The records of early literate societies offer some form of chronology, such as calculating events from the founding of a city. If these can be equated to modern calendar years, then they provide a framework into which buildings or sites can be fitted. This allows a site phase or part of a sequence to be associated with a particular era.

Dendrochronology is the study of data from tree-ring growth (see image 1). Trees lay down annual growth rings, the thickness of which reflects minor changes in climate. Trees from the same species, growing under the same conditions across a region, will show very similar growth patterns. By measuring the widths of the rings and plotting them on graphs, these patterns can be cross-matched, either visually or by a computer program. Reference chronologies can be constructed by overlapping series of matching tree rings and comparing these with trees of known date. For much of Europe, reference chronologies have been extended back to *c.* 4000 BCE; similar chronologies have been developed in the United States, and elsewhere.

The establishment of radiocarbon dating (see image 3) in the twentieth century revolutionized archaeology and other sciences. Carbon-14 is a radioactive isotope, produced by cosmic rays bombarding the upper atmosphere; since all living matter contains carbon, this isotope becomes absorbed in the same proportions into anything organic. Once that matter dies, the radioactive isotope starts to decay and reverts into the more stable form of carbon. As the half-life of carbon-14 is 5,730 years, this process is gradual. By measuring the amount of carbon-14 left in an object and comparing this to the amount now present in the atmosphere, its age at death can be calculated. All dates are expressed as statistical ranges before the present (BP), calculated from 1950: 4075 ± 38 BP, for example. The confidence levels are indicated either as 1 sigma range (68 percent probability of the date falling in the stated range) or 2 sigma (95 percent probability). Radiocarbon measurement is normally effective to 30,000 or 40,000 BP, but it is possible to date samples back to 60,000 BP.

There are periodic known fluctuations in the direction and intensity of Earth's magnetic field. When any fired-clay object begins to cool, the iron particles in its clay align themselves with the direction of that field: hence, by measuring their orientation, it should be possible to calculate the date of their last firing. This technique, known as archaeomagnetic dating, is most often used to date kilns, hearths, and ovens, but it can also be applied to river silts and marine alluvium dating back to the Mesolithic. **DE**

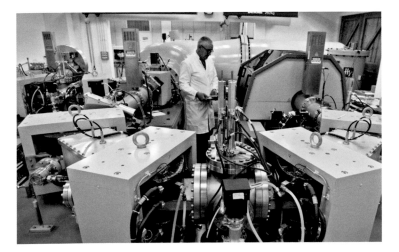

Relative Chronology: Egypt

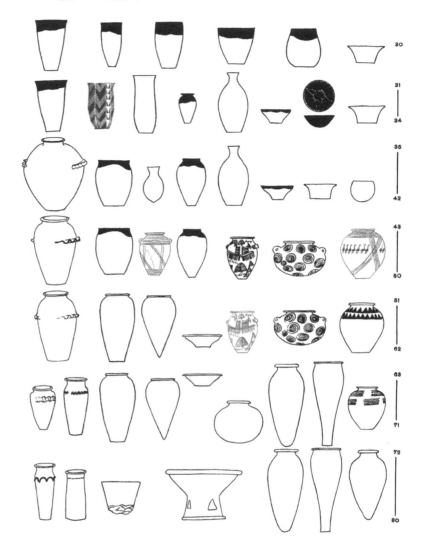

Egyptologist Flinders Petrie developed a system of ordering pottery based on style, which allowed him to "date" otherwise undatable predynastic graves that were mixed together in the same cemeteries.

At the turn of the twentieth century, Egyptologists were starting to excavate many thousands of graves belonging to the Predynastic period: the time immediately before Egypt united under one king. This posed a problem. How could the graves, each slightly different in content, be dated in the absence of writing?

British archaeologist Flinders Petrie (1853–1942) applied a statistical approach, basing his analysis on the pottery contained within the graves excavated in the Nagada cemetery in Upper Egypt. By listing the contents of each of 900 excavated graves on a separate slip of paper, he was able to develop sequence dating: a pottery typology, or classification, which could be used to define the Nagada pottery. From this he was able to group the Nagada graves and, by extension, the entire Predynastic culture, into three successive chronological phases named after a their type site: Nagada I, Nagada II, and Nagada III. Petrie's work had its limitations. In particular, it was solely based on his subjective observation of the evolving appearance of the pottery included in the Nagada graves. It ignored other factors, such as the nature of the clay used in the manufacture of the pots, and the contents of the pots. Nevertheless, his classification, modified in the light of subsequent archaeological discoveries, is still used by Egyptologists today. **JT**

⊙ FOCAL POINTS

EGYPT'S TIMEKEEPERS

Egypt's priests recorded the movements of the sun, moon, and stars so that they might make offerings to the gods at the correct time of day and night. Their observations led to the development of a calendar whose year was divided into twelve months of thirty days plus a spare five "days above the year."

MANETHO

Ptolemy II (r. 285–246 BCE) asked the priest Manetho of Sebennytos to compile a list of Egypt's kings. Manetho organized the kings into dynasties who were connected politically but not necessarily blood relatives. He started his history with the reigns of the gods and ended it with Nectanebo II, final king of the 30th dynasty. His list was expanded to include the 31st dynasty (the second Persian period), but his own age, the Ptolemaic dynasty, was never numbered.

LOST LANGUAGE

Egypt's dynastic age lasted for over 3,000 years, from the unification of the country in c. 3100 BCE until the death of Cleopatra in 30 BCE. This history was recorded in the Egyptian language, using hieroglyphic script. The use of the language was lost after the arrival of Christianity in Egypt. In 1822, when the hieroglyphic script was decoded, the true extent of Egypt's history was understood.

DATING THE PHARAOHS

The Egyptians saw time as a repeating cycle of reigns. They did not use a linear calendar, but dated events with reference to the current king: Year 1 of Tutankhamun, Year 2 of Tutankhamun and so on (above). As every new reign was a beginning, each king started his accession with a new Year 1. This can be confusing: if a wine jar labeled Year 1 is found, how can it be dated to a particular reign?

KING LIST AT ABYDOS

The dynastic and year dating system has been adopted by Egyptologists because, although it is by no means perfect, it is the most accurate way to date specific events within Egypt. So Tutankhamun (r. c. 1336–1327 BCE) is conventionally described as a late 18th dynasty king, with the 18th dynasty (c. 1550–1295 BCE) being the first dynasty of the New Kingdom (dynasties 18–20: c. 1550–1069 BCE). Specific events of Tutankhamun's reign are then dated to particular regnal years. This Egypt-centric dating method can appear baffling to non-Egyptologists and it isolates Egypt from the rest of the ancient world.

Egypt's kings needed to understand their position in history. They therefore maintained king lists, which are chronological lists of all the recognized kings and their reign lengths that were recorded on papyrus and stone, and then stored in the state and temple archives. Unfortunately these king lists were neither complete nor entirely accurate, and monarchs who were considered unacceptable, Tutankhamun and the female pharaoh Hatshepsut included, were omitted.

The best-known king list is inscribed on a wall in the Gallery of the Lists in the temple built by the 19th dynasty king Seti I (r. c. 1294–1279 BCE) at Abydos. It shows the figures of Seti I and his son Ramesses II offering to seventy-six previous rulers, starting with the legendary unifier of Egypt, Menes. The name of each king in the list is enclosed within a cartouche; an oval loop used to distinguish the names of Egypt's kings and queens. A similar king list was carved in the neighboring temple of Ramesses II.

Absolute Chronology: English Long Barrows

The entrance to Wayland's Smithy long barrow in Oxfordshire, United Kingdom. A sequence of twenty-three dates from Wayland's Smithy suggests that deposition in the first mound probably lasted for just one generation (up to fifteen years). The second mound may have been in use for at most thirty-five years.

Long barrows represent one of the main classes of funerary monument in England during the Neolithic period. When the radiocarbon dating of archaeological sites began in the 1950s, samples from excavated long barrows were submitted for determination, in the hope of building a broad chronology for these monuments. However, many of these early samples were from material from old excavations, and little thought was given as to whether they might be from residual or poorly stratified objects. By the later 1970s the conventional wisdom was that these monuments had originated during the fourth millennium BCE, but remained in use for a long time.

By the mid 1980s the use of accelerator mass spectrometry (AMS) made it possible to obtain samples from much smaller amounts of material, such as residues on potsherds. This allowed far more material to be considered for dating; but there were still a large number of different date ranges. In the following decade, the application of Bayesian chronological modeling to stratigraphic sequences allowed a statistical distribution to be imposed on a whole series of dates, and thus permit inter-site comparisons to be made. The production of high-precision calibration curves, based on wood samples dated by dendrochronology, gave much greater certainty. A program of sampling was carried out at five barrows in southern England in 2004 to 2007. Only securely stratified contexts were considered, and multiple samples were taken from these stratified sequences. This allowed chronological spans of perhaps 250 years to be narrowed to sometimes within a few decades. Not only did this demonstrate that these barrows were built within a much shorter time frame, but it suggested that their use was short-lived and intensive. **DE**

FOCAL POINTS

HOW RADIOCARBON DETERMINATIONS ARE EXPRESSED

A radiocarbon determination is expressed as a chronological date range, qualified by a probability factor. A date of 1230 ± 70 BP at 1 sigma means there was a 68 percent probability that the sample dates to between 680 and 885 cal CE; at 2 sigma probability, there is a 95 percent chance of it lying between 650 and 980 cal CE. Dates are expressed in years before the present (BP), calculated from 1950.

CALIBRATED DATE RANGES

Radiocarbon years are different from calendar years, and have always needed to be corrected for comparisons to be made. But when radiocarbon samples were taken from the precisely dated rings of ancient trees, it quickly became clear that the production of radiocarbon was not constant over time, and thus date ranges needed to be corrected by using internationally agreed calibration curves. These corrected dates are expressed as ranges such as 3600 to 3550 cal BCE (83 percent probability).

ACCELERATOR MASS SPECTROMETRY (AMS) DATING

Although AMS was first employed by scientists in 1939, it was not until 1977 that it was used to accelerate radioactive ions to an energy where a rare isotope could be separated from an abundant neighboring mass. The potential application for the separation of carbon-14 from carbon-12 in radiocarbon determinations was recognized. It required a smaller sample, and the measurements could be taken much faster—about one hour, as opposed to several days—than conventional decay counting methods.

MARINE RADIOCARBON RESERVOIR EFFECT

This arises from the difference between the carbon-14 content of the ocean and the atmosphere: the former can give marine organisms an apparent radiocarbon age of about 400 years. Samples from marine organisms, such as this shell, appear older than their terrestrial counterparts. Human populations that eat a large amount of marine fish and shellfish can give misleading radiocarbon determinations. This is often encountered in medieval samples from coastal societies and needs to be taken into account.

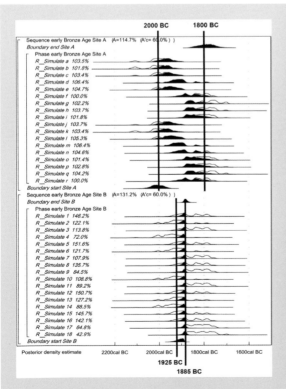

RADIOCARBON REVOLUTIONS

Radiocarbon dating has had an enormous impact on archaeology since its use was pioneered in 1949. This has caused not just one but three revolutionary steps forward, and has dramatically changed thinking—particularly in the field of prehistory.

Between 1949 and the late 1960s, the results of sampling a wide range of sites made clear that conventional chronologies based on artifact typologies and comparisons with classical societies were incorrect. Existing chronologies were often far too short, while proposed dating schemes were not substantiated by the radiocarbon dates. From the late 1960s onward, it became apparent, from comparing tree-ring dates with radiocarbon determinations taken from individual rings of known date, that the carbon-14 dates needed to be calibrated, and that there was a need for internationally agreed calibration curves. Successive curves were adopted in 1967, 1973, 1986, 1993, 1998, 2004, 2009, and 2013; this process is ongoing. This, once again, pushed certain dates back much further.

Finally, the availability of affordable AMS dating, coupled with the application of Bayesian modeling, has allowed greater precision in dating. In many cases, this has forced a major reconsideration of the dating of key classes of monuments.

SCIENTIFIC METHODS OF ANALYSIS

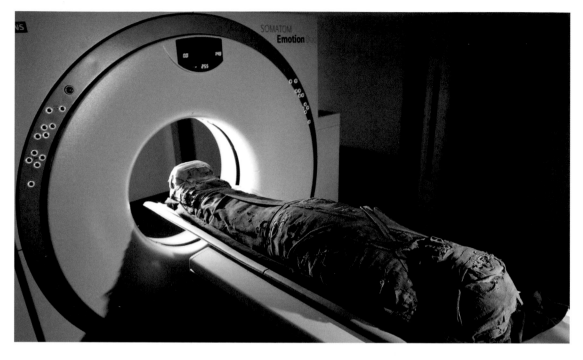

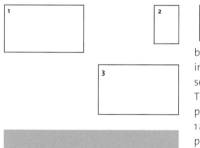

1 The 2,500-year-old mummified body of an Egyptian female known as Tahemaa is scanned at City University, London. She is thought to have lived in Luxor, Egypt, and specialists hope to ascertain how she died.

2 Samples are taken from a 1,000-year-old body from the Al-Fustat necropolis in Cairo, where members of the Fatimid dynasty were buried. The researchers use genetic analysis to study the family origins and relationships.

3 With the aid of a microscope, an archaeologist carefully cleans a gold Celtic necklace using a brush and suction device. The jewelry was excavated from a druid's grave at Glauberg near Frankfurt in Germany.

Field projects such as excavations can generate substantial volumes of records, finds, and samples, all of which need to be processed, quantified, identified, and studied for the archaeologist to make sense of what has been found and to establish its significance. This work falls into three broad interlinked categories: conventional post-excavation analysis, application of scientific analyses to inform that study, and computer analysis of the data. The first of these comprises the study of the structural sequence and its phasing, artifacts, environmental remains including human ones (see images 1 and 2), industrial and technological residues, and soil samples. All of these are processed, and the more significant studied, to establish what has been found and to place it into context. A variety of techniques is used to analyze the samples, depending on the nature of the find.

Petrological analysis and thin-sectioning is used to identify the source of stone objects and also of the grits used in ceramics, whereas a combination of neutron activation and inductively coupled plasma spectroscopy analysis may identify the clay sources used for making those ceramics. Thin coatings on pottery are examined using scanning electron microscopy, and residues from the use of vessels can be identified via lipid analysis. Most metal objects are routinely X-rayed as part of their conservation assessment because this can reveal details hidden beneath corrosion; many are also subject to microscopic examination and specialist cleaning (see image 3). X-ray fluorescence spectrometry (XRF) can be used on glazes and inlays, obsidian, and glass, and also to reveal the presence of metallic coatings.

Organic artifacts very often need careful cleaning, followed by treatment to stabilize them if recovered from waterlogged environments (see p. 546). This needs to be done before they can be handled for detailed study or placed in a museum. DNA analysis is undertaken on selective human remains (see p. 540), although its cost precludes its universal application.

Another technique is that of isotope analysis (see p. 542) of the skeleton to determine its likely area of origin. Selected skeletons can also be sampled for a radiocarbon determination to establish their probable date range. In addition to the larger pieces of hand-collected environmental material, such as human and animal bones, soil samples are usually taken to ensure that a representative sample of the smaller pieces of environmental evidence is recovered (fish bones, bird bones, plant remains, and insects, for example). These samples are wet-sieved and sometimes subject to paraffin flotation to recover as much as possible. They are then sorted and identified under microscopic examination.

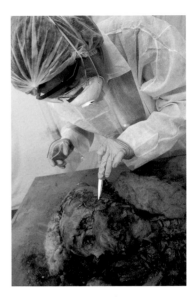

When wooden structures are discovered they are often sampled for dendrochronological assay because this may indicate a date when the timber used to make the structure was felled; it may also shed light on the general area from which the timber was sourced. Slags and other industrial residues tend to be first sorted macroscopically and separated into recognizable categories, such as diagnostic slags and residues (ore, iron smelting slag, iron smithing slag, or non-ferrous slags, for example) and non-diagnostic slags and residues (hearth or furnace lining, or baked clay, for example). Selected pieces may then be subject to archaeometallurgical analysis to characterize those slags and to understand the technology of the industry represented.

Computers are increasingly used in archaeology (see p. 544), and most field projects now include a digital archive that, in many cases, comprises several substantial databases. For larger syntheses, such as national or regional studies, it is quite common to use computers to manipulate large bodies of data—for example, the application of Bayesian analysis to help to refine chronological sequences. Statistical analyses and computer models have also been used in environmental archaeology. **DE**

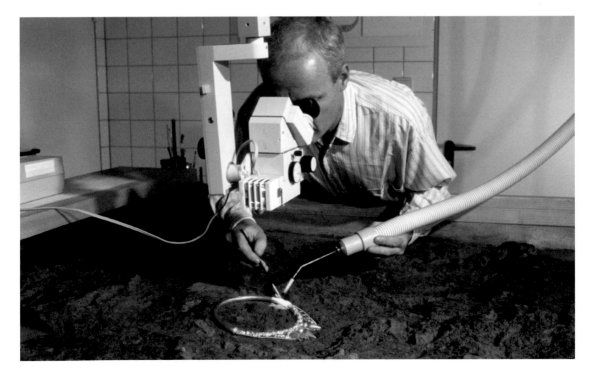

Genetic Coding: Skeleton of King Richard III

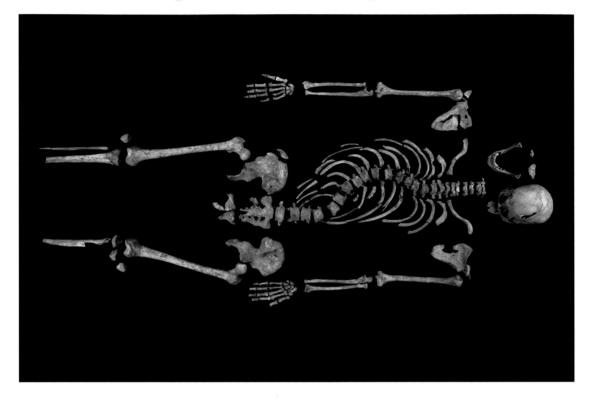

The remains of Richard III were found during the first days of the dig. Almost complete, the skeleton shows the extreme curvature of the king's spine.

In September 2012 an archaeological excavation at a parking lot in Leicester, U.K., located the choir of the medieval Greyfriars Church, and within it was uncovered a burial containing a rather gracile skeleton, with a distorted spine and several wounds. King Richard III (1452–85) had reputedly been brought to the church for burial after being killed at the Battle of Bosworth in 1485, but friary churches commonly contain large numbers of burials. Consequently, archaeologists needed to ascertain whether the remains were those of Richard III or some other individual.

First, they needed to establish whether they could use DNA and other techniques to try to confirm the likely date and sex of the skeleton. Second, if DNA happened to survive, they needed to determine whether any DNA profile obtained would match those of any of the king's modern relatives. Two samples were taken from the skeleton— one from the teeth and another from a thigh bone—and they were sent off to two separate laboratories for DNA analysis; this ruled out any risk of cross-contamination. The results showed the presence of a Y chromosome, which confirmed that the skeleton was indeed male. Although Richard himself had no direct descendants who survived his death, his sister—Anne of York (1439–76)—had an unbroken line of descendants that extends to the present day. The project team managed to track down two of her relatives and DNA samples were taken. The mitochondrial DNA from the skeleton was reassembled and compared with those from the two modern donors. It proved to be an exact match with one and differed from the other in only one single base. This is consistent with the two modern donors being related through the maternal line to the skeleton. A control check against other European databases of more than 22,000 mitochondrial DNA samples revealed no additional matches, which indicates that the possibility of a chance match would have been very small. Finally, the DNA suggested that this skeleton would probably have had blue eyes (96 percent) and (at least in childhood) blond hair (77 percent). **DE**

FOCAL POINTS

DNA AND ARCHAEOLOGY

This is the oldest excavated skeleton in the world to be identified via a genetic match with a modern descendant. More typical uses of DNA analysis in archaeology are to look for potential family relationships within cemetery groups, or to map the spread or movements of racial or tribal groups over time. For example, the Blood of the Vikings project (2000–01) discovered that 60 percent of males from the Northern Isles had Norse ancestry.

Y-CHROMOSOME DNA

Although paternal lines of descent are easier to trace through documentary research than material ones, they can be difficult to demonstrate using DNA analysis. First, the samples contain less Y-chromosome DNA, and second, an unbroken chain of descent depends a great deal on the marital fidelity of the various ancestors. Five modern descendants of Richard's family through the male line were identified, but none matched the DNA of the excavated skeleton.

MITOCHONDRIAL DNA

All living organisms contain DNA, which are the building blocks of life and act as the genetic instructions to the next generation. Human DNA contains separate instructions inherited through paternal and maternal lines. The latter is called mitochondrial DNA and is inherited by a mother's children through her egg; it can only be passed on by her daughters through their eggs. Mitochondrial DNA is much more plentiful than DNA from the paternal line, and is easier to extract from ancient bone.

CONTEXTUAL FACTORS

The location of the skeleton provided contextual clues to its identity. First, the remains lay within the friary to which the king's body was reputedly brought for burial. Second, it was found within the choir—a part of the church normally associated with higher status or significant burials. The irregular shape of the grave and the layout of the body both suggested an interment made in haste, rather than one accorded due dignity, which would fit with the circumstances after the Battle of Bosworth.

RICARDVS · III · ANG · REX ·

IDENTIFICATION

The identification of the body depended on a number of factors, some contextual, others scientific. For example, the estimated age range at death was twenty-five to thirty-four: Richard III would have been thirty-two when he died. The skeleton was also found to have severe scoliosis, a condition in which the spine is bent from side to side; this fits with some historical descriptions of the king. Furthermore, this individual had suffered a violent death: the skeleton bore eleven injuries from a variety of bladed weapons—mostly to the skull, but also to the torso. More tellingly, the radiocarbon dating of one of the ribs offered a corrected calibrated date range of cal 1475–1530 CE (at 68.2 percent probability) and cal 1430–1530 CE (at 96 percent probability). This confirms that the individual died during the later part of the friary's occupation and within the right era for Richard III's death in 1485. Isotope analysis of the skeleton demonstrated that this person had probably spent their early childhood in eastern England, but had later moved west; Richard was born in Fotheringhay (Northamptonshire), but at the age of seven moved to Ludlow (on the border between Wales and England). When combined with the results of the DNA analysis, which indicate a strong genetic link through the maternal line to two of the king's surviving relatives, these factors suggest that the probability that the skeleton is that of Richard III is in the region of 99.99 percent.

Isotope Studies: Diet and Movement

New applications of analytical chemistry are continually opening new avenues for archaeological investigation and making it possible for old bones to tell new stories. In the decades to come, such work will yield many new insights into the lives of ancient people.

The first recognition of the value of isotopes to archaeology was, of course, radiocarbon dating (see p. 532). Radioactive carbon-14, however, is not a stable isotope and eventually disappears from the organic material being studied. During the 1970s, researchers discovered that the ratios of stable isotopes, such as between carbon-13 and carbon-12 and nitrogen-15 and nitrogen-14, could provide evidence about the diet consumed by an individual. One of the earliest applications of carbon stable isotope ratios was to track the shift from a diet based on marine foods to one based on agricultural products during the transition from hunting and gathering to agriculture in Denmark and Britain.

More recently, the use of carbon and nitrogen stable isotopes has been refined to produce detailed assessments of prehistoric diets, especially during the last ten years of an individual's life. Carbon isotope ratios can distinguish among proteins obtained from marine, terrestrial, and freshwater resources, as well as between amounts of plants that use different forms of photosynthesis. For example, most plants have what is called a C_3 photosynthetic pathway, while certain ones that are economically important, such as maize and millet, have C_4 photosynthesis. Nitrogen stable isotope ratios reflect where an individual stands on the food chain, and thus a diet richer in protein results in a higher ratio. Taken together, the pattern of these isotopic ratios in a skeletal population can show the extent to which diet varied among individuals, with the possibility that some people had a better diet than others, or between communities. Other minute details are possible to ascertain with this method, such as the age at which children were weaned. **PB**

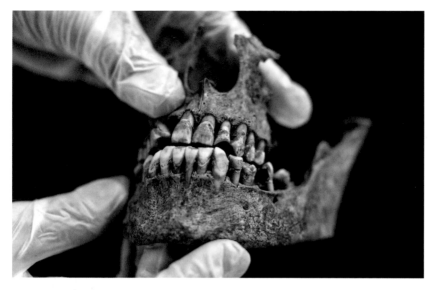

TEETH

Strontium isotopes in teeth are used to study patterns of human and animal mobility. Strontium-87 is formed through the decay of rubidium-87 in the Earth's crust, while stable strontium-86 occurs naturally. Different types of rock formations have different $^{87}Sr/^{86}Sr$ ratios. Bones and teeth develop over time. Thus differences in the $^{87}Sr/^{86}Sr$ ratio between different teeth, or between the teeth and bones of a skeleton, and between these anatomical elements and the local geological ratio, can reflect changes in where the person lived.

EGTVED GIRL

Strontium isotope analysis can be applied to skeletons that were excavated years ago. In 1921 an oak coffin under a mound in Denmark was found to contain the body of Egtved Girl, who died *c.* 1370 BCE. The strontium in the wool of her skirt showed that it probably came from southwestern Germany. Strontium in her hair, fingernails, and a molar tooth indicated that she had originally lived in the area of the Black Forest, then came to Denmark, and then moved back and forth between these two areas, returning to Denmark about a month before dying there.

TRACKING THE AMESBURY ARCHER AND GERMANIC BARBARIANS

The Amesbury Archer (see p. 136) is an example of the application of strontium isotope ratios to study movement. The Archer appears to have been born and raised somewhere in central Europe, and came to the area of Stonehenge, Wiltshire, where he died late in his life.

This analytical technique has also been brought to bear on the movements of Germanic barbarians in the 1st millennium CE in a study of nineteen individuals from an early Anglo-Saxon cemetery at Berinsfield, Oxfordshire. Most were born locally, ate food grown on local soils, and drank local water their entire lives. Four,

however, appear to have grown up elsewhere. One had strontium ratios that are a better fit to those found in southwestern Germany, while another had non-local ratios that could be traced to Germany or northeastern England. Two others had non-local ratios but that may have been from elsewhere in southern Britain. This evidence makes it seem unlikely that the arrival of Anglo-Saxons resulted in widespread replacement of the local population, but suggests that small groups of immigrants from continental Europe mingled with indigenous communities.

Data Analysis: Digital Tools

CAD software is used to aid restoration of a Roman wall painting at the Chao Samartín archaeological site in Asturias, northwest Spain.

Computers have given archaeologists a new set of powerful research tools. Even medium-sized excavations can produce thousands of finds, including stones, bones, ceramics, seeds, soil samples, and a host of excavation observations. Computers are now essential for storing and managing these large datasets. More importantly, computing offers a huge and growing suite of new analytical possibilities. Geographical information systems (GIS) permit sophisticated mapping, analyzing, and visualizing of spatial data, within sites or landscapes. Harris Matrix software is another tool for understanding spatial and temporal relationships. The program computes relationships between the layers in archaeological sites to establish the order of deposition, and therefore their relative age. Computer-aided design software (CAD) and computer graphics take visualization into the realm of 3D. Because data (such as measurements) can be built into these images, they may also function as a research tool. Other computer graphic technologies are invaluable for digital enhancement and analysis of photographs.

Aerial photography for surveying has been partly replaced by hi-res satellite images and remote sensing. These are especially useful for searching inaccessible or thickly vegetated landscapes for features such as structures and roads that are otherwise concealed. The same technology has been used for interactive websites that allow public participation in academic survey projects. Internet archaeology in general helps researchers to provide educational resources and to share their discoveries by publishing findings online. Online archives, databases, and new technologies have made information easily accessible, even for archaeologists working in the field in remote locations. **AS**

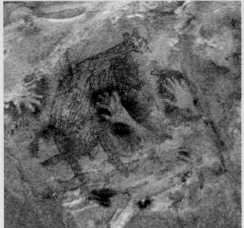

FOCAL POINTS

GEOGRAPHICAL INFORMATION SYSTEM (GIS)

GIS depends on mapped information entered as different layers that can be overlaid and compared. Layers might map features such as living sites, rivers, pottery scatters, and topography. Any combination of these can then be compared against one another, and correlations analyzed. Though a powerful tool, the value of GIS analyses depends on user understanding of how it works, and the quality of the data entered.

HARRIS MATRICES

The Harris Matrix program was developed to help establish stratigraphic sequences in excavated deposits. The program generates a diagram that shows those sequences, which would be hard to calculate without the power of the computer. It has also been useful for rock-art researchers. Rock-art sites may contain multiple overlapping and superimposed images, and it can help create a relative chronology and identify stylistic sequences.

RECONSTRUCTIONS

Archaeologists try to reconstruct the past and appreciate what ancient lives were like but, inevitably, most archaeological remains show the signs of centuries or millennia of decay. 2D or 3D computer-generated reconstructions can act as aids to the imagination. In museums they provide evocative glimpses of what things, such as mural art, now faded, or Pompeii house interiors, now ruined, might have looked like originally.

FOSSILFINDER

Using satellite images of Earth, anyone can help survey for artifacts and fossils from a home computer. The website fossilfinder.org invites people to search hi-res satellite photos of Kenya's Turkana Basin (below), home to numerous important hominin fossil finds. People scan close-ups of the ground and report finds. Crowdsourcing of this kind speeds up research and is the archaeological equivalent of "many hands make light work."

DSTRETCH DIGITAL PHOTO ENHANCEMENT

DStretch is a free plugin program for enhancing digital photographs of rock art; it can reveal details invisible to the naked eye. Available for PC, Mac, and Android devices, it works by means of an algorithm that manipulates colorspaces. Because of this color dependency, it works best for rock paintings, rather than petroglyphs. After uploading a photograph, researchers can cycle through a variety of colorspaces. Different colorspaces are useful for different photos, depending on their color range, and can be selected to enhance particular colors, such as reds or blacks. The enhancements create false colors but can hugely improve the visibility of elements of a painting. (If necessary, images can then be converted back to the standard RGB colorspace.) The brightening effect or, sometimes, revelation of imperceptible detail has potentially huge implications for identifications of subject matter, as well as the interpretations of ancient artworks that depend on basic iconography.

Ötzi the Iceman

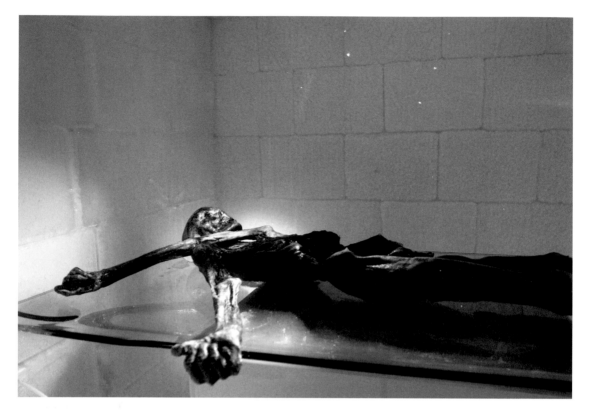

Ötzi has been exhibited at the South Tyrol Museum of Archaeology in Bolzano, Italy, since 1998. The mummy is kept in a specially devised cold cell and can be viewed only through a small window.

The frozen, desiccated corpse found by two hikers on an Alpine ridge in September 1991 was one of the most remarkable finds in the history of archaeology. More than twenty-five years after his discovery, Ötzi, or the Iceman, as he is known, continues to give up the secrets that died with him in 3300 BCE, when he perished in an icy gully. Modern analytical techniques, many not available in the 1990s, have yielded an immense amount of information about how he lived as a member of a Neolithic community and how he died, not as a result of a fall into the gully but as the victim of a stone arrow.

When Ötzi was discovered, the first task was to ascertain his basic anatomical details and to figure out how old he was. It was soon realized that the Iceman was not a recent victim of an accidental death and that he was probably a prehistoric person. A large amount of the analysis focused on the artifacts found with him, made from wood, leather, grass, and flint. A metal ax turned out to be pure copper rather than bronze, suggesting that the corpse was more than 4,000 years old. Radiocarbon dating using the still relatively new accelerator mass spectrometry (AMS) method then established the date of the Iceman's death at around 3300 BCE, toward the end of the Stone Age.

Anthropological study established that Ötzi was relatively short, approximately 5 feet 3 inches (160 cm.) tall and weighed about 110 pounds (50 kg.). Tattoos, made by rubbing charcoal dust into tiny cuts that then healed, were found on his back, knees, ankles, and left wrist. They formed groups of parallel short lines and, in one case, a cross. His teeth were worn down, but surprisingly he had no cavities. During the initial study of his corpse, it was clear that the Iceman had lived a hard life. Several of his bones had been broken and healed during his lifetime, and some joints were arthritic. His toes had been frostbitten. When his internal organs were first examined, it was immediately apparent from his blackened lungs that he had inhaled smoke throughout his life, while his arteries were clogged with plaque. **PB**

CLOTHING

Ötzi's clothing, such as his cloak made from tufts of grass, was a revelation. For the first time, archaeologists were able to determine what Stone Age people wore in cold climates. One important observation was the number of different animal species that were used for the Iceman's clothing. His cap and the soles of his shoes were made from bear fur, while a coat, leggings, and loincloth were made from goatskin. Deer hide was used for his shoe uppers, and a belt and pouch were made from calfskin.

TOOLS

Ötzi's pure copper ax was set in yew. A branch of yew about 2 feet (60 cm.) long formed the handle, while a side branch had been split to receive the axe blade, which was glued in place with birch pitch, then wrapped with leather strips. Another strip of yew was intended to be a bow but was not finished. Similarly, a quiver made from chamois skin held several arrows with viburnum shafts, but only two had points attached. The Iceman may also have been carrying a leather backpack on a wooden frame.

FURTHER INVESTIGATIONS

In 2001 a CT scan revealed a small stone arrow point embedded under Ötzi's left shoulder blade, which had been missed by previous X-rays. A tiny unhealed wound indicated where it had entered. Although the arrow was small, it did a lot of damage. Researchers believe that it ripped Ötzi's subclavian artery, and he bled to death.

While it is not known who shot Ötzi, it is possible to reconstruct his final journey through the detailed study of the contents of his intestines, particularly airborne pollen that entered his esophagus and wound up in his digestive tract. During his final two days, he was at first in a montane area of pine and spruce forest. Then he went downhill to a valley in northern Italy. In this valley, a tree called the hop hornbeam grew, which is only found south of the Alps. The hop hornbeam pollen also established that it was late spring. Several hours before he died, Ötzi ascended through the pine and spruce woods and beyond the tree line, where he ate his last meal of ibex meat, an hour or so before he died.

Recently, scientific attention has shifted to Ötzi's genome, which has been fully reconstructed. It is now known that he probably had brown eyes, belonged to blood group O, and was lactose intolerant. He had a genetic propensity to cardiovascular disease, which is corroborated by the clogged arteries observed in his first autopsy. DNA of the pathogen that causes Lyme disease was found in his body, and the bacterium *Helicobacter pylori* was identified in Ötzi's stomach, suggesting that he had a chronic inflammation. Most interestingly, the modern populations that are closest to Ötzi's genome are found on the Mediterranean islands of Sardinia and Corsica. This does not mean that he came from there, rather that more investigation into population movements is required.

ETHNOARCHAEOLOGY

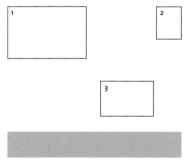

1 A researcher observes a Costa Rican clam worker to help gain insights into the construction of ancient shell middens.

2 Ethnographies of African hunter-gatherers, especially the San of the Kalahari, have long been an important source of information for archaeologists.

3 An Arrernte rock painting south of Alice Springs, Australia, apparently depicting a figure hunting a kangaroo with a spear.

Ethnoarchaeology uses observations from living or recent peoples to help interpret the archaeological record. The use of analogies with peoples practicing traditional ways of life dates to at least the early twentieth century. Anthropological or ethnographic work specifically designed to answer archaeological questions about material culture came to the fore in the 1960s and 1970s with the processual archaeology of Lewis Binford (1931–2011). He hoped to uncover "laws" of cultural behavior, with ethnographic observations potentially giving analogies a sounder scientific basis. Binford studied Alaskan Nunamiut caribou hunters, and the material remains of their subsistence activities, for comparison with European Paleolithic hunter-gatherer sites.

Although laws of cultural behavior proved elusive, ethnoarchaeology can aid understanding of the processes that produce the patterns visible in archaeological materials. Anthropological data can be used to look at spatial patterning within sites and settlements or across landscapes, or the composition of specific assemblages arising from food processing (see image 1) or stone tool making. Analogies may help elucidate what artifacts were used for, and provide insights into their manufacture, style, and social contexts of production.

Ethnoarchaeology is most effective where there are continuities between the living culture and those that produced the archaeological materials to be explained. However, using contemporary peoples as analogues for past groups carries the risk regarding them as "living fossils," prioritizing the antiquity of their ways of living over their histories and status as fully modern peoples. It neglects historical change and shifts in the use or "meaning" of artifacts or artworks. One project that could address this was launched in 1973 by William Longacre (1937–2015). This ethnoarchaeological study of the Kalinga of the

Philippines focused on the pottery made in different villages. It ran for fourteen years, generating insights into factors such as the style, variability, and sociology of ceramic production, as well as changes in the tradition over time.

Hunter-gatherer peoples have long been the subject of ethnoarchaeological enquiry and analogy. In 1903, the French scholar Salomon Reinach (1858–1932), compared European Paleolithic rock art to that made by the Australian Arrernte people, suggesting that it was made as part of sympathetic magic to increase game and hunting success. Though this turned out to be based on a misunderstanding of Arrernte art, it helped displace ideas about Paleolithic art as merely decorative or produced for aesthetic pleasure (see image 3).

Probably the most famous hunter-gatherers of all are the Kalahari Ju/'hoansi (see image 2) of Namibia and Botswana. They have been intensively studied since the 1950s for clues to the subsistence behavior of past hunter-gatherers. Butchery practices, refuse discard patterns, style in artifacts such as arrows, and the layout of campsites are some of the observations that have been useful to archaeologists interpreting much older hunter-gatherer materials that have been found around the world. Analogies with twentieth-century Kalahari hunter-gatherers and their healing trance dance, used to hypothesize that southern African prehistoric rock-art and European Paleolithic images depict shamanic visions, have proven controversial.

Information from living peoples can be useful in other ways too. Archaeologists classify stone artifacts from excavations into categories that make sense to modern analysts who are cultural outsiders. In 1972, Peter White (b. 1937) and David Thomas (b. 1945) asked informants in New Guinea to make stone tools and classify them by type. The differences between indigenous and archaeological typologies, as well as those of different groups and even individual makers, shed new light on artifact variability.

Experimental archaeology, a close relative of ethnoarchaeology, involves replicating past practices. It is used to explore a range of ancient technologies, such as stone shaping, metal smelting, and building methods, and to study the discard and spatial patterns left by manufacturing processes. It can be a useful method for testing hypotheses—for example, to answer questions about what ancient tools were used for, or how the massive Stonehenge megaliths were moved. **AS**

READING THE PAST

1 The Rosetta Stone dates to 196 BCE and bears a priestly decree concerning Ptolemy V (*c*. 210–180 BCE) in three blocks of text: hieroglyphic (fourteen lines), demotic (thirty-two lines), and Greek (fifty-four lines).

2 The first grid Michael Ventris constructed in 1951 in his efforts to decipher the Mycenaean Linear B script. The signs in a column are thought to share the same vowel, and those in a row are thought to share the same consonant.

3 An octagonal clay prism containing the annals of the Assyrian king Tiglath-pileser I (r. 1114–1076 BCE). Written in cuneiform, the text describes one of Tiglath-pileser I's military campaigns.

Writing began in Mesopotamia (see p. 142) and Egypt *c*. 3200 BCE, and was independently invented later in ancient China and Mesoamerica; writing systems developed in many other places, with or without influence from these regions. Some, like the Chinese script and the alphabet, have developed continuously, making it possible to work back from their modern descendants to read their earliest forms. Most scripts, however, have died out, so whether these can be deciphered depends on the availability of clues and aids.

A reasonable corpus of material is needed for decipherment: a single text or a number of very short texts make success unlikely. The direction of writing can often be established (see p. 554). Analyses can show how texts are segmented, which may establish word boundaries, and give clues to the nature of the underlying language. Counting the signs gives an indication of the type of script: alphabetic scripts have the fewest signs, about twenty to forty; syllabic scripts have about forty to 150; purely logographic scripts, in which signs each represent a whole word, require thousands; in practice, even scripts that have a strong logographic component generally also make use of some phonetic signs, so mixed logo-syllabic scripts, using hundreds of signs, are common, particularly in antiquity—evidence shows that even the earliest Sumerian writing made occasional phonetic use of signs. It may be hard to determine the exact number of signs in a script: separate signs must be distinguished from different ways of writing the same sign, and scripts often also include silent determinatives, which indicate the category to which a word belongs—such as "god," "place," "tree"—diacritic markings, ligatures, and other complications.

Deciphering alphabetic scripts is clearly easiest, because the number of signs to be understood is small and the results interlock: so, if a clue allows some letters to be identified, these enable words to be partially read, providing clues to identify other letters. A purely syllabic script, such as Linear B (see p. 552), similarly produces interlocking results, though the number of variables is much higher. Analyses may help, such as the grids (see image 2) that U.S. classicist Alice Kober (1906–50) and British architect Michael Ventris (1922–56) used when working on Linear B, enabling them to determine which syllabic signs shared the same consonant but had different vowels, and which had the same vowel but different consonants. Logographic scripts, however, have to be deciphered sign by sign, none giving a clue to any other, and the case is similar for logo-syllabic scripts, where words can often be written in various alternative ways, as, for example, they were by the Maya (see p. 402), greatly complicating the decipherer's task.

Knowledge of the underlying language is vital: without this, it may be possible to transliterate texts and discover the meaning of some words from their contexts, but not to go further. For example, Linear A uses signs similar to those of Linear B, probably with the same sound values, but as its language is unknown, it cannot be understood. Many scripts render a language that is now dead but that can be reconstructed from knowledge of related languages. What made it possible for French historian Jean-François Champollion (1790–1832) to decipher the Egyptian hieroglyphic script using the Rosetta Stone (see image 1) was that the underlying language was related to Coptic, a known later Egyptian language. Similarly, decipherment of Linear B succeeded when Ventris discovered that its underlying language was an early form of Greek. The Sumerian cuneiform script, rendering a dead language with no known relatives, could be deciphered because cuneiform (see image 3), which was also used to write the Akkadian language, had already been deciphered and the ancient Mesopotamians had compiled Akkadian-Sumerian dictionaries and other helpful works.

The key aid in decipherment, used in cracking Egyptian hieroglyphs, the cuneiform scripts, and many others, is a bilingual: one text, written in two different scripts (and often languages), so that the known, readable text provides the content of the text in the undeciphered script. Decipherment using a bilingual often focuses first on the names; additional clues can come from titles and formulaic expressions such as "king of kings." In the absence of a bilingual, other clues may give similar help, such as known names associated with places. German scholar Georg Friedrich Grotefend (1775–1853) began the decipherment of Persian cuneiform by looking in the Persepolis (see p. 262) inscriptions for sign sequences to match the genealogy of associated kings: "Xerxes, son of Darius" and "Darius, son of Hystaspes." Ventris successfully matched Cretan town names with some Linear B sign sequences he thought were probably place names, providing the key to deciphering the script. These techniques have enabled many scripts to be deciphered. Without them, potential progress is inevitably limited. **JM**

'B' SYLLABARY PHONETIC 'GRID' Fig. 1
1: State as of 28 Jan 51: before publication of Pylos inscriptions

Solved Scripts: Linear B

A clay tablet inscribed with Linear B script, recording a number of ewes and rams.

NAVIGATOR

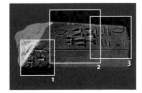

The first writing system to be developed in the Aegean was Minoan Hieroglyphic, which appeared at the time of the first Minoan palaces in *c.* 1900 BCE and was seemingly restricted to Crete. Documents in Minoan Hieroglyphic script are too few in number to offer hope of decipherment. Another script, known as Linear A, emerged at about the same time, and within the next 200 years had been adopted throughout Crete. It includes some ideograms, numerals and small groups of signs that represent words rendered syllabically. Although many of the words can be read, Linear A is not fully deciphered. Archaeological evidence suggests that Linear A was used for administration both in Crete and in the Cycladic islands in contact with Crete, for example Thera.

Another script, known as Linear B, was used from the late fourteenth to the early twelfth century BCE. Documents written in Linear B have been found on the Greek mainland and on Crete, the latter dating to the time of Mycenaean administration at Knossos (see p. 192) and Khania, and possibly elsewhere on the island. Linear B is an early form of Greek. It has just over ninety signs, each of which represents a syllable. Most syllables are a consonant plus a vowel. There are also ideograms, possibly to enable those who could not read to use the tablets. The tablets are read from left to right, with lines beginning at the left and unfilled spaces to the right.

The script was used in two main forms: painted onto coarse-ware vessels known as stirrup jars, or incised into clay tablets. The clay tablets were not preserved intentionally and have only survived as a result of fires. They were made in two forms: either long and slender, called "leaf-shaped," or rectangular, called "palm-shaped." The Linear B tablets record information of concern to the palace economies: administration, social structure, commodities, agriculture, livestock, and religion, including records of offerings and the names of deities. **GM**

👁 FOCAL POINTS

1 PLACE NAMES

The two written syllables "no-to" are likely to be part of the place name "qa-na-no-to," which may be where the animals mentioned on the tablet were kept. Although found infrequently on the surviving Linear B tablets, "qa-na-no-to" tends to be used in connection with sheep.

2 LIVESTOCK

Ideograms for different types of livestock are recorded, including goats, pigs, and cattle, distinguishing males and females. The illustration shows the ideogram for male sheep. On the tablet as a whole, the ideogram for female sheep is shown on the right.

3 NUMERALS

The majority of tablets use numerals. Units are represented by short upright lines, tens by short horizontal lines, hundreds by a circle and thousands by a circle with rays. The illustration shows the number seventy-eight; on the tablet as a whole, the numerals refer to numbers of sheep.

▲ Linear B is found painted on coarse-ware vessels known as stirrup jars. The vessels are 20 to 24 inches (50–60 cm.) tall and were used for the transport of olive oil. Most were made at Khania on Crete, and the inscriptions mainly refer to people or place names. They have been found at Knossos and Khania and several sites on the Greek mainland, particularly Thebes and Mycenae.

DECIPHERING LINEAR B

The decipherment of Linear B was largely the work of Michael Ventris, who trained as an architect. In 1936 Ventris, then aged fourteen, met archaeologist Sir Arthur Evans at an exhibition of Minoan objects at the Royal Academy in London. Reportedly, a chance remark by Evans that Linear B had not been deciphered was the inspiration for Ventris to begin his quest. He originally thought the language was related to Etruscan, publishing this suggestion in a paper in 1940. Other scholars, notably John Myres, Alice Kober, and Emmett L. Bennett had also been working on the decipherment of Linear B, aided by the discovery of an archive of Linear B tablets at the Mycenaean palace of Pylos in 1939.

In 1952 Ventris advanced the idea that Linear B was an archaic form of Greek. He published an article on the decipherment with John Chadwick in 1953, and Ventris and Chadwick's book *Documents in Mycenaean Greek* (1956) appeared three years later, shortly after the tragic death of Ventris in a car accident.

Unsolved Scripts: Indus Script

Most surviving Indus texts are on seals, which also bear an image, commonly of a unicorn. As in many ancient cultures, lumps of clay fastening packages of good were marked with seal impressions, probably to identify the owner or issuing authority and to prevent tampering in transit. Often only the seal text was impressed, so the image may have served a different role.

⬡ NAVIGATOR

When the Indus civilization was discovered in 1922 (see p. 178), its small, beautiful, inscribed steatite seals immediately drew attention. However, there was no clue to help early scholars to decipher the script, and the situation has not improved greatly since. The Indus script was written on a small range of objects, mainly seals, but also on molded tablets, copper tablets, an occasional tool, and a unique signboard from Dholavira (see p. 182). Most texts are extremely short, from one to seventeen or twenty-six signs, the majority around five. This is not a helpful corpus because the longer the texts, the greater the chance of detecting significant patterns by analysis. The signs have been counted and there are around 350 to 450. Counting was not straightforward because it is difficult to distinguish between different signs and single signs that are written in slightly different ways (allographs), and some may be ligatures of two or more separate signs. The number of signs found is far too great for an alphabetic script, too large for a purely syllabic script, and too small for a purely ideographic script. Therefore, it is probably a script in which some of the signs are used logographically (to mean a word) and some phonetically (to signify a sound): the result is a mixed, logosyllabic script, which is difficult to decipher.

Some small steps have been taken successfully toward decipherment: the direction of writing has been established as right to left; probable numbers have been identified; some patterns in the texts' layout have been detected; and plausible decipherments have been offered for a few signs. However, until the underlying language can be indubitably identified, complete decipherment is impossible. So far no claimed decipherment has offered a set of sign meanings that can be independently applied to new material to produce meaningful and consistent text, the necessary proof. **JM**

1 DIRECTION OF WRITING

Clues show the script was written from right to left. Short inscriptions have their blank portion on the left; long ones may have squashed or smaller left-hand signs; and the "handled jar" sign, usually positioned at or toward the left-hand end, is sometimes pushed onto a second line.

2 NUMBERS

One of the few interpretations on which there is limited general agreement is that of the sets of short lines, not written elevated. These are seen as numbers, written in a single row of one to five lines or in two rows, one above the other. The number in this text would be three.

3 "FISH" SIGNS

Using evidence derived from iconography and comparative religion, Asko Parpola (b. 1941), a leading scholar of the Indus script, argues that stars were regarded as fish swimming in the heavens, so the "fish" sign may signify "deity," and the various forms may represent individual deities.

4 SEGMENTATION

Sign frequency and association analyses allow seal inscriptions to be divided into segments. One of the most common is a sign or short sequence that always appears toward the right-hand end: one or two short elevated lines, or one short and one long, straight or bent.

INDUS LANGUAGE

This Mesopotamian seal belonged to Shu-ilishu, an interpreter of the Indus language who lived around 2200 BCE. Deciphering a script requires knowledge of the language it encodes, from which its phonetic signs derive their sound values. The unknown identity of the Indus language is the main problem facing the Indus script's decipherment. Suggestions offered by various scholars include an early form of Indo-Aryan (an Indo-European language ancestral to most languages now spoken in the subcontinent), a minority view; Proto-Dravidian, thought likely by many scholars (the Dravidian languages are now spoken in South India, but originally had a wider currency); or, pessimistically, an unknown and unknowable dead language.

▲ Sometimes, Indus iconography provides evidence for meaning. Images show a kneeling figure making an offering (often in the form of a simple U-shaped pot), to a sacred tree. Both figure and pot appear as signs in the script and may well represent "devotee" and "an offering" respectively. Such clues contribute tiny pieces to the jigsaw of decipherment.

GLOSSARY

absolute dating
The use of dating methods that provide ages in calendar years or as years before the present.

accelerator mass spectrometry
A method of radiocarbon dating that uses a spectrometer to count the number of carbon-14 atoms in a sample.

activity area
Part of a site where a particular activity, such as tool making, occurred

adobe
A building material, also known as mud-brick, used in constructions in various parts of the world.

aerial photography
A survey tool used to discover or study sites and structures, originally from aircraft but now also using drones and images from satellites.

agora
The civic center of an ancient Greek city, usually surrounded by official buildings and sometimes markets.

alluvium
A general term for sediment deposited by rivers; it is often organic-rich, providing fertile soils for farming.

amphitheater
An arena surrounded by semicircular bands of tiered seating.

amphora
A large, usually two-handled jar used for transporting or storing oil or wine or other liquids.

archaeology
The study of the human past, from its earliest times until yesterday, through the recovery and analysis of what has survived of material culture.

artifact
Any movable object that has been used, modified, or manufactured by humans.

assemblage
Any collection of artifacts that forms a single analytical unit, perhaps used for a particular activity.

barrow
See tumulus.

bronze
An alloy of copper with (usually) tin, used to make tools, weapons, and works of art.

Bronze Age
A period in different parts of the Old World when bronze was the main material for tools and weapons.

burnish
A polish applied to the surface of pottery or bronze for decorative purposes.

cartouche
A device in Egyptian hieroglyphics comprising an elongated oval containing the royal names of a king.

caryatid
A column carved in the form of a woman.

celadon
A kind of glazed stoneware developed in China in the ninth–fourteenth centuries AD.

cenote
A natural sinkhole or well, usually in limestone, in which the Maya often conducted rituals and sacrifices.

Chalcolithic
See Copper Age.

context
The physical or cultural associations of archaeological finds, which provide crucial information that is lost if finds are removed by looters or thieves.

Copper Age
A period in the Near East and Europe between the Neolithic and Bronze Age when copper metallurgy was adopted.

culture
The beliefs, behaviors, and customs that characterize a specific people.

ethnoarchaeology
The study of the material culture of living societies to see how and why materials enter the archaeological record.

excavation
The methodical and systematic recovery of archaeological material and information through the exposure of buried sites and artifacts.

experimental archaeology
The replication of ancient technologies and behavior to provide hypotheses that can be tested against actual archaeological data.

feature
A non-portable element of a site, such as a hearth or activity area.

forum
An open space at the heart of a Roman city, usually surrounded by shops, administrative buildings, and temples.

geomorphology
A branch of geology devoted to landscapes and their evolution.

grave goods
Objects placed inside tombs, presumably to accompany the deceased into the afterlife.

ground reconnaissance
Non-intrusive geophysical field survey techniques, such as ground-penetrating radar, used to detect or identify buried structures and materials.

hearth
A fireplace.

hieroglyphics
A pictorial script used by the ancient Egyptians, primarily for religious purposes and on public monuments.

hoard
A group of valuables (often metal) that was deliberately buried, usually in times of conflict or war, but never reclaimed.

hunter-gatherers
People whose subsistence is based on the hunting of wild animals and the gathering of wild plants.

industry
See assemblage.

ingot
A quantity of a material—usually metal—of standardized form and weight, used for trade or as currency.

Iron Age
The period in the Old World when iron metallurgy superseded the use of bronze for weapons and tools.

landscape archaeology
The study of the distribution of material culture across the landscape, and of human adaptation to the terrain.

Last Glacial Maximum
The period from c. 23,000 to 12,000 BCE when global temperatures reached the lowest levels during the last Ice Age.

material culture
The physical remains of the human-made traces of past society, which together constitute the archaeological record.

megalith
A large stone; the term also denotes a megalithic monument.

Mesolithic
The "Middle Stone Age" in the Old World, a period of transition between the end of the Paleolithic and the start of the Neolithic.

metallurgy
Techniques for the working of metal.

microlith
A small stone artifact, often used as the tip of a projectile or grouped in composite implements.

microwear analysis
The microscopic study of the surface and working edges of an artifact for signs of use or for residues.

midden
A concentration of cultural debris, such as an accumulation of shells or potsherds.

mortuary temple
An Egyptian temple, usually located near a royal tomb, and used for rites for the benefit of the dead king.

mud-brick
See adobe.

Mya
Million years ago.

Neanderthal
An archaic form of humans that inhabited parts of the Old World before anatomically modern humans became predominant.

Neolithic
The "New Stone Age," a period following the Mesolithic, characterized by ground-stone tools, pottery, and farming.

orchestra
In semicircular Greek theaters, the area at the foot of the tiered seats where the acting took place.

Paleolithic
The "Old Stone Age," the first and longest period of prehistory, which starts with the earliest stone tools and ends when the Mesolithic begins.

posthole
A hole in the ground into which a wooden post was placed; the rotted post is replaced with sediment of a different texture or color from the surrounding soil.

potsherd
A fragment of pottery.

prehistory
Any period of the past for which there is no contemporary documentary evidence.

pylon
The monumental gateway to an ancient Egyptian temple.

pyramid
In Egypt, it comprised a monumental stone structure with a square base and four straight sides converging to a point at the top; in the New World, it was a religious or funerary mound of earth or rubble, sometimes with a stone facing and a flat platform at the top.

quern
A large grindstone; in the New World the term "metate" is also used.

relative dating
Methods of dating by placing materials or events into a sequence, without linking them to calendar years.

radiocarbon dating
A technique for determining the age of organic materials, based on the radioactive decay of the carbon-14 isotope in a sample.

rockshelter
A natural cavity or hollow in a rock wall, large enough for human habitation or activities.

site
A place where there is evidence for human behavior, ranging from a single tool in the landscape to a city.

skene
In ancient Greek theaters, a building of several stories behind the orchestra, and used as a backdrop or for storage.

smelt
To separate metal from ore, by heating in a furnace or hearth.

stela
An upright stone slab, often inscribed, carved, or painted.

stoa
A multipurpose colonnaded building in ancient Greece.

stoneware
A kind of pottery of East Asia, fired at more than 1,000°C and usually gray in color.

stratigraphy
The study of the formation, composition, and sequence of sediment-layers.

stupa
A Buddhist monument, usually containing relics of the Buddha or other holy people or texts.

style
The distinctive way in which an artifact or art object is made and/or decorated.

survey
The examination of land surfaces in search of artifacts and sites, and their recording and preliminary analysis.

tell
An artificial mound in the Near East, created by the accumulation over centuries of disintegrated mud-brick walls and other cultural debris.

tesserae
Small colored cubes of stone or glass.

thermoluminescence
A dating technique used primarily on pottery and sediments; in pottery it measures the energy stored since firing.

tholos
In ancient Greece, a round stone chamber used as a tomb.

tokens
Small clay geometric objects found in Neolithic sites of western Asia.

tumulus
A mound of earth or stone, usually covering one or more burials.

typology
The classification of artifacts by dividing them into different types and subtypes based on technological, functional, or decorative attributes.

Ya
Years ago

ziggurat
A stepped, rectangular temple-tower in Mesopotamia, usually made of brick.

CONTRIBUTORS

Paul Bahn (PGB)
is a leading archaeological writer, translator, and broadcaster. He is a Contributing Editor of the Archaeological Institute of America's *Archaeology* magazine, and he has written extensively on prehistoric art. He has also authored and/or edited many books on more general archaeological subjects, including *The Cambridge World Prehistory*, *Archaeology: Theories, Methods and Practice*, and *The Penguin Archaeology Guide*. He holds a PhD from the University of Cambridge and is a Fellow of the Society of Antiquaries and a Corresponding Member of the Archaeological Institute of America. He was an advisor on the BBC's *The Making of Mankind* and a consultant on a segment of WGBH's NOVA trilogy *Human Origins*.

Caroline Bird (CB)
studied archaeology at Cambridge University before completing a PhD at the University of Western Australia. She has since had a diverse archaeological career in teaching, curriculum development, consulting, and research, and is now an independent archaeologist, based in Perth, Western Australia.

Peter Bogucki (PB)
studied archaeology at the University of Pennsylvania and Harvard University. He serves as dean for undergraduate affairs of the School of Engineering and Applied Science at Princeton University while continuing research in European prehistory. His recent books include *The Barbarians* and (as co-editor with Pam Crabtree) *European Archaeology as Anthropology: Essays in Memory of Bernard Wailes*.

Philip Duke (PD)
received degrees in archaeology from the University of Cambridge and the University of Calgary. He is a Fellow of the Society of Antiquaries. Now retired, he spends his time, among other pursuits, writing historical fiction.

Dave Evans (DE)
has been a professional archaeologist for over forty years, and served as a County Archaeologist for more than two decades. He has worked extensively on both rural and urban archaeology projects, and has published widely.

David Gill (DG)
is Professor of Archaeological Heritage and Director of Heritage Futures at the University of Suffolk, and is a Visiting Research Fellow in the School of History at the University of East Anglia. He is a former Rome Scholar at the British School at Rome, and curated the Greek and Roman antiquities at the Fitzwilliam Museum, Cambridge University, before moving to Swansea University where he was Reader in Mediterranean Archaeology. In 2012 he received the Outstanding Public Service Award from the Archaeological Institute of America for his research on cultural property.

Jane McIntosh (JM)
studied archaeology at Cambridge University, from which she received her doctorate and where she was a Senior Research Associate of the Faculty of Asian and Middle Eastern Studies. She is the author of numerous books on archaeology and prehistory and has participated in many excavations in Britain and abroad.

Georgina Muskett (GM)
is an Honorary Associate at the University of Liverpool. She was formerly Curator of Classical Antiquities at National Museums Liverpool. Previously she taught Greek art and archaeology at the University of Liverpool.

Paul Pettitt (PBP)
is Professor of Paleolithic Archaeology at the University of Durham. After reading Ancient History and Archaeology at Birmingham University, he took an MA in Archaeology at University College London, and researched aspects of the Middle Paleolithic of Southwest France for his PhD at Cambridge. Since then he has been Senior Archaeologist at the Radiocarbon Accelerator Unit, Oxford University, Research Fellow and Tutor at Keble College, Oxford. From 2003 to 2013 he was Lecturer, Senior Lecturer, and Reader at Sheffield University, and joined Durham as Professor in 2013. He researches the art and archaeology of the European Middle and Upper Paleolithic.

Patricia Plunket (PPN)
received her PhD from Tulane University in 1983. Her studies have focused on the transition from village to urban life in Mexico's central highlands, including the role volcanic disasters played in that process.

Margarete Prüch (MP)
is an art historian and archaeologist of East Asia. Her research interests focus mainly on the dynastic periods of China, Korea, and Japan, specializing in Chinese Zhanguo- and Han-period tombs.

Anne Solomon (AS)
is an archaeologist specializing in southern African rock paintings and the culture of Later Stone Age hunter-gatherers. Her research interests include the mythology and oral testimonies of the /Xam, nineteenth-century "San"-speakers from near the South African–Namibian border.

Henry Tantaleán (HT)
was born in Lima, Peru, and studied archaeology at San Marcos University, Peru. He got his Masters and PhD in Prehistoric Archaeology at the Universidad Autónoma de Barcelona, Spain. He has taught archaeology at universities in America and Europe and has published many scientific papers and books. Currently he is Staff Researcher at the Cotsen Institute of Archaeology at UCLA and Associate Researcher at the French Institute of Andean Studies in Lima. He runs a number of archaeological projects in Peru, including the Chincha Archaeological Project on Peru's southern coast. He is co-editor of the *Ñawpa Pacha* journal of archaeology of the Institute of Andean Studies.

Joyce Tyldesley (JT)
is a Senior Lecturer in Egyptology at the University of Manchester, where she teaches a suite of online courses in Egyptology. She is the author of many books on ancient Egypt.

INDEX

Page references for illustrations are indicated in **bold**

PICTURE CREDITS

The publishers would like to thank the museums, illustrators, archives and photographers for their kind permission to reproduce the works featured in this book. Every effort has been made to trace all copyright owners but if any have been inadvertently overlooked, the publishers would be pleased to make the necessary arrangements at the first opportunity.

(Key: top = t; bottom = b; left = l; right = r; centre = c; top left = tl; top right = tr; centre left = cl; centre right = cr; bottom left = bl; bottom right = br)

2 INTERFOTO/Alamy Stock Photo 8 Chronicle/Alamy Stock Photo 9 Pierre Perrin/Sygma via Getty Images 10 The Natural History Museum/Alamy Stock Photo 11 JOSEPH EID/AFP/Getty Images 12 Patrick Aventurier/Getty Images 13 Jim Hollander/Epa/REX/Shutterstock 16 Cro Magnon/Alamy Stock Photo 17t JOHN READER/SCIENCE PHOTO LIBRARY 17b Universal Images Group North America LLC/DeAgostini/Alamy Stock Photo 18 Lanmas/Alamy Stock Photo 19t Africa Media Online/Alamy Stock Photo 19b The Natural History Museum/Alamy Stock Photo 20 Lanmas/Alamy Stock Photo 21 The Natural History Museum/Alamy Stock Photo 22a © Xinhua/Photoshot 23tl The Natural History Museum/Alamy Stock Photo 23tr PMU M3887, Palaeonotological collections, Museum of Evolution, Uppsala University, Sweden 23b View Stock/Alamy Stock Photo 24 Rosino/Wikimedia Commons 25t CHRISTELLE ORLUC/LOOK AT SCIENCES/SCIENCE PHOTO LIBRARY 25b MAURICIO ANTON/SCIENCE PHOTO LIBRARY 26 Homo heidelbergensis/Natural History Museum, London, UK/Bridgeman Images 27t The Natural History Museum/Alamy Stock Photo 27b Sabena Jane Blackbird/Alamy Stock Photo 28 age fotostock/Alamy Stock Photo 29t JAVIER TRUEBA/MSF/SCIENCE PHOTO LIBRARY 29b JAVIER TRUEBA/MSF/SCIENCE PHOTO LIBRARY 30 LOIC VENANCE/AFP/Getty Images 31t CESAR MANSO/AFP/Getty Images 31b DEA/A. DAGLI ORTI/De Agostini/Getty Images 32 Joao Zilhao 33l © Stewart Finlayson/ The Gibraltar Museum 33r Paul Bahn 34 Michel Girard 35t © Marian Vanhaeren und Michèle Julien 35b © Marian Vanhaeren, Francesco d'Errico and Michèle Julien 36 ANNA ZIEMINSKI/AFP/Getty Images 37 The Natural History Museum/Alamy Stock Photo 38 PLANETOBSERVER/SCIENCE PHOTO LIBRARY 39 MISSION ARCHEOLOGIQUE DE QAFZEH/LOOK AT SCIENCES/SCIENCE PHOTO LIBRARY 40 Women Butchering Mastodon, 1998 (w/c on paper), Harlin, Greg (b.1957)/Private Collection/Wood Ronsaville Harlin, Inc. USA/Bridgeman Images 41l © Tom Uhlman/Alamy Stock Photo 41r CAROLINA BIOLOGICAL SUPPLY CO/VISUALS UNLIMITED, INC. /SCIENCE PHOTO LIBRARY 42 Barrow Island Archaeology Project, UWA 43t Barrow Island Archaeology Project, UWA 43b Barrow Island Archaeology Project, UWA 44 Photo: Don Hitchcock, donsmaps.com 45t Petr Novák/Wikimedia Commons 45b Paul Bahn 46 © Nature Picture Library/Alamy Stock Photo 47 Paul Bahn 48 PHILIPPE PSAILA/SCIENCE PHOTO LIBRARY 49 PHILIPPE PSAILA/SCIENCE PHOTO LIBRARY 50 © NHPA/Photoshot 51 SSPL/Getty Images 52 Corbis Documentary/Getty Images 53t Paul Mayall/imageBROKER/REX/Shutterstock 53b © Suzanne Long/Alamy Stock Photo 56 Hercules Milas/Alamy Stock Photo 57t Universal Images Group/Getty Images 57b Skeletons of woman and child from Bogebakken/De Agostini Picture Library/Bridgeman Images 58 Petroglyphs, including oxen and a person ploughing/Werner Forman Archive/Bridgeman Images 59t Jean-Loic Le Quellec/LOOK AT SCIENCES/SCIENCE PHOTO LIBRARY 59b Gianni Dagli Orti/REX/Shutterstock 60 Universal History Archive/UIG via Getty Images 61t Handle with animal figure, HaNahal Cave, Mt. Carmel, Natufian Culture (bone)/The Israel Museum, Jerusalem, Israel/Bridgeman Images 61b World History Archive/Alamy Stock Photo 62t World History Archive/Alamy Stock Photo 63b Gideon Hartman/Hebrew University via Getty Images 64 iStock/Getty Images Plus 65 Werner Forman/Universal Images Group/Getty Images 66 United National Photographers/REX/Shutterstock 67t John Short/Getty Images 67b National Geographic Creative/Alamy Stock Photo 68 Pecold/Shutterstock.com 69l Dusan Boric 69r akg-images/Erich Lessing 70 Granger Historical Picture Archive/Alamy Stock Photo 71 Buddy Mays/Alamy Stock Photo 72 Photo by Del Baston, courtesy Center for American Archeology 73t Phil Wahlbrink/WahlbrinkPHOTO/Alamy Stock Photo 73b Steven Patricia 74 Inga Locmele/Shutterstock.com 75l CLAUDIO SANTANA/AFP/Getty Images 75r REUTERS/Alamy Stock Photo 76 Robert Gilhooly/Alamy Stock Photo 77t Robert Gilhooly/Alamy Stock Photo 77b DeAgostini/Getty Images 78 courtesy of Mr.ONBE Shin,Office of Kumakogen –cho, Ehime Pref. 79t courtesy of Mr.ONBE Shin,Office of Kumakogen –cho, Ehime Pref. 79b Image courtesy Takao Sato 80 Universal History Archive/UIG via Getty Images 81 © Jack Golson. http://whc.unesco.org/en/list/887/gallery/ 82 Luca Mozzati/Archivio Luca Mozzati/Mondadori Portfolio/Getty Images 83 Nico Tondini/robertharding/Getty Images 84 Dr Andrew M.T. Moore 85t Human bones found at Abu Hureyra/Natural History Museum, London, UK/Bridgeman Images 85b JAMES KING HOLMES/ SCIENCE PHOTO LIBRARY 86 www.BibleLandPictures.com/Alamy Stock Photo 87b Images & Stories/Alamy Stock Photo 88 Vincent J. Musi© 2017. National Geographic Image Collection / Scala, Florence 89 Nir Alon/Alamy Stock Photo 90 gezmen/Alamy Stock Photo 91bl National Geographic Creative/Alamy Stock Photo 91br Vincent J. Musi/Getty Images 92 Portrait skull with cowrie shell eyes, Jericho, c.7th millennium BC (skull, plaster, shell), Prehistoric/Ashmolean Museum, University of Oxford, UK/Bridgeman Images 93l akg-images/Erich Lessing 93r World History Archive/Alamy Stock Photo 94 Roger Viollet Collection/Getty Images 95 DEA/A. DE GREGORIO/De Agostini/Getty Images 96 fpolat69/Shutterstock.com 97br David Tipling Photo Library/Alamy Stock Photo 98 Roger Viollet Collection/Getty Images 99l PRISMA ARCHIVO/Alamy Stock Photo 99r Bryn Mawr College: Richard S. Ellis Photographs 100 robertharding/Alamy Stock Photo 101l © The Trustees of the British Museum 101r © Illustrated London News Ltd/Mary Evans 102 Samuel Daniell/Wikimedia Commons 103t TONY KARUMBA/AFP/Getty Images 103b Paul Bahn 104 De Agostini Picture Library/Getty Images 105 DEA/G. DAGLI ORTI/Getty Images 106 JTB MEDIA CREATION, Inc./Alamy Stock Photo 107t DEA PICTURE LIBRARY/Getty Images 107b akg-images/Pictures From History 108 DEA PICTURE LIBRARY/Getty Images 109t Lou-Foto/Alamy Stock Photo 109b CTK/Alamy Stock Photo 110 Wellcome Images/Wikimedia Commons 111 INTERFOTO/Alamy Stock Photo 112 Landesamt für Archäologie Sachsen; photographer: Matthias Rummer 113l Einsamer Schütze/Wikimedia Commons 113r Landesamt für Archäologie Sachsen; photographer: Matthias Rummer 114 F1online digitale Bildagentur GmbH/Alamy Stock Photo 115t imageBROKER/Alamy Stock Photo 115b Stefano Ravera/Alamy Stock Photo 116 David Lyons/Alamy Stock Photo 117t johnbraid/Shutterstock.com 117b mark ferguson/Alamy Stock Photo 118 Michal Sikorski/Alamy Stock Photo 119t North Wind Picture Archives/Alamy Stock Photo 119b North Wind Picture Archives/Alamy Stock Photo 120 DEA/L. DE MASI/Getty Images 121t Henry Tantaleán 121b Jorge G. Marcos and Natasha Flores, from Un Sitio Llamado Real Alto, published by the Universidad Internacional del Ecuador UIDE, Quito, Ecuador 2015 122 DEA/G. DAGLI ORTI/De Agostini/Getty Images 123t DEA/A. DE GREGORIO/De Agostini/Getty Images 123b Ian Murray/imageBROKER/REX/Shutterstock 124 Edwin Baker/Alamy Stock Photo 125tr DEA/A. DAGLI ORTI/De Agostini/Getty Images 125b Fine Art Images/Heritage Images/Getty Images 126 Elzbieta Sekowska/Shutterstock.com 127t James Osmond/Getty Images 127b Hemis/Alamy Stock Photo 128 Eireann/Shutterstock.com 129l Stephen Emerson/Alamy Stock Photo 129r Pecold/Shutterstock.com 130 Skyscan Photolibrary/Alamy Stock Photo 131l Stonehenge: first phase comprising a ditch, bank and counterscarp enclosing the Aubrey Holes, 1995 (w/c on paper), Lapper, Ivan (b.1939)/Private Collection/© Historic England/Bridgeman Images 131r DEA PICTURE LIBRARY/ Getty Images 134 © Asian Art & Archaeology, Inc./CORBIS/Corbis via Getty Images 135t Chris Howes/Wild Places Photography/Alamy Stock Photo 135b INTERFOTO/Alamy Stock Photo 136 Wessex Archaeology 137t Wessex Archaeology 137b Wessex Archaeology 138 Xinhua/Alamy Stock Photo 139 DEA PICTURE LIBRARY/ De Agostini /Getty Images 140 © Hierakonpolis Expedition 141l Werner Forman/Universal Images Group/Getty Images 141r © Hierakonpolis Expedition 142 www. BibleLandPictures.com/Alamy Stock Photo 143t Leemage/Corbis via Getty Images 143b nik wheeler/Alamy Stock Photo 144 Photo Scala, Florence 145r epa european pressphoto agency b.v./Alamy Stock Photo 145b age fotostock/Alamy Stock Photo 146 Courtesy of Penn Museum, image #56378 147l www.BibleLandPictures.com/ Alamy Stock Photo 147r © 2017. Image copyright The Metropolitan Museum of Art/Art Resource/Scala, Florence 148 Anton_Ivanov/Shutterstock.com 149tr www.BibleLandPictures.com/Alamy Stock Photo 149b Realy Easy Star/Alamy Stock Photo 150 akg-images/De Agostini Picture Lib./G. Dagli Orti 151l DEA/M. SEEMULLER/Getty Images 151r Philippe Maillard/akg-images 152 Bill Curtsinger/National Geographic/Getty Images 153t Bill Curtsinger/National Geographic/Getty Images 153b Images & Stories/Alamy Stock Photo 154 Joyce Tyldesley 155t Joyce Tyldesley 155b Joyce Tyldesley 156 Mike P Shepherd/Alamy Stock Photo 157t Mike P Shepherd/Alamy Stock Photo 157b Mike P Shepherd/Alamy Stock Photo 158 Joyce Tyldesley 159b Les Stocker/Getty Images 160 Joyce Tyldesley 161t DEA PICTURE LIBRARY/De Agostini/Getty Images 161b De Agostini/S. Vannini/REX/Shutterstock 162 Joyce Tyldesley 163t Joyce Tyldesley 163b Joyce Tyldesley 164 Joyce Tyldesley 165t De Agostini Picture Library/De Agostini/Getty Images 165b Scott D. Haddow/Getty Images 166 Jim Henderson/Alamy Stock Photo 167l Joyce Tyldesley 167r Vladimir Wrangel/Shutterstock.com 168 Joyce Tyldesley 169t Joyce Tyldesley 169b iStock/Getty Images Plus 170 Cultura RM Exclusive/Kevin C Moore/Getty Images 171l florentina georgescu photography/Getty Images 171r Joyce Tyldesley 172 Hemis/Alamy Stock Photo 173t Julian Love/Getty Images 173b Joyce Tyldesley 174 Dan Breckwoldt/Alamy Stock Photo 175t Jar decorated with lion masks and cobra goddesses on lotus flowers, from Tomb 1090, Faras, Sudan, 1st-2nd century AD (painted pottery), Egyptian/Ashmolean Museum, University of Oxford, UK/Bridgeman Images 175b Andrew McConnell/Alamy Stock Photo 176 hecke61/Shutterstock.com 177t Spouted black-topped red polished jar, Classic Kerma, c.1700-1550 BC (ceramic), Nubian/Museum of Fine Arts, Boston, Massachusetts, USA/Bridgeman Images 177b Statue of Lady Sennuwy, probably for Tomb of Djefaihapu, Asyut, Egypt, found in Royal Tumulus K III, Kerma, Nubia, Sudan, Middle Kingdom, reign of Senwosret I, 1971-26 BC (grandiorite), Egyptian 12th Dynasty (1991-1786 BC)/Museum of Fine Arts, Boston, Massachusetts, USA/ Harvard University - Museum of Fine Arts Expedition/Bridgeman Images 178 Jupiterimages/Getty Images 179t DeAgostini/Getty Images 179b DeAgostini/

or late 20th century./Photo © Granger/Bridgeman Images **376** Stephen Alvarez/Getty Images **377t** Douglas Peebles Photography/Alamy Stock Photo **377b** Andoni Canela/Getty Images **378** Michele Burgess/Alamy Stock Photo **379tr** Paul Bahn **379b** John Elk/Getty Images **380** David Wall/Alamy Stock Photo **381t** paul kennedy/Alamy Stock Photo **381b** © 2017. Christie's Images, London/Scala, Florence **384** Tim Whitby/Alamy Stock Photo **385** Adrian Wojcik/Alamy Stock Photo **386** Jesse Kraft/Alamy Stock Photo **387t** Paul Thompson Images/Alamy Stock Photo **387b** Sergi Reboredo/Alamy Stock Photo **388** wening/Alamy Stock Photo **389r** Gianni Dagli Orti/REX/Shutterstock **390** Danita Delimont/Alamy Stock Photo **391t** Ryszard Stelmachowicz/Alamy Stock Photo **391b** Gianni Dagli Orti/REX/Shutterstock **392** Eye Ubiquitous/UIG via Getty Images **393** trappy76/Shutterstock.com **394** David South/Alamy Stock Photo **395l** Vladimir Korostyshevskiy/Shutterstock.com **395r** Gino's Premium Images/Alamy Stock Photo **396** Kenneth Garrett/National Geographic/Getty Images **397r** John Mitchell/Alamy Stock Photo **398** Archivo del proyecto "La pintura mural prehispánica en México", Instituto de Investigaciones Estéticas, UNAM. Foto: Ricardo Alvarado Tapia, 2008. **399b** age fotostock/Alamy Stock Photo **400** Vessel with a Procession of Warriors, Late Classic Period, c.750-850 (polychromed ceramic), Mayan/Kimbell Art Museum, Fort Worth, Texas, USA/Bridgeman Images **401t** Presentation of Captives to a Maya Ruler, Late Classic Period, c.785 (limestone with traces of paint), Mayan, (8th century AD)/Kimbell Art Museum, Fort Worth, Texas, USA/Bridgeman Images **401b** Arterra Picture Library/Alamy Stock Photo **402** Peabody Museum Expedition: Teobert Maler, 1899-1900. © President and Fellows of Harvard College, Peabody Museum of Archaeology and Ethnology, PM# 00-36-20/C2740 **403t** Photograph © Justin Kerr **403b** Universal History Archive/Contributor **404** ton koene/Alamy Stock Photo **405** Richard A. Cooke/Getty Images **406** National Geographic Creative/Alamy Stock Photo **407l** National Geographic Creative/Alamy Stock Photo **407r** Carver Mostardi/Alamy Stock Photo **408** Buddy Mays/Alamy Stock Photo **409l** George H.H. Huey/Alamy Stock Photo **409r** George H.H. Huey/Alamy Stock Photo **410** Naumenko Aleksandr/Shutterstock.com **411t** PavleMarjanovic/Shutterstock.com **411b** Serg Zastavkin/Shutterstock.com **412** dinosmichail/Alamy Stock Photo **13l** Ayhan Altun/Alamy Stock Photo **413r** Lestertair/Shutterstock.com **414** Artur Bogacki/Shutterstock.com **415t** Mehmet Cetin/Shutterstock.com **415b** david pearson/Alamy Stock Photo **416** Joana Kruse/Alamy Stock Photo **417t** akg-images/Erich Lessing **417b** CM Dixon/Print Collector/Getty Images **418** REUTERS/Alamy Stock Photo **419bl** World History Archive/Alamy Stock Photo **419br** World History Archive/Alamy Stock Photo **420** Associated Newspapers /REX/Shutterstock **421l** REX/Shutterstock **421r** World History Archive/Alamy Stock Photo **422** DeAgostini/Getty Images **423** Dish, Abbasid period (750-1258) (earthenware), Mesopotamian (9th century)/Ashmolean Museum, University of Oxford, UK/Gift of Sir Alan Barlow/Bridgeman Images **424** Steve Heap/Shutterstock.com **425t** Deviatov Aleksei/Shutterstock.com **425b** Gianni Dagli Orti/REX/Shutterstock **427t** Vittoriano Rastelli/Getty Images **427b** REUTERS/Alamy Stock Photo **428** Werner Forman/Universal Images Group/Getty Images **429t** Werner Forman/Universal Images Group/Getty Images **429b** Rolf_52/Alamy Stock Photo **430** John Sherbourne/Associated Newspapers/REX/Shutterstock **431t** C M Dixon/AAA Collection/Alamy Stock Photo **431b** York Archaeological Trust. **432** imageBROKER/Alamy Stock Photo **433t** Torbenbrinker/Wikimedia Commons, CC-BY-SA-3.0 **433b** Robert Clark **434** Ivy Close Images/Alamy Stock Photo **435t** Phil Degginger/Alamy Stock Photo **435b** Photo: Werner Karrasch/Copyright: The Viking Ship Museum, Denmark **436** Angelika Warmuth/DPA/PA Images **437t** MOLA/Getty Images **437b** © Historical Picture Archive/CORBIS/Corbis via Getty Images **438** Peter Thompson/Heritage Images/Getty Images **439t** Andrew Melbourne/Alamy Stock Photo **439b** Loop Images Ltd/Alamy Stock Photo **440** akg-images/Sputnik **441t** SPUTNIK/SCIENCE PHOTO LIBRARY **441b** Dzmitry Huletski/Shutterstock.com **442** Peter Horree/Alamy Stock Photo **443t** Ann Ronan Pictures/Print Collector/Getty Images **443b** The Photolibrary Wales/Alamy Stock Photo **444** Wolfgang Kaehler/LightRocket via Getty Images **445t** Heritage Image Partnership Ltd/Alamy Stock Photo **445b** The Print Collector/Getty Images **446** Izzet Keribar/Getty Images **447t** ATTILA KISBENEDEK/AFP/Getty Images **447b** Tarik Kaan Muslu/Alamy Stock Photo **448** Santi Rodriguez/Alamy Stock Photo **449bl** LeoPatrizi/Getty Images **449br** Peter Eastland/Alamy Stock Photo **450** Jorg Hackemann/Shutterstock.com **451t** Dmitry Rukhlenko - Photos of India/Alamy Stock Photo **451b** IndiaPictures/UIG via Getty Images **452** INTERFOTO/Alamy Stock Photo **453tr** Maria Heyens/Alamy Stock Photo **453br** Maria Heyens/Alamy Stock Photo **454** robertharding/Alamy Stock Photo **455t** Anton_Ivanov/Shutterstock.com **455b** Eastland Photo/Alamy Stock Photo **456** JTB Photo/UIG via Getty Images **457t** National Museum of Korea, Seoul/Wikimedia Commons **457b** Yuriko Nakao/Getty Images **458** Jeremy Horner/LightRocket via Getty Images **459t** Werner Forman/Universal Images Group/Getty Images **459b** akg-images **460** IMAGEMORE Co, Ltd./Getty Images **461l** Ivan Vdovin/Alamy Stock Photo **461r** Stock Connection/REX/Shutterstock **462** Savvapanf Photo/Shutterstock.com **463** Richardfabi/Wikimedia Commons, CC-BY-SA-3.0 **464** riNux/Wikimedia Commons, CC-BY-SA-2.0 **465tr** Yooniq Images/Alamy Stock Photo **465br** DeAgostini/Getty Images **466** JTB MEDIA CREATION, Inc./Alamy Stock Photo **467t** Tamamushi shrine from the Horyu Ji Temple, depicting the story of Buddha in a previous incarnation, c.650, Japanese school, (7th century)/Nara, Japan/Bridgeman Images **467b** akg-images/Pictures From History **468** KPG Payless2/Shutterstock.com **469t** Footstool, with ivory inlay, Nara, Japanese School/Shoso-in Treasure House, Japan/Bridgeman Images **469b** Kyodo News via Getty Images **470** David Cumming/Eye Ubiquitous/UIG via Getty Images **471t** RSMultimedia/Alamy Stock Photo **471b** DeAgostini/Getty Images **472** Alexey Stiop/Shutterstock.com **473t** Westend61/Getty Images **473b** N M/EyeEm/Getty Images **474** Peter Dennis/Getty Images **475t** Sabena Jane Blackbird/Alamy Stock Photo **475b** Roger de la Harpe/Getty Images **476** Lynn Y/Shutterstock.com **477t** Colin Hoskins/Alamy Stock Photo **477b** Carved soapstone bird, Zimbabwean, 13th-15th century (steatite), Zimbabwean/Private Collection/Photo © Heini Schneebeli/Bridgeman Images **478** John Warburton-Lee Photography/Alamy Stock Photo **479t** Ulrich Doering/Alamy Stock Photo **479b** Christine Osborne Pictures/Alamy Stock Photo **480** Gabrielle Therin-Weise/Getty Images **481t** Paul Strawson/Alamy Stock Photo **481b** Paul Strawson/Alamy Stock Photo **482** Wolfgang Kaehler/LightRocket via Getty Images **483t** Ellen Mack/Getty Images **483b** John Elk III/Alamy Stock Photo **484** © The Trustees of the British Museum **485t** AA World Travel Library/Alamy Stock Photo **485b** © The Trustees of the British Museum **486** Kylie Ellway/Alamy Stock Photo **487t** DC Premiumstock/Alamy Stock Photo **487b** Matyas Rehak/Shutterstock.com **488** High angle view of the old ruins of a temple, Templo Mayor, Mexico City, Mexico/De Agostini Picture Library/G. Dagli Orti/Bridgeman Images **489l** DEA PICTURE LIBRARY/Getty Images **489r** Universal Images Group North America LLC/Alamy Stock Photo **490** Stefano Ravera/Alamy Stock Photo **491t** INTERFOTO/Alamy Stock Photo **491b** Stephen Bay/Alamy Stock Photo **492** Tim Whitby/Alamy Stock Photo **493t** Alex Bramwell/Alamy Stock Photo **493b** Yadid Levy/robertharding/Getty Images **494** Jarno Gonzalez Zarraonandia/Shutterstock.com **495t** Armando Frazao/Shutterstock.com **495b** Ralf Broskvar/Shutterstock.com **498** Stephen Foote/Alamy Stock Photo **499t** B.O'Kane/Alamy Stock Photo **499b** Alexander Tolstykh/Shutterstock.com **500** Sipa Press/REX/Shutterstock **501t** Sandra van der Steen/Alamy Stock Photo **501b** An assorted lot of 'Nanking Cargo' porcelain, mid 18th century (porcelain), Chinese School, (18th century)/Private Collection/Photo © Christie's Images/Bridgeman Images **502** SSPL/Getty Images **503** DEA/G. NIMATALLAH/De Agostini/Getty Images **504** 19th era/Alamy Stock Photo **505t** LEON NEAL/AFP/Getty Images **505b** G.11631.B.L. Catalogue page from 'Mr. William Shakespeare's Comedies, Histories and Tragedies', edited by J. Heminge and H. Condell, 1623 (print), English School, (17th century)/British Library, London, UK/© British Library Board. All Rights Reserved/Bridgeman Images **506** Danita Delimont/Alamy Stock Photo **507t** Geography Photos/UIG via Getty Images **507b** Arco Images GmbH/Alamy Stock Photo **508** Rolf Richardson/Alamy Stock Photo **509t** P A Thompson/Getty Images **509b** Rolf Richardson/Alamy Stock Photo **510** imageBROKER/Alamy Stock Photo **511t** Markus Matzel/ullstein bild via Getty Images **511b** MICHAEL URBAN/AFP/Getty Images **512** GraphicaArtis/Getty Images **513l** Granger Historical Picture Archive/Alamy Stock Photo **513r** Wikimedia Commons **514** Nagel Photography/Shutterstock.com **515** Bill Bachman/Alamy Stock Photo **516** Heritage Image Partnership Ltd/Alamy Stock Photo **517** Stuart Black/Alamy Stock Photo **518** akg-images/ullstein bild **519** DeAgostini/Getty Images **520** PASQUALE SORRENTINO/SCIENCE PHOTO LIBRARY **522** Science History Images/Alamy Stock Photo **523** SSPL/Getty Images **524** fotolincs/Alamy Stock Photo **525t** Radharc Images/Alamy Stock Photo **525b** Pool DEVILLE/AFSM/Gamma-Rapho via Getty Images **526** © LBI ArchPro, Wolfgang Neubauer **527t** © LBI ArchPro, Geert Verhoeven **527b** National Geographic Creative/Alamy Stock Photo **528** "Arlen F. Chase, Diane Z. Chase, John F. Weishampel, Jason B. Drake, Ramesh L. Shrestha, K. Clint Slatton, Jaime J. Awe, and William E. Carter. "Airborne LiDAR, Archaeology, and the Ancient Maya Landscape at Caracol, Belize. Journal of Archaeological Science 38: 87-398." **529t** "Arlen F. Chase, Diane Z. Chase, Jaime J. Awe, John F. Weishampel, Gyles Iannone, Holley Moyes, Jason Yaeger, M. Kathryn Brown, Ramesh L. Shrestha, William E. Carter, and Juan Fernandez Diaz. ""Ancient Maya Regional Settlement and Inter-Site Analysis: The 2013 West-Central Belize LiDAR Survey. Remote Sensing 6(9): 8671-8695." **529b** Yann Arthus-Bertrand/Getty Images **530** SPUTNIK/SCIENCE PHOTO LIBRARY **531t** Agencja Fotograficzna Caro/Alamy Stock Photo **531b** Vito Arcomano/Alamy Stock Photo **532** JS Photo/Alamy Stock Photo **533t** Lanmas/Alamy Stock Photo **533b** JAMES KING-HOLMES/SCIENCE PHOTO LIBRARY **534** Flinders Petrie, Diospolis Parva (1901) **535t** Joyce Tyldesley **535b** Mike P Shepherd/Alamy Stock Photo **536** David Lyons/Alamy Stock Photo **537t** JAMES KING-HOLMES/SCIENCE PHOTO LIBRARY **537b** The Times of Their Lives project **538** Leon Neal/AFP/Getty Images **539t** PASCAL GOETGHELUCK/SCIENCE PHOTO LIBRARY **539b** VOLKER STEGER/SCIENCE PHOTO LIBRARY **540** University of Leicester/REX/Shutterstock **541t** University of Leicester/REX/Shutterstock **541b** DEA PICTURE LIBRARY/Getty Images **542** JAMES KING-HOLMES/SCIENCE PHOTO LIBRARY **543t** Carl Court/Getty Images **543b** DEA PICTURE LIBRARY/De Agostini/Getty Images **545** Carlos Mora/Alamy Stock Photo **545tr** Paul Bahn **545cr** Paul Bahn **545bl** Marion Kaplan/Alamy Stock Photo **546** Andrea Solero/AFP/Getty Images **547t** Fragments from a loose sleeveless cloak found with the Oetzi Iceman (woven grass), Copper Age, (4th millennium BC)/South Tyrol Museum of Archaeology, Bolzano, Italy/Wolfgang Neeb/Bridgeman Images **547b** Objects found with the Oetzi Iceman, Copper Age, (4th millennium BC)/South Tyrol Museum of Archaeology, Bolzano, Italy/Wolfgang Neeb/Bridgeman Images **548** Barbara Voorhies **549t** Neil Harris/Alamy Stock Photo **549b** imageBROKER/Alamy Stock Photo **550** © The Trustees of the British Museum **551t** Granger Historical Picture Archive/Alamy Stock Photo **551b** PHAS/UIG via Getty Images **552** Garstang Museum, The University of Liverpool **553t** DEA/G. DAGLI ORTI/Contributor **553b** Express/Stringer **554** Copyright Harappa Archaeological Research Project/Harappa.com, courtesy Dept. of Archaeology and Museums, Govt. of Pakistan. **555bl** Kharbine-Tapabor/REX/Shutterstock **555br** Larry Burrows/The LIFE Picture Collection/Getty Images